SCHOOLS FOR SPECIAL NEEDS

2011–2012

SEVENTEENTH EDITION

SCHOOLS FOR SPECIAL NEEDS 2011–2012

The complete guide to special needs education in the United Kingdom

Gabbitas Education
CONSULTANTS SINCE 1873

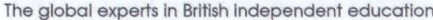
The global experts in British independent education

KoganPage

LONDON PHILADELPHIA NEW DELHI

Photographs on front cover supplied with kind permission of (top) Cotswold Chine School, (left to right) RNIB Pears Centre for Specialist Learning, St John's Catholic School for the Deaf and New College Worcester.

First published in 1995
This seventeeth edition published in 2011

120 Pentonville Road
London N1 9JN
United Kingdom
www.koganpage.com

1518 Walnut Street,
Suite 1100
Philadelphia PA 19102
USA

4737/23 Ansari Road
Daryaganj
New Delhi 110002
India

© Gabbitas and Kogan Page, 2011

British Library Cataloguing in Publication Data

A CIP record for this book is available from the British Library

ISBN   978 0 7494 6417 2
E-ISBN   978 0 7494 6416 5

Typeset by AJS DataSolutions Ltd., Huddersfield
Print production managed by Jellyfish
Printed and bound in Great Britain by CPI Antony Rowe

Contents

PART 2:
SPECIAL SCHOOLS AND COLLEGES –
INDEPENDENT AND NON-MAINTAINED

PART 3:
SPECIAL SCHOOLS AND COLLEGES – MAINTAINED

PART 4:
INDEPENDENT MAINSTREAM SCHOOLS
WITH SPECIALIST PROVISION

PART 5:
REFERENCE SECTION

Special Needs – Guidance for Parents

Introduction

Gabbitas Educational Consultants

Choosing the right school for your child is one of the most important decisions you will ever make. For parents of children with special needs, finding the right school may well involve various stages of assessment and the views of the child's teachers, the Local Authority and a range of education and health professionals.

Schools for Special Needs is designed specifically for parents, offering step-by-step guidance on all aspects of finding the right provision for a child with special educational needs. It also offers a valuable resource for teachers and other education professionals. As well as information on legal and practical issues, the Guide includes details of special schools throughout the UK together with information on special needs provision at mainstream independent schools.

Part 1

Part 1 offers extensive guidance written by experts on the many aspects of assessment, statementing and provision, as well as on choice of schools, admissions procedures, special arrangements for examinations, education planning at 16+, social security benefits for children and carers, and advice for parents overseas.

Part 2

Part 2 gives information about special schools, including a comprehensive directory of independent and non-maintained special schools, plus details of colleges and other establishments providing training and support services for students aged 16+. This is followed by more detailed listings contributed by schools and an index of schools under specific types of provision.

Part 3

Part 3 includes a complete directory of maintained special schools in each UK education authority.

Part 4

Part 4 contains a directory of special provision available at mainstream independent schools plus listings contributed by individual schools and an index of schools under specific types of provision.

Each entry includes contact details and basic information about school type and pupil age ranges. Information about special needs provision is divided into three categories: Learning Difficulties; Behavioural, Emotional and Social Disorders; and Physical Impairment and Medical Conditions. Within each category schools are asked to indicate the type of provision available. This may vary widely from one school to another. Some schools offer extensive specialist support in specific areas, most commonly learning difficulties, while others may have more limited resources. Schools are also asked to indicate in each category whether they currently have pupils who have been diagnosed with certain types of learning difficulty or disability.

Part 5

Part 5 offers suggestions for further reading, an extensive list of useful addresses and associations and details of schools registered under CReSTeD (Council for the Registration of Schools Teaching Dyslexic Pupils).

We are indebted to all those who have helped in the preparation of this Guide, as advisers and authors. A special mention goes to the Heads and Principals who have contributed information about their schools, colleges and support services; without which publication would not have been possible.

We should particularly like to acknowledge with thanks the support provided by the following:

AFASIC

Association for Spina Bifida and Hydrocephalus (ASBAH)

Christine Betts, Senior Lawyer, Veale Wasbrough Vizards Lawyers

Dr Steve Chinn, maths learning difficulties consultant

CReSTeD (Council for the Registration of Schools Teaching Dyslexic Pupils)

Cystic Fibrosis Trust

Priya Dhingra, BA, MA, Cert Ed, MSc, C. Psychol

Disability Alliance

Down's Syndrome Association

Dyslexia Action

The Dyspraxia Foundation

Epilepsy Action

John Friel, Barrister-at-Law, Gray's Inn, Member of the Dyslexia Council, Former Chair of the Advisory Centre for Education Council, Chair of the Special Needs Group of the Educational Law Society

Professor Philip Garner (SEN & Inclusion)

Joint Council for Qualifications

Dr Richard Lansdown, Chartered Psychologist

Liz Malcolm, Chartered Educational Psychologist PSI (UK) Ltd

Muscular Dystrophy Campaign

National Association for Gifted Children

The National Autistic Society

Royal Association for Disability and Rehabilitation

Royal National Institute for the Blind (RNIB)

SCOPE

Skill (National Bureau for Students with Disabilities)

David Urani, Chartered Educational Psychologist

Gabbitas Educational Consultants

Established for over 130 years, Gabbitas is uniquely placed to offer parents a wealth of professional expertise, an understanding of their concerns and a personal knowledge of independent schools throughout the UK. Each year Gabbitas helps thousands of parents and students in the UK and abroad seeking guidance at all stages of education. Our expertise covers:

- choice of independent preparatory and senior boarding and day schools;
- choice of independent sixth form or further education colleges;
- educational assessment services;
- sixth form options – A levels, International Baccalaureate, Pre-U, vocational courses;
- university and degree choices and UCAS applications;
- careers assessment and guidance.

Gabbitas also advises on specialist areas such as transferring into the British education system from overseas, and guardianship for international students attending boarding schools in the UK.

Educational Psychologists

Educational Psychologists (EPs) whether in independent practice or employed by local authorities are concerned with children's learning and emotional development. They work closely with schools, teachers and parents, to carry out a wide range of tasks with the aim of enhancing children's learning. The service offered includes assessment, support and advice to enable teachers to more effectively help children. An awareness of the range of social and curriculum factors affecting both teaching and learning informs their involvement with young people, which often ranges from pre-school age to 19 years old. The main strands of professional practices are:

- assessment and intervention;
- consultation and problem solving;
- research;
- training;
- personal and group support and counselling.

Child and adolescent mental health focused support

Where there are particular concerns relating to a child's emotional development or wellbeing, help may be sought through teams often known as Child and Adolescent Mental Health Services (CAMHs). A number of professionals work together with parents and families to help with special needs including ADHD, BESD and other problems such as sleep disorders, depression, anxiety and eating disorders. The professional teams may include clinical psychologists, child psychotherapists, a child psychiatrist, social workers and community psychiatric nurses. Individual treatment, group or family therapy may be offered depending on requirements.

In addition to offering appointments, some CAMHs professionals can see you and your child at home if it is difficult to meet elsewhere. They may accept direct contact from parents but in the majority of cases a referral from a GP, school teacher or other professional is required. Again, a number of clinicians work in independent practice. Further information is available from the Royal College of Psychiatrists at www.rcpsych.ac.uk.

Advice and information (voluntary groups)

There are a number of voluntary groups that exist to provide information for parents and to signpost useful resources. Every local authority has a list. Each also has a Parent Partnership Service (parentpartnership.org.uk) which is established to provide advice and support to parents of children with special educational needs (SEN). They can be contacted through the local authority office or website. Details for some of the more prominent voluntary groups can be found in the Useful Addresses and Associations section in Part 5.

Therapists

The health therapists that families are most likely to have contact with are physiotherapists, speech and language therapists, occupational therapists and dieticians. Therapists are based in hospitals or health centres and can be contacted through a GP, health visitor or paediatrician referral. Some also operate as independent practitioners.

Physiotherapists

Physios, as they are often known, treat people with physical problems caused by illness or accident that can give rise to associated special educational needs. They aim to help people improve their range of movement in order to promote health and wellbeing. In particular, physiotherapists concentrate on problems that affect muscles, bones, the heart, circulation and lungs. Physiotherapy involves a range of treatments, including manipulation, massage, exercise, electrotherapy and hydrotherapy.

Speech and language therapists

Children who have difficulty producing and using speech, understanding or using language, may need the help of a speech and language therapist. These professionals are also frequently sought to help children who stammer or have other voice problems. The therapists' expertise can also be employed to help children who have problems with feeding, chewing or swallowing. Treatments are generally provided as individual therapy sessions and programmes that can be implemented in school.

Occupational therapists

Occupational therapists work with individuals who suffer from mentally, physically, developmentally, or emotionally disabling conditions. They use specific, purposeful activity to develop, recover or maintain the daily living, learning and work skills of their patients. Occupational therapists provide help to perform all types of activities, from using a computer to caring for daily needs such as dressing, cooking and eating. Work is based in hospitals, community settings or in a child's home setting.

Dieticians

Dieticians help promote good health through proper eating. Their work involves: supervision of the preparation and service of food, development of modified diets and education about good nutritional habits. A key part of their approach when helping children with special educational needs is dietary modification to address issues involving dietary intake.

Professional independent assessment of your child's progress

Gabbitas offers

- Assessment with a qualified educational psychologist
- Educational experience combined with insight from chartered ed psychs
- Review of support provided at your child's present school
- Recommendations of next steps to take, including appropriate school choices
- Full written report following assessment and consultation

The completely impartial and objective assessment of our son was very valuable and indentified a number of things we didn't know about his developmental needs. Your service provided us with a clear idea of exactly which school would suit him best.

Mrs S, Kent

+44 (0)20 7734 0161

agc@gabbitas.co.uk

www.gabbitas.co.uk

A Guide to the Classification of Special Needs

Attention Deficit Hyperactivity Disorder

(Priya Dhingra, BA, MA, Cert Ed, MSc, C. Psychol)

It is not uncommon to come across children who get distracted by things around them, cannot sit still and get constant comments from teachers to say that they need to focus and concentrate. Some may also need continual supervision for homework and music practice, have high energy levels all day long, shout out during discussions in the classroom and talk persistently. It is also quite usual to see children who do not wait their turn during conversations with peers and adults, and find it hard to play games nicely in recreational time. As a child matures some of these behaviours tend to reduce or change. However, when high levels of impulsivity, hyperactivity and inattention interfere with daily functioning at home and school, there is a possibility that a child might have Attention Deficit Hyperactivity Disorder (ADHD).

ADHD is a condition that affects an individual's ability to control attention and behaviour in an optimal and adaptive manner. It is a childhood disorder that continues through adolescence and adulthood which is frequently associated with educational underachievement, antisocial behaviour and poor psychosocial adjustment.

What should you do if you suspect a child has ADHD?

If parents suspect that their child has ADHD, they can raise it with their family doctor or GP. Teachers should raise concerns with the Special Educational Needs Coordinator (SENCo) and a meeting with parents is recommended to explore whether such behaviours are noticed at home too. If parents and teachers are in agreement, a referral needs to be made for a developmental assessment by a paediatrician. Sometimes an Educational Psychologist is involved to conduct observations at home and school to gather additional information concerning behaviour and learning, for the diagnostic assessment.

As a word of caution, many pre-schoolers and young children are very active at one time or another and develop at different rates. They may be very immature at one point, and go through a developmental spurt and calm down later. If difficulties with hyperactivity, impulsivity, and inattention are seen over time, it may be wise to get a medical opinion. However, other factors such as language, learning, emotional and social aspects of a child's development need to be explored too, as they can sometimes present as ADHD features.

ADHD and age

It should also be noted that ADHD presents differently depending on a child's age, maturity and as the environment requirements for sustained self-control change (Taylor and Sonuga-Barke, 2008). In a pre-school child hyperactivity may involve incessant and demanding extremes of activity. During school years a child may make excessive movements during situations when they are expected to be calm. During adolescence hyperactivity may present as excessive fidgetiness rather than whole body movement. Often inattention diminishes and attention span usually increases with age, but there still tends to be a lag when compared to unaffected individuals and the level needed for everyday attainments.

Diagnosing ADHD

A diagnosis of ADHD should only be made by a specialist psychiatrist, paediatrician or other appropriately qualified healthcare professionals with training and expertise in the diagnosis of ADHD. Initially a full clinical and psychosocial assessment is made of the child or young person. This includes discussion about behaviour and symptoms across home and school settings. Observations, rating scales, schedules, and questionnaires are used to gather information from the family, child, where appropriate, and from relevant school staff.

The two main diagnostic criteria in current use are – the International Classification of Mental and Behavioural Disorders 10th revision (ICD-10) and the Diagnostic and Statistical Manual of Mental Disorders 4th edition (DSM-IV). ICD-10 uses a narrower diagnostic category, which includes people with more severe symptoms and impairment. DSM-IV has a broader, more inclusive definition, which includes a number of different ADHD subtypes.

The National Institute of Heath and Clinical Excellence (NICE) guidelines are also used by practitioners in the United Kingdom. The diagnostic criteria for ADHD in DSM-IV require that symptoms of inattention or hyperactivity should be displayed (to some degree) in at least two settings (ie home and school), and have persisted for at least six months to a degree that is maladaptive and out of line with age expectation. Children meet the criteria for the disorder if they have six or more symptoms of inattention, hyperactivity/impulsivity, or both. According to the DSM-IV, there are three main subtypes of ADHD:

1. the primarily 'hyperactive-impulsive' type;

2. the primarily 'inattentive' type;

3. the combined type 'combination of hyperactivity, impulsivity, and inattention'.

Some of these signs should have been recognized before the age of 7 years and there needs to be clear evidence of significant impairment in social, academic, and daily living functioning.

ADHD should be considered in all age groups, with symptom criteria adjusted for age-appropriate changes in behaviour.

ADHD tends to co-occur with other developmental disorders such as Oppositional Defiant Disorder, Conduct Disorder, Mood Disorders, Anxiety Disorders, Dyslexia and Specific Learning Difficulties. According to DSM-IV the prevalence rate for ADHD is around 3–5 per cent of children of primary school age.

Symptoms of ADHD in children

Children who have symptoms of inattention may:

- be easily distracted, miss details, forget things, and frequently switch from one activity to another;
- have difficulty focusing on one thing;
- become bored with a task after only a few minutes, unless they are doing something enjoyable;
- have difficulty focusing attention on organizing and completing a task or learning something new;
- have trouble completing or turning in homework assignments, often losing things (eg, pencils, toys, assignments) needed to complete tasks or activities;
- not seem to listen when spoken to;
- daydream, become easily confused, and move slowly;
- have difficulty processing information as quickly and accurately as others;
- struggle to follow instructions.

Children who have symptoms of hyperactivity may:

- fidget and squirm in their seats;
- talk nonstop;
- dash around, touching or playing with anything and everything in sight;
- have trouble sitting still during dinner, school, and story time;
- be constantly in motion;
- have difficulty doing quiet tasks or activities.

Children who have symptoms of impulsivity may:

- be very impatient;
- blurt out inappropriate comments, show their emotions without restraint, and act without regard for consequences;
- have difficulty waiting for things they want or waiting their turn in games;
- often interrupt conversations or activities of others.

Cause of ADHD

The main cause of ADHD is unknown. Many studies suggest that genes play a large role based on the research in twin studies. Like other disorders, ADHD probably results from a combination of factors. In addition to genetics, researchers are looking at possible environmental factors such as cigarette smoking and alcohol consumption during pregnancy, brain injuries, and the social environment.

Managing ADHD

It is important that appropriate steps are taken to help a child or young person with ADHD, as inappropriate treatment and management can lead to poor self-esteem, academic under-achievement and social isolation. A one-size-fits-all approach for the management of ADHD does not exist. Each child presents differently and a clear plan needs to be put in place depending on the presenting profile. Some of the commonly used strategies for managing ADHD are:

● Medication

The most common type of medication used for treating ADHD is called a 'stimulant'. Although it may seem unusual to treat ADHD with a medication considered a stimulant, it actually has a calming effect on children with ADHD. For many children, ADHD medications reduce hyper-activity and impulsivity and improve their ability to focus, work, and learn. Any child taking medication must be monitored closely and carefully by parents or caregivers and doctors. As there are side effects to medication, the benefits and risks should be considered carefully.

● Management at school and home

Establishing appropriate learning environments – A child with ADHD should be seated away from obvious distractions in the classroom such as doors and windows. Seating a child near the teacher's desk or in the front row of the classroom might help. Allow children to work in pairs rather than groups where possible. Often they find unstructured times difficult and they might need careful supervision at transition times in class or in less structured lessons such as Art and Music. During homework time ensure that the learning environment is free from distractions such as music, television and posters.

Language and instructions – Make eye contact while giving instructions. Keep instructions concise and clear. Encourage repeating back of instructions to check understanding. Often explicit instructions help. Use a calm but firm voice.

Organization and structure – Provide a clear and uncomplicated structure for the day, lesson and activity. Use visual information to support understanding of structure. Give plenty of warning of any change in routine, eg 'In 5 minutes it will be play time.' Use consistent routines; model and teach these routines. Ensure all materials and equipment are available for the student to avoid wandering around searching and getting distracted. A homework or com-munication book will ensure that the right homework is written down and can also be used for communication with parents. Timers can be used in the classroom and at home to manage tasks and improve attention span. Tasks need to be short and structured. Increase length and complexity slowly.

When attentional drifts occur, use it as a sign that the child might need extra support or a short break. Students cope better when the task is broken down into manageable parts. For example if the teacher wants the class to write a page, a student with ADHD might be asked to write 5 lines first which is reviewed before continuing. Tasks need to be varied during lessons and homework time, ie an easy task after a very challenging task. Short breaks for physical activity such as a movement break or water break will help in lessons that involve prolonged periods of being seated. Lists and daily task sheets will help a student remember useful information.

Managing behaviour – Adults need to remain calm and should employ pre-established consequences for unacceptable behaviour. Keep in mind that it is not always the child's fault if things are not going well; ADHD can make it difficult for an individual to regulate their behaviour. As different adults have different expectations and boundaries, clear expression and consistency are of paramount importance. Clearly set out your expectations of desired behaviour at the beginning of a session. For example, not 'be good today' but 'finish half a page of writing in 15 minutes'. When setting limits, be clear, calm and concise. Also consider rewarding positive behaviours with an appropriate token. Avoid shouting, sarcasm or anger – some children find this reinforcing and will continue the unwanted behaviour. Countdowns are often useful, eg 'Simon, I want you to stop shouting or you will need time out ...1...2...3...4... well done for listening.' Never make threats that cannot be carried through or sanctions that are unrealistic. Use choices and distractions to avoid confrontations. Whole class rewards can be used to encourage peer support.

Involve the child in their own management plan; this is empowering and helps to develop their self awareness. Give frequent feedback and always try to frame it positively. Feedback such as praise and rewards should be given immediately to be most effective. Ignore minor silly behaviour or disruptions where possible. Provide 'chill out' areas for a child to remove themselves from a situation. This encourages controlled self time-out. Parents and teachers will benefit from the support an Educational or Clinical Psychologist when considering appropriate strategies to manage behaviour at school and home.

Social skills and understanding – Children with ADHD often misinterpret social cues and language. Thus clear language needs to be used and clarified where necessary. Avoid the use of ambiguous language. A child will benefit from developing awareness of their own physiological responses to triggers, to manage and monitor their behaviour where required. Visual charts and a Feelings Thermometer can be used to regulate and manage behaviour. The practice of self-talk will help children calm down and take control. Deep breathing, counting backwards and visualization will also help in situations where children need to regulate their behaviour. Social skills training can focus on turn taking, listening and conversation skills, to avoid interruptions and to introduce scripts for 'social graces'.

Reframing technique – Use of the reframing technique by parents and teachers may help them to see the child with ADHD as having lots of potentially positive characteristics rather than associating the child with largely undesirable behaviours. Reframing involves finding new and positive ways of thinking about a child's problem behaviour to help the family, teacher and child to break cycles of negativity. For example, here are some negative and positive ways of framing characteristics associated with ADHD, with some positive comments to try out:

Negative	Positive	Reframing in action
Distractible eg off task	High level of environmental awareness	'You notice so many things going on around you. Let's see how we can use those skills in this activity.'
Impatient eg calling out	Goal orientated	'You're so keen to contribute and get started. I can't wait to hear your ideas when I've finished talking.'
Acts without considering consequences eg getting involved in arguments/ sticking up for peer who is in trouble	Willing and able to take risks	'It's good that you're helping out your friend. Maybe we can think of different ways and times you can use that skill while teachers sort out the classroom problems.'

Reframing may help reduce levels of parent and teacher stress because they spend less time being angry, exasperated and frustrated and more time thinking positively about the child. This technique is likely to enhance the child's self esteem and motivation. Children, like adults, are more likely to show positive behaviours and form positive relationships with those who behave in a consistent and positive way towards them.

Parents and teachers can feel exhausted, irritated and angry with a child with ADHD as they feel that all the difficulties lie with the child. However, it should be noted that environmental changes and appropriate management strategies can help relieve adult stress, child frustration, and give a sense of control. ADHD is a manageable childhood disorder if the right strategies are put in place at school and home.

References

American Psychiatric Association (2000) *Diagnostic and Statistical Manual of Mental Disorders: Text revision* (4th edn, text revision), American Psychiatric Association, Washington, DC
Hulme, C and Snowling, M J (2009) *Developmental Disorders of Language Learning and Cognition*, Wiley-Blackwell, West Sussex, UK
National Institute for Health and Clinical Excellence (2009) *Attention Deficit Hyperactivity Disorder – Diagnosis and management of ADHD in children, young people, and adults*, British Psychological Society and The Royal College of Psychiatrists, Leicester.
Taylor, E and Sonuga-Barke, E (2008) *Disorders of Attention and Activity in Rutter's Child and Adolescent Psychiatry* (5th edn) (eds M Rutter, E Taylor, J S Stevenson, et al), Blackwell, London
World Health Organization (1992) *The ICD-10 Classification of Mental and Behavioural Disorders: Clinical descriptions and diagnostic guidelines*, World Health Organization, Geneva

Autism

(Information supplied by The National Autistic Society)

Autism (including Asperger syndrome) is a complex developmental disability that affects social and communication skills. People with autism can often have accompanying learning disabilities, but everyone with the condition shares a difficulty in making sense of the world.

In most children with autism, some types of skills will be better than others, so their development will not only be slower than usual but will also be uneven and different from that of other children with learning disabilities.

Autism is a life-long disability and is not, at present, curable, but there are ways of helping, especially if a child is diagnosed and receives appropriate intervention early in life. Specialized education and structured support can really make a difference to a child's life, helping to maximize skills, minimize any behaviour problems and achieve full potential in adulthood.

Autism affects the way a child communicates and relates to people around him or her. Being a spectrum condition means that, while all children with autism share three main areas of difficulty, their condition will affect them in different ways. The three main areas of difficulty (sometimes known as the 'triad of impairments') are:

● social interaction (includes difficulty with recognizing and understanding other people's feelings and managing their own. Not understanding how to interact with other people can make it hard to form friendships);

● social communication (includes difficulty with using and understanding verbal and non-verbal language, such as gestures, facial expressions and tone of voice);

● social imagination (includes difficulty in the development of imaginative play and having a limited range of imaginative activities, which can be copied and pursued rigidly and repetitively).

In addition to this triad, repetitive behaviour patterns and a resistance to change in routine are notable features. People with autism may also experience over- or under-sensitivity to sounds, touch, tastes, smells, light or colours.

Particular points about autism are worth noting:

● the severity of difficulties differs from person to person, and different aspects of behaviour are more obvious at some ages than others;

● three-quarters of children with autism also have mild or severe learning disabilities;

● a child's personality, education and social environment can also markedly affect their behaviour;

● children with autism may also have other associated disabilities and learning difficulties, including epilepsy, ADHD, cerebral palsy, dyslexia and dyspraxia.

Asperger syndrome is a form of autism. People with Asperger syndrome are usually at the 'higher-functioning' end of the autism spectrum. Most are of average or above average intelligence and generally have fewer problems with language, often speaking fluently, though their words can sometimes sound formal or stilted. Unfortunately, because their disability is often less obvious, a person with Asperger syndrome may be more vulnerable. They can, sadly, be an easy target for teasing or bullying at school.

The causes of autism are still being investigated. Many experts believe that the pattern of behaviour from which autism is diagnosed may not result from a single cause. There is strong evidence to suggest that autism can be caused by a variety of physical factors, all of which affect brain development, and that genetic factors are responsible for some forms of autism. Scientists have been attempting to identify which genes might be implicated in autism for some years. Autism is likely to have multiple genes responsible rather than a single gene. The difficulty of establishing gene involvement is compounded by the interaction of genes and by their interaction with environmental factors. Autism cannot be caused by emotional deprivation or the way a person has been brought up.

It is crucial that autism is recognized early in a child's life to enable effective intervention and management of the condition. Early diagnosis and intervention are also essential to ensure that families and carers have access to appropriate services and professional support.

In most cases, the triad of impairments emerges in the first two to three years of life. Indeed, there are often indications of developmental problems within the first year. However, because autism is a complex condition it is easy to miss important clues.

Autism is a pattern of abnormal development that unfolds over time, so diagnosis depends on obtaining a detailed history of the child's development and a careful assessment of skills and abilities.

In infancy one of the most important indications that autism could be present is the absence, or very delayed development, of drawing the attention of parents and others to objects or events. In typical childhood development, by 12–18 months children are usually pointing at things and trying to engage the interest of the person they are with to invite them to look too. They can also gain attention by bringing toys and making eye contact when doing so. If this behaviour does not occur or begins very late and is limited to the child's own interests, an autism spectrum disorder should be suspected.

If you suspect that autism is present, it is essential that you refer the child for a specialist diagnosis and assessment as early as possible – either to your local GP, the Child Development Centre or Child and Adolescent Mental Health Service, or, if you are a teacher, to your local authority's educational psychologist.

The National Autistic Society is the UK's leading charity for people affected by autism. We were founded in 1962 by a group of parents passionate about ensuring a better life for their children. Today we have just under 20,000 members, over 100 branches and provide a wide range of advice, information, support, specialist community and educational services to 100,000 people each year. For more information about autism and education please contact The National Autistic Society. Call 020 7833 2299 or e-mail: nas@nas.org.uk. Website: www.autism.org.uk. Autism Helpline (Mon–Fri, 10am–4pm): 0845 070 4004.

Behavioural, Emotional and Social Difficulty (BESD)

(Philip Garner Professor of Education, SEN and Inclusion)

Behavioural, Emotional and Social Difficulty (BESD) in schools is one of the most high-profile special needs in the United Kingdom, both in terms of the level of attention it receives in the general media, and also in terms of the concerns expressed about it by teachers and other professionals. Over the last 20 years both groups have continually expressed concern over a perceived rising level of challenging behaviour in schools in the United Kingdom. For instance, very few general elections go by without there being mention, by all political parties, of concerns regarding deteriorating standards of 'discipline' in schools. And when statutory guidance and sponsored research by UK governments are considered, it is obvious that there is an ongoing preoccupation with this complex area of special needs.

What is BESD?

The term BESD is one which incorporates a continuum of severity of behaviours. A succinct explanation is provided in Circular 9/94 by the English government, stating that 'Such difficulties lie on the continuum between behaviour which challenges teachers but is within the normal, albeit unacceptable, bounds and that, which is indicative of serious mental illness'.

It is not uncommon to encounter pupils who achieve to a very high standard in certain curriculum areas, but yet frequently display unacceptable behaviour, sometimes of an aggressive nature. More usually, however, BESD is associated with academic underperformance, which causes some to ask whether unwanted behaviour is a result of the child's frustration with his failure to learn. But there can be no doubt that BESD is a special need which presents a barrier to learning, and becomes a cause of serious concern when a range of interventions and strategies employed by mainstream schools does not produce a change in the level of unacceptable behaviour or, as stated in the *Code of Practice*, 2001, the pupil 'presents persistent emotional or behavioural difficulties which are not ameliorated by the behaviour management techniques usually employed in the school' (p 53).

The *Code of Practice* in England (2001) provides a currently applicable official working definition of BESD, stating that:

> 'Pupils with behavioural, emotional and social difficulties cover the full range of ability and continuum of severity. Their behaviours present a barrier to learning and persist despite the implementation of an effective school behaviour policy and personal/social curriculum. They may be withdrawn or isolated, disruptive and disturbing, hyperactive and lack concentration, have immature social skills or present challenging behaviours' (p 93).

As stated, BESD refers to a spectrum of behaviours along a continuum. At the milder end are pupils who have difficulties with social interaction and find it difficult to work in a group or cope in unstructured time. They may have poor concentration, temper outbursts and be verbally and/or physically aggressive to peers. Some pupils display similar signs of low esteem, under achievement and inappropriate social interaction, but do not have behavioural outbursts. They will be withdrawn, quiet and difficult to communicate with. Many children at one time or another will display at least some of these behaviours, although these will be isolated instances usually associated with the various stages of emotional and social development they are passing through at the time. It is when such behaviour starts to become a dominant feature in the child's life, and is more pronounced or prolonged, that more specialized interventions are needed.

Further along the continuum are pupils who are inclined to be confrontational or openly defiant, sometimes physically aggressive towards their peers or adults and who often present as resentful of authority or angry. Such pupils will more often be unable to concentrate on formal learning, and will sometimes have a low self-esteem. In spite of the severity of their behaviour they do not take responsibility for it or recognize its negative impact.

Finally, there are a smaller number of pupils whose behaviour is such that they are unable to function as part of a classroom or group. Their behaviour is persistent and sometimes physically violent, requiring the use of authorized restraint techniques. Such pupils will also present the full range of achievement levels, although again dominated by those who have a history of chronic underachievement.

The continuum, expressed in these general terms, encompasses a range of individual 'conditions'. These include *Oppositional Defiant Disorder* (or ODD, which is especially common in younger children and is characterized by temper tantrums, disobedience, arguing with teachers, parents or other significant adults), *Tourette's Syndrome* (a condition which begins in early childhood and is manifested by both motor and verbal 'tics', the latter sometimes involving repetitive verbal obscenities), *Obsessive Compulsive Disorder* (or OCD, characterized by obsessional thoughts and compulsive behaviours, often with attendant anxiety and depression) and *Bullying* (which often involves pupils with BESD as perpetrators or as victims, the latter often being pupils who are withdrawn, isolated and who are sometimes referred to as the "silent 'E'" in BESD'.

The principal issue raised by the current term 'BESD' is the variety of interpretations given to it – whilst there may be broad agreement on its basic characteristics, the United Kingdom does not have an explicitly applied definition which is consistently utilized. Variations exist from LA to LA, from school to school. Moreover, what is regarded as a 'serious' BESD by one school can be interpreted very differently in another. So, when determining the severity of BESD, teachers and other professionals will normally be informed by such considerations as the nature, persistence, negative impact on the child's learning and on the learning of others.

In terms of incidence, it is difficult to estimate precise numbers of pupils presenting BESD. Cooper (2001) for example estimates that '...currently at least 10 per cent (and possibly 20 per cent) of school age children in England and Wales experience clinically significant levels of social, emotional and behavioural difficulties'.

What are the causes of BESD?

Because BESD is essentially a 'broad spectrum' special need, encompassing a variety of behaviours, it follows that underlying causes comprise a diverse set of catalysts and explanations. There is certainly evidence in the literature of professionals citing quite different causal factors based on their own training, experience and perspective. It is most often the case that multi-factorial causes are implicated, making subsequent intervention a complicated and long-term process.

Pupils with BESD can be characterized as 'troubled and troubling' children as a result of biological, psychological or social factors; they can be either long-term, chronically present issues or more immediate triggers for unwanted problem behaviour. All three are interrelated and each will vary in its impact on the child over time. Unpacking the relative importance of each of these is of crucial importance, given that an understanding of cause is more likely to result in a more appropriate intervention.

In the case of biological or physical causes, a number of genetic abnormalities, diseases or problems occurring as a result of pre-natal or post-natal complications can be implicated. A range of psychological factors will also be present, associated with temperament, self-esteem, insecurity and a lack of resilience to social stressors. Social explanations for BESD are common and comprise a wide variety of factors. They will include both family-related and school-related contexts. Amongst the former are such things as divorce or separation, bereavement, unemployment, poor housing and unsatisfactory social relationships.

Ultimately, however, it is important to re-emphasize the interrelationships between the three broad groups of causes highlighted. One of the implications of this is that resulting intervention will invariably comprise a multi-professional approach, involving specialist strategies and skills.

Recognition of the links between the three groups of causal factors is central to the application of the so-called 'ecosystemic' interpretation of BESD (Bronfenbrenner, 1979). When applied to pupil behaviour this attempts to locate an understanding and intervention within a linked set of domains: the 'micro' system (which refers to the pupil in the classroom); the 'meso' system (the whole school); the 'exo' system (which relates to the wider context of family, community and inputs from supporting professionals); and finally, the 'macro' system (which broadly refers to the perceptions, beliefs and cultures of society which define its overall perception of pupils and their behaviour). And more recently it has become popular to link 'behaviour' with 'learning' and associate success in both areas with an ability to establish positive relationships. This has recently formed the basis of government advice regarding the management of BESD in mainstream schools in England.

How do schools manage pupils with BESD?

Considerable attention has been directed towards addressing the needs of pupils experiencing BESD in mainstream schools in the United Kingdom, as well as in alternative specialist settings. A number of major reports and sets of policy guidance have been published in the last decade, most notably those from the committee chaired by Sir Alan Steer (DCSF, 2008; 2009). These place an emphasis on generic behaviour problems, rather than those formally ascertained as BESD. However, 47 separate recommendations are made, stressing the importance of early intervention as well as further professional development in behaviour management skills for teachers. Moreover, the pivotal role of whole-school procedures and policies, as well as effective liaison with parents, community and other professionals are regarded as being essential features of those schools which are successful in meeting the needs of learners who have BESD.

What is apparent from the Steer Report and most other sets of guidance, as well as recent academic research, is that there has been a consistently similar set of advice directed towards teachers and schools which has really changed very little for several decades. In 1989, the Elton Report, *Discipline in Schools*, recommended a set of strategies for dealing with problematic behaviour. These included most of the guidelines set out 20 years later by Steer. They include an emphasis upon:

- recognizing the link between behaviour, learning and the quality of teaching;

- an agreed whole-school policy on behaviour with clear guidelines regarding rules and sanctions;

- understanding that there is no single solution to the problem of poor behaviour, but that consistency is a key element in behaviour management;

- respect has to be given in order to be received: all stakeholders need to operate in a culture of mutual regard;

- support for schools from parents based on a clear understanding of the rights and responsibilities of each;

- the critical role of school-leaders in establishing high standards of learning, teaching and behaviour.

Alongside these generic approaches are a set of strategies and interventions which are utilized by teachers and other professionals who have specific roles in managing BESD, especially in those instances where serious concerns are expressed. These include such approaches as restorative justice, behaviour contracting, person-centred therapy, solution focused brief therapy and motivational interviewing.

What provision is available for pupils with more severe BESD?

Pupils who present the most serious challenges to schools on account of the extreme nature of their behaviour and its persistence over time are statistically the most likely to be excluded from mainstream schools. There is, nevertheless, a legal requirement to provide full-time education for such pupils up until 16 years of age. As a result, a range of alternative provision exists. Off-site provision or pupil referral units (PRUs) are intended for short-term strategic placement of BESD pupils, in the expectation that a return to mainstream schooling will follow a period of intensive input to address the priority behaviours identified. Most LAs have PRUs, and the teachers in them work collaboratively with specialist professionals (educational psychologists, therapists, social workers and staff from other behaviour-related agencies) as well as the mainstream schools from which the pupils have been excluded. In some instances dual enrolment forms part of the overall strategy; a pupil receives part of his education in a mainstream school and the remainder in an off-site facility.

Separate special schools for pupils with BESD have long been a common feature of the educational landscape. In part this is a recognition that pupils who present the most serious challenging behaviour are unlikely to be included in mainstream schools. They have a number of advantages. Firstly, such schools are geared towards meeting specific behavioural needs, and have the skills and experience to manage extreme and disturbing behaviour. Furthermore, they are able to plan the curriculum in a more individualized way, in order to meet the needs of specific pupils – in mainstream settings there is always a concern that such adjustments will affect the learning of others and the external profile and reputation of the school.

Some concluding points

Any consideration of pupils who present characteristics of 'BESD' has to take account of certain contextual issues; recognition of these will serve to ensure that such an emotive and distressing issue, which too frequently evokes unhelpful and even damaging responses, can be tackled in ways which offer more likelihood of adjustment and behaviour change. Thus teachers, parents and others need to understand that pupils identified as having BESD do not behave unacceptably all of the time – there may be extended periods when the pupil demonstrates compliant behaviour. They also need to be aware that 'spontaneous remission', whereby a young person 'grows out' of the unwanted behaviour, is also common. And finally there should be a recognition that BESD is not a condition where instant 'cures' exist – behaviour change takes time.

Further information

A wide range of useful resources is available electronically. These include:
Behaviour for Learning (http://www.behaviour4learning.ac.uk/Index.aspx)

Behaviour in Schools (Wales)
(http://wales.gov.uk/consultations/education/behaviourinschools/?lang=en)
Behaviour in Scottish Schools
(http://www.scotland.gov.uk/Publications/2009/11/20101438/0)
The National Strategies
(http://nationalstrategies.standards.dcsf.gov.uk/inclusion/behaviourattendanceandseal)
School Discipline and Promoting Positive Behaviour (Northern Ireland)
(http://www.deni.gov.uk/index/21-pupils-parents-pg/21-pupils_parents_school_
discipline_promoting_positive_behaviour-pg.htm)
Social, Emotional and Behavioural Difficulties Association
(http://www.sebda.org/resources.asp)
Teachernet (http://www.teachernet.gov.uk/wholeschool/behaviour/)

References

Bronfenbrenner, U (1979) *The Ecology of Human Development*, Harvard University Press, Cambridge
Cooper, P (2001) *Dealing with Disruptive Students in the Classroom*, Kogan Page, London
DCSF (2008) *Behaviour Review* (The Steer Report), DCSF, London
DCSF (2009) *Review of Pupil Behaviour. Interim Report 4* (The Steer Report), DCSF, London
DES (1989) *Discipline in Schools* (The Elton Report), HMSO, London

Cerebral palsy

(Information supplied by SCOPE, formerly The Spastics Society)

Cerebral palsy is not a disease or an illness. It is the description of a physical impairment that affects movement. The movement problems vary from barely noticeable to extremely severe. No two people with cerebral palsy are the same – it is as individual as people themselves.

Cerebral palsy is most commonly the result of failure of the part of the brain to develop, either before birth or in early childhood. This is sometimes because of bleeding or blocked blood vessels, complications in labour, or extreme prematurity. Infections during pregnancy, eg rubella, or in infancy or early childhood, eg meningitis or encephalitis, can also lead to cerebral palsy. Very occasionally it is due to an inherited disorder. In such cases genetic counselling may be helpful. However, it is rare for cerebral palsy to be caused by a genetic link. It is sometimes possible to identify the cause of cerebral palsy, but not always.

The main effect of cerebral palsy is difficulty in movement. Many people with cerebral palsy are hardly affected, others may have problems walking, feeding, talking or using their hands. Some people, for example, are unable to sit up without support and need constant enabling.

Sometimes other parts of the brain are also affected, resulting in sight, hearing perception and learning difficulties, and some people are also affected by epilepsy.

People with cerebral palsy often have difficulty controlling their movement and facial expressions. This does not necessarily mean that their mental abilities are in any way impaired. Some are of higher than average intelligence, other people with cerebral palsy have moderate or severe learning difficulties.

Cerebral palsy includes a variety of conditions. The three main types correspond to injuries on different parts of the brain and many people will have a mixture of the following types and effects:

● People with spastic cerebral palsy find that some of the muscles become very stiff and weak, especially under effort. This can affect their control of movement.

● People with athetoid or dyskinetic cerebral palsy have some loss of control of their posture, and tend to make unwanted movements.

● People with ataxic cerebral palsy usually have problems with balance. They may also have shaky hand movements and irregular speech.

Many people with cerebral palsy will have a combination of the above types. The needs of children with cerebral palsy are very wide and often very complex. Some are able to integrate into mainstream schools with minimal support, while others require the help of a welfare assistant, special furniture and adaptations to the environment. The mainstream experience can vary greatly according to the individual challenges faced by each child, the available expertise, resources and environment, and the commitment of all involved. However, the needs of some children cannot easily be met with integrated mainstream provision.

In many cases, it is the complexity of needs as a result of cerebral palsy, for example communication, visuo-motor and visual perceptual problems, physical ability, learning difficulties and medical conditions such as epilepsy and dietary needs that lead parents to seek out specialist education.

It is now widely agreed that early intervention is very important. The early diagnosis of a disability, coupled with appropriate specialist intervention, can do much to lessen its effects upon the development of children, and thus reduce the potential of the disability to result in functional handicap. This is no less true in the case of cerebral palsy than of any other disability.

The effectiveness of such a strategy in the early years is enhanced greatly by the active participation of the parents and family of a disabled child. Their involvement is central to the success of such programmes. During recent years, there has been a recognition of the role of parents as the prime educators of young children with whom other professional groups must work in genuine partnership.

Access to the National Curriculum is enhanced when children with cerebral palsy have opportunities to develop stable sitting, head control, hand–eye coordination, gross/fine motor skills, effective communication, independence in standing, walking and self-help skills.

Many children need additional time to achieve writing and manipulation activities and, in order to keep pace with their peers, require up-to-date micro-technology and/or communication aids to support their learning.

Methods of teaching vary and professionals from many disciplines can be involved, eg teachers, occupational therapists, physiotherapists, conductors, nursery nurses, speech and language therapists, psychologists, as well as a variety of medical professionals. There are traditional educational methods within mainstream and special schools. Some mainstream schools have special units attached. Multidisciplinary teams of staff are involved in teaching and providing for the needs of individual children. Children attending a mainstream school will usually require time out to attend therapy sessions. This may be within the school or can involve attendance at a child development centre.

Children attending a special school will usually receive their therapy support in the school. Some therapists see the children in their classroom as well as for individual sessions.

An option for some children can be Conductive Education, developed by Professor Andra Peto in Hungary. Conductive Education is a holistic learning system that incorporates teaching and learning, and may help some children with cerebral palsy to become as independent as possible, encompassing all their learning needs.

For further information on cerebral palsy and SCOPE, contact SCOPE Response, SCOPE, PO Box 833, Milton Keynes MK12 5NY; tel: 0808 800 3333 (freephone).

Cystic fibrosis

(Information supplied by the Cystic Fibrosis Trust)

Cystic fibrosis (CF) is one of the UK's most common life-threatening inherited diseases, affecting over 8,500 children and young people. It is caused by a single faulty gene that controls the movement of salt and water through cells in the body. In people with CF the internal organs, especially the digestive system, become clogged with thick, sticky mucus. As recently as the 1960s children with CF did not live very long. However, better understanding and treatment means that today most live into adulthood and half live beyond 38, with the condition kept under control. Cystic fibrosis affects children in different ways and can vary in severity from one month to the next, so it is important to examine the special needs of each child on an individual basis.

One person in 25 is a carrier of the faulty gene that can cause CF in their children. Carriers are, however, completely healthy because they also have a normal gene that overrides the defective gene. If both parents are carriers of CF, any child they have has a 25 per cent chance of having CF (by inheriting faulty genes from both parents), a 50 per cent chance of being completely healthy but being a carrier (by inheriting a faulty gene from one parent and a healthy gene from the other) and a 25 per cent chance of being completely unaffected (by inheriting normal genes from both parents). Screening is now possible to enable prospective parents to find out if either is a carrier and is recommended if there is any history of CF in the family.

Medical complications

The abnormally thick mucus produced in the lungs of children born with CF can block smaller airways and cause infections, leading to long-term damage. The most noticeable effect is a persistent cough which is non-infectious but may cause distress in front of classmates, particularly if severe, and may lead to coughing up mucus. Digestive problems, in widely varying degrees, may be caused as a result of damage to the pancreas, which produces insulin to regulate sugar levels in the blood and enzymes that aid digestion.

Other less common health problems associated with CF include sinus infections, nasal polyps, osteoporosis, diabetes and liver problems. Sexual maturity may be delayed and boys with CF may become infertile (but not impotent).

Treatment for cystic fibrosis

Treatment for CF aims to keep the lungs functioning as normally as possible. Physiotherapy and breathing exercises to clear the lungs of thick mucus that attracts infection are a vital part of each child's daily routine. Many will require it two or three times a day, from 15 minutes to an hour at a time, depending on the child's needs. Parents are taught to do physiotherapy as soon as CF is diagnosed, but older children can do part of the treatment themselves and often become completely independent.

Physiotherapy may be combined with nebuliser treatment, in which liquid medication is converted to a fine mist which is inhaled and works directly in the lungs. Antibiotics are also taken regularly to prevent or treat infections. Digestive problems can be alleviated by enzyme treatments taken with meals to aid good absorption of food.

Special educational needs

A child with CF may have special educational needs if the condition prevents or hinders him or her from making use of educational facilities of a kind provided for children of the same age in schools covered by the Local Authority. Most children with CF can be provided for within a mainstream school without the need for a statement. Schools should, of course, involve parents and seek their views at all stages.

All schools have the service of a medical officer or equivalent, but not always on site. Teachers, therefore, must be willing to allow parents or other helpers to come into school when a child requires treatment. The school's medical room or another suitable room will need to be made available.

Teachers may also need to arrange supervision at mealtimes to ensure that children eat well and take any necessary medication and food supplement capsules.

Cystic fibrosis does not affect a child's intellectual or academic abilities but may mean long periods away from school because of chest infections or hospital stays. However, schools may be able to set work to be done at home or in the hospital if the child is well enough. Physical exercise is usually very good for children with CF because it helps to loosen mucus in the lungs, but teachers should be aware that children may feel unusually tired after a cold or chest infection. Teachers should remember that children with CF may need to use the toilet urgently and more frequently than other pupils. Therefore, consideration should be made for them to leave the classroom for privacy to cough and visit the toilet. As children with CF can pick up CF-related infections from others diagnosed with the condition, it is advisable for them to avoid such contact where possible.

Children with CF may be teased at school because of their persistent cough and the fact that they may be small for their age. Some may also find it embarrassing to take medication in front of their classmates. Friends must be supportive and encouraged to understand the importance of physiotherapy sessions which may sometimes interfere with the social timetable. The adolescent years can be particularly traumatic. Some teenagers may display rebellious behaviour by neglecting physiotherapy and diet and refusing to recognize the potential seriousness of the condition. Sympathetic counselling can be valuable to help teenagers cope with the stresses associated with delayed sexual maturity, to advise girls of the risks associated with pregnancy and to offer support to boys who face possible infertility.

The pressures of coping with CF can place great strain on family life and relationships. Brothers and sisters may feel resentment at the attention given to their sibling with CF and may feel guilty as a result. This can give rise to bad behaviour, withdrawal or other problems at school. All members of the family will be affected by the psychological pressures arising from the severe nature of CF, uncertainty about the future, genetic aspects and tiring routines. Families may also have to face the prospect of death. Medical advice, support and bereavement counselling are available to help families cope with these pressures.

Teachers can help by meeting parents before a child comes into class and by understanding the problems that may arise within the family. They may be able to offer practical help by administering medication or supervising children taking it. There are no national guidelines for teachers on giving medication to children at school and teachers are not obliged to do so. If parents consent, however, there is no reason why teachers should not help in this way, provided they are insured by their employer. Teachers can also explain to classmates the reasons for coughing, physiotherapy and so on, and encourage a positive attitude.

Special arrangements can be made for candidates with CF taking examinations. Additional time and supervised breaks may be allowed, or permission given for candidates to take examinations in hospital or at home.

For further information parents should contact the Cystic Fibrosis Trust, 11 London Road, Bromley, Kent BR1 1BY; tel: 020 8464 7211, fax: 020 8313 0472, e-mail: enquiries@ cftrust.org.uk, website: www.cftrust.org.uk.

Deafness/hearing impairment

(Information provided by the National Deaf Children's Society (NDCS))

Types of deafness

Conductive deafness is the most common type. It means that sounds cannot pass efficiently through the outer and middle ear to the cochlea and auditory nerve. This is often caused by fluid in the middle ear – a condition known as glue ear or otisis media that affects about one in five children.

Sensori-neural deafness, or nerve deafness as it is sometimes called, usually means that the cochlea is not processing the sound effectively. Often the cause of sensori-neural deafness is not known, but hereditary factors are often present. Few children are totally deaf. Most children will have some hearing at some frequencies if the sound made is loud enough.

Causes of permanent deafness

Causes before birth (pre-natal causes)

Around half of all deaf children born in the UK are deaf as a result of inherited genetic factors. Deafness can be passed down in families, even though there is no immediately apparent family history of deafness. Approximately 70 per cent of these deaf children will encounter no other difficulties arising from their genetic problem. However, the remaining 30 per cent may have disabilities or health problems resulting from the underlying genetic cause of deafness.

Causes in early childhood (post-natal causes)

Premature birth can increase the risk of a child being deaf or becoming deaf. Babies born prematurely are often prone to infections that can cause deafness. Severe jaundice or a lack of oxygen at some point can cause deafness. Infections later on during early childhood, such as meningitis, measles and mumps, can also be responsible for a child becoming deaf. Although less frequently occurring, deafness can be caused by head injury or exposure to loud noises.

Communication methods

Children naturally try to learn a language that enables them to be understood. The communication method used by a deaf child will depend on a number of factors, such as the level of his or her hearing loss and which method he or she feels most comfortable with. The most common types of communication used by deaf children are summarized below.

Auditory-oral approaches. Auditory-oral approaches aim to develop listening skills and spoken language in deaf children. They emphasize the use of hearing aids, radio aids and cochlear implants to maximize the use of any residual hearing a child has. Most auditory-oral approaches also use lip-reading to help the child's understanding. These approaches are used with children with all levels of deafness, from mild to profound. Auditory-oral approaches do not use sign language or fingerspelling to support understanding of spoken language. The main aim of these approaches is to allow deaf children to develop good, effective speech.

Sign-bilingualism. A sign-bilingual approach uses sign language and spoken language. In England the main languages are usually British Sign Language (BSL) and English. If a family speaks another language, children may learn that as a second language, with or without English. When they have become confident in BSL, they can use this as a medium to learn English. BSL also allows them access to the Deaf community. Learning English as a second language is essential for children to develop reading and writing, as there is no written form of BSL. The aim of using a sign-bilingual approach is to allow your child to communicate using language and to develop skills in their home language.

Total communication. Total communication uses a combination of methods to communicate with deaf children. The aim of the approach is to communicate and teach vocabulary in any way that works. Deaf children and their families are encouraged to use sign language, fingerspelling, natural gestures, lip-reading, body language, speech and amplification (hearing aids or radio aids), to help them communicate effectively.

Lip-reading. Lip-reading is the ability to read words from the lip and face patterns of the speaker. Deaf children naturally try to lip read when they are communicating. It's estimated that about 30–40 per cent of speech sounds can be lip-read under the best conditions – with a quiet environment and good lighting.

British Sign Language (BSL) is the language of the British Deaf community. Over 70,000 people use the officially recognized language as their first or preferred language. BSL is a visual language, using hand shapes, facial expressions, gestures and body language to communicate, which has developed over hundreds of years. It has a structure and grammar different from that of written and spoken English. The complete language is independent of any other, with a unique vocabulary. Like other languages it has evolved over time and developed regional and national dialects. **Fingerspell** is used as a part of sign language. It uses the hands to spell out words. Each letter of the alphabet can be indicated using the fingers and palm – specific patterns create individual words.

Deafness itself is not defined as a Special Educational Need. However, there are needs arising from deafness, whether it is temporary or permanent that may require special educational provision. For example, deaf children's language and communication development can often be affected by their deafness. They may need extra provision in the form of support from a specialist teacher of deaf children, support from a communication support worker (CSW) or regular speech and language therapy. Specialist equipment such as a radio aid system is also often required. There are various issues to consider when a deaf child attends a school, such as: appropriate teaching methods, technical support, language and communication support, as well as social and emotional development.

Teaching of deaf children

Teachers of deaf children support them in a variety of ways:

- Home visits to newly diagnosed and pre-school children to help parents develop involvement in their child's early education and social development.

- The development of language, whether signed or spoken or both (as in Total Communication approaches).

- Checking of audiological equipment (though parents, support staff and young deaf people could be taught to check hearing and radio aids).

- Advising and training school staff to identify and meet the needs of individual deaf children.

Speech and language therapy

Speech and language therapists have specialist knowledge about speech and language development (which goes beyond teaching the child to articulate sound) and may work with oral or signing children to develop some competence in lip-reading or British Sign Language (BSL). Some may use Sign Supported English, which is where a sign is used to follow the significant words in an English sentence.

Specialist equipment

There is a range of technical support now available for deaf children. Such technology can be used to make the teaching and learning process easier. At school a deaf child may use a radio aid system with their hearing aid or cochlea implants to help them pick out the teacher's voice and cut out background noise.

An acoustically treated environment

The layout and type of classroom can make it easier or harder for a deaf child to learn. An acoustically treated environment is particularly important. Background noise makes it difficult for pupils who use hearing aids or cochlea implants, because their microphone amplifies all noise.

It is very important that there is a whole-school approach to the education of deaf children. This means that all members of staff need to be aware of the needs of deaf children and how to meet these needs. It is also essential that there is a commitment within the school to ensuring that a deaf child has an equal opportunity to participate in every aspect of school life.

Deaf Friendly Schools and *Deaf Friendly Teaching* are booklets produced by the National Deaf Children's Society (NDCS) for teachers and governors. They provide information and guidance about working with deaf children. If you would like a copy, please contact the NDCS Freephone helpline.

For further information, please contact:

The National Deaf Children's Society
Freephone helpline: 0808 800 8880 (voice and text)
Open 10 am–5 pm, Monday–Friday
Fax: 020 7251 5020
E-mail: helpline@ndcs.org.uk
Website: www.ndcs.org.uk

Down's syndrome

(Information provided by the Down's Syndrome Association)

Down's syndrome is the most common form of learning disability. It is caused by an accident before or around the time of conception, which gives rise to an extra number 21 chromosome in each of the person's cells. Instead of the usual 46 chromosomes, a person with Down's syndrome has 47 chromosomes. This results in a disruption of the growth of the developing embryo, and a degree of developmental delay in the child.

The presence of the extra chromosome also gives rise to a number of physical character-istics, which are often shared by people who have the condition. These include:

- short stature;

- eyes that slant upward and outward – the eyelids often have an extra fold of skin (epicanthic fold) which appears to exaggerate the slant (this does not mean there is anything wrong with the eyes – they just look different);

- small ears;

- short fingers;

- poor general muscle tone, although this tends to improve as the child grows.

The presence or absence of these characteristics bears no relation to the child's intellectual ability. It cannot be stressed enough that each child will have his or her own personality and traits of character, just like any other child.

Certain medical problems are more common among people with Down's syndrome than in the rest of the population. These include:

Hearing loss

Children with Down's syndrome are particularly prone to colds and often find them more difficult to 'shake off'. The Eustachian tubes, which connect the ear to the nose, can be particularly narrow in children with Down's syndrome and become easily blocked with mucus. This, in turn, can lead to middle ear infections (otitis media) and cause temporary deafness. Usually, when the cold gets better, the Eustachian tube clears and the mucus that caused the infection drains away.

Sometimes, however, a single infection, or repeated upper respiratory infections such as colds, or infected or enlarged adenoids, can cause more long-term obstruction of the middle ear space which never drains away. Glue ear, as this is known, can occur in all children, but is more frequent in children with Down's syndrome.

Vision problems

Many children with Down's syndrome also have a degree of visual impairment. As with other pupils who wear glasses, teachers must make sure that the child actually does wear them when necessary. Visually impaired children have a partial or total lack of vision in both eyes. Most Local Authorities employ advisory teachers for visually impaired students, and these specialists will be able to give guidance to teachers in mainstream schools. It is estimated that 75–80 per cent of classroom activities are based on vision, so a child who is visually disadvantaged will need considerable support.

Lack of muscle tone

Many babies with Down's syndrome have poor muscle tone and tend to be 'floppy' (hypotonic). In most cases, this characteristic reduced muscle tone improves as the child grows. However, in some children, it can contribute to a delay in acquiring fine and/or gross motor skills. This means that skills such as running, skipping, throwing and catching may cause a child with Down's syndrome more difficulty than the other children in the class, but there is nothing to prevent that child from acquiring these skills eventually. As with all children, the opportunity to practise these skills is necessary and it is important not to restrict such opportunities because the child is perceived to have certain limitations.

Poor muscle tone can also affect fine motor skills such as writing. Again, most children will eventually be able to write quite well, but may take longer to acquire such skills.

Heart defects

It is estimated that about 40 per cent of children born with Down's syndrome also have a heart defect. Such defects can range from relatively minor problems to severe malformations of the heart, which can require surgery and/or medication. Most children of school age who have an operable defect should already have undergone surgery. Successful treatment will allow the child to lead as active a life as he/she wants.

Speech and language problems

Nearly all children with Down's syndrome have significant delay in language acquisition and understanding. This is caused by a combination of factors, some of which are purely physical and some due to the overall developmental delay that usually accompanies the condition.

The main physical obstacle is the ratio of the size of the tongue to the size of the mouth. Many children with Down's syndrome have a small mouth cavity, which means that their tongue seems too big for their mouth. This, along with poor muscle tone in the tongue and mouth, can cause children varying degrees of difficulty in actually producing the sounds required for talking clearly.

Other speech and language problems of children with Down's syndrome stem from delayed understanding of language or difficulty in processing words. It is common for children with Down's syndrome to have problems with auditory short-term memory, which has limited capacity for storing and processing information they hear. This difficulty can sometimes make the child seem disobedient or stubborn when, in fact, he or she has been given too much information at once and is unable to process it. This can be helped in a number of ways, principally by breaking down information into smaller units which the child can deal with more easily, giving him or her time to process the information and respond. Speech and language therapists will be able to suggest strategies for improving any language problems.

Since the 1981 Education Act, the trend has been towards the integration of children with Down's syndrome into ordinary schools rather than special schools. However, a significant number of children with Down's syndrome are successfully placed in special schools and some will spend time in both.

The variance in the abilities of children with Down's syndrome means that they are as individual as other members of the population and should be assessed as such when a choice of school is made.

Dyscalculia

(Information supplied by Dr Steve Chinn, maths learning difficulties consultant)

With the publication (Butterworth, 2003) of Brian Butterworth's Screening Test for Dyscalculia and the inclusion of dyscalculia as a specific learning difficulty in the DfE (formerly DCSF) consultation document for the 2004 SEN census, dyscalculia became of interest to educators. This section sums up my thinking about dyscalculia as I try to make sense of all those factors that influence the maths learning outcomes of children and adults.

Dyscalculia is not a simple psychological construct. There are many reasons why a person may be bad at maths. It is unlikely that there are any instant or simple 'cures' because it is unlikely that there is a single reason behind the problem of the many, many people who fail to master maths and it is unlikely that all of the reasons are dyscalculic.

In order to start the debate I think we have to look at definitions, or at least descriptions, which can then be discussed and rewritten without the levels of academic aggression directed at dyslexia. This topic is in its infancy, being some 20 years behind our knowledge of language/dyslexia.

Definitions and labels

As a (lapsed) physicist I have a scientist's concept of what makes a definition. In physics one can control the variables and do pretty reliable experiments. People are difficult to control (especially as teenagers). In this respect I view some definitions as descriptions.

Here is a small sample of definitions. The first is from a DfE booklet (2001) on supporting pupils with dyslexia and dyscalculia in the National Numeracy Strategy (NNS).

> Dyscalculia is a condition that affects the ability to acquire mathematical skills. Dyscalculic learners may have difficulty understanding simple number concepts, lack an intuitive grasp of numbers, and have problems learning number facts and procedures. Even if they produce a correct answer or use a correct method, they may do so mechanically and without confidence.

> Very little is known about the prevalence of dyscalculia, its causes, or treatment. Purely dyscalculic learners who have difficulties only with numbers will have cognitive and language abilities in the normal range and may excel in non-mathematical subjects. It is more likely that difficulties with numeracy accompany the language difficulties of dyslexia.

The second definition dates from 1970 and is attributed to Kosc.

Developmental dyscalculia is a structural disorder of mathematical abilities which has its origin in a genetic or congenital disorder of those parts of the brain that are the direct anatomico-physiological substrate of the maturation of the mathematical abilities adequate to age, without a simultaneous disorder of general mental functions.

Sharma (1990) explains dyscalculia and acalculia as:

Dyscalculia refers to a disorder in the ability to do or to learn mathematics, ie, difficulty in number conceptualisation, understanding number relationships and difficulty in learning algorithms and applying them. (An irregular impairment of ability.)

Acalculia is the loss of fundamental processes of quantity and magnitude estimation. (A complete loss of the ability to count.)

What distinguishes dyscalculia from just problems with maths? What do we mean by 'problems with maths'? How big is the problem?

We don't know the answers to these three key questions. Obviously the answers will depend to a large extent on the definition. Many people have a 'difficulty' with maths. Like all skills, if you cease to practise you lose the skill, and few adults practise maths, especially a topic such as fractions or algebra, after leaving school. So the extent of the problem could well increase in adults. A study done in 1995 on behalf of the Basic Skills Agency on 1,714 adults aged 35 years found that just under one-quarter had very low numeracy skills at a level that would make it difficult to complete everyday tasks successfully. The consensus of opinion from papers suggest around 3–6 per cent of the population are dyscalculic.

Dyscalculia introduces another word into the vocabulary of special needs. Some see these words as labels and thus as descriptors of a person. That would not be helpful. At my former school, Mark College, an independent school for boys who have been diagnosed as dyslexic, the results for GCSE maths were significantly above national average. Usually at least 75 per cent of grades were at C and above, compared to the national average of around 50 per cent. Obviously I believe that if the teaching is appropriate, then a learning difficulty does not necessarily mean lack of achievement.

What is maths?

As for maths, well there is the maths you need for everyday life. This rarely includes algebra, fractions (other than ¼ and ½), coordinates or indeed much of what is taught in secondary schools. It does include a lot of money, measurement, some time and the occasional percentage. Take, as an example of a real-life maths exercise, paying for a family meal in a restaurant. It needs estimation skills, possibly accurate addition skills, subtraction skills if using cash, and percentage skills for the tip.

The Russian psychologist Krutetskii listed the components of mathematical ability that could act as a description of what a learner needs to be 'good at maths' and thus also act as a guide as to what may be the deficits that handicap the learner failing to be good at maths:

1. An ability to formalize maths material (to abstract oneself from concrete numerical relationships).

2. An ability to generalize and abstract oneself from the irrelevant.

3. An ability to operate with numerals and other symbols.

4. An ability for sequential segmented logical reasoning.

5. An ability to shorten the reasoning process.

6. An ability to reverse a mental process.

7. Flexibility of thought.

8. A mathematical memory.

9. An ability for spatial concepts.

It must be possible for a person to be good at some areas of maths and a failure in other topics. Would a learner have to fail in all topics to be dyscalculic?

In terms of subject content, early maths is mostly numbers. Later it becomes more varied with new topics introduced such as measure, algebra and spatial topics. Up to GCSE, despite the different headings, the major component remains number. So the demands of maths can appear quite broad, but number is the dominant part of early learning experiences. We have to consider the match between the demands of the task and the skills of the learner.

In terms of approach, maths can be a written subject or a mental exercise. It can be formulaic or it can be intuitive. It can be learned and communicated in either way or in a combination of ways by the learner, and it can be taught and communicated in either way or in a combination of ways by the teacher.

Maths can be concrete, but fairly quickly moves to the abstract and symbolic. It has many rules and a surprising number of inconsistencies.

In terms of judgement, feedback and appraisal, maths is quite unique as a school subject. Work is usually a blunt 'right' or 'wrong' and it has to be done quickly. This results in anxiety and attitude being more significant than in many other subjects.

Even on this brief overview it is obvious that the demands of maths are varied. The importance placed on speed of working could also be another key issue, as many special needs learners are slow processors.

Memory

I often pose the question in my lessons 'What does the learner bring to maths?' I am sure that short-term and working memory are vital for mental arithmetic, particularly for those sequential, formula-based maths thinkers. There is also a need for long-term, mathematical memory. However, if maths is taught as an exercise in memory, a significant number of children fail.

Counting on and on

The first number test on the Butterworth Dyscalculia Screener (Butterworth, 2003) is for subitizing. This means an ability to look at a random cluster of dots and know how many are there, without counting. Most adults do this at 6 plus or minus 1.

A person who has to rely entirely on counting for addition and subtraction is severely handicapped in terms of speed and accuracy. Such a person is even more handicapped when trying to use counting for multiplication and division. Often their page is covered in endless tally marks and often they are just lined up, not grouped as ++++, that is, in fives. Maths is done in counting steps of one. If you show them patterns of dots or groups, they prefer to see lines.

Good skills in numeracy are not just the ability to 'see' and use fives. It's the ability to see 9 as one less than 10, to see $6 + 5$ as $5 + 5 + 1$, to count on in twos, tens and fives, especially if the pattern is not the basic one of 10, 20, 30. . . but 13, 23, 33, 43. . ., to see the relationship between the four operations $(+, \times, -$ and $\div)$. It's the ability to go beyond counting in ones by seeing the patterns and relationships in numbers (Ashcroft and Chinn, 2003).

Garden variety or what?

How do we distinguish between a 'garden variety' poor reader and a dyslexic (Stanovich, 1991)? How do we distinguish between a 'garden variety' poor mathematician and a dyscalculic?

I think the answer has a lot to do with persistence of the difficulty in the face of skilled, varied and appropriate intervention.

Can you be a good reader and still be a dyslexic? Can you be good at some areas of maths and still be dyscalculic? My guess is that the answer to both questions is 'Yes', but for maths it is partly because maths is made up of topics, some of which make quite different demands (and for both questions, good appropriate teaching can make such a difference).

Teaching

Throughout my years of teaching and research I have developed a philosophy and range of practical processes for teaching dyslexic pupils (Chinn and Ashcroft, 1998; Chinn, 2004). I suspect that these will also be effective with dyscalculic pupils. Indeed, I have taught many pupils who have a combination of dyslexia and dyscalculia.

For a final thought in this section, I ask 'What is the influence of the style of the curriculum?' I know, for example, from a European study in which I was involved, that the design of the maths curriculum certainly affects thinking style in maths.

Back to definitions and descriptions

I have added some extra notes into the DfES (now DfE)/NNS definition, which may then be better seen as a description (and thus not a label).

> *Dyscalculia is a perseverant condition that affects the ability to acquire mathematical skills* despite appropriate instruction. *Dyscalculic learners may have difficulty understanding simple number concepts* (such as place value and the use of the four operations $+$, $-$, $\times$ and $\div$), *lack an intuitive grasp of numbers* (including the value of numbers and understanding and using interrelationship numbers), *and have problems learning, retrieving and using quickly number facts* (for example multiplication tables) *and procedures* (for example long division). *Even if they produce a correct answer or use a correct method, they may do so mechanically and without confidence* (and have no way of knowing or checking that the answer is correct).

The NNS definition focuses on number, which makes sense to me. It mentions memory and it includes those who present as competent in some areas, but whose performance has no underlying understanding of number. An addendum could list some of the key contributors, such as:

> *A learner's difficulties with maths may be exacerbated by anxiety, slow processing, poor short-term memory, inability to use and understand symbols, and inflexible learning style.*

Finally, there are many pupils out there who may present dyscalculic as young learners. It's what happens next that confirms or challenges that description.

References

Butterworth, B (2003) *The Dyscalculia Screener*, NFER-Nelson, London

Chinn, S (2004) *The Trouble with Maths: A practical guide to helping learners with numeracy difficulties*, RoutledgeFalmer, London

Chinn, S J and Ashcroft, J R (1992) in *Dyslexia and Mathematics,* 2nd edn, ed T R Miles and E Miles, RoutledgeFalmer, London

Chinn, S J and Ashcroft, J R (1998) *Mathematics for Dyslexics: A teaching handbook*, 2nd edition, Whurr Publishers Ltd, London

Chinn, S J and Ashcroft J R (2003) *Mathematics for Dyslexia and Dyscalculia*, 3rd edition, Wiley-Blackwell, London

Chinn, S J and Ashcroft, J R (2007) *Mathematics for Dyslexics: Including Dyscalculia*, 3rd edn, Wiley, Chichester

DCSF (2001) *The National Numeracy Strategy. Guidance to support pupils with dyslexia and dyscalculia*, DfES 0512/2001, London

Kosc, L (1970) *Psychology and psychopathology of mathematical abilities, Studia psychologica*, **12** 159–62

Kosc, L (1986) Dyscalculia, *Focus on Learning Problems in Mathematics*, **8** (3, 4)

Sharma, M (1990) Dyslexia, dyscalculia and some remedial perspectives for mathematics learning problems, *Math Notebook*, **8**, nos 7–10

Stanovich, K E (1991) The theoretical and practical consequences of discrepancy definitions of dyslexia, in *Dyslexia: Integrating theory and practice*, eds M Snowling and M Thomson, Whurr, London

Dyslexia

(Information supplied by Dyslexia Action)

Dyslexia causes difficulties in learning to read, write and spell. Short-term memory, mathematics, concentration, personal organization and sequencing may also be affected.

Dyslexia usually arises from a weakness in the processing of language-based information. Biological in origin, it tends to run in families, but environmental factors also contribute.

Dyslexia can occur at any level of intellectual ability. It is not the result of poor motivation, emotional disturbance, sensory impairment or lack of opportunities, but it may occur alongside any of these. The effects of dyslexia can be largely overcome by skilled specialist teaching and the use of compensatory strategies.

Tiny neurological differences in specific areas of the brain of dyslexic people create difficulties in processing information. Differences occur in lower levels, where sensory informa-tion is coming into the brain, and in higher levels, where languages and codes are being organized, sequenced and retrieved. Pre-school dyslexic children will often have difficulties with spoken language. They may be late in learning to talk and in learning common sequences, and may confuse sounds. Typically, at five years of age, dyslexic children will have problems with letter knowledge, in linking sounds with symbols and in blending letters. They are also likely to have difficulty in learning by heart such things as the months of the year and songs and rhymes, and in carrying out sequential activities like learning tables. They may become increasingly reluctant to go to school during the first few years, or may develop emotional or behavioural problems.

Unidentified early problems persist and become more complex as they undermine the learning process. Children with dyslexia are puzzling to their parents and to their teachers. Often they appear (because they are) much more able than their work suggests and occasionally it is only the more complex writing and comprehension tasks required at secondary school that expose the problems.

Dyslexia affects some people more severely than others, depending on the amount of neurological difference and the effectiveness of the support they receive. The greater the difference, the greater the help required. The later the condition is identified, the greater its impact is likely to be.

The effects of dyslexia can be alleviated by skilled specialist teaching and committed learning. All children benefit from well-structured, phonically based early learning at school, and from practice to make the learning permanent. For dyslexic children this type of teaching is essential, and because of their difficulties, a multi-sensory approach that integrates seeing, hearing and doing is critical to them. If by the age of six a child is failing to gain early reading, writing and spelling skills (or earlier if dyslexia exists in the family), a psychologist's assessment should be considered. An assessment by an experienced specialist teacher can be very valuable in the early years. The aim is to identify strengths and weaknesses and make recommendations for appropriate helping strategies.

The majority of dyslexic children can, and should, be educated in ordinary schools alongside their peers. They will benefit from specialist teaching to enable them to reach their full potential. Only a tiny minority with severe and complex problems, which are frequently exacerbated by other conditions such as attention deficit disorder or dyspraxia, need to be educated in specialist schools. The key is the quality of teaching by the specialist teacher. Wherever possible dyslexic children should be placed in schools that can nurture their latent talents, as they frequently have strong creative and lateral thinking abilities. If their education is well managed and they are prepared to work hard, they can, and do, succeed in a wide range of careers.

Dyspraxia

(Information supplied by the Dyspraxia Foundation)

The Dyspraxia Foundation defines dyspraxia as 'an impairment or immaturity of the organization of movement and, in many individuals, there may be associated problems with language, perception and thought'.

The term normally used is Developmental Dyspraxia or Developmental Co-ordination Disorder.

The condition is thought to affect up to 6 per cent of the population in varying degrees. It is probable that there is at least one dyspraxic child in every classroom requiring access to a specific treatment programme.

Symptoms are evident from an early age. Youngsters are generally irritable from birth and many exhibit significant feeding problems. They are slow to achieve expected developmental milestones, often not sitting independently by the age of eight months. Many fail to go through the crawling stage as babies, preferring to 'bottom shuffle' and then walk. Children with dyspraxia usually avoid tasks that require good manual dexterity and depend upon well-developed perceptual skills. Inset puzzles, Lego and jigsaws are difficult.

Between the ages of three and five, children with dyspraxia may demonstrate the following types of behaviour:

- Very high levels of motor activity, including feet swinging and tapping when seated, hand clapping or twisting and an inability to stay in one place for more than five minutes.

- High levels of excitability, with a loud/shrill voice. Children may be easily distressed and prone to temper tantrums.

- Awkward movement. Children may constantly bump into objects and fall over. Associated mirror movements, hands flap when running.

- Difficulty pedalling a tricycle or similar toy.

- Poor figure and ground awareness. Children may lack any sense of danger, illustrated, for example, by jumping from an inappropriate height.

- Continued messy eating. Children may spill liquid from drinking cups and prefer to eat with their fingers.

- Avoidance of constructional toys, such as jigsaws or building blocks.

- Poor fine motor skills, demonstrated by difficulty in holding a pencil or using scissors. Drawings may appear immature.

- Lack of imaginative play. Children may show little interest in 'dressing up' or playing appropriately in a home or Wendy House.

- Limited creative play.

- Isolation within the peer group. Rejected by peers, children may prefer adult company.

- Laterality still not established. Problems crossing the mid-line.

- Persistent language difficulties. Children are often referred to a speech therapist.

- Sensitivity to sensory stimulation, including high levels of noise, being touched or wearing new clothes.

- Limited response to verbal instruction. Children may exhibit a slower response time and have problems with comprehension.

- Limited concentration. Tasks are often left unfinished.

If the condition is not identified, problems can persist throughout school life, causing increasing frustration and a lowering of self-esteem.

Between the ages of five and seven, behaviour may include the following traits:

- problems adapting to a more structured school routine;

- difficulties with PE (Physical Education);

- slow at dressing and inability to tie shoe laces;

- barely legible handwriting;

- immature drawing and copying skills;

- limited concentration and poor listening skills;

- literal use of language;

- inability to remember more than two–three instructions;

- slow completion of class work;

- continued high levels of motor activity;

- motor stereotypes – hand flapping or clapping when excited;

- tendency to become easily distressed and emotional;

- problems coordinating a knife and fork;

- inability to form relationships with other youngsters, isolation in class;

- sleeping difficulties, including wakefulness at night and nightmares;

- reporting of physical symptoms, such as migraine, headaches or feeling sick.

Poor handwriting is one of the most common symptoms of dyspraxia, and as the child progresses through the education system, requirement for written work increases. By the age of about eight or nine the children may have become disaffected and poor school attendance is much in evidence in secondary education.

With access to appropriate treatment, the majority of dyspraxic youngsters can have their needs accommodated within a mainstream setting.

Parents concerned about their children should refer to their GP or health visitor if the child is aged under five or to the special needs coordinator if the child is in full-time schooling. A referral may then be made to an outside professional, for example a paediatrician, educational psychologist, physiotherapist, occupational therapist or speech therapist for assessment.

When an appointment has been made, write down all your concerns. In an unfamiliar setting your child may not behave in the expected manner or give sufficient attention to the tasks set. Assessment usually involves giving a detailed account of your child's developmental history, examination of gross and fine motor skills, and a test of intellectual ability.

Treatment is available from specialists in health and education when the condition has been identified. Movement programmes may be offered by therapists and additional support can be made available in school.

If you require further information about dyspraxia or how to help your child, contact the Dyspraxia Foundation, 8 West Alley, Hitchin, Herts SG5 1EG; tel: 01462 454986, website: www.dyspraxiafoundation.org.uk.

Epilepsy

(Information supplied by Epilepsy Action)

Epilepsy is defined as a tendency to have recurrent seizures (sometimes called fits). A seizure is caused by a sudden burst of excess electrical activity in the brain, causing a temporary disruption in the normal message passing between brain cells. This disruption results in the brain's messages becoming halted or mixed up.

The brain is responsible for all the functions of the body, so what is experienced during a seizure will depend on where in the brain the epileptic activity begins and how widely and rapidly it spreads. For this reason, there are many different types of seizure and each person will experience epilepsy in a way that is unique to them.

Epilepsy can begin at any age, but the incidence is higher in childhood. Sometimes the reason epilepsy develops is clear. It could be because of brain damage caused by a difficult birth, a severe blow to the head, a stroke which starves the brain of oxygen, or an infection of the brain such as meningitis. Epilepsy with a known cause is called 'symptomatic' epilepsy. For most people there is no known cause and this is called 'idiopathic' epilepsy.

Children with uncomplicated epilepsy (without additional learning difficulties or physical disabilities) have the same range of intelligence and abilities as children without epilepsy. Many children with the condition are educated in mainstream schools, usually without additional educational support. However, some young people experience behavioural problems and/or learning difficulties. Behavioural problems and learning difficulties in children with epilepsy can have many different causes, including the following.

- The severity of the epilepsy. If seizures are occurring frequently a child's everyday life may be affected.

- Any damage to the brain could cause a number of symptoms. These can include seizures, learning difficulties and behavioural problems.

- The area of the brain in which epileptic activity is occurring. For example, if it is in the part of the brain concerned with memory, then learning difficulties may be experienced.

- The type of seizure. For example, when someone is experiencing a complex partial seizure they may appear to others as if their behaviour is strange or abnormal.

- Sub-clinical seizure activity. This refers to continuous epileptic activity which disrupts brain activity, without a seizure happening. This type of activity is quite rare. It can impair the brain's ability to process, although the child might appear not to be affected.

- The duration of seizures. Prolonged seizure activity may be accompanied by confusion, inappropriate behaviour etc.

- Anti-epileptic medication. Some anti-epileptic drugs can have a negative effect on a child's behaviour.

- Psychological and social factors, such as family and peer attitudes as well as self-image.

There is also research that suggests that some children with epilepsy experience learning difficulties in specific subject areas, most notably mathematics and reading. The educational psychologist has a role to play in suggesting ways that these can be overcome in order for the child to achieve their full potential.

Some children with severe epilepsy may need to attend a special school. There are very few schools that specifically cater for children with epilepsy. However, schools in this category include The National Centre for Young People with Epilepsy (NCYPE), St Piers Lane, Surrey, tel: 01342 832243; St Elizabeth's School, Herts, tel: 01279 844270; and the David Lewis School, Cheshire, tel: 01565 640066.

Further information about epilepsy and education can be obtained from Epilepsy Action's epilepsy Helpline, freephone: 0808 800 5050, e-mail: helpline@epilepsy.org.uk, text: 07797 805390 or from our website: www.epilepsy.org.uk.

Gifted children and high ability

(Information provided by the National Association for Gifted Children)

Giftedness should not be seen as a property present in a few children but absent from the many; it is broadly the upper 10 per cent of the ability spectrum. However, it is possible that within the top 2 per cent there are individuals whose rapid development can dissociate them from their peers, socially, academically and intellectually. The *challenge of gifted children* is that of creating learning opportunities appropriate to their ability, age and maturity while at the same time supporting them emotionally and socially within their peer structure. For this to be successful parents and teachers need to work in partnership.

The first issue must be identifying the child who has unusual abilities. Growing knowledge of the brain's complexity and increasing understanding of how learning takes place has led to less reliance being placed on measures that put groups of children in order, high to low. Describing human ability by a single measurement such as a quotient or a score is now seen as simplistic. At least 80 working definitions of giftedness and high ability were developed during the 20th century; each created with its own defined purpose. These include selecting adults for particular high-level tasks, selecting students to attend enrichment programmes, diagnosing reasons for particular pupil behaviours and assessing progress. Hence, for the identification of highly able children there is no one all-embracing definition of what giftedness is, and there are many strategies and diagnostic tests that can be used and that vary across the age range.

Identification

Some parents will have been sorely tested by the insatiable curiosity of their very young child.

For children in the pre-school phase, parents are the people best-placed to observe whether they are developing skills and talents significantly in advance of their peers. Early talking, unusual levels of concentration, and the ability to make creative connections of ideas are good indicators. Parents may encounter problems at toddler group, playgroup or pre-school nursery because staff do not recognize that the child can easily do the things the other children are enjoying doing and so is quickly bored and becomes behaviourally challenging. This should best be managed by discussion between parents and staff as to how adaptable the activities can be.

Once at school some aspects change but others do not. The child is now of an age when an educational assessment can give added professional insight. But as giftedness or high ability does not legally fall in the category of educational special needs, there are limited additional resources available for a child assessed as highly able. If issues have developed, if the child does not want to go to school, is bored at school, is unhappy or has become withdrawn, then parents need to work in partnership with the school, the class teacher and the Head to expose the issues in a non-confrontational way. The appropriateness and purpose of an assessment can then be discussed. A case for a LA assessment might be made if behaviour difficulties have developed. If parents are willing to have a private assessment undertaken, then this is best done with the full knowledge of the school and an understanding of what will happen in the school as a result of the findings.

If, after discussions with the school, parents feel that they need to know more about how they can manage their child, but the school is not willing to proceed, they can still undertake a private assessment. This will provide the parents with additional information about their child's intellectual ability and potential. Parents can then make an informed decision on the way forward, accepting that this may be limited by the school's position.

Schools should have a written policy on how they manage their most able children and it should be openly available on request. It should include how children are identified and what measures are put in place to stretch and challenge them. The policy should have the full support of the staff, the governors and parents.

Identifying older children as having unrecognized abilities, gifts and talents is always a sad occurrence, for it represents a waste of earlier opportunities. If the abilities are not recognized and encouraged early, there is the risk that the child will become withdrawn, or will merge into the crowd, or will develop a disruptive pattern of behaviour, all of which would detract attention from his or her ability that may go on undetected for many years. It is often when schools undertake a formal assessment on the basis of poor behaviour that the truth is revealed – the child is a high-ability low performer!

Providing the learning for highly able children

Once identified, the highly able child needs challenging learning experiences. The roles of parents and of schools are of equal importance in building this provision. Through parents the child has access to evening, weekend and holiday time activities, and so can be involved with a wide range of ages and expertise that is not found within the school system. This helps to ground the child's emotional and social development.

How learning experiences are managed within school will depend on the child's age as well as the Key Stage of the National Curriculum and the resources available in the school. Teachers in primary schools are used to managing groups of children of widely different abilities, can plan individual extension or enrichment activities for every lesson for the gifted child and can involve him/her in determining appropriate enrichment activities. Where the curriculum allows it, the child can work with other staff or older classes on agreed activities, always remembering that what can happen easily one year may be difficult to secure the next. For some parents the easy solution would appear to be to accelerate the child one or two years. This needs to be viewed with the utmost caution, for older children can be hostile to a younger child being joined to their peer group and also because there are major issues to be faced at the transition from Primary to Secondary phase.

The structure of the secondary school gives additional scope for differentiating the curriculum and locating pupils in ability sets, but the highly able child still needs to have enrichment activities built into each lesson. The strategies available to a school depend on its unique circumstances, but much good practice has been built up over recent years. Besides a 'Gifted and Talented' policy, schools are expected to have a G and T coordinator, and school inspectors expect that there will be evidence that shows that the policy is working. There has been an ongoing series of Government-sponsored projects aimed at enriching the learning experiences of the most able pupils and more information about these can be found on the National Association for Gifted Children's website at www.nagcbritain.org.uk or from the NAGC helpline (tel: 0845 450 0221).

Information on Excellence in Cities and Excellence Clusters is also available from the DCSF website (www.dcsf.gov.uk), which gives the most up-to-date information. These projects are not universal but are targeted on areas of specific educational need. Every state school is expected to have a Gifted Coordinator and a direct approach to the school is needed to make contact with them. In addition, most LAs have an officer who carries a direct responsibility for Gifted and Talented education, and a telephone call to the Local Education Office will reveal who this is.

The British Psychological Society (tel: 0116 254 9568; www.bps.org.uk) publishes lists of chartered psychologists who are able to carry out private educational assessments. You can obtain a leaflet with guidance on how to choose an Educational Psychologist from the NAGC (tel: 0845 450 0221).

Loss of, or damage to, limbs

(Information supplied by the Royal Association for Disability and Rehabilitation)

Children may be born without a limb or part of one (limb deficiency), or they may lose all or part of a limb as a result of an accident, or through medical necessity (amputation).

Artificial limbs (prostheses) are usually provided for young children, both to encourage development of strength in the muscles and patterns of movement and, perhaps most importantly, to encourage independence. Learning to use artificial limbs is self-evidently not a natural process and takes time and practice, according to the motivation and skills of each child. Some may need encouragement, while others may need help to prevent them being too ambitious. For children born with digits missing or who have a partial hand, prostheses are not available or appropriate.

Staff will need to be aware of a child's needs before he or she starts school. Parents will be able to advise on the medical aspects of the limb loss and in most instances a child will be able to explain his or her own needs, eg how he or she operates the arm, what he or she can and cannot do and how much help might be needed. It is important for a pupil to be given the opportunity to say when he or she prefers to wear or remove the artificial limb, for example for PE, or during hot weather when the residual limb may become uncomfortably hot in the prosthesis.

A child who is fitted with a prosthesis will be in regular contact with a prosthesist, who will be able to advise on any problems in using the prosthesis, or in new tasks to be learned. As children grow, prostheses need to be replaced regularly. If the child has had an amputation, he or she may need surgery from time to time to check the growth of the residual limb.

There are no learning difficulties specifically associated with limb deficiency or amputa-tion. However, teachers may have to seek extra time for students sitting examinations if it is considered that the student's writing speed is affected by the limb loss. Written forms of language can be produced on typewriters, personal computers or a voice-activated computer system, and access to word-processing can be tailored to the requirements of the pupil. Other solutions include accessing the word processor via single or multiple switches, which may be in the form of rollerballs or joysticks.

The artificial arms usually supplied to children are made from metal or plastic and have a grasp mechanism. They are normally covered in foam and toning plastic to improve the appearance. With practice pupils develop the skills needed to use the arm and grasp mechanism. Most children do not learn to write with their artificial arm. Some prefer to use their own ways of managing instead of, or as well as, using an artificial arm. A pupil's preference is important but it is also advisable to check with the parents, prosthesist and/or occupational therapist to ensure a consistent approach.

Children with no upper limbs who do not use artificial arms have to learn methods of managing their own personal needs. Initially they may require assistance, but with time many of them develop the skills needed to be fully independent. Children who have lost one or both legs, above or below the knee, will be able to use artificial limbs, but are still likely to have some mobility difficulties. Some may use sticks or crutches and some may use a wheelchair. Mobility needs should be taken into account when considering emergency procedures.

Children who have limb deficiency should be encouraged to take part in PE as far as possible. Physical fitness is as important for these pupils as for all others. Children will often develop strategies for participating within their limits but may need encouragement. If advice is needed, a physiotherapist will be able to help. If the child chooses to participate without the artificial limb, it is important it is stored safely and securely. If the limb is hidden as a prank, this can be very distressing for the child.

Children who lose a limb following an accident or through medical necessity often find it difficult to adjust to their impairment and changed body image. They, their parents and possibly siblings may need counselling to help them work through the emotional stress of the loss of a limb. Emotional stress is an almost universal experience among amputees, their families and carers.

Any child who is physically 'different' is at risk of being teased. It may be helpful to ensure that the child concerned has a simple explanation and is ready to satisfy the curiosity of his or her peers. A matter-of-fact attitude on the part of the adults will help to reduce any embarrassment felt by a pupil and his or her peer group.

Good communication between parents, professionals and the pupil must be encouraged to ensure proper resources are in place. The expertise of parents and pupil should be utilized, and inter-agency collaboration will help smooth the way for the pupil's academic and social development. The transition from school to adult life can often be a stressful time and the process of transitional planning is therefore essential.

Further information is available from:

The National Coordinator
REACH – Association for Children with Hand or Arm Deficiency
PO Box 54
Helston
Cornwall
TR13 8WD
Tel: 0845 130 6225

Limbless Association
Roehampton Rehabilitation Centre
Roehampton Lane
London
SW15 5PR
Tel: 020 8788 1777

Muscular dystrophy

(Information supplied by the Muscular Dystrophy Campaign)

Muscular dystrophy (MD) is a name given to many different conditions that have in common the breakdown of muscle fibres, leading to weak and wasted muscles. More than 60,000 children and adults in the UK have MD or a related neuromuscular condition. A further 300,000 people in the UK are indirectly affected as relations or carers.

Each of these neuromuscular conditions has a different cause; they are mostly genetic, but some are autoimmune (where a person's immune system attacks healthy cells within the body itself). Symptoms of some disorders show very early on, even at birth, but in others symptoms may only start to show later in childhood or adulthood. Severity is variable: several conditions are very disabling or life-threatening; the rest can cause moderate or mild disability. Most of the conditions cause progressive weakening of the muscles but some remain stable. Different conditions affect different muscles and various other body systems. The inheritance risks vary. There can also be a wide variation in the degree of severity not only between one type of dystrophy and another but also between individuals with the same type.

In some conditions, particularly Duchenne muscular dystrophy (DMD) and myotonic dystrophy, some individuals may have a degree of intellectual impairment. This may be reflected particularly in poor reading ability, word comprehension and memory skills. This intellectual impairment is not directly related to muscle weakness, however, and is not progressive.

Children's educational needs depend, of course, on the individual concerned and the nature of their condition and disability. Some children may need to attend special schools but many will be able to continue with mainstream schooling right through to college or university. Help needed within school will also vary widely, depending on the physical limitations of the individual. Many children with a significant disability will need a great deal of support.

Some conditions also have other complications which need to be carefully monitored, such as heart and breathing problems and allergy to anaesthesia. Muscle weakness can also cause additional mobility problems such as contractures (tightening of joints) and scoliosis (curvature of the spine).

Anyone can be affected by these conditions. They are usually inherited from the parent(s) but can appear out of the blue, in a family with no history of the condition. Males and/or females can be affected, depending on the genetic cause of the condition. For example, DMD is usually inherited from the mother by the son. Apart from very rare exceptions females are the only carriers of DMD and can themselves be manifesting carriers. In myotonic dystrophy either the mother or the father is affected and can pass the gene on. In spinal muscular atrophy neither parent is affected but both must carry the faulty gene for it to be passed on to their children. The conditions are not infectious.

It is not possible to 'catch' muscular dystrophy or any of the related conditions. However, if someone is found to be affected, their relatives might also have the condition because the disrupted gene may run in the family.

Although there are as yet no treatments or cures available for the majority, physiotherapy is helpful and symptoms can be alleviated through careful management. However, it is possible to treat the symptoms of myotonia congenita effectively. Immunological treatment is possible for polymyositis, dermatomyositis, myasthenia gravis and other immunological neuromuscular conditions. These treatments may involve the use of immunosuppressive drugs such as steroids, plasma exchange and intravenous immunoglobin.

Researchers are trying to find treatments and cures for other conditions. Where the cause is genetic, identification of the genetic fault is the first vital step towards understanding the condition and then finding a treatment. Muscular Dystrophy Campaign researchers are at the forefront of international research; they already know the genetic faults responsible for several conditions and are investigating several possible treatments.

Guidance for primary and secondary schools entitled 'Inclusive education for children with muscular dystrophy and other neuromuscular conditions' is available from the Muscular Dystrophy Campaign, 61 Southwark Street, London SE1 0HL; tel: 020 7803 4800; freephone: 0800 652 6352; e-mail: info@muscular-dystrophy.org; website: www.muscular-dystrophy.org.

Speech and language difficulties

(Information supplied by Afasic)

The ability to use language and communicate effectively is the basis of all learning and social interaction. Without these skills, education would not achieve its goals. It follows that the development of language and communication skills is central to all education.

The vast majority of children with special educational needs have one or other kind of communication difficulty. There is also a group of children who do not develop language skills normally, irrespective of any obvious intellectual or physical disability. These children are often said to have a specific or primary speech or language impairment, which may be in isolation or alongside another disability.

It is estimated that 1 in 500 school-age children will have severe long-term impairments, while at least 6 per cent will experience some degree of difficulty at some time that could interfere with their educational progress.

Characteristics

Some children are unable to understand or express themselves clearly, while others have near normal understanding but experience difficulty in speaking intelligibly. Some may not be able to form words and sentences correctly, have limited vocabulary, may produce strings of unintelligible sounds or repeat spoken language correctly without knowing the meaning of what they are saying. Some will have difficulty with the beginnings and endings of words. Others may display 'autistic tendencies'.

Identification of difficulties

Any of the following can be an indication of a language impairment:

● late onset of speech;

- a discrepancy between verbal and non-verbal skills or between receptive and expressive language;

- lack of concentration;

- history of 'glue-ear';

- difficulty with fine and/or gross motor skills;

- poor short-term memory;

- word-finding difficulties;

- poor interaction with peers.

As language skills develop very rapidly in the early years, much is gained if difficulties are identified as early as possible. Two to three years of age is not too early. Where help is provided at this age, a child is often able to join a mainstream school at five years of age. If the difficulties are not tackled in the early years, and the child struggles through primary schooling, difficulties can be seriously compounded by the time secondary age is reached. In a mainstream school the child is unlikely to be able to master the necessary conceptual understanding and complex social interactions expected in such a setting and may well become confused, disorientated, suffer emotional stress and succumb to bullying. Special schooling is then likely to be the only way to begin to provide effective help.

Assessment of difficulties

If there is cause for concern and a speech and language therapist has not already been seen, referral should be arranged following discussion with the parent(s). It is obviously important to identify a child's particular strengths and weaknesses at the first possible opportunity. Speech and language therapists have the skills to undertake such an assessment and to advise how any weakness may be overcome. Where a child's difficulties are particularly severe it is likely that a full assessment has taken place, or is under way, and that a statement has been drawn up.

Ways to help

Those with severe difficulties are best helped in a special school or language unit or class, with teachers and speech and language therapists working very closely in partnership. In the latter, intensive language work can take place with integration into the host school as and when appropriate. There are about 400 such units throughout the country, but few, as yet, are available for secondary-aged pupils.

Even where difficulties are not said to be severe, input from a speech and language therapist is recommended, as different approaches and programmes can be discussed, the most appropriate selected and queries clarified. Advice from an occupational therapist and/or physiotherapist should be sought for those with coordination difficulties.

Because these children do not acquire language spontaneously as others do, they need to be taught appropriate skills in a structured setting.

- A planned approach should be used to teach speaking and listening skills and reading and writing for all pupils.

- Activities should encourage the development of turn-taking, rhythms and rhyme, and the building up of self-esteem and confidence.

- Where a child has difficulty in learning the order of a task, it helps to structure the sequence of skills and to simplify each step.

- The use of computers and a combination of sight, sound, touch or movement can be valuable.

- Small group work (four–eight pupils) is essential to achieve National Curriculum targets successfully.

- Social skills and the use of social or functional language must be developed.

It can be especially helpful to relate work to a child's own interests or family.

For further information please send a stamped, addressed envelope to Afasic, 2nd Floor, 50–52 Great Sutton Street, London EC1V ODJ.

Spina bifida and/or hydrocephalus

(Information supplied by the Association for Spina Bifida and Hydrocephalus)

What is spina bifida?

Spina bifida is a congenital condition that affects babies very early in pregnancy. It is a fault in the development of the spine, when one or more vertebrae fail to close properly. Spina bifida usually affects the lower limbs, where there may be a lack of sensation of pain and temperature and perhaps problems with circulation. Many people with spina bifida will have continence problems, which need to be managed effectively if self-image is not to be damaged.

What is hydrocephalus?

Hydrocephalus happens when the fluid in the brain cannot drain away into the bloodstream because the pathways are blocked. The excess pressure must be relieved quickly to minimize damage.

New drainage pathways are opened, either by inserting a fine tube (called a shunt) inside a space in the brain or by making a small hole in the floor of one of these spaces. This operation is called a ventriculostomy.

Many people with spina bifida also have hydrocephalus, but it can occur by itself, especially in babies born prematurely, or after meningitis, a head injury or stroke.

Hydrocephalus may affect motor skills, vision, speech and language, and behaviour.

Neither spina bifida nor hydrocephalus is associated with any particular level of general intelligence.

Educational issues for children with spina bifida and/or hydrocephalus

Time off in hospital

Children with spina bifida and/or hydrocephalus may require repeated admission to hospital or hospital visits as out-patients. During prolonged stays in hospital, arrangements will probably need to be made for formal education to be continued.

Physical access

Consideration must be given to access issues, especially wheelchair access, or access to the curriculum through specialist equipment or classroom assistance before a child starts at a particular school. Accessible toilet facilities may also be necessary. For pupils with spina bifida who manage their own continence, or need assistance with this, the privacy of toilet facilities must also be considered.

Learning

Hydrocephalus, whether it has or has not been shunted, may affect 1) a child's co-ordination and visual-spatial perception, 2) short-term memory, concentration and the ability to solve problems, and to conceptualize, and 3) social and emotional development and peer relationships.

1. Coordination and perception

Some children appear to be clumsy and have balance problems. Many tire very easily. Hand–eye coordination may be poor, and there is often a weak handgrip.

Visuo-spatial perception may be affected, resulting in a distorted view of the world. There may, for instance, be difficulty in distinguishing between a step and a line drawn on the ground. Many children have squints, some may have tunnel vision, or nystagmus. Work in mathematics, especially abstract concepts, and geography may be affected.

Careful observation is needed to identify ways in which visual problems (squints, tunnel vision) may be affecting children's performance, eg in copying from the board and organizing their belongings, as they may have poor organizational skills.

Help and understanding may be needed in the following situations:

- walking long distances and walking up and down stairs;

- colouring-in and hand-writing; using scissors and other tools; fastening buttons; tying laces;

- moving in crowded spaces without bumping into furniture or other people;

- 'finding' objects that are mixed up with other objects, interpreting diagrams and maps;

- noticing things on their desk/table that are immediately in front or to one side;

- 'tuning in' to one voice, against a background of chatter and hypersensitivity to noises like clapping, laughter or lawn mowers.

2. Memory, problem-solving and conceptualization

Long-term memory for details of events is usually very good. However, many children have short-term memory problems, especially in retaining spoken words long enough to understand what they mean. The perceived 'verbal' ability of many children can lead others to presume that they understand the instructions and conversations when this may not be so. Most children will have short concentration spans. Many will have problems in self-correcting, expressing observations and giving explanations, and these children will find it difficult to 'make connections' between different items of information. Most children will need extra time and help to learn new ideas, and to develop the thinking strategies they need to deal with unfamiliar information.

Again for some children, some abilities can improve if appropriate experiences are provided. However, unless they are also helped to recognize their own competencies and what is expected of them, many will still experience a great deal of anxiety in relatively unfamiliar situations, which may include formal tests.

Help and understanding may be needed in the following situations:

- concentrating on tasks, and self-monitoring;

- switching from one activity to another;

- finding their way in an unfamiliar environment;

- understanding and remembering verbal instructions;

- giving clear accounts – there can be a tendency to focus on isolated, unconnected details;

- self-organization – where to start, what to do next;

- problem-solving – reluctance to engage in 'difficult' work without help;

- thinking ahead – a tendency to act or speak before they think.

3. Social and emotional behaviour

Hydrocephalus is sometimes linked with developmental delay in physical development in infancy and also in language development.

Although some children with hydrocephalus are very 'sociable', they may have problems in adjusting their own behaviour to different social contexts. Some can tend to treat everyone as a 'friend'. Some may be very shy, or overly domineering with their peers. Lack of self-esteem is common and some people become withdrawn and depressed, while others show challenging behaviours.

Children with hydrocephalus can be helped to learn social skills and have more confidence in themselves, and the chances of this teaching being effective are greater if begun before the beginning of Key Stage 2.

Help may be needed to develop skills in the following areas:

- self-inhibition, eg learning to wait their turn to speak;

- addressing different people in appropriate ways;

- peer relationships;

- anticipating unfamiliar situations;

- participating in family and classroom chores;

- initiation of discussion.

Support in mainstream schools

Open and trusting relationships between parents and teachers are essential, as is a problem-solving approach to any perceived difficulties.

Good school–home partnerships will ensure that information relating to possible medical problems and physical difficulties is shared and understood, and that the 'strategies' to be used to solve behavioural problems are consistent. Behavioural problems may be evident in school but not at home, and vice versa. It is important not to attribute blame in either context. No strategy will succeed unless the child is also involved.

If learning support assistant time is available in class, target it on developing the skills the children will need to work and socialize independently. Independent skills should be encouraged; eg as children develop the ability to listen to whole-class instructions and carry them out, the assistant may begin to use prompts instead of repeating the whole instructions on a one-to-one basis.

Make a point of observing and noting the outcomes of the approaches that are used, and to modify them as necessary after discussions. If the children can begin to think positively about the skills and knowledge they are developing, this will provide the confidence for more difficult tasks.

ASBAH produces books titled *Hydrocephalus and You* and *Your Child and Hydrocephalus*. These are available from: Helpline and Information, ASBAH House, 42 Park Road, Peterborough PE1 2UQ; tel/helpline: 0845 450 7755, e-mail: info@asbah.org, website: www.asbah.org.

Visual impairment

(Information supplied by the Royal National Institute for the Blind)

There are an estimated 25,000 blind and partially sighted children and young people under the age of 16 in the UK today. Approaching 50 per cent of this number have additional sensory, physical or learning needs that affect their education.

While visual impairment is a 'low-incidence' disability with only about two children in every thousand being blind or partially sighted, these children have very individual and important information and support needs.

Although a few children have no sight at all, most have some vision. For example, some can tell the difference between light and dark, some have central vision and can only see things in front of them, while others can see objects to one side but are unable to see the detail of things directly in front of them.

Some children see everything as a vague blur, others as a patchwork of blanks and defined areas. Some see better in bright light, some when it is darker, others find it difficult to adjust between light and dark.

Some children's vision is affected not by a problem with the eyes themselves, but with the processing of visual information in the brain. This is known as cerebral visual impairment (CVI) and can make it difficult for children to interpret and understand what they are seeing. Ongoing functional vision assessment (observing the child's response to different visual stimuli) can be helpful in understanding the impact of CVI on a child's ability to see.

Children who are blind or partially sighted but have no other significant additional needs

The majority of blind and partially sighted children whose main disability is visual impairment attend mainstream schools. For most of these children, inclusion will be appropriate throughout their education.

Whilst mainstream education for blind and partially sighted children is now the norm, some may need a certain level of special school education. A small number of specialist schools cater specifically for blind and partially sighted children. However, of the blind and partially sighted children who attend special schools, most attend local authority special schools that cater for diverse ranges of special educational need and disability.

Each child should be assessed as soon as possible so that the level of educational support needed can be planned in conjunction with the local authority (LA) visual impairment specialist. RNIB can provide names of LA visual impairment specialists and also offers a wide variety of assessment services.

Whether in a mainstream or special school, a child with a visual impairment will need some specialized materials, equipment, or adaptations to the resources and materials used by their fully sighted peers. This is required in order to maximize their learning potential and to provide access to the National Curriculum.

Children with some residual vision may be able to use enlarged materials, whether enlarged on a photocopier or specially printed in a larger print size. All examination boards provide pre-enlarged exam papers, and all Key Stage test papers are available in both enlarged and modified enlarged formats. Many diagrams, maps, photos and pictures in learning materials will need to be simplified or presented in an alternative way for children with sight problems.

If visual impairment prevents children from reading enlarged print, they may learn to read and write braille and may also make extensive use of audio material. In addition there are organizations, including RNIB, which can offer advice and information on a range of access technology solutions. Examples include:

- a closed-circuit television (CCTV). This enables a student to place a regular piece of print underneath a small moving camera, while the CCTV shows the enlarged print on a monitor. The student can then move the camera across a page and read a whole page of standard print;

- computer packages that can convert words on a computer screen into synthesized speech, and read computer files back to a blind or partially sighted student;

- devices that can be attached to a computer and allow the user to have a braille display of what is on the computer screen;

- packages that can convert computer text into a braille printout;

- portable braille note-takers, which allow individuals to braille information into a small machine and retrieve it later by connecting it to a computer. Print copies can then be produced for a sighted teacher.

RNIB offers advice, in-service training, curriculum advice and support and help in setting up new inclusion schemes to LA staff. For individual schools and pupils, RNIB has facilities for trying out special equipment and can help with particular aspects of the curriculum. For more information, visit rnib.org.uk/curriculum.

The decision on what type of school is appropriate depends on many factors and not just the extent of a child's vision or how well he or she uses this. The ability of a school to include a child socially is as important as meeting their educational needs within the national curriculum.

Blind and partially sighted children with additional needs

Owing to the range of causes of visual impairment, approximately 50 per cent of children with a sight problem may also have a hearing impairment, learning difficulty, physical difficulty or a combination of impairments.

A full multidisciplinary assessment of all of the child's educational needs will determine whether a special or mainstream school is most appropriate. It is very important that the LA visual impairment teaching service is included in this assessment process.

Most children with complex needs and visual impairment go to special schools within their local authority. In exceptional circumstances, however, children sometimes attend residential schools further from home. Each local authority has its own approach to educating children with sight problems and complex needs.

There are a small number of special schools for blind and partially sighted children with additional needs, including two RNIB schools.

Technology is also used extensively with blind and partially sighted children with additional needs, particularly in the form of multi-sensory rooms using lights and sounds to stimulate the child. Touch screens, communication aids with adapted tactile access and switch technology can also help develop communication skills and provide access to the National Curriculum.

A large number of books, DVDs and factsheets have been published by RNIB and others about the education of blind and partially sighted children, many of which are available from RNIB. For details of any aspect of the education of a blind or partially sighted child, including the services mentioned above, please contact the RNIB Helpline Telephone: 0303 123 9999 or e-mail: children@rnib.org.uk.

The Special Educational Needs Code of Practice

John Friel, Barrister-at-law, Gray's Inn

The Special Educational Needs (SEN) Code of Practice was introduced as part of a substantial reform by the 1993 Education Act. For parents of children with special educational needs, the 1993 Act gave both parents and children new specific rights, including rights of appeal. Alongside those rights of appeal was the Code of Practice, which provided guidance to all schools. The initial Code, to be used by parents and all concerned, was issued in 1994. It was replaced by a revised Code of Practice in November 2001.

The 1996 Education Act clarified previous Education Acts, but has now been subject to later variations. These include the Learning Skills Act 2000 and the Special Educational Needs and Disability Discrimination Act 2001.

The purpose of the Code of Practice is to give practical guidance on the discharge of functions in relation to children with special educational needs (under the Education Act 1996), to LAs, governing bodies of all maintained schools, teachers, parents and all interested parties. The Code sets out guidance on policies and procedures aimed at enabling pupils with special educational needs to reach their full potential.

The Code makes it clear that the vast majority of children will be assisted in a mainstream setting. In addition, some children at some time will require further help from SEN services and other agencies.

A small minority of children who have special educational needs of a severe or complex nature will need Statements. The basic intention behind the Code is to set out guidelines in order to ascertain:

- whether children have special educational needs;
- whether they require special educational provision;
- if so at what level;
- and if a Statement is eventually or immediately necessary, provide guidance on this issue.

Editor's note: A nationwide consultation on approaches to special educational needs and disability began in 2011, which could affect legislation and/or the Code of Practice. Although it is unlikely that such changes will take effect before the publication of the next edition (18th) we would like to note that any that do will not be reflected in the editorial of this 17th edition. For further details on the consultation please visit www.education.gov.uk/schools/pupilsupport/sen.

Principles of the Code of Practice

The Code is intended to help schools and LAs obtain the best value from the considerable resources and expertise they invest in helping children with special educational needs. It considers the rights and duties introduced by the 2001 Act and Regulations, as well as the Learning Skills Act 2000.

Fundamental principles

The general principles are that:

- Children with special educational needs should have their needs met.

- The special educational needs of children will normally be met in mainstream schools or settings.

- The view of the child should be sought and taken into account.

- Parents have a vital role to play in supporting a child's education.

- Children with special educational needs should be offered full access to a broad, balanced and relevant education, including an appropriate curriculum at foundation stage and the National Curriculum.

The Code sets out a number of critical success factors, which are as follows:

- All resources in a school setting should be managed and deployed to ensure that all children's needs are met.

- LA schools and settings should work together to ensure that any child's special educational needs are identified early.

- LA schools and settings should exploit best practice when devising their interventions.

- The wishes of the child concerned should be taken into account in the light of his or her age and understanding.

- Parents and professionals should work in partnership.

- The views of individual parents should be taken into account.

- Interventions for each child should be reviewed regularly and assessed for their impact and effectiveness.

- There should be close cooperation between all relevant agencies together with a multidisciplinary approach.

- LAs should meet the prescribed time limits set out in the Regulations.

● Where children require Statements these should be clear and detailed; the LA should meet the prescribed time limits and should monitor the arrangements and review the Statement annually.

The Code of Practice defines the role of the LA and its statutory duties extensively. Equally, it defines the role of the school governing body and its statutory duties. It considers SEN policies in early education settings at schools and includes a useful table (paragraph 1.39) of roles and responsibilities.

The current Code is far more detailed and complex than the earlier Code. The 1994 Code provided a clear five-stage assessment of children with special educational needs. Stages 1 and 3 were the school-based interventions (Stage 3 bringing in outside intervention). Stages 4 and 5 were statutory assessment and a Statement. The current Code introduces the idea of School Action and School Action Plus, which are much vaguer concepts than a five-stage Code of Practice.

The Code is divided into a number of sections. The first defines principles and policies and thereafter outlines the system of identification and intervention. It begins with identification, assessment and provision in early education settings, then in the primary phase and finally in the secondary sector. Statutory assessments are dealt with in Chapter 7 of the Code. Statements of Special Educational Needs are dealt with in Chapter 8 and annual reviews in Chapter 9. Chapter 10 describes working in partnership with other agencies, including where a child transfers from the school sector into further education.

Overall, the Code seeks to make schools more accountable for children with special educational needs and the funds invested in them. The previous Code could be described as far more precise about intervention on behalf of the child and more concerned with ensuring that some definition of his or her learning difficulties is set out. The current Code has abandoned the useful detailed guidance on certain learning difficulties contained in Chapter 3 of its predecessor.

Significant criticisms were made of the current Code of Practice in its draft form, and it was withdrawn in draft on a number of occasions. Some of these criticisms were valid. First, it is too complicated for parents and for teachers. Second, it uses unnecessarily complicated language. Overall, the document is far more concerned with administration and accountability than the first Code.

The current Code places greater obligations than the previous version on all schools to make sure that the Special Educational Needs Coordinator (SENCo) in primary and secondary schools is given a substantial management role and has sufficient time to carry out the required duties. In seeking greater levels of accountability and clearer evidence of intervention, the Code is likely to create problems in cases where schools do not comply with its requirements. Local Authorities may well claim in cases where parents seek Statements of Special Educational Needs that there is insufficient information. However, the legal position is that a Statement depends not on the availability of information, but on whether a Statement is necessary for the child (Section 323, the assessment provisions, and Section 324, the Statement provisions of the 1996 Act, make this quite clear).

School Action and School Action Plus

The Code incorporates a two-stage procedure: School Action and School Action Plus. Although the criteria for primary and for secondary level differ slightly, the overall principles are the same.

School Action depends on the identification by the SENCo or a member of staff that the child requires an intervention additional to, or different from, that normally provided by the school. The criteria outlined at secondary level are that the child:

- makes little or no progress even when teaching approaches are targeted particularly at a pupil's identified area of weakness;
- shows signs of difficulty in developing literacy or mathematics skills that result in poor attainment in some curriculum areas;
- has persistent emotional and/or behavioural difficulties that are not ameliorated;
- has sensory or physical problems and continues to make little or no progress despite specialist equipment;
- has communication and/or interaction difficulties and continues to make little or no progress despite the provision of a differentiated curriculum.

The Code provides for consultation and cooperation with parents. It also requires an individual education plan, examples of which are found in the *SEN Toolkit*, an associated document published by the Department for Education. The Individual Education Plan should include information about:

- the short-term targets set for or by the pupil;
- teaching strategies to be used;
- provision to be put in place;
- when the plan is to be reviewed;
- success and/or exit criteria;
- outcomes.

The next stage is School Action Plus. This stage follows a review of intervention under School Action, which would normally bring in, when needed, external support services provided by the LA and/or outside agencies. The triggers for this are defined in the Code of Practice at secondary level (Chapter 6.64) as being that the child:

- continues to make little or no progress in specific areas over a long period;
- continues working at National Curriculum level substantially below that expected of pupils of a similar age;
- continues to have difficulty in developing literacy and mathematics skills;
- has emotional or behavioural difficulties that substantially and regularly interfere with his or her own learning and/or that of the class group despite intervention;
- has sensory or physical needs that require additional specialist equipment or regular advice or visits providing direct intervention of pupil or staff;
- has ongoing communication or social interaction difficulties that impede the development of social relationships and cause substantial barriers to learning.

The Code of Practice allows that for a very small number of pupils the help given by schools through Action Plus may not be sufficient to enable the pupil to make adequate progress.

Schools can now themselves seek a statutory assessment. The terms upon which they can seek such an assessment are defined on pages 72 and 73 of the Code of Practice (Chapter 6.72).

It should be noted that the expectation of the Code of Practice is for a very complex and sophisticated intervention at Action Plus. Practical experience suggests that this may not be available in all cases. For example, where children or staff require specific help or disability equipment, they may in reality only be provided with aids as a result of a Statement or a statutory assessment under Section 323. The current Code of Practice expects an enormous amount of schools. It remains to be seen whether schools can deliver such a sophisticated service.

Statutory assessment and Statement

Chapter 7 of the Code deals with the statutory assessment of special educational needs, the evidence to be provided by the school or the early education setting and referral by another agency. Considerations for parents who wish to request an assessment are important in this section (pages 78–79 of the Code, Chapter 7.21 to 7.29). Many of the parents consulting this Guide will be considering making such a request.

Chapter 7.23 sets out the principles on which parents should request an assessment. First, parents should believe that their child's needs are not being met through school-based intervention or that the needs are so substantial that a mainstream school could not meet them effectively without the use of outside resources. The Code points out that parents should clearly set out the reasons for their request. They should also provide information about the provision that the child has already received. However, the Code is silent on issues arising from certain cases that frequently come to the attention of LAs, and the Special Educational Needs Tribunal. These are cases where children have not received any or adequate intervention because their problems have been underestimated or missed altogether.

The previous Code included detailed criteria for dealing with individual categories of disability, ie emotional and behavioural difficulties and specific learning difficulties, including dyslexia. The current Code does not address matters in similar detail. However, the previous Code omitted some obvious categories.

The current Code provides an improvement on the previous version in that it includes a section on children who need an immediate referral for a statutory assessment. Obviously this refers to children with the most severe difficulties, and this new, more substantial section of the Code is a welcome addition.

Evidence in deciding whether to make a statutory assessment

Pages 81–89 of this Code cover the evidence that a LA should consider before making a decision to conduct a statutory assessment. This includes, with guidance, some considera-tion of certain learning difficulties, but not in the same detail or complexity as the previous Code.

The evidence to be considered by the LA includes:

- Evidence that the school has responded appropriately to requirements of the National Curriculum especially in relation to inclusion.

- Evidence provided by the child's school, parents and other professionals involved with the child as to the nature, extent and cause of the child's learning difficulties.

- Evidence of action already taken by the child's school to meet and overcome those difficulties.

- Evidence of the rate and style of the child's progress.

- Evidence that where some progress has been made, it has been the result only of additional efforts and instruction at a sustained level not usually commensurate with provision through School Action Plus.

The Code clearly requires specific evidence of attainment and requires LAs to seek clear, recorded evidence of the child's academic attainment. Overall, the LA should consider the case for a statutory assessment where the balance of evidence presented to, and assessed by, it suggests that the child's learning difficulties:

- have not responded to relevant and purposeful measures taken by the school or by an external specialist;

- may call for special educational provision that could not reasonably be provided within the resources normally available to mainstream maintained schools and settings in the area.

The new document improves on the previous Code by seeking the child's views. It also points out that each child is unique and that the questions asked by the LA should reflect the particular circumstances of the child.

The Code then covers some areas of strengths and difficulties such as: communication and interaction; vocation and learning behaviour; emotional and social development; sensory and/or physical needs; and medical conditions. However, it covers these issues in a much broader sense than the previous Code and the guidance it gives is far more general. For example, autism, dyslexia, dyspraxia and hearing impairment are covered in Chapter 7.55 to 7.57. The previous Code covered specific learning difficulties including dyslexia very effectively and accurately in greater depth.

Criteria for considering intervention

In dealing with children with, for example, dyslexia, dyspraxia, language delay, other learning difficulties or language and communication problems, the types of intervention are set out as follows:

- Flexible teaching and arrangements.

- Help in acquiring, comprehending and using language.

- Help in articulation.

- Help in acquiring literacy skills.

- Help in using augmentative and alternative means of communication.

- Help to use different means of communication confidently and competently for a range of purposes, including formal situations.

- Help in organizing and coordinating oral and written language.

- Support to compensate for the impact of communication difficulty on learning in English as an additional language.

- Help in expressing, comprehending and using the child's own language, where English is not his or her first language.

The Code goes on to state that if some or all of these programmes can be provided for a child by the school in collaboration with the LA or external services, then the LA may conclude that intervention should be provided at School Action Plus and be monitored to see if that action is effective. It would then be appropriate for the LA to conclude that a statutory assessment was not necessary. If, on the other hand, the school support and services had already provided these interventions through School Action Plus and the child had not made acceptable progress, then a statutory assessment should be considered.

There is one difficulty with the Code worth noting here. It makes no reference to the necessity of a Statement in cases where there has been no intervention and where there is evidence that sufficient support is not available. In most such cases a Statement should be necessary, but the Code does not address this point.

If one turns to the provision for Statements in Chapter 8 of the Code, particularly the criteria for deciding to draw up a Statement, and contrasts this with the provisions relating to a statutory assessment, it is clear that where children will require greater intervention than is normally available, a Statement should be made. There is therefore a clear internal conflict in the Code between cases in which there is lack of evidence of adequate intervention by the school together with insufficient evidence that there will be future adequate intervention, and cases where the LA is bound to draw up a Statement.

Generally speaking, the Code seems to overemphasize the requirement of a school to provide detailed compliance documentation, and places insufficient emphasis to the child's interest. The law, however, lies clearly in the other direction. The statutory considerations in Sections 323 and 324 are based on the whole child *R v Secretary of State for Education ex parte E* (1992) FLR p377.

The test as outlined by the Court of Appeal in that leading case is far more simple. As *Balcombe LJ in ex parte E* pointed out, the real test is whether the school, with or without assistance on assessment from the LA, can provide from its own resources (which include the resources normally provided to the school through LA services) adequate intervention to deal with the child's needs. If so, no Statement is necessary. If, however, outside intervention over and above that which is normal is required, then a Statement is necessary.

The current Code has made the test extremely complex, and to some degree ignores the guidance of the Courts on these issues.

In outlining considerations for a Statement, the Code accurately sets out the law. A Statement makes a diagnosis of the child's learning difficulties and the prescription to meet his or her needs. If the LA can provide what is needed together with the school within the normal resources, no Statement is necessary. If it cannot, then a Statement is necessary. Normally, of course, Statements are required, as the Code makes clear, for children with severe and complex learning difficulties, but a Statement can be required for a child solely with a severe learning difficulty or a complex learning difficulty.

Chapter 10 of the Code discusses partnership with other agencies and covers future progress. It is to be noted that the Connexions service brought in under the Learning Skills Act is an important development. The intention of this chapter is to make sure that for children with Statements there is smooth cooperation between other agencies, particularly for the more disabled child who will require continuous support, and for those who will require support well into further and higher education. To this extent, again the Code is a great improvement.

Criteria for residential placement

The current Code does provide clearer guidance which overall is of considerable assistance to parents who are seeking a residential school or a specialist independent school. Many of the schools in this guide provide for children with greater disabilities, and for such schools the changes in the Code of Practice that relate to these issues are extremely important.

In essence, the Code takes the following approach:

1. If a child requires multi-professional intervention by Health, Social Services and the Education Authority, the Code requires that specific arrangements are put in place.

2. If a parent is seeking a residential placement, the Code states that if the child's needs cannot be met in local day provision, or the child requires a consistent programme both during and after school hours that cannot be provided by parents with support from other agencies, these are the main factors in considering a residential placement.

In practice this means that where it is accepted or established that a consistent programme after school hours is needed (a waking day curriculum), where a local authority has not established the existence of combined provision from Social Services and Health, the parent is entitled to rely on these provisions of the Code. In particular, the Code provides at pages 104–105, paragraphs 8:44 to 8:48 that the Statement should set out the non-educational needs that the LA either proposes to meet or is satisfied will be met by arrangement or by other action with Health Services, Social Services or some other body. The provision should also be set out in the Statement, but can only be set out if the Local Authority is satisfied that it will be made available by either Social Services or Health or the LA proposes itself to make such provision available (paragraph 8:44).

When looking at the criteria, a parent who has care of their child where there is not joint funding for an independent placement with Health and/or Social Services should consider that the important issues are:

1. Is it established that the child has severe or multiple special educational needs that cannot be met in local day provision?

2. Is it established that the child has severe or multiple needs that require a consistent programme during the waking day, which cannot be provided by parents with support from other agencies.

First, the child's needs for a waking day curriculum must be established. In considering such cases, it is extremely important to examine the extent of Health support, Social Services support, its competence and consistency. Ultimately, these are issues for the Special Educational Needs and Disability Tribunal.

Disability Discrimination Act 1995 – Code of Practice

The Code of Practice on disability discrimination is available from the Disability Rights Commission. It is to be read together with the Code of Practice Special Educational Needs. However, for the purposes of this book, the Disability Code of Practice has applied fully in education since September 2002. It is frankly of minor importance, because parents who are seeking a specialist placement will not normally wish to bring proceedings in disability discrimination. However, the Code is of some relevance, particularly if parents wish to establish a case for an alternative school, and that the current school is making an unlawful provision that is discriminatory for their child.

The structure of the Code

The Code is divided into some 10 chapters, explaining the different aspects of disability discrimination.

Prior to the coming into force of the 2001 Act, disability discrimination was excluded from education. However, for parents, the provisions of the 1995 Act in relation to discrimination in relation to goods, facilities and services is probably the most relevant. Section 19 declares that it is unlawful for the provider of services to discriminate against a disabled person in the ways provided in the Section. For the purposes of the Act, a school/Local Authority or independent school is a provider of services, ie school holidays, outings, equipment, sports, etc.

A good example of a breach of the provisions of the Act is the case DRC/00/138: refusal of permission to go on school trips to a young person who suffered from diabetes. The young person, who was 15 years old, suffered from diabetes and had recently had a hypoglycaemic attack while away on a school trip. The school took the view that the attack was a result of his mismanagement of his diabetes. They banned him from future school trips merely as a result of one attack. The young person's paediatrician stated that she had never come across such poor treatment by a school of a diabetic pupil. The young person's lawyers argued that he had been treated unfairly, and had suffered detriment. The court awarded damages on the basis that the young person had been discriminated against on both counts, and made a declaration of discrimination and an award of damages under the Act. Damages were quite substantial, totalling in fact £3,000 for the denial of a school trip.

Disability discrimination in primary and secondary education

It is now unlawful for those responsible for a school, including an independent school, to discriminate against a disabled person:

1. in the arrangements it makes for determining an admission to the school as a pupil;

2. in the terms in which it offers to admit a child to the school as a pupil;

3. by refusing or deliberately omitting to accept an application of admission to the school as a pupil;

4. in the education or associated services provided or offered to pupils at school;

5. in exclusions.

The Disability Code of Practice states in summary that education or associated services cover all aspects of school life including:

1. preparation for entry into school;

2. the curriculum;

3. teaching and learning;

4. classroom and organization;

5. timetabling;

6. grouping of pupils;

7. homework;

8. access to school facilities;

9. activities to supplement the curriculum, eg a drama group;

10. school sport;

11. school policies;

12. breaks and lunchtimes;

13. the serving of school meals;

14. interaction with peers;

15. assessment of exam arrangements;

16. school discipline and sanctions;

17. school clubs and activities;

18. school trips;

19. the school's arrangements for working with other agencies;

20. preparation of pupils for the next phase of education.

The responsible body is in relation to a maintained school, the LA or the governing body. In relation to student referral units the LA is the responsible body, as it is in relation to nursery schools. In relation to independent schools, it is the proprietor. The definition of discrimination and the test of discrimination are complex and are not set out in detail in this work. A claim for damages can be made in relation to provision of services as set out above, but aside from further and higher education, the Act restricts the right to redress to certain statutory bodies. In relation to admissions, the body would normally be the admissions of appeal panel, and in relation to exclusions it would be the exclusions appeal panel set up by statute. As regards other acts of discrimination that are not concerned with the provision of services, the normal body to determine these issues is the Special Educational Needs and Disability Tribunal, which covers discrimination by all responsible educational bodies, with (as set out above) the exception of claims relating to admissions, or permanent exclusions which are dealt with by the relevant independent panels.

The Tribunal has a limited jurisdiction, but if it considers a claim is well founded, it may declare that a person has been unlawfully discriminated against, and if it does so it may make such an order as it considers reasonable in all the circumstances of the case. The power to make such orders is intended to be exercised with a view to obviating or reducing the adverse effects of the discrimination, rather than, as in failure to provide services, compensation by way of damages, which also applies in further and higher education. The Tribunal's jurisdiction, thus, is limited.

Overall, such claims will have a limited role in relation to parents reading this work and seeking a school that offers specialist education or specialist facilities.

Children with Special Educational Needs – The Legal Implications

John Friel, Barrister-at-law, Gray's Inn

The Special Educational Needs and Disability Act 2001 has made some amendments to rights and duties in relation to children in this field. In particular, it brings into play the Disability Rights Commission and the provisions of the Disability Discrimination Act 1995 in education, when education has previously been exempt.

There is a Code of Practice on disability discrimination in education, but in relation to the issues arising for parents reading this Guide disability discrimination issues will normally not be particularly relevant. The 2001 Act effectively:

● Strengthens the specific duty to educate in a mainstream school, if the child can be so educated, and if the parents so wish.

● Creates a needed mediation system, to which parents may have recourse when they are in dispute with a Local Authority over a Statement. However, the mediation system should not delay or deny an appeal.

● Brings in rights to raise disability discrimination issues in exclusion appeals. Parents who are paying fees for an independent school education may note that these schools are now subject, like state schools, to claims that they have discriminated against disabled children. While damages cannot be claimed, extensive changes may be required by the school to meet a disability discrimination claim.

● Brings the full weight of the Disability Discrimination Act into further and higher education, an area in which it is likely to have a long-term substantial effect.

How do you enforce your rights?

Despite alterations to the law, and two new Codes of Practice, the principles as to how parents can obtain adequate assistance for their children remain unchanged. In some cases, the new

Code of Practice may be of assistance, for example if a school is discriminating against particular disabilities by making no provision for them. Therefore the Code of Practice on Disability Discrimination should not be ignored and should be obtained. However, the chief concern for parents reading this Guide is clearly the enforcement of their child's rights.

For parents of children with more severe disabilities there will probably be no debate about whether or not a Statement is required. The issue in this case will be how the child's difficulties are to be addressed, and where he or she should be educated. For parents of children who have obviously severe and complex learning difficulties (but not profound and multiple handicaps), and who will go on, if assisted properly, to take a role in normal life, the situation will not be the same as for a severely disabled child. The school may, of course, identify the child's problem, but it may not. Thus the parent may be seeking a statutory assessment under s.323, or alternatively, having reached the point where everybody agrees a Statement is necessary, be seeking to argue that they require much more for their child than the LA is prepared to offer.

The principles upon which parents should prepare a case are exactly the same whether the issue concerns the necessity of a Statement or its content. However, the considerations and the level of preparation will be different if there is no Statement.

Preparation of your case

Before a parent or an Education Authority can know whether there is a legal obligation to make provision (under the Education Act 1996, s.324) for a Statement of Special Educational Needs or even for a statutory assessment, the child's needs must first be assessed.

Identification of children with special educational needs

The Code of Practice and the 1996 Act require a LA to exercise its powers with a view to securing or identifying that those children who have special educational needs and for whom it is necessary for the authority to determine the special educational provision required are so identified. If the authority forms the opinion that the child's special educational needs require, or probably require, a Statement, then they will conduct an assessment. The school itself can now request an assessment.

However, a major problem arises where the LA has failed to identify children with special educational needs. Many requests for Statements still come from parents. Thus where a parent requests statutory assessment, unless that parent has evidence that it is required, the LA will inevitably refuse. The terms of the new Code of Practice make it clear that the LA will be entitled to refuse unless the request is supported by substantial evidence.

The 2001 Act allows schools to request a statutory assessment as well as permitting LAs to conduct an assessment under s.323. Therefore it is likely to be more rather than less difficult for parents to obtain a statutory assessment and/or a Statement in circumstances where neither the LA nor the school has requested an assessment. Regrettably, this can only be done if the case is prepared properly by the parent.

Preparing a request for an assessment

If possible, a parent who can afford independent advice should consider such advice essential. Where there is no support or little support by a school for a statutory assessment and evidence that the school has simply not fulfilled its role adequately, or where the LA requires clearly identified intervention by the school and there is none, parents will not be able to obtain a Statement or even a statutory assessment unless they are prepared to obtain adequate independent reports.

Regrettably, for parents who have limited means, this is difficult. For those who are on Income Support, the legal help scheme (available from some specialist solicitors) provides a means whereby independent reports can be obtained. However, parents seeking such advice should ideally use specialist education solicitors because the Legal Services Commission has changed matters and procedure in legal aid cases. Legal aid is now only available from approved solicitors. For parents with very limited means (ie those on Income Support), this remains one route.

Another route for those with limited income is the National Health Service. A number of hospitals – for example the Munro Centre, 66 Snowsfields, London SE1 3SS and Liverpool Alder Hey – have clinical/educational psychologists who can provide a detailed and appropriate report. There are also some charities that provide assessments or funds for them. An example is the Dyslexia Institute Bursary Fund, which will provide funds for an assessment. However, this and other charities do not generally provide such assessments for the purposes of seeking a statutory assessment but in order to establish a level of need. IPSEA (the Independent Panel of Special Needs Advisors) remains a valuable service.

On the assumption that adequate funds are available, reports must be obtained. It should be remembered that experts need to earn a living but are not, in comparison with other services today, generally expensive. Independent experts should be used.

Parents should also bear in mind that they are asking the LA to provide, in the form of a Statement, a potential substantial and valuable benefit. The cost of education at the state schools listed in this Guide or the independent schools with specialist help is considerable. All these schools provide a sophisticated, expensive and complex service to assist children with varying learning difficulties. Nobody would approach a claim where, for example, they had been run over in the street and suffered substantial damages, on the basis of amateur and inadequate preparation. Parents must take great care to prepare their child's case adequately.

Many children with special educational needs have conditions that require medical treatment or the supervision of doctors. In all such cases medical reports should be obtained. For those with physical difficulties and associated brain damage, that may include reports from a paediatrician, physiotherapist, occupational therapist and speech therapist. However, it should be borne in mind that increasingly NHS speech therapy reports do not advise on the child's level of need, but rather what is on offer from the Local Health Service. Because provision from Local Health Services varies nationally, the advice also varies in quality. In some cases it is excellent; in others the authority may only say what will be made available, not what is needed.

The legal duty of the Local Authority is to provide for the special educational needs of the child. Thus what is on offer from the Health Service is not necessarily what a Local Authority is obliged to provide. In cases of Statements of Special Educational Needs, the law requires the LA to pay for a provision irrespective of resources. If provision is not locally available, the LA must pay for the provision to be made from elsewhere: see *East Sussex County Council ex parte T* (1998) Education Law Reports p198. The House of Lords differentiated the duties in education from duties in social services.

The Courts have strengthened parents' rights in this field. A Statement must have a diagnosis of and a prescription of the child's special educational needs: see *R v Secretary of*

State for Education ex parte E (1992) Family Law Reports p377. Further Statements must be specific so that provision in a Statement is ascertainable, identifiable and quantified. Although the Code of Practice and the Regulations make this point quite clearly, the major failing by LAs is to so identify the provision. In *L v Clarke & Somerset* (1998) Education Law Reports p128 and *Bromley v The SENT* (1999) Education Law Reports p260 CA, both the High Court and the Court of Appeal confirmed that Statements must be detailed, quantified and specific.

This is an important consideration in dealing with a child's learning difficulties. Parents will need to seek evidence – both at the assessment stage and at the statementing stage – that the intervention is detailed, sufficiently quantified, and sufficiently specific to ameliorate the child's learning difficulties. Evidence that such intervention is not available provides grounds for a case for a statutory assessment and means that it should succeed, irrespective of the vagueness of the Code of Practice on this issue. It should also establish a case for the parent on an appeal against a Statement.

Thus the expert must address the following questions:

- What are the child's needs in the area of expertise required? For example, an educational psychologist will need to comment on requirements for specialist reports, eg from speech therapists, occupational therapists, etc.

- What is the provision required to meet the needs?

- What provision is available at the local school?

- What provision is required for the child? If this is an assessment case, is this likely to be available in the local school or LA?

- What provision does the expert advise?

As far as occupational therapists, physiotherapists, speech therapists, paediatricians and other specialists are concerned, the same questions arise within their area of expertise. In cases of autistic children or children with emotional and behavioural problems or mental health problems, a report from a consultant child psychiatrist or child and adolescent psychiatrist can be essential. Regrettably, there are few good experts available nationally. However, in cases where such a skill is involved, attention should be given to such reports.

Involvement of the child and the role of Social Services and educational welfare services

The Code of Practice now requires the views of the child to be sought. While this is a good and appropriate development, it can lead to difficulties. Parents may be understandably over-anxious. At the same time there is a risk that schools and LAs may put pressure on children to make statements in support of the institution.

Where children are capable of expressing their views – and some children may not be able to do so – use of the guidance given in the Children Act for the interviewing of young people by the LA is essential. This guidance is to ensure that children are not over-influenced by the interviewer, or pressurized into saying things with which they do not agree. Recent experience has shown that attempts have been made both by parents and by local authorities to influence children in expressing their views. Children with special educational needs are generally vulnerable and may well be unduly subject to pressure.

Regrettably, Social Services intervention is often notable by its absence. Children with considerable learning difficulties who are likely to be disabled for life or for a substantial period often have no Social Services care plan or intervention in place for them. Section 17 of the Children Act provides a general power to assess children who are in need. Assessment provisions of the Act normally require that children should be assessed at the same time as a Statement of Special Educational Needs is put into place or a statutory assessment takes place.

In *London Borough of Bromley v The SENT* (1999) Education Law Reports p260 the Court of Appeal emphasizes that there is no border between Social Services needs, medical needs and educational needs that are clear and defined. Children who require a waking day curriculum or a 24-hour curriculum may be as much in need of a whole multi-professional approach (educational, medical and practical) as they are in need of education. Less able children will develop independence skills and communication skills but may never be fully independent or fully able to communicate, and thus the working day curriculum is educational.

If available, reports should be sought from Social Services. In more complex cases involving children with severe and complex difficulties, an independent social worker's report may be required if the Social Services reports are inadequate or if there has been no Social Services intervention.

What is a Statement?

A Statement is a document that clearly defines a child's educational needs and the intervention to meet those needs. It must be specific, quantified and effective. Case law in this area has been considered above.

The process of assessment

The process of assessment is governed by Regulation. The LA should normally seek:

- educational advice;
- advice from an educational psychologist;
- advice from Social Services;
- medical advice;
- advice from any specialist services providing assistance to the child.

The Act creates a definite timetable that is often dishonoured. The Code of Practice timetable is set out at the end of this section and is laid out clearly in the current Regulations and in the Code of Practice. The Education (Special Educational Needs) England Consolidation Regulations 2001 SI 3455 clearly state the time limits. Once a Local Authority has completed an assessment it is under obligation to serve a draft Statement. The parent then has the right to require meetings and representations. It is at this time, once a Statement has been finalized, that mediation should be considered. The time limits for an appeal to the Tribunal are extremely strict. Appeals should be made within two months of the date of service of the final Statement, and it is only in exceptional circumstances that a Tribunal can extend the time.

The structure of the Act requires the parent to prepare the case in advance. If the parent is seeking to catch up, difficulties will ensue.

Experts

A major difficulty of seeking expert advice is that even though there are a large number of psychologists available for private consultation, few are prepared to assist in special educational needs appeal cases. Some who offer their services in these instances do not have the forensic skills to do so. Parents seeking to put forward a case in support of an application for a place at one of the schools in this Guide are well advised to seek expert legal guidance. If that is not available to them, advice from charities that have good working knowledge of complex difficulties should be sought. For example, the British Dyslexia Association provides an advisory and representation service, as does the National Autistic Society. Parents should appreciate that these are complex, difficult and sophisticated cases which normally require expert preparation and support.

Experience suggests that the documents from the Special Educational Needs Tribunal indicating that parents can easily prepare a case and can represent themselves are unrealistic. Children who require a Statement will normally have complex difficulties. Although it is possible for parents to prepare cases properly, experience has shown that the task is often substantially underestimated. Many appeals to the High Court have arisen where parents were unrepresented, and for that reason the Tribunal has not been able to address key issues in their case and consequently has made quite substantial mistakes. The Tribunal system is obviously designed to hear very complex cases and decide them quickly. It does so without great cost in comparison to normal cases of this complexity and importance. However, because the documentation of the Tribunal attempts to help parents – and ensure that cases are decided quickly and efficiently in the child's interest – it disguises the basic complexity of many cases. Some cases will be simple, but a parent reading this publication would require expensive specialist provision. Cases of this nature are not easy, and few parents have been able to come away from a Tribunal feeling that they have handled cases on their own adequately. A number have complained after the hearing that the Tribunal publications on this issue are misleading and that they did not understand the difficulty and complexity of cases. For the reader of this Guide cases should be presented either with legal assistance, or at least with assistance from one of the major charities that provide representation of an experienced and competent nature.

A surprising number of appeals to the High Court are settled, resulting in a rehearing. If argued, they have usually resulted in a remission to the Special Educational Needs Tribunal. The overall experience indicates that parents are better at preparing cases like this with professional legal advice and with adequate reports than they are attempting to prepare without such guidance. The Tribunal carries out good work, in difficult circumstances, to the best of its ability.

The Code of Practice timetable

The LA must decide whether or not to make a statutory assessment within six weeks of the date that the request was lodged. The LA then has 10 weeks to undertake the statutory assessment process. The decision about whether or not to make a Statement must be finalized within two weeks of completing the statutory assessment, allowing eight weeks to gather information, seek professional advice and make a decision. The LA then has a further two weeks to notify the parents of its decision and to make a proposed Statement if appropriate. Otherwise a note in lieu, explaining why the Statement was refused, must be provided. A final Statement must be agreed within eight weeks of the issue of the proposed Statement.

Enforcing your rights – the SEN Tribunal

The 1996 Education Act, as amended by the 2001 Act, provides parents with a right of appeal to the Special Educational Needs and Disability Tribunal. Most relevant to the present Act are the appeal rights as follows:

1. It provides the parents with an appeal against a refusal to make a statutory assessment.

2. It provides the parents with a right of appeal where the authority has conducted an assessment and has either refused to make a Statement, or has refused to amend a Statement. The powers of the Tribunal when a Statement has been refused are different from the powers when a Statement is amended or when one is refused following assessment. In one case the Tribunal can order a Statement to be made or reconsidered, in the other they can order the Statement to be amended.

3. Appeal against the contents of the Statement, including the school.

4. In certain limited circumstances, an appeal providing a right to change the name of the school contained in the Statement so long as the parent wishes to change the name to another state-operated school of whatever type.

5. If a parent claims disability discrimination against a school, but not damages.

Although there are a number of charities that assist parents with the preparation of a case, such as the British Dyslexia Association, and IPSEA, in general, because of the financial costs of independent specialist education, or even of specialist state education, parents are advised to seek specialist legal advice in this field if possible. If they cannot access such advice, then they should obtain at least specialist help and assistance from one of the recognized charities. While a Tribunal does its best to assist unrepresented parents, the major criticism from unrepresented parents and indeed from a number of charitable representatives, is that the Tribunal is not listening sufficiently to the lay person. From my personal experience, normally Tribunals do their best to ensure fair play. But handling difficult cases, for children with special educational needs, many of whom have severe difficulties, is a very onerous task, the more so if you present a case for your own child. Generally, the view is that the parents are assisted by representation, if possible legal representation, and that a specialist can assist preparation of the case greatly. Equally, parents will be advised if their hopes are unrealistic. I do not intend in this chapter to promote the interest of lawyers, but it is necessary to point out that a constant feeling of parents who have appeared on their own in Tribunals is how difficult presenting the case has been.

I would, however, comment that the Tribunal's own material suggests to parents that the procedure is relatively easy, parent friendly and not over-legalistic. This description is certainly considered by most to be over optimistic, though well intentioned. There is no doubt that taking a case to a Tribunal involves a difficult personal decision as well as a great deal of time, effort and work.

Disability Discrimination – How Relevant?

John Friel, Barrister-at-law, Gray's Inn

Introduction

The current work is a guide intended for parents. The Disability Discrimination Act (DDA) has made some useful reforms, although those reforms give rights within the school environment that are much more limited than the rights given in higher education. However, it is another matter altogether whether those rights have any great relevance to the main issue involved in this work, the choice of school and appropriate provision, other than as a means of redress such as a negligence action.

For the purposes of the parent of a child with learning difficulties, a major point to be remembered is that the definition of disability in the DDA is not the same as a learning difficulty that requires a Statement of Special Educational Needs as defined by Section 312 of the Education Act 1996. The words 'disability' and 'disabled persons' (which are the subject of the DDA 1995 as extended) are defined in Part 1 of the 1995 Act, Sections 1–3 and Schedules 1 and 2. A person is classified as disabled if he or she has a disability. A person has a disability if he or she has a physical or mental impairment that has a substantial and long-term adverse effect on his or her ability to carry out normal day-to-day activities. These provisions are supplemented by regulations.

The burden of proof that a complainant was a disabled person at the time of an alleged act of discrimination lies with the complainant. Although not many claims have been made against schools in the Special Educational Needs and Disability Tribunal, most of them have failed because the Tribunal has determined that there is not sufficient evidence of a disability. Most parents need to produce expert evidence showing that the child or young person's learning difficulty has an effect which amounts to a physical or mental impairment that has a substantial and long-term adverse effect on him or her. Clearly, severe dyslexia will affect a person all his or her life. A milder or less severe form of dyslexia might not. Similarly, other learning difficulties, such as Asperger's syndrome, might require a Statement but not fall within this definition.

If a child or young person suffers from a recognized mental illness, such as autism, attention deficit hyperactivity disorder (ADHD) or attention deficit disorder (ADD), the

Employment Appeal Tribunal ruling in *Goodwin v The Patent Office* 1999, IRLR pg 4, is relevant. This recommended that reference should be made to the World Health Organization International Classification of Diseases.

A second factor to take into account is that the rights of disabled children and young persons in relation to education often have to be enforced within the existing statutory appeal system. The relevant legal provisions are set out below. 'Discrimination' is defined as an action by a responsible body that discriminates against a disabled person for a reason that relates to his or her disability; that is, it treats him or her less favourably than it treats, or would treat, others for whom that reason does not or would not apply. In addition, the action must not be justified. Further, Section 28C provides that pupils are not to be substantially disadvantaged as a result of their disability and discrimination.

I set out below the areas covered by the new statutory provisions. However, in the educational sector, independent schools and state schools often provide services for which, should they discriminate, there is no right of recovery of damages through the Special Educational Needs and Disability Tribunal. To some degree, the matters are more concerned with schools than with the parent and child. The various routes of redress are considered in more detail below. It must be borne in mind, however, that in relation to applications to the Special Educational Needs Tribunal, the Tribunal cannot order compensation, although it has a wide power to order action to be taken. In many cases compensation may be an issue.

Although many of the issues considered below have become major matters of concern for independent schools because of the Disability Discrimination Act, the existence of the Act itself, and the fact that there are now new rights given under it, will very probably be influential in other areas where there is a breach of the Act. For example, a failure to identify disability needs after admission, when they ought to have been identified, would result in a claim for damages in negligence: see *Phelps v Hillingdon* 2001 AC p 618, House of Lords. In addition, the fact that a child was the victim of discrimination would in many cases give rise to an action for damages on the grounds that the school had behaved either unprofessionally or unfairly, and was therefore in breach of contract. Some of these issues certainly would not have been in the mind of parents prior to the existence of the Act. Thus the Act not only creates new rights that did not exist before, but makes it more likely that old established rights of action can be used.

The issues

1. Admissions.

2. Identification of special educational needs (SEN) after admission.

3. Exclusions.

4. Organization of the school for disabled persons.

Relevant legal provisions

Section 5, which is important, is not reproduced. Some of the provisions below apply only to state schools, but most of them are relevant to all schools, as the principles are of general application.

28A   *Discrimination against disabled pupils and prospective pupils*

(1)   It is unlawful for the body responsible for a school to discriminate against a disabled person:
  (a)   in the arrangements it makes for determining admission to the school as a pupil;
  (b)   in the terms on which it offers to admit him or her to the school as a pupil; or
  (c)   by refusing or deliberately omitting to accept an application for his or her admission to the school as a pupil.

(2)   It is unlawful for the body responsible for a school to discriminate against a disabled pupil in the education or associated services provided for, or offered to, pupils at the school by that body.

(3)   The Secretary of State may by regulations prescribe services that are, or services that are not, to be regarded for the purposes of subsection (2) as being:
  (a)   education; or
  (b)   an associated service.

(4)   It is unlawful for the body responsible for a school to discriminate against a disabled pupil by excluding him or her from the school, whether permanently or temporarily.

(5)   The body responsible for a school is to be determined in accordance with Schedule 4A, and in the remaining provisions of this chapter is referred to as the 'responsible body'.[1]

28B   *Meaning of 'discrimination'*

(1)   For the purposes of Section 28A, a responsible body discriminates against a disabled person if:
  (a)   for a reason that relates to his or her disability, it treats him or her less favourably than it treats or would treat others to whom that reason does not or would not apply; and
  (b)   it cannot show that the treatment in question is justified.

(2)   For the purposes of Section 28A, a responsible body also discriminates against a disabled person if:
  (a)   it fails, to his or her detriment, to comply with Section 28C; and
  (b)   it cannot show that its failure to comply is justified.

(5)   Subsections (6) to (8) apply in determining whether, for the purposes of this section:
  (a)   less favourable treatment of a person, or
  (b)   failure to comply with Section 28C is justified.

(6)   Less favourable treatment of a person is justified if it is the result of a permitted form of selection.

---

[1]   By virtue of Schedule 4A to the Disability Discrimination Act 1995, the responsible body for a maintained school is either the Local Authority or governing body, according to which has the function in question. In the present case, the responsible body is the governing body.

(7) Otherwise, less favourable treatment, or a failure to comply with Section 28C, is justified only if the reason for it is both material to the circumstances of the particular case and substantial.

(8) If, in a case falling within subsection (1):
   (a) the responsible body is under a duty imposed by Section 28C in relation to the disabled person, but
   (b) it fails without justification to comply with that duty

   its treatment of that person cannot be justified under subsection (7) unless that treatment would have been justified even if it had complied with that duty.

28C Disabled pupils not to be substantially disadvantaged

(1) The responsible body for a school must take such steps as it is reasonable for it to have to take to ensure that:
   (a) in relation to the arrangements it makes for determining the admission of pupils to the school, disabled persons are not placed at a substantial disadvantage in comparison with persons who are not disabled; and
   (b) in relation to education and associated services provided for, or offered to, pupils at the school by it, disabled pupils are not placed at a substantial disadvantage in comparison with pupils who are not disabled.

(2) That does not require the responsible body to:
   (a) remove or alter a physical feature (for example, one arising from the design or construction of the school premises or the location of resources); or
   (b) provide auxiliary aids or services.

(4) In considering whether it is reasonable for it to have to take a particular step in order to comply with its duty under subsection (1), a responsible body must have regard to any relevant provisions of a code of practice issued under Section 53A.

28K Admissions

(1) If the condition mentioned in subsection (2) is satisfied, this section applies to a claim in relation to an admissions decision that a responsible body:
   (a) has discriminated against a person (A) in a way which is made unlawful under this chapter; or
   (b) is by virtue of Section 58 to be treated as having discriminated against a person (A) in such a way.

(2) The condition is that arrangements (appeal arrangements) have been made:
   (a) under Section 94 of the School Standards and Framework Act 1998, or
   (b) (are not relevant), enabling an appeal to be made against a decision by A's parent.

(3) The claim must be made under the appeal arrangements.

(4) The body hearing the claim has powers in relation to an appeal under the appeal arrangements.

(5)   An admissions decision means:
    (a)   the decision of a kind mentioned in Section 94(1) or (2) of the School Standards and Framework Act 1998,
    (b)   (is not relevant).

29L   Exclusions

(1)   If the conditions mentioned in subsection (2) are satisfied, this section applies to a claim in relation to an exclusion decision if the responsible body:
    (a)   has discriminated against a person (A) in a way that is made unlawful under this chapter; or

(2)   The condition is that the appeal arrangements have been made:
    (a)   under Section 67 of the School Standards and Framework Act;
    (b)   under an agreement entered into between the responsible body for an academy or the Secretary of State.

Summary of duties where they affect independent schools

It is unlawful for the body responsible for the school to discriminate against a disabled person in:

- the arrangements it makes for determining admission to the school as a pupil;

- the terms on which it offers to admit him or her to the school as a pupil; or

- refusing or deliberately omitting to accept an application for his or her admission to the school as a pupil.

It is also unlawful for the body responsible for the school to discriminate against a disabled pupil in the education or associated services provided for or offered to the pupil by the school or that body.

The Schools' Code of Practice, paragraphs 4.23–4.26, defines education and associated services without intending to be exhaustive as including preparation for entry to the school, curriculum, teaching and learning, classroom organization, timetabling, grouping of pupils, homework, access to school facilities, activities to supplement the curriculum (such as groups visiting the school or going outside), school sports, school politics, breaks and lunchtimes, school meals, interaction with peers, assessment and exam arrangements, school discipline and sanctions, exclusion procedures, clubs and activities, trips, working with agencies and preparation for further education.

Responsible body

This is either the governing body or the LA. The responsible body in an independent school not maintained by the LA is the proprietor of the school as defined in the Education Act 1996, Section 579.

What is discrimination?

The basis of an allegation of discrimination by a school is that it discriminated against the child because:

- owing to a reason that relates to his or her disability, it treated him or her less favourably than it treats others to whom that reason does not or would not apply;

- it cannot show that the treatment in question was justified.

The key question to be decided is what are the characteristics of the others to whom the reason does not or would not apply? In employment law, where the Disability Discrimination Act uses the same terms as in education, the courts have taken a very strict view of the definition of discrimination. Applying logic and looking at the definition in Section 5(1) of the Act, as against Section 28B1(a), two questions arise:

- Does the act complained of relate to the disability?

- If the answer is yes, does the school treat the applicant less favourably than it would treat others to whom the reason does not or would not apply?

It is settled law in the employment context that the first of these questions is a question of fact: *Clark v TDG Ltd* 1999 ICR pg 951 at pg 961H. In answering this question, it should be noted that in the expression of a reason that relates to the disabled person's disability in Section 5 of the Act and Section 28, the description of the causative link has been broadened from that used in other discrimination acts (those concerned with sex discrimination and race discrimination). It therefore includes wider causative links than those that would have fallen within the expression 'on the ground of or by reason of the disability': *Rowden v Dutton Gregory* 2002 ICR 971 at 973E–974A.

The next question is, what is the comparator? The comparator is a pupil who is neither disabled nor badly behaved. See *Clark v TDG Ltd* 1999 ICR P 951, at 926D–F, 963C–F and 965B–A. This issue was considered in educational terms by the High Court, by Silber J in a case decided on 11 December 2003: EWHC 3045 (Admin.), *McAuley Catholic High School v Special Educational Needs and Disability Tribunal*.

That case is particularly important. First, it applied the normal comparator in employment law (the employee with no disability) to education law. Therefore the comparator was taken to be a pupil with no disability. The implications of this are extremely serious. The head teacher at McAuley Catholic High was assaulted by the pupil on whose behalf this case was brought, as were members of the staff. The child was not excluded but was suspended for a substantial period and did not return to school. While most of the allegations were dismissed, the tribunal nonetheless found discrimination in relation to the failure to support the child over a period before the child eventually was suspended and thereafter moved out of the school.

However, the school had treated the child more favourably rather than less favourably than other pupils who had misbehaved. A non-disabled pupil who had assaulted staff would have been excluded, but because the child in question was severely autistic he was not excluded. Thus, by treating the child more favourably than other children who had behaved in a serious manner, the school was found to have discriminated.

Reasonable adjustments

A responsible body also discriminates against a disabled person if it fails, to his or her detriment, to comply with the duty to make reasonable adjustments and cannot show that the failure to comply is justified. The duty is anticipatory and continuing in that the school is required to take reasonable steps to ensure that in an education admission or thereafter in the school or the associated services provided in education, the child is not disadvantaged.

Knowledge of disability

If the responsible body did not know, or could show that at the time it could not reasonably have been expected to know, that the child was disabled, and its failure to take a step was attributable to that lack of knowledge, then that is a defence. However, the defence involves the word 'reasonable', and therefore incompetence or negligence or failing to act in accordance with normal practice would not be an excuse.

A further defence is justification.

Accessibility, strategies and plans

In implementing the anti-discrimination provisions of the Act as they affect schools, there are new provisions placing duties on LAs and schools, including independent schools, to develop an accessibility plan. The responsible body is again the proprietor of the independent school, and the plan is a plan for:

- increasing the extent to which disabled pupils can participate in the school's curriculum;

- improving the physical environment of the school for the purpose of increasing the extent to which disabled pupils are able to take advantage of the education and associated services provided or offered by the school; and

- improving the delivery to disabled pupils of information that is provided in writing for pupils who are not disabled, within a reasonable time and in ways that are determined after taking account of their disability and any preferences expressed by them or their parents.

Such a plan must be in writing and provided within a prescribed period. In the regulations for prescribed periods for accessibility, strategies and plans for schools in England in force from September 2002, the prescribed period ended on 31 March 2006. Independent schools must provide a copy of the plan to the Secretary of State or the National Assembly if they ask for such a copy. The plan must be available for inspection.

The implications

For the purposes of admissions in relation to an independent school, the Act is somewhat simpler than in the state system but in some ways more difficult. In the state system, exclusions and admissions claims are to be made within those proceedings, but in relation to independent schools, claims fall within Sections 28B and 28C even if there are contractual appeal arrangements. This arises because both sections dealing with admissions and exclusions refer to the statutory scheme.

The Code of Practice issued by the Disability Discrimination Council gives a number of examples, which are not set out here. This document can be obtained or downloaded from the Disability Discrimination Council.

Obviously, less favourable treatment will be justified if a child with a disability is not admitted to a school, but the school does not have the ability to cope, because the child's needs are too complex. Just as it is permissible for state schools to refuse to select a child without the relevant abilities (as is done in grammar schools), the same principles apply. It is in the cases where the school's admission procedure, or the school itself through its structure and services, discriminates that a claimant will be successful.

If a bright dyslexic or a child with Asperger's syndrome is refused admission on the basis that the admissions procedure does not make adequate allowances for the disability, or is excluded because inadequate planning and allowances have been made, it would obviously be discrimination. If such a child is admitted and adjustments are not made, resulting in exclusion or withdrawal of the child, then equally there could be a case made for discrimination.

As far as the organization of schools for disabled persons is concerned, the fourth duty obviously is also subject to the structure of the building and practicality. Many schools are located in historic buildings, and it may not be possible to adapt or organize the school to accommodate those with some types of disability. It obviously will be possible to organize the school for others.

The most difficult issue is the identification of special needs after admission. To some degree, the question arises whether staff should have identified a child's special needs, and whether any failure to do so can be considered to be one of professional negligence: see *Phelps v Hillingdon* 2001 2 AC pg 618. However, if staff do not exercise their duties in accordance with a reasonable standard, and the child suffers, that probably amounts to disability discrimination as well as negligence. Once an identification of a disability takes place, if no adjustments are made or inadequate adjustment is made, which is the more common situation, then serious issues arise.

Remedies

In England and Wales the provisions applying to schools are enforceable in the Special Educational Needs and Disability Tribunal. A claim that a responsible body has discriminated against a person in a way that is unlawful can be made by the parents under Section 28(i). The Tribunal's powers, if it considers that the claim is well founded, are very wide indeed. It can make a declaration and such order as it considers reasonable in all the circumstances: see Section 28(i)(3). Such an order can be made with a view to reducing the adverse effect of the disability on the person concerned, or regarding any matter on which the claim relates. It does not include the power to order compensation.

However, in the case of independent schools, a power to order compensation does exist by reason of Section 19. Section 19 applies to discrimination in relation to the provision of goods, facilities and services. It provides that it is unlawful for a provider of services to discriminate against the disabled person in:

- refusing to provide, or deliberately not providing, to the disabled person any service that is provided, or the provider is prepared to provide, to the public;

- failing to comply with any duty imposed by Section 21;

- the standard of service provided to a disabled person or the manner in which it is provided; or

- the terms on which the services are provided to the disabled person.

The provider of services is defined as a person concerned with the provision of services to the public or to a section of the public. Clearly it will include education.

Some claims have been made to the county court and substantial sums awarded in damages for minor acts of discrimination. No major claim has yet been decided. It must, however, be remembered, that alongside disability discrimination claims, lie claims in breach of contract against independent schools. In a case involving a college of further education, *Buckingham & Others v Rycotewood College*, Judge Harris QC, transcript 28 February 2003, Oxford County Court, damages were awarded for:

1. Breach of contract.

2. Expenses incurred.

3. Disappointment as a result of failure to provide a satisfactory education.

Damages in respect of discrimination involve sums awarded by way of aggravated damages. It must also be remembered that damages can be claimed for breach of contract itself, which will now include damages for disappointment. As actions under Section 19 are to be brought in the county court, it is likely that the claim will be pleaded by any competent lawyer to include breach of contract and possibly inappropriate claims for professional negligence.

The post-16 Code of Practice suggests that services might include teaching, including classes, lectures or seminars and practical sessions; curriculum design; examination and assessments; field trips and outdoor education; arranging study abroad or work placements; outings or trips; short courses; items of equipment and materials; careers advice; catering facilities, residential accommodation and the like. Clearly for pre-16 pupils the list is less extensive, and a school will provide fewer services to them.

The finding of discrimination by the Special Educational Needs and Disability Tribunal therefore may well found another claim for damages. Alternatively, there is no reason in relation to an independent school, where the child has actually been admitted to the school, why the claim cannot be made for damages under Section 19, as opposed to the tribunal. Even if a claim is made to the tribunal as an initial step, these proceedings can be difficult and expensive.

Conclusion

Given the small number of cases referred to the Special Educational Needs and Disability Tribunal, and the low number of cases actually reported by the Disability Rights Commission (whose website normally reports such cases), this area of law remains unexplored. It may well be that disabled students are able to get better compensation and redress in an action for damages concerning further and higher education than would be available to a child or young person in a school. For that reason it may well be that there is not so much activity in this field. However, as knowledge of the law grows, it is likely that more applications will take place. But the main object of parental concern is to see that the child achieves appropriately. This will normally result in less concern about matters that have gone wrong, and more concern about getting matters put right. This is as it should be, therefore this legislation may not be as important as other rights.

A Parents' Guide to Admissions Procedures for Children with Special Educational Needs

Veale Wasbrough Lawyers

For all parents, getting their child into their first choice of school can seem complicated and challenging. For parents of children with special educational needs (SEN) it can be even more so. This article examines procedures for children who have Statements of SEN and for those with SEN, but no Statement, who are seeking admission to maintained schools, special schools or independent schools.

Special educational needs provision is not, as many people believe, a matter just for special schools. It should be possible for the needs of most children with SEN to be met in ordinary ('mainstream') schools.

It might be assumed that the term 'mainstream school' refers to any school that is not a special school. In fact the Education Act 1996 defines a mainstream school as any school that is not a special school or an independent school. City Technology Colleges, City Colleges for the Technology of the Arts, and Academies are classified as independent schools but all count as mainstream schools for these purposes, as do Pupil Referral Units.

Ever since the Warnock Committee Report in 1978, one of the main principles of SEN policy is that children with special educational needs should be educated in mainstream schools whenever possible. This is reinforced by legislation and the SEN Code of Practice.

General law regarding admissions

Under the School Standards and Framework Act 1998, Local Authorities (LA) must make arrangements to allow parents: a) to express a preference as to the maintained school, City Technology College or Academy, at which they wish education be provided for their child; and

b) to give reasons for this preference. The LA also has a duty to provide advice and assistance to parents to help with this process. Under the 2009 School Admissions Code, LAs must put in place a scheme to co-ordinate all admissions (including in year admissions) by 2011/2012. However this does not apply to nursery schools or special schools. The Admission Authority of the school must comply with the parental preference, subject to certain conditions (see below). The admissions procedures for children with Statements are different. So how does the law on admissions procedures affect children with SEN? This is dependent on whether or not the child has a Statement of Special Educational Needs and on the representations the parents make as to where their child should be educated.

SEN – children without a Statement of Special Educational Needs

In the maintained sector, children who have SEN but do not have a Statement must be educated in mainstream schools, except in very specific circumstances as outlined below. The School Admissions Code 2009 states that pupils with SEN but without Statements must be treated in at least the same way as all other applicants, but protocols must include arrangements for ensuring that, where there is prior need for particular support or reasonable adjustments, such children are placed quickly. The admission authority must consider all such applications on the basis of the school's published admission criteria as part of the normal admissions procedures. In fact, many LAs and schools give priority to children with SEN in their admission oversubscription criteria.

Despite the clear direction for children with SEN to be educated in mainstream schools, there may be a small number of exceptional cases where a child has SEN but does not have a Statement, where it is more appropriate for the child to attend a special school. These exceptional circumstances are set out in section 316A(2) of the Education Act 1996 and include situations where an assessment for a Statement is taking place or where a child is a hospital patient and is admitted to a hospital school, which is classed as a special school.

SEN – children with a Statement of Special Educational Needs

Again, in the maintained sector, if a child who would normally attend school has a Statement, that child must be educated in a mainstream school unless: a) this is contrary to the wishes of the parents; or b) it is incompatible with the provision of efficient education for other children. These are the only reasons why the LA can refuse to arrange mainstream education. The LA needs to take reasonable steps to prevent 'incompatibility' in a particular school or across its mainstream schools. Efficient education means providing for each child a suitable and appropriate education in terms of a child's age, ability, aptitude and any SEN that he or she may have.

Cases must be considered on their individual merits. For example, if a child's needs are such that they pose a threat to the safety of other children or if the education of other children is seriously affected, this would be incompatible with the efficient education of other children but only if reasonable steps had been taken and had not been effective. The term 'other children' means children with whom the child with the Statement would be likely to come into contact on a regular day-to-day basis, such as the child's class if in primary school or the tutor group and subject classes if in secondary school. 'Other children' does not mean children in other schools or pupils who will only occasionally come into contact with the child.

OFSTED monitors how admission authorities operate their procedures in relation to children with SEN, and the Secretary of State can act if it is believed that the maintained school or the LA is acting unreasonably by refusing to admit children with SEN. Reasonable steps might include one-to-one support, counselling, special equipment or occasional sessions in a special needs unit. Whether one of these steps is 'reasonable' will depend on a number of factors including cost and practicality. School numbers – maintained schools named on a Statement cannot refuse to take a child because the school is full. However, before naming a school, the LA should consider whether the school is already nominally full. Admitting children over the planned number may be incompatible with the provision of efficient education or the efficient use of resources.

LAs also have to ensure that they comply with the legislation on infant class sizes. The Schools Standards Framework Act 1998 imposes a limit of 30 pupils per infant class. Children with a Statement that specifies a school and who are admitted outside the normal admission round (that is, for example, in the middle of a term or at the start of the Spring term), do not have to be counted as part of this maximum limit. Also, pupils who are registered at a special school or who are usually educated in a special unit but come into the mainstream school for certain classes are not to be counted for these purposes.

Expressing a preference

Parents of a child with a Statement have the right to express a preference as to where their child is educated and to give reasons for their preference. This preference will affect the duties on the LA when naming a school in the child's Statement.

Mainstream provision

1. *Expressing a preference for a maintained mainstream school.*
   If the parents of a child with a Statement express a preference for a maintained school, the LA has a duty to name the parents' preferred school unless: (a) the school is unsuitable to the child's age, ability or aptitude or to his or her special educational needs; or (b) the attendance of the child at the school would be incompatible with the provision of efficient education for the children with whom the child would be educated, or the efficient use of resources. LAs must explain to parents the arrangements that allow them to express their preference. Before naming a maintained school in a child's Statement, the LA must consult the school and send it a copy of the draft Statement. If the school is outside the LA area, then the LA must also consult the LA responsible for the school. Consultation does not mean that either the school or the other LA has a veto. If a maintained school is named in a child's Statement, the school must admit the child.

2. *When parents do not express a preference for an individual mainstream school.*
   Where parents request mainstream education for their child but do not express a preference for a particular school, the LA must decide which mainstream school should

be named in the Statement. All the mainstream schools in that area will be reviewed. Mainstream education can be refused in only a small number of cases by using the efficient education ground as set out above.

3. *When parents make representations for an independent mainstream school.*
   Under the Education Act 1996, City Technology Colleges, City Colleges for the Technology of the Arts, and Academies are classed as independent mainstream schools. Other independent schools are not considered to be mainstream for this purpose. When parents have asked for an independent mainstream school to be named in their child's Statement, the LA must consider the request in the light of Section 9 of the Education Act 1996. This sets out the general principle, now reinforced by the Human Rights Act 1998, that pupils must be educated in accordance with their parents' wishes so far as this is compatible with: (a) the provision of efficient instruction and training; or (b) the avoidance of unreasonable public expenditure.

Before naming an Academy in a child's Statement, the LA has to consult the Academy concerned. The Academy's funding agreement with the Secretary of State will usually provide for the Academy to consent to being named in a Statement except where admitting the child would be incompatible with the provision of efficient education for other children and where no reasonable steps may be made to secure compatibility. Where there is a disagreement between an Academy and the LA over the proposal to name an Academy in a Statement, the matter can be referred to the Secretary of State who can direct the Academy to admit the child. Other independent mainstream schools should also admit the child providing that the usual admission requirements have been satisfied. Where the LA does not name the preferred independent mainstream school in the Statement, it must name another mainstream school.

Non-mainstream provision

Where a child has a Statement and the child's parents do not want him or her to go to a mainstream school, the duty of the LA to provide a place in a mainstream school does not apply, although the LA still has the option to name a mainstream school in the child's Statement. The parents can appeal against such a decision to the First-Tier Tribunal (Health, Education and Social Care (SEND Tribunal)). There should be strong and clear reasons for going against the parents' wishes.

1. *Where parents express a preference for a maintained special school.*
   The LA must name the parents' preferred choice of maintained special school in the child's Statement unless the school is unsuitable or the child's inclusion would be incompatible with efficient education (see above).
      The LA must consult the school before naming it in a Statement, including sending the school a copy of the draft Statement. Where a maintained special school is named in a child's Statement, the school must admit the child. Where the LA does not name the parents' preferred choice of special school in the Statement, the LA must consider the request for special school education in the light of the general duty set out in Section 9 of the Education Act 1996 (see above).

2. *Where parents make representations for an independent or non-maintained school.*
   Although parents are able to express a preference for an independent school or a

non-maintained special school to be named in their child's Statement and the LA must consider such a request, it is unusual for the LA to agree, as costs will usually be high. The LA must be satisfied that the child's interests require education at a non-maintained school and that education at the particular school is appropriate. When an LA names an independent or non-maintained special school in a child's Statement, it must pay all the fees. If the LA does not agree to name the independent or non-maintained special school in the child's Statement, it must name another school, mainstream or special, and the parents have the right of appeal to the SEND Tribunal.

Parents who have children with a Statement of SEN have the right to educate their child, at their own expense, at an independent school or non-maintained special school if they so choose and it is agreed with the school. Even if the parents are paying for their child to be educated at an independent school, the LA still has a duty to ensure that the child is receiving efficient SEN provision and that the Statement is reviewed on an annual basis.

Parents should look to the individual non-maintained school's admission policy for details of that school's admissions criteria. Under the Education (Independent Schools Standards) (England) Regulations 2003, it is now mandatory for independent schools to have an admissions policy, which should include a section on equal treatment and must be compliant with the Disability Discrimination Act 1995, discussed elsewhere in this Guide.

3. *Where parents do not express a preference for an individual special school.*
   If parents tell the LA that they do not want their child to be educated in mainstream provision but do not indicate a preferred choice of school, the LA must decide which school should be named in the child's Statement.

Parents' right of appeal

Under the 1996 Education Act, parents have the right of appeal to the SEND Tribunal if they disagree with the school named in Part 4 of their child's Statement or with Part 2 describing the child's SEN and Part 3 stating the special educational help that the LA thinks that the child should get. For children with SEN but no Statement, the usual admissions appeals procedures for maintained schools apply as set out in the School Admissions Code.

Where the LA refuses the parent's request to name an Academy in the Statement, the parent can appeal to the SEND Tribunal, although (as is the case with other independent schools) the Tribunal has no power to direct the Academy to admit the child. If the Tribunal does name an Academy, the Secretary of State expects the child to be admitted and is likely to issue a direction to that effect if the Academy is still reluctant to agree. If an independent school refuses admission to a child with SEN, there is no access to an Independent Appeal Panel as in the maintained sector. However, it may be possible to make a claim for disability discrimination to the SEND Tribunal. If discrimination is found, the Tribunal has the power to order the school to admit the child. Very few cases have been brought so far. Other sections in this Guide provide more details of the process for appeal to the SEND Tribunal.

Sources

For further details:

- School Admissions Code 2009.

- School Admission Appeals Code 2010.
- DCSF SEN Code of Practice, DfES/0581/2001.
- DCSF SEN Toolkit, DfES/0558/2001.
- Inclusive Schooling – Children with SEN, DfES/0774/2001.
- Removing Barriers to Achievement, DfES/0117/2004.

Legislation

- Education Act 1996.
- Schools Standards and Framework Act 1998.
- Special Educational Needs and Disability Act 2001.
- Education (Infant Class Sizes) (England) Regulations 1998.
- Education (Independent School Standards) (England) Regulations 2003.
- Education and Skills Act 2008.

Independent Schools and Special Educational Needs

Veale Wasbrough Lawyers

Most children with special educational needs (SEN) are educated in 'mainstream' state or independent schools, alongside children without special needs.

Section 146 of the Education and Skills Act 2008 (in force as of 1 September 2009) has removed the need for an independent school to obtain the approval of the Secretary of State before it can admit a child who has a Statement of Special Educational Needs. Schools admitting a child without a Statement are still required by general law to detect when a child has learning difficulties and deal with them appropriately.

Unlike a state school where legal relationships are regulated by *public law*, the legal relationships in the independent sector are governed by a private contract between the school and the parents. This is known as the 'parent contract'. Good examples of these contracts will include a form that seeks full information (in confidence) from parents about:

- any learning difficulty, disability, medical condition or allergy affecting the child;

- any learning difficulty affecting other members of the family, since certain conditions are often inherited.

Parents are encouraged to provide the school with as much information as possible, whether or not the forms ask about these matters, and to have confidence that the information will be used constructively to ensure the child receives the right support and can integrate successfully. Conversely, to withhold information or play down the extent of a child's needs can undermine the essential working relationship between parents and school.

The admission process to an independent school will vary according to whether a school is more or less academically selective. Most independent schools set entry tests, and a school that is oversubscribed will often use the test results to produce a rank order for interviews. The law now requires a school to make reasonable adjustments to its admission procedures to ensure that a child with SEN or a disability is not disadvantaged any more than necessary during the admissions process. Therefore, parents applying for a place should let the school know in good time if their child will need special arrangements, such as wheelchair access to the examination room, large-print or Braille test papers, quick access to a toilet or extra time to complete the test. An application of this kind should be backed up by written evidence, such as the report of an educational psychologist sent in advance in good time. The twin themes of *'full information'* and *'as much notice as possible'* run throughout this Guide and apply most of all to the admissions process.

Both state and independent schools have the same responsibility to recognize when a child may have a learning difficulty or disability (SEN) and to refer the child or provide appropriately for the difficulty. Methods may differ between the sectors:

- A state school is expected to follow each stage of the SEN Code of Practice and to make and maintain a Statement where that is necessary.

- An independent school will normally carry out screening tests and then consult with parents if there are indications that a further assessment is needed. The assessment may be carried out by the school's SEN Coordinator (SENCo), or the child may be referred to an educational psychologist.

- The LA remains responsible for ensuring that the needs of a statemented child at a mainstream independent school are being met, and the LA has a statutory right to enter school premises at any reasonable time for the purpose of monitoring the SEN provision being made for that child.

There are many cases where parents have not disclosed – or have not realized – that their child has a special need or learning difficulty, which starts to manifest itself in the first term or perhaps later on. Symptoms may include deteriorating or violent behaviour, loss of concentration or motivation in class and poor quality homework. Schools and parents need to recognize that this kind of behaviour may be a symptom of a special educational need or disability that must be referred for assessment. Not doing this and treating the behaviour solely as a disciplinary matter is potentially an error that can lead to litigation.

The expert who assesses the child's needs should be asked to make clear recommendations as to future provision and management. Sometimes the expert's report discloses a level of SEN or disability that a mainstream independent school cannot provide for, even after making reasonable adjustments. The same may be true of the psychologist's list of recommendations.

An independent school faced with this problem, and often being pressed by parents to persevere, must consider whether it is going to be able to meet the child's needs as diagnosed and assessed. Careful consideration should be given to the evidence and the reasonable adjustments that can be made to the school's regime and the cost of making those adjustments. There should be consultation with the parents and the parents should refer the child to the LA for assessment for a Statement.

There are cases when the head of an independent school makes a conscientious decision that the child must leave because the school cannot cope with his or her needs but the parents wish to challenge the Head's judgement. The parents should ask for a copy of the school's complaints procedure or seek legal advice on whether the school has operated its own procedures correctly.

Parents who consider that their child has a disability and has been treated differently from other children, without justification, have the right to apply to the First-Tier Tribunal (Health, Education and Social Care (SEND Tribunal)).

In a recent case, a boy's behaviour at an independent school was disruptive over a long period of time. The school had provided a great deal of support and employed a number of strategies but even so his behaviour was affecting the education of other children to an unacceptable degree and he was excluded. His parents applied to the Tribunal claiming the school had discriminated against their son on grounds of his behavioural disorder, which was a disability. The tribunal held:

- in most respects the school had done all it could. The exclusion, although discriminatory, was justified and therefore lawful, but

- detentions imposed on the boy for failure to hand in homework on time were *unjustified* discrimination because his lack of personal organization was a symptom of his disorder and the school had not provided any support systems that might have helped him to overcome this.

A mainstream independent school is likely to find that the greatest difficulty arises with behavioural disorders such as attention deficit hyperactivity disorder (ADHD) and also behavioural, emotional and social disorders (BESD). In the interests of the child as much as the school, assessments should be carried out when the symptoms become apparent. It will normally be a condition of attendance at an independent school that parents pay the cost of tests and assessments. If they are unwilling to cooperate in having their child assessed or following recommendations it may become necessary for an independent school, after consultation and appropriate warnings, to require them to remove their child.

How Parents Can Help

John Peake, Southwestlaw

John Peake works within the Education Law team at Southwestlaw, a Bristol-based firm of public law solicitors. He represents parents at SENDIST, Admission and Exclusion hearings and here he offers parents some practical advice on managing the educational system in a non-confrontational and positive manner.

All references etc to the Code are the 2001 SEN Code of Practice unless otherwise stated. Figures in brackets are the paragraph number within the Code.

Being a parent is one of the most difficult jobs in the world! As a parent you want what is best for your child and when your child has, or you believe that he or she has, special educational needs, then this becomes even more difficult.

You want an education that meets all of your child's needs. But what you as a parent may believe are your child's needs or what are the best ways to meet them may well not be shared by your local authority or school. It is important to remember this. Just because you as a parent believe something about your child does not necessarily mean that the experts or teachers will feel the same way.

The first thing to remember is that your child has the right to be educated and if your child has special needs then that education should address and meet those needs.

Some parents take the view that they are not going to leave their children to the uncertainty of the state sector and that they will pay privately for their child's education. This is not an option to be undertaken lightly since the cost of a placement at a school catering for students with special needs can be very expensive. Remember also that this is not a one off payment but an ongoing commitment as long as the child remains within the private sector. Generally speaking it is cheaper to place a child at the most expensive private school than in a specialist school.

Most parents will not be in the position where they can consider funding a place at a private school. That said, a number of schools offer subsidised places or bursaries so it is definitely worth investigating and contacting the school or college to find out.

Most parents however will be dependant on the local authority to pay for the specialist provision. All local authorities are under considerable pressure to keep costs to a minimum and more often than not this will be by educating the child either within a mainstream school with support, or at a special school or placement run by the local authority. There is normally resistance to a child being placed at a special private school where that place will have to be funded by the local authority.

At the same time they are required to identify and meet children's needs with appropriate provision. All LAs therefore have clear mechanisms to manage the SEN process based on law and regulation. This chapter aims to give you a basic framework to manage the process for your child. There are sources of help out there. They are heavily oversubscribed but keep on trying. We shall start at the beginning of the process; don't worry if you come to it part way through. Your job will be to work within the SEN process by managing and directing it to produce the outcome you desire. The professionals with whom you will come into contact have considerable knowledge of the SEN process. It is essential to ensure that, as far as possible, you have equal knowledge.

The essentials

It is essential you are sure about your child's needs. In particular what is your child's disability or what is it that means he or she has special needs. How does this show and what needs does your child have? For instance does your child have difficulty concentrating, finds it hard to process information or is there a physical disability. Different conditions require different types of support or help so it is important to know your starting point.

In relation to the practice and procedure knowledge equals power, so you must get a copy of the *Special Educational Needs Code of Practice*, DfE reference DfES/581/2001 and *SEN Toolkit*, DfES/558/2001, both available free from the DfE publications branch on 0845 602 2260 or from the DfE website. You need to find out as much as possible about the law, the Code, the procedures involved and your child's learning difficulties and/or disabilities. Good books to start with are *Taking Action* by John Wright and David Ruebain and *Children with Special Educational Needs – Caught in the Act* by John Friel. Talk to the helplines run by the national charities specifically for your child's needs. A more general organization dealing with school problems is Advisory Centre for Education (ACE). Ask for a copy of a typical statement or IEP (Individual Education Plan), so you will at least have an idea of what everyone else is talking about.

Practical points

Local Authorities have a legal duty to meet the needs of all children within their area. They have to be seen to manage the process equally for all parents and their processes are largely paper based. You need to be organized to manage this information. The following may help:

● Keep a large ring binder file with all reports and correspondence in date order. Don't subdivide it. If you want to identify all the Individual Education Plans (IEPs), use coloured tags. Do not be tempted to stuff everything in a drawer! It's not unusual to have at least one completely full lever arch folder.

● Send letters to confirm in writing what has been said at meetings and on the phone and keep paper copies both on paper and on a PC. But remember that PCs have a habit of breaking down just when you need a particular document. So keep a paper copy.

- Keep a diary. We advise getting an A4 Date-a-Day diary.
  - Keep the top third of each page as a diary – who you spoke to, what you agreed, when they were going to action that point.
  - Try to keep notes of all telephone calls – who you spoke to, what you agreed, when they were going to action that point.

- If there is going to be a delay, for whatever reason, agree the new date and bring that forward in the diary.
  - In the bottom part of the diary run a behaviour log. Keep it brief and to the point. What you need is a short daily comment about how your child has fared that day. What's gone well, what's gone badly, what caused it? Make notes of the things your child says about his or her problems.

Meetings

Prepare for meetings. It is a good idea to send a letter beforehand, saying what you would like to discuss at the meeting. If possible agree an agenda. Give the school copies of any evidence in advance. There is no point asking people to comment on new information in a meeting when they have not had time to consider it. The focus of the meeting should be your child. It is very easy to get distracted by a discussion about who said what and when or delays in the procedure, and find that you have not said anything about what really worries you about your child's difficulties. The diary also helps here because it is clear and unambiguous. If at all possible take someone with you to make sure the meeting sticks to the point and to help you keep calm. It is also nice to know you have someone there on your side. Take notes. At times you may feel angry or upset but try to stay calm. Send a letter afterwards noting what was said and agreed.

You have a right to express your concerns and your views should be heard. Get in contact with the LA Parent Partnership Officer, who will give you impartial advice as to how the SEN process works within your LA (Chapter 2 of the Code). They should be able to help by offering an Independent Parental Supporter to work with you throughout the time that your child has SEN.

You have a right to enter into dispute resolution with an independent conciliator (Chapter 2). They will try to help you reach agreement with the LA or school as to how to proceed. Use of this service will not at any time prejudice your right of access to the Special Educational Needs Tribunal. It is free to use.

You know your child. You cannot solve all of his or her problems on your own, but you can do your best to make sure that all those difficulties are fully understood and that he or she receives the right sort of help. So how do you achieve this?

First concerns

Whatever the triggers are for the concerns you may have about your child's progress you should always seek to talk to the child's tutor or class teacher. Schools should be 'open and responsive to parents' concerns (5.14). Many teachers misunderstand parents at this stage and believe that parents are saying that they are bad teachers. You must be very careful in what you say and how you say it. You need to be clear about your child's exact difficulties and what you want the school to do to address these difficulties. Even at this early stage it is important to be as clear as possible about what difficulties you think he or she has and why you are worried. Research the disability with the relevant national charity and get their advice on how to present the information effectively. If you are not sure you have all the information about the child, you can ask for a copy of the school files on your child, with certain exceptions. The request should be in writing and the school has to provide the information within 15 working days. There are strict charging limits for this information. Go to: www.informationcommissioner.gov.uk and enter 'access to education records' into the search engine. That should get you to 'Subject Access – Right of access to education records in England'.

All schools should provide special help within the normal curriculum framework and monitor and review the effectiveness of this additional help. This is done through an Individual Education Plan (IEP). You have a right to be involved in the formulation of the IEP and must sign each one to say that you have seen it. If you do not agree with the plan, write 'Not Agreed' and sign and date it rather than not sign at all. This stops any discussion at a later point as to whether you have seen the IEP before. This stage is known as School Action.

When the action that the school has carried out at this stage has not been effective, then the school draws on the external specialists within the Local Authority, eg educational psychologists, advisory teachers, etc. This stage is called School Action Plus. Parents should contribute to the information gathered (2.2). The school must inform you that your child has special educational needs (Section 317A, 1996 Education Act).

Independent reports, for example from an educational psychologist or speech and language therapist, stating that your child has severe Special Educational Needs, should be taken seriously by the school and by the local authority. If not, you should write to the school asking why they disagree with professional advice about both your child's difficulties and the help he or she needs. Insist on a reply in writing. Local authorities must have due regard to the private advice; they cannot ignore it. It is usually, but not always, easier to find agreement on a child's difficulties than the sort of help he or she should have. School governors have a statutory duty to 'use their best endeavours to secure that if any registered pupil has special educational needs the special educational provision which his learning difficulty calls for is made' (Section 317, 1996 Education Act).

If your child needs more help than they can get at Action Plus they may need the extra help that comes through having a statement of Special Educational Needs. A statement describes all your child's difficulties and the help that they must get to meet those difficulties. Not all children will have first received help through Action Plus before a statement is needed. It may be clear from birth or at an early stage in your child's life that they will need a lot more help than most children. Or your child may suddenly need a lot of extra help after an accident, major upset or illness. If the local education authority thinks your child may need a lot of support to learn or make use of school facilities they must carry out a statutory assessment.

The statutory assessment

This means the local authority will find out about your child's learning difficulties and work out what help is needed. If the local authority then thinks it necessary, it will write a statement. If a school makes a request for statutory assessment and the local authority refuses this assessment, the parents have a right of appeal to the Special Needs Tribunal (now SEND

Tribunal) against the decision. Regulations state that the local authority has to make its decision within six weeks of the request. If the parents make the request, then the local authority only has to comply with the request to start a statutory assessment 'if it is necessary'. Your view of what is necessary and theirs may well be some distance apart. It is not enough to write a polite letter asking for an assessment. You must gather evidence and demonstrate that it is really needed, that everything else has been tried and that your child needs help that his or her school cannot provide. Once you write the letter asking for an assessment you are on a strict timeline. Make sure you have the information first rather than trying to find it out later.

If the school makes the request, the local authority will have a form to be completed by the Head. Try to work with the school to complete this form. Get as much information as possible to support your case. Make sure that the rate of progress through the IEP is included, eg '6 months progression reading comprehension over 18 months with 3 hours of 1:1 support throughout this time'. Make sure that all of the additional help that the school is providing is included. It is important to describe in detail all the difficulties you know your child experiences. If he or she has difficulties with reading, for example, describe these very precisely. What happens when he or she can't read a word? Does he or she guess wildly? Or attempt to work it out? How successfully? In continuous reading, does your child make errors; eg miss words or syllables (beginning, middle, and end)? Can he or she read for information? A bus timetable? A computer game manual? The *TV Times*? Does your child seem to be concentrating so hard on decoding, or reading so slowly, that he or she can't remember what he or she has read? Can he or she remember/understand a sentence/page/chapter? What strategies does he or she use to avoid reading? What help does your child need? If certain activities at home are helpful, say so, eg 'If I read the textbook to him, he can do the homework'. Examples of a child's work are useful evidence. Make sure that any examples submitted by the school are unaided work, ie not rehearsed or 'helped' with. You may find it helpful to use headings to describe each of your child's difficulties.

An example of possible headings is given below in the section about analysing a statement. Don't rely on your independent evidence to speak for you. Use it instead to back up what you say. Think carefully about the help your child needs and say why. Say also why his or her local school cannot provide it. Remember that you are describing a 'difficulty in learning' or a disability that 'prevents or hinders' your child from making use of educational facilities, not simply his or her scores on certain tests (Section 312, Education Act 1996).

Once the local authority has agreed to start the assessment it will seek more advice from parents, educational advice from the child's school, medical advice and the advice of a psychologist. The local authority psychologist must consult with other psychologists involved with the child, including your independent psychologist. The quality of advice varies enormously, but The Education (Special Educational Needs) (England) (Consolidation) Regulations 2001, printed at the back of the Code of Practice, are quite specific:

The Regulations (Section 7(2)) state that advice, including parents' advice, shall relate to:

1. the educational, medical, psychological or other features of the case (according to the nature of the advice sought) that appear to be relevant to the child's educational needs (including his or her future needs);
2. how these features could affect the child's educational needs; and
3. the provision that is appropriate for the child in the light of those features of the child's case.

When you receive the advice you should check that it has properly detailed what your child's difficulties are and that it specifies the help he or she needs. If it does not, you should challenge the view in writing immediately.

If, after making the assessment, the local authority decides that an ordinary school can meet your child's needs, it may decide not to make a statement. In this case they will issue a 'note in lieu' saying what his or her needs are and the help he or she requires. If you do not accept that this amount of help is adequate, you have a right to appeal to the First-Tier Tribunal.

Analysing the Statement

Once the local authority has decided 'it is necessary' for it to make a Statement, it will first send you a proposed Statement, with all the advice gathered during the assessment. You have a right to make representations and to have a meeting to discuss the Statement (Schedule 27, 1996 Education Act). The Code is very specific about what is required within a Statement (8.29 and 8.32/8.33 forward). A judge has described Part two of the Statement, which covers the special educational needs or difficulties, as a 'diagnosis' and Part three, which specifies provision, as a 'prescription'. Part two must therefore describe 'all the child's needs'. All means all – each and every one of the needs, not just the one that the school can easily manage. Where behaviour is an issue, then it should explain how the behaviour is going to be managed. Part three must make provision 'for each and every one' of the needs described in Part two. Provision, how the needs shall be met, should normally be quantified (eg in terms of hours of provision, staffing arrangements, etc) (8.37). Local authorities are not allowed to have blanket policies on not detailing provision.

A good Statement is one that enables anyone reading it, eg a supply teacher who does not know your child, to understand what his or her special educational needs are and makes it clear what sort of help he or she will receive. There should be no doubt about what is going to happen, who is going to do it and how often. It is essential to analyse the proposed Statement carefully.

There are two ways of doing this, a paper method or using a PC spreadsheet; the methodology is the same. First make a copy of the Statement and all reports. You need one working copy. Put the original away in a safe place. Number the pages on the working copy. Then take three different coloured highlighter pens. Go through all the reports, including the one you wrote yourself and your independent evidence. With one colour, highlight any descriptions of your child's experiences. With another, highlight any proposed provision. With the third, colour anything with which you disagree. Assign a number alongside each high-lighted point. It does not matter that the numbers on the page are in sequence. You have now created a reference system so that you can refer to each point quickly in the future, eg 15 /2, page 15, highlighted item 2. Use a separate sheet of paper for each of your child's special educational needs and give each a heading. For example, for a dyslexic or dyspraxic child they may be: reading, writing, spelling, maths, memory, organization, motor skills, language skills, social skills, self-esteem, confidence, behaviour and abilities. Other learning difficulties or disabilities will have similar characteristics that your child may or may not share. Fold the paper in half, so that you have one half for descriptions of difficulties (SEN) and one half for the suggested provision for that particular difficulty or aspect of the disability. Go through all the reports again. Copy each highlighted phrase of a description of difficulty on to the relevant page and similarly any advice about provision (noting the reference number). You may also wish to note who said what. Don't worry if the same need or provision appears in two different columns. You now have a list of what everyone says about each of your child's educational needs and the help they say that he or she requires. Check this list against the Statement. This preparation will be invaluable when you meet with the local authority. You can also, using the vocabulary from the reports, draft a proposed statement of your own to be used as the basis of discussion. You will be asked to state a preference for a maintained school. You have the right to make representations for an independent school. The local authority in that case, only has to support your request if it cannot meet your child's needs in a maintained school (mainstream). You need to prove that a mainstream maintained school cannot meet those needs. The local authority has eight weeks in which to finalise the Statement. You have a right to meet with a local authority officer to discuss the draft Statement. If, after trying to negotiate, you find you still disagree with the Statement, you have a right to appeal to the First-Tier Tribunal (see Parts 1.4 and 1.5) about the description of needs and/or provision and the name of the school.

Reviews

A Statement has to be reviewed at least annually. That means every 12 months, not 15 or18 months. The Code of Practice describes what should happen at the review. Most of this is endorsed by Regulations, printed on the back of the Code. You will be asked to give your views. Reports should be considered at the Annual Review. They should be disclosed ahead of the meeting although often this is not the case. If you do feel that the statement is not adequate or wish to move to an independent school, you will need to think about your report in much the same way as described for the statutory assessment. The review report, written after the meeting, should recommend amendments to the Statement. The local authority does not have to follow this advice but it does have to explain to you and the school why it has failed to follow it. If the Statement is amended, but you are still not satisfied, you have a right to appeal to the First-Tier Tribunal about the contents of the Statement, including the name of the school (see Parts 1.4 and 1.5 of this Guide for further information).

And finally!

Keep encouraging your child and give him or her plenty of support. Home is where your child should be safe and happy, however hard things may be at school. Try to keep any frustrations or anxieties to yourself and allow yourself to escape from the pressure sometimes. Join a support group!

An Introduction to Assessment

Dr Richard Lansdown MA, PGCE, DipPsych, PhD, FBPsS,

The psychological assessment of a child thought to have special educational needs is an exercise in problem-solving.

First, one has to pose a 'why' question, examples of which are:

- Why is he or she not reading as well as we expect?

- Why is he or she unable to get on well with other children?

- Why is he or she having such difficulty with written work?

The problem then is to answer these questions in a way that will give indications for the child's educational future.

The first step

The very first step is to gather some general information, which involves taking a brief medical, social and educational history, usually from parents. Information on milestones like walking and talking, hearing and vision, serious illnesses or accidents is essential. Whether there is a history of learning difficulties of any kind in the family may be relevant, and details on how many schools have been attended are also sought.

Next comes current information: what do the present teachers say about the child's attainment and behaviour? Is there any specific concern, eg maths or reading, or is the worry more general? What are the child's interests? What is the child's behaviour like at home? Are there any problems with sleeping or eating or with making and keeping friends?

At this stage it is usually helpful to have some formal rating of a child's behaviour. This can be obtained from standardized questionnaires, which allow one to compare the child in question with others of the same age.

Equally important, especially in view of the Code of Practice that was published in 2001, is to listen to the child. For example, what does he or she see as a problem? What are the good or bad points about the school?

The first hypothesis

Once this information has been gathered, a preliminary hypothesis can be made. For example, consider these five nine-year-olds:

- Peter Doe was born after a difficult delivery and he has always been slow in his milestones. His hearing and vision are normal but he has not been able to keep up with his peers in school work and has been kept down a year in primary school. He prefers to play with younger children. He used to sleep well but now says that it is hard to get to sleep, especially in term time.

- Mary Doe was a normal toddler, very bubbly and outgoing as a young child, who has always had a wide circle of friends. She was a little late in talking but is very agile and swims like a fish. She has recently been reluctant to go to school, complaining of headaches or tummy aches, and her reports have been encouraging but consistent in pointing to a difficulty with reading and spelling.

- Jenny Doe has severe cerebral palsy and has no speech. She can swipe at an object with a closed fist but cannot hold or manipulate a pencil. Her parents report that she seems able to understand a great deal but they admit that they may be biased.

- John Doe is described as having been a good baby, but not at all cuddly, with normal motor milestones, no illnesses but some language delay. He is solitary at school and has only one friend in the neighbourhood who shares his interest in trains. By choice, he reads nothing but train books, including out-of-date timetables, and will spend hours at a station. He hates change of any kind.

- Michael Doe was adopted when he was five years old. When with his birth parents, he was neglected and abused physically and mentally. He is now aggressive, very active with a short concentration span and finds it hard to make friends. His teachers say he is bright but they cannot get him to stay on task long enough.

Each of these yields a different hypothesis. The next step is to test them, using tests and/or observations.

Testing the hypotheses

An intelligence test is the usual starting point for children with learning difficulties of any kind. Two are commonly used in the UK: the Wechsler Scales and the British Ability Scales. Both follow the same pattern of asking that children undertake a range of tasks, which include verbal and non-verbal reasoning, memory, general knowledge, vocabulary and so on. The results are then aggregated to yield an IQ, with 100 as an average score. About 80 per cent of children score between 80 and 120. As a very rough rule of thumb, a score below 70 is an indication of learning difficulties, but it is of the utmost importance to note that this is only an indication, not a ticket to a special school.

There has been much criticism of intelligence tests, and it is true that they have to be used with caution, especially with children from cultures different from that on which the test was standardized. Caution has to be exercised also when quoting an overall IQ, since this can mask significant differences between verbal and non-verbal skills. What is more, an IQ is not as precise a measure as height or weight: there is an expected variation of plus or minus about 6 points, so a given IQ of 100 could be seen to represent a 'true' score of between 94 and 106.

It should be remembered that the tests have been devised for and standardized on able-bodied children, so if one is assessing a child with disabilities one is comparing that child with children without disabilities.

Much can be learned from the scores on such a test, but also from the way the child approaches the task. Does he rush at everything, showing no sense of planning or reflection on what he is doing? Does she persist, even when the tasks are getting hard? How does he react to failure?

But an IQ is only a beginning. One needs next to look at other relevant areas, depending on the question being asked.

Peter: global or specific problems?

Peter's history suggests global difficulties, but to check on this one would supplement the intelligence test with others that look at reading and maths, writing and drawing. If they all point in the same direction, one begins to firm up on a diagnosis of learning difficulty, but it may be helpful also to consider his behaviour. Here rating scales completed by parents and teachers are useful.

Mary: dyslexia?

Mary is reported to have problems with reading and spelling, so one must test those skills. Here we run into the difficulty of defining what we mean by reading. Some tests simply look at the child's ability to read single words out of context; this is useful as a screen, but if there are difficulties it should be supplemented with a test of reading comprehension: how well does the child understand what is read? How much can he or she use context to guess at difficult words or phrases? Spelling mistakes can also give a clue to the next area of investigation: a child who writes 'mite' for 'might' and 'dun' for 'done' may have a weakness in visual memory.

If Mary's reading and/or spelling are poor when compared with her IQ, and if there are no reasons in her educational, medical or social history to explain the discrepancy, then the hypothesis of specific reading difficulty or dyslexia is likely to be upheld. It is common at this stage to assess the child's phonological awareness, which means in essence finding out how well he or she copes with language-related sounds. There are batteries of tests to examine this, most of which include asking the child to detect words that rhyme, picking out words according to their ending sound or saying as many words as possible that begin with a certain letter in a short time. The rationale is that children diagnosed as dyslexic have often been found to have a weakness in such skills.

If it is thought that the child has a memory weakness, then there are tests that examine his or her memory, differentiating between visual and auditory channels.

A rating of Mary's behaviour may also be helpful, but equally important may be to look at how she sees herself. Here one uses a self-concept scale, which gives some idea of whether she perceives herself as socially or academically a success, or possibly whether she feels supported at home.

A note on dyscalculia. Much is made of dyslexia, less of the maths equivalent, which is known as dyscalculia. Relatively little work has been done in this area. There is some suggestion that it is related to spatial skills. The approach is similar to that used for dyslexia, with more detailed assessments of mathematical knowledge being carried out.

Jenny: a test for the tester?

Jenny is quite a different matter. There are no tests standardized on children with cerebral palsy and so one normally uses instruments devised for the able-bodied and interprets them in the light of the child's disability. At first it may seem impossible even to begin testing a child with no language and no hand control, but much can be learned if the child can point, and swiping with a fist is often enough. For example, the British Picture Vocabulary Test consists of a series of pages with four pictures on each. The tester says a word and the child has to indicate the appropriate picture on that page. In this way one can assess vocabulary even in a child who has no speech at all. There are similar tests for spatial skills, and even one new scale that claims to assess general intelligence.

The interpretation of such tests is very much a matter of experience, for one has to take into account the fact that children with physical disabilities have not had the opportunities to learn that their able-bodied peers have.

John: autism?

From his history, John is possibly autistic. Here one starts not with any formal testing but with a careful and detailed consideration of what he has done in the past and what he does now. Observations from teachers and parents are all important. One approach is to take the criteria for autism given in one of the classification systems[1] and to look to see to what extent the child's behaviour matches them.

Once it has been established that a child can be so classified, tests can be useful, and indeed are essential, to allow recommendations for the type of school that will be the best. Standard intelligence and attainment tests can often be used, although it may be necessary to rely on non-verbal scales for some children.

Behaviour ratings are also helpful, especially those that focus on activity levels, for autistic children are often overactive.

Michael: brain injury?

Michael's history is one of neglect and trauma. It is now known that adverse environmental conditions in the first two years of life can affect the actual structure of the brain, and even if he does not have any established injury his behaviour is consistent with someone who does.

In his case it is advisable to give the standard battery of tests of intelligence, memory, reading and maths but also to look carefully at what is known as his executive functioning, by which is meant how well, or badly, he organizes himself, how impulsive he is, how well he seems to be able to learn from mistakes and so on. There are questionnaires for parents and teachers to complete and individually administered tests as well.

---

[1] There are two classification systems in use in the UK. DSM IV is a US system; ICD X is European. They both give detailed lists of criteria for the whole range of psychiatric disorders.

This is a relatively new area but already ways of helping such children are being developed.

These five examples have been chosen to show that not only are different tests used according to the question put but different weights are assigned to test or assessment approaches as well. The art of assessment is not simply in coming up with answers; it lies crucially in asking the right question.

Some miscellaneous points

1. *A note on IQ (intelligence quotient) and reading age.* Psychologists usually report the results of intelligence tests using an IQ or standard score. This computation allows an age correction to be applied to children's responses: a six-year-old answering 20 out of 30 items correctly is clearly brighter than a nine-year-old who has the same raw score. Reading test results are sometimes expressed as standard scores as well (and the purists say they should be), but they are often given as a reading age that indicates the level reached by an average child of those years.

2. *What effect is there when a child feels unwell, or if he or she does not like the psychologist?* It is unwise to test a child who is unwell, and most unwise to rely on scores of one who is emotionally upset. The personality of the psychologist can make a difference, but if he or she has been properly trained this should be relatively small.

3. *Are scores stable over time?* The older the child, the more stable the IQ will be. But a test is a snapshot, taken at one time, giving a picture of a child on that occasion, and although large changes are relatively unusual in older children, they can occur and a retest after two years is advisable.
   NB There can also be a practice effect on tests; that is, if a child is given the same test again within a few weeks, the scores on the second occasion tend to be higher by up to 8 points on the full-scale IQ.

4. *Is IQ that important in explaining school success or failure?* Yes and no. There is no doubt that, in general, children with high IQs do better in school than those at the lower end, which is hardly surprising. But factors within children such as motivation, organization and persistence play a major part, as do good teaching and support from home.

5. *Do all intelligence tests give similar IQ scores?* Again, yes and no. They are likely to give more or less similar scores but the variation can be considerable. The IQ is basically a figure derived from a comparison of the child being tested with the sample on whom the test was standardized. So test A, standardized on group A, will not necessarily give the same results as test B, standardized on group B. Of relevance here is the fact that tests get out of date and should be restandardized every 20 years or so.

6. *What does an IQ of 100 really mean?* When a test standardized on a British population is used, it indicates that the child has scored at an average level when compared with a sample of children chosen to be representative of the whole of the UK, geographically, ethnically and socially.

7. *Why are IQ scores generally preferred to mental ages?* Mental ages are sometimes helpful but they can be misleading. Say three children have a mental age of a nine-year-old. There is all the difference in the world between a four-year-old, a nine-year-old and a fifteen-year-old with that mental age.

8. *Does IQ predict success in areas other than the academic?* Not really; many other factors come into play, like the ability to get on with other people and creative ability.

9. *Should we, then, talk of many different types of intelligence?* It is reasonable to distinguish between practical and academic abilities: one person may be outstanding at running a greengrocery business, always giving the right change and managing to balance the books, but may have been hopeless at the more sophisticated maths at school. Some people are brilliant at school work but hopeless socially. Musical or artistic skills also seem frequently to be distinct, ie a child can be very talented in either of these areas but will not necessarily do well in mainstream school subjects.

Choosing a School for Your Child's Special Educational Needs

David Urani, Consultant Educational Psychologist

The Special Educational Needs Code of Practice defines special educational needs in the following way:

'Children have special educational needs if they have a learning difficulty which calls for special educational provision to be made for them'.

In recent years the general thrust in special needs education has been one of 'inclusion': the belief that the majority of children with special needs will and can be catered for within a mainstream school setting.

This, however, is not always the case. Situations do arise whereby a child's special educational needs cannot be effectively met within a mainstream context, due to the complexity or unique nature of the needs involved. In such a situation, a range of more specialist provision will need to be considered.

Types of specialist provision

Special needs units

Units are based on mainstream school sites. They enable children to access specialist support from the unit, as well as having the possibility of regular integration into a mainstream class. In some cases children can be enrolled in the unit, but in fact spend most of their time in a mainstream setting.

Local Authority special schools

Some children may require the intensive and specialist support provided by special schools. LA special schools (including grant maintained special schools) offer smaller class sizes, teachers with specialist training, high levels of one to one and small group support, and on-site input from therapists and other professionals where necessary. Special schools usually have the resources to cater for children with more severe learning, emotional/behavioural or medical needs.

Special schools fall into two broad categories. Some specialize in dealing with a specific need, for example dyslexia or autism. Other schools cater for a variety of children who may have different specific diagnoses but broadly fit a more general description, such as moderate learning difficulties (MLD) or severe learning difficulties (SLD).

In the main, LA special schools are day provisions where the child can continue to live at home. In exceptional circumstances, where the special need is relatively rare, complex or the appropriate school is not near the child's home, residential provision can be offered.

Depending on the child's progress, some children in special schools can be given the opportunity to integrate into local mainstream schools with support. In a few cases, it is possible for the child to return to full-time mainstream education with support.

Independent special schools

There are a smaller number of independent special schools in the UK that offer specialist provision for children with special educational needs.

Being independent, fees are charged for children to attend. While some schools will accept private fee-paying students, in the main the costs are too prohibitive for most parents. Many independent special schools have a policy of only considering children who have a Statement of Special Educational Needs, where the child's LA is prepared to fund the placement. In some instances, funding may be arranged through other agencies such as Social Services or Health, depending on the specific needs and circumstances of the child.

Independent special schools are designated by the Secretary of State for Education, and are recognized by LAs as providing for a particular aspect of special needs education. In cases where the school does not have official approval to take a certain category of special need child, LAs will not be in a position to support the placement. In exceptional circumstances, it is possible to gain permission from the Secretary of State for a child to attend a non-designated school.

Another category of independent special school, Non-Maintained Special Schools, are also approved by the Secretary of State but are wholly funded by charitable organizations (eg Barnardo's, National Autistic Society).

Alternative provisions

In very exceptional circumstances, such as chronic illness, some children's learning needs cannot be met in a school setting. With prior approval from the LA, tuition can be offered at home or in hospital. Tuition, however, is often only provided on a part-time basis, and is seen as a short-term arrangement.

Some parents choose to implement an intensive home-based programme, supervised by a non-LA organization. An example of this is the Lovaas/Applied Behavioural Analysis interventions used for young autistic children. These programmes are either funded by parents, or can be funded by the LA through a child's Statement.

Parents should be aware, however, that most LAs are reluctant to fund such programmes, commonly referred to as 'education otherwise'. It is frequently the LA's view that most children with special needs can be catered for from within the Authority's own maintained provision.

Selecting a school

Parents are frequently in the position of having to assess the suitability of a school in meeting their child's special needs. The decision as to which school to choose can be a daunting task. The following are some aspects to consider prior to contacting a potential school:

- What is the LA recommending as suitable to your child's needs? Is there a choice? Do you accept that the school/s being offered are appropriate?

- What are the opinions of professionals such as teachers, educational psychologists, therapists or medical consultants regarding the type of school needed for your child?

- Many support groups or professional organizations (eg Royal Institute for the Blind, National Autistic Society) are there to help parents and are able to offer advice in their area of expertise.

- Consulting organizations such as Gabbitas or IPSEA for a list of possible schools can be a good place to start a search.

- Schools often publish a prospectus for parents. Many schools have their own website.

- Has the school had a recent Ofsted inspection and is the report available for you to see? (Ofsted publishes its reports on the internet at www.ofsted.gov.uk.)

Once you have narrowed down the schools you think may be suited to your child's needs, the next step is to visit the schools and see what they have to offer. It is advisable not to take your child on an initial visit, as it may create unrealistic expectations within the child of attending the school.

The following are a few things to consider:

- Don't limit your list to only one school. The more schools you see, the greater your chances are of finding the most appropriate one for your child.

- The most vital question to ask before taking things further is whether the school actually has a place to offer. Many schools are often full, or may have a waiting list.

- How far is the school from home? Will transport be an issue? Will boarding need to be considered?

- Does the school only cater for your child's specific area of need (eg visual impairment) or is it more generalist (eg MLD)? What are the special needs of the other children in the school?

- What is the physical learning environment like? Is the school modified for children with physical impairments? Is the playground safe and easy to supervise?

- Is the school well resourced in terms of learning materials and teaching aids? What level of access is there to computers?

- What are the class sizes and the adult to child ratio? What is the training expertise of the teaching and supporting staff? Is there access to other professionals such as psychologists and speech and language therapists if needed?

● Are there opportunities for mainstream integration? If so, are there children in the school who are on an integration programme?

● Were you able to see children in a lesson? If so, did the children appear to be stimulated and interested? How did the teacher deal with unforeseen circumstances such as a child misbehaving?

● What are the residential facilities like for boarding pupils? Are there extra-curricular activities on offer?

● With older children, is there a work experience/life skills component to the curriculum? What links does the school have with post-secondary colleges?

It is more than likely that you will have further questions to ask after seeing a school for the first time. A second visit is always a good idea, especially if you're unsure. If you feel certain of your choice, take your child along. Ultimately he or she is the one who will be attending and it may well be that you haven't considered some aspect of the school from his or her perspective. For support, it is also helpful to take a friend or a trusted professional who knows your child and can provide a more objective opinion.

Making an application to a school

If as parents you are paying the fees, the application process is relatively uncomplicated and is made directly to the school.

With a Statemented child the situation is very different. You will need to ascertain if the LA is prepared to fund a place in the school you have chosen. Even when you have found a school, and the school is prepared to offer a place, the LA is under no legal obligation to support the placement if it believes an appropriate provision can be found from within its own resources.

Disagreements between parents and LAs regarding school placement can arise. In some instances this can lead to an appeal by parents to an independent First-Tier Tribunal (Health, Education and Social Care (SEND Tribunal)). This can be a very drawn out and expensive option, and should be seen as a last resort.

Advice from professionals such as educational solicitors or independent educational psychologists experienced in Tribunal appeals is strongly recommended before proceeding with this route.

1.12

Social Security Benefits

Rundip Thind from the Disability Alliance

Many families with a child with special needs are not aware of how the social security system could help them. This chapter is a brief introduction to the benefits that you may be able to claim if your child has a physical disability, a learning disability, developmental delays or behavioural problems.

Getting advice

The benefits system need not be daunting or confusing. You can get information and advice from a number of sources. In the first instance you could contact your local Jobcentre Plus office, or call the Benefit Enquiry Line on 0800 882200 (a national telephone helpline about benefits for people with disabilities).

You can get independent advice from a Citizens Advice Bureau, DIAL (Disability Information and Advice Line) or local advice centre. There are also a number of books that give information or advice about benefits. The Disability Alliance provides information about the social security benefits and tax credits that disabled people can claim. It publishes the *Disability Rights Handbook* and a range of other publications every year (see useful addresses at the end of the book).

The information in this chapter uses the benefit rates current from April 2011.

Benefits for your child

Child Benefit

You are entitled to receive Child Benefit for any dependent child, regardless of your other income or savings. You do not have to be the child's parent, but you have to be responsible for them. You can receive Child Benefit for a child aged under 16, or a young person aged under 20 if they are in full-time, non-advanced education (ie more than 12 hours a week at school or college) or in approved unwaged training. A 19 year old can only be included if they started such education or approved training before their 19th birthday. You may not be entitled to Child Benefit if your child is in local authority care for more than eight weeks (unless the child regularly stays with you for at least a day a week, midnight to midnight), or if you receive a fostering allowance for that child. Child Benefit is administered by HM Revenue & Customs.

Amounts
Only or eldest child   £20.30
Each other child   £13.40

To claim Child Benefit, contact the Child Benefit helpline (0845 302 144; textphone 0845 302 1474).

Child Tax Credit

Child Tax Credit is paid to families both in and out of work. It is paid *in addition* to Child Benefit. Although Child Tax Credit is affected by your family income, it is by no means aimed only at low-income families. A family with one child would receive some Child Tax Credit as long as their gross income is less than £45,000 a year (and this figure could be even higher if there is at least one disabled child in the family). HM Revenue & Customs administers Child Tax Credit. You can claim it on form TC600 (which can also be used to claim Working Tax Credit), available from your local Jobcentre Plus office, or by calling the HM Revenue & Customs helpline (0845 300 3900; textphone 0845 300 3909).

Child Tax Credit will be replaced by the Universal Credit after 2013.

Disability Living Allowance

The most important benefit for anyone looking after a disabled child is Disability Living Allowance. It is assessed purely on the child's needs; your financial circumstances are irrelevant. It is not means-tested or taxable, and it is paid on top of any other benefits you may receive. In fact, your other benefits or tax credits may actually be increased when your child receives Disability Living Allowance. The benefit is assessed and paid in two parts. The 'care component' helps with the extra costs of providing personal care, and the 'mobility component' helps with the extra costs of going out.

The care component can be paid if your child needs extra attention (in connection with his or her bodily functions) or supervision (to maintain his or her safety). Obviously, all children need different amounts of attention or supervision at different stages in their development. However, to get the care component you have to show that your child needs attention or supervision that is *'substantially in excess'* of that normally needed by other children of the same age and sex. The care component can be claimed at any age, but your child must have needed the extra attention or supervision for at least three months before any benefit is paid. The care component is paid at three different rates, depending on whether the extra attention or supervision is needed for just a portion of the day, throughout the day or night, or around the clock. A simple way of building up a picture of your child's extra needs would be to make a short diary. This diary could provide details of a typical day or week in your child's life, outlining all the things that you need to do for him or her, why you need to do them and how long they take. You could include a copy of the diary with the claim form, to provide a clearer account of your child's extra attention and supervision needs.

The mobility component is paid at two different rates and is designed to help with the costs of going out and getting around. The higher rate can be paid from the age of three.

Amounts

Care component		Mobility component	
Highest	£73.60	Higher	£51.40
Middle	£49.30	Lower	£19.55
Lowest	£19.55		

Your child will normally be awarded Disability Living Allowance for a fixed period. You will need to re-apply before the award expires: a renewal form should be sent to you automatically. It is common for benefit to be renewed at *milestone* ages – 5, 11 and 16 – when you will need to re-apply.

If you think your child may be entitled to Disability Living Allowance, you should make a claim. You can phone the Benefit Enquiry Line on 0800 882200 and ask them to send you a claim-pack (the DLA1: Child). If you are awarded benefit, it can be paid from the date of this phone call. You can also claim online (www.direct.gov.uk/disability-dla). The claim-pack that you will receive can seem quite complicated, so seek advice if you are not sure how to fill it in.

It is also worthwhile to get the support of any professionals who are involved with your child, in particular paediatricians, nurses or GPs. There is a page in the claim-pack that they can complete. If you have made a diary of your child's extra care or supervision needs, you should provide them with a copy, in case they are approached later to provide further information.

If your child gets the higher rate of mobility component, you will also be entitled to exemption from road tax for one car, and you may be able to hire or buy a car under the Motability scheme (telephone 0845 456 4566). You can also apply to your local authority for a Blue Badge for concessionary parking. Even if your child doesn't get the higher rate mobility component, you may still be able to get a Blue Badge if your child has *'a permanent and substantial disability which causes inability to walk or very considerable difficulty in walking'* or is registered blind.

The Government intends to replace Disability Living Allowance with a new benefit, the 'Personal Independence Payment.' From 2013–14, existing claimants of Disability Living Allowance between the ages of 16 and 64 will be tested under the benefit and moved onto it if they pass the conditions. As yet there are no plans to extend the Personal Independence Payment to children under 16. However, migration may occur at a later date.

Benefits your child can claim at age 16

On reaching the age of 16, a young disabled person can claim benefit in his or her own right. If he or she receives benefit, they will cease to be your dependant for benefit purposes and you will no longer be able to claim Child Benefit or Child Tax Credit for them. Any benefits will be paid in his or her name, though if the young person is unable to handle their own claim, you may apply to be their 'appointee' and act for him or her.

Employment and Support Allowance

Employment and Support Allowance (ESA) is the new benefit for people whose ability to work is limited by their disability or illness. There are two types of the benefit; contributory ESA and income-related ESA.

Contributory ESA

Contributory ESA can generally only be paid if the young disabled person has paid enough

National Insurance contributions or satisfies the rules for ESA in youth. ESA in youth can be paid to a young person whose limited capability for work began before the age of 20. It is important that they claim before their 20th birthday, because after that age they will only be able to receive contributory ESA if they have been employed and paid sufficient National Insurance contributions. There is some protection for young people in education or training to allow them to make a claim under these rules up to the age of 25. To be protected, their course of education or training must have begun at least three months before their 20th birthday, and they must claim ESA within two years of the course ending.

Contributory ESA cannot usually be paid to a student under 19 who is at school or college and is attending classes for 21 hours or more a week. When calculating the 21 hours you should ignore any time spent in study that would not be suitable for a person of the same age who does not have a physical or mental disability. So, if a young disabled person receives a lot of support to follow a course, or if the course is taught in such a way that would make it unsuitable for a non-disabled person, then he or she may still be entitled to contributory ESA.

From April 2012 ESA in youth will be abolished for new claimants. When this happens, those already getting ESA in youth will be able to remain on it, but entitlement will be limited to one year from the time entitlement began.

Income-related ESA

Income-related ESA can be paid if the young disabled person has no other income or only a small income. It can be paid by itself, or it can top up contributory ESA if the young person is also entitled to that. It cannot be paid to a young person who has more than £16,000 savings; any savings between £6,000 and £15,999 will reduce the amount of benefit paid.

Income-related ESA can include extra amounts called premiums which are paid to more severely disabled people. The enhanced disability premium is payable to a person receiving the highest-rate care component of Disability Living Allowance; the severe disability premium is payable to a person living alone receiving the middle or highest-rate care component of Disability Living Allowance (as long as no one is getting Carer's Allowance for looking after them).

If a disabled young person receives income-related ESA, he or she can also apply for help from the Social Fund for certain one-off expenses.

Income-related ESA will be replaced by the Universal Credit after 2013.

Claiming ESA

A claim for ESA can be started by calling the Jobcentre Plus claim-line (0800 055 6688; textphone 0800 023 4888). Online claims can made at www.dwp.gov.uk/eservice. Paper claim-forms (ESA1) can be obtained from Jobcentre Plus offices.

A medical certificate will be needed. A young person will only be entitled to contributory ESA after they have had a limited capability for work for 28 weeks. It is possible for these weeks to be before their 16th birthday, so that they can claim as soon as they reach the age of 16. They will need a fit note from their GP, and if ESA is to start right away, it should be backdated to cover the 28 weeks prior to the claim. It is also possible for a new claim for ESA to be backdated for up to three months, as long as the claimant would have qualified for it at that time, but this extra time must additionally be covered on any backdated fit note (ie on top of the 28 weeks).

The first 13 weeks of the claim will be an assessment period. During this time ESA will be paid at a lower level. A 'work-focused interview' will take place after about 8 weeks. At this interview a personal adviser will discuss work prospects with the young person. Also during the assessment period a 'Work Capability Assessment' will take place. This assessment will usually start with a form (the ESA50) being sent to the young person to complete. They should seek advice if they are not sure how to fill this in. A follow-up medical may then be arranged. The work capability assessment will determine whether the young person stays on ESA and, if they do, which of two groups of claimants they will be placed in: the 'support group' or the 'work-related activity group'. If they are placed in the support group, they do not have to undertake work-related activities, although they can volunteer to do so. They receive a higher rate of ESA than if they are in the work-related activity group. If they are placed in the work-related activity group, they must meet work-related conditions, including attending six work-focused interviews; if they fail to meet the conditions, their ESA payment may be reduced.

If the young disabled person is found not to have a limited capability for work at the Work Capability Assessment, they will no longer be able to claim ESA. They can either claim Jobseeker's Allowance instead, or they can appeal against the decision. An appeal will be heard by an independent tribunal. Appeal forms (the GL24) can be obtained from Jobcentre Plus offices.

Amounts

Assessment period

(aged under 25)	£53.45
(aged 25 or over)	£67.50

After 13 weeks

Work-related activity group	£94.25
Support group	£99.85

Premiums (income-related ESA)

Enhanced disability premium	£14.05
Severe disability premium	£55.30

Benefits for carers

Carer's Allowance

You can claim Carer's Allowance if your child receives Disability Living Allowance care component at the middle or highest rate. You must be looking after him or her for at least 35 hours every week. You can claim even if you have a partner who is in full-time work.

You cannot receive Carer's Allowance if you are in full-time education (21 hours or more of study per week) or earning above £100 net per week. It does not matter for how many hours you work, as long as you are below this earnings limit and you are still caring for your child for at least 35 hours per week. To calculate your net earnings, deduct tax, National Insurance contributions and half of your contributions towards an occupational or personal pension. You are also allowed to deduct care costs up to a maximum of half your net earnings. This includes care for the disabled person for whom you claim Carer's Allowance, or for any child under 16 for whom you claim Child Benefit, as long as the care is not provided by a close relative of yours or of the person cared for. There is no upper age limit for new claims for Carer's Allowance.

Carer's Allowance is paid at £55.50 per week, and while you are receiving the allowance your National Insurance contribution record will be protected. Your Carer's Allowance will be taken into account if you (or your partner) are also claiming Income Support, Income-related Employment and Support Allowance or income-based Jobseeker's Allowance, but these benefits will also be increased by an additional carer's premium. To claim Carer's Allowance, get a claim form from your local Jobcentre Plus office, call the DWP Benefit Enquiry Line freephone on 0800 882200 or claim online (www.direct.gov.uk/carers-ca).

Other benefits

National Insurance contributory benefits

If you are unable to work, unemployed, widowed, pregnant or retired, you may be entitled to some benefits through the payment of National Insurance contributions. Employment and Support Allowance, contribution-based Jobseeker's Allowance, Maternity Allowance and State Pension can be payable if you have paid enough contributions. In the case of bereavement benefits (for widows, widowers and surviving civil partners), your late husband's, wife's or civil partner's contributions are relevant.

If you qualify, these benefits are paid to you as an individual. It does not matter if you have savings, or (except for bereavement benefits) a partner who is in full-time work. However, if these benefits are your family's only or main source of income, you will usually need to claim a top-up from a means-tested benefit, such as Income Support, as well (Employment and Support Allowance has its own means-tested element). To claim any of these benefits call the Jobcentre Plus claim-line 0800 055 6688 (or textphone 0800 023 4888).

Income Support, Income-based Jobseeker's Allowance and Pension Credit

Income Support and income-based Jobseeker's Allowance are the benefits for people who do not have enough money to live on and who are not in full-time work. You will not be entitled to these benefits if you have savings or capital above £16,000. If you have savings or capital of more than £6,000, your benefit will be reduced. Pension Credit is the equivalent benefit for claimants who are aged 60 or over.

Income Support can be paid to lone parents with a child under 7 (reduced to 5 from January 2012) or carers. Some people from abroad, who are not entitled to other benefits, may be entitled to a reduced rate of Income Support. If you do not fit into any of the categories for which Income Support can be paid, you will have to claim income-based Jobseeker's Allowance (if you are able to work) or income-related Employment and Support Allowance (if you are not) instead. To claim Income Support call the Jobcentre Plus claim-line 0800 055 6688 (or textphone 0800 023 4888).

Income-based Jobseeker's Allowance is paid to people who are required to be available for, and actively seeking, work. You can be sanctioned, and have your benefit reduced or taken away altogether, if you refuse the offer of a job or leave a job without 'just cause'. To claim income-based Jobseeker's Allowance call the Jobcentre Plus claim-line 0800 055 6688 (or textphone 0800 023 4888).

Income support and income-based Jobseeker's Allowance will be replaced by the Universal Credit after 2013.

Pension Credit can be paid to people who have reached state pension age (which is being increased from 60 to 66 between 2010 and 2020). To find out your exact state pension age, call the Pension Service on 0845 6060265 or visit www.direct.gov.uk/pensions. Pension credit consists of a 'guarantee credit', which is similar to Income Support, and a top-up 'savings credit' for those aged 65 or over. There is no upper capital limit above which you cannot claim Pension Credit. To claim Pension Credit contact the Pension Service application line (0800 99 1234).

If you own your home, Income Support, income-based Jobseeker's Allowance, income-related Employment and Support Allowance and the guarantee credit of Pension Credit are particularly important as they are the only benefits that provide any direct help with your mortgage costs.

If you receive Income Support, income-related Employment and Support Allowance or income-based Jobseeker's Allowance, you will be entitled to free school meals, vouchers for milk, fresh fruit or vegetables for children under four, free prescriptions, NHS dental treatment and vouchers for glasses, wigs and fabric supports. You can also claim a refund of your fares to hospital. Additionally, you can apply for grants and loans from the Social Fund for one-off expenses.

Housing Benefit and Council Tax Benefit

These benefits are administered by your local council. You can claim them whether you are working or on benefits. Housing Benefit helps with your rent if you are a tenant. Council Tax Benefit helps with your Council Tax bill (it does not matter whether you are an owner-occupier or a tenant).

If you are on Income Support, income-related Employment and Support Allowance, income-based Jobseeker's Allowance or the guarantee credit of Pension Credit, you will be entitled to the maximum allowable Housing and Council Tax Benefit. Otherwise the amount of help you get will depend on the level of your family's income. The amount you get may be reduced if you have any other adults living with you. Contact your Local Council for their claim forms.

Health benefits

If you receive Income Support, income-related Employment and Support Allowance, income-based Jobseeker's Allowance or the guarantee credit of Pension Credit, you will automatically qualify for help with prescription charges, hospital travel costs, dental treatment and glasses.

If you receive Working Tax Credit or Child Tax Credit, you may get assistance with the above medical costs, depending on how your Tax Credit has been worked out – if you are entitled to help you should be sent a Tax Credit exemption certificate.

If you are not in receipt of these benefits, you can still claim help with medical costs on grounds of low income. Ask for form HC1, which you can get from your local Jobcentre Plus office, or by calling the Prescription Pricing Division: 0845 850 1166.

Working Tax Credit

You can claim Working Tax Credit if you are working for 16 hours or more a week and you have at least one dependent child. Working Tax Credit is also available to disabled workers and some other groups of workers who do not have childcare responsibilities (including anyone aged 25 or over working for 30 hours or more a week). The amount that you receive depends on your family circumstances and the level of your earnings. Working Tax Credit and the related Child Tax Credit are administered by HM Revenue & Customs. They are calculated and awarded on an annual basis.

You can obtain claim forms for either Tax Credit from your local Jobcentre Plus office, or by calling the Tax Credit helpline on 0845 300 3900, which can also advise you on how much you may be entitled to.

Working Tax Credit will be replaced by the Universal Credit after 2013.

Would you be better off in work?

If you are thinking about coming off benefit and claiming Working Tax Credit instead, you can visit a Citizens Advice Bureau or any other local advice centre to ask for a 'better off' calculation, comparing your current rate of benefit with what you could be entitled to once you start work. You will need to know roughly how much you would be earning, and how much your weekly rent and Council Tax bills are. When you make your decision remember to take into account your extra expenses and costs of going out to work, as well as other factors such as the possible loss of free school meals and milk vouchers, and the loss of access to grants and loans from the Social Fund. If you own your own home, remember that Income Support, income-related Employment and Support Allowance, income-based Jobseeker's Allowance and the guarantee credit of Pension Credit are the only benefits that provide any help with mortgage interest.

Getting further advice

This chapter can only give a very brief introduction to the benefits and tax credits that you may be entitled to. If you would like to find out more, contact a local Citizens Advice Bureau, DIAL or other advice centre. If you believe that the Department for Work and Pensions has made a mistake about your benefit, you should contact them and explain why you think the decision is wrong. You could ask them to reconsider the decision and you may also be able to appeal to an independent tribunal, but there are very strict time limits – get independent advice.

Access Arrangements, Reasonable Adjustments and Special Consideration

The document *Access Arrangements, Reasonable Adjustments and Special Consideration* is produced by the Joint Council for Qualifications (JCQ). The rules and regulations are designed to facilitate access to qualifications for candidates who are eligible for adjustments in examinations. The regulations in force as at September 2011 are valid for the academic year 1 September 2011–31 August 2012. They apply to General and Vocational qualifications. The regulations are reviewed throughout the year and revised annually before publication in September. There are three categories of adjustment:

1. *Access Arrangements.* These are agreed before an examination or assessment. They allow candidates with special educational needs, disabilities or temporary injuries to access the examination(s).

   Access arrangements allow candidates to show what they know and can do without changing the demands of the assessment; examples include, provision of readers, scribes or word processors.

   An access arrangement which meets the need of a disabled candidate would be a 'reasonable adjustment' for that candidate.

2. *Reasonable Adjustments.* A reasonable adjustment required by a candidate will usually be an access arrangement, but it may include other adjustments that are not included in the JCQ document. Reasonable adjustments should be applied for in the same way as access arrangements. Where a candidate has significant needs, advice must be sought from the relevant awarding body.

3. *Special Consideration.* This may be given after an examination or assessment to ensure that a candidate with a temporary illness, injury or indisposition at the time of the assessment is given some recognition of the difficulty he or she faced.

It should be noted that the information shown here is necessarily only a very brief introduction. For a copy of the document, which includes examples of how Access Arrangements might apply, visit the JCQ website at www.jcq.org.uk. Day-to-day enquiries about interpretation of the Regulations should be made to the JCQ. Subject specific enquiries or advice on the suitability of a particular specification should be made to the individual awarding body concerned.

Assessment and Qualifications Alliance (North)
Devas Street
Manchester M15 6EX
Tel: 0161 953 1180
Fax: 0161 455 5444
Website: www.aqa.org.uk

Assessment and Qualifications Alliance (South)
Stag Hill House
Guildford
Surrey GU2 5XJ
Tel: 01483 506506
Fax: 01483 300152
Website: www.aqa.org.uk

Council for the Curriculum Examinations and Assessment (CCEA)
29 Clarendon Road
Belfast BT1 3BG
Tel: 02890 261200
Fax: 02890 261234
Website: www.ccea.org.uk

Edexcel
One90 High Holborn
London WC1V 7BH
Tel: 0844 576 0025 (GCE)
0844 576 0027 (GCSE)
0844 576 0026 (BTEC & NVQ)
Website: www.edexcel.org.uk

JCQ
Veritas House
125 Finsbury Pavement
London EC2A 1NQ
Tel: 020 7638 4137

OCR
Syndicate Buildings
1 Hills Road
Cambridge CB1 2EU
Tel: 01223 553998
Fax: 01223 553051
Website: www.ocr.org.uk

Welsh Joint Education Committee
245 Western Avenue
Cardiff CF5 2YX
Tel: 02920 265000
Website: www.wjec.co.uk

1.14

Children with Special Educational Needs – Guidance for Families Overseas[1]

Leaving the UK

Parents leaving the UK, for example on a temporary posting, face key decisions about their children's education, including whether their child should accompany them or, alternatively, remain at a boarding school in the UK. In cases where a child has special educational needs, wider issues must also be considered. If you expect to live overseas for a period, the following points may be helpful in planning your child's education.

Whether your child will accompany you or remain in the UK for his or her education depends on many factors, including:

- your individual circumstances;
- expected length of stay outside the UK;
- continuity – are you likely to move again before returning to the UK?
- your child's age;
- the nature and severity of your child's special needs;
- availability and accessibility of suitable education provision and, where appropriate, medical provision and therapy in the UK and in the host country;
- your child's ability to cope with change.

It is also wise to ensure that you have a thorough understanding of the culture and attitudes towards special needs or disabilities in the country in which you will be living. You may also wish to check the general levels of physical access available to people with mobility difficulties; some travel guides provide good information on this point.

---

[1] This chapter has been updated with the kind assistance of Lydia Parbury, Special Needs and Disability Adviser at the Diplomatic Service Families Association.

If your child has a Statement of Special Educational Needs, check with your Local Authority (LA) the position with reference to the maintenance of that Statement. This may vary from one LA to another and according to your child's individual circumstances. If your child has been attending a day school, for example, will the LA maintain a place for him or her while you are away from the UK? What happens upon your return? Depending on circumstances, funding may be shared between the LA and Local Health Authority, and arrangements may be complex. It is wise to send a copy of your child's annual review, or its equivalent, back to the LA for their records while you are away. Remember too that your child would normally have a Transition Review at age 14, which will influence the next vital years in education. You should be aware that your child will not be able to have this review if he or she is abroad.

If you plan to take your child with you, life in your host country may offer a number of advantages and disadvantages. The benefits might include:

- better salary and employment conditions;
- better climate;
- availability of domestic help;
- good provision for your child's particular needs;
- local tax concessions;
- higher welfare benefits;
- better housing;
- travel opportunities that will broaden your child's horizons and experiences;
- better medical provision.

Against this, however, there may be drawbacks, including:

- isolation;
- absence of support groups;
- lack of family support;
- language barriers;
- loss of welfare benefits;
- limited special needs provision;
- lack of facilities for the disabled;
- climate;
- housing (perhaps in a flat with no garden);
- setbacks in your child's progress;
- lack of networking opportunities to share help and ideas;
- poorer medical provision.

Above all, avoid making hasty decisions. Give yourself time to make an informed choice and to consider the benefits and drawbacks for the whole family.

Points to remember

1. If your child is having extra help at school, make sure you take an up-to-date Individual Education Plan (IEP) with you. The IEP can then be adjusted at any new school abroad.

2. Find out as much as you can with reference to the host country in which you expect to live, for example:

- What provision is available for your child's needs? Consider any medical care as well as educational provision.

- Is there an appropriate centre/support group where you can obtain information and advice?

- Is your child/are you entitled to any state benefits or tax concessions?

Some countries may offer highly advanced provision, others almost none. Your support group in the UK, if one exists, may be able to advise you or put you in touch with 'sister groups' in the host country or with other members of the association who have lived abroad. If experienced in working in the host country, your employer/your partner's employer may be able to guide you. It may also be worth consulting international organizations such as the European Dyslexia Association or the British Embassy/High Commission or the British Council office in your host city/country for any other useful information.

The internet offers a wealth of information. Most schools now have prospectuses and information available online. Use the schools' websites to find out about those which might be of interest to you.

3. If you know the area in which you will be living, try to make contact with sources of help, such as:

- a local doctor or hospital;

- local authority or equivalent;

- any English-speaking organization, for example an expatriates' club. There may also be a local special needs group online;

- any organization for the disabled. Even if it does not focus specifically on your child's particular needs, it may still be able to offer support and direct you to other appropriate organizations.

4. You may wish to consider educating your child at home. If so, make sure you have all the support you need before committing yourself. The internet is a good source of help, but check whether you will have access to it in your new destination. At the time of writing there are several useful website addresses with details of the National Curriculum and support groups. For general information try the website of the Department for Education at www.education.gov.uk.

5. Talk over the move and possible changes in routine with your child. Take care also to talk to siblings about their concerns.

6. Keep a written record of the help you seek, names and contact numbers.

7. Try to obtain some basic training in the treatment of the type of special needs presented by your child and research why your child has the condition or learning difficulty.

8. Keep your employer and/or your partner's employer fully briefed about your child's special needs. Most companies now have a Family Friendly Policy. Might either employer offer any help to meet additional costs associated with your child's education?

9. Take with you any reference books about the condition or learning difficulty that affects your child, or make a note of useful website addresses.

10. Join any organization in your home country that can keep you up to date with developments and improvements in provision for the special needs your child has.

11. State clearly what you want and need for your child. Do not assume that friends and colleagues understand the kind of help and support you and your child require. Remember too that you will not be alone: at least 20 per cent of children will at some time in their lives present special needs in some form.

12. Remember to take with you all relevant and up to date papers concerning your child's special needs. Also ensure you update your records whilst abroad.

13. Finally, be realistic about the level of involvement you have had with your child's needs and the extent of support given by the school and other sources. How will your child cope under different circumstances?

Returning to the UK

If you are returning to the UK after being resident abroad, it is wise to contact in advance the LA for the area in which you intend to live and ask for an assessment of your child's needs. However, be aware that you will need to confirm your address in the UK before the LA can discuss schools with you or make an assessment, and that the reintegration process back into UK education may be a difficult process taking a number of weeks. At the same time, contact your support group in the UK to ensure that you are fully up to date with DFE regulations on special needs provision.

Educating your child in the UK

If you live overseas, either as a British expatriate or as a citizen of another country, but wish to have your child educated in the UK, there are a number of points to consider.

The UK offers a variety of boarding education options. The independent (fee-paying) sector offers a wide choice of boarding education with varying levels of provision for special needs. Few mainstream independent schools have children with Statements of Special Educational Needs. Many, however, have children with mild or moderate specific learning difficulties. Some schools have dedicated units to cater for children requiring special tuition and usually operate on a withdrawal basis, which means that children are withdrawn from certain lessons during the school day to have special tuition for their particular needs. Other schools offer more limited assistance, for example through extra lessons from a visiting teacher. Annual fees at independent boarding schools in 2010–2011 generally range from £12,000 to £20,000 at preparatory level and from £18,000 to £25,000+ at senior level.

Where a child's needs are more complex or severe, and where a child has a Statement of Special Educational Needs, a special school may be more appropriate. Residential special schools usually provide for a particular type of special need. Because of the highly specialist teaching and facilities offered by independent special schools, fees are often substantial. Where the LA agrees that a child should attend a particular school, it will normally pay the fees (sometimes in conjunction with Social Services or Health Services), provided that the school is one that has been approved by the Secretary of State for Education and Skills. In some cases, the fees are paid by parents. Parents with no right of abode in the UK should expect to meet the full cost of fees.

State-maintained boarding schools are few in number and are open only to UK and EU nationals and others with a right of residence in the UK. Fees are charged only for the cost of boarding at these schools, while tuition is free. Annual fees are therefore generally no more than £6,000 and in some cases considerably less. As indicated above, parents should take care to find out exactly how much help will be offered to a child with special needs.

In most cases, parents based overseas should expect to meet the cost of the fees for a boarding place. A boarding allowance is made for British parents employed by the Foreign & Commonwealth Office or by HM Forces. British parents living overseas *may* be eligible for LA support for a child being educated in the UK, but are strongly advised to take independent advice in accordance with their individual circumstances.

Non-British children of statutory school age, who are nationals of a member state of the European Union (EU) or of Iceland, Norway or Liechtenstein and who are being educated in the UK (whether accompanied by their parents or not), have the same rights to education in the UK as British citizens. Under reciprocal arrangements within the EU, those who hold the equivalent of a Statement of Special Educational Needs made in another EU country may be eligible for support from the LA covering the area of the UK in which they will be living, but parents should seek advice according to their particular circumstances. In practice, children who come to the UK unaccompanied may be more likely to attend a boarding school in the independent sector, for which parents will normally be required to meet the fees.

Unaccompanied children of statutory school age who do not have a right of abode in the UK are not normally allowed entry to take up a place at a state-maintained school. Entry to the UK for purposes of receiving an education is only permitted if the student can demonstrate that he or she has been accepted for a course of study at an independent educational institution.

It may be helpful to obtain a clear assessment of a child's needs in the home country for use in finding suitable UK schools. Some schools will reassess the child before offering a place.

Points to remember about boarding education in the UK for parents resident overseas

The choice of a suitable boarding school requires careful research. As well as providing suitable provision for your child's special needs, the school must meet your child's wider needs and offer an environment in which he or she will feel happy and at home. Find out as much as possible about schools in which you are interested and visit them before making a choice. Consider in particular:

- **Your child's academic background**
  If your child has been educated in the British system, it should not be difficult to join a school in the UK. Entry from a different national system is possible but may be less straightforward.

- **Your child's level of English**
  Is additional support required?

- **Length of stay**
  If the stay in the UK is expected to be relatively short, an international school may be more appropriate.

- **Location**
  You may prefer a location that enables your child to be near friends or relatives, but most parts of the UK are well served by air, road and rail links, so it is not necessary to limit your search to schools close to major airports.

Further advice on the choice of a suitable mainstream school is given in Part 4.1.

Also bear in mind the following points:

- If your child is attending a boarding school in the UK while you are overseas, he or she must have a guardian in the UK, preferably living near the school, who will take responsibility for your child at weekends and other times when your child is out of school. While some residential special schools offer 52-week placements, most schools have three school holidays plus half-term holidays and exeats (weekends out of school). You may have friends or relatives in the UK able to care for your child during these periods, but this arrangement is not always suitable and may limit your choice of schools. If you have no contacts in the UK, talk to a reputable guardianship service provider such as Gabbitas who can find a family able to offer your child a safe and welcoming home-from-home and take care of other travel and administrative arrangements.

- Your child may require an escort during travel, which will incur additional costs. Some airlines issue a card to travellers who require special care and will provide the facilities requested free of charge each time a booking is made. Children with parents in the Forces may be entitled to have escorts provided by the British Red Cross or the Soldier, Sailor and Airforce Families Association (SSAFA).

- While you should receive regular progress reports from your child's school and guardian, communication with your child on a day-to-day basis may be difficult if his or her special needs give him or her limited or no speech unless he or she can use e-mail.

Children accompanying their parents to the UK

Children accompanying parents who have the right of abode in, or leave to enter, the UK will normally be treated as dependants. Upon taking up residence in the UK, overseas parents living in the UK have the same right as anyone else with a right of abode in the UK to apply for a place at a maintained school. They also, therefore, have the same entitlement to have their child's educational needs met by their LA.

Whatever your requirements, you are strongly advised to seek specialist guidance in accordance with your own individual circumstances and the specific needs of your child. Further information may be available from your child's school, from any parents' support group to which you currently belong or from one of the associations listed at the back of this book.

Education and Training for Young People with Disabilities or Learning Difficulties After Age 16

Skill (National Bureau for Students with Disabilities)

If you are nearly 16 years old, you will probably be thinking about education and training options ahead. You will need to consider what you are best at and what you would most like to do. You may also need to consider any extra support that you may need because of your disability or learning difficulty. This chapter explains the options available to you and the support you can expect because of your disability or learning difficulty.

What choices are available at 16?

School sixth form

You may be able to stay at your current school if it has a sixth form or you might want to go to a different sixth form for a particular course or better support. At sixth form you can take an academic course such as A levels, or a work-based course such as a National Vocational Qualification (NVQ). Your school should be able to give you advice about your options. If you are leaving your school, your Connexions Personal Adviser (PA) can help you to find a new place to learn or train (see below).

Link courses

Many schools offer 'link courses'. These courses are based at school, but students attend a local further education college for part of their studies.

Further education (FE) colleges

You may find that your local FE college offers a wider range of courses than is available at your school. These might include:

- Academic courses (GCSEs, A and AS levels).

- Work-based or work-related courses (National Vocational Qualifications (NVQs), including RSA, Edexcel or City & Guilds Institute qualifications).

- General courses to prepare you for adult life. These courses may not always lead to a qualification.

It is important to find a course that you like and to ensure that the college can offer you any extra support you need because of your disability or learning difficulty.

Specialist colleges

You may find that your support needs cannot be met in a local school or college. If this is the case, there are specialist colleges that have extensive experience of teaching students with a particular type of disability or a range of different disabilities. These colleges are located around the country and recruit nationally, so you may have to travel to get there. Many specialist colleges are residential and can help you to learn to live away from home. Some colleges offer a range of education options, including those listed above under further education colleges.

Information on specialist residential colleges is given in part 2.4 of this guide and the COPE Directory (of post-16 residential education and training for young people with special educational needs). Your local careers/Connexions service should have a copy of the COPE Directory and they should be able to help you find the best college. You can also contact the Association of National Specialist Colleges (NATSPEC) for details of their colleges.

Higher education

Once you have completed A levels or an equivalent qualification you may want to go on to higher education to study for a Higher National Certificate (HNC), Higher National Diploma (HND) Foundation Degree (FD) or a degree. Your school or college should be able to give advice on how to apply for higher education.

Work-based learning opportunities

Work-based learning for young people is organized by the Local Authority. Young people are able to take up these opportunities when they leave school at 16 or 17.

- **Employment preparation**, which does not necessarily lead to a particular qualification, eg life skills training.

- **Entry to Employment (E2E)**, which provides high-quality work-based learning below NVQ Level 2 for young people at the pre-apprenticeship stage.

- **Apprenticeships**, which give school leavers training while they work within an industry. There are different levels of Apprenticeship available but they all lead to **National Vocational Qualifications (NVQs)**, **Key Skills** qualifications and, in most cases, a technical certificate such as a **BTEC** or **City & Guilds**.

Your local careers/Connexions service can give you information on work-based learning opportunities in your area. If you want to know more about apprenticeships you should contact the National Apprenticeship Service (NAS), www.apprenticeships.org.uk. For information on training programmes for adults contact your local Jobcentre Plus.

Paid time off for study or training

You can get 'reasonable' paid time off from work to study if you are 16 or 17 and employed but do not yet have a Level 2 qualification. The types of qualification you could study for include GCSEs, NVQs and BTECs. The study or training could be at a local college, by distance learning or in the workplace. Contact your local careers/Connexions service for further information.

How do I find out what's available? Can anyone help me?

Careers education at school

You should be given help to prepare for your future in Year 9. There may be a teacher who is responsible for careers education. There may also be a Connexions PA who comes into your school. The school should have access to careers information, such as books and leaflets about further education, training and careers. This information should be given to you in your preferred format. For example, if you read Braille, you should be given access to this information in Braille.

Guidance on careers and future learning

From Year 9 onwards you may need independent information, advice and guidance on your future work or learning. This information is available from your local careers/Connexions service.

In **England** every young person aged 13–19 should have access to a Connexions Personal Adviser (PA). If you have a disability you can continue to use Connexions until the age of 25. Connexions support young people at all times, especially at times of transition. Connexions services have access to a wide range of information about careers, employment and further study. Connexions PAs can help you to write a Career Action Plan, which includes your goals in education and employment and the steps you need to take to get there. They can advise you about different jobs available and the type of training or course required for the job of your choice. They can also tell you about courses in local schools and colleges and can direct you to your local careers library.

Transition plan

If you have a Statement of Special Educational Needs (SEN), it should be reviewed every year. When you are 14 you should be involved in writing a transition plan that will help you think about what to do when you reach 16. Your Connexions PA or careers adviser should be able to assist you in finding another school, college, or training course if you are unable to stay at your school after 16. It is important that your Connexions PA or careers adviser helps you look at all of your options to choose what is most appropriate for you. Your Connexions PA or careers adviser should also attend your transition review meeting, which will be held at school. Your Connexions PA can help if you are having problems getting the support you need from your school or Local Authority (LA). Your parents or guardians should also be involved in ensuring that there is a good transition plan.

If you have a Statement of Special Educational Needs (SEN), your LA has a duty to arrange for you to have a Section 139a assessment. If you do not have a Statement of SEN but have a disability or learning difficulty and are likely to go on to college, training or university, your LA has the power to arrange a Section 139a assessment for you. Section 139a will set out your learning needs and the provision required to meet those needs.

How do I contact my local Connexions/careers service?

Your school or college can help you find your local Connexions or careers service and you should also find them listed in the telephone directory. For your Local Connexions service you can search online at www.connexions-direct.com.

Social Services and Health Authority support

Arrangements for personal and medical care comes from different sources. If you have a Statement of SEN your LA must work with the local Social Services and local Health Authority to meet your needs. This is particularly important when your transition plan is written and again when you are due to leave school.

Local Social Services or social work departments are required to provide certain services to young people and adults with disabilities. If you are worried that the department is not getting involved in your transition plan, you can contact your local Social Services or the social work department directly. Your Connexions PA can also speak to the different agencies involved and ensure that everything is paid for before you begin your course.

How do I find out about courses?

National Database of Accredited Qualifications

This is a searchable online database of qualifications accredited by the regulators of external exams, in England (Ofqual), Wales (DCELLS) and Northern Ireland (CCEA), www.accredi-tedqualifications.org.uk. You should be able to use this database at your local careers/ Connexions service.

Learndirect freephone (0800 100 900)

This is a free telephone helpline set up by the Government. The helpline can give information about course providers and qualifications needed to pursue particular careers. They can also tell you where you can get careers advice in your local area. See also www.learndirect.co.uk.

Will I get the support or help I need because of my disability or learning difficulty?

What happens to my Statement when I reach age 16?

A Statement of Special Educational Needs (SEN) sets out the type of educational support you need at school. The school has a legal duty to provide the support specified in your statement.

When you reach 16 your Statement will only continue to be a legal document if you stay at school. If you go to college, your Statement will no longer give you a legal right to the support it sets out. But your college will have a legal duty to assess your needs and provide you with the support you need.

School

If you stay on in the same school or move to a different school, your Statement of SEN will continue to be a legal document and you should continue to get the support you had previously. As long as you remain at a school, your Local Authority (LA) must ensure that you receive the support you need.

Local further education (FE) colleges

Local FE colleges receive money from their funding bodies to pay for additional support needed by students with disabilities or learning difficulties, for example additional study support for dyslexia students, an interpreter for deaf students or materials in alternative formats. Most FE colleges also offer study programmes specifically for people with learning difficulties, which include specialist help. These may be Basic Skills courses, which aim to develop numeracy and literacy skills, or Independent Living Skills courses that prepare students generally for adult life. Disability or Learning Support Coordinators are available at local FE colleges and their job is to coordinate disability support within the college. Before you start your course the college should look at what you will need to take part in the course. Sometimes you may need to have an assessment to find out what support suits you best. You should contact the college Disability or Learning Support Coordinator to discuss your individual support arrangements.

Specialist further education (FE) colleges

Specialist FE colleges provide education exclusively for people with disabilities. Some specialist colleges provide education for students with any type of disability, while others provide education for students with specific disabilities. Going to a specialist college can give you access to specialist equipment, support and teaching that your local college may be unable to provide.

Work-based learning

If you want to take up work-based learning when you leave school, you should be given enough support to enable you to take part in and complete successfully the training outlined in your Individual Training Plan. When you attend college, the college must ensure that you have the support you need to make the most of your studies. Your college also has a duty to ensure that you have the support you need while on work placements. If you are on an apprenticeship, you can apply for Access to Work to help meet the costs of any support you need while at work. For further information, contact the National Apprenticeship Agency (NAS).

The Disability Discrimination Act (DDA) 1995

The DDA provides legal rights for disabled people in education. Part 4 of the DDA gives legal duties to schools, including school sixth forms, under the pre-sixteen section, and further education colleges, sixth-form colleges and universities under the post-16 section. Work-based learning held at a private training provider is covered by Part 3 of the DDA. For more information on the DDA you can contact the Skill Information Service or the Equality and Human Rights Commission's disability helpline.

How is education and training after the age of 16 funded?

Education up to 19

Sources of funding for education up to the age of 19 vary according to the type of education chosen.

School

Your Local Authority will pay for your education if you stay at a school until you are 19. If you have a Statement of SEN you should continue to receive the support it sets out.

Local further education (FE) colleges

In **England**, your Local Authority will also pay for your education up to the age of 19 at local or specialist FE colleges. If you have a Section 139a assessment, your Local Authority can pay for your education up to the age of 25. Courses for adult learners will be funded by the Skills Funding Agency (SFA).

In **Wales,** the Department for Education, Lifelong Learning and Skills (**DELLS**) funds all further education.

In **England** and **Wales** you will not have to pay any tuition fees if you are studying full time at a further education college and are aged 16–19 years or up to 25 if you are studying for your first full Level 3 qualification, or at any age if you are studying for your first Level 2 qualification.

In **Scotland**, further education colleges receive funding from the Scottish Further Education Funding Council (SFEFC). You will not pay fees if you are a full-time student and meet the residency conditions. A college should not accept you unless it can offer the support that you need because of your disability or learning difficulty and must provide any equipment or extra support services you need. An assessment may be needed to find out exactly what is required.

Education over 19

Funding for education should not stop when you reach 18 or 19. If you start a full-time course before you are 19, you should be funded until the end of your course. If you start a course once you are over 19, you may still be exempt from paying tuition fees. Colleges operate a fee-waiver scheme, whereby students on certain means-tested benefits do not have to pay tuition fees. Sometimes individual colleges will also waive or reduce the fees for students who do not receive any of these benefits but who nevertheless find it difficult to meet their course fees.

Independent specialist colleges

If your disability-related needs can be met at a local FE college, then it is unlikely that you will receive government funding for a place at a specialist college. However, the Local Authority will fund a specialist place for a student up to the age of 25 if they have a Section 139a assessment and their needs cannot be met at a local college. When applying for funding you will need to provide certain forms of evidence that your needs cannot be met in a local FE college. Your Connexion PA can approach the funding bodies on your behalf.

Social Services may also pay or contribute towards a specialist place where the provision includes a strong care component.

In **Scotland** you may be able to obtain funding for a placement in an independent college through a bursary from the education department of your local council.

Transport help and costs

Local Authorities (LAs) must publish an integrated transport plan and transport policy for learners aged 16-19. They also have a duty to make financial support or transport services provision available to students aged 16-18 and those aged 19 or over if they continue to attend a course they began before they were 19. This is to ensure they are not prevented from attending school or college because their fares are too high or because transport provision is inadequate. LAs are also required to produce a transport policy statement for post-19 disabled learners. When creating this policy they must consider their duty to provide suitable education and training that meets the reasonable needs of disabled learners aged 19 to 25.

To search for your local transportation policy, visit www.direct.gov.uk. LAs cannot refuse to help with transport costs on policy grounds without considering your individual circumstances.

Social Services also have the power to pay for transport, but may take their resources into account when deciding whether to provide transport.

FE colleges have Learner Support Funds (LSF) for students who face financial hardship. If your transport costs are very high, you can apply to the LSF for extra money.

In **Scotland** you should contact your college to see if you could get help with travel costs through a bursary. Learner Support Funds may be asked to contribute some of your EMA (see below).

Benefits

When you are 16, you may be able to claim certain benefits in your own right, even if you are still studying. These include:

- Employment and Support Allowance (ESA)

- Disability Living Allowance (DLA)

If you need help with the calculations or what you can claim, you should contact a local welfare rights unit or Citizens Advice.

Bursary scheme

From September 2011, the Educational Maintenance Allowance will be replaced with a new bursary scheme. Students aged between 16 and 19 years facing financial hardship while in full-time education may be eligible for bursary.

Schools, colleges and training providers will be responsible for awarding bursaries. In most cases they decide on the amount, when it is paid and whether it's linked to behaviour or attendance, although there are exceptions. For example, those most in need (those in care, care leavers or those claiming income support) are guaranteed a bursary of £1,200.

Applying to Higher Education – Guidance for Disabled People

Skill (National Bureau for Students with Disabilities)

For many people the prospect of entering higher education is becoming more attractive. Everyone considering entry to college or university should ask questions about courses and facilities. However, disabled students are likely to have other concerns too. These might include, for example, provision of learning materials in accessible formats such as Braille, wheelchair access to lecture halls or the extent to which an institution will understand the difficulties encountered by a student with dyslexia.

What is higher education?

Higher education is any course that leads to a certain level of qualification. It includes the following:

Undergraduate studies leading to:

- a first degree (BSc, BA, BEd, LLB, BDS, MBBS, BEng, BMus, or at some Scottish universities BMed);

- undergraduate master's degree (MEng, MSci, MPharm, MPhys, MA in Scotland);

- a National Vocational Qualification (NVQ4 or 5) linked with a degree, a diploma of higher education (DipHE) or job-related courses such as Diploma in Nursing;

- a Higher National Diploma (HND) or Higher National Certificate (HNC), often more work related than other undergraduate qualifications;

- foundation degree or other vocational courses.

Postgraduate studies leading to:

- a master's degree (MA, MSc, MEd, MPhil);

- a doctorate (PhD or DPhil);

- a Postgraduate Certificate of Education (PGCE);

- other postgraduate diplomas.

These courses are offered in universities and colleges around the country. Some further education colleges also offer higher education courses.

Higher education – is it for me?

You could go into higher education for a number of reasons. This might be in preparation for a chosen career, for the experience, to study a subject you enjoy or to develop a new interest. Higher education can also offer opportunities to take up other activities, gain independence and meet new people.

Will I get the funding I need?

Money is a big issue for all students. If you have study-related needs because of your disability, you may be eligible for Disabled Students' Allowances to help pay for additional costs such as equipment, non-medical helper support or travel. Contact Skill for further information on funding disabled students in higher education and claiming Disabled Students' Allowances.

How do I choose the right course?

You should start your search for a university or college like any other student – by choosing a course to study. There are several questions to consider, including:

- Is the course essential for your proposed work or career plans? Would it be helpful?

- Could you still pursue your ambitions with a degree or HND in any subject?

- What subjects are you interested in? Does the content of your course reflect your interests?

- Would you prefer to study full time or part time?

- Which teaching methods are used?

- Which assessment methods are used?

- What level of course do you require?

- Can you fulfil the entry requirements? Is there a related course with different require-ments?

- Are you seeking a course that includes work experience or study abroad?

Where should I study?

You may be tempted to apply only to institutions that have good provision for disabled students. But choosing the right institution and course for you as an individual is very important. A good way to start is to prepare a list of places that offer the courses that interest you. Then think through the following issues:

Academic considerations:	Facilities and reputation of the college? Academic support, eg personal tutor? Library facilities?
Location:	Near home, or away from home? Campus or city site? Near to transport?
Money:	How much are the fees? What bursaries and scholarships are available?
Student community:	How many students are there? What age groups?
Recreation and leisure:	Town facilities, sports, hobbies, students' union?
Access:	To lecture theatres and teaching rooms? To the library, photocopier, etc? To a parking space? To the bar and canteen? To sports facilities? In other ways, eg induction loops, clear signs, good lighting?
Experience:	Other disabled students? Staff attitude to you as a disabled person?
Accommodation:	Is it accessible? Would you be integrated with other students? Could equipment be installed or adaptations made? Would a room be provided for your personal assistant? What are the fire procedures for disabled students?
Disability support:	Talk to the disabled student's adviser about the support available. Is there a suitable centre available locally for medical treatment? Any particular facilities for disabled students, eg Braille embosser, dyslexia support tutor, sign language interpreter unit, campus minibus, note-takers? If these are not available, can they be arranged in time for the start of your course?

How do I find out more about a college or university?

Website and prospectus

All colleges and universities have websites where you can find listings of courses and information on student services, visits and open days.

Prospectuses are produced which provide information about the general facilities as well as course details. Most also give some details of facilities for disabled students. They may also give a contact name for the disability coordinator.

Disability equality scheme

All higher education institutions are required to produce a disability equality scheme that sets out how they intend to improve disability equality for staff and students. The scheme can also give information on the general support provided for disabled people. You could ask for a copy to be sent along with the prospectus, or read it on the institution's website.

Student union or association

The student union or association may produce its own information about the college or university and may have its own disability support structures and policy.

Making contact

If your questions are not answered by the prospectus, website or other written information, you could contact the institution. For information on disability-related provision contact the disability coordinator, who is responsible for services for disabled students.

Skill's 'Into Higher Education'

You can search this online database for the contact details of disability coordinators and the disability equality scheme at the institutions you are interested in. See: www.skill.org.uk.

Making a visit

The best way to find out what a university or college is like is to visit. Many places welcome early informal 'information visits'. Try to visit during term time or semester, when you are more likely to meet other students and will be able to form a more accurate picture.

How do I apply?

The application form

Applications for most courses are made through the Universities and Colleges Admissions Service (UCAS). Most UCAS applications are now made online.

Your disability

As part of UCAS online applications you are asked to choose a disability category. Some people worry that disclosing a disability at this stage may leave them vulnerable to discrimination. However, Part 4 of the Disability Discrimination Act (DDA) 1995 exists to protect disabled people against discrimination in education. (It is worth remembering that if you do experience discrimination, you will only be protected by the DDA 1995 if the university or college knows or 'could reasonably have known' about your disability. For more information about the DDA, contact Skill.) You may also wish to consider the following when making your mind up about disclosing your disability:

- If you need additional disability-related support from the university or college, you may wish to disclose your disability at an early stage to ensure that the support is in place from the beginning of the course.

- You may have had an unusual academic career because of your disability, eg taking exams later than usual. Disclosing your disability may help to explain this.

- Your disability may not affect your study. Similarly, if you are receiving support from a source other than the university or college, you may feel that disclosing your disability is unnecessary.

- If you choose not to disclose your disability at application stage, you should still be given opportunities to do so once you have been accepted on to the course.

The decision about what to write is yours and you must feel comfortable with it. Beware of using terms that admissions tutors may not understand. The institution is interested in two things: how your disability may affect your studies and what kind of support you will need.

If you cannot fill in the form yourself because of your disability, ask someone to type or write your answers for you. Your referee can explain in his or her confidential report the method used and the reasons for it.

Selection interviews

If you are invited to attend an interview, let the institution know if you need any particular access arrangements. You may be asked about your disability, for example about adapting course material to suit your needs. Be prepared to speak clearly and confidently about potential problems and solutions. It is best if these points have already been discussed during your information visit.

Admissions tests

Some institutions have introduced admissions tests for their most popular subjects. If you are required to sit an admissions test you may want to discuss your access needs with the institution's disability coordinator.

Offers

Admissions tutors decide whether to offer you a place and the offer will usually be a conditional offer. This means that your exam results must meet the UCAS point and grade requirements of the course.

Rejections

Institutions rarely give reasons for a rejection. If you think you have been rejected because of your disability, contact the institution to request the reason. If you believe you have been discriminated against you have the right to make a complaint. Contact Skill for more information on how to proceed. If the institution is unable to meet your needs, UCAS will allow you to substitute another choice of institution.

Do I need support?

Do not be afraid to use support. It does not make you different from other students; it is intended to enable you to study and participate with other students. You can always change your support arrangements, eg if your needs change or if the support turns out to be unsuitable.

How do I find out more?

There are many websites and directories containing information about higher education courses. A list of suggested titles is given in the Bibliography in Part Five. These can be found in careers, and local libraries.

For further information about higher education for disabled people, contact Skill's information service on 0800 328 5050 (voice) or 0800 068 2422 (text) Tuesday 11.30am–1.30pm, Thursday 1.30pm–3.30pm; or write to Skill at:

Skill
Unit 3, Floor 3, Radisson Court
219 Long Lane
London SE1 4PR

Alternatively visit the Skill website at www.skill.org.uk or e-mail: info@skill.org.uk.

Editor's note: Expert, personal guidance on issues of interest to any student planning to enter higher education, including choice of courses and universities, gap year options, UCAS applications and interview techniques, is also available from:

Gabbitas Educational Consultants
Norfolk House, 30 Charles II Street, London SW1Y 4AE
Tel: 020 7734 0161   Fax: 020 7437 1764
E-mail: info@gabbitas.co.uk   Website: www.gabbitas.co.uk

SPECIAL SCHOOLS AND COLLEGES – INDEPENDENT AND NON-MAINTAINED

2.1

Notes on the Directory

Type of school

Part 2 of *Schools for Special Needs* contains two directories covering establishments in England, Scotland, Northern Ireland and Wales:

1. *Independent and non-maintained schools*
2. *Colleges and other provision at 16+*

Independent and non-maintained schools

The term 'special school' covers a wide range of different types of school. Special schools that are provided by a Local Authority (LA) (maintained special schools) are listed in Part 3. 'Non-maintained special school' is a technical term which is often abbreviated as NMSS. These schools take pupils with Statements and must comply with detailed regulations. Matters covered in the regulations include admission arrangements, governing body, teaching staff and many other aspects. They must be constituted as registered charities and, although they are not funded directly by a Local Authority, all or most of their pupils are placed by the LA under a Statement, and the LA pays all fees. Some of these schools provide residential accommodation. Where this is for 52 weeks in the year, the school will be registered as a Children's Home and will be inspected by Ofsted accordingly. Independent special schools may be charities but are not required to be. They may be owned either by an individual or by a limited company or group of companies. The proportion of children placed by parents or by LAs will vary from school to school. These schools are classified as 'Independent Schools' and will be equipped to take children with particular types of special needs, whether they have a Statement or not.

Colleges and other provision at 16+

These are divided between maintained, non-maintained and independent. Maintained provision is listed in Part 3. Some establishments will be residential communities registered under the Care Standards Act and will provide care and educational opportunities for people from 16 until well into adulthood.

Entries in the directory

Every effort has been made to compile a comprehensive list of schools and provision at 16+. Each entry includes the school name, address, and web address (where available), and the age range and gender of students accepted. Schools may be independent or Non-maintained, or in Scotland Voluntary Aided or Grant Aided. The status of each school is given where known. Entries also indicate whether or not the school offers 52-week care.

The types of need for which a school or college makes provision are shown in abbreviated form. A key to the abbreviations used is given below. The principal types of special needs catered for, are shown in bold.[1] Please note that this information is intended as a guide only. For further information contact schools direct.

Key to abbreviations used in the directory

Special needs provision

ADD	Attention Deficit Disorder	EPI	Epilepsy
ADHD	Attention Deficit Hyperactivity Disorder	HEA	Health Problems (eg heart defect, asthma)
ASD	Autistic Spectrum Disorder	HI	Hearing Impairment
ASP	Asperger's Syndrome	IM	Impaired Mobility
BESD	Behavioural, Emotional and Social Disorders	MLD	Moderate Learning Difficulties
		PMLD	Profound and Multiple Learning Difficulties
CB	Challenging Behaviour		
CP	Cerebral Palsy	SLD	Severe Learning Difficulties
DOW	Down's Syndrome	SP&LD	Speech and Language Difficulties
DYC	Dyscalculia	TOU	Tourette's Syndrome
DYP	Dyspraxia	VI	Visual Impairment
DYS	Dyslexia		

Wheelchair access

W	Wheelchair access (unspecified)	WA3	No permanent access for wheelchairs; temporary ramps available
WA1	School is fully wheelchair accessible in all areas		
WA2	Main teaching areas are wheelchair accessible		

---

[1] In addition to catering for the special needs specified, all schools and colleges recognize their responsibilities under the Disability Discrimination Act 1995 to consider the needs of all disabled children and to make reasonable adjustments to facilitate the admission of such children to the school.

Symbols

+   Registered with CReSTeD (see Part 5.1)
*   School profile later in this section

2.2

Directory of Independent and Non-Maintained Special Schools

England

BEDFORDSHIRE

ASHMEADS
Montague House, Bedford,
Bedfordshire MK40 2DN
Type: Boys Day Only 11–16
Special needs: ADD ADHD ASD
ASP **BESD** CB DYP DYS HEA
MLD TOU VI

BERKSHIRE

ANNIE LAWSON SCHOOL
Nine Mile Ride, Crowthorne,
Berkshire RG45 6BQ
Type: Co-educational Boarding
and Day 11–19
Special needs: ASD **ASP** CB CP
EPI HEA HI **PMLD SLD** SP&LD VI
Wheelchair access: W
Independent Special

ELLESMERE COLLEGE
Hermitage, Thatcham, Berkshire
RG18 9NU
Website: www.priorscourt.org.uk
Type: Co-educational Boarding
and Day 5–19
Special needs: ADHD ASD **ASP**
CB EPI HEA MLD SLD SP&LD
Wheelchair access: WA2
Independent Special

HEATHERMOUNT SCHOOL
Devenish Road, Ascot, Berkshire
SL5 9PG
Type: Co-educational Boarding
and Day 3–19
Special needs: **ASD** ASP
Wheelchair access: W
Non-maintained

HIGH CLOSE SCHOOL
(BARNARDO'S)*
Wiltshire Road, Wokingham,
Berkshire RG40 1TT
Website: www.barnardos.org.uk/
highcloseschool
Type: Co-educational Boarding
and Day 9–16
Special needs: **ADD ADHD** ASD
ASP **BESD CB** DYC DYP DYS
HEA MLD SP&LD
Non-maintained

MARY HARE SCHOOL FOR
THE DEAF
Arlington Manor, Newbury,
Berkshire RG14 3BQ
Website: www.maryhare.org.uk
Type: Co-educational Boarding
and Day 11–19
Special needs: **HI**
Wheelchair access: WA2
Non-maintained

PRIORS COURT SCHOOL*
Thatcham, Berkshire RG18 9NU
Website: www.priorscourt.org.uk
Type: Co-educational Boarding
and Day
Special needs: ASD CB EPI MLD
SLD SP&LD
Wheelchair access: WA2
Independent Special

BRISTOL

BELGRAVE SCHOOL
10 Upper Belgrave Road, Clifton,
Bristol BS8 2XH
Website: www.belgrave-school.org
Type: Co-educational Day Only
5–13
Special needs: ADD ASD ASP
DYC DYP **DYS** SP&LD
Wheelchair access: WA3
Independent Special

ST CHRISTOPHER'S SCHOOL
Carisbrooke Lodge, Westbury
Park, Bristol BS6 7JE
Website: www.st-christophers.
bristol.sch.uk
Type: Co-educational Boarding
Only 5–19
Special needs: ASD CB CP EPI
PMLD SLD
Wheelchair access: WA1
Independent Special
52-week care

SHEILING SCHOOL,
CAMPHILL COMMUNITY
THORNBURY
Thornbury Park, Thornbury,
Bristol BS35 1HP
Website: www.sheilingschool.
org.uk
Type: Co-educational Boarding
and Day 7–19
Special needs: ADD ADHD ASD
ASP BESD CP DOW DYP EPI
HEA MLD SLD SP&LD
Wheelchair access: WA2

BUCKINGHAMSHIRE

MACINTYRE WINGRAVE SCHOOL*
Leighton Road, Aylesbury, Buckinghamshire HP22 4PA
Website: www.macintyrecharity. org
Type: Co-educational Boarding and Day 10–19
Special needs: ASD CB EPI PMLD **SLD** SP&LD
Independent Special
52-week care

PENN SCHOOL*
Church Road, High Wycombe, Buckinghamshire HP10 8LZ
Website:
www.pennschool.bucks. sch.uk
Type: Co-educational Boarding and Day 11–19
Special needs: **ASD** ASP HI SP&LD
Non-maintained

WALNUT TREE LODGE SCHOOL
Avenue Farm Lane, Buckinghamshire MK44 2PY
Type: Co-educational Day Only 11–16
Special needs: BESD
Independent Special

CAMBRIDGESHIRE

CHARTWELL HOUSE SCHOOL
Goodens Lane, Wisbech, Cambridgeshire PE13 5HQ
Website: www.thechartwellgroup. co.uk
Type: Boys Boarding Only 10–16
Special needs: ADD ADHD ASP **BESD** CB DYC DYP DYS MLD TOU
Wheelchair access: WA2
Independent Special
52-week care

DOWNHAM LODGE SCHOOL
1 Second Drove, Ely, Cambridgeshire CB6 2UD
Type: Boys Boarding and Day 10–16
Special needs: BESD

STATION SCHOOL
5 Station Approach, March, Cambridgeshire PE15 8SJ
Type: Co-educational Day Only 11–16
Special needs: BESD
Wheelchair access: W

CHESHIRE

ACORNS SCHOOL
19b Hibbert Lane, Stockport, Cheshire SK6 7NN
Type: Co-educational Day Only 5–16
Special needs: BESD

CHAIGELEY SCHOOL
Lymm Road, Warrington, Cheshire WA4 2TE
Type: Boys Boarding and Day 8–16
Special needs: ADD ADHD **BESD**
Wheelchair access: W
Non-maintained

CORNERSTONES
2 Victoria Road, Warrington, Cheshire WA4 2EN
Type: Boys Day Only 8–18
Special needs: **ASD ASP BESD CB EPI SLD** SP&LD
Wheelchair access: WA3
52-week care

THE DAVID LEWIS SCHOOL
Mill Lane, Nr Alderley Edge, Cheshire SK9 7UD
Website: www.davidlewis.org.uk
Type: Co-educational Boarding and Day 7–19
Special needs: ASD **ASP CP EPI PMLD SLD** SP&LD
Wheelchair access: WA1
Non-maintained
52-week care

DELAMERE FOREST SCHOOL
Blakemere Lane, Warrington,
Cheshire WA6 6NP
Type: Co-educational Boarding
and Day 6–17 (Jewish boarders
only)
Special needs: ADD ADHD **ASD**
ASP BESD DOW DYP DYS EPI
HEA **MLD** SP&LD TOU

HALTON SCHOOL
31 Main Street, Runcorn,
Cheshire WA7 2AN
Type: Co-educational Day Only
7–14
Special needs: ADD ADHD
BESD CB DYC DYP DYS MLD
Wheelchair access: W

**LAMBS GRANGE
RESIDENTIAL AND DAY
EDUCATION AND CARE**
Forest Road, Cuddington,
Cheshire CW8 2EH
Website: www.lambs-group.co.uk
Type: Co-educational Boarding
and Day 14–19
Special needs: ASD **ASP** CB EPI
PMLD SLD SP&LD
Wheelchair access: W
52-week care

**ROYAL SCHOOL
MANCHESTER**
Stanley Road, Cheadle, Cheshire
SK8 6RQ
Website: www.seashelltrust.org.uk
Type: Co-educational Boarding
and Day 2–22
Special needs: ASD **ASP** CB CP
DOW EPI HEA **HI IM PMLD SLD**
SP&LD VI
Wheelchair access: WA2
Non-maintained
52-week care

**THE ST JOHN VIANNEY
SCHOOL**
(Lower School), Stockport,
Cheshire SK4 2AA
Website: www.stjohnvianney.co.uk
Type: Co-educational Day Only
5–11
Special needs: **ADD** ADHD ASD
ASP CP **DOW** DYP **MLD** SP&LD
Wheelchair access: W

CUMBRIA

APPLETREE SCHOOL
Natland, Kendal, Cumbria
LA9 7QS
Website: www.appletreeschool.
co.uk
Type: Co-educational Boarding
Only 6–12
Special needs: **ADD ADHD**
BESD CB DYP DYS **MLD** SP&LD
Wheelchair access: WA2
Independent Special
52-week care

EDEN GROVE SCHOOL
Appleby, Cumbria CA16 6AJ
Website: www.priorygroup.com
Type: Boys Boarding and
Day 8–19
Special needs: **ADHD** ASD ASP
BESD CB MLD SP&LD TOU
Wheelchair access: W
Independent Special
52-week care

WHINFELL CARE
Kendal, Cumbria
Website: www.whinfellschool.
co.uk
Type: Boys Boarding Only 11–19
Special needs: **ADD ADHD ASD**
ASP BESD CB DYP DYS MLD
SLD SP&LD **TOU**
Wheelchair access: WA3
52-week care

WINGS SCHOOL
Whassett, Milnthorpe, Cumbria
LA7 7DN
Website: www.wingsschool.co.uk
Type: Co-educational Boarding
Only 11–17
Special needs: ADD ADHD ASP
BESD DYP DYS MLD
Wheelchair access: WA3
Independent Special
52-week care

WITHERSLACK HALL*
Grange-over-Sands, Cumbria
LA11 6SD
Website:
www.witherslackhallschool.co.uk
Type: Boys Boarding Only 11–19
Special needs: **ADD ADHD ASD**
ASP BESD CB DYP DYS **MLD**
SP&LD
Independent Special
52-week care

DERBYSHIRE

ALDERWASLEY HALL SCHOOL AND CALLOW PARK COLLEGE*
Belper, Derbyshire DE56 2SR
Website: www.alderwasleyhall.com
Type: Co-educational Day and Boarding 5–19
Special needs: ADD ADHD **ASD ASP CB DYC DYP** DYS EPI HEA HI SP&LD VI
Independent Special
52-week care

EASTWOOD GRANGE SCHOOL
Milken Lane, Nr Chesterfield, Derbyshire S45 0BA
Website: www.priorygroup.com
Type: Boys Day and Boarding 11–16
Special needs: **ADD** ADHD **BESD CB**
Wheelchair access: W
Independent Special
52-week care

NEW DIRECTION SCHOOL
Ringer Lane, Chesterfield, Derbyshire S43 4BX
Type: Co-educational 11–16
Special needs: ASD ASP BESD MLD SLD
Independent Special

PEGASUS SCHOOL*
Caldwell Hall, Caldwell, Derbyshire DE12 6RS
Website: www.pegasusschool uk.com
Type: Co-educational Day and Boarding 8–19 (Places for up to 23 students.)
Special needs: **ADD ADHD** ASD **ASP** BESD **CB** DOW DYP **EPI HEA HI IM** MLD **PMLD SLD** SP&LD **TOU** VI
Wheelchair access: WA3
Independent Special
52-week care

ROYAL SCHOOL FOR THE DEAF DERBY*
Ashbourne Road, Derby, Derbyshire DE22 3BH
Website: www.rsd-derby.org.uk
Type: Co-educational Boarding and Day 3–19
Special needs: **HI**
Wheelchair access: WA1
Non-maintained

THE TRUST CENTRE*
C/O Alderwasley Hall School, Derbyshire DE56 2SR
Website: www.thetrustcentre.com
Type: Co-educational Day and Boarding 9–19
Special needs: **BESD CB** CP **EPI HEA HI IM** SP&LD VI W
Independent Special
52-week care

DEVON

CHELFHAM MILL SCHOOL*
Barnstaple, Devon EX32 7LA
Website: www.chelfhammillschool.co.uk
Type: Boys Boarding and Day 9–16
Special needs: ADD **ADHD ASD ASP BESD CB** DYS EPI MLD TOU
Independent Special
52-week care

CHELFHAM SENIOR SCHOOL
Yelverton, Devon PL20 7EX
Website: www.prioryeducation.com
Type: Boys Boarding and Day 7–19
Special needs: **ADD ADHD** ASD ASP **BESD** CB MLD SP&LD **TOU**
Independent Special
52-week care

DAME HANNAH ROGERS SCHOOL
Woodland Road, Ivybridge, Devon PL21 9HQ
Website: www.damehannah.com
Type: Co-educational Boarding and Day 5–19
Special needs: **CP** EPI HEA IM **MLD PMLD SLD** SP&LD VI W
Wheelchair access: WA1
Non-maintained
52-week care

NAS BROOMHAYES SCHOOL*
The National Autistic Society, Bideford, Devon EX39 4PL
Website: www.autism.org.uk/broomhayes
Type: Co-educational Day and Boarding 10–21 (Students can be admitted up to the age of 18 years but there is provision for residential accommodation up to 23.)
Special needs: **ASD ASP**
Independent Special
52-week care

ROYAL WEST OF ENGLAND SCHOOL FOR THE DEAF
50 Topsham Road, Exeter, Devon EX2 4NF
Website: www.rsd-exeter.ac.uk
Type: Co-educational Boarding and Day 3–19
Special needs: BESD CP **HI** MLD SLD VI

TRENGWEATH SCHOOL
Hartley Road, Plymouth, Devon
PL3 5LP
Type: Co-educational Boarding
and Day 8–19
Special needs: CP **PMLD** SLD

VRANCH HOUSE SCHOOL
Pinhoe Road, Exeter, Devon
EX4 8AD
Type: Co-educational Day Only
2–12
Special needs: **CP** MLD PMLD
SP&LD
Wheelchair access: W

**THE WEST OF ENGLAND
SCHOOL AND COLLEGE FOR
PUPILS WITH LITTLE OR NO
SIGHT**
Countess Wear, Exeter, Devon
EX2 6HA
Website: www.westengland.
org.uk
Type: Co-educational Boarding
and Day 2–22
Special needs: VI
Wheelchair access: W

WHITSTONE HEAD SCHOOL
Holsworthy, Devon EX22 6TJ
Website: www.
whitstoneheadschool.ik.org
Type: Co-educational Boarding
and Day 10–16
Special needs: **ADD ADHD ASD
ASP BESD** DYS HEA MLD TOU
Wheelchair access: WA3
Non-maintained

WOLSDON STREET SCHOOL
Wolsdon Street, Plymouth, Devon
PL1 5EH
Type: Co-educational Boarding
Only 14–18
Special needs: BESD

**WYCHBURY HOUSE
RESIDENTIAL SCHOOL**
22 Cleveland Road, Torquay,
Devon TQ2 5BE
Type: Boys Boarding Only 9–16
Special needs: BESD MLD
52-week care

DORSET

THE FORUM SCHOOL*
Shillingstone, Dorset DT11 0QS
Website: www.cambiangroup.
com
Type: Co-educational Boarding
Only 7–19 (Mixed gender 7–19
years)
Special needs: **ASD CB** EPI HEA
MLD SP&LD
*Independent Special
52-week care*

LANGSIDE SCHOOL
Langside Avenue, Poole, Dorset
BH12 5BN
Type: Co-educational Day Only
2–18
Special needs: CP EPI HEA
PMLD SLD VI
Wheelchair access: WA1

**PHILIP GREEN MEMORIAL
SCHOOL**
Boveridge House, Wimborne,
Dorset BH21 5RU
Website: www.pgmschool.org.uk
Type: Co-educational Boarding
and Day 11–19
Special needs: ADD ASD ASP
BESD CB DOW DYP EPI HEA HI
MLD SLD SP&LD
Independent Special

PORTFIELD SCHOOL*
Parley Lane, Christchurch,
Dorset BH23 6BP
Website: www.twas.org.uk
Type: Co-educational Boarding
and Day 3–19
Special needs: ASD
*Non-maintained
52-week care*

PURBECK VIEW SCHOOL*
Northbrook Road, Swanage,
Dorset BH19 1PR
Website: www.cambiangroup.
com
Type: Co-educational Boarding
Only 9–19 (Mixed gender 9–19
years)
Special needs: **ASD CB** EPI HEA
MLD SP&LD
*Independent Special
52-week care*

**VICTORIA EDUCATION
CENTRE**
12 Lindsay Road, Poole, Dorset
BH13 6AS
Type: Co-educational Day and
Boarding
Special needs: **CP DYP** DYS EPI
HEA HI **MLD** SLD SP&LD
Wheelchair access: WA1
Non-maintained

ESSEX

DOUCECROFT SCHOOL
Abbotts Lane, Colchester, Essex
CO6 3QL
Website: www.essexautistic.
org.uk
Type: Co-educational Boarding
and Day 2–19
Special needs: **ASD ASP**
Wheelchair access: W

JACQUES HALL
Harwich Road, Manningtree,
Essex CO11 2XW
Website: www.priorygroup.com
Type: Co-educational Boarding
and Day 11–18
Special needs: **ADD ADHD** ASD
BESD CB MLD SP&LD TOU
Wheelchair access: W
Independent Special
52-week care

THE RYES COLLEGE &
COMMUNITY
Ryes Lane, Sudbury, Essex
CO10 7EA
Website: www.theryescollege.
org.uk
Type: Co-educational Boarding
Only 7–16
Special needs: **ADD ADHD ASD
ASP BESD CB** CP DYS EPI HEA
MLD PMLD SLD SP&LD **TOU**
Independent Special
52-week care

ST JOHN'S RC SCHOOL
Turpins Lane, Woodford Green,
Essex IG8 8AX
Type: Co-educational Day Only
5–19
Special needs: **MLD** SLD SP&LD

WOODCROFT SCHOOL
Whitakers Way, Loughton, Essex
IG10 1SQ
Website: www.woodcroftschool.
net
Type: Co-educational Day Only
2–12
Special needs: ADD ADHD ASD
ASP CB DYP DYS EPI HEA MLD
SLD SP&LD TOU
Wheelchair access: WA3
Independent Special

GLOUCESTERSHIRE

COTSWOLD CHINE SCHOOL*
Near Stroud, Gloucestershire
GL6 9AG
Website: www.cotswold-chine.
org.uk
Type: Co-educational Boarding
and Day 9–19 (and exceptionally
from 8)
Special needs: **ADD ADHD ASD
ASP BESD** CB DYP DYS EPI
MLD SLD SP&LD TOU
Independent Special

MARLOWE EDUCATION UNIT
Hartpury Old School, Hartpury,
Gloucestershire GL19 3BG
Type: Co-educational Day Only
8–16
Special needs: **BESD**

ST ROSE'S SCHOOL
Stroud, Gloucestershire GL5 4AP
Website: www.stroses.org.uk
Type: Co-educational Boarding
and Day 2–19
Special needs: ASP **CP** DOW
DYP EPI HEA HI **IM MLD PMLD**
SLD SP&LD VI W
Wheelchair access: WWA1WA2
Non-maintained

WILLIAM MORRIS HOUSE
CAMPHILL COMMUNITY
William Morris House,
Stonehouse, Gloucestershire
GL10 3S
Special needs: ASD ASP DOW
MLD

HAMPSHIRE

COXLEASE SCHOOL
High Coxlease House, Lyndhurst, Hampshire SO43 7DE
Website: www.coxleaseschool.co.uk
Type: Boys Boarding and Day 9–18
Special needs: **ADD ADHD** ASD ASP **BESD** CB MLD TOU
Wheelchair access: W
Independent Special
52-week care

GRATELEY HOUSE SCHOOL*
Andover, Hampshire SP11 8TA
Website: www.cambiangroup.com
Type: Co-educational Boarding and Day 9–19
Special needs: ADHD **ASP CB** DYC DYP DYS EPI MLD SP&LD **TOU**
Independent Special

HILL HOUSE SCHOOL*
Lymington, Hampshire SO41 8NE
Website: www.cambiangroup.com
Type: Co-educational Boarding Only 11–19 (Mixed gender 11–19 years)
Special needs: ASD **CB EPI** HEA **MLD SLD** SP&LD
Independent Special
52-week care

HOPE LODGE SCHOOL
22 Midanbury Lane, Southampton, Hampshire SO18 4HP
Website: www.has.org.uk
Type: Co-educational Boarding and Day 4–19
Special needs: **ASD ASP** SLD SP&LD
Wheelchair access: WA2
Independent Special
52-week care

LODDON SCHOOL
Wildmoor, Hook, Hampshire RG27 0JD
Website: www.Loddon-school.co.uk
Type: Co-educational Boarding Only 8–18
Special needs: **ADD ADHD** ASD **ASP** BESD CB DOW **EPI SLD** SP&LD VI
52-week care

ROSEWOOD SCHOOL
The Bradbury Centre, Southampton, Hampshire SO16 5NA
Website: www.roseroad.co.uk
Type: Co-educational Day Only 2–19
Special needs: CP EPI HEA HI IM **PMLD** SLD SP&LD VI
Wheelchair access: WA1

ST EDWARD'S SCHOOL*
Melchet Court, Romsey, Hampshire S051 6ZR
Website: www.melchetcourt.com
Type: Boys Boarding and Day 10–17
Special needs: ADD ADHD ASD ASP BESD DYS MLD SP&LD
Independent Special

STANBRIDGE EARLS SCHOOL*+
Stanbridge Lane, Romsey, Hampshire SO51 0ZS
Website: www.stanbridgeearls.co.uk
Type: Co-educational Boarding and Day 10–19
Special needs: **DYC DYP DYS** SP&LD

THE SHEILING SCHOOL RINGWOOD
Horton Road, Ringwood, Hampshire BH24 2EB
Website: www.sheilingschool.co.uk
Type: Co-educational Boarding and Day 6–19
Special needs: ADD ADHD ASD BESD CB CP DOW DYP EPI HEA IM MLD **SLD** SP&LD
Wheelchair access: WA2
Independent Special

SOUTHERN ENGLAND PSYCHOLOGICAL SERVICES
Fair Oak, Eastleigh, Hampshire SO50 7DE
Website: www.drludwigfredlowenstein.com
Type: Co-educational Boarding and Day 5–16
Special needs: ADD ADHD **ASD ASP BESD** DOW **DYC DYP DYS** MLD **SLD**
Wheelchair access: W
Independent Special

SOUTHLANDS SCHOOL*
Vicar's Hill, Lymington, Hampshire S041 5QB
Website: www.cambiangroup.com
Type: Boys Boarding and Day 7–16
Special needs: **ASP** CB DYC DYP DYS EPI HEA SP&LD TOU
Independent Special

TADLEY HORIZON
Tadley Common Road, Basingstoke, Hampshire RG26 3TB
Website: www.priorygroup.com
Type: Co-educational Boarding and Day 5–19
Special needs: ADD ADHD ASD **ASP** CB EPI MLD SP&LD
Wheelchair access: W
Independent Special
52-week care

TRELOAR SCHOOL*
London Road, Hampshire
GU34 4EN
Website: www.treloar.org.uk
Type: Co-educational Boarding
and Day 9–19
Special needs: **CP** DYP DYS EPI
HEA HI IM MLD SLD SP&LD VI
Non-maintained

HEREFORDSHIRE

BARRS COURT SCHOOL
Barrs Court Road, Hereford,
Herefordshire HR1 1EQ
Website: www.
barrscourtschool.ik.org
Type: Co-educational Day Only
11–19
Special needs: **PMLD SLD**
Wheelchair access: W

QUEENSWOOD SCHOOL
Callow Hills Farm, Ledbury,
Herefordshire HR8 2PZ
Website: http://www.priorygroup.
com/
Type: Co-educational Boarding
Only
Special needs: **BESD**
Wheelchair access: W
Independent Special
52-week care

ROWDEN HOUSE SCHOOL*
Rowden, Bromyard,
Herefordshire HR7 4LS
Website: www.rowdenhouse.com
Type: Co-educational Boarding
and Day 11–19 (Individualized
care and education programmes
for children and young adults.)
Special needs: **ADD ADHD ASD**
ASP **BESD CB CP DOW DYC**
DYP EPI HEA HI IM **MLD PMLD**
SLD SP&LD **TOU** VI
52-week care

HERTFORDSHIRE

MELDRETH MANOR*
Fenny Lane, Nr Royston,
Hertfordshire SG8 6LG
Website: www.scope.org.uk/
education
Type: Co-educational Boarding
and Day 9–19
Special needs: CP IM **PMLD**
Independent Special
52-week care

**NAS RADLETT LODGE
SCHOOL***
The National Autistic Society,
Radlett, Hertfordshire WD7 9HW
Website: www.autism.org.uk/
radlettlodge
Type: Co-educational Day and
Boarding 4–19
Special needs: **ASD ASP** EPI
SLD TOU
Wheelchair access: WA2
Independent Special

ST ELIZABETH'S SCHOOL*
Much Hadham, Hertfordshire
SG10 6EW
Website: www.stelizabeths.
org.uk
Type: Co-educational Boarding
and Day 5–19
Special needs: **ASD CB EPI** MLD
PMLD **SLD**
Non-maintained

ISLE OF WIGHT

ST CATHERINE'S SCHOOL*
Grove Road, Ventnor, Isle of
Wight PO38 1TT
Website: www.stcatherines.
org.uk
Type: Co-educational Boarding
and Day 11–19
Special needs: ADD ADHD ASD
ASP CB DYC DYP DYS EPI HEA
HI MLD SP&LD VI
Independent Special

KENT

BASTON HOUSE SCHOOL*
Baston Road, Bromley, Kent
BR2 7AB
Website: www.bastonhouseschool.
org.uk
Type: Co-educational Day Only
2–16
Special needs: ASD **ASP**
Independent Special

BREWOOD SECONDARY
SCHOOL
86 London Road, Deal, Kent
CT14 9TR
Type: Co-educational Day Only
7–16
Special needs: ADD ADHD ASP
BESD DYC DYP DYS HI **MLD**
SP&LD TOU VI
Wheelchair access: WA2

BROWN'S SCHOOL+
Cannock House, Chelsfield, Kent
BR6 7PH
Website: www.brownsschool.
co.uk
Type: Co-educational Day Only
6–12
Special needs: **DYP DYS**

CALDECOTT COMMUNITY
Ashford, Kent TN25 6SP
Website:
www.caldecottfoundation.
co.uk
Type: Co-educational Boarding
and Day 5–16
Special needs: ADHD **BESD** DYS
MLD

DORTON HOUSE SCHOOL
Royal London Society for the
Blind, Sevenoaks, Kent TN15 0ED
Website: www.rlsb.org.uk
Type: Co-educational Boarding
and Day 5–16
Special needs: VI

EAST COURT SCHOOL+
Ramsgate, Kent CT11 8ED
Website: www.eastcourtschool.
co.uk
Type: Co-educational Boarding
and Day 7–13
Special needs: DYC DYP **DYS**
Wheelchair access: WA3

GREAT OAKS SMALL SCHOOL
Ebbsfleet Farmhouse, Minster,
Kent CT12 5DL
Type: Co-educational Day Only
18–11
Special needs: **ADD ADHD ASD
ASP**
Wheelchair access: W
Independent Special

HEATH FARM SCHOOL
Heath Farm, Ashford, Kent
TN27 0AX
Type: Co-educational Day Only
5–18
Special needs: **BESD**

HYTHE HOUSE EDUCATION
Power Station Road, Sheerness,
Kent ME12 3AB
*Website:*www.
hythehousesupport.co.uk
Type: Boys Day Only 6–16
Special needs:
Wheelchair access: WA2

LEARNING OPPORTUNITIES
CENTRE PRIMARY
Canterbury, Kent CT4 6HE
Type: Co-educational Day Only
7–12
Special needs: ADD ADHD ASP
BESD DYP DYS

LEARNING OPPORTUNITIES
CENTRE SECONDARY
Deal, Kent CT14 8DW
Type: Co-educational Day Only
11–16
Special needs: ADD ADHD ASP
BESD

LITTLE ACORNS SCHOOL
London Beach Farm, Tenterden,
Kent TN30 6SR
Type: Co-educational Boarding
Only 5–11
Special needs: **ADD ADHD** ASD
ASP **BESD** CB DYP DYS HI MLD
SLD SP&LD TOU VI
Wheelchair access: W
Independent Special
52-week care

MEADOWS SCHOOL (BARNARDO'S)*
London Road, Southborough, Kent TN4 0RJ
Website: www.barnardos.org.uk/meadowsschool
Type: Co-educational Boarding and Day 11–19
Special needs: **ADD ADHD ASD BESD MLD**

NAS HELEN ALLISON SCHOOL*
The National Autistic Society, Meopham, Kent DA13 0EW
Website: www.autism.org.uk/helenallison
Type: Co-educational Boarding and Day 5–19
Special needs: **ASD** ASP EPI TOU

NASH COLLEGE
Croydon Road, Bromley, Kent BR2 7AG
Type: Co-educational Boarding and Day 18–25
Special needs: **CP** EPI **PMLD** VI
Wheelchair access: W

THE NEW SCHOOL AT WEST HEATH*
Ashgrove Road, Sevenoaks, Kent TN13 1SR
Website: www.westheathschool.com
Type: Mixed Residential and Day 11–19
Special needs: ADD **ADHD ASD ASP BESD HEA** SP&LD **TOU**
Independent Special

THE OLD PRIORY SCHOOL
Priory Road, Ramsgate, Kent CT11 9PG
Type: Boys Day Only 11–16
Special needs: **BESD**
Wheelchair access: WA3

THE QUEST SCHOOL FOR AUTISTIC CHILDREN
The Old Stables, West Malling, Kent ME19 5NX
Type: Co-educational Day Only 5–14
Special needs: **ASD ASP**
Wheelchair access: WA1

RIPPLEVALE SCHOOL
Chapel Lane, Deal, Kent CT14 8JG
Website: www.ripplevaleschool.co.uk
Type: Boys Boarding and Day 7–16
Special needs: **ADD** ADHD **ASD ASP BESD CB DYC DYP DYS** EPI HEA HI **MLD** SP&LD **TOU**
Wheelchair access: WA3
Independent Special

THE ROYAL SCHOOL FOR DEAF CHILDREN MARGATE*
Victoria Road, Margate, Kent CT9 1NB
Website: www.townsendtrust.com
Type: Mixed Residential and Day 4–16
Special needs: ADD ADHD ASD ASP BESD CB CP DOW DYP DYS EPI HEA **HI** IM MLD PMLD SLD SP&LD TOU VI W
Wheelchair access: WA2
Non-maintained

TRINITY SCHOOL+
13 New Road, Rochester, Kent ME1 1BG
Website: www.trinityschool.info
Type: Co-educational Day Only 6–16
Special needs: ADD **ASD ASP DYC DYP DYS** SP&LD
Wheelchair access: WA1
Independent Special

WESTWOOD SCHOOL
479 Margate Road, Broadstairs, Kent CT10 2QA
Website: www.actionforchildren.org.uk
Type: Co-educational Day Only 11–16
Special needs: ADHD ASD ASP **BESD CB** MLD
Wheelchair access: WA2
Non maintained

LANCASHIRE

APPLEGATE
51–53 Albert Rd, Colne, Lancashire BB8 0BP
Website: www.northern-care.co.uk
Type: Boys Boarding Only 11–17
Special needs: **BESD CB**

BEECH TREE
Meadow Lane, Preston, Lancashire PR5 8LN
Website: www.scope.org.uk
Type: Co-educational Boarding and Day 8–17
Special needs: ADHD ASD **ASP CB** DOW EPI HI **PMLD SLD** SP&LD TOU
Wheelchair access: WA1
Independent Special
52-week care

BELFORD COLLEGE
Grange Avenue, Oldham, Lancashire OL8 4EL
Type: Co-educational Day Only 16–99

BELMONT SCHOOL
Hasligdon Road, Rawtenstall, Lancashire BB4 6RX
Website: www.belmont-school.co.uk
Type: Boys Boarding and Day 8–16
Special needs: **BESD**
Non-maintained

THE BIRCHES
106 Breck Rd, Poulton le Fylde, Lancashire FY6 7HT
Website: www.northern-care.co.uk
Type: Boys Boarding Only 11–17
Special needs: **BESD CB**

BIRTENSHAW SCHOOL
Darwen Road, Bolton, Lancashire BL7 9AB
Website: www.birtenshaw.org.uk
Type: Co-educational Day Only 3–19 (3–19yrs)
Special needs: **ADD** ADHD **ASD ASP CB CP DOW EPI HEA** HI **IM PMLD SLD** SP&LD VI W
Wheelchair access: WWA1WA2
Non-maintained
52-week care

CEDAR HOUSE SCHOOL*
Kendal Road, via Carnforth, Lancashire LA6 2HW
Website:
www.cedarhouseschool.co.uk
Type: Co-educational Boarding and Day 7–16
Special needs: ADD ADHD ASD ASP **BESD CB** CP DYC DYP DYS EPI HEA MLD SP&LD TOU
Independent Special

CROOKHEY HALL SCHOOL
Garstang Road, Lancaster, Lancashire LA2 0HA
Type: Boys Day Only 11–16
Special needs: **ADD ADHD ASD** ASP **BESD CB DYS MLD PMLD SLD**
Wheelchair access: WA3
Independent Special

CUMBERLAND SCHOOL*
Church Road, Preston, Lancashire PR5 6EP
Website:
www.cumberlandschool.co.uk
Type: Co-educational 11–16
Special needs: ADHD ASP **BESD** MLD
Independent Special

EMMANUEL CHRISTIAN SCHOOL
Fylde Community, Blackpool, Lancashire FY3 0BE
Type: Co-educational Day Only 5–16

MILL HOUSE
Farington Moss, Leyland, Lancashire PR26 6PS
Website: www.northern-care.co.uk
Type: Boys Boarding Only 11–17
Special needs: **BESD CB**

THE NOOK SCHOOL
The Nook, Colne, Lancashire BB8 8HH
Website: www.northern-care.co.uk
Type: Boys Boarding Only 8–13
Special needs: **BESD** CB
52-week care

NUGENT HOUSE SCHOOL
Carr Mill Road, St Helens, Lancashire WN5 7TT
Website: www.nugenthouse.co.uk
Type: Boys Boarding Only 7–19
Special needs: ADD ADHD ASD **ASP BESD CB** DYP **DYS** TOU
Wheelchair access: W
Independent Special
52-week care

OLIVER HOUSE
Hallgate, Chorley, Lancashire PR7 1XA
Type: Co-educational 6–19
Special needs: ASD DYC DYP DYS EPI SLD
Independent Special

PENNSYLVANIA HOUSE
1 Barclay Avenue, Blackpool, Lancashire FY3 4HH
Website: www.northern-care.co.uk
Type: Boys Boarding Only 11–17
Special needs: **BESD CB**

PONTVILLE SCHOOL*
Black Moss Lane, Ormskirk, Lancashire L39 4TW
Website: www.pontville.co.uk
Type: Co-educational Boarding and Day 5–19
Special needs: ADD ADHD **ASD ASP** DYP EPI HEA MLD SP&LD
Wheelchair access: W
Independent Special

PRIMROSE COTTAGE
Hudcar Lane, Bury, Lancashire
Website: www.northern-care.co.uk
Type: Girls Boarding Only 11–17
Special needs: **BESD CB**

PROGRESS SCHOOL
Suites 1 - 5 Centurion House, Leyland, Lancashire PR25 3GR
Website: www.progressschool.co.uk
Type: Co-educational Boarding Only 7–19
Special needs: CB SLD
52-week care

RED ROSE SCHOOL
28 - 30 North Promenade, Lytham St Annes, Lancashire FY8 2NQ
Type: Co-educational Day Only 7–16
Special needs: **ADHD ASD ASP DYC DYP DYS** SP&LD **TOU**
Wheelchair access: WA2

RIDGWAY PARK SCHOOL
Jenny Browns Point, Carnforth, Lancashire LA5 0UA
Type: Co-educational Boarding Only 11–16
Special needs: ADHD ASD **BESD**
Wheelchair access: WA3
52-week care

ROSSENDALE SCHOOL
Ramsbottom, Lancashire BL0 0RT
Website: www.priorygroup.com
Type: Co-educational Boarding and Day 8–16
Special needs: **ADD ADHD ASD ASP BESD CB DYP** DYS EPI TOU
Wheelchair access: WA3
Independent Special

UNDERLEY GARDEN SCHOOL
Carnforth, Lancashire LA6 2DZ
Website: www.underleygardenschool.co.uk
Type: Co-educational Boarding Only 9–19
Special needs: ADD **ADHD** ASD **ASP BESD CB** DOW DYC DYP DYS EPI HEA HI **MLD SLD** SP&LD TOU VI
Wheelchair access: WA2
Independent Special
52-week care

UNDERLEY HALL SCHOOL
Carnforth, Lancashire LA6 2HE
Website: www.underleyhallschool.
co.uk
Type: Co-educational Boarding
and Day 9–19
Special needs: **ADD ADHD** ASP
BESD CB DYP DYS **MLD** SP&LD
Wheelchair access: WA3
Independent Special
52-week care

WATERLOO LODGE SCHOOL
Preston Road, Chorley,
Lancashire PR6 7AX
Type: Co-educational Day Only
11–16
Special needs: **ADHD** ASD
BESD CB DYP DYS HI SP&LD
Wheelchair access: WA3

WESTMORLAND SCHOOL*
Weldbank Lane, Chorley,
Lancashire PR7 3NQ
Website: www.
westmorlandschool.co.uk
Type: Co-educational Day Only
5–11 (32 Day pupils,
co-educational)
Special needs: **BESD**
Independent Special

LEICESTERSHIRE

LEWIS CHARLTON SCHOOL
North Street, Ashby-de-la-Zouch,
Leicestershire LE65 1HU
Type: Co-educational Day Only
11–16
Special needs: **BESD**
Wheelchair access: WA2

SKETCHLEY HORIZON
Manor Way, Burbage,
Leicestershire LE10 3HT
Website: www.prioryeducation.
com
Type: Co-educational Day Only
8–16
Special needs: ASD **ASP**
Wheelchair access: WA3

LINCOLNSHIRE

KISIMUL SCHOOL – OLD VICARAGE*
The Old Vicarage, Swinderby,
Lincolnshire LN6 9LU
Website: www.kisimul.co.uk
Type: Co-educational Boarding
and Day 8–19
Special needs: ASD **CB** DOW
EPI HI **SLD** SP&LD
Independent Special
52-week care

NORTH LINCOLNSHIRE

NEW OPTIONS (BARTON) SCHOOL
Barrow Road, Barton upon Humber, North Lincolnshire DN18 6DA
Website: www.optionsgroup.co.uk
Type: Co-educational Boarding and Day 8–19
Special needs: ADD ADHD **ASD ASP** CB EPI HEA SLD
Wheelchair access: W
Independent Special
52-week care

LONDON

ABINGDON HOUSE SCHOOL+
4–6 Abingdon Road, London W8 6AF
Website: www.abingdonhouseschool.co.uk
Type: Co-educational Day Only 4–11
Special needs: **ADD ADHD ASD DYC DYP DYS**
Wheelchair access: W
Independent Special

BLOSSOM HOUSE SCHOOL+
8A The Drive, London SW20 8TG
Website: www.blossomhouseschool.co.uk
Type: Co-educational Day Only 3–16
Special needs: ASD ASP DYP DYS SP&LD
Wheelchair access: WA2
Independent Special

CENTRE ACADEMY*+
92 St John's Hill, London SW11 1SH
Website: www.centreacademy.net
Type: Co-educational Day Only 8–19
Special needs: **ADD ADHD ASD ASP DYP DYS MLD** SP&LD

THE CHELSEA GROUP OF CHILDREN
The Gatehouse, London SW18 3NP
Type: Co-educational Day Only 4–11
Special needs: ADD ADHD ASD **ASP** CB DYC DYP DYS **MLD** SP&LD
Independent Special

FAIRLEY HOUSE SCHOOL*+
30 Causton Street, London SW1P 4AU
Website: www.fairleyhouse.org.uk
Type: Co-educational Day Only 5–14 (Junior Department – Year 2–5 Senior Department – Year 6–9)
Special needs: **ADD DYC DYP DYS** EPI HEA SP&LD

FREDERICK HUGH HOUSE*
48 Old Church Street, London SW3 5BY
Website: www.frederickhughhouse.com
Type: Co-educational Day Only (Currently registered for children aged 4–11 years with special needs but with a vision to take our children through to 18 years old.)
Special needs: **ADD ADHD ASD ASP CP DOW DYC DYP DYS EPI IM MLD** SP&LD TOU W
Wheelchair access: WA1 WA2
Independent Special

HOME SCHOOL OF STOKE NEWINGTON
46 Alkham Road, London N16 7AA
Type: Co-educational Day Only 11–16
Special needs: **ASD** ASP **DYP DYS**

HORNSEY CONDUCTIVE EDUCATION CENTRE
54 Muswell Hill, London N10 3ST
Website: www.hornseytrust.org.uk
Type: Co-educational Day Only
Special needs: **CP**
Wheelchair access: WA1

KESTREL HOUSE SCHOOL
104 Crouch Hill, London N8 9EA
Type: Co-educational Day Only
2–12
Special needs: ADD ADHD **ASD
ASP** DYP MLD SLD SP&LD
Wheelchair access: WA3
Independent Special

KISHARON DAY SCHOOL
1011 Finchley Road, London
NW11 7HB
Website: www.kisharon.org.uk
Type: Co-educational Day Only
5–19 (Jewish pupils only)
Special needs: ADHD ASD **ASP**
BESD CP **DOW MLD** SP&LD

**THE LONDON CENTRE FOR
CHILDREN WITH CEREBRAL
PALSY**
54 Muswell Hill, London N10 3ST
Website: www.cplondon.org.uk
Type: Co-educational Day Only
Special needs: **CP IM**
Wheelchair access: W
Independent Special

THE MOAT SCHOOL+
Bishop's Avenue, London
SW6 6EG
Website: www.moatschool.
org.uk
Type: Co-educational Day Only
11–16
Special needs: **DYC DYP DYS**
Wheelchair access: W
Independent Special

PARAYHOUSE SCHOOL
New Kings School Annex,
London SW6 4LY
Website: www.parayhouse.com
Type: Co-educational Day Only
7–16
Special needs: ADD ADHD ASD
ASP BESD CB DOW DYP DYS
EPI HEA HI **MLD** SP&LD TOU
Wheelchair access: WA3
Non-maintained

THE PRIORY LODGE SCHOOL
Priory Lane, London SW15 5JJ
Website: www.priorygroup.com
Type: Co-educational Day Only
7–19
Special needs: ADHD **ASD ASP**
Independent Special

**THE SPEECH, LANGUAGE &
HEARING CENTRE**
1–5 Christopher Place, London
NW1 1JF
Website: www.speech-lang.
org.uk
Type: Co-educational Day Only
Special needs: ADD ADHD ASD
ASP BESD CB DYP **HI** MLD
SP&LD
Wheelchair access: WA1
Independent Special

TREE HOUSE
The TreeHouse Trust, London
N10 3JA
Type: Co-educational Day Only
3–11
Special needs: ASD **ASP** SP&LD

GREATER MANCHESTER

AIM HABONIM
401 Bury Road, Greater
Manchester M7 2RT
Type: Co-educational Day Only
Special needs: SLD
Independent Special

DIDSBURY SCHOOL
611 Wilmslow Road, Manchester,
Greater Manchester M20 6AD
Website: www.
advancedchildcare.co.uk
Type: Co-educational Boarding
and Day
Special needs: ADHD **BESD**
MLD

INSCAPE HOUSE SALFORD
Silkhey Grove, Worsley, Greater
Manchester M28 7FG
Type: Co-educational Day Only
5–19
Non-maintained

LIMES MEADOWS
73 Taunton Rd, Ashton under
Lyne, Greater Manchester
OL7 9DU
Website: www.northern-care.
co.uk
Type: Boys Boarding Only 11–17
Special needs: **BESD CB**

**THE ST JOHN VIANNEY
SCHOOL**
Stretford, Greater Manchester
M16 0EX
Website: www.
stjohnvianneyschool.ik.org
Type: Co-educational Day Only
5–19
Special needs: **MLD**
Wheelchair access: W
Independent Special

TAXAL EDGE SCHOOL
Macclesfield Road, High Peak,
Greater Manchester SK23 7DR
Type: Co-educational Day Only
11–16
Special needs: **BESD**

MERSEYSIDE

CLARENCE HIGH SCHOOL
West Lane, Formby, Merseyside L37 7AZ
Website: http://www.nugentcare.org/index.php/clarence_high_school_frontpage/
Type: Co-educational Boarding and Day 9–19
Special needs: ADD ADHD **ASP BESD** CB **DYS** TOU
Wheelchair access: W
Independent Special

LAKESIDE SCHOOL*
Naylors Road, Liverpool, Merseyside L27 2YA
Website: www.lakesideschool.co.uk
Type: Co-educational Day Only 5–13
Special needs: ADD **ADHD ASD ASP** BESD **CB** DOW **DYC DYP DYS** EPI HEA HI IM MLD SP&LD TOU VI
Independent Special
52-week care

PETERHOUSE SCHOOL
Preston New Road, Southport, Merseyside PR9 8PA
Website: www.autisminitiatives.org
Type: Co-educational Boarding and Day 5–19
Special needs: **ASD ASP**
Wheelchair access: WA2
Non-maintained
52-week care

ROYAL SCHOOL FOR THE BLIND
Church Road North, Liverpool, Merseyside L15 6TQ
Website: www.rsblind.org.uk/index.
Type: Co-educational Boarding and Day 2–19
Special needs: BESD **MLD PMLD SLD** VI
Wheelchair access: W
Independent Special

ST VINCENT'S SCHOOL, A SPECIALIST SCHOOL FOR SENSORY IMPAIRMENT AND OTHER NEEDS
Yew Tree Lane, Liverpool, Merseyside L12 9HN
Website: www.stvin.com
Type: Co-educational Boarding and Day 4–19
Special needs: ASD ASP CP DYS EPI HI MLD SP&LD VI W
Wheelchair access: WWA2
Non-maintained

WALTON PROGRESSIVE SCHOOL
European Lifestyles Education Sevices, Liverpool, Merseyside L9 1NR
Type: Co-educational Day Only 8–19
Special needs: **ADD ADHD ASD ASP CB EPI** HI **IM** PMLD **SLD** SP&LD VI
Wheelchair access: WA1
Independent Special

WARGRAVE HOUSE SCHOOL
449 Wargrave Road, Newton-le-Willows, Merseyside WA12 8RS
Website: www.wargravehouse.com
Type: Co-educational Boarding and Day 5–19
Special needs: **ASD ASP**

WEST KIRBY RESIDENTIAL SCHOOL*
Meols Drive, Wirral, Merseyside CH48 5DH
Type: Co-educational Boarding and Day 5–18
Special needs: **ADD ADHD ASD ASP BESD CB** DYP DYS EPI HI MLD SP&LD TOU VI
Non-maintained

MIDDLESEX

HILLINGDON MANOR SCHOOL
Moorcroft Complex, Uxbridge, Middlesex UB8 3HD
Type: Co-educational Day Only 6–19
Special needs: ASD **ASP** SLD
Independent Special

NAS SYBIL ELGAR SCHOOL*
The National Autistic Society, Southall, Middlesex UB2 4NY
Website: www.autism.org.uk/sybilelgar
Type: Co-educational Day and Boarding 8–19
Special needs: **ASD ASP** SP&LD
Independent Special

PIELD HEATH SCHOOL
Pield Heath Road, Uxbridge, Middlesex UB8 3NW
Type: Co-educational Boarding and Day 7–19
Special needs: ADD ASD ASP CP DOW DYP EPI HEA **MLD** PMLD **SLD** SP&LD VI

RNIB SUNSHINE HOUSE SCHOOL AND CHILDREN'S HOME*
33 Dene Road, Northwood, Middlesex HA6 2DD
Website: www.rnib.org.uk/sunshinehouse
Type: Co-educational Day and Boarding 2–11 (Children from the ages of 5 to 14 years can board Monday to Thursday for up to 50 weeks per year.)
Special needs: CP EPI HEA HI IM **PMLD SLD** SP&LD **VI** W
Wheelchair access: WA1
Non-maintained

NORFOLK

EAGLE HOUSE – NORFOLK SCHOOL
Andrews Furlong, Norwich, Norfolk NR16 2HU
Website: www.eaglehousenorfolk.co.uk
Type: Co-educational Boarding and Day 4–19
Special needs: ADD ADHD ASD **ASP** CB EPI MLD SLD SP&LD
Wheelchair access: WA3
Independent Special
52-week care

SHERIDAN SCHOOL
Thetford Road, Thetford, Norfolk IP26 5LQ
Website: http://www.priorygroup.com/Locations/East-Anglia/Sheridan-School.aspx
Type: Co-educational 10–19
Special needs: ADD ADHD ASP **BESD CB** DYS MLD SP&LD
Wheelchair access: WA3
Independent Special
52-week care

NORTHAMPTONSHIRE

POTTERSPURY LODGE SCHOOL*
Potterspury Lodge, Towcester, Northamptonshire NN12 7LL
Website: www.potterspurylodge.co.uk
Type: Boys Boarding and Day 8–18
Special needs: **ADD ADHD ASD ASP BESD** CB DYP DYS MLD SP&LD TOU
Independent Special

THORNBY HALL THERAPEUTIC COMMUNITY
Naseby Road, Thornby, Northamptonshire NN6 8SW
Type: Co-educational Boarding Only 12–18
Special needs: BESD CB
Wheelchair access: WA3
Independent Special
52-week care

NORTHUMBERLAND

NUNNYKIRK CENTRE FOR DYSLEXIA+
Morpeth, Northumberland
NE61 4PB
Type: Co-educational Boarding and Day 7–16
Special needs: **DYS**

NOTTINGHAMSHIRE

GLENDALE HOUSE
255 Tamworth Rd, Long Eaton, Nottinghamshire NG10 1AS
Website: www.northern-care.co.uk
Type: Co-educational Boarding Only 11–17
Special needs: **BESD CB**

HOPE HOUSE SCHOOL
Barnby Road, Nottinghamshire NG24 3NE
Website: www.hopehouseschool.co.uk
Type: Co-educational 5–14
Special needs: ASD **ASP**
Independent Special

I CAN'S DAWN HOUSE SCHOOL*
Helmsley Road, Mansfield, Nottinghamshire NG21 0DQ
Website: www.ican.org.uk
Type: Co-educational Boarding and Day 5–19
Special needs: SP&LD
Non-maintained

ORCHARD SCHOOL
South Leverton, Retford, Nottinghamshire DN22 0DJ
Website: www.orchardspecial.shropshire.sch.uk
Type: Co-educational Day Only 2–16
Special needs: ASD DYS SLD

RUTLAND HOUSE SCHOOL
1 Elm Bank, Nottingham, Nottinghamshire NG3 5AJ
Website: www.scope.org.uk/rutland
Type: Co-educational Boarding and Day 5–19
Special needs: **CP EPI** HI IM PMLD SP&LD VI
Wheelchair access: WA2
Independent Special
52-week care

SUTHERLAND HOUSE SCHOOL (CARLTON)
Sutherland Road, Nottingham, Nottinghamshire NG3 7AP
Website: www.sutherlandhouse.org.uk
Type: Co-educational Day Only 3–19
Special needs: ASD **ASP**
Wheelchair access: WA2
Non-maintained

SUTHERLAND HOUSE SCHOOL (SECONDARY DEPARTMENT)
"Westward", Mapperley Park, Nottinghamshire NG3 5ED
Type: Co-educational Day Only 11–16
Special needs: ASD **ASP**

WINGS EAST SCHOOL
Kirklington Hall, Nottinghamshire NG22 8NB
Website: www.wingseastschool.co.uk
Type: Co-educational Boarding Only 11–17
Special needs: **ADD ADHD ASD BESD DYP DYS MLD**
Independent Special
52-week care

OXFORDSHIRE

ACTION FOR CHILDREN PARKLANDS CAMPUS*
Action for Children, Abingdon, Oxfordshire OX13 5QB
Website: www.actionforchildren.org.uk/schools
Type: Co-educational Boarding and Day 11–16
Special needs: **ADD ADHD BESD CB**
Non-maintained
52-week care

ACTION FOR CHILDREN PENHURST SCHOOL*
New Street, Chipping Norton, Oxfordshire OX7 5LN
Website: www.actionforchildren.org.uk/schools
Type: Co-educational Boarding and Day 5–19
Special needs: CP EPI HI IM **PMLD** SLD SP&LD VI
Non-maintained
52-week care

CHILWORTH HOUSE SCHOOL*
Thame Road, Oxfordshire OX33 1JP
Website: www.chilworthhouseschool.com
Type: Co-educational Day Only 5–14
Special needs: **ADD ADHD ASD ASP BESD CB DYS MLD**
Independent Special

CHILWORTH HOUSE UPPER SCHOOL*
Grooms Farm, Oxfordshire OX33 1JP
Website: www.witherslackgroup.co.uk/chilworth-house-upper-school
Type: Co-educational 11–16
Independent Special

HILLCREST PARK SCHOOL
Southcombe, Chipping Norton, Oxfordshire OX7 5QH
Type: Co-educational Day Only 8–16
Special needs: ADD ADHD **BESD CB** MLD SLD
Wheelchair access: W

MULBERRY BUSH SCHOOL
Abingdon Road, Witney, Oxfordshire OX29 7RW
Website: www.mulberrybush.oxon.sch.uk
Type: Co-educational Boarding Only 5–12
Special needs: **ADD ADHD BESD CB** HEA HI MLD
Wheelchair access: WA2
Non-maintained

SWALCLIFFE PARK SCHOOL TRUST*
Swalcliffe, Banbury, Oxfordshire OX15 5EP
Website: www.swalcliffepark.oxon.sch.uk
Type: Boys Boarding and Day 11–19
Special needs: ADD ADHD **ASD ASP** BESD CB DYC DYP DYS MLD SP&LD TOU
Non-maintained

THE UNICORN SCHOOL*+
20 Marcham Road, Abingdon, Oxfordshire OX14 1AA
Website: www.unicorndyslexia.co.uk
Type: Co-educational Day Only 6–13
Special needs: ADD ADHD **DYC DYP DYS** SP&LD
Independent Special

RUTLAND

THE GRANGE THERAPEUTIC SCHOOL
Oakham, Rutland LE15 8LY
Type: Boys Boarding and Day 8–16
Special needs: **BESD**
Wheelchair access: W
Independent Special

SHROPSHIRE

CRUCKTON HALL*
Shrewsbury, Shropshire SY5 8PR
Website: www.cruckton.com
Type: Boys Boarding and Day
8–19
Special needs: **ADD ADHD ASD
ASP BESD** CB DYC DYP **DYS**
EPI HI MLD
52-week care

HIGHLEA SCHOOL
Astbury Lane, Bridgenorth,
Shropshire WV16 6AX
Type: Co-educational

LEARNING FOR LIFE
Station Road, Bridgnorth,
Shropshire WV16 6SS
Type: Co-educational Day Only
11–16

**NEW OPTIONS (HIGFORD)
SCHOOL**
Shifnal, Shropshire TF11 9ET
Website: www.optionsgroup.
co.uk
Type: Co-educational Boarding
Only 8–19
Special needs: ADD ADHD **ASD
ASP** CB EPI HEA HI IM SLD
SP&LD VI
Wheelchair access: W
Independent Special

OVERLEY HALL SCHOOL
Wellington, Shropshire TF6 5HE
Website: www.overleyhall.com
Type: Co-educational Boarding
Only 9–19
Special needs: ADHD ASD **ASP**
CB DOW **EPI** HI PMLD **SLD**
SP&LD
Wheelchair access: WA2
Independent Special
52-week care

SOMERSET

**EDINGTON AND SHAPWICK
SCHOOL+**
Shapwick Manor, Shapwick,
Somerset TA7 9NJ
Website: www.edingtonshapwick.
co.uk
Type: Co-educational Boarding
and Day 8–18
Special needs: DYC DYP **DYS**
Wheelchair access: WA3
Independent Special

FARLEIGH COLLEGE
Newbury, Somerset BA11 3RG
Website: www.priorygroup.com
Type: Co-educational Boarding
and Day 10–16
Special needs: ADD ADHD **ASD**
ASP CB DYC DYP DYS
Wheelchair access: WA2
Independent Special

THE LIBRA SCHOOL
Edgemoor Court, South Molton,
Somerset EX36 3LN
Type: Co-educational Day Only
8–18
Special needs: BESD
Independent Special

**THE MARCHANT-HOLLIDAY
SCHOOL***
Templecombe, Somerset
BA8 0AH
Website: www.marchantholliday.
co.uk
Type: Boys Boarding and Day
5–15
Special needs: **ADD ADHD** ASD
ASP BESD CB DYC DYP DYS
HEA IM MLD SLD SP&LD TOU
Independent Special

MARK COLLEGE+
Mark, Highbridge, Somerset
TA9 4NP
Website: www.markcollege.
somerset.sch.uk
Type: Co-educational Boarding
and Day 10–19
Special needs: ADD **DYC DYP
DYS** SP&LD
Wheelchair access: WA2
Independent Special

MERRYHAY ACADEMY
Merryhay House, Ilminster,
Somerset TA19 9DU
Type: Co-educational Day and
Boarding 11–16
Special needs: **ADD ADHD** ASD
ASP BESD CB DYP DYS MLD
Wheelchair access: WA3
Independent Special
52-week care

STAFFORDSHIRE

BLADON HOUSE SCHOOL*
Newton Solney, Burton upon
Trent, Staffordshire DE15 0TA
Website: www.bladonhouse.com
Type: Co-educational Day and
Boarding 5–19
Special needs: **ADD ADHD** ASD
ASP BESD **CB** CP **DOW DYC
DYP EPI** HEA **HI** IM **MLD PMLD
SLD** SP&LD **TOU**
Wheelchair access: WA3
Independent Special
52-week care

DRAYCOTT MOOR COLLEGE
Draycott Old Road, Stoke-on-
Trent, Staffordshire ST11 9AH
Type: Co-educational Day Only
11–16
Special needs: BESD
Independent Special

MAPLE HAYES SCHOOL
Abnalls Lane, Lichfield,
Staffordshire WS13 8BL
Website: www.dyslexia.gb.com
Type: Co-educational Day Only
7–17
Special needs: **DYS**
Wheelchair access: W
Independent Special

ROACHES SCHOOL
Tunstall Road, Stoke On Trent,
Staffordshire ST8 7AB
Type: Co-educational Boarding
and Day 5–16
Special needs: **BESD**
52-week care

RUGELEY HORIZON SCHOOL
Blithbury Road, Rugeley,
Staffordshire WS15 3JQ
Website: www.prioryeducation.
com
Type: Co-educational Boarding
and Day 4–19
Special needs: ASD **ASP**
Wheelchair access: WA1
Independent Special

STOKE

AIDENSWOOD
47 Liverpool Rd East, Stoke
SY10 9DD
Website: www.northern-care.
co.uk
Type: Boys Boarding Only 11–17
Special needs: **BESD CB**

SUFFOLK

BRAMFIELD HOUSE
Walpole Road, Halesworth,
Suffolk IP19 9AB
Type: Boys Boarding and Day
10–16
Special needs: BESD MLD

**CENTRE ACADEMY EAST
ANGLIA+**
Church Road, Suffolk IP7 7QR
Website: www.centreacademy.
net
Type: Co-educational Day and
Boarding 8–16
Special needs: **ADD ADHD ASD
ASP DYC DYP DYS MLD** SP&LD
Independent Special

SURREY

CORNFIELD SCHOOL
53 Hanworth Road, Redhill,
Surrey RH1 5HS
Type: Girls Boarding and Day
11–18
Special needs: BESD
Wheelchair access: WA1
Independent Special
52-week care

**EAGLE HOUSE SCHOOL
MITCHAM**
224 London Road, Mitcham,
Surrey CR4 3HD
Website: www.
eaglehouseschool.co.uk
Type: Co-educational Day Only
4–19
Special needs: ADD ADHD **ASD
ASP** DYP MLD SLD SP&LD
Wheelchair access: WA3
Independent Special

GRAFHAM GRANGE SCHOOL
Grafham, Guildford, Surrey
GU5 0LH
Website: www.ggset.co.uk
Type: Boys Day and Boarding
10–18
Special needs: ADD ADHD ASD
ASP **BESD CB** DYS MLD SP&LD
Wheelchair access: W
Non-maintained

I CAN'S MEATH SCHOOL*
Brox Road, Ottershaw, Surrey
KT16 0LF
Website: www.ican.org.uk
Type: Co-educational Day and
Boarding 4–11
Special needs: ADD ASP DYP
DYS EPI HI MLD SP&LD
Non-maintained

THE JIGSAW SCHOOL
Dunsfold Park, Cranleigh, Surrey
GU6 8TB
Type: Co-educational Day Only
4–16
Special needs: ASD **ASP**
Independent Special

**KISIMUL SCHOOL –
WOODSTOCK HOUSE***
Woodstock Lane North, Long
Ditton, Surrey KT6 5HN
Type: Co-educational Boarding
Only 8–19
Special needs: ASD **CB** DOW
EPI **SLD** SP&LD
Wheelchair access: W
Independent Special

KNOWL HILL SCHOOL+
School Lane, Pirbright, Surrey
GU24 0JN
Website: www.knowlhill.org.uk
Type: Co-educational Day Only
7–16
Special needs: DYC DYP **DYS**
Wheelchair access: W

THE LINK PRIMARY SCHOOL
138 Croydon Road, Croydon,
Surrey CR0 4PG
Website: www.link.ik.org
Type: Co-educational Day Only
6–12
Special needs: ASD ASP DOW
DYP DYS MLD SP&LD
Wheelchair access: WA3
Non-maintained

**THE LINK SECONDARY
SCHOOL**
82–86 Croydon Road,
Beddington, Surrey CR0 4PD
Website: www.link-sec.sutton.
sch.uk
Type: Co-educational Day Only
11–19
Special needs: ASD ASP SP&LD
Wheelchair access: WA2

LITTLE DAVID'S SCHOOL
(Timebridge Centre), Croydon,
Surrey CR0 9AZ
Type: Co-educational Day Only
3–12
Special needs: **ADD ADHD** ASD
ASP BESD CB DYS **MLD PMLD
SLD** SP&LD
Wheelchair access: WA3
Independent Special

**MOON HALL COLLEGE AND
BURYS COURT+**
Flanchford Road, Reigate, Surrey
RH2 8RE
Website: www.moonhall.surrey.
sch.uk
Type: Co-educational Boarding
and Day 11–16
Special needs: **DYS**
Wheelchair access: WA3

MOON HALL SCHOOL
Feldemore, Dorking, Surrey
RH5 6LQ
Website: www.belmont-school.
org
Type: Co-educational Boarding
and Day 2–13
Special needs: DYC DYP DYS
Independent Special

MOOR HOUSE SCHOOL
Oxted, Surrey RH8 9AQ
Website: www.moorhouse.surrey.
sch.uk
Type: Co-educational Boarding
Only 7–16
Special needs: DYC DYP DYS
SP&LD

MORE HOUSE SCHOOL+
Moons Hill, Farnham, Surrey
GU10 3AP
Type: Boys Boarding and Day
9–18
Special needs: **DYC DYP DYS**
SP&LD

MRCS EDUCATIONAL UNIT
61 Lodge Road, Croydon, Surrey
CR20 2PH
Type: Boys Day Only 11–16
Special needs: **ADD ADHD
BESD DYS HEA MLD SLD**
SP&LD **TOU**

RUTHERFORD SCHOOL
1A Melville Avenue, South
Croydon, Surrey CR2 7HZ
Website: www.
garwoodfoundation.org.uk
Type: Co-educational Day Only
2–19
Special needs: **CP EPI HEA HI
IM PMLD SLD** VI W
Wheelchair access: WWA1WA2
Independent Special

ST DOMINIC'S SCHOOL
Hambledon, Godalming, Surrey
GU8 4DX
Website: www.
stdominicsschool.org.uk
Type: Co-educational Boarding
and Day 8–16
Special needs: ADD ADHD ASD
ASP DYC DYP DYS EPI HEA
SP&LD
Wheelchair access: W
Non-maintained

**ST PIERS SCHOOL, THE
NATIONAL CENTRE FOR
YOUNG PEOPLE WITH
EPILEPSY (NCYPE)**
St Piers Lane, Lingfield, Surrey
RH7 6PW
Website: www.ncype.org.uk
Type: Co-educational Boarding
and Day 5–19
Special needs: ADHD ASD ASP
BESD CB DOW **EPI** HI MLD
PMLD SLD SP&LD TOU
Wheelchair access: WA1
Independent Special
52-week care

**THE SCHOOL FOR PROFOUND
EDUCATION***
The Children's Trust, Tadworth,
Surrey KT20 5RU
Website: www.thechildrenstrust.
org.uk/profoundeducation
Type: Co-educational Boarding
and Day 5–19 (There is additional
college provision for 19 to 25 year
olds.)
Special needs: **CP EPI HEA HI
IM PMLD** VI W
Wheelchair access: WA1
Non-maintained
52-week care

UNSTED PARK SCHOOL
Mustead Heath Road,
Godalming, Surrey GU7 1UW
Website: www.prioryeducation.
com
Type: Co-educational Boarding
and Day 7–16
Special needs: ASD ASP
Wheelchair access: WA2
Independent Special

EAST SUSSEX

CHAILEY HERITAGE SCHOOL*
Haywards Heath Road, Nr
Lewes, East Sussex BN8 4EF
Website: www.chs.org.uk
Type: Co-educational Day and
Boarding 3–19 (The school also
offers a Young Adults' Transition
Service for young disabled adults
aged 19–25.)
Special needs: ASD **CP** EPI **HEA**
HI **IM** MLD PMLD SLD SP&LD
VI W
Wheelchair access: WA1 WA2
Non-maintained
52-week care

THE FIRS
2 The Green, St Leonards on Sea,
East Sussex
Website: www.northern-care.
co.uk
Type: Boys Boarding Only 11–17
Special needs: **BESD CB**

FREWEN COLLEGE+
Brickwall, Rye, East Sussex
TN31 6NL
Website: www.frewencollege.
co.uk
Type: Co-educational Boarding
and Day 5–16
Special needs: ASP **DYC DYP
DYS** SP&LD
Wheelchair access: W
Independent Special

**HAMILTON LODGE SCHOOL
FOR DEAF CHILDREN**
Walpole Road, Brighton, East
Sussex BN2 0LS
Website: hamiltonlodgeschool.
co.uk
Type: Co-educational Boarding
and Day 5–18
Special needs: **HI**
Wheelchair access: WA2
Non-maintained

THE LIONCARE SCHOOL
c/o The Lioncare Group, Hove,
East Sussex BN3 3WL
Website: www.lioncare.co.uk
Type: Co-educational Day Only
7–16
Special needs: **ADD ADHD ASD**
ASP **BESD CB DYS** HEA HI **MLD
PMLD** SLD SP&LD VI
Wheelchair access: WA3
Independent Special
52-week care

NORTHEASE MANOR+
Lewes, East Sussex BN7 3EY
Website: www.northease.co.uk
Type: Co-educational Boarding
and Day 10–17
Special needs: DYC DYP **DYS**

OWLSWICK SCHOOL
Newhaven Road, Lewes, East
Sussex BN7 3NF
Website: www.owlswickschool.
co.uk
Type: Co-educational Boarding
Only 10–18
Special needs: ADD **ADHD**
BESD DYS **MLD**
52-week care

**ST JOHN'S SCHOOL &
COLLEGE**
Firle Road, Seaford, East Sussex
BN25 2HU
Website: www.st-johns.co.uk
Type: Co-educational Boarding
and Day 7–22
Special needs: ADD ASD ASP
BESD DOW **MLD SLD** TOU
Non-maintained

**ST MARY'S WRESTWOOD
CHILDREN'S TRUST***
Wrestwood Road, Bexhill-on-Sea,
East Sussex TN40 2LU
Website: www.st-marys.bexhill.
sch.uk
Type: Co-educational Boarding
and Day 7–19
Special needs: ADD ASD **ASP**
CP DOW DYP DYS EPI HEA HI
IM **MLD** SP&LD TOU VI
Wheelchair access: WA1
Non-maintained

WEST SUSSEX

BRANTRIDGE SCHOOL
Staplefield Place, Haywards
Heath, West Sussex RH17 6EQ
Website: www.brantridge-school.
co.uk
Type: Boys Boarding 6–11
Special needs: ADD ADHD ASD
ASP **BESD** CB MLD SP&LD
Wheelchair access: W
Non-maintained

FARNEY CLOSE SCHOOL
Bolney Court, Haywards Heath,
West Sussex RH17 5RD
Website: www.farneyclose.co.uk
Type: Co-educational Boarding
and Day 11–16
Special needs: ADD ADHD ASP
BESD MLD

HILLCREST SLINFORD*
Stane Street, Nr Horsham, West
Sussex RH13 0QX
Type: Boys Boarding Only 11–16
Special needs: ADD **ADHD**
BESD CB
52-week care

INGFIELD MANOR SCHOOL*
Ingfield Manor Drive,
Billingshurst, West Sussex
RH14 9AX
Website: www.scope.org.uk
Type: Co-educational Day and
Boarding 3–19
Special needs: **CP** IM SP&LD
Independent Special

**KINGS MANOR COMMUNITY
COLLEGE**
Kingston Lane, Shoreham-by-
Sea, West Sussex BN43 6YT
Website: www.kingsmanor.w-
sussex.sch.uk
Type: Co-educational Boarding
Only 11–16
Special needs: ADD **ADHD**
BESD **DYP** DYS EPI HEA MLD

MUNTHAM HOUSE SCHOOL
Barns Green, Horsham, West
Sussex RH13 7NJ
Website: www.munthamhouse.
w-sussex.sch.uk
Type: Boys Boarding and Day
8–18
Special needs: ADD **ADHD** ASD
ASP **BESD CB**
Wheelchair access: WA3

**PHILPOTS MANOR SCHOOL
AND FURTHER TRAINING
CENTRE***
West Hoathly, East Grinstead,
West Sussex RH19 4PR
Website: www.
philpotsmanorschool.co.uk
Type: Co-educational Boarding
and Day 7–19
Special needs: ADD ADHD **ASD**
ASP BESD **CB** DYC DYP **DYS**
EPI HEA **MLD** SP&LD **TOU**
Independent Special

SOUTHWAYS SCHOOL
The Vale House, Worthing, West
Sussex BN14 0RA
Website: families-for-children.
co.uk
Type: Co-educational Day Only
7–11
Special needs: **BESD**
Wheelchair access: W
Independent Special

TYNE AND WEAR

NORTHERN COUNTIES SCHOOL
Great North Road, Newcastle-Upon-Tyne, Tyne and Wear NE2 3BB
Website: www.northern-counties-school.co.uk
Type: Co-educational Boarding and Day 3–19
Special needs: **HI** MLD **PMLD** VI
Wheelchair access: W

PARKSIDE HOUSE SCHOOL
Station Road, Backworth, Tyne and Wear NE27 0AB
Type: 11–16
Special needs: BESD MLD
Independent Special

PERCY HEDLEY SCHOOL
Station Road, Newcastle-upon-Tyne, Tyne and Wear NE12 8YY
Website: www.percyhedley.org.uk
Type: Co-educational Day and Boarding 3–19
Special needs: ADHD ASD ASP **CP** DYP HI IM SP&LD VI
Wheelchair access: WA1
Non-maintained

TALBOT HOUSE SPECIAL SCHOOL
Hexham Road, Newcastle Upon Tyne, Tyne and Wear NE15 8HW
Website: www.talbothouseschool.org
Type: Co-educational Day and Boarding 7–18
Special needs: **ADD ADHD BESD CB** DYP MLD TOU
Wheelchair access: WA2
Non-maintained
52-week care

THORNHILL PARK SCHOOL
21 Thornhill Park, Sunderland, Tyne and Wear SR2 7LA
Type: Co-educational Boarding and Day 2–19
Special needs: **ASD ASP**
Wheelchair access: W
52-week care

WARWICKSHIRE

ARC SCHOOL
Church End, Nr Nuneaton, Warwickshire CV10 0QR
Type: Co-educational Day Only 11–16
Special needs: BESD
Independent Special

THE OLD SCHOOL
Church End, Nr Nuneaton, Warwickshire CV10 0QR
Type: Co-educational Day Only 11–16
Special needs: **BESD**

RNIB PEARS CENTRE FOR SPECIALIST LEARNING*
Wheelwright Lane, Warwickshire CV7 9RA
Website: www.rnib.org.uk/pearscentre
Type: Co-educational Boarding and Day 4–19
Special needs: ASD BESD CB CP DOW EPI HEA HI **IM PMLD SLD** SP&LD VI W
Wheelchair access: WA1
52-week care

WATHEN GRANGE SCHOOL
C/O Complete Care (Warks) Ltd, Leamington Spa, Warwickshire CV32 5YY
Type: Co-educational Day and Boarding 12–16
Special needs: **BESD** CB
Wheelchair access: WA1
Independent Special
52-week care

WEST MIDLANDS

NATIONAL INSTITUTE OF CONDUCTIVE EDUCATION
Cannon Hill House, Birmingham, West Midlands B13 8RD
Website: www.conductive-education.org.uk
Type: Co-educational Day Only 1–11
Special needs: ASD **CP** DYP HEA IM MLD SP&LD
Wheelchair access: WA2
Independent Special

NEW HALL PROJECT 20/20
The Huntingtree Park Centre, Halesowen, West Midlands B63 4HY
Type: Co-educational Day Only 14–16

QUEEN ALEXANDRA COLLEGE OF FURTHER EDUCATION*
Court Oak Road, Birmingham, West Midlands B17 9TG
Website: www.qac.ac.uk
Type: Mixed Residential and Day
Special needs: ASD **ASP** CP DOW DYP DYS EPI HI IM **MLD** SP&LD VI
Wheelchair access: WA1

THE ROYAL WOLVERHAMPTON SCHOOL+
Penn Road, Wolverhampton, West Midlands WV3 0EG
Website: www.theroyalschool.co.uk
Type: Co-educational Boarding and Day 2–18
Special needs: ADD ADHD DYP **DYS**

SECOND CHANCES AT THE VINE TRUST WALSALL
33 Lower Hall Lane, Walsall, West Midlands WS1 1RR
Type: Co-educational Day Only 14–16
Wheelchair access: W

SUNFIELD SCHOOL*
Clent Grove, Stourbridge, West Midlands DY9 9PB
Website: www.sunfield.org.uk
Type: Co-educational Boarding and Day 6–19
Special needs: **ADHD ASD CB SLD**
Independent Special
52-week care

WILTSHIRE

APPLEFORD SCHOOL+
Elston Lane, Salisbury, Wiltshire SP3 4HL
Website: www.applefordschool.org
Type: Co-educational Boarding and Day 7–14
Special needs: ADD ADHD **DYC** DYP **DYS** MLD SP&LD
Wheelchair access: WA3
Independent Special

BELMONT SCHOOL
School Lane, Salisbury, Wiltshire SP1 3YA
Type: Co-educational Day Only 11–16
Special needs: **BESD**
Wheelchair access: WA3

BURTON HILL SCHOOL
Malmesbury, Wiltshire SN16 0EG
Website: www.shaftesburysoc.org.uk/burtonhill
Type: Co-educational Boarding and Day 11–20
Special needs: ASD **CP** HEA HI **IM MLD PMLD SLD** SP&LD VI
Wheelchair access: WA1
Non-maintained

CALDER HOUSE SCHOOL+
Thickwood Lane, Chippenham, Wiltshire SN14 8BN
Website: www.calderhouseschool.co.uk
Type: Co-educational Day Only 5–13
Special needs: DYC **DYP DYS** HEA SP&LD
Wheelchair access: WA3

COTSWOLD COMMUNITY
Spine Road West, Swindon, Wiltshire SN6 6QU
Website: www.actionforchildren.org.uk/schools
Type: Boys Boarding and Day 9–18
Special needs: ADD ADHD ASP **BESD** CB DYS HI MLD
Wheelchair access: WA1
Independent Special
52-week care

TUMBLEWOOD PROJECT SCHOOL
The Laurels, Westbury, Wiltshire BA13 4LF
Type: Girls Day Only 11–18
Special needs: **BESD**
Wheelchair access: WA2
52-week care

WESSEX COLLEGE
Wessex House, Warminster,
Wiltshire BA12 9JN
Type: Co-educational Day Only
11–16
Special needs: BESD

WORCESTERSHIRE

NEW COLLEGE WORCESTER*
Whittington Road, Worcester,
Worcestershire WR5 2JX
Website: www.
newcollegeworcester.co.uk
Type: Co-educational Boarding
and Day 11–19
Special needs: ASP DYP DYS
HEA HI IM VI W
Wheelchair access: WA2
Independent Special

NORTH YORKSHIRE

BRECKENBROUGH SCHOOL*
Sandhutton, Thirsk, North
Yorkshire YO7 4EN
Website: www.breckenbrough.
org.uk
Type: Boys Boarding and Day
9–17
Special needs: ADD ADHD ASD
ASP BESD CB DYP
Non-maintained

**SPRING HILL SCHOOL
(BARNARDO'S)***
Palace Road, Ripon, North
Yorkshire HG4 3HN
Website: www.barnardos.org.uk/
springhillschool
Type: Co-educational Day Only
9–19
Special needs: **ADD ADHD ASD
ASP BESD CB** DOW DYP DYS
EPI HEA HI **MLD** SLD SP&LD
TOU VI
Non-maintained
52-week care

SOUTH YORKSHIRE

**DONCASTER SCHOOL FOR
THE DEAF***
Leger Way, Doncaster, South
Yorkshire DN2 6AY
Website: www.deaf-school.co.uk
Type: Co-educational Boarding
and Day 5–16
Special needs: ADHD BESD CP
DYS **HI** MLD PMLD SLD SP&LD
VI
Wheelchair access: WA1
Independent Special
52-week care

FULLERTON HOUSE SCHOOL
off Tickhill Square, Doncaster,
South Yorkshire DN12 4AR
Website: www.hesleygroup.co.uk
Type: Co-educational Boarding
Only 8–19
Special needs: ASD EPI SLD
SP&LD

**NAS ROBERT OGDEN
SCHOOL***
The National Autistic Society,
Rotherham, South Yorkshire
S63 0BG
Website: www.autism.org.uk/
robertogden
Type: Co-educational Boarding
and Day 7–19
Special needs: **ASD ASP** MLD
PMLD SLD
Independent Special
52-week care

**PACES CONDUCTIVE
EDUCATION**
Pack Horse Lane, Sheffield,
South Yorkshire S35 3HY
Website: www.paces-school.
org.uk/
Type: Co-educational
Special needs: **CP** HEA HI MLD
SLD SP&LD VI W
Non-maintained

WILSIC HALL SCHOOL
Doncaster, South Yorkshire
DN11 9AG
Website: www.wilsichallschool.
co.uk
Type: Co-educational Boarding
Only 11–19
Special needs: ASD **ASP** CB SLD
SP&LD
Wheelchair access: WA3
Independent Special
52-week care

WEST YORKSHIRE

DENBY GRANGE SCHOOL
Off Stocksmoor Road, Wakefield,
West Yorkshire WF4 4JQ
Type: Co-educational Day Only
11–16
Special needs: ADD ADHD
BESD CB MLD
Wheelchair access: WA1
Independent Special

HOLLY BANK SCHOOL
Roe Head, Mirfield, West
Yorkshire WF14 0DQ
Website: www.hollybanktrust.
com
Type: Co-educational Boarding
and Day 5–19
Special needs: **CP** EPI **IM** MLD
PMLD SLD SP&LD VI
Wheelchair access: WA2
Non-maintained
52-week care

NORSETT HOUSE
West View, Halifax, West
Yorkshire HX3 6PG
Website: www.northern-care.
co.uk
Type: Boys Boarding Only 11–17
Special needs: **BESD CB**

**ST JOHN'S CATHOLIC
SCHOOL FOR THE DEAF***
Church Street, Boston Spa, West
Yorkshire LS23 6DF
Website: www.stjohns.org.uk
Type: Co-educational Boarding
and Day 4–19
Special needs: ADHD ASD ASP
CP DYP DYS EPI **HI** IM MLD
SP&LD VI
Non-maintained

**WILLIAM HENRY SMITH
SCHOOL**
Brighouse, West Yorkshire
HD6 3JW
Website: www.whsschool.org.uk
Type: Boys Boarding and Day
8–16
Special needs: ADD ADHD
BESD CB DYS
Wheelchair access: WA2
Non-maintained

YORK

NEW HAVEN
3 Wilton Rd, Hornsea, York
HU18 1QU
Website: www.northern-care.
co.uk
Type: Boys Boarding Only 11–17
Special needs: **BESD CB**

SCOTLAND

ABERDEENSHIRE

CAMPHILL SCHOOL ABERDEEN
Central Office, Aberdeen, Aberdeenshire AB15 9EP
Website: www.camphillschools.org.uk
Type: Co-educational Boarding and Day 3–19
Special needs: ADD ADHD **ASD ASP BESD** CP DOW DYP DYS EPI HEA HI **MLD PMLD SLD** SP&LD TOU VI
Wheelchair access: WA2
Independent Special

LINN MOOR RESIDENTIAL SCHOOL
Aberdeen, Aberdeenshire AB14 0PJ
Website: www.linnmoorschool.co.uk
Type: Co-educational Boarding. Only 5–18
Special needs: ASD ASP CB **MLD** PMLD SLD
Wheelchair access: WA1
52-week care

OAKBANK SCHOOL
Midstocket Road, Aberdeen, Aberdeenshire AB15 5XP
Type: Co-educational Boarding and Day 12–18
Special needs: ADHD **BESD**

NORTH AYRSHIRE

GEILSLAND SCHOOL
Beith, North Ayrshire KA15 1HD
Type: Boys Boarding Only 14–18
Special needs: **BESD** MLD

SEAFIELD SCHOOL
86 Eglinton Road, Ardrossan, North Ayrshire KA22 8NL
Type: Boys Boarding and Day 7–17
Special needs: ADD ADHD ASP **BESD** DYS MLD
Wheelchair access: W

EAST AYRSHIRE

NAS DALDORCH HOUSE SCHOOL*
The National Autistic Society, Catrine, East Ayrshire KA5 6NA
Website: www.autism.org.uk/daldorch
Type: Co-educational Boarding and Day 5–25 (Primary and secondary education for students up to 18, and continuing education and supported living up to 25.)
Special needs: ASD **ASP**
Wheelchair access: W
52-week care

CLACKMANNANSHIRE

NEW STRUAN SCHOOL
A Centre for Autism, Alloa, Clackmannanshire FK101NP
Website: www.autism-in-scotland.org.uk
Type: Co-educational Boarding and Day 5–19
Special needs: **ASD ASP**
Wheelchair access: WA1

DUMFRIES & GALLOWAY

WOODLANDS SCHOOL
Merton Hall, Wigtownshire, Dumfries & Galloway DG8 6QL
Type: Boys Boarding Only 7–17
Special needs: ADD ADHD
BESD MLD SP&LD

FALKIRK

BARNARDO'S LECROPT
School & Family Support Service,
Camelon, Falkirk FK1 4HS
Type: Co-educational Day Only
5–12
Special needs: ADD **ADHD** ASD
ASP **BESD CB** DYC DYP DYS
SP&LD TOU
Wheelchair access: WA1

FIFE

FALKLAND HOUSE SCHOOL
Falkland Estate, Cupar, Fife
KY15 7AE
Website: www.
falklandhouseschool.org
Type: Boys Boarding and Day
Special needs: ADHD ASP BESD
TOU
Independent Special

HILLSIDE SCHOOL
Aberdour, Fife KY3 0RH
Type: Boys Boarding Only 11–16
Special needs: ADD ADHD BESD
DYS MLD
Wheelchair access: WA3
52-week care

STARLEY HALL
Aberdour Road, Burntisland, Fife
KY3 0AG
Website: www.starleyhallschool.
co.uk
Type: Co-educational Boarding
Only 11–16
Special needs: **ADD ADHD** ASP
BESD TOU
52-week care

SYCAMORE SCHOOL
6 Bellyeoman Road, Dunfermline,
Fife KY1 3HD
Special needs: ASD **BESD**

GLASGOW

EAST PARK SCHOOL
1092 Maryhill Road, Glasgow
G20 9TD
Type: Co-educational Boarding
and Day 5–19
Special needs: ADHD ASD **ASP
CB** CP **EPI HEA** IM **PMLD** SLD
SP&LD VI
Wheelchair access: WA1
52-week care

ST FRANCIS DAY BOY UNIT
1190 Edinburgh Road,
Springboig, Glasgow G33 4EH
Type: Boys Day Only 14–16
Special needs: BESD MLD

SPRINGBOIG ST JOHN'S
1190 Edinburgh Road, Glasgow
G32 4EH
Type: Boys Boarding Only 14–17
Special needs: BESD

LANARKSHIRE

PARK VIEW
73 Grange St, Clayton le Moors,
Lanarkshire BB5 5PJ
Website: www.northern-care.
co.uk
Type: Boys Day Only 11–17
Special needs: **BESD CB**

NORTH LANARKSHIRE

ST PHILLIP'S SCHOOL
Plains, Airdrie, North Lanarkshire
ML6 7SF
Website: www.
stphilipsschoolplains.org.uk
Type: Boys Boarding and Day
10–16
Special needs: ADD ADHD
BESD MLD

SOUTH LANARKSHIRE

**STANMORE HOUSE
RESIDENTIAL SCHOOL**
Lanark, South Lanarkshire
ML11 7RR
Type: Co-educational Boarding
and Day 2–18
Special needs: **CP** EPI PMLD
SLD

LOTHIAN

**DONALDSON'S COLLEGE FOR
THE DEAF**
Edinburgh, Lothian EH12 5JJ
Website: www.donaldsons.
org.uk
Type: Co-educational Boarding
and Day 3–19
Special needs: **ASD** ASP **HI**
SP&LD
Wheelchair access: W

HARMENY SCHOOL
45 Mansfield Road, Balerno,
Lothian EH14 7JY
Website: www.harmeny.org.uk
Type: Co-educational Day and
Boarding 6–13
Special needs: ADD **ADHD** ASP
BESD CB DYC DYS MLD SP&LD
Wheelchair access: WA3
52-week care

MOORE HOUSE SCHOOL
Edinburgh Road, Bathgate,
Lothian EH48 1EX
Type: Co-educational Day and
Boarding 11–16
Special needs: **ADHD BESD CB**
MLD
Wheelchair access: W
Independent Special
52-week care

THE ROYAL BLIND SCHOOL, EDINBURGH
Craigmillar Park, Edinburgh,
Lothian EH16 5NA
Website: www.royalblind.org
Type: Co-educational Boarding
and Day 5–19
Special needs: ADD ASD ASP
BESD CB CP DOW DYS EPI HEA
HI IM MLD PMLD SLD SP&LD VI

PERTH AND KINROSS

OCHIL TOWER (RUDOLF STEINER) SCHOOL
140 High Street, Auchterarder,
Perth and Kinross PH3 1AD
Website: www.ochiltowerschool.
org.uk
Type: Co-educational Boarding
and Day 5–18
Special needs: ADD ADHD ASD
ASP BESD CB DOW DYC DYP
DYS **MLD** PMLD **SLD** SP&LD
TOU
Independent Special

SEAMAB HOUSE SCHOOL
Rumbling Bridge, Kinross, Perth
and Kinross KY13 0PT
Type: Co-educational Boarding
and Day 5–12
Special needs: **BESD** CB
Wheelchair access: WA2
52-week care

PERTHSHIRE

THE NEW SCHOOL
Butterstone, Dunkeld, Perthshire
PH8 0HJ
Website: http://www.
thenewschool.co.uk
Type: Co-educational Boarding
and Day 12–20
Special needs: **ADD ADHD ASD
ASP DYC DYP DYS EPI** HEA
MLD TOU W
Independent Special

RENFREWSHIRE

GOOD SHEPHERD CENTRE
Greenock Road, Bishopton,
Renfrewshire PA7 5PF
Website: www.
goodshepherdcentre.co.uk
Type: Girls Boarding and Day
12–16
Special needs: **BESD** MLD
Wheelchair access: W
52-week care

KIBBLE CENTRE
Goudie Street, Paisley,
Renfrewshire PA3 2LG
Website: www.kibble.org
Type: Boys Boarding and Day
12–17
Special needs: ADD ADHD ASD
ASP **BESD** CB DYP DYS EPI
MLD TOU
Wheelchair access: WA2
52-week care

STIRLING

BALLIKINRAIN RESIDENTIAL SCHOOL
Fintry Road, Stirlingshire, Stirling
G63 0LL
Website: www.ballikinrain.org
Type: Boys Boarding and Day
8–14
Special needs: ADD ADHD ASD
ASP **BESD CB** DYC DYP DYS
MLD
Wheelchair access: WA3
Independent Special
52-week care

SNOWDON SCHOOL
31 Spittal Street, Stirling FK8 1DU
Type: Girls Boarding Only 12–18
Special needs: ADD ADHD ASD
ASP **BESD** CB DYS
Wheelchair access: WA3
Independent Special
52-week care

STRATHCLYDE

CORSEFORD SCHOOL
Kilbarchan, Strathclyde PA10 2NT
Type: Co-educational Day and
Boarding

WALES

CARDIFF

CRAIG-Y-PARC SCHOOL*
Heol y Parc, Pentyrch, Cardiff
CF15 9NB
Website: www.scope.org.uk
Type: Co-educational Boarding
and Day 3–19
Special needs: **CP** EPI HI **PMLD**
SLD SP&LD VI

PENGWERN COLLEGE*
Rhuddlan, Denbighshire
LL18 5UH
Type: Mixed Residential Only
16–25
Special needs: ADD ASD ASP
CB CP DOW EPI HI IM MLD
PMLD SLD SP&LD

DENBIGHSHIRE

THE BRANAS SCHOOL
Branas Isaf, Corwen,
Denbighshire LL21 0TA
Type: Boys Day Only 10–17

DYFED

YSGOL RHYDYGORS+
Llanstephan Road, Carmarthen,
Dyfed SA31 3NQ

FLINTSHIRE

**NEW OPTIONS (KINSALE)
SCHOOL**
Kinsale Hall, Holywell, Flintshire
CH8 9DX
Website: www.optionsgroup.
co.uk
Type: Co-educational Boarding
and Day 8–19
Special needs: ADD ADHD **ASD**
ASP CB **EPI** MLD SP&LD
Wheelchair access: W
Independent Special
52-week care

GWYNEDD

ARAN HALL SCHOOL*
Dolgellau, Gwynedd LL40 2AR
Website: www.senadgroup.com/
aran
Type: Mixed Residential Only
11–19 (38 to 52 week residential
care available.)
Special needs: **ADD ADHD** ASD
ASP BESD CB CP DOW DYC
DYP EPI HEA HI IM MLD PMLD
SLD SP&LD **TOU**
Wheelchair access: W
Independent Special
52-week care

MONMOUTHSHIRE

TALOCHER SCHOOL
Talocher Farm, Monmouth,
Monmouthshire NP25 4DN
Website: www.priorygroup.com
Type: Co-educational Day Only
11–18
Special needs: **BESD**
Wheelchair access: W
Independent Special
52-week care

PEMBROKESHIRE

ST DAVID'S EDUCATION UNIT
Pembroke House,
Haverfordwest, Pembrokeshire
SA62 6NP
Type: Co-educational Day Only
8–17

POWYS

HILLCREST PENTWYN
SCHOOL*
Clyro, Hereford, Powys HR3 5SE
Website: www.hillcrestcare.co.uk
Type: Boys Boarding Only 11–17
Special needs: ADD ADHD
BESD CB DYC DYP **DYS**
Independent Special
52-week care

**MACINTYRE WOMASTON
SCHOOL***
Womaston School, Presteigne,
Powys LD8 2PT
Type: Co-educational Boarding
Only 14–19
Special needs: ADD ADHD ASD
ASP CB CP DOW DYP EPI IM
MLD **PMLD SLD**
Independent Special
52-week care

VALE OF GLAMORGAN

**ACTION FOR CHILDREN
HEADLANDS SCHOOL***
2 St Augustines Road, Penarth,
Vale of Glamorgan CF64 1YY
Website: www.
actionforchildren.org.uk/schools
Type: Co-educational Boarding
and Day 8–19
Special needs: **ADD ADHD ASD
ASP BESD CB DYP DYS** MLD
SP&LD **TOU**
Independent Special

WREXHAM

**PROSPECTS CENTRE FOR
YOUNG PEOPLE**
Bersham Road, Wrexham
LL14 4HS
Website: www.prospectscare.
co.uk
Type: Co-educational Day and
Boarding 11–16

**WOODLANDS CHILDREN'S
DEVELOPMENT CENTRE**
27 Pentrefelyn Road, Wrexham
LL13 7NB
Website: www.
woodlandslimited.com
Type: Boys Day Only 11–17

2.3

Profiles of Independent and Non-Maintained Special Schools

Symbol key

Gender

● Girls
● Boys
● Coed

Accommodation

🏠 Boarding only
🏠 Boarding and Day
🏠 Day and Boarding
🏠 Day only

CReSTeD

◆ Yes (CReSTeD Registered)

Action for Children

Action for Children Headlands School

2 St Augustines Road, Penarth, Vale of Glamorgan CF64 1YY
T: (029) 2070 9771 **F**: (029) 2070 0515 **E**: headlands.school@actionforchildren.org.uk
W: www.actionforchildren.org.uk/schools

Principal Mr M Burns   **Founded** 1918
School status Co-educational boarding and day
Religious denomination Non-denominational
Member of NAS, NASEN
Special needs provision ADD, ADHD, ASD, ASP, BESD, CB, DYP, DYS, MLD, SP&LD, TOU
Age range 8–19; *boarders from 8*
No of pupils 43; *(boarding)* 10; *(weekly boarding)* 10
Sixth Form 8; Girls 6; Boys 37
Teacher:pupil ratio 1:7 **Average class size** 7

We strongly believe that 'expectations are everything'. This means that we hold high expectations of our learners and staff and what they can achieve together. We base our approach on attachment theories, which means we believe that building positive and trusting relationships with learners is critical to their success. Action for Children Headlands School helps children and young people who are having difficulty learning as a result of challenging behaviour, including those with behavioural, emotional and social difficulties (BESD), Autistic Spectrum Disorder (ASD) and Asperger's Syndrome. Education, activities and residential care are provided onsite and children may attend as boarders or as day students. We have a comprehensive wellbeing curriculum which is designed to support pupils' social, emotional and behavioural needs at our school. Residential care is provided on a weekly, fortnightly and term-time basis.

Action for Children Parklands Campus

Action for Children, Near Appleton, Abingdon, Oxfordshire OX13 5QB
T: (01865) 390436 **F**: (01865) 390688 **E**: parklands.campus@actionforchildren.org.uk
W: www.actionforchildren.org.uk/schools

Principal Mr Raymond Wilson
School status Co-educational non-maintained boarding and day
Religious denomination Non-denominational
Member of NASS
Special needs provision ADD, ADHD, BESD, CB
Age range 11–16; *boarders from 11*

Action for Children Parklands Campus is a new special school, opening September 2011. We will be providing an integrated and holistic approach to education and care. Day, residential, fostering and outreach services will be available. Our aim is to help young people with Behavioural, Emotional and Social Difficulties, Autistic Spectrum Disorder, Asperger's Syndrome and Complex Needs to build positive relationships in a safe environment. Our teaching supports the individual in achieving to their full potential.

We create and tailor programmes of study for the individual to help engage and motivate within a structured pathway. Positive outcomes are achieved through appropriate leadership in the provision of a partnership approach, flexible package options, transition support (and other specialist support) and by careful reintegration into the parental home. The innovative approach to teaching and learning at Parklands makes use of the latest ICT to ensure that best practice is shared and that students, parents and carers are engaged in the learning process.

Action for Children Penhurst School

New Street, Chipping Norton, Oxfordshire OX7 5LN
T: (01608) 642559 **F**: (01608) 647029 **E**: penhurst.school@actionforchildren.org.uk
W: www.actionforchildren.org.uk/schools

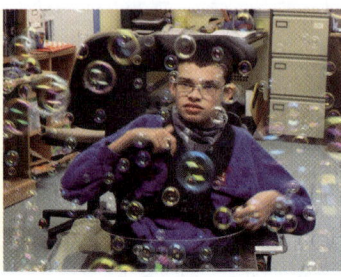

Principal Mr Derek Lyseight-Jones   **Founded** 1902
School status Co-educational non-maintained boarding and day
Religious denomination Non-denominational
Member of BILD, EQUALS, NASS
Special needs provision CP, EPI, HI, IM, **PMLD**, SLD, SP&LD, VI
Age range 5–19; with additional adult provision up to 25 years;
boarders from 5
No of pupils 21; *(boarding)* 26; *(full boarding)* 26; *Girls* 4; *Boys* 17
Average class size 5

We provide an outstanding and award-winning environment where all children and young people benefit from an individual approach to their learning needs from our experienced and caring teams. Action for Children Penhurst School caters for boys and girls who have complex disabilities associated with profound and multiple learning difficulties. The school age range is from 5 to 19 years, with additional adult provision up to 25 years. Education, therapy and care are provided onsite and children may attend as boarders or as day students. Residential care is provided for a standard 51/52-week placement.

We provide an individualized and enriching extended curriculum in a purpose-built, well-equipped environment through sensory education programmes, integrated therapy and year-round care package. The holistic needs of students are met by our education, care and specialist support staff. Each of our four residential houses has highly skilled staff contributing to the 24-hour curriculum needs of our students.

Barnardo's

High Close School (Barnardo's)

Wiltshire Road, Wokingham, Berkshire RG40 1TT

T: (0118) 978 5767 **F**: (0118) 989 4220 **E**: high.close@barnardos.org.uk **W**: www.barnardos.org.uk/highcloseschool

Principal Zoe Lattimer **Founded** 1939
School status Co-educational non-maintained prep and senior boarding and day
Member of BILD, ENGAGE, NAHT, SWALSS
Special needs provision ADD, ADHD, ASD, ASP, **BESD, CB**, DYC, DYP, DYS, HEA,
MLD, SP&LD
Age range 9–16; *boarders from* 10 **Average class size** 6

High Close is a school for pupils with social, emotional, behavioural and associated learning difficulties. The school is campus-based with four purpose-built residential units and a unit for day pupils, which provides a breakfast club and pastoral support. The social care was graded as 'Outstanding' by Ofsted in 2009. A newly built sports hall offers excellent indoor facilities. A team of field social workers provides 52-week support to parents. Staff also continue to work with ex-pupils for six months after they leave. The full range of the National Curriculum is taught with up to seven GCSE and Entry Level subjects. Vocational courses are delivered both onsite and via links with local colleges. We also offer professional support provided by a speech and language therapist, an educational psychologist, a dyslexia specialist, a counsellor and an occupational therapist. An extensive range of after-school activities, including the Duke of Edinburgh Award scheme, is also offered.

Meadows School (Barnardo's)

London Road, Southborough, Kent TN4 0RJ

T: (01892) 529144 **F**: (01892) 527787 **E**: meadows@barnardos.org.uk
W: www.barnardos.org.uk/meadowsschool

Principal Mr Mike Price
School status Co-educational boarding and day
Special needs provision ADD, ADHD, ASD, BESD, MLD
Age range 11–19 **No of pupils** 64

Meadows School is a co-educational, non-maintained school for pupils with severe social, emotional, behavioural and associated learning difficulties offering GCSE and vocational courses at Year 11. The school has purpose-built education facilities with two onsite residential units for boys and one offsite unit for girls. A new 16+ off-site for KS5 pupils provides supported education for functional skills, access courses and social/life skill development. Meadows can provide speech and language support, individual counselling and has a Service Level Agreement with the local CAMHS.

Spring Hill School (Barnardo's)

Palace Road, Ripon, North Yorkshire HG4 3HN

T: (01765) 603320 **F**: (01765) 607549 **E**: springhill.school@barnardos.org.uk **W**: www.barnardos.org.uk/springhillschool

Principal Mrs Linda Nelson **Founded** 1950
School status Co-educational non-maintained day only
Religious denomination Non-denominational
Member of BILD, NAHT
Special needs provision ADD, ADHD, ASD, ASP, BESD, CB, DOW, DYP, DYS,
EPI, HEA, HI, **MLD**, SLD, SP&LD, TOU, VI
Age range 9–19; *boarders from* 9; *(full boarding)* 40; *(day)* 6 **Average class size** 6

Spring Hill is a residential, non-maintained special school for boys and girls aged 9 to 19. Spring Hill caters for pupils who have moderate/severe learning difficulties and challenging behaviour. There is accommodation for 40 residential pupils in 6 purpose built cottages, with boarding provision for both 38 and 52-week care. There is also extra provision for day pupils. The school has pupils with a range of needs including autism, Asperger's syndrome, ADHD, emotional difficulties, issues around mental wellbeing and global developmental delay. The school follows the National Curriculum modified to meet the needs of pupils. Post-16 students follow a broad academic curriculum with emphasis on vocational education in preparation for adult life.

Baston House School

Baston Road, Hayes, Bromley, Kent BR2 7AB
T: (0208) 4621010 **E**: info@bastonhouseschool.org.uk **W**: www.bastonhouseschool.org.uk

Principal Mr Steve Vincent BA (Hons), PGCE
School status Co-educational
Special needs provision ASD, **ASP**
Age range 2–16

Baston House School is an independent special school for children aged between 3 1/2 and 19 years, whose Statement of Special Educational Needs describes their Primary need as being on the Autism Spectrum. Our goal is to break down the barriers to learning that our students encounter and to help them to equip themselves for as independent a life as possible outside school. Our approach is based on an eclectic fusion of child-centred and autism-specific strategies and techniques, with a clear focus on improving communication and interaction skills through positive interventions.

Breckenbrough School

Sandhutton, Thirsk, North Yorkshire YO7 4EN
T: (01845) 587238 **F**: (01845) 587385 **E**: office@breckenbrough.org.uk **W**: www.breckenbrough.org.uk

Headmaster Mr G Brookes
Founded 1937
School status Boys' non-maintained boarding and day
Religious denomination Quaker
Member of IAPS, ISBA
Special needs provision ADD, ADHD, ASD, **ASP**, **BESD**, CB, DYP
Age range 9–17; *boarders from* 9
No of pupils 36; *(boarding)* 30; *(full boarding)* 10; *(weekly boarding)* 20;
Senior 36
Average class size 5

Breckenbrough School is a residential boarding school with newly established sixth form provision, for 40 pupils aged 9 to 19 who exhibit emotional and behavioural difficulties and have high academic potential. Our pupils have repeatedly struggled with the structure and ethos of mainstream education where their eccentricities and needs have never been adequately met. They have in effect learning differences that deserve the opportunity to be developed. In recent years, we have developed expertise and success with boys diagnosed with Asperger's, ADHD, ADD and dyslexia and offer support, advice and training on conflict resolution and restorative justice. The school, a non-profit-making charitable trust, is housed in a Victorian country house, together with an attached classroom block, sports field, pond and motorbike track. The governors are appointed by the Yorkshire General Meeting of the Society of Friends (Quakers).

Cambian Group

The Forum School

Shillingstone, Blandford Forum, Dorset DT11 0QS
T: (0800) 288 9779 **F**: (020) 87356151 **E**: education@cambiangroup.com **W**: www.cambiangroup.com

Head Mr Adrian J A Wylie BEd PG DIP (Autism) NPQH
School status Co-educational boarding only. Mixed gender 7–19 years
Religious denomination Non-denominational
Member of BILD, EQUALS, NASS
Special needs provision ASD, **CB**, EPI, HEA, **MLD**, SP&LD
Age range 7–19 (Mixed gender 7–19 years); *(boarding)* 57

The Forum School was deemed to be an outstanding school for Autistic Spectrum Disorders, as determined by Ofsted in their June 2009 report. The Forum School is a co-educational, 38 and 52 week boarding school specializing in the education and care of students who have autism. We have a very positive approach to behaviour and with support from our clinical psychology assistant practitioners we have consistent behaviour plans drawn up to support all students. Understanding the condition and how students with ASD view the world is essential when dealing with unpredictable behaviours that may challenge. Classes are broadly based on age, although the high-functioning students are also streamlined in order to address individual need. The Curriculum is broad and balanced, encompassing the National Curriculum using modified or differentiated programmes of study where appropriate. Vocational Educational training, Individual Social Skills and Life Skills Independence are also part of our teaching and learning. A Parent Liaison Officer is available to discuss, in confidence, a young person's specific needs.

Grateley House School

Grateley, Andover, Hampshire SP11 8TA
T: (0800) 288 9779 **F**: (020) 87356151 **E**: education@cambiangroup.com **W**: www.cambiangroup.com

Head Mrs Sue King BA (Hons) PGCE DAE(SEN) NPQH
School status Co-educational boarding and day. Mixed gender 9–19 years
Religious denomination Non-denominational
Special needs provision ADHD, **ASP**, **CB**, DYC, DYP, DYS, EPI, MLD, SP&LD, **TOU**
Age range 9–19 (Mixed gender 9–19 years); *(full boarding)* 47

Grateley House School is a 38-week residential school for young people aged 9 to 19 who are experiencing difficulties as a result of Asperger Syndrome (AS) and other associated difficulties. Admission can take place at any time during the school year and throughout KS 2, 3, 4 or in preparation for post-16. For students living close to the school there is flexibility for day provision. We are a part of the Cambian Group, the largest provider of specialist residential education and care for young people with Autistic Spectrum Disorders in the United Kingdom. Students have full access to the National Curriculum with teaching appropriately differentiated to meet the needs of our young people. Grateley draws upon a proven programme of Specialist Education, specialist 24-hour care and a wide range of clinical and therapeutic inputs, including speech and language therapy, behavioural therapy, occupational therapy, psychiatry and psychology. Multi-disciplinary teams and high staff ratios ensure intensive individual support. We offer extensive community-based programmes, vocational training and further education opportunities. Please contact us as above. A Parent Liaison Officer is available to discuss, in confidence, a young person's specific needs and we are delighted to help with any questions or to arrange a visit to the school.

Hill House School

Rope Hill, Boldre, Lymington, Hampshire SO41 8NE
T: (0800) 288 9779 **F**: (020) 87356151 **E**: education@cambiangroup.com **W**: www.cambiangroup.com

Head Ms Jenny Wright BEd, ADV DIP SEN, MA(Ed), NPQH
Founded 1992
School status Co-educational boarding only. Mixed gender 11–19 years
Religious denomination Non-denominational
Special needs provision ASD, **CB**, **EPI**, HEA, **MLD**, **SLD**, SP&LD
Age range 11–19 (Mixed gender 11–19 years); *(boarding)* 18

Hill House School is one of the leading residential schools for young people with autism in the United Kingdom. Our students often have some of the most complex needs and challenging behaviours on the autistic spectrum and will also have associated learning difficulties. The school was rated as 'Outstanding' by Ofsted in March 2009. The report can be downloaded from our website above. Admission can take place at any time during the school year. We are a part of the Cambian Group, the largest provider of specialist residential education and care for young people with Autistic Spectrum Disorders in the United Kingdom. Hill House offers a unique, personalized approach to each student's learning and care needs. An individualized behavioural curriculum is implemented alongside an academic curriculum. We believe in a non-aversive positive approach; we do not believe in punishment in any form. Hill House draws upon a proven programme of specialist education, specialist 24-hour care and a wide range of clinical and therapeutic inputs, including speech and language therapy, behavioural therapy, occupational therapy, psychiatry and psychology. Multi-disciplinary teams and high staff ratios ensure intensive individual support. A Parent Liaison Officer is available to discuss, in confidence, a young person's specific needs.

Purbeck View School

Northbrook Road, Swanage, Dorset BH19 1PR
T: (0800) 288 9779 **F**: (020) 87356151 **E**: education@cambiangroup.com **W**: www.cambiangroup.com

Head Mrs Susan Harvey Certificate in Qualified Social Work, Executive Diploma in Management Level 7
School status Co-educational boarding only. Mixed gender 9–19 years
Religious denomination Non-denominational
Special needs provision ASD, **CB**, **EPI**, HEA, **MLD**, SP&LD
Age range 9–19 (Mixed gender 9–19 years); *(boarding)* 51; *(full boarding)* 51

Purbeck View School is a residential school specializing in the care and education of students with a diagnosis of autism, or whose difficulties place them on the autistic continuum. Our students often have complex needs, associated learning difficulties and challenging behaviours. Purbeck offers both 38 and 52 week placements for 63 students between the ages of 9 and 19. Admission can take place at any time during the school year. Purbeck View is a part of the Cambian Group, the largest provider of specialist residential education and care for young people with Autistic Spectrum Disorders in the United Kingdom. Purbeck View draws upon a proven programme of specialist education, specialist 24-hour care and a wide range of clinical and therapeutic inputs, including speech and language therapy, behavioural therapy, occupational therapy, psychiatry and psychology. Multi-disciplinary teams and high staff ratios ensure intensive individual support. We offer extensive community-based programmes, vocational training and further education opportunities. A Parent Liaison Officer is available to discuss, in confidence, a young person's specific needs and we are delighted to help with any questions or to arrange a visit to the school.

Southlands School

Vicar's Hill, Boldre, Lymington, Hampshire SO41 5QB
T: (0800) 288 9779 **F**: (020) 87356151 **E**: education@cambiangroup.com **W**: www.cambiangroup.com

●♠

Head Ms Naomi Clarke BEd, Dip Ed, SEN, AMBDA
School status Boys' prep and senior boarding and day. Boys 7–16 years
Religious denomination Non-denominational
Special needs provision ASP, CB, DYC, DYP, DYS, EPI, HEA, SP&LD, TOU
Age range 7–16 (Boys 7–16 years); *(boarding)* 48; *(full boarding)* 48

In 1995, Southlands School established itself as the first residential school in the United Kingdom for students with Asperger Syndrome. Today, we continue to lead with innovative teaching methods, access to the full National Curriculum and new Information Communication Technologies in classrooms. For students living close to the school there is flexibility for day provision. We are a part of the Cambian Group, the largest provider of specialist residential education and care for young people with Autistic Spectrum Disorders in the United Kingdom. Southlands offers a 38-week residential programme for boys. Admission can take place at any time during the school year and day provision is available for students living close to the school. Southlands draws upon a proven programme of specialist education, specialist 24-hour care and a wide range of clinical and therapeutic inputs, including speech and language therapy, behavioural therapy, occupational therapy, psychiatry and psychology. Multi-disciplinary teams and high staff ratios ensure intensive individual support. We offer extensive community-based programmes, vocational training and further education opportunities. Southlands is located in the village of Boldre, near Lymington in Hampshire. A Parent Liaison Officer is available to discuss, in confidence, a young person's specific needs.

Symbol key

Gender

● Girls
● Boys
● Coed

CReSTeD

◆ Yes (CReSTeD Registered)

Accommodation

♠ Boarding only
♠ Boarding and Day
♠ Day and Boarding
♠ Day only

Centre Academy London

92 St John's Hill, Battersea, London SW11 1SH
T: (020) 7738 2344 **F**: (020) 7738 9862
E: info@centreacademy.net
W: www.centreacademy.net

Principal Dr D J Rollo BA, MA, PhD	**Member of** ADHD Alliance BDA, ECIS, CReSTeD, LISA, NASN
Founded 1974	**Special needs provision ADD, ADHD, ASD, ASP, DYP, DYS,**
Headteacher London Vikki Langford BA, MA	**MLD**, SP&LD
Head of School East Anglia Kim Salthouse BA, MED	**Age range** 8–19
Founded 1974	**No of pupils** CA London 60; *Prep* 30; *Senior* 30
School status Co-educational independent	CA East Anglia 40; *Pre-Prep* 5; *Prep* 25; *Senior* 10
Religious denomination Non-denominational	**Teacher:pupil ratio** 1:3
	Average class size 5

Centre Academy East Anglia

Church Road, Brettenham, Suffolk IP7 7QR
T: (01449) 736404 **F**: (01449) 737881
E: admin@centreacademy.net
W: www.centreacademy.net

The Centre Academy Schools enable students with a variety of learning difficulties to reclaim their futures. We do so by teaching the skills and coping strategies that students with SP&LD, Dyslexia, ADHD and other learning challenges require in order to succeed.

With exceptionally small classes, significant one-on-one instruction and dedicated and experienced faculty members, the Centre Academy Schools make it possible for their students to work to their fullest potential. Following testing and evaluation, we design a programme of instruction to meet the student's individual needs.

We are able to cater to the strengths of the individual student rather than being limited to a 'one size fits all' approach. This is achieved by offering both the British National Curriculum through GCSE and the American High School Diploma. The Diploma, seen as the gateway to university, involves a system of continual assessment, thus reducing pressure and anxiety that so frequently accompany exams. We have never had a diploma graduate who has failed to gain admission to university.

At both schools, English and maths form the core of a student's studies. Other key areas involve history, science, ICT, music, drama, art, geography, modern foreign languages, PSHE and RE. The efforts of our teaching staff are complemented by a coterie of specialists, including speech and language, occupational therapy, reading and counselling.

At CA London, our co-educational day school, we are able to use the capital's cultural, artistic and historic possibilities as our own personal classroom. The Houses of Parliament, the National Gallery, the Natural History Museum, the Science Museum and many other sites are easily accessible to us. We are well served by all forms of public transportation.

Offering both boarding and day programmes, CA East Anglia is located on the edge of a small rural village, 40 minutes from Cambridge and one hour by train from London. Our 10-acre campus comprises elegant classroom buildings and excellent residential facilities for both boys and girls. There are excellent facilities for sport, art and drama. All boarding students are supported by highly trained staff members and by an experienced Head of Care.

Parents are invited to ring either school for a prospectus and to arrange a visit.

Chailey Heritage School

Haywards Heath Road, North Chailey, Nr Lewes, East Sussex BN8 4EF
T: (01825) 724444 **F**: (01825) 723773 **E**: schooloffice@chs.org.uk **W**: www.chs.org.uk
We welcome visits to the school – please contact the School Office to arrange an appointment

Principal Mrs Sylvia Lamb BA Hons, PGCE, MA
Headteacher Mr Simon Yates BA Hons, PGCE, NPQH
Founded 1903
School status Co-educational non-maintained day only
Religious denomination Non-denominational
Member of EQUALS, NAHT, NASS, NASEN
Special needs provision ASD, **CP**, EPI, **HEA**, HI, **IM**, MLD, PMLD, SLD,
SP&LD, VI, W
Age range 3–19 (The school also offers a Young Adults' Transition
Service for young disabled adults aged 19–25)
No of pupils 74; *(52 weeks)* 5; *(boarding)* 19; *(full boarding)* 8; *(weekly boarding)* 6; *Girls* 38; *Boys* 36

Chailey Heritage School is a special school for children and young people, aged 3 to 19+, with complex physical, communication, sensory and learning difficulties and health needs. As a registered Children's Home, the school can offer residential care packages for up to 52 weeks a year. Judged 'Outstanding' by Ofsted, the school offers a broad and balanced curriculum adapted for each pupil. It shares its location with specialist clinical team, Chailey Heritage Clinical Services (CHCS), part of the South Downs Health NHS Trust. Pupils' clinical needs are overseen by specialists in paediatric conditions, neurological problems and long-term disabilities. CHCS therapists form part of a multidisciplinary team, enabling the school to integrate education and therapy. Communication and mobility are especially important and are supported by skilled staff and pioneering technology.

Chailey Heritage School is a registered charity no 1075837.

Chelfham Mill School

Chelfham, Barnstaple, Devon EX32 7LA
T: (01271) 850448 **F**: (01271) 850235 **E**: enquiries@chelfhammillschool.co.uk **W**: www.chelfhammillschool.co.uk

Principal Mrs K Roberts BEd, BPhil (EBD) RMA   **Founded** 1966
School status Boys' prep and senior boarding and day
Religious denomination Non-denominational
Member of BILD, NAHT
Special needs provision ADD, **ADHD**, **ASD**, **ASP**, **BESD**, **CB**, DYS, EPI, MLD, TOU
Age range 9–16
No of pupils 33 **Average class size** 5

The school considers all types of emotional and behavioural problems in children, with a particular expertise in helping children who exhibit more challenging types of behaviour, eg Asperger's, Tourette.

Placements: 52-week, 38-week and 38-week with respite.

Specialist facilities/services: single rooms, music room/recording studio, IT suite, CDT, construction, horti-culture, social skills, self esteem building, objective-based teaching all provided.

The Principal is qualified in education and CBT. The founder/director is an educational psychologist and CB therapist. Another part-time CB therapist is employed along with a full-time art/play therapist. CB therapeutic drama and Nature Quest therapy are special to the school as is the unique anger management programme. Chelfham is set in 60 acres, four miles from the regional market town of Barnstaple in picturesque North Devon, close to its beautiful coastline and to Exmoor. Parents are encouraged to visit where they are advised on behaviour management in the home.

Cotswold Chine School

Box, Near Stroud, Gloucestershire GL6 9AG
T: (01453) 837550 **F**: (01453) 834970 **E**: info@novalis-trust.org.uk **W**: www.cotswold-chine.org.uk

Headteacher Ms M Smith MA(Ed) AMBDA
Founded 1954
School status Co-educational boarding and day
Religious denomination Christian
Member of BILD
Special needs provision ADD, ADHD, ASD, ASP, BESD, CB, DYP, DYS, EPI, **MLD**, SLD, SP&LD, TOU
Age range 9–19; *boarders from 9*
No of pupils 50; *(boarding)* 40; *(full boarding)* 42; *Girls* 20; *Boys* 22
Teacher:pupil ratio 1:2/3
Average class size 7

Cotswold Chine School is an independent day and residential therapeutic special school (DfE Registered). The School offers outstanding education and care for vulnerable students with a range of complex learning needs. These include, but are not limited to, moderate to severe learning disabilities, autistic spectrum including Asperger's syndrome, ADHD, epilepsy, attachment disorders, communication needs and associated challenging behavioural, emotional and social difficulties.

Many of the young people at the school have experienced difficulties in previous educational settings, but once settled they generally find that the School's holistic approach to education and care provides them with an environment in which they can make progress and achieve both socially and academically.

Registration is for co-educational provision for students aged 9 to 19 years. Students board from 39 to 52 weeks a year; a small number of day places are available. The school has eight housegroups, including several semi-independent living units.

'Cotswold Chine School provides an outstanding quality of education that fully meets its aims, maintaining its high standards from the previous inspection. Students make outstanding progress because the quality of the curriculum, teaching and assessment is outstanding' (Ofsted 2010).

The School offers full access to the National Curriculum and students leave school with a wide range of externally accredited qualifications including Unit Awards, Entry Level Certificates, Duke of Edinburgh, ASDAN, COPE, Work Related Learning and GCSEs, with some students gaining at Grade C and above. Additionally, students have access to an extensive craft and vocational curriculum which enables them to develop a wide range of practical and artistic skills.

The School's recent Ofsted report (2010) highlighted the "many curriculum pathways open to KS 4 and post 16 students" and the "lively pace and frequent changes of activity so that students attend well and remain absorbed" as being particularly outstanding features of the School's educational provision. Education is delivered through a multi-disciplinary approach, with all staff working together to ensure each student achieves their potential.

Educational accommodation includes seven well-resourced classrooms with excellent ICT facilities, a design/technology/art room, food technology room, music room (with recording facilities), library and school hall. The School is currently developing specialist science facilities. There are extensive grounds, access to the nearby common as well as to an area of woodland, which provides an excellent resource for outdoor education in a range of subject areas.

Cotswold Chine School Continued...

Teaching staff are well qualified and able to provide additional communication aids/strategies such as visual aids and a structured approach to teaching, where appropriate.

Within the residential accommodation "Young people benefit from enthusiastic staff who feel supported in their professional development through excellent training opportunities. Young people enjoy the activities available and the individual support to meet their social and academic targets and to develop their life skills" (Ofsted 2010).

Our comprehensive facilities also include therapy and psychology support from a range of in-house professionals, speech and language assessment, high staff to student ratio and health promotion/support via a dedicated school nurse.

Cotswold Chine was founded in 1954 and is administrated by Novalis Trust, a charitable organization based on the principles of care and education of Rudolf Steiner.

Head Teacher: Maureen Smith MA(Ed), Admissions: Rebecca Benson, 01453 837550

Cruckton Hall

Cruckton, Shrewsbury, Shropshire SY5 8PR
T: (01743) 860206 **F**: (01743) 860941 **E**: admissions@kisimul.co.uk **W**: www.cruckton.com

Head Master Mr P D Mayhew
School status Boys' boarding and day
Religious denomination Broadly Christian
Member of NAS, NASEN
Special needs provision ADD, ADHD, ASD, ASP, BESD, CB, DYC, DYP, DYS, EPI, HI, MLD
Age range 8–19
No of pupils 92; *(full boarding)* 84

Cruckton Hall School offers an integrated residential education for boys aged 8–19 years of age who have been diagnosed with Autism Spectrum Disorders. Placements are offered from day up to 52 weeks of the year. Structured individual programmes are devised to meet students' specific needs and these are met in small group settings with a high staffing ratio. A broad and balanced waking day curriculum is provided that enables students' to acquire the knowledge and skills to sit GCSE examinations. In addition, the school offers ECDL, AQA Skills for Life Awards and a variety of Entry Level Certificates. The whole experience provides outstanding outcomes and opportunities for the young people to lead a meaningful adult life within society.

Doncaster School for the Deaf

Leger Way, Doncaster, South Yorkshire DN2 6AY
T: (01302) 386710 **F**: (01302) 361808 **E**: principal@ddt-deaf.org.uk **W**: www.deaf-school.co.uk

Executive Principal Mr A W Robinson
School status Independent (special), co-educational boarding and day
Type of School Mixed – full/flexible/weekly and 52 week provision (Enrolment
throughtout the year. Please contact us to arrange an informal visit.)
Religious denomination Non-denominational
Member of BILD
Special needs provision AHDH, BESD, CP, DYS, **HI**, MLD, PMLD, SLD,
SP&LD, VI, WA1
Age range 5–16
No of pupils 17; *(full boarding)* 1; *(weekly boarding)* 1; *(day)* 15; *Girls* 6;
Boys 11

We offer a broad and balanced curriculum which is accessible to all our pupils, providing smooth progression and continuity through all Key Stages. We provide the most appropriate curriculum for every pupil, based on an assessment of their needs.

We are committed to a Bilingual, Language and Communication Policy which includes British Sign Language (BSL). The School has a full-time Audiologist, Speech Therapist and a team of Learning Support Assistants as well as a visiting doctor and an onsite fully qualified nurse.

Qualifications include GCSE, Entry Level Certificate of Achievement, ASDAN, CoPE (Certificate of Personal Effectiveness), Signature Qualifications and Unit Awards. KS4 access vocational course as part of a 14–16 curriculum resource onsite via Doncaster College for the Deaf.

Fairley House School

30 Causton Street, London SW1P 4AU
T: (020) 7976 5456 **F**: (020) 7976 5905 **E**: office@fairleyhouse.org.uk **W**: www.fairleyhouse.org.uk
The Junior Department is located at 218-220 Lambeth Road, SE1 7YJ

Principal Miss J Murray BA (Hons) MEd DipPsychol MSc Dip RSA (SpLD) HPC Reg
Educational Psychologist
Founded 1982
School status Co-educational independent Junior Department – Year 2–5 Senior
Department – Year 6–9
Religious denomination Non-denominational
Member of AGBIS, BDA, CReSTeD, ISA, NAHT; **Accredited by** ISA
Special needs provision ADD, DYC, DYP, DYS, EPI, HEA, SP&LD
Age range 5–14 (Junior Department – Year 2–5 Senior Department – Year 6–9)
No of pupils 179; *Girls* 39; *Boys* 140
Teacher:pupil ratio 1:3.5 **Average class size** 12

Curriculum: The primary aim is to transform the lives of children with specific learning difficulties. We do this by improving their literacy, numeracy and self-confidence and providing a full and rich curriculum. We will bring out any talents a child might have. There is a structured, multi-sensory approach. Speech and language and occupational therapy are integrated with education. The National Curriculum is followed throughout the school with emphasis on ICT, Science, Art and DT. Most children usually remain for two to three years and are carefully prepared for a return to mainstream education. Eighty-five per cent of children achieve this goal. The trans-disciplinary team includes full-time speech and language and occupational therapists. The Principal is a fully qualified educational psychologist. All class teachers and special provision staff are experienced in teaching SPLD children and the majority hold a recognized SPLD qualification. We are a training centre for teachers who can complete the nationally recognized OCR Certificate in specific learning difficulties with us.

Entry requirements: Fairley House School 2-day assessment.

Frederick Hugh House

48 Old Church Street, London SW3 5BY
T: (0207) 3498833 **F**: (0207) 3526821 **E**: info@frederickhughhouse.com **W**: www.frederickhughhouse.com

Headmistress Ms Tanya Jamil
Founded 2010
School status Co-educational
Religious denomination Christian
Member of NASEN
Special needs provision ADD, ADHD, ASD, ASP, CP, DOW, DYC, DYP, DYS, EPI, IM, MLD, SP&LD, **TOU, W**
Age range (Currently registered for children aged 4–11 years with special needs but with a vision to take our children through to 18 years old.)
No of pupils 4; *Pre-prep* 4; *Girls* 2; *Boys* 2
Teacher:pupil ratio 1:4
Average class size 8

About the school

An exciting New Special Needs Primary School in Chelsea, Frederick Hugh House is an innovative and unique special needs primary school in the Royal Borough of Kensington and Chelsea, for children with learning difficulties.

At Frederick Hugh House every child benefits from a tailor-made therapeutic programme. This includes in-house speech, occupational and physiotherapists who work closely with our teaching staff, integrating each child's targets into all aspects of the school day. As well as 1:1 sessions, our therapists are involved in all aspects of the school day, taking lessons and joining play-times.

All facets of teaching and learning are supported by multi-sensory state of the art facilities, including an interactive multi-sensory theatre, enabling each child to access the curriculum whatever their learning style. In addition to our broad, holistic curriculum we are proud of the exciting experiences we are able to share with our children, including horse riding, pottery classes and dance and drama workshops.

Our regular shopping, park and community trips all contribute to making learning fun and meaningful. Our ethos is to discover and nurture the talents or passion of every child, so that they may fulfil their potential.

An important strength is the impact made by the various therapists employed by the school. The full-time speech therapist develops pupils' speaking and language skills effectively both in individual therapy sessions and when working alongside subject teachers. (Ofsted, 2011)

Arrangements for the welfare, health and safety of pupils are outstanding. Staff care exceptionally well for pupils and pay very good attention to their well-being. (Ofsted, 2011)

For more information please visit www.frederickhughhouse.com

The Hesley Group
Enhancing Lives

Hillcrest Care

Hillcrest Pentwyn School

Clyro, Hereford, Powys HR3 5SE
T: (01497) 821420 **F**: (01497) 821591 **E**: headpentwyn@yahoo.co.uk **W**: www.hillcrestcare.co.uk

Headteacher Mr D Davidson
Founded 1983
School status Boys' boarding only
Religious denomination Non-denominational
Member of ISA, ISC, NAHT
Special needs provision ADD, ADHD, **BESD**, **CB**, **DYC**, DYP, **DYS**
Age range 11–17
No of pupils 15; *(boarding)* 15; *(full boarding)* 15; *Boys* 15
Average class size 4

Hillcrest Pentwyn School is registered and approved by the Welsh Assembly Government as a residential special school for boys with significant social, emotional and behavioural difficulties. The school is also a registered home with the Care & Social Services Inspectorate for Wales (CSSIW). Hillcrest Pentwyn offers both 39- and 52-week placements for a maximum of 15 boys aged 11–17.The school is a fully registered Examination Centre with the OCR Examination Board and offers a secondary curriculum to all pupils who are taught in small groups of no more than four. The pupils have the opportunities to sit a wide range of accredited subjects and vocational courses including GCSEs, ELQs and ASDAN. Hillcrest Pentwyn also has access to a wide range of local outdoor activity centres.

Hillcrest Slinford

Stane Street, Slinford, Nr Horsham, West Sussex RH13 0QX
T: (01403) 790939 **F**: (01403) 790954 **E**: slinford@hillcrestcare.co.uk

Head of Education Miss N Forsyth
School status Boys' prep and senior boarding only
Religious denomination Non-denominational
Special needs provision ADD, **ADHD**, **BESD**, **CB**
Age range 11–16
No of pupils 21; *(full boarding)* 21; *Boys* 21

Hillcrest Slinfold comprises an Ofsted registered school and three registered children's homes for boys aged 11–17 yrs, offering 52-week care and education.

A holistic model of care and education has been designed to help boys take control of their lives. We endeavour to teach our young men how to achieve their potential and to prepare to manage their future.

Focus is on outcome-based education and accreditation and there is a strong emphasis on improving literacy, numeracy and ICT skills and building students' personal and social skills whilst meeting the demands of the National Curriculum. There is also growing vocational provision including: Brick laying, Carpentry, Woodwork, Horticulture and General Skills. On-going co-operation between the school and the three houses ensures the young people's needs are met at all times.

I CAN

8 Wakley Street, London EC1V 7QE   Tel: (0845) 225 4071   Fax: (0845) 225 4072
E-mail: info@ican.org.uk   Website: www.ican.org.uk

I CAN is the children's communication charity. I CAN works to develop speech, language and communication skills for all children. I CAN's particular focus is children who find communication hard.

I CAN's Dawn House School

Helmsley Road, Rainworth, Mansfield, Nottinghamshire NG21 0DQ
T: (01623) 795361 **F**: (01623) 491173 **E**: dawnhouse@ican.org.uk **W**: www.ican.org.uk

Headteacher Angela Child
School status Co-educational non-maintained boarding and day
Special needs provision SP&LD
Age range 5–19
No of pupils 82; *(boarding)* 30; *(weekly boarding)* 30; *Girls* 20; *Boys* 62

Dawn House School provides intensive and specialist support for pupils aged 5 to 19 years who have severe and complex communication difficulties and Asperger's. The school aims to support pupils' development in speech and language, thinking and reasoning, self-confidence and independence. Education, therapy and care programmes are tailored to meet the needs of each pupil. Teaching and therapy are supported by up-to-date technology and Paget Gorman Signed Speech. Joint planning by our highly qualified and experienced staff ensure that the school provides a fully integrated language environment. It is a very effective school, where teaching and learning are very good, and for the past two years it has been cited by Ofsted in its annual list of England's outstanding schools. The school works in partnership with parents. They are involved in planning and reviewing their child's programme and in informal and social activities in the school. Independent living skills are highly valued and are fostered through the curriculum and care programmes. The Further Education Department provides a highly inclusive programme for students from 16 to 19 years. Three pathways enable students to choose a programme suitable for their abilities and aspirations.

I CAN's Meath School

Brox Road, Ottershaw, Surrey KT16 0LF
T: (01932) 872302 **F**: (01932) 875180 **E**: meath@meath-ican.org.uk **W**: www.ican.org.uk

Headteacher Janet Dunn
Founded 1982
School status Co-educational non-maintained residential and day
Member of NAHT, NASS
Special needs provision ADD, ASP, DYP, DYS, EPI, HI, MLD, SP&LD
Age range 4–11; *boarders from* 5
No of pupils 52; *(boarding)* 4; *(weekly boarding)* 4; *Girls* 15; *Boys* 37
Average class size 10

Meath School provides a multi-professional, integrated and collaborative approach to the teaching, therapy and care of children (and families) whose primary difficulty is speech, language and communication, including Asperger's Syndrome. Children with additional or associated difficulties – including some degree of learning difficulty, attention control, motor coordination problems, mild visual or hearing impairments, and social interaction problems – can also benefit. Specialist practice and programmes enable full access to the National Curriculum teaching. Classes have a teacher, speech and language therapist and a teaching assistant. An occupational therapy department provides individual and group sessions. A life skills programme is offered in the residential setting; this reinforces a 24-hour curriculum.

Ingfield Manor School

Ingfield Manor Drive, Five Oaks, Billingshurst, West Sussex RH14 9AX
T: (01403) 782294/784241 **F**: (01403) 785066 **E**: ingfield.manor@scope.org.uk **W**: www.scope.org.uk

Headteacher Mrs Catherine Allison
Founded 1961
School status Non maintained special school, co-educational day and weekly boarding
Special needs provision CP, IM, SP&LD
Age range 3–19; *(boarding)* 8; *(weekly boarding)* 8

Ingfield Manor is acknowledged as one of the leading centres for Conductive Education in the United Kingdom. It has a national reputation for the development of communication work with pupils. The school is a day and weekly boarding school for children with cerebral palsy. It has established a new Pre-School and Assessment Service for children with physical disabilities and associated learning difficulties. The main school has recently expanded to include pupils past the age of 16. Ofsted have concluded that: 'The work in Conductive Education by pupils and staff is outstanding'. This is a centre of excellence for an alternative approach to the education of children with cerebral palsy. The Dame Vera Lynn Trust School for Parents is a unique free service for families of young children with cerebral palsy and other disabilities. Parents and children learn daily living skills together using the principles of Conductive Education. The School for Parents is run in partnership with The Dame Vera Lynn Trust for Children with Cerebral Palsy. Ofsted described it as 'outstanding provision' and a 'centre of excellence'.

Kisimul School – Old Vicarage

The Old Vicarage, High Street, Swinderby, Lincolnshire LN6 9LU
T: (01522) 868279 **F**: (01522) 866000 **E**: admissions@kisimul.co.uk **W**: www.kisimul.co.uk

Director Mr Danny Carter
Founded 1977
School status Co-educational boarding and day
Religious denomination Non-denominational
Member of BILD, EQUALS
Special needs provision ASD, **CB**, DOW, EPI, HI, **SLD**, SP&LD
Age range 8–19; *boarders from* 8
No of pupils 70
Average class size 6

Kisimul School specializes in providing high quality care and education for children and young adults with severe learning difficulties and challenging behaviour, for up to 52 weeks of the year. We provide a caring, consistent, safe and supportive environment in which our pupils can flourish and develop their skills, in order to fully realize their individual potential. The 24-hour curriculum, with residential and school staff working closely together, enables pupils to progress in their personal development and promotes their confidence, self-esteem and independence. Classes are small, with a staffing ratio of 1:1. Alongside the National Curriculum, Adult Pre-Entry Curriculum Framework (post-16) and Foundation Learning we also offer a wide range of therapeutic and developmental programmes, collectively designed to meet the diverse sensory needs of our pupils.

Kisimul School – Woodstock House

Woodstock Lane North, Long Ditton, Surrey KT6 5HN
T: (0208) 3352570 **F**: (0208) 3352571 **E**: admissions@kisimul.co.uk **W**: www.kisimul.co.uk

Director Mr Danny Carter
Founded 1977
School status Co-educational boarding only
Religious denomination Non-denominational
Member of BILD, EQUALS
Special needs provision ASD, **CB**, DOW, EPI, **SLD**, SP&LD, W
Age range 8–19; *boarders from 8*
Average class size 6
No of pupils 60

Woodstock House specializes in providing high quality care and education for children and young adults with severe learning difficulties and challenging behaviour, for up to 52 weeks of the year. We provide a caring, consistent, safe and supportive environment in which our pupils can flourish and develop their skills, in order to fully realize their individual potential. The 24-hour curriculum, with residential and school staff working closely together, enables pupils to progress in their personal development and promotes their confidence, self-esteem and independence. Classes are small, with a staffing ratio of 1:1. Alongside the National Curriculum, Adult Pre-Entry Curriculum Framework (Post-16) and Foundation Learning we also offer a wide range of therapeutic and developmental programmes, collectively designed to meet the diverse sensory needs of our pupils.

MacIntyre Schools

MacIntyre Wingrave School

Leighton Road, Wingrave, Aylesbury, Buckinghamshire HP22 4PA
T: (01296) 681274 **F**: (01296) 681091 **E**: wingrave@macintyrecharity.org **W**: www.macintyre-education.org

Principal Mr D Miller QTS - NPQH
Head of Care Miss M Tole NVQ 4 Registered Manager Award
School status Co-educational boarding and day
Religious denomination Non-denominational
Member of NAS, NASS
Special needs provision ASD, CB, EPI, PMLD, **SLD**, SP&LD
Age range 10–19; *boarders from* 10
No of pupils 43; *(full boarding)* 40; *Senior* 14; *Sixth Form* 29;
Girls 3; *Boys* 40
Teacher:pupil ratio 1:6 **Average class size** 6

MacIntyre Wingrave School provides education and care for young people with complex learning difficulties aged 10 to 19 years in a purpose built school situated in a beautiful village in Buckinghamshire. Rated 'Good' by OFSTED, we specialize in an individualized approach and believe in maximizing the potential of all our students. Our services include: Full-time, day and residential placements for young people with a range of severe learning disabilities, including Autism, and a behaviour support team working across education and residential settings. We have an excellent reputation for providing a safe and positive environment for our students that helps to minimize behaviours that challenge. Speech and language therapy, physiotherapy, occupational therapy, music therapy and clinical psychology are onsite. Transition support is through the MacIntyre My Way service, where dedicated brokers work with young people leaving the school to identify suitable solutions for the next stage of their lives.

MacIntyre Womaston School

Womaston School, Walton, Presteigne, Powys LD8 2PT
T: (01544) 230308 **F**: (01544) 231317 **E**: womaston@macintyrecharity.org **W**: www.macintyre-education.org

Principal Mr M J Bertulis
Founded 1986
School status Co-educational senior boarding only
Religious denomination Non-denominational
Special needs provision ADD, ADHD, **ASD**, ASP, **CB**, CP, DOW, DYP,
EPI, IM, MLD, **PMLD**, SLD
Age range 14–19; *boarders from* 14
No of pupils 16; *(full boarding)* 16; *Girls* 5; *Boys* 11
Average class size 5

A proven track record in providing person-centred learning for young people with severe and complex learning difficulties and challenging behaviour. Flexible packages of care and education provide an exciting new model of transition planning and delivery, experienced integrated education and care teams. OCN and OCR accreditation and a good range of support professionals, with learning in meaningful contexts. Womaston provides flexibility within clear boundaries. The development of communication and achievement allows students to re-engage with learning, improve self-image, independence and make great progress in many areas.

Planned approach to transition, through MacIntyre My Way, where skilled brokers work with young people to plan suitable solutions for adult life.

The Marchant-Holliday School

North Cheriton, Templecombe, Somerset BA8 0AH
T: (01963) 33234 **F**: (01963) 33432 **E**: office@marchant-holliday.co.uk **W**: www.marchantholliday.co.uk

Headteacher Mr T Kitts MEd, BEd (Hons), DPSE SEN
Founded 1952
School status Boys' flexible boarding and day
Religious denomination Non-denominational
Member of ISBA, NASS, NASEN, SEBDA
Special needs provision ADD, ADHD, ASD, ASP, BESD, CB,
DYC, DYP, DYS, HEA, IM, MLD, SLD, SP&LD, TOU
Age range 5–15
No of pupils 32
Teacher:pupil ratio 1:3
Average class size 6

The school provides a 'unique, highly specialized and therapeutic level of care to children who present a range of educational and behavioural challenges' (Ofsted, 2010). It is situated in beautiful countryside surroundings and consists of a large country house in 13 acres of woodland, field and gardens. It is readily accessible from London, Bristol, Southampton, the South and West and all areas of the home counties. The school aims to offer positive learning experiences within a secure and caring environment which will enable each child to develop his full potential for social, emotional, physical and intellectual growth. There are a wide range of facilities and residential accommodation is homely with single and double rooms, the majority being en suite.

National Autistic Society (NAS)

NAS Broomhayes School

The National Autistic Society, Kingsley House, Alverdiscott Road, Bideford, Devon EX39 4PL
T: (01237) 473830 **F**: (01237) 421097 **E**: broomhayes@nas.org.uk **W**: www.autism.org.uk/broomhayes

Principal Mr B Higgins
Founded 1985
School status Co-educational independent boarding and day
Students can be admitted to Broomhayes up to the age of 18 years but there is provision for residential accommodation up to 23 years of age.
Religious denomination Non-denominational
Special needs provision ASD, ASP
Age range 10–21; *boarders from* 10
No of pupils 25

NAS Broomhayes School and Children's Centre provides high quality education for children and young people on the autism spectrum in a stimulating, safe, and structured environment. With our specialist support your child will learn new skills, develop social relationships and enjoy a broad and balanced education based on the National Curriculum. Every student has an individual plan reflecting their needs and abilities. Their plan makes sure they enjoy their learning and reach their full potential. Recent developments onsite include a new purpose-built post-16 college, residential block and independent living home. Here students will build their confidence and independence and expand their horizons in preparation for transition to an adult placement. Broomhayes is set in spacious grounds and students live in small groups on the campus. We emphasize community access and our curriculum outside the classroom is varied and exciting.

NAS Daldorch House School

The National Autistic Society, Sorn Road, Catrine, East Ayrshire KA5 6NA
T: (01290) 551666 **F**: (01290) 553399 **E**: daldorch@nas.org.uk **W**: www.autism.org.uk/daldorch

Principal Mrs S Pinkerton
Founded 1998
School status Co-educational independent boarding and day
We offer primary and secondary education for students up to the age of 18, and continuing education and supported living for young people up to the age of 25.
Special needs provision ASD, ASP, W
Age range 5–25
No of pupils 64

Learning is an ongoing process at Daldorch. The development of communication and social and life skills compliments our work within the Curriculum for Excellence. All our students have access to a broad and balanced curriculum which is individually designed to reflect their abilities and meet their needs. We enrich each student's learning by capitalizing on their interests and expanding their understanding of the world. Learning opportunities are present across 365 days of the year. Our purpose is to support students to become successful learners, confident individuals, responsible citizens and effective contributors. We offer primary and secondary education for students up to the age of 18, and continuing education and supported living for young people to the age of 25.

NAS Helen Allison School

The National Autistic Society, Longfield Road, Meopham, Kent DA13 0EW

T: (01474) 814878 **F**: (01474) 812033 **E**: helen.allison@nas.org.uk **W**: www.autism.org.uk/helenallison

Principal Dr J Ashton Smith
Founded 1968
School status Co-educational independent boarding and day
Religious denomination Non-denominational
Special needs provision ASD, ASP, EPI, TOU
Age range 5–19
No of pupils 70

At NAS Helen Allison School we deliver a high quality, relevant and autism-specific education that meets the needs of children and young adults with autism and Asperger syndrome within a structured and safe environment. We believe that education is fun, but we have ambitions for each child and focus on their strengths. We have small classes with expert teaching, delivering an individual programme to each student that reflects their needs and abilities enabling them to reach their potential. These programmes are developed and monitored by a multi-disciplinary team including educationalists, Speech & Language Therapists, Psychologist and Occupational Therapist. We enrich our main curriculum with a wide range of community-based learning and social activities enabling every student to maximize their educational experience and ultimately to become active and equal members of adult society. Our further education (post-16) department and residential units are in nearby Gravesend, giving students easy access to a range of colleges, leisure activities, work experience opportunities, shops, amenities and public transport.

NAS Radlett Lodge School

The National Autistic Society, Harper Lane, Radlett, Hertfordshire WD7 9HW

T: (01923) 854922 **F**: (01293) 859922 **E**: radlett.lodge@nas.org.uk **W**: www.autism.org.uk/radlettlodge

Principal Mrs L Perry
Founded 1974
School status Co-educational independent boarding and day
Religious denomination Non-denominational
Special needs provision ASD, ASP, EPI, SLD, TOU, WA2
Age range 4–19
No of pupils 49

At NAS Radlett Lodge School our students learn new skills, develop social relationships and enjoy a broad and balanced education thanks to our structured and supportive learning environment. Our curriculum meets the specific needs of pupils with autism and emphasizes communication and social skills. Each student's individual programme takes into account their needs and abilities and enables them to reach their full potential. Our high staff to student ratio enables them to access all areas of the National Curriculum at an appropriate level. To prepare students for adult life we encourage them to enjoy activities in the local community, improving their social and independent living skills. We have strong links with the wider community and some students visit other local schools for specific sessions.

NAS Robert Ogden School

The National Autistic Society, Clayton Lane, Thurnscoe, Rotherham, South Yorkshire S63 0BG
T: (01709) 874443 **F**: (01709) 870701 **E**: robert.ogden@nas.org.uk **W**: www.autism.org.uk/robertogden

Principal Mrs G Roberts
Founded 1976
School status Co-educational boarding and day
Religious denomination Non-denominational
Special needs provision ASD, ASP, MLD, PMLD, SLD
Age range 7–19
No of pupils 98

NAS Robert Ogden School is one of the largest schools in the United Kingdom for children and young people with autism. Our stable, structured and nurturing environment helps children and young people to see school as an enjoyable, positive place where they are welcome. At the appropriate Key Stage children and young people access the National and Vocational Curriculum in a way that is specifically geared to their educational needs and abilities. We provide specialist academic and leisure facilities that motivate children and young people to build social confidence, learn new skills and enjoy the benefits of a broad and balanced education. In particular, our curriculum takes into account the specific challenges that our children face in the area of language, communication and social awareness. We help the whole child develop from primary through to further education.

NAS Sybil Elgar School

The National Autistic Society, Havelock Road, Southall, Middlesex UB2 4NY
T: (020) 8813 9168 **F**: (020) 8571 7332 **E**: sybil.elgar@nas.org.uk **W**: www.autism.org.uk/sybilelgar

Principal C Phillips
Founded 1965
School status Co-educational independent boarding and day
Religious denomination Non-denominational
Special needs provision ASD, ASP, SP&LD
Age range 8–19
No of pupils 87

At NAS Sybil Elgar School we treat every child as an individual and listen to, and respect their values and views. We put their needs and wellbeing before anything else. We gear our curriculum to the needs of children and young people with autism, nurturing their communication and social skills. We cater for a wide range of abilities and needs through: individual educational programmes; our high staff to student ratio; and enriched multi-disciplinary teams, including Speech & Language Therapy, Psychology and Occupational Therapy. Every student receives a broad, balanced and relevant education based on the National Curriculum and, where appropriate, an extended curriculum of activities. Our students especially enjoy our creative and expressive arts programme. From 16 students move into our specialist further education department. We are known for being innovative and progressive, and our school is a dynamic place for young people on their way to adulthood, enabling them to access their wider community.

New College Worcester

Whittington Road, Worcester, Worcestershire WR5 2JX
T: (01905) 763933 **F**: (01905) 763277 **E**: liaison@newcollegeworcester.co.uk
W: www.newcollegeworcester.co.uk

Principal Mrs M Smith
Founded 1866
College status Co-educational boarding and day
Special needs provision ASP, DYP, DYS, HEA, HI, IM, VI, W
Age range 11–19; *boarders from* 11
No of pupils 78; *(full boarding)* 78; *Senior* 37
Sixth Form 41; *Girls* 39; *Boys* 39
Average class size 3

New College Worcester is a residential college for blind and partially sighted students aged 11 to 19. Every student receives an individual programme of education, mobility and Independent Living Skills to support them in reaching their full potential both in and outside the classroom. As well as an extensive range of GCSE, AS and A level courses, we offer ASDAN courses and a broad range of outdoor and leisure activities. Staff members are all specialists in their subject and additionally qualified to teach visually impaired young people. We encourage all interested students and their families to visit prior to booking an assessment. Funding of places is usually via the student's Local Authority.

The New School at West Heath

Ashgrove Road, Sevenoaks, Kent TN13 1SR
T: (01732) 460553 **F**: (01732) 456734 **E**: principal@westheathschool.com **W**: www.westheathschool.com

Principal Christina Wells BA (Hons)
Founded 1998
School status Co-educational boarding and day
Special needs provision ADD, **ADHD**, **ASP**, **BESD**, **HEA**, SP&LD, **TOU**
Age range 11–19; *boarders from* 11
No of pupils 123; *(boarding)* 36; *(weekly boarding)* 36; *Girls* 36; *Boys* 76
Average class size 8

We offer an exciting broad and balanced curriculum with specialist subjects tailored to the individual. The most recent Ofsted inspection found that "The outstanding curriculum provides a very wide range of experiences and is matched closely to the specific learning needs of students."

The school's motto "rebuilding lives through education" is reflected in the approach of nurturing and educating young people in a safe and highly supportive environment. Teaching is supported by in-house communication, speech and language programmes, and an emotional literacy curriculum. Our students often respond very well to the additional support provided, achieving good GCSE and A level grades.

"We believe in our students until they believe in themselves."

Pengwern College

Sam Lane, Rhuddlan, Denbighshire LL18 5UH
T: (01745) 592300 **F**: (01745) 591736 **E**: pengwern.college@mencap.org.uk **W**: www.mencap.org.uk/pengwern

Principal Pauline Rowland
College status Co-educational independent boarding and day
Special needs provision ADD, ASD, ASP, CB, CP, DOW, EPI, HI, IM, MLD, PMLD, SLD, SP&LD
Age range 16–25

Pengwern College is an Independent Specialist College, providing education and care for students aged 16–25 with moderate to severe learning disabilities. The college is situated in a rural environment in Rhuddlan, North Wales and attracts students from all areas of the country. We offer both day and residential placements.

We pride ourselves on our commitment to providing high-quality education. The college helps students gain the confidence and skills they need to move on to the next stage of their lives; whether that is gaining employment, moving towards independent living or progressing on to further study.

The aim of our curriculum is to provide opportunities that enable students to develop their functional, vocational and personal skills.

Each student has a programme tailored to meet their needs and aspirations. Their progress is guided through person-centred goals, with the specialist support they need.

Penn School

Church Road, Penn, High Wycombe, Buckinghamshire HP10 8LZ
T: (01494) 812139 **F**: (01494) 811400 **E**: office@pennschool.bucks.sch.uk **W**: www.pennschool.bucks.sch.uk

Headteacher Mrs M N Richardson BA (Hons) PGCE, MEd AdDip BPhil
(Speech and Language Difficulties) PGC Aspergers NCSL
Founded 1921
School status Co-educational non-maintained day and weekly residential
Religious denomination Non-denominational
Member of EQUALS, NAHT, NAS, NASS
Special needs provision ASD, ASP, HI, SP&LD
Age range 11–19
Average class size 7

Penn School provides a multi-professional, integrated and collaborative approach to the teaching, therapy and care of pupils (and families) whose primary difficulty is speech, language and communication/ASD/ASP/HI. Children with additional or associated difficulties, including some degree of learning difficulty, attention control, motor coordination problems and mild visual problems, can also benefit. Emphasis is placed on work related learning and living skills in the 14–19 years curriculum and in the waking hours curriculum (residential). The pupils follow the broader National Curriculum and obtain examination certificates in a range of subjects at Entry 1 and 2. GCSEs are available in ICT, Art, English, and Maths for more able students. Each child has an Individual Education Plan addressing their SEN, which is jointly devised by the specialist teacher, the speech and language therapist and the occupational therapist who offer a sensory integration approach. Our aim is to develop the full potential of each individual pupil in a happy safe environment.

Philpots Manor School and Further Training Centre

West Hoathly, East Grinstead, West Sussex RH19 4PR
T: (01342) 810268 **F**: (01342) 811363 **E**: jill.roberts@philpotsmanorschool.co.uk
W: www.philpotsmanorschool.co.uk

Education Co-ordinator L Churnside
Founded 1959
School status Co-educational boarding and day
Religious denomination Christian
Member of Steiner Waldorf Schools Fellowship
Special needs provision ADD, ADHD, **ASD**, **ASP**, **BESD**, **CB**, DYC, DYP,
DYS, EPI, HEA, **MLD**, SP&LD, **TOU**
Age range 7–19; *boarders from* 7
No of pupils 46; *(boarding)* 31; *(day)* 15; *Girls* 12; *Boys* 34
Average class size 6

Philpots Manor School is based on the education principles of Rudolf Steiner. The school admits children who present a broad range of emotional and behavioural difficulties. The academic ability of the children ranges from high average to moderate learning difficulties. Children are eligible providing they have the capacity to function in a classroom situation where children are helped to reach their full potential within the Steiner curriculum. GCSEs, Entry Level and OCN qualifications are taken.

Portfield School

Parley Lane, Christchurch, Dorset BH23 6BP
T: (01202) 573808 **F**: (01202) 580532 **E**: portfield-school@twas.org.uk **W**: www.twas.org.uk

Director of services Andrew Thomas
School status Non-maintained special school (NMSS), day, 39 and 52 week boarding.
Flexible boarding and respite care also available
Religious denomination Non-denominational
Member of NAS, NASS
Special needs provision ASD
No of pupils 60
Average class size 5–6

The Wessex Autistic Society is a voluntary organization which aims to ensure that people with Autism receive appropriate education, care, support and individual development services.

Education

Portfield School in Dorset is committed to achieving the highest standards of education and care for children and young people with autism. Providing an individualized approach to learning and personal development, each child's personal curriculum and care plan reflects their ability, not just their disability. In a context of security, enjoyment and respect, the intention is that Portfield School will prepare young people to enter adulthood equipped to maximize their independence and quality of life and to engage in their communities as active citizens.

Purpose-built facilities

Built in 2002, Portfield School takes a holistic approach to the education and care of children on the autism spectrum, and is equipped with specialist teaching facilities to make learning a success. The school boasts state of the art leisure facilities including an indoor therapy pool, soft play and sensory rooms.

Residential facilities

Portfield is registered by OFSTED as a children's home and offers personalized and flexible boarding options from 39 to 52 weeks a year. Four purpose-built boarding houses are located on the main school site with one additional Post-16 residential house located within the community. All students have their own bedrooms as well as benefitting from homely communal spaces and an excellent range of learning and leisure resources.

Life skills department for post-16 students

Promoting independence through learning is particularly evident of the School's Life Skills Service for older students aged 16–19. Students continue to work on their academic skills, alongside a number of practical activities such as work experience, meal planning and preparation, and running a Young Enterprise project. A range of pracitcal skills lessons aim to ensure that students develop the ability to integrate within society while maximizing their independence.

Quotes

'*Pupils enjoy school and attend well because they feel very safe and because the curriculum provides a good range of stimulating experiences for them to develop their personal and communication skills. This enables every pupil to gain nationally recognized qualifications for their work by the time they leave.*' (OFSTED 2010)

'*Students at the school benefit from outstanding provision for protecting and promoting their welfare.*' (OFSTED 2010)

'*My child is treated with the utmost respect at all times. His confidence and independence has soared. The staff really encourage his self-esteem.*' (Parent 2010)

Potterspury Lodge School

Potterspury Lodge, Towcester, Northamptonshire NN12 7LL
T: (01908) 542912 **F**: (01908) 543399 **E**: mail@potterspurylodge.co.uk **W**: www.potterspurylodge.co.uk
●♠

Principal Mr J W D Brown
Founded 1956
School status Boys' boarding and day
Member of NASS, NASEN, SCA
Special needs provision ADD, ADHD, ASD, ASP, BESD, CB,
DYP, DYS, MLD, SP&LD, TOU
Age range 8–18; *boarders from* 8
No of pupils 64; *(boarding)* 20; *(full boarding)* 2; *(weekly
boarding)* 18; *Prep* 5; *Senior* 44; *Sixth Form* 3; *Boys* 64
Teacher:pupil ratio 1:3
Average class size 8

Potterspury Lodge prides itself on its commitment and dedication to pupils with special needs, aiming to provide them with a wide range of opportunities to experience success. We aim to help them progress towards being better integrated into society and ultimately to go on to meet the demands of independent adult life.

Class sizes are around 8 or 9 students and in addition to the subject teachers there is a strong team of learning support assistants to ensure each child gets the help and support they need. We employ an experienced Speech and Language Therapist, an Education Psychologist and a part-time Occupational Therapist, specializing in sensory difficulties.

From year 10, pupils follow an accredited life skills programme, helping to prepare them for their future. In year 11, some students are able to take part in work-based training and all year 10 and year 11 students undertake two week-long periods of work experience.

Boarders live in small groups of 5 or 6 in self contained hostels. Inspectors comment that the school's ethos and underpinning philosophy is strong throughout, ensuring pupils live in a supportive and caring community within which boarders feel valued and safe.

All meals are prepared by our Head Chef, using fresh ingredients wherever possible. Much of the fruit and most of the vegetables we use are grown in our own garden without the use of chemicals

Provision for students in years 12 and 13 is in The Stables Further Education Centre. Education and Residential support managers enable students to follow programmes of education and training according to their individual needs, using our own resources and those of local colleges, amenities and workplace training providers.

The school enables children to develop and grow in a caring and supportive atmosphere, and gives them the perfect opportunity to socialize and enjoy life. We organize regular trips for the students, including an annual skiing holiday in Italy and outdoor pursuits expeditions in the United Kingdom and France. Last year a group of students also visited the First World War Battlefield sites in France and Belgium.

The grounds are wonderful for sports and outdoor games, particularly when the weather is nice. A wide range of evening clubs is offered, including badminton, pottery, football, computers, practical skills and technology. Extensive use is made of local leisure and recreational facilities; some students attend an Army Cadets Corps and others are members of our own Scout Troop.

Priors Court School

Hermitage, Thatcham, Berkshire RG18 9NU
T: (01635) 247202 **F**: (01635) 247203 **E**: mail@priorscourt.org.uk **W**: www.priorscourt.org.uk

Principal Stephen Bojdala-Brown
School status Independent Specialist School. 38, 44 and 52 weeks. Co-educational boarding and day
Special needs provision ASD, CB, EPI, MLD, SLD, SP&LD, WA2
Age range 5–19
No of pupils 54
Teacher:pupil ratio 1:1, 2:1, 1:2
Average class size 6

Prior's Court offers specialist education and care for young people with autism, learning difficulties and complex needs. The school is set in 50 acres of beautiful grounds with outstanding facilities. Experienced, highly trained staff and a large onsite therapeutic team work in partnership with parents to enable students to develop communication, independent living and social skills, choice-making and advocacy and learn to self-manage behaviour. Each pupil has an individual programme of learning with a Waking Day curriculum which is adapted to ensure it is meaningful and functional and built around each student's interests and abilities. Skills are extended with a rich and varied range of activities at school and out in the community. Vocational development is encouraged by projects such as horticulture and animal husbandry with onsite and offsite work placements.

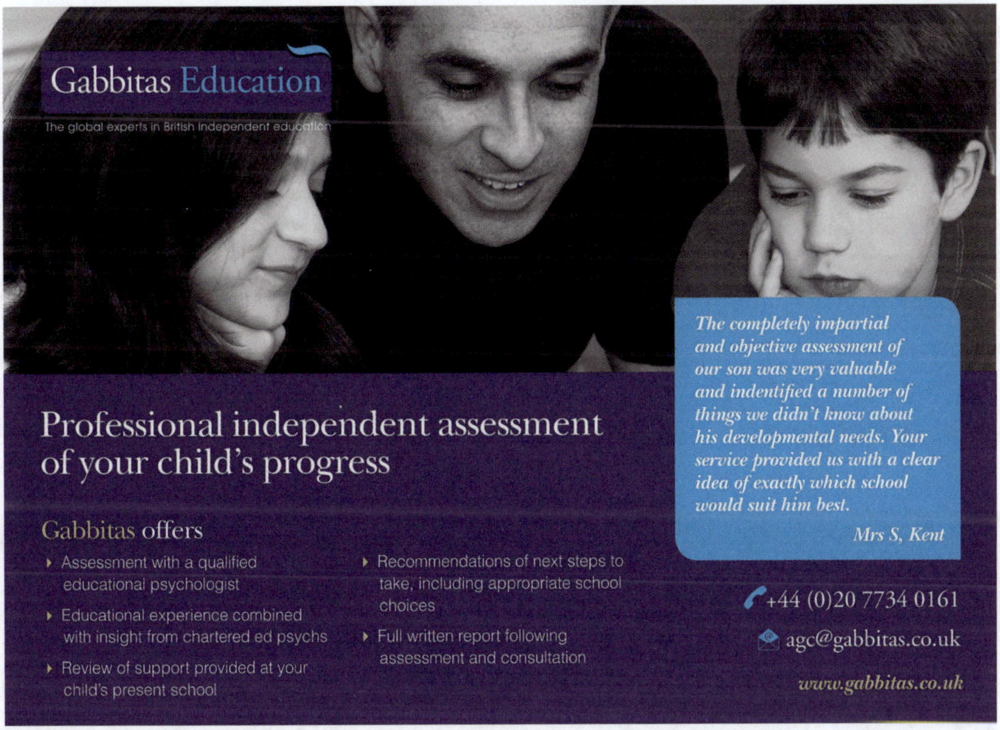

Integrated Pathways

Priory Education Services is the country's leading independent provider of specialist education and care for children and young people from age five and upwards.

We offer a unique integration of education, care and therapy to young people with a variety of complex needs including:

- **Asperger's Syndrome**
- **Autistic spectrum disorders**
- **Behavioural, emotional and social difficulties**
- **Specific learning difficulties and language disorders**

The group includes 30 specialist schools, colleges and care homes nationwide, together with an emergency placement service and fostering services.

Options include:

- **Day and extended day**
- **Up to 52 week residential**
- **Post 16**
- **Emergency placements**
- **Weekly boarding**
- **Respite care**

To request an information pack, arrange a visit or to make a referral please contact us:

0845 2 774679

education@priorygroup.com   www.priorygroup.com/education

Unique services for unique young people

Asperger's Syndrome (AS)	Gender	Age	Placement	Placement type
Farleigh College Frome, Somerset	Mixed	11-19	Term time	Residential and day
North Hill House, Somerset	Boys	7-18	Term time	Residential and day
Unsted Park School, Surrey	Mixed	7-19	Term time	Residential and day
Farleigh FE College Frome, Somerset	Mixed	16-25	Term time	Residential and day
Priory Coleg North Wales, Wrexham	Mixed	16-25	Term time	Residential and day
Priory Coleg Wales, Pontypool	Mixed	16-25	Term time	Residential and day
Farleigh FE College Swindon, Wiltshire	Mixed	16-25	Term time	Residential and day

Autism with emotional and behavioural difficulties	Gender	Age	Placement	Placement type
Chelfham Senior School, Devon	Mixed	7-19	Up to 52 weeks	Residential and day
Priory Hurworth House, Darlington	Mixed	7-19	Term time	Day/extended day
Rossendale School, Lancashire	Mixed	8-16	Term time	Residential and day
Troup House School, Aberdeenshire	Mixed	8-16	52 weeks	Day/extended day

Autistic spectrum disorder (ASD)	Gender	Age	Placement	Placement type
Oliver House, Lancashire	Mixed	6-19	Up to 52 weeks	Residential and day
Rugeley Horizon School, Staffordshire	Mixed	5-19	Up to 52 weeks	Residential and day
Sketchley Horizon School, Leicestershire	Mixed	8-19	Day term time	Day/extended day
Tadley Horizon School, Hampshire	Mixed	5-19	Up to 52 weeks	Residential and day
The Priory Lodge School, London	Mixed	7-19	Day term time	Day/extended day

Behavioural, emotional and social difficulties (BESD)	Gender	Age	Placement	Placement type
Coxlease School, Hampshire	Mixed	9-18	Up to 52 weeks	Residential and day
Eastwood Grange, Derbyshire	Boys	11-16	Up to 52 weeks	Residential and day
Eden Grove School, Cumbria	Boys	8-19	Up to 52 weeks	Residential and day
Jacques Hall, Essex	Mixed	11-18	Up to 52 weeks	Residential and day
Queenswood School, Herefordshire	Mixed	11-19	Up to 52 weeks	Residential and day
Sheridan School, Norfolk	Mixed	10-19	Up to 52 weeks	Residential and day
Talocher School, Monmouthshire	Mixed	11-18	Up to 52 weeks	Residential and day

Specific learning difficulties - language disorder, dyslexia	Gender	Age	Placement	Placement type
Mark College, Somerset	Mixed	10-19	Term time	Residential and day

Emergency placements	Gender	Age	Placement	Placement type
Coxlease Abbeymead, Hampshire	Mixed	9-16	Up to 12 week assessments	Residential and day

Complex psychological disorders	Gender	Age	Placement	Placement type
Priory Pines House, Darlington	Mixed	7-16	Up to 52 weeks	Residential, day and respite care

Fostering	Gender	Age		
Priory Fostering Services	Mixed	0-18		

Post 19 austistic spectrum disorders (ASD)	Gender	Age	Placement	Placement type
The Bakehouse, Lancashire	Mixed	16-25	Up to 52 weeks	
Highfields Road, Staffordshire	Mixed	18-25	Residential	Residential
The Gatehouse, Hampshire	Mixed	16-25	Residential	Residential

Post 19 Asperger's Syndrome (AS)	Gender	Age	Placement	Placement type
Rookery Hove, East Sussex	Mixed	18-35	Residential	Residential
Rookery Radstock, Somerset	Mixed	18-25	Residential	Residential

RNIB Pears Centre for Specialist Learning

Formerly RNIB Rushton School and Children's Home

Wheelwright Lane, Ash Green, Coventry, Warwickshire CV7 9RA
T: (024 76) 36 95 00 **F**: (024 76) 36 95 01 **E**: pearscentre@rnib.org.uk **W**: www.rnib.org.uk/pearscentre
Contact Liz Gutteridge to discuss places or arrange an informal visit

Headteacher Mr A Moran
Principal Manager: Care & Wellbeing Ms V Tyler
Founded 1957
School status Co-educational boarding and day
Religious denomination Non-denominational
Member of EQUALS, NAHT, NASS, NASEN
Special needs provision ASD, BESD, CB, CP, DOW, EPI, HEA, HI, **IM**, **PMLD**, **SLD**, SP&LD, VI, W
Age range 4–19
No of pupils 30; *(boarding)* 19; *(full boarding)* 19; *Girls* 8; *Boys* 11
Average class size 7

RNIB Pears Centre for Specialist Learning (formerly known as RNIB Rushton School and Children's Home) offers individually tailored education, care, healthcare and therapies to young people with complex needs who are blind or partially sighted. Building on over 50 years of expert care and education, RNIB Pears Centre offers a stimulating and supportive environment for young people to reach their full potential for learning, independence and fulfilment. Residential and day places are available. We welcome visits from parents, carers, children, other family members and professionals.

Learning: We recently became the only non-maintained special school in England to be awarded specialist SEN status for cognition and learning. Our broad, balanced and relevant curriculum is differentiated to meet individual needs and learning styles. National Curriculum core and foundation subjects are highly personalized to the needs of each student. From the age of 14, students follow a theme-based curriculum which focuses on life skills, vocational studies and work experience. Students also participate in the Duke of Edinburgh's Award scheme.

Living: We offer up to 52-week residential care from new purpose-built bungalows with gardens and outdoor play areas. Each young person staying with us has their own bedroom which is made safe and personal to them. We work in partnership with parents, carers and families to ensure that they are closely involved at each step of their child's journey. Our team promotes achievement in personal development, independence, communication, mobility and socialization. We actively support transition to ensure that all young people attending RNIB Pears Centre get the very best start to their adult life.

Therapies and healthcare: We offer an in-house team of therapists and health care consultants, including specialist learning disability nurses, physiotherapists, and speech and language therapists. Water and music therapies are also part of our provision. Support is also available from clinical psychology, habilitation and occupational therapists. All young people receive the highest level of healthcare with access to a GP, paediatrician and other community health services.

Where we are: Located in a pleasant residential area with excellent transport links (near M6, M1 and M69 motorways), RNIB Pears Centre is easily accessible from many areas of the United Kingdom. From 2011 new Modern facilities will enhance our specialist services as part of a major redevelopment.

Queen Alexandra College of Further Education

Court Oak Road, Harborne, Birmingham, West Midlands B17 9TG
T: (0121) 428 5050 **F**: (0121) 428 5045 **E**: info@qac.ac.uk **W**: www.qac.ac.uk

Principal Hugh J Williams CEng MIET MIMechE MCMI BSc (Eng)
Founded 1858
College status Independent FE College. Mixed residential and day 16+.
Learners with visual impairment, MLD, Asperger Syndrome and other
disabilities aged 16+
Religious denomination Non-denominational
Special needs provision ASD, **ASP**, CP, DOW, DYP, DYS, EPI, HI, IM,
MLD, SP&LD, **VI**, WA1; *boarders from* 16
No of pupils 150; *(boarding)* 75; *(full boarding)* 75; *Girls* 65; *Boys* 85
Average class size 8

Queen Alexandra College (QAC) in Birmingham is a leading specialist residential college for people aged 16+ with disabilities. QAC has a particular expertise in visual impairment but also welcomes people with a range of other disabilities including Asperger Syndrome. Learners may work at entry level or gain BTEC qualifications at Levels 1, 2 or 3. Skills for independent living and an active sports, leisure and social programme are an important part of the extended curriculum. Speech and language therapy and specialist skills training, such as the use of assistive technology, Braille and in orientation and mobility are provided. Our education and residential teams support learners to develop independence and confidence. An experienced transitions team helps leavers maximize their opportunities for successful progression to continuing education or employment. QAC is a small and friendly college located in a residential area of a vibrant city.

The Royal School for Deaf Children Margate

Victoria Road, Margate, Kent CT9 1NB
T: (01843) 227561 **F**: (01843) 227637 **E**: enquiries@royalschoolfordeaf.kent.sch.uk
W: www.townsendtrust.com

headteacher Mrs W Eadsforth
School status Co-educational non-maintained boarding and day
Religious denomination Non-denominational
Member of EQUALS, NASS, NATSPEC
Special needs provision ADD, ADHD, ASD, ASP, BESD, CB, CP, DOW,
DYP, DYS, EPI, HEA, **HI**, IM, MLD, PMLD, SLD, SP&LD, TOU, VI, W
Age range 4–16; *boarders from* 4
No of pupils 44; *(boarding)* 33; *(weekly boarding)* 33; *Pre-prep* 3; *Prep*
3; *Senior* 38; *Girls* 14; *Boys* 30
Teacher:pupil ratio 1:2 **Average class size** 6

We educate and care for deaf children and young people with communication difficulties, who may have additional needs, for a positive future within work and their communities.

The Royal School for Deaf Children Margate is a non-maintained school offering residential and day provision for pupils from 4–16 years. Pupils and students attending the school are deaf or have communication difficulties. Many have additional learning and physical disabilities, mental health and associated challenging behaviours. Communication modes include speech, BSL, SSE, PECS symbols and objects of reference.

Royal School for the Deaf Derby

Ashbourne Road, Derby, Derbyshire DE22 3BH
T: (01332) 362512 **F**: (01332) 299708 **E**: principal@rsdd.org.uk **W**: www.rsd-derby.org.uk

Principal C Ford
Founded 1893
School status Co-educational non-maintained boarding and day
Religious denomination Non-denominational
Special needs provision HI
Age range 3–19; *boarders from* 5
No of pupils 135; *(weekly boarding)* 54; *(day)* 81; *Nursery* 7;
Pre-prep 6; *Prep* 23; *Senior* 73; *Sixth Form* 26; *Girls* 40; *Boys* 95

RSD Derby values the languages and cultures of both deaf and hearing people. The National Curriculum is delivered through English and BSL and is adapted to individual needs by personalized learning programmes. The school promotes a positive sense of identity for each pupil, preparing them for the opportunities of adult life and full participation in their local community. The foundation group offers free places to deaf children from age 3 to 5. Subject specialist teachers of the deaf work in small class groups with examinations offered including GCSE, DIDA and Entry Levels. Post-16 students follow individual, supported programmes of study at mainstream colleges with courses ranging from vocational options through to A levels and Level 3 BTEC National. Key Skills, Wider Key Skills and Skills for Life are delivered by teachers of the deaf at base. Weekly and part-time boarders benefit from a 24-hour curriculum which includes developing life skills and managing money. The residential houses are designed to promote a feeling of belonging and security while living away from home.

St Catherine's School

Grove Road, Ventnor, Isle of Wight PO38 1TT
T: (01983) 852722 **F**: (01983) 857210 **E**: general@stcatherines.org.uk **W**: www.stcatherines.org.uk
Our facility for 16+ is Grove Hill Further Education Centre – The direct telephone number 01983 857206.

Principal Mr B Carleton (Acting)
Founded 1983
School status Co-educational boarding and day
Religious denomination Church of England
Member of NAHT, NASS, NASEN
Special needs provision ADD, ADHD, ASD, ASP,
CB, DYC, DYP, DYS, EPI, HEA, HI, MLD, SP&LD, VI
Age range 11–19; *boarders from* 11
No of pupils 56; *(boarding)* 40; *(full boarding)* 23; *(weekly boarding)* 17; *Senior* 33; *Sixth Form* 23; *Girls* 20;
Boys 36
Teacher:pupil ratio 1:8
Average class size 6

St Catherine's School provides for learners between the ages of 11 and 19 who have speech and language impairments and associated difficulties. St Catherine's is a residential centre of excellence for education, speech and language therapy. Each learner has his/her own individual educational programme integrating learning and language therapy. This work is supported by our highly skilled care, occupational therapy and medical teams. Our holistic approach ensures each and every learner has access to high quality learning and personal development relevant to their needs. Education for 16+ is offered at Grove Hill Further Education Centre.

St Edward's School

Melchet Court, Sherfield English, Romsey, Hampshire S051 6ZR
T: (01794) 885252 **F**: (01794) 885253 **E**: enquiries@melchetcourt.com **W**: www.melchetcourt.com

Head Master Mr L P Bartel BEd
Deputy Head Mr Philip Rogers MA Ed
Founded 1963
School status Boys' boarding and day
Religious denomination Non-denominational
Member of NASS
Special needs provision ADD, ADHD, ASD, ASP, BESD, DYS, MLD, SP&LD
Age range 10–17; *boarders from* 10
No of pupils 52; *(boarding)* 41; *(weekly boarding)* 41; *Prep* 33; *Senior* 14
Sixth Form 5
Average class size 5

St Edward's is recognized as a high quality provision for boys who have behavioural, emotional and social difficulties (BESD).

Specialist facilities and additional services include anger management coaching, outreach and home visits, and support at the early stages of pupils' placements. Pupils' outcomes are tracked in accord with the ECM Agenda.

St Edward's school is a Member of NASS and user of National Contract. It has been commended for the excellent relationships evident between pupils and staff and offers the Full National Curriculum. GCSE courses are available in eight subjects, as well as BTEC courses for Key Stage 4 and beyond Sport (Outdoor Education), Living Skills and Public Services. Excellent vocational opportunities (LCCI) in painting and decorating, horticulture, design technology, brickwork, working in a motor vehicle area and work experience programme in Years 10, 11 and 12 are also available.

Qualified staff offer a wide range of activities, including motorcycling, kayaking and canoeing, snowboarding, swimming, football, art, music, roller hockey, sub-aqua, golf, fishing and sailing (not exhaustive). We offer field trips and outdoor pursuits expeditions, home and abroad and excellent sports facilities, and have high-quality residential and recreational accommodation.

'Oustanding' Ofsted outcomes in 2008/2010.

Aims and Philosophy: St Edward's School Charitable Trust aims to foster each boy's personal and social growth.

The overall Ofsted quality rating is outstanding. (Ofsted, 2011). Here are just a few of the comments from this year's report:
- Pupils are educated and cared for in an environment where respect for each other has a strong presence.
- The effectiveness of behavioural management systems is exceptional. The emphasis placed on recording and reporting on individual pupil's assessed needs, provides very clear and concise leads for negotiating the appropriate... intervention.
- All staff work harmoniously to give pupils the best of opportunities to engage in culture, environment and citizenship activities.
- Pupils are continuously involved in decision-making processes. They are also supported in an environment where a broad range of diverse needs are met without prejudice or judgement.

St Elizabeth's School

South End, Much Hadham, Hertfordshire SG10 6EW
T: (01279) (844270) **F**: (01279) (843903) **E**: school@stelizabeths.org.uk **W**: www.stelizabeths.org.uk

Principal Mr B Sainsbury
Founded 1904
School status Co-educational non-maintained boarding and day
Religious denomination Roman Catholic
Member of BILD, EQUALS, NASS
Special needs provision ASD, CB, EPI, MLD, PMLD, **SLD**
Age range 5–19
No of pupils 51; *(boarding)* 51; *(full boarding)* 51; *Girls* 19; *Boys* 32
Average class size 6

St Elizabeth's is an outstanding, non-maintained special residential and day school registered with the Department for Education. We are located in a 68 acre parkland setting in rural Hertfordshire which we share with St Elizabeth's College (post-19) and St Elizabeth's Adult Home, providing excellent continuity of provision. All school buildings are single storey and fully ramped. The Living and Learning building which opened in 2007 caters for students aged 16–19 and comprises small groups of en-suite bedrooms built around dedicated study facilities. At St Elizabeth's we believe that every student is uniquely valuable. We use our expertise and multi-disciplinary approach to cater for pupils who present with a profile of complex learning and medical needs, including epilepsy, autism and associated social and communication difficulties, some challenging behaviours and moderate and severe learning needs.

St John's Catholic School for the Deaf

Church Street, Boston Spa, West Yorkshire LS23 6DF
T: (01937) 042144 **F**: (01937) 541471 **E**: info@stjohns.org.uk **W**: www.stjohns.org.uk
St John's is a SEN Specialist School.

Head Teacher Mrs A M Bradbury
Founded 1870
School status Co-educational non-maintained boarding and day
Religious denomination Roman Catholic
Special needs provision ADHD, ASD, ASP, CP, DYP, DYS, EPI, **HI**, IM, MLD, SP&LD, VI
Age range 4–19
No of pupils 79; *Girls* 31; *Boys* 48
Average class size 6

St John's is a residential and day school offering an excellent oral education to children aged from 4 to 19 years. A strong Christian ethos permeates all aspects of school life and children of all denominations are welcomed. The curriculum is broad and balanced and provides the opportunity for pupils to take GCSEs, Entry Level qualifications and a wide range of vocational courses. In addition to 20+ qualified Teachers of the Deaf, support is available from speech and language therapists, an audiologist, highly qualified care staff and a school nurse. St John's is a SEN Specialist School in the field of sensory and physical impairment.

St Joseph's Specialist School & College

Amlets Lane, Cranleigh, Surrey GU6 7DH
T: (01483) 272449 **F**: (01483) 276003 **E**: office@st-josephscranleigh.surrey.sch.uk
W: www.st-josephscranleigh.surrey.sch.uk

Headteacher Mrs M E Fawcett   **Founded** 1906
College status Co-educational non-maintained boarding and day
Religious denomination Roman Catholic
Member of BILD, CES, NAS, NASS, NASEN
Special needs provision ADD, **ADHD**, **ASD**, ASP, **CB**, CP, **DOW**, DYP, EPI, HEA, HI, IM, **MLD**, **SLD**, SP&LD, TOU, VI
Age range 5–19; *boarders from 7*
No of pupils 78; *(boarding)* 39; *(full boarding)* 38; *(weekly boarding)* 31; *Girls* 20; *Boys* 58
Average class size 6

Set in 23 acres of beautiful Surrey countryside, St Joseph's provides day and residential facilities for learners with ASD moderate, complex and severe learning difficulties. We have achieved specialist status in communication and interaction. We provide speech and language therapy, occupational therapy and arts psychotherapy (music and art) from a team of HPC registered professional therapists supported by dedicated speech and language and occupational therapy assistants. Our school buildings are well resourced and equipped, and facilities include a heated swimming pool, sensory room and chapel. Students have the opportunity to undertake nationally accredited courses including Entry Level GCSEs, Asdan and Equals. Our post-16 and residential departments are judged 'outstanding' by Ofsted. They focus on learning to promote personal, social and adult independence.

St Mary's Wrestwood Children's Trust

Wrestwood Road, Bexhill-on-Sea, East Sussex TN40 2LU
T: (01424) 730740 **F**: (01424) 733575 **E**: adm@st-marys.bexhill.sch.uk **W**: www.st-marys.bexhill.sch.uk

Chief Executive Ms Gail Pilling
Headteacher Mrs Joanna Whiteman
Founded 1922
School status Co-educational non-maintained boarding and day
Religious denomination Christian
Member of BILD, NAS, NASS, NASEN, NATSPEC
Special needs provision ADD, **ASD**, ASP, CP, DOW, DYP, DYS, EPI, HEA, HI, IM, **MLD**, SP&LD, TOU, VI
Age range 7–19; *boarders from 7*
No of pupils 137; *(boarding)* 110; *(full boarding)* 35; *(weekly boarding)* 75; *Prep* 9; *Senior* 63
Sixth Form 65; *Girls* 53; *Boys* 84
Average class size 8

Curriculum: We follow the National Curriculum, differentiated where necessary, plus individual learning programmes and a comprehensive life skills programme. We have a team of speech and language therapists, an art psychotherapist, a counselling psychologist, physiotherapists, occupational therapists, a specialist teacher for hearing-impaired pupils and a high ratio of qualified and experienced care and nursing staff.

Entry requirements: Formal assessments and interview. Referrals are normally made through local education departments. Private referrals are also considered.

St Mary's is a DCSF non-maintained special school, situated in a semi-rural location in East Sussex near the sea. St Mary's Wrestwood Children's Trust is a registered charity that exists to provide high-quality education, therapy and care in a residential setting, for boys and girls with special educational needs.

The School for Profound Education

The Children's Trust, Tadworth Court, Tadworth, Surrey KT20 5RU
T: (01737) 365810 **F**: (01737) 365819 **E**: profoundeducation@thechildrenstrust.org.uk
W: www.thechildrenstrust.org.uk/profoundeducation

The School for Profound Education
education, care & therapy for learners with pmld

formerly St Margaret's School, Tadworth

Headteacher Mrs J Cunningham ANEA Cert. Ed M Ed
Founded 1985
School status Co-educational non-maintained boarding and day
The school admits learners aged 5 to 19 years old. There is additional college provision for 19 to 25 year olds.
Member of NAHT, NASS, NASEN
Special needs provision CP, **EPI**, **HEA**, **HI**, **IM**, **PMLD**, VI, W
Age range 5–19 (The school admits learners aged 5 to 19 years old. There is additional college provision for 19 to 25 year olds.); *boarders from* 5
No of pupils 39; *(boarding)* 30; *(full boarding)* 30; *Girls* 16; *Boys* 23
Average class size 7

The School for Profound Education (formerly known as St Margaret's School) is one of the few special schools in the United Kingdom that works exclusively with pupils with profound and multiple learning difficulties (PMLD) and complex health needs. The school is a non-maintained residential special school that provides education, care and therapy in a safe, caring and happy environment in which each learner's needs can be met. The school has its own doctor and small team of nurses, and provides 24-hour medical cover. The school has developed particular expertise in catering for learners with Rett syndrome and acquired brain injury.

All learners use The Profound Education Curriculum, which has been specially developed by the school. It is a broad, balanced curriculum designed to be relevant to individual needs, delivered to a 24-hour model.

SCOPE

Craig-y-Parc School

Heol y Parc, Pentyrch, Cardiff CF15 9NB **T**: (029) 2089 0397 **F**: (029) 2089 1404 **E**: cyp@scope.org.uk **W**: www.scope.org.uk

Principal Anthony Mulcahy
School status Co-educational boarding and day
Religious denomination Non-denominational
Special needs provision CP, **IM**, **PMLD**
Age range 3–19; *(boarding)* 13; *(full boarding)* 6; *(weekly boarding)* 7 **Average class size** 6

Craig-y-Parc School is a place where pupils come to learn, live and get the most out of life. Situated on the outskirts of Cardiff, we combine a range of educational, therapeutic, social activities and residential care for pupils with cerebral palsy and other complex support needs. We work with pupils to focus on learning, ability and independence. With classroom space for 56 pupils, the school is both well-equipped and expertly staffed.

Meldreth Manor

Fenny Lane, Meldreth, Nr Royston, Hertfordshire SG8 6LG
T: (01763) 268000 **F**: (01763) 268099 **E**: meldreth.manor@scope.org.uk
W: www.scope.org.uk/education

Principal Mr R Gale
School status Co-educational boarding and day
Religious denomination Non-denominational   **Age range** 9–19
Special needs provision CP, EPI, HI, **PMLD**, SLD, SP&LD, VI
No of pupils 33; *(full boarding)* 33; *Girls* 8; *Boys* 25

Our education philosophy is founded on teaching disabled children and young adults to use communication techniques to develop skills that they will use in adult life. Our school, based in Cambridgeshire, welcomes pupils on a day, weekly or full board basis who have a statement of special needs. We offer a creative approach to a multi-sensory curriculum, which promotes the child's physical, social, emotional and intellectual development which are addressed simultaneously through a range of therapies including: speech and language therapy, occupational therapy, physiotherapy, music therapy and imaginative use of ICT. Read Suzanne Little, specialist teacher at Meldreth, on multi-sensory environments.

SENAD Group

Alderwasley Hall School and Callow Park College

Alderwasley, Belper, Derbyshire DE56 2SR
T: (01629) 822586 **F**: (01629) 826661 **E**: info@alderwasleyhall.com **W**: www.alderwasleyhall.com
Please contact the School directly or SENAD Group central office on Tel:01332 378840

Head Teacher Mrs Angela Findlay NPQH MEd Cert Ed
School status Co-educational residential and day
Religious denomination Non-denominational
Member of NAHT, NAS, NASS
Special needs provision ADD, ADHD, **ASD**, **ASP**, **CB**, **DYC**, **DYP**, DYS, EPI, HEA, HI, SP&LD, VI
Age range 5–19

We provide day and 38–52 week residential education placements for young people with Autism, Asperger's Syndrome and specific language disorders, all of whom experience complex speech, language and communication needs (SLCN).

We provide a broad and balanced curriculum, along with programmes to develop students' life skills. We support students' development in speech and language, thinking and reasoning, self confidence and independence and operate an interdisciplinary model of working. This model enables the identification of the optimum teaching methods, environments and therapies to meet students' needs. As well as qualified Teachers, Care Managers and Support Assistants our interdisciplinary staff team includes a large number of Speech and Language Therapists and Occupational Therapists. Therapists work closely with Teachers, Parents and Key Care Workers (residential placements) and assess and prepare targeted intervention plans for each student. This plan includes one to one, paired and group sessions as appropriate to meet students' needs. They also provide class support where necessary.

Aran Hall School

Rhydymain, Dolgellau, Gwynedd LL40 2AR
T: (01341) 450641 **F**: (01341) 450637 **E**: info@aranhall.com **W**: www.aranhall.com
Please contact the school directly or call SENAD Group central office on Tel: 01332 378840

Principal Mr Duncan Pritchard Cert Ed Dip App SS BSc(Hons) MSc(Psych) MSc(ABA)
School status Co-educational residential
We provide 38 to 52 week residential care with education to children and young people with a range of learning disabilities and autistic spectrum disorders both with associated severe challenging behaviour.
Religious denomination Non-denominational
Member of BILD, NASS
Special needs provision ADD, ADHD, ASD, ASP, BESD, CB, CP, DOW, DYC, DYP, EPI, HEA, HI, IM, MLD, PMLD, SLD, SP&LD, **TOU**
Age range 11–19

We provide residential care with education to students with a range of learning difficulties and autism, both with associated severe challenging behaviour. We use evidence-based practices, which improve psychological wellbeing, independence and educational ability. Our education, care and behavioural management programmes follow these evidence-based practice models, enabling us to demonstrate students' achievements. To enable students to access education we have a behavioural management programme developed by our Consultant Psychologist. Students receive an individualized education plan. ASDAN qualifications are the main focus of the curriculum. Students are taught in small groups by qualified Teachers and Assistants. Teaching is divided into formal classroom settings and community-based activities. Post16 students are encouraged to attend college to experience an educational setting outside the school.

Bladon House School

Newton Solney, Burton upon Trent, Staffordshire DE15 0TA
T: (01283) 563787 **F**: (01283) 510980 **E**: info@bladonhouse.com **W**: www.bladonhouse.com
Please contact the School directly or call SENAD Group central office on Tel:01332 378840

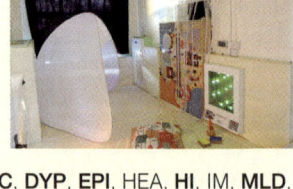

Head Teacher Mrs Kate Britt Cert Ed MA Educ Management
School status Co-educational residential and day
Bladon House School specializes in moderate to severe learning difficulties, autism, speech and language disorders and associated behavioural difficulties. We work with students aged 5 to 19 years and offer day and residential placement options.
Religious denomination Non-denominational
Member of BILD, EQUALS, NAHT, NAS, NASS
Special needs provision ADD, ADHD, ASD, ASP, BESD, **CB**, CP, **DOW, DYC, DYP, EPI**, HEA, **HI**, IM, **MLD, PMLD, SLD**, SP&LD, **TOU**
Age range 5–19

Our education provision is rated as 'Outstanding' by Ofsted. Our curriculum is designed to meet the statemented needs of individual students, whilst being based on the National Curriculum. Students study ICT, PE, Music and Food Technology in small class sizes by specialist qualified teachers. There is an emphasis on practical, functional activities incorporating skills for life, enterprise and work related learning. We offer a range of National Framework Accredited courses including NVQ Horticulture, GCSE, Entry Level Qualifications, ASDAN and OCR. The Duke of Edinburgh Award is also an established part of our provision. Our multi-disciplinary team includes experts in Care, Education and Therapy. This team sets targets and identifies progress across academic and non academic areas and is supported by our Behaviour Consultant and Forensic Psychologist.

Pegasus School

Caldwell Hall, Main Street, Caldwell, Derbyshire DE12 6RS
T: (01283) 761352 **F**: (01283) 761312 **E**: info@pegasusschooluk.com **W**: www.pegasusschooluk.com
Please contact the school directly or call SENAD Group central office on Tel:01332 378840

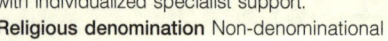

Head Mr Hugh Rodger BEd, Cert Ed in hearing impaired education, MBA in education management
School status Co-educational residential and day
We provide education and care for children and young people between the ages of 8 and 19 years, who have challenging behaviour and complex communication and learning difficulties. We have places for up to 23 students, all of whom are provided with individualized specialist support.
Religious denomination Non-denominational
Member of BILD, EQUALS, NAHT, NAS, NASS
Special needs provision ADD, ADHD, ASD, ASP, BESD, **CB**, DOW, DYP, **EPI, HEA, HI, IM**, MLD, **PMLD, SLD**, SP&LD, **TOU**, VI, WA3
Age range 8–19

We work with students who have Autism, challenging behaviour and severe communication and learning difficulties. An individual education and care programme is developed for each student. This is based on their developmental levels, motivation and understanding and generalization skills and is developed by our multi-disciplinary team. Education, therapy (Speech and Language and Occupational) and care all focus on the development of interactive skills and the self management of behaviours, giving students the ability to communicate effectively and increase their motivation and confidence. This allows them to access the wider curriculum which includes daily living skills, leisure skills, personal care, cognitive and vocational development. We offer accreditation programmes for all students. We have a Health Promotion Manager and access to a Psychologist, Paediatrician and Psychiatrist.

Rowden House School

Rowden, Bromyard, Herefordshire HR7 4LS
T: (01885) 488096 **F**: (01885) 483361 **E**: info@rowdenhouse.com **W**: www.rowdenhouse.com
Please contact the school directly or call SENAD Group central office on Tel: 01332 378840

Head Teacher Mr Ian Gateley NPQH (National Professional Qualification for Head Teachers), BMet (Hons), Metallurgy BA (Hons)
School status Co-educational day and residential
Rowden House School provides individualized care and education programmes for children and young adults aged 11 to 19 years, with severe learning disabilities and challenging behaviour.
Religious denomination Non-denominational
Member of BILD, NASS
Special needs provision ADD, **ADHD**, **ASD**, ASP, **BESD**, **CB**, **CP**, DOW, DYC, DYP, **EPI**, **HEA**, **HI**, IM, **MLD**, **PMLD**, **SLD**, SP&LD, **TOU**, VI
Age range 11–19

We work with young people with severe learning disabilities and challenging behaviour. Our facilities and expertise enable us to guide young people through programmes of formal and informal education and development. We encourage all our students to develop a positive self image, promoting their ability to express their personal preferences through informed choice. This develops confidence, enabling them to realize their full potential and grow into happy and healthy adults. Our approach to education ensures that learning experiences extend beyond the classroom to encompass every opportunity for students to develop to their full potential. Education programmes develop the young person as a whole and help them to reduce their need to use challenging behaviours as a form of communication or as an expression of frustration.

The Trust Centre

c/o Alderwasley Hall School, Alderwasley, Belper, Derbyshire DE56 2SR
T: (01629) 821480 **F**: (01629) 826661 **E**: janetteashworth@thetrustcentre.com **W**: www.thetrustcentre.com
The Trust Centre is an independent unit which shares its site with Alderwasley Hall School.

Principal Ms Angela Findlay NPQH, MEd, Cert Ed
Head of the Trust Centre Mrs Janette Ashworth BA Honours English Literature Post Graduate Certificate in Education, Post Graduate Diploma in Education
Founded 2011
School status Co-educational day and residential
Religious denomination Non-denominational
Special needs provision BESD, **CB**, CP, **EPI**, **HEA**, **HI**, **IM**, SP&LD, VI, W
Age range 9–19

The Trust Centre is a unique education facility offering bespoke programmes which integrate rehabilitation principles into an education curriculum for young people with an acquired brain injury. Following assessment and admission, an individualized programme will be developed for each student. Assessment will be ongoing with short and long term goals established and regularly reviewed. The '24 hour curriculum' model adopted by the Centre means that the interdisciplinary team will ensure that learning and development doesn't stop at the end of the school day. The team includes a Qualified Teacher, Registered Manager, Occupational Therapists and Speech and Language Therapists who work closely together and with the young person to make sure that skills acquired or developed are monitored and extended during social and leisure time.

Stanbridge Earls School

Stanbridge Lane, Romsey, Hampshire SO51 0ZS
T: (01794) 529400 **F**: (01794) 511201 **E**: admin@stanbridgeearls.co.uk **W**: www.stanbridgeearls.co.uk

The Headmaster Mr PJA Trythall BA
Founded 1952
School status Co-educational independent boarding and day
Religious denomination Inter-denominational
Member of BDA, CReSTeD, ISC, SHMIS; **Accredited by** SHMIS
Special needs provision DYC, DYP, DYS, SP&LD
Age range 10–19; *boarders from* 10
No of pupils 192; *(full boarding)* 162; *Senior* 192; *Sixth Form* 45; *Girls* 35;
Boys 157
Teacher:pupil ratio 1:6
Average class size 10

Curriculum: The National Curriculum, up to the end of Key Stage 4, is enhanced by a daily activities programme to develop the strengths and interests of every pupil. Many pupils are dyslexic and all take GCSEs. The school has excellent facilities for all academic subjects and has recently opened a new ICT Cisco academy Media suite, Sports Hall and indoor heated swimming pool. Sixth-formers are offered a wide choice of courses at Advanced level as well as GCSE retakes. The Accelerated Learning Centre, with 16 experienced specialist teachers for those with literacy difficulties, the Mathematics Skills Centre with nine specialist staff, six speech and language specialists, two occupational therapists and two EAL specialists ensure that all pupils get the right level of specialist support.

Leisure: Large sports hall, heated indoor swimming pool, fitness suite, squash court, tennis courts, vehicle engineering workshop and playing fields in over 50 acres of ground.

Entry: Educational psychologist's report, school report, interview.

Registered charity number: 30742.

Symbol key

Gender

● Girls
● Boys
● Coed

CReSTeD

◆ Yes (CReSTeD Registered)

Accommodation

🏠 Boarding only
🏠 Boarding and Day
🏠 Day and Boarding
🏠 Day only

Sunfield School

Clent Grove, Woodman Lane, Stourbridge, West Midlands DY9 9PB
T: (01562) 882253 **F**: (01562) 883856 **E**: sunfield@sunfield.org.uk **W**: www.sunfield.org.uk

●🏠

Principal Mrs Amanda Jones
Founded 1930
School status Co-educational boarding and day
Religious denomination Non-denominational
Member of BILD, EQUALS, NAHT, NASS, NASEN, SCA
Special needs provision ADHD, ASD, CB, SLD
Age range 6–19; *boarders from* 6
No of pupils 65; *(full boarding)* 65; *Girls* 10; *Boys* 55
Teacher:pupil ratio 1:5
Average class size 5

From its pioneering inception in 1930, Sunfield, a registered charity, continues to lead the way in providing the highest quality residential care, education and therapy for children and young people with severe learning needs and Autism Spectrum Disorder.

- Children with severe learning difficulties and Autism Spectrum Disorder.
- Extensive onsite specialist and pioneering facilities.
- Structured teaching, routine and supportive environment.

Our new school buildings and teaching approaches ensure structure, routine and a learning environment in which students truly flourish and achieve. Sunfield's comprehensive 24-hour curriculum approach has inspired others nationally and internationally. Strengths include: 'Small group houses with single bedrooms', 'Personalized development programmes' and 'Outstanding resources'.

Sunfield has ten residential houses, each accommodating six or seven students on the basis of their age and needs. Houses are fully self-contained with their own garden. Each house also has a dedicated team of qualified and experienced staff led by a team leader and every child has their own key worker. Sunfield has numerous facilities within its 58 acre parkland site including: a farm and horticultural areas, nature trails, an adventure playground, a superb sensory integration suite, sensory rooms and outdoor specialist sensory play equipment and trampolines. In nearby towns we access swimming, bowling, cinemas, riding, clubs and other community-based leisure activities. Our fleet of buses, people carriers and cars ensure students' opportunities for community integration are maximized for learning as well as leisure pursuits.

- Comprehensive assessment and planning.
- Total communication approach.
- Integrated occupational, music, play.
- Sensory integration therapy and psychology.

On admission to Sunfield every student undergoes a comprehensive three-month assessment period led by our Therapies Department. Following this assessment we put in place a personalized plan that spans learning, care, therapy and health targets. We meet regularly with families to celebrate achievement and outcomes, review the plan and set new targets.

- Family-centered approach.
- Family accommodation.
- Sibling support programme.

Sunfield offers a real family-focused approach embracing all those who are significant. Sibling events, parent support, training and fantastic family accommodation are all part of the Sunfield offer to support working in partnership. We welcome informal enquiries and do visit our website where you can download or request our prospectus. We also welcome visitors by prior appointment and will enjoy showing you around our great school.

RNIB Sunshine House School and Children's Home

33 Dene Road, Northwood, Middlesex HA6 2DD
T: (01923) 822538 **F**: (01923) 826227 **E**: shsadmin@rnib.org.uk **W**: www.rnib.org.uk/sunshinehouse

Executive Head Teacher Mr John Ayres National Leader of Education (NLE)
Founded 1948
School status Co-educational Non-maintained. Children aged 2 to 11 years
can attend the school. With 30 places available, we support both boys and
girls. Children from the ages of 5 to 14 years can stay overnight Monday to
Thursday for up to 50 weeks per year. Children do not need to attend the
school in order to access the Children's Home facilities.
Religious denomination Non-denominational
Member of EQUALS, NASS, NASEN
Special needs provision CP, EPI, HEA, HI, IM, **PMLD**, **SLD**, SP&LD, **VI**, W
Age range 2–11 Children can stay overnight from aged 5 years.
No of pupils 30 (12 weekly overnight stay places)
Teacher:pupil ratio 2:3 **Average class size** 8

RNIB Sunshine House is a specialist primary school, children's home and service for families in Northwood,
Middlesex.

Located down a leafy private road and set within extensive grounds boasting a range of specialist indoor and
outdoor facilities, Sunshine House provides a safe and supportive environment for blind and partially sighted
children with significant learning difficulties and disabilities to meet their full potential.

Everyone at Sunshine House is treated as an individual with their own set of needs and learning goals. Working
together with parents and specialists we ensure that achievements go beyond the classroom into everyday life.

Our specialist primary school educates blind and partially sighted children with significant learning difficulties
and disabilities between the ages of two and 11 years.

Each class has no more than eight children with a minimum support ratio of two adults for every three children.
Our skilled staff assess each child, delivering tailored programmes matched to their individual needs, interests
and abilities.

Our team of therapists are on hand to provide support both within the classroom and in dedicated sessions
with individuals. Therapies and specialist facilities include speech and language therapy, physiotherapy,
occupational therapy, mobility and orientation training, music and creative therapy, sensory garden and
playground with interactive fountain, hydrotherapy pool, soft play room, library and dark areas in every classroom for visual light training. We also have a paediatric community nurse who visits daily, working with staff to
ensure that all medical needs are met.

Children aged over five can stay with us overnight up to four nights per week (Monday to Thursday) during the
school term and for periods during the school holidays.

Learning and development continue in a relaxed and informal environment, making full use of the school's
facilities. Activities also take place away from Sunshine House within the local community and beyond with
shopping trips, meals out and theatre visits.

In addition to our day staff, waking night staff visit the children every 15 minutes, so you can be sure that your
child is receiving the specialist care needed within a homely environment.

We welcome visits from parents, carers, children, other family members and professionals. You can get in
touch by calling 01923 82 25 38 or e-mailing shsadmin@rnib.org.uk. Alternatively you can find out more and
download our prospectus online at rnib.org.uk/sunshinehouse.

Swalcliffe Park School Trust

Swalcliffe, Banbury, Oxfordshire OX15 5EP
T: (01295) 780302 **F**: (01295) 780006 **E**: admin@swalcliffepark.co.uk **W**: www.swalcliffepark.co.uk

Principal Mr Kiran Hingorani **Founded** 1965
School status Boys' non-maintained boarding and day
Religious denomination Non-denominational
Member of NAHT, NASEN
Special needs provision ADD, ADHD, **ASD**, **ASP**, BESD, CB, DYC, DYP, DYS, MLD, SP&LD, TOU
Age range 11–19; *boarders from* 11
No of pupils 62; *(boarding)* 57; *(full boarding)* 57; *Sixth Form* 4; *Boys* 62
Average class size 6

Swalcliffe Park School is a non-maintained charitable trust providing specialist residential education and care for up to 57 secondary age boys (11-19 years). All students have a diagnosis of Autistic Spectrum Disorder (ASD) – mainly Asperger Syndrome, with many having additional needs arising from other diagnoses including ADHD, Dyslexia, Dyspraxia and language impairment.

Placements are funded by Local Authorities from across the United Kingdom for a 38-week school year and on a two weekly boarding basis.

The school offers a wide range of learning opportunities both within the school day as well as in the evenings and weekends. These are designed to promote academic achievement (through GCSE and other nationally recognized qualifications), social inclusion, independence and personal well-being. The school has strong links with local colleges, community based organizations and a variety of local work experience placements.

In order to support best outcomes for the students, the school has well qualified and trained Teachers, Learning Support Assistants and Residential Care Staff who work collaboratively with a specialist therapeutic team which includes professionals from Speech and Language Therapy, Educational Psychology, Nursing, Psychiatry, Occupational Therapy and Massage Therapy.

Treloar School

London Road, Holybourne, Alton, Hampshire GU34 4EN
T: (01420) 547425 **F**: (01420) 542708 **E**: admissions@treloar.org.uk **W**: www.treloar.org.uk

Treloar's Principal Mrs Amanda Quincey ACiB, MDip, BPhil (Sen), Cert Ed
Vice Principal Mr Tim Harding Msc Ed Certd
School status Co-educational non-maintained boarding and day
Religious denomination Non-denominational
Member of NASS
Special needs provision CP, DYP, DYS, EPI, HEA, HI, IM, MLD, SLD, SP&LD, VI
Age range 9–19; *boarders from* 9
No of pupils 77; *(boarding)* 49; *(full boarding)* 11; *(weekly boarding)* 38; *Girls* 41; *Boys* 36

For over 100 years, Treloar's has offered education, independence training, medical support, therapy and first-class care to young people with physical disabilities. Many students have sensory impairments, communication difficulties and additional learning disabilities. Treloar's offers the full National Curriculum, carefully differentiated according to need. In addition to individual therapy sessions, physiotherapists, speech and language therapists, occupational therapists, assistive technology engineers and technicians work with teachers and care staff to achieve a truly multidisciplinary approach. Students study GCSEs, Entry Level examinations, ASDAN awards, the National Skills Project and ALL (Accreditation for Life and Living Skills), with facilities for sport, music, art and design, and drama. Students are encouraged to develop personal interests and there are extensive off-site trips. Treloar's is flexible and adaptable. FlexiOptions allows the school's resources to be accessed at any time during the individual's 'learner journey', and tailor-made offers can include full-time placement, part-time placement, limited-time placement, short-break packages, seconded services, etc.

The Unicorn School

20 Marcham Road, Abingdon, Oxfordshire OX14 1AA
T: (01235) 530222 **F**: (01235) 536889 **E**: info@unicorndyslexia.co.uk **W**: www.unicorndyslexia.co.uk

Principal Mrs J Vaux
Founded 1991
School status Co-educational
Member of BDA, CReSTeD, The Dyspraxia Foundation
Special needs provision ADD, ADHD, **DYC**, **DYP**, **DYS**, SP&LD
Age range 6–13
No of pupils 67; *Girls* 10; *Boys* 57
Average class size 10

The aims and philosophy of the Unicorn School are to provide specialist education for dyslexic children, from both the independent and the maintained sector, and to teach strategies and skills to enable them to return to mainstream education as soon as possible. A structured, multi-sensory programme, including an appropriately differentiated National Curriculum, is followed with extensive use of word processors and encouragement to develop creative talents. Educational and emotional needs are met on an individual basis as well as through a friendly atmosphere and community spirit. Close liaison is maintained with the local education authority; parents are supported throughout the time they are associated with the Unicorn and are helped to find suitable schools for their children to move on to.

West Kirby Residential School

Meols Drive, West Kirby, Wirral, Merseyside CH48 5DH
T: (0151) 632 3201 **F**: (0151) 632 0621 **E**: garethwilliams@wkrs.co.uk

Principal Mr G W Williams MEd
Founded 1881
School status Co-educational non-maintained boarding and day
Religious denomination Non-denominational
Member of BILD, NAHT
Special needs provision ADD, **ADHD**, **ASD**, **ASP**, **BESD**, **CB**, DYP,
DYS, EPI, HI, MLD, SP&LD, TOU, VI
Age range 5–18; *boarders from 6*
No of pupils 91; *(weekly boarding)* 12; *(flexible boarding)* 14; *(primary)*
11; *(secondary)* 62; *(Post-16)* 18; *Girls* 12; *Boys* 79
Average class size 8

The school's priority is to provide a structured, supportive and controlled learning environment for each pupil. By actively encouraging children to develop their inner control and social skills, staff can help them to overcome their own individual behavioural difficulties. Pupils are able to learn and grow in situations that will help them achieve their maximum potential. Specially trained staff assist pupils in developing an awareness both of themselves as individuals and within a group, increasing their own respect for others, their self-esteem, emotional stability and acceptability. Young people at WKRS are continually presented with a wide range of challenges, in education and life skills, to help nurture their unique talents and prepare them for adult life. The school is located on the Wirral Peninsula in a pleasant residential area about 200 yards from the beach, with access to a range of outdoor and cultural pursuits in nearby Chester, Liverpool and North Wales.

Cedar House School

Cedar House School, Cumbria
Complex learning needs with challenging behaviour
Mixed, ages 7-16 years, Residential & Day School
Tel: 01524 271181

Lakeside School

Lakeside School, Liverpool
Complex learning and communication needs with
challenging behaviour
Mixed, ages 5-13 years, Day School
Tel: 0151 4877211

Chilworth House School

Chilworth House School, Oxford
Complex learning and communication needs with
challenging behaviour
Mixed, ages 5-11 years, Day School
Tel: 01844 339077

Pontville School

Pontville School, Ormskirk
Speech, language and social communication impairment
Mixed, ages 5-19 years, Residential & Day School
Tel: 01695 578734

Chilworth House Upper School

Chilworth House Upper School, Oxford
Complex learning and communication needs with
challenging behaviour
Mixed, ages 11-16 years, Day School
Tel: 01844 337720

Westmorland School

Westmorland School, Chorley
Behavioural, emotional and social difficulties with associated
learning needs
Mixed, ages 5-11 years, Day School
Tel: 01257 278899

Cumberland School

Cumberland School, Preston
Behavioural, emotional and social difficulties with associated
learning needs
Mixed, ages 11-16 years, Day School
Tel: 01772 284435

Witherslack Hall School

Witherslack Hall School, Cumbria
Complex learning needs with challenging behaviour
Boys, ages 11-19 years, Residential & Day School
Tel: 015395 52397

Belle Vue House
Assessment & Development Centre

Belle Vue House Assessment
& Development Centre
Independent assessment and development centre
for individuals with communication difficulties
or Autism Spectrum Disorders
Tel: 01695 578558

Witherslack Care & Education Initiatives
52-week care, education and therapy
Mixed, ages 9-18 years
Tel: 0844 8806520

For information please contact individual establishment or visit
www.witherslackgroup.co.uk

Witherslack Group

Witherslack Group

Cedar House School

Kendal Road, Kirkby Lonsdale, via Carnforth, Lancashire LA6 2HW
T: (01524) 271181 **F**: (01524) 271910 **E**: schooloffice@cedarhouseadmin.co.uk
W: www.cedarhouseschool.co.uk

Cedar House School

Headteacher Mrs G Ridgway BEd ALCM
Founded 1976
School status Co-educational prep and senior boarding and day
Member of NAHT, NASS, NASEN
Special needs provision ADD, ADHD, ASD, ASP, **BESD**, **CB**, CP, DYC, DYP, DYS, EPI, HEA, MLD, SP&LD, TOU
Age range 7–16; *boarders from* 7
No of pupils 74; *(boarding)* 58; *(weekly boarding)* 58; *Prep* 20; *Senior* 54; *Girls* 24; *Boys* 50
Teacher:pupil ratio 1:8 **Average class size** 8

Cedar House is a 38 week residential and day special school, which caters for boys and girls between the ages of 7–16. The school provides pupils with a safe, secure and caring environment, within which personal growth and development is promoted. 52 week care provision is available via local Witherslack Care Children's Homes.

Specialist facilities

We have excellent amenities, including a separate primary teaching base with well-equipped specialist facilities for science, information technology, art and craft.

Support services provided

Each class group has a class tutor who is available to discuss individual education related issues. Class tutors also give feedback to pupils about their behaviour and their grades each week. All pupils have a Keyworker, and the opportunity for regular timetabled one-to-one sessions when individual concerns and difficulties can be discussed and personal success can be celebrated. The school has a permanent Educational Psychologist who provides support and advice to pupils and staff regarding a wide range of issues including behaviour management, classroom organization and specific requirements for individual pupils. There is access to a Speech and Language Therapist and a School Mental Health Worker, who is linked to the Morecambe Bay Primary Health Care Trust CAMHS Service, and a psychotherapist who works with individual pupils on a weekly basis. The school has excellent links with psychiatrists having clinical responsibility for pupils who receive medication.

Home school links

Parents are welcome and are encouraged to attend school events. Home visits by the Pastoral Care Manager and other contacts are arranged to help develop a mutually supportive link.

General environment

Cedar House was originally a small mansion house to which has been added purpose-built dining, assembly, teaching and residential units. The school is situated close to the centre of Kirkby Lonsdale, an old market town within easy reach of the Yorkshire Dales and the Lake District.

Aims and philosophy

Cedar House School is committed to providing quality care and education, creating an environment to foster resilience, ensure success and provide opportunities for achievement, enabling every child over time to reach their potential as responsible citizens. The social and educational curriculum has been adapted to interest pupils, capture their imagination and enable them to reinforce their learning in realistic settings. A focus on active learning along with the excellent use of local community facilities brings the curriculum to life. The School provides access to the National Curriculum and a range of external exams are offered at GCSE and entry level. Cedar House School is rated as an outstanding provider by Ofsted.

Staff qualification and selection

All staff are recruited through a high quality selection procedure and their suitability checked through the Criminal Records Bureau at Enhanced Level.

Chilworth House School

Thame Road, Wheatley, Oxford, Oxfordshire OX33 1JP
T: (01844) 339077 **F**: (01844) 339088 **E**: admin@chilworthhouseschool.com
W: www.chilworthhouseschool.com

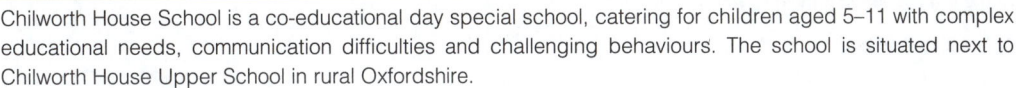
Chilworth House School

Principal Mr R Marchbank
Head Teacher Mrs S N Garner B Ed (Hons), M Ed (Oxon), NPQH
School status Co-educational
Member of NAHT, NASS, SEBDA
Special needs provision ADD, ADHD, ASD, ASP, BESD, CB, DYS, MLD
Age range 5–14
No of pupils 42; *Prep* 24; *Senior* 18; *Boys* 42
Average class size 6

Chilworth House School is a co-educational day special school, catering for children aged 5–11 with complex educational needs, communication difficulties and challenging behaviours. The school is situated next to Chilworth House Upper School in rural Oxfordshire.

Special needs catered for

Pupils will primarily have needs associated with complex educational needs, communication difficulties and challenging behaviours.

Specialist facilities

Our high quality provision comprises of classrooms, therapy/1:1 rooms, quiet areas, library area, hall, dining hall and outside facilities including an all-weather pitch. The school is well resourced and modern technology is used to enhance the pupils' education. Each classroom has an interactive whiteboard and we have a suite of laptop computers and wireless access throughout the building. Chilworth House is a Forest Schools site.

Support services provided

We receive regular input from visiting therapists and an Educational Psychologist.

Home school links

Parents are welcome and are encouraged to attend school events. Home visits and other contacts are arranged to help develop a mutually supportive link.

General environment

The school benefits from 3.24 acres of grounds, situated in a rural environment near Oxford which enhances our educational opportunities.

Aims and philosophy

We are committed to providing a happy, welcoming and motivating learning environment where the whole school enjoy their learning experiences and are encouraged to achieve their potential. As a school we have put in place a curriculum model which offers pupils' a broad, balanced, relevant and differentiated curriculum that has 'values education' and the development of social and emotional skills at its core. Our curriculum aims to be relevant, improve self-esteem, foster motivation and achievement, develop skills for adult life and engage pupils in their learning. This is achieved through cross-curricular learning which helps pupils to make links across the subjects. Regular offsite visits support the curriculum model. At Chilworth House School we place a strong emphasis on establishing stable and trusting relationships between pupils and staff, offering support to both pupils and parents at school and at home.

Staff qualification and selection

All staff are recruited through a high quality selection procedure and their suitability is checked through the Criminal Records Bureau at Enhanced Level.

Chilworth House Upper School

Grooms Farm, Thame Road, Wheatley, Oxfordshire OX33 1JP
T: (01844) 337720 **F**: (01844) 734927 **E**: admin.upper@chilworthhouseschool.com
W: www.witherslackgroup.co.uk

Principal Mr B Marchbank
Head Teacher Mr Kevin Larsen
School status Co-educational
Member of NASS
Special needs provision ADD, ADHD, ASD, ASP, BESD, CB, DYS, MLD
Age range 11–16
No of pupils 36

Chilworth House Upper School is a co-educational day special school, catering for children aged 11–16 with complex educational needs, communication difficulties and challenging behaviours. The school situated next to Chilworth House School in rural Oxfordshire.

Specialist Facilities

Our high quality provision comprises of classrooms, Science, Design Technology, Art and therapy/1:1 rooms, and outside facilities including bike track and forest schools. The school is well resourced and modern technology is used to enhance the pupils' education. Each classroom has an interactive whiteboard.

Support services provided

We receive regular input from visiting therapists and an Educational Psychologist.

Home school links

At Chilworth House Upper School we place a strong emphasis on establishing stable and trusting relationships between pupils and staff, offering support to both pupils and parents at school and at home. Parents are welcome and are encouraged to attend school events. Home visits and other contacts are arranged to help develop a mutually supportive link.

General environment

Situated in a rural environment near Oxford, the fantastic school grounds enhance educational opportunities for the pupils.

Aims and philosophy

At Chilworth House Upper School we are committed to providing a happy, welcoming and motivating learning environment where the whole school enjoy their learning experiences and are encouraged to achieve their potential.

As a school we have put in place a curriculum model that offers pupils a broad, balanced, relevant and differentiated curriculum that has 'values education' and the development of social and emotional skills at its core.

Our curriculum aims to be relevant, improve self-esteem, motivation and achievement, develop skills for adult life and engage pupils in their learning. This is achieved through cross-curricular learning which helps pupils to make links across the subjects. Regular offsite visits support the curriculum model.

Staff qualification and selection

All staff are recruited through a high quality selection procedure and their suitability is checked through the Criminal Records Bureau at Enhanced Level.

Cumberland School

Cumberland School

Church Road, Bamber Bridge, Preston, Lancashire PR5 6EP
T: (01772) 284435 **F**: (01772) 338136 **E**: office@cumberlandschool.co.uk **W**: www.cumberlandschool.co.uk

Head Teacher David Barden M.Ed DASE (SEN) Cert. Ed
School status Co-educational prep and senior
Member of NASS
Special needs provision ADHD, ASP, **BESD**, MLD
Age range 11–16

Cumberland School is a day school for girls and boys aged 11–16 who have behavioural, emotional, social and associated learning difficulties, which can hinder their academic progress. The school aims to provide a quality secondary curriculum to young people who need a more specialized environment in order to meet their potential academic and social development.

Specialist facilities

All pupils are taught in small class groups, which together with a high staff:pupil ratio, ensures their educational progress and personal development. There is continual use of information and communication technology across the curriculum, with the latest specification computers and interactive whiteboards in many of the classrooms. The pupils' use of ICT is encouraged in all aspects of school life, and the excellent modern facilities for Design Technology, Food Technology, Art, and Science are amongst the best in secondary schools of this type.

Support services provided

Through the BEST curriculum our young people receive regular one-to-one support from experienced pastoral staff. Pupils with specific difficulties and those with delayed literacy and numeracy benefit from individual tuition and support. As a staff team with a wealth of experience and qualifications and the input from our own educational psychologist, councillor, speech and language and occupational therapist, we are able to provide comprehensive individual programmes which run alongside class teaching to help our pupils.

Home school links

The Pastoral Care system is a major strength of the school. A team of four highly experienced staff support the pupils both inside and outside the classroom, and close liaison between school and the pupils' homes is a central feature of the care and welfare provided by the school.

General environment

The school is ideally located in Bamber Bridge, at the junctions of the M6, M61 and the M65. The main part of the school is a Grade II listed building, whilst the new classroom areas are modern, bright, air-conditioned and well-equipped. Opened in April 2008, Cumberland School (Bamber Bridge) along with Westmorland School (Chorley) and Cumberland Upper (Blackburn) is part of the Witherslack Group's South Lancashire cluster of schools. The cluster offers continuous education for day pupils from 5 through to 16, including children and young people who are residents within Witherslack Children's Homes.

Aims and philosophy

The school prides itself in providing the highest levels of education, care, supervision and support for its pupils, based on the theory of 'Resilience' and on the school's motto, which is simply: 'Respect'. At Cumberland School, we support children in their developmental and social progress, as well as their academic achievements. The key to a young person's success at school is enjoyment in their education. Cumberland School provides a happy and caring environment in which achievements are recognized and rewarded, and in which each student is encouraged to feel a positive sense of belonging. Students are constantly encouraged to meet and overcome challenges and to reach their maximum potential.

Staff qualification and selection

All staff are recruited through a high quality selection procedure and their suitability is checked through the Criminal Records Bureau at Enhanced Level.

Special Schools and Colleges – Independent and Non-Maintained

Lakeside School

Lakeside School

Naylors Road, Liverpool, Merseyside L27 2YA
T: (0151) 487 7211 **F**: (0151) 487 7214 **E**: admin@lakesideschool.uk.com **W**: www.lakesideschool.co.uk

Headteacher Mrs V I Size BEd (Hons)
School status Co-educational day only
Member of NASS
Special needs provision ADD, **ADHD**, **ASD**, **ASP**, BESD, **CB**, DOW, **DYC**, **DYP**, **DYS**, EPI, HEA, HI, IM, MLD, SP&LD, TOU, VI
Age range 5–13
No of pupils 22; *Girls* 4; *Boys* 18
Teacher:pupil ratio 1:3 **Average class size** 6

Lakeside School caters for children aged 5–13 with complex learning and communication difficulties. The school adopts a holistic approach towards children and provides a high level of quality education within a broad, balanced and stimulating curriculum, promoting the spiritual, moral, cultural, mental and physical development of the pupils.

Special needs catered for
Key Stage 1, 2 and in some cases Key Stage 3 pupils who exhibit complex learning and communication difficulties with associated challenging behaviours.

Specialist facilities
The school offers full access to the National Curriculum, differentiated and modified where appropriate. The school is particularly well resourced and all classrooms have access to the very latest technology, including interactive whiteboards.

Support services provided
A resident clinical team with access to therapeutic services, including educational psychology, occupational therapy and speech and language therapy.

Home school links
The Pastoral Care of all children at Lakeside School is within the supervision of the Deputy Head, Head of Pastoral Care who maintains a close liaison with parents and other primary carers as well as statutory authorities.

General environment
The school is situated in a rural environment on the outskirts of Liverpool within a few minutes of the major motorway junction between the M57 and M62. The building is a converted farmhouse and is located within attractive grounds including a lake, which can be used for educational purposes.

Aims and philosophy
In partnership with parents/carers and Children's Services Authorities we aim:
1. To strive for the highest quality of education and care through which every child will achieve their full potential, both academically and personally.
2. To provide a happy, secure and caring environment where children are valued equally and can develop their confidence and self-esteem, independence, self discipline and respect and concern for others.
3. To offer a broad, balanced and stimulating curriculum, that meets the individual needs of each child.
4. To develop positive links between home, school and the wider community in order to support children's learning.
5. To encourage the development of teaching and non-teaching staff, enabling them to work together as a team, sharing expertise and valuing each other's strengths.

Staff qualification and selection
The staff are recruited from mainstream and special education. All teachers are well qualified and experienced, and all staff are encouraged to develop professionally. The school has established an excellent reputation and a recent Ofsted inspection reported extremely favourably upon the quality of teaching and learning. The welfare, health and safety of pupils was judged to be outstanding as was their spiritual, moral, social and cultural development.

Pontville School

Black Moss Lane, Ormskirk, Lancashire L39 4TW
T: (01695) 578734 **F**: (01695) 579224 **E**: office@pontville.co.uk **W**: www.pontville.co.uk

Pontville School

Head Mr I Sim BSc PGCE MEd ToD
School status Co-educational boarding and day
Religious denomination Non-denominational
Member of NASS
Special needs provision ADD, ADHD, **ASD**, **ASP**, DYP, EPI, HEA, MLD, SP&LD
Age range 5–19; *boarders from* 5
Teacher:pupil ratio 1:2
Average class size 4

Pontville School is a co-educational day and residential school for children and young people between the ages of 7–19. The specialized school meets the needs of pupils who have a range of Social Communication Difficulties and associated learning difficulties. 52 week care provision is available via local Witherslack Care Children's Homes.

Specialist facilities

The full National Curriculum is offered through uniquely modified schemes of work delivered by specialist teachers in specialized accommodation. The school has specifically resourced areas for ICT, Science, Home Economics, Physical Education, Vocational Subjects and Functional Skills. Pontville also has a College Unit offering a vocational curriculum for students aged 14–19. Courses include basic education, social and life skills, woodwork, construction, catering, vehicle maintenance, animal husbandry, horticultural studies and IT. Accreditation includes Entry Level Certification, NVQ and BTEC.

Support services provided

All young people at the school have a keyworker. This is a personally identified member of staff who works with the young person on individual targets and programmes. The school places an emphasis on the development of social communication skills across its curriculum. It provides highly differentiated schemes of work for pupils with communication deficit and associated complex needs. It also provides additional therapy input in Speech and Language, Educational Psychology, Occupational Therapy, Music and Play, based on identified need.

Home school links

Parents are welcome and are encouraged to attend school events. Home visits by the Pastoral Care Manager and other contacts are arranged to help develop a mutually supportive link.

General environment

The school is located in the historic market town of Ormskirk in Lancashire. This gives the school excellent links for activities during the day and the evening, enabling us to integrate and include our young people into the wider community.

Aims and philosophy

Pontville School is rated as Outstanding in all areas of its provision by Ofsted (2009). The School has a long and successful history of providing support for children with special educational needs. Accreditation includes Life Skills Certification, Entry Level Awards and GCSE's.

Staff qualification and selection

All staff are recruited through a high quality selection procedure and their suitability checked through the Criminal Records Bureau at Enhanced Level.

Westmorland School

Weldbank Lane, Chorley, Lancashire PR7 3NQ
T: (01257) 278899 **F**: (01257) 265505 **E**: office@westmorlandschool.co.uk
W: www.westmorlandschool.co.uk

●🏠

Westmorland School

Head Teacher Mrs S M Asher BSc Hons, PGCE, NPQH   **Founded** 2000
School status Co-educational day
Religious denomination Non-denominational
Member of NASS, NASEN
Special needs provision BESD
Age range 5–11 (32 Day pupils, co-educational); *Prep* 32
Teacher:pupil ratio 1:3 **Average class size** 8

Westmorland School is a co-educational day special school for children aged 5–11 with behavioural, emotional and social difficulties (BSED), communication difficulties and various other special educational needs.

Specialist facilities

All pupils are taught in small class groups, which together with a high staff:pupil ratio, ensures their educational progress and personal development. The warm, stimulating and caring environment includes a dedicated therapy room.

Support services provided

Children receive high standards of support and care, through our well structured day equipping them with the skills to succeed, building their self esteem and confidence. Our qualified and dedicated staff team support pupil's needs, using continuous assessment and supportive advice from our multi disciplinary professionals. We have the support of two Educational Psychologists, a Psychotherapist, a Speech and Language Therapist and we are currently offering Art Psychotherapy. The majority of our Year 6 pupils take the SATS tests and achieve results which are comparable with mainstream schools.

Home school links

Parents are welcome and are encouraged to attend school events. Home visits by the Pastoral Care Manager and other contacts are arranged to help develop a mutually supportive link.

General environment

We are situated central to Chorley, Lancashire with easy access to the M6, M61 and the M65.

Children attend from a wide radius of home destinations. Westmorland School (Chorley), along with Cumberland School (Bamber Bridge) and Cumberland Upper (Blackburn) is part of the Witherslack Group's South Lancashire cluster of schools. The cluster offers continuous education for day pupils from 5 through to 16, including children and young people who are resident with in Witherslack Children's homes.

Aims and philosophy

Westmorland School is a creative, innovative learning environment where children are given the opportunities to successfully engage in their education. The School vision statement is: "*We learn to live together, together we live to learn*" and there is a pleasant, caring and purposeful working atmosphere where pupils feel confident to ask questions. We provide a broad and balanced curriculum with opportunities for enrichment activities through lunchtime clubs, which include badminton, craft club, gardening club, visits and field trips, off-site activities such as trampolining and swimming lessons.

Staff qualification and selection

All staff are recruited through a high quality selection procedure and their suitability checked through the Criminal Records Bureau at Enhanced Level.

Witherslack Hall

Witherslack, Grange-over-Sands, Cumbria LA11 6SD
T: (01539) 552397 **F**: (01539) 552419 **E**: admin@whs.uk.com
W: www.witherslackhallschool.co.uk

Witherslack Hall School

Headteacher Mrs Tina McIntosh MBA
School status Boys' boarding only
Member of NASS, NASEN, SEBDA
Special needs provision ADD, ADHD, ASD, ASP, BESD, CB, DYP, DYS, MLD, SP&LD
Age range 11–19
No of pupils 72; *(full boarding)* 72; *Boys* 72

Witherslack Hall School is a well established and highly effective independent 38 week residential and day school. The school caters for boys, aged 11–19, who have complex learning needs and challenging behaviour. We aim to develop resilience in our young people through teaching the skills of emotional literacy and through building confidence, self-esteem and trust within a supportive environment. 52 week care provision is available via local Witherslack Care Children's Homes.

Specialist facilities

All areas of the National Curriculum are taught within specialist areas. A range of vocational subjects are offered by specialist instructors including Motor Vehicle Engineering, construction and Environmental Studies. Residential provision provides high quality independent living areas within the school grounds. All rooms are furnished and decorated to a high standard. The school offers higher dependency provision both educationally and residentially for a variety of complex needs.

Support services provided

Witherslack Hall School provides the services of an onsite school nurse, speech and language therapist, educational psychologist and counsellor-psychotherapist. A 'Buddy System' is also provided for new boys starting at Witherslack Hall.

Home school links

Parents are always welcome and are encouraged to attend school events. Home visits and other contacts are arranged to help develop a mutually supportive link. Weekend leave patterns are negotiable.

General environment

The school is located in a mansion house which was built as a hunting lodge in 1874, and is situated between the Lakeland Villages of Witherslack and Bowland Bridge. It has extensive playing fields, woodlands and a fishing lake.

School ethos

The overall ethos of the school is geared towards providing a safe, secure and caring environment within which personal growth and development is promoted. Opportunities to experience success, learn from mistakes, and build trusting relationships serve to enhance confidence and self-esteem. Extensive individual programmes are provided within education and care, which allows this ethos to be implemented. The school offers an extensive range of nationally recognised academic and vocational qualifications and a high quality activity programme catering for a variety of needs.

Staff qualifications and selection

All staff are recruited through a high quality selection procedure and their suitability checked through the Criminal Records Bureau. All care staff are supported through their NVQL3 Caring for Children and Young People. Ongoing staff training occurs weekly and staff are encouraged to further their knowledge and skills.

2.4

Directory of Colleges and Other Special Provision at 16+

England

BERKSHIRE

PRIOR'S COURT COTTAGES*
Prior's Court Foundation,
Thatcham, Berkshire RG18 9NU
Website: www.priorscourt.org.uk
Type: Mixed Residential and Day
16–25
Special needs: ADD ADHD ASD
CB EPI MLD SLD SP&LD W
Independent Special
52-week care

BRISTOL

CINTRE COMMUNITY
54 St John's Road, Bristol
BS8 2HG
Type: Mixed Residential Only
16–35
Special needs: ASD BESD DOW
DYS EPI MLD

CAMBRIDGESHIRE

SENSE EAST
72 Church Street, Peterborough,
Cambridgeshire PE6 8AL
Type: Mixed Residential Only
Special needs: **HI** MLD PMLD
SLD VI
Wheelchair access: W

CHESHIRE

BRIDGE COLLEGE
Curzon Road, Stockport,
Cheshire SK2 5DG
Website: www.bgws.org.uk
Type: Mixed Day Only 16–23
Special needs: ADD ADHD **ASD**
ASP BESD CB CP DOW EPI HEA
HI IM MLD PMLD **SLD** SP&LD VI
Wheelchair access: WA2

CUMBRIA

**LINDETH COLLEGE OF
FURTHER EDUCATION**
The Oaks, Bowness-on-
Windermere, Cumbria LA23 3NH
Type: Mixed Residential and Day
16–25
Special needs: ADD ADHD ASD
ASP DOW DYS EPI HI **MLD** SLD
SP&LD VI
Wheelchair access: WA2
Independent Special

DEVON

EXETER COLLEGE
Hele Road, Exeter, Devon
EX4 4JS
Type: Mixed Day Only
Special needs: ADD ADHD ASD
ASP BESD CP DOW DYC DYP
DYS EPI HI MLD SLD SP&LD
TOU VI
Wheelchair access: W

**EXETER ROYAL ACADEMY
FOR DEAF EDUCATION**
50 Topsham Road, Exeter, Devon
EX2 4NF
Website: www.
exeterdeafacademy.ac.uk
Type: Mixed Residential and Day
5–23
Special needs: ADHD ASD ASP
BESD CP DYS EPI **HI** IM MLD
SLD SP&LD VI W
Wheelchair access: WA2
Non-maintained

**EXETER ROYAL ACADEMY
FOR DEAF EDUCATION**
FE College, Exeter, Devon
EX2 4NF
Website: www.
exeterdeafacademy.ac.uk
Type: Mixed Day and Residential
16–25
Special needs: ADHD ASD BESD
EPI **HI** SLD SP&LD VI
Wheelchair access: WA2
Independent Special

OAKWOOD COURT
7–9 Oak Park Villas, Dawlish,
Devon EX7 0DE
Website: www.
oakwoodcourtcollege.co.uk
Type: Mixed Residential Only
16–25
Special needs: ADHD ASD ASP
BESD CP DOW DYP DYS EPI
MLD SLD SP&LD TOU
Wheelchair access: W

RNIB MANOR HOUSE
Middle Lincombe Road, Torquay,
Devon TQ1 2NG
Type: Mixed Residential and Day
Special needs: CP DYS EPI HI VI
Wheelchair access: W

THE WEST OF ENGLAND COLLEGE FOR STUDENTS WITH LITTLE OR NO SIGHT
Countess Wear, Exeter, Devon
EX2 6HA
Type: Mixed Residential and Day
16–22
Special needs: MLD VI
Wheelchair access: W

DORSET

FORTUNE CENTRE OF RIDING THERAPY
Avon Tyrrell, Christchurch,
Dorset BH23 8EE
Website: www.fortunecentre.org
Type: Mixed Residential Only
16–25
Special needs: ADD ADHD ASP
BESD CB CP DOW DYP EPI HI
MLD SP&LD VI
Wheelchair access: W

IVERS INCLUSIVE LEARNING PROJECT
Hains Lane, Sturminster Newton,
Dorset DT10 1JU
Type: Mixed Day and Residential
18–40
Special needs: ASD BESD CB
DOW EPI **MLD** SLD SP&LD
Wheelchair access: WA2
52-week care

THE WING CENTRE*
126 Richmond Park Road,
Bournemouth, Dorset BH8 8TH
Website: www.cambiangroup.
com
Type: Boys Residential and Day
16–19 (Boys 16–19 years)
Special needs: **ASP** CB DYC
DYP DYS EPI HEA SP&LD
Independent Special

COUNTY DURHAM

FINCHALE TRAINING COLLEGE
Durham, County Durham
DH1 5RX
Website: www.finchalecollege.
co.uk
Type: Mixed Residential and Day
Special needs: ASP CP DYC DYP
DYS EPI HEA HI MLD VI
Wheelchair access: WA1

ESSEX

HOPEWELL SCHOOL
Harmony House, Essex RM9 6XN
Type: 11–16
Special needs: BESD MLD
Independent Special

GLOUCESTERSHIRE

NATIONAL STAR COLLEGE
Ullenwood Manor, Cheltenham,
Gloucestershire GL53 9QU
Website: www.natstar.ac.uk
Type: Mixed Residential and Day
16–25
Special needs: ASP **CP** DYP EPI
HEA PMLD SP&LD VI
Wheelchair access: WA1

HAMPSHIRE

ENHAM
Andover, Hampshire SP11 6JS
Website: www.enham.org.uk
Type: Mixed Residential and Day
Special needs: ASD CP DYP DYS
EPI MLD SP&LD
Wheelchair access: WA1
52-week care

TRELOAR COLLEGE*
London Road, Hampshire
GU34 4EN
Website: www.treloar.org.uk
Type: Mixed Residential and Day
16–25
Special needs: **CP** DYP DYS EPI
HEA HI IM MLD SLD SP&LD VI
Wheelchair access: WA1
Non-maintained

HEREFORDSHIRE

**THE ROYAL NATIONAL
COLLEGE FOR THE BLIND
(RNCB)***
College Road, Hereford,
Herefordshire HR1 1EB
Website: www.rncb.ac.uk
Type: Mixed Residential and Day
16–65
Special needs: ASP AUT BESD
CP DYC DYP DYS EPI HEA HI IM
MLD SP&LD TOU **VI**+

KENT

DORTON COLLEGE OF FURTHER EDUCATION
Royal London Society for the Blind, Sevenoaks, Kent TN15 0AH
Website: www.rlsb.org.uk
Type: Mixed Residential and Day
Special needs: MLD VI
Wheelchair access: WA1
Independent Special

NASH COLLEGE OF FURTHER EDUCATION
Croydon Road, Bromley, Kent BR2 7AG
Website: www.nash.ac.uk
Type: Mixed Residential and Day 16–25
Special needs: **CP** DOW DYP DYS EPI HEA HI IM **PMLD** SLD SP&LD VI
Wheelchair access: W

SHALOM PLACE
Hawthorne Farm, West Kingsdown, Kent TN15 6YA
Website: www.shalomplace.co.uk
Type: Mixed 8–16
Special needs: ASD **ASP**
Independent Special

WESTGATE COLLEGE FOR DEAF PEOPLE
Westcliff House, Westgate, Kent CT8 8QP
Website: www.westgate-college.org.uk
Type: Mixed Residential and Day 16–25
Special needs: ADD ASD ASP BESD CB DOW DYC DYP DYS EPI HEA **HI** IM MLD PMLD SLD SP&LD TOU VI
Wheelchair access: WA2
52-week care

LANCASHIRE

BEAUMONT COLLEGE OF FURTHER EDUCATION
Slyne Road, Lancaster, Lancashire LA2 6AP
Type: Mixed Residential and Day
Special needs: CP EPI MLD SLD SP&LD

LEICESTERSHIRE

HOMEFIELD RESIDENTIAL COLLEGE
42 St Mary's Road, Loughborough, Leicestershire LE12 7TL
Type: Mixed Residential and Day
Special needs: ASD HI MLD SLD

RNIB COLLEGE LOUGHBOROUGH*
Radmoor Road, Loughborough, Leicestershire LE11 3BS
Website: www.rnibcollege.ac.uk
Type: Mixed Residential and Day 16–63
Special needs: ADD ADHD ASD ASP BESD CB CP DOW DYC DYP DYS EPI HEA HI IM MLD PMLD SLD SP&LD TOU VI
Wheelchair access: WA1
Independent Special

LINCOLNSHIRE

BROUGHTON HOUSE COLLEGE*
Brant Broughton, Lincolnshire
LN5 0SL
Website: www.cambiangroup.
com
Type: Mixed Residential Only
16–25 (Mixed gender 16–25
years)
Special needs: **ASD CB EPI MLD
SLD** SP&LD
52-week care

LINKAGE COLLEGE
Toynton Campus, Spilsby,
Lincolnshire PE23 5AE
Website: www.linkage.org.uk
Type: Mixed Residential and Day
16–25
Special needs: **ADD ADHD ASD
ASP CP DOW** DYP DYS **EPI** HEA
HI MLD SLD SP&LD **TOU** VI
Wheelchair access: WA3

NORTH EAST LINCOLNSHIRE

LINKAGE COLLEGE
Weelsby Campus, Grimsby,
North East Lincolnshire
DN32 9RU
Type: Mixed Residential and Day
16–25
Special needs: ADD ADHD ASD
ASP CP **DOW** DYP DYS EPI HEA
HI **MLD SLD** SP&LD TOU VI
Wheelchair access: W
Independent Special

NORTH LINCOLNSHIRE

AALPS COLLEGE (NORTH)
Winterton Road, Nr Scunthorpe,
North Lincolnshire DN15 0BJ
Website: www.optionsgroup.
co.uk
Type: Mixed Residential Only
16–30
Special needs: ADD ADHD **ASD
ASP** CB EPI HEA HI IM MLD SLD
SP&LD TOU VI
Wheelchair access: W
52-week care

GREATER MANCHESTER

**FOURWAYS ASSESSMENT
UNIT**
Cleworth Hall Lane, Tyldesley,
Greater Manchester M29 8NT
Type: Mixed Residential and Day
18–25
Wheelchair access: W

NORFOLK

EAGLE LIFE COLLEGE
Andrew's Furlong, Banham,
Norfolk NR16 2HH
Website: www.eaglelifecollege.
co.uk
Type: Mixed Residential and Day
19–25
Special needs: ADD ADHD ASD
ASP CB DYP EPI MLD SLD
SP&LD
Wheelchair access: WA2

NORTHAMPTONSHIRE

HILL FARM COLLEGE
CastleCare Education Ltd,
Rothwell, Northamptonshire
NN14 6BQ
Website: www.castlecaregroup.
co.uk
Type: Boys
52-week care

HINWICK HALL COLLEGE
Hinwick, Wellingborough,
Northamptonshire NN29 7JD
Website: www.hinwick.demon.
co.uk
Type: Mixed Residential and Day
16–25
Special needs: ASD CP **DOW** HI
MLD **PMLD SLD** SP&LD
Wheelchair access: WA1

SOLDEN HILL HOUSE
Banbury Road, Daventry,
Northamptonshire NN11 6UA
Type: Mixed Residential Only
Special needs: **MLD**

NORTHUMBERLAND

**DILSTON COLLEGE OF
FURTHER EDUCATION**
Dilston Hall, Corbridge,
Northumberland NE45 5RJ
Type: Mixed Residential and Day
16–25
Special needs: ASD ASP DOW
EPI HI MLD SLD SP&LD

NOTTINGHAMSHIRE

PORTLAND COLLEGE
Nottingham Road, Mansfield,
Nottinghamshire NG18 4TJ
Type: Mixed Residential and Day
16–25
Special needs: CP DYC DYP DYS
EPI HI MLD SP&LD
Wheelchair access: W

OXFORDSHIRE

KINGHAM HILL SCHOOL+
Kingham, Chipping Norton,
Oxfordshire OX7 6TH
Website: www.kingham-hill.oxon.
sch.uk
Type: Mixed Residential and Day
11–18
Special needs: DYC DYP DYS
SP&LD

SHROPSHIRE

DERWEN COLLEGE
Oswestry, Shropshire SY11 3JA
Website: Derwen@enterprise.net
Type: Mixed Residential Only
Special needs: ASP CP DOW
DYS EPI HI MLD SLD SP&LD VI
Wheelchair access: W

FARLEIGH FURTHER EDUCATION COLLEGE CONDOVER
Condover Hall, Shrewsbury,
Shropshire SY5 7HA
Website: www.
farleighcollegecondover@
priorygroup.com
Type: Mixed Residential and Day
14–19
Special needs: ADD ADHD **ASD
ASP** BESD CB MLD
Wheelchair access: WA1
Independent Special

LOPPINGTON HOUSE FURTHER EDUCATION & ADULT CENTRE
Wem, Shropshire SY4 5NF
Website: www.loppingtonhouse.
co.uk
Type: Mixed Residential Only
18–25
Special needs: ASD BESD CP
DOW EPI HI MLD SLD SP&LD VI
Wheelchair access: WA2
52-week care

YOUNG OPTIONS COLLEGE
Lamledge Lane, Shropshire
TF11 8SD
Website: www.optionsgroup.
co.uk
Type: Mixed Residential Only
9–16
Special needs: **BESD**
Wheelchair access: W
Independent Special
52-week care

SOMERSET

LUFTON COLLEGE OF FURTHER EDUCATION
Lufton, Yeovil, Somerset
BA22 8ST
Type: Mixed Residential and Day
16–25
Special needs: MLD SLD
Wheelchair access: WA2

NORTH HILL HOUSE
Fromefield, Frome, Somerset
BA11 2HB
Website: www.nhh4as.co.uk
Type: Boys Residential and Day
7–18
Special needs: **ASD ASP**
Wheelchair access: W
Independent Special

BATH & NORTH EAST SOMERSET

RNID CARE SERVICES
Watery Lane, Bath, Bath & North
East Somerset BA2 1RN
Website: www.rnid.org.uk
Type: Mixed Residential Only
Special needs: HI SP&LD VI
Wheelchair access: W

ROOKERY RADSTOCK
Rookery House, Radstock, Bath
& North East Somerset BA3 3RS
Website: www.priorygroup.com
Type: Mixed Residential Only
18–30
Special needs: ADD ADHD **ASD
ASP** BESD CB
Wheelchair access: WA3
Independent Special
52-week care

STAFFORDSHIRE

STRATHMORE COLLEGE
38/40 Dimsdale Parade,
Staffordshire, Staffordshire
ST5 8BU
Website: www.
strathmoresupportservices.co.uk
Type: Mixed Residential and Day
Special needs: ADD ADHD ASD
ASP BESD DOW DYP EPI **MLD
SLD** SP&LD
Wheelchair access: WA2
52-week care

SURREY

EAGLE HOUSE SCHOOL – SUTTON
95 Brighton Road, Sutton, Surrey
SM2 5SJ
Website: www.eaglehousesutton.
co.uk
Type: Mixed Day Only 11–19
Special needs: ADD ADHD ASD
ASP CB DYP MLD SLD
Wheelchair access: WA3
Independent Special

THE GRANGE CENTRE FOR PEOPLE WITH DISABILITIES
Bookham, Surrey KT23 4DZ
Website: www.grangecentre.
org.uk
Type: Mixed Residential and Day
Special needs: ASD ASP BESD
CP DOW EPI HI MLD SP&LD VI
Wheelchair access: W

QUEEN ELIZABETH'S FOUNDATION
Leatherhead Court, Leatherhead,
Surrey KT22 0BN
Website: www.qef.org.uk
Type: Mixed Residential Only
16–35
Special needs: BESD EPI MLD
SP&LD VI
Wheelchair access: W

SEEABILITY (FORMERLY ROYAL SCHOOL FOR THE BLIND)
SeeAbility House, Epsom, Surrey
KT19 8SQ
Website: www.seeability.org
Type: Mixed Residential and Day
Special needs: BESD CP EPI HI
MLD PMLD SLD VI
Wheelchair access: W

EAST SUSSEX

THE MOUNT CAMPHILL COMMUNITY
Faircrouch Lane, Wadhurst, East
Sussex TN5 6PT
Type: Mixed Residential and Day
10–25
Special needs: ASD ASP BESD
DOW MLD SLD
Wheelchair access: WA3

ROOKERY HOVE
22–24 Sackville Gardens, Hove,
East Sussex BN3 4GH
Type: Mixed Residential Only
18–35
Special needs: ADD ADHD **ASD
ASP** BESD CB
Wheelchair access: WA1
Independent Special
52-week care

TYNE AND WEAR

THORNBECK COLLEGE
14 Thornhill Park, Sunderland,
Tyne and Wear SR2 7LA
Website: www.tawas.org.uk
Special needs: ASD ASP

WEST MIDLANDS

HEREWARD COLLEGE
Bramston Crescent, Coventry,
West Midlands CV4 9SW
Website: www.hereward.ac.uk
Type: Mixed Residential and Day
Special needs: **ASD** ASP CP
DOW DYC DYP DYS EPI HEA HI
MLD SLD SP&LD TOU VI

WILTSHIRE

FAIRFIELD FARM COLLEGE
Dilton Marsh, Westbury, Wiltshire
BA13 4DL
Type: Mixed Residential and Day
16–23
Special needs: ASD ASP DOW
DYP EPI MLD SLD SP&LD

WORCESTERSHIRE

AALPS COLLEGE (MIDLANDS)
Riverside House, Hanley Castle,
Worcestershire WR8 0AD
Website: www.optionsgroup.
co.uk
Type: Mixed Residential Only
16–25
Special needs: ADD ADHD **ASD
ASP** CB EPI HEA HI IM MLD
SP&LD TOU VI
Wheelchair access: W
52-week care

NORTH YORKSHIRE

HENSHAWS COLLEGE
Bogs Lane, Harrogate, North
Yorkshire HG1 4ED
Website: www.henshaws.org.uk/
college
Type: Mixed Residential and Day
Special needs: CP DOW DYP EPI
HI IM **MLD SLD** SP&LD VI
Wheelchair access: WA1
Independent Special

SOUTH YORKSHIRE

DONCASTER COLLEGE FOR THE DEAF*
Leger Way, Doncaster, South Yorkshire DN2 6AY
Website: www.deaf-trust.co.uk
Type: Mixed Residential and Day 16–60
Special needs: ASP **BESD** CP DYS **HI** MLD PMLD SLD SP&LD VI
Wheelchair access: WA1

WEST YORKSHIRE

PENNINE CAMPHILL COMMUNITY
Wood Lane, Wakefield, West Yorkshire WF4 3JL
Website: www.pennine.org.uk
Type: Mixed Residential and Day 16–25
Special needs: ADD ADHD ASD ASP BESD CB CP DOW DYC DYP DYS EPI HEA HI MLD SLD SP&LD VI
Wheelchair access: WA2

SCOTLAND

ABERDEENSHIRE

**EASTER AUGUSTON
TRAINING FARM**
Peterculter, Aberdeen,
Aberdeenshire AB14 0PJ
Website: www.easteranguston.
org
Type: Mixed Residential Only
Special needs: **DOW MLD**
SP&LD

LOTHIAN

RNIB SCOTLAND
Employment and Learning
Centre, Edinburgh, Lothian
EH15 2NJ
Website: www.rnib.org.uk
Type: Mixed Residential and Day
16–65
Special needs: BESD CB DYS
MLD VI
Wheelchair access: W

STIRLING

**CAMPHILL BLAIR DRUMMOND
TRUST**
Blair Drummond House, Stirling,
Stirling FK9 4UT
Website: www.camphill.org.uk
Type: Mixed Residential and Day
16–30
Special needs: ASD **ASP** BESD
CB **DOW** EPI HEA HI MLD PMLD
SLD SP&LD
Wheelchair access: W
52-week care

WALES

BRIDGEND

BRIDGEND COLLEGE
Cowbridge Road, Bridgend,
Bridgend CF31 3DH
Website: www.bridgend.ac.uk
Type: Mixed Residential Only
16–25
Special needs: ADD ASP CP
DOW DYP DYS EPI HI MLD VI
Wheelchair access: W

YSGOL BRYN CASTELL
Llangewydd Road, Bridgend,
Bridgend CF31 4JP
Type: Mixed Day Only 8–19
Special needs: ADHD ASD ASP
BESD DOW DYS EPI HI **MLD**
SLD SP&LD TOU
Wheelchair access: WA3

CARMARTHENSHIRE

COLEG ELIDYR
Llandovery, Carmarthenshire
SA20 0NL
Website: www.colegelidyr.com
Type: Mixed Residential Only
18–25
Special needs: ADD ASD BESD
DOW EPI **MLD SLD**
Wheelchair access: W
Independent Special

GWYNEDD

BRYN MELYN GROUP
Llandderfel, Bala, Gwynedd
LL23 7RA
Website: www.brynmelyngroup.
com/foundation/
Type: Mixed Residential Only
12–19
Special needs: ADD BESD DYP
EPI MLD

2.5

Profiles of Colleges and Other Special Provision at 16+

Cambian Group

Broughton House College

Brant Broughton, Lincolnshire LN5 0SL
T: (0800) 288 9779 **F**: (020) 87356151 **E**: education@cambiangroup.com **W**: www.cambiangroup.com

Head of Service Ms Carole Guy BA (Hons) PGCE DMS RNLD
Founded 1993
College status Co-educational boarding only. Mixed gender 16–25 years
Religious denomination Non-denominational
Member of NATSPEC
Special needs provision ASD, CB, EPI, MLD, SLD, SP&LD
Age range 16–25 (Mixed gender 16–25 years); *(boarding)* 27; *(full boarding)* 27

Broughton has built a reputation over the past 10 years as a leading post-16 residential place of education and care for young people with autism and severe learning disabilities, often accompanied by complex needs and challenging behaviours. Admission can take place at any time during the school year. We are a part of the Cambian Group, the largest provider of specialist residential education and care for young people with Autistic Spectrum Disorders in the United Kingdom. Broughton has 150 staff providing specialist education and care for up to 30 young people, aged 16 to 25 years. The goal for most of our young people is to return to their local community in supported living. Broughton draws upon a proven programme of Specialist Education, Specialist 24-hour Care and a wide range of Clinical and Therapeutic Inputs, including Speech & Language Therapy, Behavioural Therapy, Occupational Therapy, Psychiatry and Psychology. Multi-disciplinary teams and high staff ratios ensure intensive individual support. During the programme, young people move within Broughton to progressively more independent living facilities. These planned moves reinforce behavioural improvements and life skills in new settings, leading to the goal of returning to their local community. A Parent Liaison Officer is available to discuss, in confidence, a young person's specific needs.

The Wing Centre

126 Richmond Park Road, Bournemouth, Dorset BH8 8TH
T: (0800) 288 9779 **F**: (020) 87356151 **E**: education@cambiangroup.com **W**: www.cambiangroup.com

Head Ms Janette Morgan MA BA NPQH Post Graduate Certificate in Asperger Syndrome, Chartered Member CIPD
School status Young mens' senior boarding and day. Young men 16–19 years
Member of NATSPEC
Special needs provision ASP, CB, DYC, DYP, DYS, EPI, HEA, SP&LD
Age range 16–19 (Young men 16–19 years); *(full boarding)* 36

The Wing Centre is a leading residential special college for young men of 16–19 years who have Asperger Syndrome. The college offers a 38-week residential programme and day provision is available for students living close to the school. Admission can take place at any time during the school year. We are a part of the Cambian Group, the largest provider of specialist residential education and care for young people with Autistic Spectrum Disorders in the United Kingdom. Students have full access to the national curriculum with teaching appropriately differentiated to meet the needs of our young people. We draw upon a proven programme of Specialist Education, Specialist 24-hour Care and a wide range of Clinical and Therapeutic Inputs, including Speech & Language Therapy, Behavioural Therapy, Occupational Therapy, Psychiatry and Psychology. Multi-disciplinary teams and high staff ratios ensure intensive individual support. We offer extensive community-based programmes, vocational training, further education opportunities and programmes at local FE colleges. The Centre's main campus is in the village of Boldre, near Lymington, Hampshire, with several independent living houses for older students nearby. Please contact us as above. A Parent Liaison Officer is available to discuss, in confidence, a young person's specific needs and we are delighted to help with any questions or to arrange a visit to the Centre.

Doncaster College for the Deaf

Leger Way, Doncaster, South Yorkshire DN2 6AY
T: (01302) 386710 **F**: (01302) 361808 **E**: principal@ddt-deaf.org.uk **W**: www.deaf-trust.co.uk

Executive Principal Mr A W Robinson
College status Independent FE college mixed residential and day (Enrolment throughout the year. Please contact us to arrange an informal visit)
Religious denomination Non-denominational
Special needs provision ADHD, **BESD**, CP, DYS, **HI**, MLD, PMLD, SLD, SP&LD, VI, WA1
Age range 16–60
No of pupils 137; *(full boarding)* 109; *(day)* 28; *Girls* 52; *Boys* 85

Doncaster College for the deaf is a Residential, National Specialist College, providing Lifelong learning opportunities, with expertise in education and training deaf and hearing-impaired people, and those with additional communication or complex needs from 16-60 years.

The College's Total Communication (TC) policy allows students to use their preferred method of communication – British Sign Language (BSL), Signed Supported English (SSE) or a mixture of speech and lip-reading.

There is a complete support system on campus for students, incorporating Key Workers, Educational Support Workers, Speech and Language Therapy, Medical and Audiology.

Programmes of Learning include: Foundation and Life Skills, Media and Office Technology, Catering and Hospitality, Construction, Design and Technology, Hair and Beauty, Health Education and Social Studies, Motor Vehicle Engineering, Sport, Recreation and Leisure Studies.

Prior's Court Cottages

Prior's Court Foundation, Hermitage, Thatcham, Berkshire RG18 9NU
T: (01635) 247202 **F**: (01635) 247203 **E**: mail@priorscourt.org.uk **W**: www.priorscourt.org.uk

Manager Ms R Over
School status Independent Specialist Residential 52 weeks
Special needs provision ADD, ADHD, ASD, CB, EPI, MLD, SLD, SP&LD, W
Age range 16–25

Prior's Court has built a worldwide reputation over the past 13 years as a leading provider of specialist education and care for young people with autism, learning difficulties and complex needs. Prior's Court Cottages is a supportive living and learning environment which aims to provide young adults with autism with a toolkit of essential skills enabling them to lead a fulfilling and purposeful life, and prepare them for greater inclusion within their local community. The specialist environment offers a mix of small group homes and flats with an onsite Learning Centre and ten acres of grounds for leisure, horticulture, animal husbandry and vocational work. Through individualized, person-centred planning and Prior's Court's unique and successful approach each individual is supported in a wide range of areas including self care, daily living, leisure skills, communication, choice-making and managing their own behaviour. A strong emphasis is placed on developing vocational skills with opportunities for work placements in the community. Open days, visits and admissions information throughout the year.

RNIB College Loughborough

Radmoor Road, Loughborough, Leicestershire LE11 3BS
T: (01509) 611077 **F**: (01509) 232013 **E**: enquiries@rnibcollege.ac.uk **W**: www.rnibcollege.ac.uk

Principal Mr Tony Warren
Founded 1989
College status Co-educational boarding and day
Member of NATSPEC
Special needs provision ADD, ADHD, ASD, ASP, BESD, CB, CP, DOW, DYC, DYP, DYS, EPI, HEA, HI, IM, MLD, PMLD, SLD, SP&LD, TOU, VI, WA1
Age range 16–63; *boarders from* 16
Average class size 5

RNIB College Loughborough is an independent specialist college for people with sight loss and other disabilities. Students learn the skills to access education, work and housing, and to enjoy a healthy lifestyle and positive relationships.

We are a small friendly college offering residential and day programmes to people with a wide range of disabilities from many social and ethnic backgrounds. We share a campus with the mainstream Loughborough College which means the range of subjects and course levels we can offer goes from Foundation Learning all the way to A Levels or equivalent. We have a flexible curriculum and will agree an individual learning programme based on your needs and goals with progress regularly monitored and celebrated.

We are experts at what we do. Our staff are highly skilled at meeting needs and our buildings and facilities are second to none. Ofsted rate us as one of the top specialist colleges in the country and our learners have a big say in how the college is run.

In-house programmes are taught in small supportive classes, and are designed to get learners to where they want to be in life, whether that is the next stage in their education, finding a job or living independently. Programmes are based on our innovative and exciting enterprise-led curriculum, developing learners' skills in a practical setting. Enterprises include catering, retail, office work and an arts enterprise.

We also offer two progression programmes. The Bridge Programme is designed for learners who have finished their education and want to focus on progressing into independent or supported living. This programme offers a stepping stone between home, a residential school and supported/independent living. The Young People's Employment Programme is designed for people wanting to progress into employment whilst developing their independence skills.

RNIB College shares a campus with mainstream Loughborough College. We work in close partnership so that learners have the option, if they wish, to study a very wide range of mainstream courses. Programmes on offer include A Levels, vocational courses including business, care and health, leisure, travel and tourism, music, performing arts and sport, exercise and fitness.

Residential and day learners have access to a weekly programme of social, sporting and leisure activities that take place outside of the College day. The programme aims to develop learners' confidence, social and independence skills. Regular activities include: youth club, ten pin bowling, karaoke, gym training, shopping trips, drama club, sport and beauty and pampering sessions. Learners can be part of the student committee and can become members of Loughborough Students' Union with its numerous clubs and societies.

Why not come to one of our visit days and see for yourself what we can offer?

The Royal National College for the Blind (RNCB)

College Road, Hereford, Herefordshire HR1 1EB
T: (01432) 376621 **F**: (01432) 376628 **E**: info@rncb.ac.uk **W**: www.rncb.ac.uk
To arrange a visit or to request a prospectus call our Enquiry line on 01432 376621 or info@rncb.ac.uk

Principal Mr G Draper
Founded 1872
College status Independent Specialist College FE
Religious denomination Non-denominational
Member of NATSPEC, National Network of Assessment Centres
Special needs provision ASP, AUT, BESD, CP, DYC, DYP, DYS, EPI, HEA, IM, MLD, SP&LD, TOU, **VI+**
Age range 16–65; *boarders from* 16; *(boarding)* 200
Average class size 8

At RNCB we provide a wide range of full time academic and vocational programmes designed to prepare both young people and adults for Further Education, university and the world of work but most importantly – independent living.

In our Care Standards Ofsted Inspection, RNCB's overall quality rating for support was acclaimed as 'Outstanding.' Ofsted found the standard of provision to be 'exceptionally high.'

All students follow individualised programmes which are recognised by universities and employers both here in the United Kingdom and abroad. Students can study:

- A Levels
- Administration and Skills for the Working Office
- Art and Design
- Braille and Braille Technology
- Business
- Foundation Courses
- ICT
- Language Skills
- Massage and Complementary Therapy
- Media and Music Technology
- Performing Arts
- Sport, Recreation and Leisure

These are further supported with training in Literacy and Numeracy, Communication and Study Skills, Assistive Technology, Independent Living Skills, Mobility and Transitional Skills.

Developing Independence

Improving independence through learning and living is central to our provision. Students are offered intensive individual support with mobility and daily living skills to help develop the confidence and skills they need to move on to a much more independent future within their home communities.

Sport, leisure and recreation facilities

At RNCB, social and recreational activities are as important as class-based learning and students are encouraged to make the most of their College experience with a diverse range of timetabled and extra-curricular activities, events and excursions on offer.

On campus there are excellent facilities for recreational arts, sport and socialising. Regular social events are organised by the Student Union, there is a student common room and internet café as well as thePoint4, our state of the art sport and complementary therapy centre which houses a student gym, two spas, a hydrotherapy pool, indoor and outdoor sports pitches. thePoint4 also has a Bistro, hairdressing and beauty salons, and a wide range of group exercise classes are on offer.

Learner Support

Medical, counselling, residential and student support services are provided by qualified staff at all times. 24 hour support is always available in Halls of Residence. All students have a dedicated Personal Tutor.

Treloar College

London Road, Holybourne, Alton, Hampshire GU34 4EN
T: (01420) 547425 **F**: (01420) 542708 **E**: admissions@treloar.org.uk **W**: www.treloar.org.uk

Treloar's Principal Ms Amanda Quincey ACiB, MDip, BPhil (Sen), Cert Ed
Vice Principal Mr Tim Harding MSc Ed Certd
Founded 1907
College status Co-educational non-maintained boarding and day
Religious denomination Non-denominational
Member of NASS, NATSPEC
Special needs provision CP, DYP, DYS, EPI, HEA, HI, IM, MLD, SLD,
SP&LD, VI, WA1
Age range 16–25; *boarders from* 16
No of pupils 164; *(full boarding)* 164; *Girls* 73; *Boys* 91
Teacher:pupil ratio 1:6
Average class size 6

Treloar College is a specialist college of further education for young people aged 16 or over with physical disabilities, associated disorders, complex needs and also students with degenerative or life-limiting conditions, from all over the United Kingdom and overseas. Treloar College offers a broad range of courses from Entry and below, through to Level 3, with pathways in Art & Design, Horticulture, ICT, Media, Photography, Sport & Leisure Studies and Travel & Tourism. As well as the courses offered onsite, we have a partnership with nearby Alton College and two other partner colleges where students have the opportunity to study as part of a tailored programme. Therapists and residential support staff work with students, alongside the teachers to focus on removing any barriers to learning to give students the best possible opportunities to learn and develop.

2.6

Index of Independent and Non-Maintained Special Schools and Colleges Classified by Special Need

ASPERGER'S SYNDROME

AALPS College (Midlands), Hanley Castle
AALPS College (North), Nr Scunthorpe
Action for Children Headlands School, Penarth
Alderwasley Hall School and Callow Park College, Belper
Aran Hall School, Dolgellau
Ashmeads, Bedford
Ballikinrain Residential School, Stirlingshire
Barnardo's Lecropt, Camelon
Baston House School, Bromley
Belgrave School, Clifton
Birtenshaw School, Bolton
Bladon House School, Burton upon Trent
Blossom House School, London
Brantridge School, Haywards Heath
Breckenbrough School, Thirsk
Brewood Secondary School, Deal
Bridge College, Stockport
Bridgend College, Bridgend
Camphill School Aberdeen, Aberdeen
Cedar House School, via Carnforth
Centre Academy, London
Centre Academy, East Anglia
Chartwell House School, Wisbech
Chelfham Mill School, Barnstaple
Chelfham Senior School, Yelverton
Chilworth House School, Oxford
Chilworth House Upper School, Oxford
Clarence High School, Formby
Cornerstones, Warrington
Cotswold Chine School, Near Stroud
Cotswold Community, Swindon
Coxlease School, Lyndhurst
Crookhey Hall School, Lancaster
Cruckton Hall, Shrewsbury
Cumberland School, Preston
Delamere Forest School, Warrington
Derwen College, Oswestry
Dilston College of Further Education, Corbridge
Donaldson's College for the Deaf, Edinburgh
Doncaster College for the Deaf, Doncaster
Doucecroft School, Colchester
Eagle House School – Sutton, Sutton
Eagle House School Mitcham, Mitcham

Sheridan School, Thetford
Snowdon School, Stirling
Snowflake School, London
Southern England Psychological Services, Eastleigh
Southlands School, Lymington
Spring Hill School (Barnardo's), Ripon
St Catherine's School, Ventnor
St Dominic's School, Godalming
St Edward's School, Romsey
St John's Catholic School for the Deaf, Boston Spa
St John's School & College, Seaford
St Joseph's Specialist School & College, Cranleigh
St Mary's Wrestwood Children's Trust, Bexhill-on-Sea
St Piers School, The National Centre for Young People with Epilepsy (NCYPE), Lingfield
St Rose's School, Stroud
St Vincent's School, A Specialist School for Sensory Impairment and Other Needs, Liverpool
Starley Hall, Burntisland
Strathmore College, Staffordshire
Swalcliffe Park School Trust, Banbury
Tadley Horizon, Basingstoke
The Chrysalis School for Autism, Hitchin
The Grange Centre for People with Disabilities, Bookham
The Jigsaw School, Cranleigh
The Link Primary School, Croydon
The Link Secondary School, Beddington
The Lioncare School, Hove
The Marchant-Holliday School, Templecombe
The Mount Camphill Community, Wadhurst
The New School, Dunkeld

The New School at West Heath, Sevenoaks
The Priory Lodge School, London
The Quest School for Autistic Children, West Malling
The Royal Blind School, Edinburgh, Edinburgh
The Royal National College for the Blind (RNCB), Hereford
The Royal School for Deaf Children Margate, Margate
The Ryes College & Community, Sudbury
The Speech, Language & Hearing Centre, London
The St John Vianney School, Stockport
The Wing Centre, Bournemouth
Thornbeck College, Sunderland
Thornhill Park School, Sunderland
Tree House, London
Tregynon Hall School, Newtown
Trinity School, Rochester
Underley Garden School, Carnforth
Underley Hall School, Carnforth
Unsted Park School, Godalming
Walton Progressive School, Liverpool
Wargrave House School, Newton-le-Willows
West Kirby Residential School, Wirral
Westgate College for Deaf People, Westgate
Westwood School, Broadstairs
Whinfell Care, Kendal
Whitstone Head School, Holsworthy
William Morris House Camphill Community, Stonehouse
Wings School, Milnthorpe
Witherslack Hall, Grange-over-Sands
Woodcroft School, Loughton
Ysgol Bryn Castell, Bridgend

ATTENTION DEFICIT DISORDER

AALPS College (Midlands), Hanley Castle
AALPS College (North), Nr Scunthorpe

Action for Children Headlands School, Penarth

New Options (Higford) School, Shifnal
New Options (Kinsale) School, Holywell
Nugent House School, St Helens
Ochil Tower (Rudolf Steiner) School, Auchterarder
Owlswick School, Lewes
Parayhouse School, London
Pegasus School, Caldwell
Pengwern College, Rhuddlan
Pennine Camphill Community, Wakefield
Philip Green Memorial School, Wimborne
Philpots Manor School and Further Training Centre, East Grinstead
Pield Heath School, Uxbridge
Pontville School, Ormskirk
Potterspury Lodge School, Towcester
Prior's Court Cottages, Thatcham
Ripplevale School, Deal
RNIB College Loughborough, Loughborough
Rookery Hove, Hove
Rookery Radstock, Radstock
Rossendale School, Ramsbottom
Rowden Hill School, Near Welshpool
Rowden House School, Bromyard
Seafield School, Ardrossan
Sheiling School, Camphill Community Thornbury, Thornbury
Sheridan School, Thetford
Snowdon School, Stirling
Southern England Psychological Services, Eastleigh
Spring Hill School (Barnardo's), Ripon
St Catherine's School, Ventnor
St Dominic's School, Godalming
St Edward's School, Romsey
St John's School & College, Seaford
St Joseph's Specialist School & College, Cranleigh
St Mary's Wrestwood Children's Trust, Bexhill-on-Sea

St Phillip's School, Airdrie
Starley Hall, Burntisland
Strathmore College, Staffordshire
Swalcliffe Park School Trust, Banbury
Tadley Horizon, Basingstoke
Talbot House Special School, Newcastle Upon Tyne
The Chelsea Group of Children, London
The Lioncare School, Hove
The Marchant-Holliday School, Templecombe
The New School, Dunkeld
The New School at West Heath, Sevenoaks
The Royal Blind School, Edinburgh, Edinburgh
The Royal School for Deaf Children Margate, Margate
The Royal Wolverhampton School, Wolverhampton
The Ryes College & Community, Sudbury
The Sheiling School Ringwood, Ringwood
The Speech, Language & Hearing Centre, London
The St John Vianney School, Stockport
The Unicorn School, Abingdon
Tregynon Hall School, Newtown
Trinity School, Rochester
Underley Garden School, Carnforth
Underley Hall School, Carnforth
Walton Progressive School, Liverpool
West Kirby Residential School, Wirral
Westgate College for Deaf People, Westgate
Whinfell Care, Kendal
Whitstone Head School, Holsworthy
William Henry Smith School, Brighouse
Wings School, Milnthorpe
Witherslack Hall, Grange-over-Sands
Woodcroft School, Loughton
Woodlands School, Wigtownshire

ATTENTION DEFICIT HYPERACTIVITY DISORDER

AALPS College (Midlands), Hanley Castle
AALPS College (North), Nr Scunthorpe

Action for Children Headlands School, Penarth

Witherslack Hall, Grange-over-Sands
Woodcroft School, Loughton

Woodlands School, Wigtownshire
Ysgol Bryn Castell, Bridgend

AUTISTIC SPECTRUM DISORDER

AALPS College (Midlands), Hanley Castle
AALPS College (North), Nr Scunthorpe
Action for Children Headlands School,
    Penarth
Alderwasley Hall School and Callow Park
    College, Belper
Annie Lawson School, Crowthorne
Aran Hall School, Dolgellau
Ashmeads, Bedford
Ballikinrain Residential School, Stirlingshire
Barnardo's Lecropt, Camelon
Baston House School, Bromley
Beech Tree, Preston
Belgrave School, Clifton
Birtenshaw School, Bolton
Bladon House School, Burton upon Trent
Blossom House School, London
Brantridge School, Haywards Heath
Breckenbrough School, Thirsk
Bridge College, Stockport
Broughton House College, Brant Broughton
Burton Hill School, Malmesbury
Camphill Blair Drummond Trust, Stirling
Camphill School Aberdeen, Aberdeen
Cavendish School, London
Cedar House School, via Carnforth
Centre Academy, London
Centre Academy, East Anglia
Chailey Heritage School, Nr Lewes
Chelfham Mill School, Barnstaple
Chelfham Senior School, Yelverton
Chilworth House School, Oxford
Chilworth House Upper School, Oxford
Cintre Community, Bristol
Coleg Elidyr, Llandovery
Coombe House, Crediton
Cornerstones, Warrington
Cotswold Chine School, Near Stroud
Coxlease School, Lyndhurst
Cruckton Hall, Shrewsbury

Dilston College of Further Education,
    Corbridge
Doucecroft School, Colchester
Eagle House – Norfolk School, Norwich
Eagle House School – Sutton, Sutton
Eagle House School Mitcham, Mitcham
Eagle Life College, Banham
East Park School, Glasgow
Eden Grove School, Appleby
Ellesmere College, Thatcham
Enham, Andover
Exeter College, Exeter
Exeter Royal Academy for Deaf Education,
    Exeter
Exeter Royal Academy for Deaf Education,
    Exeter
Fairfield Farm College, Westbury
Farleigh College Condover, Shrewsbury
Farleigh Further Education College
    Condover, Shrewsbury
Frederick Hugh House, London
Fullerton House School, Doncaster
Grafham Grange School, Guildford
Great Oaks Small School, Minster
Heathermount School, Ascot
High Close School (Barnardo's), Wokingham
Hill House School, Lymington
Hillingdon Manor School, Uxbridge
Hinwick Hall College, Wellingborough
Homefield Residential College,
    Loughborough
Hope House School, Nottinghamshire
Hope Lodge School, Southampton
Ivers Inclusive Learning Project, Sturminster
    Newton
Jacques Hall, Manningtree
Kestrel House School, London
Kibble Centre, Paisley
Kisharon Day School, London
Kisimul School – Old Vicarage, Swinderby

St John's Catholic School for the Deaf, Boston Spa

St John's School & College, Seaford

St Joseph's Specialist School & College, Cranleigh

St Mary's Wrestwood Children's Trust, Bexhill-on-Sea

St Piers School, The National Centre for Young People with Epilepsy (NCYPE), Lingfield

St Vincent's School, A Specialist School for Sensory Impairment and Other Needs, Liverpool

Strathmore College, Staffordshire

Summerhayes School, Devon

Sunfield School, Stourbridge

Sutherland House School (Carlton), Nottingham

Sutherland House School (Secondary Department), Mapperley Park

Swalcliffe Park School Trust, Banbury

Sycamore School, Dunfermline

Tadley Horizon, Basingstoke

Teaseldown School, Halstead

The Chelsea Group of Children, London

The Chrysalis School for Autism, Hitchin

The David Lewis School, Nr Alderley Edge

The Forum School, Shillingstone

The Grange Centre for People with Disabilities, Bookham

The Jigsaw School, Cranleigh

The Link Primary School, Croydon

The Link Secondary School, Beddington

The Lioncare School, Hove

The Marchant-Holliday School, Templecombe

The Mount Camphill Community, Wadhurst

The New School, Dunkeld

The Priory Lodge School, London

The Quest School for Autistic Children, West Malling

The Royal Blind School, Edinburgh, Edinburgh

The Royal National College for the Blind (RNCB), Hereford

The Royal School for Deaf Children Margate, Margate

The Ryes College & Community, Sudbury

The Sheiling School Ringwood, Ringwood

The Speech, Language & Hearing Centre, London

The St John Vianney School, Stockport

Thornbeck College, Sunderland

Thornhill Park School, Sunderland

Tree House, London

Tregynon Hall School, Newtown

Trinity School, Rochester

Underley Garden School, Carnforth

Unsted Park School, Godalming

Walton Progressive School, Liverpool

Wargrave House School, Newton-le-Willows

Waterloo Lodge School, Chorley

West Kirby Residential School, Wirral

Westgate College for Deaf People, Westgate

Westwood School, Broadstairs

Whinfell Care, Kendal

Whitstone Head School, Holsworthy

William Morris House Camphill Community, Stonehouse

Wilsic Hall School, Doncaster

Witherslack Hall, Grange-over-Sands

Woodcroft School, Loughton

Ysgol Bryn Castell, Bridgend

BEHAVIOURAL, EMOTIONAL & SOCIAL DISORDERS

Acorns School, Stockport

Action for Children Headlands School, Penarth

Action for Children Parklands Campus, Abingdon

Aidenswood, Stoke

Applegate, Colne

Appletree School, Kendal

Aran Hall School, Dolgellau

Arc School, Nr Nuneaton

Ashmeads, Bedford

Ballikinrain Residential School, Stirlingshire

Barnardo's Lecropt, Camelon

Belmont School, Rawtenstall

Belmont School, Salisbury

Bladon House School, Burton upon Trent

Bramfield House, Halesworth

Brantridge School, Haywards Heath

Breckenbrough School, Thirsk

Brewood Secondary School, Deal

Bridge College, Stockport

Bryn Melyn Group, Bala

Caldecott Community, Ashford

Camphill Blair Drummond Trust, Stirling

Camphill School Aberdeen, Aberdeen

Cavendish School, London

Cedar House School, via Carnforth

Chaigeley School, Warrington

Chartwell House School, Wisbech

Chelfham Mill School, Barnstaple

Chelfham Senior School, Yelverton

Chilworth House School, Oxford

Chilworth House Upper School, Oxford

Cintre Community, Bristol

Clarence High School, Formby

Coleg Elidyr, Llandovery

Coombe House, Crediton

Cornerstones, Warrington

Cornfield School, Redhill

Cotswold Chine School, Near Stroud

Cotswold Community, Swindon

Coxlease School, Lyndhurst

Crookhey Hall School, Lancaster

Cruckton Hall, Shrewsbury

Cumberland School, Preston

Delamere Forest School, Warrington

Denby Grange School, Wakefield

Didsbury School, Manchester

Doncaster College for the Deaf, Doncaster

Doncaster School for the Deaf, Doncaster

Downham Lodge School, Ely

Draycott Moor College, Stoke-on-Trent

Eastwood Grange School, Nr Chesterfield

Eden Grove School, Appleby

Exeter College, Exeter

Exeter Royal Academy for Deaf Education, Exeter

Exeter Royal Academy for Deaf Education, Exeter

Falkland House School, Cupar

Farleigh Further Education College Condover, Shrewsbury

Farney Close School, Haywards Heath

Fortune Centre of Riding Therapy, Christchurch

Geilsland School, Beith

Glendale House, Long Eaton

Good Shepherd Centre, Bishopton

Grafham Grange School, Guildford

Halton School, Runcorn

Harmeny School, Balerno

Heath Farm School, Ashford

High Close School (Barnardo's), Wokingham

Hillcrest Park School, Chipping Norton

Hillcrest Pentwyn School, Hereford

Hillcrest Slinford, Nr Horsham

Hillside School, Aberdour

Hopewell School, Essex

Ivers Inclusive Learning Project, Sturminster Newton

Jacques Hall, Manningtree

Kibble Centre, Paisley

Kings Manor Community College, Shoreham-by-Sea

Kisharon Day School, London

Lakeside School, Liverpool

Learning Opportunities Centre Primary, Canterbury

Learning Opportunities Centre Secondary, Deal

Lewis Charlton School, Ashby-de-la-Zouch

Limes Meadows, Ashton under Lyne

Little Acorns School, Tenterden

Little David's School, Croydon

Loddon School, Hook

Loppington House Further Education & Adult Centre, Wem

Marlowe Education Unit, Hartpury

Meadows School (Barnardo's), Southborough

Merryhay Academy, Ilminster

Mill House, Leyland

Moore House School, Bathgate

MRCS Educational Unit, Croydon

The Ryes College & Community, Sudbury
The Sheiling School Ringwood, Ringwood
The Speech, Language & Hearing Centre, London
The Trust Centre, Derbyshire
The Westside Independent School, London
Thornby Hall Therapeutic Community, Thornby
Tregynon Hall School, Newtown
Tumblewood Project School, Westbury
Underley Garden School, Carnforth
Underley Hall School, Carnforth
Walnut Tree Lodge School, Buckinghamshire
Waterloo Lodge School, Chorley
Wathen Grange School, Leamington Spa
Wessex College, Warminster

West Kirby Residential School, Wirral
Westgate College for Deaf People, Westgate
Westmorland School, Chorley
Westwood School, Broadstairs
Whinfell Care, Kendal
Whitstone Head School, Holsworthy
William Henry Smith School, Brighouse
Wings School, Milnthorpe
Witherslack Hall, Grange-over-Sands
Wolsdon Street School, Plymouth
Woodlands School, Wigtownshire
Wychbury House Residential School, Torquay
Young Options College, Shropshire
Young Options College, Shifnal
Ysgol Bryn Castell, Bridgend

CEREBRAL PALSY

Action for Children Penhurst School, Chipping Norton
Annie Lawson School, Crowthorne
Aran Hall School, Dolgellau
Beaumont College of Further Education, Lancaster
Birtenshaw School, Bolton
Bladon House School, Burton upon Trent
Bridge College, Stockport
Bridgend College, Bridgend
Burton Hill School, Malmesbury
Camphill School Aberdeen, Aberdeen
Cedar House School, via Carnforth
Chailey Heritage School, Nr Lewes
Craig-y-Parc School, Pentyrch
Dame Hannah Rogers School, Ivybridge
Derwen College, Oswestry
Doncaster College for the Deaf, Doncaster
Doncaster School for the Deaf, Doncaster
East Park School, Glasgow
Enham, Andover
Exeter College, Exeter
Exeter Royal Academy for Deaf Education, Exeter
Finchale Training College, Durham

Fortune Centre of Riding Therapy, Christchurch
Frederick Hugh House, London
Henshaws College, Harrogate
Hereward College, Coventry
Hinwick Hall College, Wellingborough
Holly Bank School, Mirfield
Hornsey Conductive Education Centre, London
Ingfield Manor School, Billingshurst
King's Bruton and Hazlegrove, Bruton
Kisharon Day School, London
Langside School, Poole
Linkage College, Spilsby
Linkage College, Grimsby
Loppington House Further Education & Adult Centre, Wem
MacIntyre Womaston School, Presteigne
Meldreth Manor, Nr Royston
Nash College, Bromley
Nash College of Further Education, Bromley
National Institute of Conductive Education, Birmingham
National Star College, Cheltenham
Oakwood Court, Dawlish

Ovingdean Hall School, Brighton
Paces Conductive Education, Sheffield
Pengwern College, Rhuddlan
Pennine Camphill Community, Wakefield
Percy Hedley School, Newcastle-upon-Tyne
Pield Heath School, Uxbridge
Portland College, Mansfield
Queen Alexandra College of Further
    Education, Birmingham
RNIB College Loughborough,
    Loughborough
RNIB Manor House, Torquay
RNIB Pears Centre for Specialist Learning,
    Warwickshire
RNIB Sunshine House School and Children's
    Home, Northwood
Rosewood School, Southampton
Rowden Hill School, Near Welshpool
Rowden House School, Bromyard
Royal School Manchester, Cheadle
Royal West of England School for the Deaf,
    Exeter
Rutherford School, South Croydon
Rutland House School, Nottingham
seeABILITY (formerly Royal School for the
    Blind), Epsom
Sheiling School, Camphill Community
    Thornbury, Thornbury
St Christopher's School, Westbury Park
St John's Catholic School for the Deaf,
    Boston Spa

St Joseph's Specialist School & College,
    Cranleigh
St Mary's Wrestwood Children's Trust,
    Bexhill-on-Sea
St Rose's School, Stroud
St Vincent's School, A Specialist School for
    Sensory Impairment and Other Needs,
    Liverpool
Stanmore House Residential School, Lanark
The David Lewis School, Nr Alderley Edge
The Grange Centre for People with
    Disabilities, Bookham
The London Centre for Children with Cerebral
    Palsy, London
The Royal Blind School, Edinburgh,
    Edinburgh
The Royal National College for the Blind
    (RNCB), Hereford
The Royal School for Deaf Children Margate,
    Margate
The Ryes College & Community, Sudbury
The School for Profound Education,
    Tadworth
The Sheiling School Ringwood, Ringwood
The St John Vianney School, Stockport
The Trust Centre, Derbyshire
Treloar College, Hampshire
Treloar School, Hampshire
Trengweath School, Plymouth
Victoria Education Centre, Poole
Vranch House School, Exeter

CHALLENGING BEHAVIOUR

AALPS College (Midlands), Hanley Castle
AALPS College (North), Nr Scunthorpe
Action for Children Headlands School,
    Penarth
Aidenswood, Stoke
Alderwasley Hall School and Callow Park
    College, Belper
Annie Lawson School, Crowthorne
Applegate, Colne
Appletree School, Kendal
Aran Hall School, Dolgellau

Ashmeads, Bedford
Ballikinrain Residential School, Stirlingshire
Barnardo's Lecropt, Camelon
Beech Tree, Preston
Birtenshaw School, Bolton
Bladon House School, Burton upon Trent
Brantridge School, Haywards Heath
Breckenbrough School, Thirsk
Bridge College, Stockport
Broughton House College, Brant Broughton
Camphill Blair Drummond Trust, Stirling

RNIB Scotland, Edinburgh
Rookery Hove, Hove
Rookery Radstock, Radstock
Rossendale School, Ramsbottom
Rowden Hill School, Near Welshpool
Rowden House School, Bromyard
Royal School Manchester, Cheadle
Seamab House School, Kinross
Sheridan School, Thetford
Snowdon School, Stirling
Southlands School, Lymington
Spring Hill School (Barnardo's), Ripon
St Catherine's School, Ventnor
St Christopher's School, Westbury Park
St Elizabeth's School, Much Hadham
St Joseph's Specialist School & College, Cranleigh
St Piers School, The National Centre for Young People with Epilepsy (NCYPE), Lingfield
Sunfield School, Stourbridge
Swalcliffe Park School Trust, Banbury
Tadley Horizon, Basingstoke
Talbot House Special School, Newcastle Upon Tyne
The Birches, Poulton le Fylde
The Chelsea Group of Children, London
The Firs, St Leonards on Sea
The Forum School, Shillingstone
The Lioncare School, Hove

The Marchant-Holliday School, Templecombe
The Nook School, Colne
The Royal Blind School, Edinburgh, Edinburgh
The Royal School for Deaf Children Margate, Margate
The Ryes College & Community, Sudbury
The Sheiling School Ringwood, Ringwood
The Speech, Language & Hearing Centre, London
The Trust Centre, Derbyshire
The Wing Centre, Bournemouth
Thornby Hall Therapeutic Community, Thornby
Tregynon Hall School, Newtown
Underley Garden School, Carnforth
Underley Hall School, Carnforth
Walton Progressive School, Liverpool
Waterloo Lodge School, Chorley
Wathen Grange School, Leamington Spa
West Kirby Residential School, Wirral
Westgate College for Deaf People, Westgate
Westwood School, Broadstairs
Whinfell Care, Kendal
William Henry Smith School, Brighouse
Wilsic Hall School, Doncaster
Witherslack Hall, Grange-over-Sands
Woodcroft School, Loughton
Young Options College, Shifnal

DOWN'S SYNDROME

Aran Hall School, Dolgellau
Beech Tree, Preston
Birtenshaw School, Bolton
Bladon House School, Burton upon Trent
Bridge College, Stockport
Bridgend College, Bridgend
Camphill Blair Drummond Trust, Stirling
Camphill School Aberdeen, Aberdeen
Cintre Community, Bristol
Coleg Elidyr, Llandovery
Delamere Forest School, Warrington

Derwen College, Oswestry
Dilston College of Further Education, Corbridge
Easter Auguston Training Farm, Aberdeen
Exeter College, Exeter
Fairfield Farm College, Westbury
Fortune Centre of Riding Therapy, Christchurch
Frederick Hugh House, London
Henshaws College, Harrogate

Hereward College, Coventry
Hinwick Hall College, Wellingborough
Ivers Inclusive Learning Project, Sturminster Newton
Kisharon Day School, London
Kisimul School – Old Vicarage, Swinderby
Kisimul School – Woodstock House, Long Ditton
Lakeside School, Liverpool
Lindeth College of Further Education, Bowness-on-Windermere
Linkage College, Spilsby
Linkage College, Grimsby
Loddon School, Hook
Loppington House Further Education & Adult Centre, Wem
MacIntyre Womaston School, Presteigne
Nash College of Further Education, Bromley
Oakwood Court, Dawlish
Ochil Tower (Rudolf Steiner) School, Auchterarder
Overley Hall School, Wellington
Parayhouse School, London
Pegasus School, Caldwell
Pengwern College, Rhuddlan
Pennine Camphill Community, Wakefield
Philip Green Memorial School, Wimborne
Pield Heath School, Uxbridge
Queen Alexandra College of Further Education, Birmingham
RNIB College Loughborough, Loughborough
RNIB Pears Centre for Specialist Learning, Warwickshire

Rowden Hill School, Near Welshpool
Rowden House School, Bromyard
Royal School Manchester, Cheadle
Sheiling School, Camphill Community Thornbury, Thornbury
Southern England Psychological Services, Eastleigh
Spring Hill School (Barnardo's), Ripon
St John's School & College, Seaford
St Joseph's Specialist School & College, Cranleigh
St Mary's Wrestwood Children's Trust, Bexhill-on-Sea
St Piers School, The National Centre for Young People with Epilepsy (NCYPE), Lingfield
St Rose's School, Stroud
Strathmore College, Staffordshire
The Grange Centre for People with Disabilities, Bookham
The Link Primary School, Croydon
The Mount Camphill Community, Wadhurst
The Royal Blind School, Edinburgh, Edinburgh
The Royal School for Deaf Children Margate, Margate
The Sheiling School Ringwood, Ringwood
The St John Vianney School, Stockport
Underley Garden School, Carnforth
Westgate College for Deaf People, Westgate
William Morris House Camphill Community, Stonehouse
Ysgol Bryn Castell, Bridgend

DYSCALCULIA

Alderwasley Hall School and Callow Park College, Belper
Appleford School, Salisbury
Aran Hall School, Dolgellau
Ballikinrain Residential School, Stirlingshire
Barnardo's Lecropt, Camelon
Belgrave School, Clifton
Bladon House School, Burton upon Trent
Brewood Secondary School, Deal

Brown's School, Orpington
Bruern Abbey School, Chesterton
Burys Court School and Moon Hall College, Reigate
Calder House School, Chippenham
Cedar House School, via Carnforth
Centre Academy, East Anglia
Chartwell House School, Wisbech
Cruckton Hall, Shrewsbury

DYSLEXIA

St Mary's Wrestwood Children's Trust, Bexhill-on-Sea

St Vincent's School, A Specialist School for Sensory Impairment and Other Needs, Liverpool

Stanbridge Earls School, Romsey

Swalcliffe Park School Trust, Banbury

The Chelsea Group of Children, London

The Link Primary School, Croydon

The Marchant-Holliday School, Templecombe

The Moat School, London

The New School, Dunkeld

The Old Rectory School, Ipswich

The Royal Blind School, Edinburgh, Edinburgh

The Royal National College for the Blind (RNCB), Hereford

The Royal School for Deaf Children Margate, Margate

The Royal Wolverhampton School, Wolverhampton

The Ryes College & Community, Sudbury

The Unicorn School, Abingdon

The Wing Centre, Bournemouth

Tregynon Hall School, Newtown

Treloar College, Hampshire

Treloar School, Hampshire

Trinity School, Rochester

Underley Garden School, Carnforth

Underley Hall School, Carnforth

Victoria Education Centre, Poole

Waterloo Lodge School, Chorley

West Kirby Residential School, Wirral

Westgate College for Deaf People, Westgate

Whinfell Care, Kendal

Whitstone Head School, Holsworthy

William Henry Smith School, Brighouse

Wings School, Milnthorpe

Witherslack Hall, Grange-over-Sands

Woodcroft School, Loughton

Ysgol Bryn Castell, Bridgend

DYSPRAXIA

Action for Children Headlands School, Penarth

Alderwasley Hall School and Callow Park College, Belper

Appleford School, Salisbury

Appletree School, Kendal

Aran Hall School, Dolgellau

Ashmeads, Bedford

Ballikinrain Residential School, Stirlingshire

Barnardo's Lecropt, Camelon

Belgrave School, Clifton

Bladon House School, Burton upon Trent

Blossom House School, London

Breckenbrough School, Thirsk

Brewood Secondary School, Deal

Bridgend College, Bridgend

Brown's School, Chelsfield

Browns School, Orpington

Bruern Abbey School, Chesterton

Bryn Melyn Group, Bala

Burys Court School and Moon Hall College, Reigate

Calder House School, Chippenham

Camphill School Aberdeen, Aberdeen

Cedar House School, via Carnforth

Centre Academy, London

Centre Academy, East Anglia

Chartwell House School, Wisbech

Cotswold Chine School, Near Stroud

Cruckton Hall, Shrewsbury

Delamere Forest School, Warrington

Doncaster College for the Deaf, Doncaster

Eagle House School – Sutton, Sutton

Eagle House School Mitcham, Mitcham

Eagle Life College, Banham

East Court School, Ramsgate

Edington and Shapwick School, Shapwick

Enham, Andover

Exeter College, Exeter

Fairfield Farm College, Westbury

Fairley House School, London

The Royal National College for the Blind (RNCB), Hereford
The Royal School for Deaf Children Margate, Margate
The Royal Wolverhampton School, Wolverhampton
The Sheiling School Ringwood, Ringwood
The Speech, Language & Hearing Centre, London
The St John Vianney School, Stockport
The Unicorn School, Abingdon
The Wing Centre, Bournemouth
Tregynon Hall School, Newtown
Treloar College, Hampshire

Treloar School, Hampshire
Trinity School, Rochester
Underley Garden School, Carnforth
Underley Hall School, Carnforth
Victoria Education Centre, Poole
Waterloo Lodge School, Chorley
West Kirby Residential School, Wirral
Westgate College for Deaf People, Westgate
Whinfell Care, Kendal
Wings School, Milnthorpe
Witherslack Hall, Grange-over-Sands
Woodcroft School, Loughton

EPILEPSY

AALPS College (Midlands), Hanley Castle
AALPS College (North), Nr Scunthorpe
Action for Children Penhurst School, Chipping Norton
Alderwasley Hall School and Callow Park College, Belper
Annie Lawson School, Crowthorne
Aran Hall School, Dolgellau
Beaumont College of Further Education, Lancaster
Beech Tree, Preston
Birtenshaw School, Bolton
Bladon House School, Burton upon Trent
Bridge College, Stockport
Bridgend College, Bridgend
Broughton House College, Brant Broughton
Bryn Melyn Group, Bala
Camphill Blair Drummond Trust, Stirling
Camphill School Aberdeen, Aberdeen
Cedar House School, via Carnforth
Chailey Heritage School, Nr Lewes
Chelfham Mill School, Barnstaple
Cintre Community, Bristol
Coleg Elidyr, Llandovery
Cornerstones, Warrington
Cotswold Chine School, Near Stroud
Cruckton Hall, Shrewsbury
Dame Hannah Rogers School, Ivybridge

Delamere Forest School, Warrington
Derwen College, Oswestry
Dilston College of Further Education, Corbridge
Eagle House – Norfolk School, Norwich
Eagle Life College, Banham
East Park School, Glasgow
Ellesmere College, Thatcham
Enham, Andover
Exeter College, Exeter
Exeter Royal Academy for Deaf Education, Exeter
Exeter Royal Academy for Deaf Education, Exeter
Fairfield Farm College, Westbury
Fairley House School, London
Farleigh College Condover, Shrewsbury
Finchale Training College, Durham
Fortune Centre of Riding Therapy, Christchurch
Frederick Hugh House, London
Fullerton House School, Doncaster
Grateley House School, Andover
Henshaws College, Harrogate
Hereward College, Coventry
Hill House School, Lymington
Holly Bank School, Mirfield
I CAN's Meath School, Ottershaw

Strathmore College, Staffordshire
Tadley Horizon, Basingstoke
The David Lewis School, Nr Alderley Edge
The Forum School, Shillingstone
The Grange Centre for People with
    Disabilities, Bookham
The Royal Blind School, Edinburgh,
    Edinburgh
The Royal National College for the Blind
    (RNCB), Hereford
The Royal School for Deaf Children Margate,
    Margate
The Ryes College & Community, Sudbury
The School for Profound Education, Tadworth

The Sheiling School Ringwood, Ringwood
The Trust Centre, Derbyshire
The Wing Centre, Bournemouth
Tregynon Hall School, Newtown
Treloar College, Hampshire
Treloar School, Hampshire
Underley Garden School, Carnforth
Victoria Education Centre, Poole
Walton Progressive School, Liverpool
West Kirby Residential School, Wirral
Westgate College for Deaf People,
    Westgate
Woodcroft School, Loughton
Ysgol Bryn Castell, Bridgend

HEALTH PROBLEMS

AALPS College (Midlands), Hanley Castle
AALPS College (North), Nr Scunthorpe
Alderwasley Hall School and Callow Park
    College, Belper
Annie Lawson School, Crowthorne
Aran Hall School, Dolgellau
Ashmeads, Bedford
Birtenshaw School, Bolton
Bladon House School, Burton upon Trent
Bridge College, Stockport
Burton Hill School, Malmesbury
Calder House School, Chippenham
Camphill Blair Drummond Trust, Stirling
Camphill School Aberdeen, Aberdeen
Cedar House School, via Carnforth
Chailey Heritage School, Nr Lewes
Coombe House, Crediton
Dame Hannah Rogers School, Ivybridge
Delamere Forest School, Warrington
East Park School, Glasgow
Ellesmere College, Thatcham
Fairley House School, London
Finchale Training College, Durham
Hereward College, Coventry
High Close School (Barnardo's), Wokingham
Hill House School, Lymington
Kings Manor Community College,
    Shoreham-by-Sea
Lakeside School, Liverpool

Langside School, Poole
Linkage College, Grimsby
Linkage College, Spilsby
MRCS Educational Unit, Croydon
Mulberry Bush School, Witney
Nash College of Further Education, Bromley
National Institute of Conductive Education,
    Birmingham
National Star College, Cheltenham
New College Worcester, Worcester
New Options (Barton) School, Barton upon
    Humber
New Options (Higford) School, Shifnal
Paces Conductive Education, Sheffield
Parayhouse School, London
Pegasus School, Caldwell
Pennine Camphill Community, Wakefield
Philip Green Memorial School, Wimborne
Philpots Manor School and Further Training
    Centre, East Grinstead
Pield Heath School, Uxbridge
Pontville School, Ormskirk
Purbeck View School, Swanage
Ripplevale School, Deal
RNIB College Loughborough, Loughborough
RNIB Pears Centre for Specialist Learning,
    Warwickshire
RNIB Sunshine House School and Children's
    Home, Northwood

HEARING IMPAIRMENT

IMPAIRED MOBILITY

AALPS College (Midlands), Hanley Castle
AALPS College (North), Nr Scunthorpe
Action for Children Penhurst School, Chipping Norton
Aran Hall School, Dolgellau
Birtenshaw School, Bolton
Bladon House School, Burton upon Trent
Bridge College, Stockport
Burton Hill School, Malmesbury
Chailey Heritage School, Nr Lewes
Craig-y-Parc School, Pentyrch
Dame Hannah Rogers School, Ivybridge
East Park School, Glasgow
Exeter Royal Academy for Deaf Education, Exeter
Frederick Hugh House, London
Henshaws College, Harrogate
Holly Bank School, Mirfield
Ingfield Manor School, Billingshurst
Lakeside School, Liverpool
MacIntyre Womaston School, Presteigne
Nash College of Further Education, Bromley
National Institute of Conductive Education, Birmingham
New College Worcester, Worcester
New Options (Higford) School, Shifnal
Pegasus School, Caldwell
Pengwern College, Rhuddlan
Percy Hedley School, Newcastle-upon-Tyne
Queen Alexandra College of Further Education, Birmingham
RNIB College Loughborough, Loughborough
RNIB Pears Centre for Specialist Learning, Warwickshire
RNIB Sunshine House School and Children's Home, Northwood
Rosewood School, Southampton
Rowden Hill School, Near Welshpool
Rowden House School, Bromyard
Royal School Manchester, Cheadle
Rutherford School, South Croydon
Rutland House School, Nottingham
St John's Catholic School for the Deaf, Boston Spa
St Joseph's Specialist School & College, Cranleigh
St Mary's Wrestwood Children's Trust, Bexhill-on-Sea
St Rose's School, Stroud
The London Centre for Children with Cerebral Palsy, London
The Marchant-Holliday School, Templecombe
The Royal Blind School, Edinburgh, Edinburgh
The Royal National College for the Blind (RNCB), Hereford
The Royal School for Deaf Children Margate, Margate
The School for Profound Education, Tadworth
The Sheiling School Ringwood, Ringwood
The Trust Centre, Derbyshire
Treloar College, Hampshire
Treloar School, Hampshire
Walton Progressive School, Liverpool
Westgate College for Deaf People, Westgate

MODERATE LEARNING DIFFICULTIES

AALPS College (Midlands), Hanley Castle
AALPS College (North), Nr Scunthorpe
Action for Children Headlands School, Penarth
Appleford School, Salisbury
Appletree School, Kendal
Aran Hall School, Dolgellau
Ashmeads, Bedford
Ballikinrain Residential School, Stirlingshire
Beaumont College of Further Education, Lancaster
Bladon House School, Burton upon Trent

The Grange Centre for People with Disabilities, Bookham
The Link Primary School, Croydon
The Lioncare School, Hove
The Marchant-Holliday School, Templecombe
The Mount Camphill Community, Wadhurst
The New School, Dunkeld
The Royal Blind School, Edinburgh, Edinburgh
The Royal National College for the Blind (RNCB), Hereford
The Royal School for Deaf Children Margate, Margate
The Ryes College & Community, Sudbury
The Sheiling School Ringwood, Ringwood
The Speech, Language & Hearing Centre, London
The St John Vianney School, Stockport
The St John Vianney School, Stretford
The West of England College for Students with Little or No Sight, Exeter

The Westside Independent School, London
Treloar College, Hampshire
Treloar School, Hampshire
Underley Garden School, Carnforth
Underley Hall School, Carnforth
Victoria Education Centre, Poole
Vranch House School, Exeter
West Kirby Residential School, Wirral
Westgate College for Deaf People, Westgate
Westwood School, Broadstairs
Whinfell Care, Kendal
Whitstone Head School, Holsworthy
William Morris House Camphill Community, Stonehouse
Wings School, Milnthorpe
Witherslack Hall, Grange-over-Sands
Woodcroft School, Loughton
Woodlands School, Wigtownshire
Wychbury House Residential School, Torquay
Young Options College, Shifnal
Ysgol Bryn Castell, Bridgend

PROFOUND & MULTIPLE LEARNING DIFFICULTIES

Action for Children Penhurst School, Chipping Norton
Annie Lawson School, Crowthorne
Aran Hall School, Dolgellau
Barrs Court School, Hereford
Beech Tree, Preston
Birtenshaw School, Bolton
Bladon House School, Burton upon Trent
Bridge College, Stockport
Burton Hill School, Malmesbury
Camphill Blair Drummond Trust, Stirling
Camphill School Aberdeen, Aberdeen
Chailey Heritage School, Nr Lewes
Craig-y-Parc School, Pentyrch
Crookhey Hall School, Lancaster
Dame Hannah Rogers School, Ivybridge
Doncaster School for the Deaf, Doncaster
East Park School, Glasgow
Hinwick Hall College, Wellingborough
Holly Bank School, Mirfield

Lambs Grange Residential and Day Education and Care, Cuddington
Langside School, Poole
Linn Moor Residential School, Aberdeen
Little David's School, Croydon
MacIntyre Wingrave School, Aylesbury
MacIntyre Womaston School, Presteigne
Meldreth Manor, Nr Royston
NAS Robert Ogden School, Rotherham
Nash College, Bromley
Nash College of Further Education, Bromley
National Star College, Cheltenham
Northern Counties School, Newcastle-Upon-Tyne
Ochil Tower (Rudolf Steiner) School, Auchterarder
Overley Hall School, Wellington
Pegasus School, Caldwell
Pengwern College, Rhuddlan
Pield Heath School, Uxbridge

RNIB College Loughborough, Loughborough
RNIB Pears Centre for Specialist Learning, Warwickshire
RNIB Sunshine House School and Children's Home, Northwood
Rosewood School, Southampton
Rowden Hill School, Near Welshpool
Rowden House School, Bromyard
Royal School for the Blind, Liverpool
Royal School Manchester, Cheadle
Rutherford School, South Croydon
Rutland House School, Nottingham
seeABILITY (formerly Royal School for the Blind), Epsom
Sense East, Peterborough
St Christopher's School, Westbury Park
St Elizabeth's School, Much Hadham
St Piers School, The National Centre for Young People with Epilepsy (NCYPE), Lingfield
St Rose's School, Stroud
Stanmore House Residential School, Lanark
The David Lewis School, Nr Alderley Edge
The Royal Blind School, Edinburgh, Edinburgh
The Royal School for Deaf Children Margate, Margate
The Ryes College & Community, Sudbury
The School for Profound Education, Tadworth
Trengweath School, Plymouth
Vranch House School, Exeter
Walton Progressive School, Liverpool
Westgate College for Deaf People, Westgate

SEVERE LEARNING DIFFICULTIES

AALPS College (North), Nr Scunthorpe
Action for Children Penhurst School, Chipping Norton
Aim Habonim, Greater Manchester
Annie Lawson School, Crowthorne
Aran Hall School, Dolgellau
Barrs Court School, Hereford
Beaumont College of Further Education, Lancaster
Beech Tree, Preston
Birtenshaw School, Bolton
Bladon House School, Burton upon Trent
Bridge College, Stockport
Broughton House College, Brant Broughton
Burton Hill School, Malmesbury
Camphill Blair Drummond Trust, Stirling
Camphill School Aberdeen, Aberdeen
Chailey Heritage School, Nr Lewes
Coleg Elidyr, Llandovery
Coombe House, Crediton
Cornerstones, Warrington
Cotswold Chine School, Near Stroud
Crookhey Hall School, Lancaster
Dame Hannah Rogers School, Ivybridge
Derwen College, Oswestry
Dilston College of Further Education, Corbridge
Doncaster College for the Deaf, Doncaster
Doncaster School for the Deaf, Doncaster
Eagle House – Norfolk School, Norwich
Eagle House School – Sutton, Sutton
Eagle House School Mitcham, Mitcham
Eagle Life College, Banham
East Park School, Glasgow
Ellesmere College, Thatcham
Exeter College, Exeter
Exeter Royal Academy for Deaf Education, Exeter
Exeter Royal Academy for Deaf Education, Exeter
Fairfield Farm College, Westbury
Fullerton House School, Doncaster
Henshaws College, Harrogate
Hereward College, Coventry
Hill House School, Lymington
Hillcrest Park School, Chipping Norton
Hillingdon Manor School, Uxbridge
Hinwick Hall College, Wellingborough
Holly Bank School, Mirfield
Homefield Residential College, Loughborough

The Sheiling School Ringwood, Ringwood
Treloar College, Hampshire
Treloar School, Hampshire
Trengweath School, Plymouth
Underley Garden School, Carnforth
Victoria Education Centre, Poole

Walton Progressive School, Liverpool
Westgate College for Deaf People, Westgate
Whinfell Care, Kendal
Wilsic Hall School, Doncaster
Woodcroft School, Loughton
Ysgol Bryn Castell, Bridgend

SPEECH & LANGUAGE DIFFICULTIES

AALPS College (Midlands), Hanley Castle
AALPS College (North), Nr Scunthorpe
Action for Children Headlands School,
    Penarth
Action for Children Penhurst School,
    Chipping Norton
Alderwasley Hall School and Callow Park
    College, Belper
Annie Lawson School, Crowthorne
Appleford School, Salisbury
Appletree School, Kendal
Aran Hall School, Dolgellau
Barnardo's Lecropt, Camelon
Beaumont College of Further Education,
    Lancaster
Beech Tree, Preston
Belgrave School, Clifton
Birtenshaw School, Bolton
Bladon House School, Burton upon Trent
Blossom House School, London
Brantridge School, Haywards Heath
Brewood Secondary School, Deal
Bridge College, Stockport
Broughton House College, Brant Broughton
Bruern Abbey School, Chesterton
Burton Hill School, Malmesbury
Calder House School, Chippenham
Camphill Blair Drummond Trust, Stirling
Camphill School Aberdeen, Aberdeen
Cedar House School, via Carnforth
Centre Academy, London
Centre Academy, East Anglia
Chailey Heritage School, Nr Lewes
Chelfham Senior School, Yelverton
Coombe House, Crediton
Cornerstones, Warrington

Cotswold Chine School, Near Stroud
Dame Hannah Rogers School, Ivybridge
Delamere Forest School, Warrington
Derwen College, Oswestry
Dilston College of Further Education,
    Corbridge
Donaldson's College for the Deaf,
    Edinburgh
Doncaster College for the Deaf, Doncaster
Doncaster School for the Deaf, Doncaster
Eagle House – Norfolk School, Norwich
Eagle House School Mitcham, Mitcham
Eagle Life College, Banham
East Park School, Glasgow
Easter Auguston Training Farm, Aberdeen
Eden Grove School, Appleby
Ellesmere College, Thatcham
Enham, Andover
Exeter College, Exeter
Exeter Royal Academy for Deaf Education,
    Exeter
Exeter Royal Academy for Deaf Education,
    Exeter
Fairfield Farm College, Westbury
Fairley House School, London
Farleigh College Condover, Shrewsbury
Fortune Centre of Riding Therapy,
    Christchurch
Frederick Hugh House, London
Frewen College, Rye
Fullerton House School, Doncaster
Grafham Grange School, Guildford
Grateley House School, Andover
Harmeny School, Balerno
Henshaws College, Harrogate
Hereward College, Coventry

St John's Catholic School for the Deaf, Boston Spa
St John's RC School, Woodford Green
St Joseph's Specialist School & College, Cranleigh
St Mary's Wrestwood Children's Trust, Bexhill-on-Sea
St Piers School, The National Centre for Young People with Epilepsy (NCYPE), Lingfield
St Rose's School, Stroud
St Vincent's School, A Specialist School for Sensory Impairment and Other Needs, Liverpool
Stanbridge Earls School, Romsey
Strathmore College, Staffordshire
Swalcliffe Park School Trust, Banbury
Tadley Horizon, Basingstoke
The Chelsea Group of Children, London
The David Lewis School, Nr Alderley Edge
The Forum School, Shillingstone
The Grange Centre for People with Disabilities, Bookham
The Link Primary School, Croydon
The Link Secondary School, Beddington
The Lioncare School, Hove
The Marchant-Holliday School, Templecombe
The New School at West Heath, Sevenoaks
The Royal Blind School, Edinburgh, Edinburgh

The Royal National College for the Blind (RNCB), Hereford
The Royal School for Deaf Children Margate, Margate
The Ryes College & Community, Sudbury
The Sheiling School Ringwood, Ringwood
The Speech, Language & Hearing Centre, London
The St John Vianney School, Stockport
The Trust Centre, Derbyshire
The Unicorn School, Abingdon
The Wing Centre, Bournemouth
Tree House, London
Tregynon Hall School, Newtown
Treloar College, Hampshire
Treloar School, Hampshire
Trinity School, Rochester
Underley Garden School, Carnforth
Underley Hall School, Carnforth
Victoria Education Centre, Poole
Vranch House School, Exeter
Walton Progressive School, Liverpool
Waterloo Lodge School, Chorley
West Kirby Residential School, Wirral
Westgate College for Deaf People, Westgate
Whinfell Care, Kendal
Wilsic Hall School, Doncaster
Witherslack Hall, Grange-over-Sands
Woodcroft School, Loughton
Woodlands School, Wigtownshire
Ysgol Bryn Castell, Bridgend

TOURETTE'S SYNDROME

AALPS College (Midlands), Hanley Castle
AALPS College (North), Nr Scunthorpe
Action for Children Headlands School, Penarth
Aran Hall School, Dolgellau
Ashmeads, Bedford
Barnardo's Lecropt, Camelon
Beech Tree, Preston
Bladon House School, Burton upon Trent
Brewood Secondary School, Deal
Camphill School Aberdeen, Aberdeen

Cedar House School, via Carnforth
Chartwell House School, Wisbech
Chelfham Mill School, Barnstaple
Chelfham Senior School, Yelverton
Clarence High School, Formby
Cotswold Chine School, Near Stroud
Coxlease School, Lyndhurst
Delamere Forest School, Warrington
Eden Grove School, Appleby
Exeter College, Exeter
Falkland House School, Cupar

VISUAL IMPAIRMENT

WHEELCHAIR ACCESS

Please see the Glossary of Abbreviations, Part 5.4, page 553, for further details.

PART THREE

Special Schools and Colleges – Maintained

3.1

Index of Education Authorities

State maintained schools are listed by Local Authority. Since 1996 a number of new unitary authorities have been created in addition to existing two-tier structures. The index below (for England) lists each local authority under the county of which it is deemed a part, and is designed to help you identify the local authorities responsible for schools in your area. Turn to the page number shown against each to find the schools within the authority. Schools in Northern Ireland, Scotland and Wales are listed by Local Authority only.

ENGLAND

Special Schools and Colleges – Maintained

Special Schools and Colleges – Maintained

Special Schools and Colleges – Maintained

WALES

Special Schools and Colleges – Maintained

3.2

Notes on the Directory

Maintained schools by Local Authority

Maintained schools are listed by Local Authority. An index of Local Authorities and their corresponding page entries appears on pages 309–14.

Every effort has been made to compile a comprehensive list of schools. Each entry includes the school name, address, and web adresses where available, the age range and sex of students accepted.

The types of need for which a school or college makes provision are shown in abbreviated form. A key to the abbreviations used is given below. The principal types of special needs catered for, where known, are shown in bold[1]. Please note that this information is intended as a guide only. For further information and details of auxiliary aids and services contact schools direct.

Key to abbreviations used in the directory

Special needs provision

ADD	Attention Deficit Disorder	EPI	Epilepsy
ADHD	Attention Deficit Hyperactivity Disorder	HEA	Health Problems (eg heart defect, asthma)
ASD	Autistic Spectrum Disorder	HI	Hearing Impairment
ASP	Asperger's Syndrome	IM	Impaired Mobility
BESD	Behavioural, Emotional and Social Disorders	MLD	Moderate Learning Difficulties
		PMLD	Profound and Multiple Learning Difficulties
CB	Challenging Behaviour		
CP	Cerebral Palsy	SLD	Severe Learning Difficulties
DOW	Down's Syndrome	SP&LD	Speech and Language Difficulties
DYC	Dyscalculia	TOU	Tourette's Syndrome
DYP	Dyspraxia	VI	Visual Impairment
DYS	Dyslexia		

[1] In addition to catering for the special needs specified, all schools and colleges recognize their responsibilities under the Disability Discrimination Act 1995 to consider the needs of all disabled children and to make reasonable adjustments to facilitate the admission of such children to the school.

Wheelchair access

W   Wheelchair access (unspecified)

WA1   School is fully wheelchair accessible in all areas

WA2   Main teaching areas are wheelchair accessible

WA3   No permanent access for wheelchairs; temporary ramps available

Symbol

+   Registered with CReSTeD (see Part 5.1)

3.3

Directory of Maintained Schools by Local Authority

England

BEDFORDSHIRE

Bedfordshire Education Offices

County Hall
Cauldwell Street
Bedford
Bedfordshire
MK42 9AP
Email: education@
bedscc.gov.uk

GLENWOOD SCHOOL
Beech Road, Dunstable,
Bedfordshire LU6 3LY
Type: Co-educational Day Only
2–11
Special needs: ASD **ASP PMLD SLD**
Wheelchair access: WA1

GRANGE SCHOOL
Halsey Road, Kempston,
Bedfordshire MK42 8AU
Type: Co-educational Day Only
7–16
Special needs: ASD **MLD**
Wheelchair access: WA2

HILLCREST SCHOOL
Regis Education Centre, Regis,
Bedfordshire LU5 5PX
Type: Co-educational Day Only
11–19
Special needs: ASD PMLD **SLD**
Wheelchair access: W

HITCHMEAD SCHOOL
Hitchmead Road, Biggleswade,
Bedfordshire SG18 0NL
Type: Co-educational Day Only
7–16

OAK BANK SCHOOL
Sandy Lane, Leighton Buzzard,
Bedfordshire LU7 8BE
Type: Boys Boarding Only 11–16
Special needs: **BESD**

RAINBOW SCHOOL
Chestnut Avenue, Bedford,
Bedfordshire MK43 8HP
Type: Co-educational Day Only
5–13
Special needs: ASD **ASP** SLD
Wheelchair access: W

RIDGEWAY SCHOOL
Hill Rise, Bedford, Bedfordshire
MK42 7EB
Type: Co-educational Day Only
2–19
Special needs: VI
Wheelchair access: WA1

ST JOHNS SCHOOL
Austin Canons, Bedford,
Bedfordshire MK42 8AA
Website: www.st-johns-school.
co.uk
Type: Co-educational Day Only
2–19
Special needs: ASD **ASP HI**
PMLD SLD VI
Wheelchair access: WA1

SUNNYSIDE SCHOOL
The Baulk, Biggleswade,
Bedfordshire SG18 0PT
Type: Co-educational Day Only
2–19
Special needs: ASD **ASP PMLD SLD**
Wheelchair access: WA1

WEATHERFIELD SCHOOL
Brewers Hill Road, Dunstable,
Bedfordshire LU6 1AF
Website: www.weatherfield.beds.
sch.uk
Type: Co-educational Day Only
7–16
Special needs: **ADD ADHD ASD
ASP BESD CB CP DOW DYP
DYS EPI HEA HI IM MLD SLD**
SP&LD **TOU** VI
Wheelchair access: WA3

Luton Borough Council

Town Hall
George Street
Luton
LU1 2BQ

LADY ZIA WERNER SCHOOL
Ashcroft Road, Luton,
Bedfordshire LU2 9AY
Type: Co-educational Day Only
2–11
Special needs: CP DOW **HEA
PMLD SLD** SP&LD
Wheelchair access: WA1

RICHMOND HILL SCHOOL
Sunridge Avenue, Luton,
Bedfordshire LU2 7JL
Type: Co-educational Day Only
5–11
Special needs: ASD **ASP** HI
PMLD SLD

**WOODLANDS SECONDARY
SCHOOL**
Northwell Drive, Luton,
Bedfordshire LU3 3SP
Type: Co-educational Day Only
11–19
Special needs: ASD ASP HI
PMLD SLD VI

BERKSHIRE

Bracknell Forest Education Department

Seymour House
38 Broadway
Bracknell
Berkshire
RG12 1AU

KENNEL LANE SCHOOL
Kennel Lane, Bracknell,
Berkshire RG42 2EX
Website: www.kennellaneschool.
com
Type: Co-educational Day Only
2–19
Special needs: ASD MLD PMLD
SLD

Reading Borough Council

Civic Centre
Reading
Berkshire
RG1 7TD

THE AVENUE SCHOOL
Basingstoke Road, Reading,
Berkshire RG2 0EN
Type: Co-educational Day Only
2–19
Special needs: BESD CP EPI
HEA MLD PMLD SP&LD VI
Wheelchair access: W

HOLY BROOK SCHOOL
145 Ashampstead Road,
Reading, Berkshire RG30 3LT
Type: Co-educational Day Only
5–11
Special needs: ADD ADHD
BESD

Slough Borough Council

Town Hall
Bath Road
Slough
Berkshire
SL1 3UQ

ARBOUR VALE SCHOOL
Farnham Road, Slough,
Berkshire SL2 3AE
Website: www.arbourvale.slough.
sch.uk
Type: Co-educational Day Only
2–19
Special needs: ASD **ASP** HI **MLD
PMLD SLD** VI
Wheelchair access: WA1

LITTLEDOWN SCHOOL
Queen's Road, Slough, Berkshire
SL1 3QW
Type: Co-educational 5–11
Special needs: BESD

West Berkshire Council

Avonbank House
West Street
Newbury
Berkshire
RG14 1BZ

BROOKFIELDS SCHOOL
Sage Road, Reading, Berkshire
RG31 6SW
Type: Co-educational Day Only
Special needs: ASD **MLD PMLD
SLD**
Wheelchair access: W

THE CASTLE SCHOOL
Love Lane, Newbury, Berkshire
RG14 2JG
Website: www.castle.westberks.
org
Type: Co-educational Day Only
2–19
Special needs: **ASD ASP DOW
MLD PMLD SLD**
Wheelchair access: WA2

Windsor & Maidenhead Education Authority

Town Hall
St Ives Road
Maidenhead
Berkshire
SL6 1RF

MANOR GREEN SCHOOL
Elizabeth Hawkes Way, Maidenhead, Berkshire SL6 3EQ
Website: www.manorgreenschool.org
Type: Co-educational Day and Boarding 2–19
Special needs: ADD ADHD **ASD ASP** BESD CB **CP DOW** DYC DYP DYS **EPI** HEA HI IM **MLD PMLD SLD** SP&LD TOU VI
Wheelchair access: W

Wokingham Education Department

PO Box 150
Shute End
Wokingham
Berkshire
RG40 1WQ

ADDINGTON SCHOOL
Loddon Bridge Road, Reading, Berkshire RG5 4BS
Type: Co-educational Day Only 2–19
Special needs: ASD **ASP MLD PMLD SLD**
Wheelchair access: WA1

SOUTHFIELD SCHOOL
Gipsy Lane, Wokingham, Berkshire RG40 2HR
Website: www.southfield.wokingham.sch.uk
Type: Co-educational Day and Boarding 11–16
Special needs: **BESD**
Wheelchair access: WA2

BRISTOL

Bristol Education and Lifelong Learning

PO Box 57
Council House
College Green
Bristol
BS99 7EB

BRIARWOOD SCHOOL
Briar Way, Bristol BS16 4EA
Type: Co-educational Day Only 3–19
Special needs: ASD **ASP PMLD SLD**
Wheelchair access: W

THE BRISTOL GATEWAY SCHOOL
Stafford Road, St Werburghs, Bristol BS2 9UR
Type: Boys Day Only 11–14
Special needs: **BESD**

CLAREMONT SCHOOL
Henleaze Park, Bristol BS9 4LR
Website: www.claremontspecial.ik.org
Type: Co-educational Day Only 2–19
Special needs: **PMLD**
Wheelchair access: WA1

ELMFIELD SCHOOL
Greystoke Avenue, Bristol BS10 6AY
Type: Co-educational Day Only 3–16
Special needs: **HI**
Wheelchair access: WA1

FLORENCE BROWN COMMUNITY SCHOOL
Leinster Avenue, Bristol BS4 1NN
Type: Co-educational Day Only 7–19
Special needs: ADHD **BESD** IM **MLD** SP&LD
Wheelchair access: WA1

KINGSDON MANOR SCHOOL
Kingsdon, Somerton, Bristol TA11 7JZ
Type: Boys Boarding Only 10–16
Special needs: **BESD** MLD

NEW FOSSEWAY SCHOOL
New Fosseway Road, Bristol BS14 9LN
Type: Co-educational Day Only 3–19
Special needs: PMLD SLD
Wheelchair access: W

NOTTON HOUSE
28 Notton, Lacock Nr Chippenham, Wiltshire SN15 2NP
Type: Boys Boarding Only 9–16
Special needs: ADD ADHD ASP **BESD** DYP DYS

WOODSTOCK SCHOOL
Courtney Road, Bristol BS15 9RL
Type: Co-educational Day Only 7–11
Special needs: **BESD**

BUCKINGHAMSHIRE

Buckinghamshire County Council

County Hall
Aylesbury
Buckinghamshire
HP20 1UA

ALFRISTON SCHOOL
Penn Road, Beaconsfield,
Buckinghamshire HP9 2TS
Type: Girls Day and Boarding
11–18
Special needs: **MLD**
Wheelchair access: WA2

BOOKER PARK SCHOOL
Booker Park, Aylesbury,
Buckinghamshire HP21 9ET
Type: Co-educational Day Only
2–11
Special needs: ADD ADHD ASD
ASP BESD CP DOW DYC DYP
DYS EPI **MLD PMLD SLD** SP&LD
VI
Wheelchair access: WA1

CHILTERN GATE SCHOOL
Verney Avenue, High Wycombe,
Buckinghamshire HP12 3NE
Type: Co-educational Day Only
Special needs: ADD ADHD ASD
ASP BESD CP DOW DYP EPI
HEA HI IM **MLD** SP&LD TOU VI
Wheelchair access: WA2

FURZE DOWN SCHOOL
Verney Road, Winslow,
Buckinghamshire MK18 3BL
Type: Co-educational Day Only
5–18
Special needs: ADHD ASD ASP
DYC DYP DYS EPI HI **MLD** SLD
SP&LD

HERITAGE HOUSE SCHOOL
Cameron Road, Chesham,
Buckinghamshire HP5 3BP
Website: www.
heritagehouseschool.co.uk
Type: Co-educational Day Only
2–19
Special needs: ASD **ASP** CP EPI
HEA IM **PMLD SLD** VI W
Wheelchair access: WA1

KYNASTON SCHOOL
Stoke Leys Close, Aylesbury,
Buckinghamshire HP21 9ET
Type: Co-educational Day Only
5–11
Special needs: **BESD**

THE LADY ADRIAN SCHOOL
Courtney Way, Cambridge,
Cambridgeshire CB4 2EE
Type: Co-educational 7–16
Special needs: ADHD ASP BESD
EPI **MLD** SLD TOU
Wheelchair access: W

MAPLEWOOD SCHOOL
Faulkner Way, High Wycombe,
Buckinghamshire HP13 5HB
Type: Co-educational Day Only
3–19
Special needs: **PMLD SLD**
Wheelchair access: WA1

MEADOWGATE SCHOOL
Meadowgate Lane, Wisbech,
Cambridgeshire PE13 2JH
Website: www.meadowgate.
cambs.sch.uk
Type: Co-educational Day Only
2–19
Special needs: ASD **ASP MLD
PMLD SLD**
Wheelchair access: WA1

PEBBLE BROOK SCHOOL
Churchill Avenue, Aylesbury,
Buckinghamshire HP21 8LZ
Type: Co-educational Day and
Boarding 11–18
Special needs: **MLD**

PRESTWOOD LODGE SCHOOL
FOR BOYS
Nairdwood Lane, Great
Missenden, Buckinghamshire
HP16 0QQ
Type: Boys Boarding and Day
11–16
Special needs: **BESD**

ROMANS FIELD SCHOOL
Shenley Road, Bletchley,
Buckinghamshire MK3 7AW
Type: Co-educational Day and
Boarding 5–11
Special needs: **BESD**
Wheelchair access: WA2

SAMUEL PEPYS SCHOOL
Cromwell Road, St Neots,
Cambridgeshire PE19 2EZ
Type: Co-educational Day Only
3–19
Special needs: ASD **ASP PMLD
SLD**
Wheelchair access: WA1

STOCKLAKE PARK SCHOOL
Stocklake, Aylesbury,
Buckinghamshire HP20 1DP
Type: Co-educational Day Only
11–19
Special needs: ASD **ASP** CP
DOW **MLD PMLD SLD** VI
Wheelchair access: WA1

STONY DEAN SCHOOL
Orchard End Avenue,
Amersham, Buckinghamshire
HP7 9JW
Website: www.stonydean.
bucks.sch.uk
Type: Co-educational Day Only
11–18
Special needs: ASD ASP DYS
MLD SP&LD
Wheelchair access: WA3

WENDOVER HOUSE SCHOOL
Church Lane, Aylesbury,
Buckinghamshire HP22 6NL
Type: Boys Boarding and Day
Special needs: **BESD**

WESTFIELD SCHOOL
Highfield Road, High Wycombe,
Buckinghamshire SL8 5BE
Type: Co-educational
Special needs: **BESD**
Wheelchair access: W

WHITE SPIRE SCHOOL
Rickley Lane, Milton Keynes,
Buckinghamshire MK3 6EW
Website: www.whitespire.
milton-keynes.sch.uk
Type: Co-educational 5–18
Special needs: **MLD**
Wheelchair access: WA2

Milton Keynes Council

Saxon Court
502 Avebury Boulevard
Milton Keynes
MK9 3HS

THE GATEHOUSE SCHOOL
Crosslands, Milton Keynes,
Buckinghamshire MK14 6AX
Type: Boys Boarding and Day
12–16
Special needs: **BESD**
Wheelchair access: W

THE REDWAY SCHOOL
Farmborough, Milton Keynes,
Buckinghamshire MK6 4HG
Website: www.theredway.net
Type: Co-educational Day Only
2–19
Special needs: ASD **PMLD SLD**
Wheelchair access: WA1

SLATED ROW SCHOOL
Old Wolverton Road, Milton
Keynes, Buckinghamshire
MK12 5NJ
Type: Co-educational Day Only
4–19
Special needs: **MLD**
Wheelchair access: WA1

THE WALNUTS SCHOOL
Admiral Drive, Milton Keynes,
Buckinghamshire MK8 0PU
Website: www.walnuts.
milton-keynes.sch.uk
Type: Co-educational Boarding
and Day 4–19
Special needs:
Wheelchair access: WA1
52-week care

CAMBRIDGESHIRE

Cambridgeshire LEA

Shire Hall
Castle Hill
Cambridge
CB3 0AP

THE HARBOUR SCHOOL
Station Road, Ely,
Cambridgeshire CB6 3RR
Type: Co-educational Boarding
and Day 5–14
Special needs: **BESD**

HIGHFIELD SCHOOL
Downham Road, Ely,
Cambridgeshire CB6 1BD
Type: Co-educational Day Only
2–19
Special needs: ADD ASD ASP
CP DOW DYP EPI HI MLD PMLD
SLD SP&LD TOU VI
Wheelchair access: WA1

Peterborough City Council

Town Hall
Bridge Street
Peterborough
PE1 1QT

THE CAUSEWAY SCHOOL
Park Lane, Peterborough,
Cambridgeshire PE1 5GZ
Type: Co-educational Day Only
Special needs: ADD ADHD
BESD

HELTWATE SCHOOL
North Bretton, Peterborough,
Cambridgeshire PE3 8RL
Type: Co-educational Day Only
5–16
Special needs: ASD HI **MLD SLD**
SP&LD
Wheelchair access: WA2

MARSHFIELDS SCHOOL
Eastern Close, Peterborough,
Cambridgeshire PE1 4PP
Type: Co-educational Day Only
9–18
Special needs: BESD **MLD**
SP&LD
Wheelchair access: W

THE PHOENIX SCHOOL
Orton Goldhay, Peterborough,
Cambridgeshire PE2 5SD
Type: Co-educational Day Only
2–19
Special needs: ASD DOW EPI HI
PMLD SLD SP&LD VI
Wheelchair access: WA1

CHANNEL ISLANDS

Guernsey Education Department

Grange Road
St Peter Port
Guernsey
Channel Islands
GY1 3AU

LONGFIELD CENTRE
Maurepas Road, Guernsey,
Channel Islands GY1 2DS
Type: Co-educational Day Only
3–7
Special needs: ADHD ASD EPI
HI **MLD** SP&LD
Wheelchair access: W

MONT VAROUF SCHOOL
Le Neuf Chemin, Guernsey,
Channel Islands GY7 9FG
Type: Co-educational Day Only
3–19
Special needs: ASD DOW EPI
PMLD SLD SP&LD VI

OAKVALE SCHOOL
Collings Road, Guernsey,
Channel Islands GY1 1FW
Type: Co-educational Day Only
11–19
Special needs: **MLD**
Wheelchair access: WA1

States of Jersey

PO Box 142
Jersey
Channel Islands
JE4 8QJ

D'HAUTREE HOUSE SCHOOL
St Saviour, Jersey, Channel
Islands JE2 4QP
Type: Co-educational Day Only
11–16
Special needs: ADHD **BESD**
MLD

MONT A L'ABBE SCHOOL
Jersey, Channel Islands JE2 3FN
Type: Co-educational Day Only
3–18
Special needs: ASD CB MLD
PMLD SLD
Wheelchair access: WA1

ST JAMES' SCHOOL
Le Breton Lane, Jersey, Channel
Islands JE2 4QN
Type: Co-educational
Special needs: **BESD**

CHESHIRE

Cheshire Education and Community Education Department

County Hall
Chester
Cheshire
CH1 1SF

ADELAIDE SCHOOL
Adelaide Street, Crewe, Cheshire
CW1 3DT
Type: Co-educational Day Only
Special needs: **BESD**

CAPENHURST GRANGE SCHOOL
Chester Road, Great Sutton,
Cheshire CH66 2NA
Type: Co-educational Boarding
Only 11–16
Special needs: ADHD **BESD**
MLD

CLOUGHWOOD SCHOOL
Stones Manor Lane, Northwich,
Cheshire CW8 1NU
Type: Boys Boarding Only
Special needs: **BESD**

DEE BANKS SCHOOL
Sandy Lane, Chester, Cheshire
CH3 5UX
Type: Co-educational Day Only
2–19
Special needs: ASD PMLD **SLD**
Wheelchair access: WA1

DORIN PARK SCHOOL
Wealstone Lane, Upton-by-
Chester, Cheshire CH2 1HD
Website: www.dorinpark.org.uk
Type: Co-educational Day Only
Special needs: PMLD

GREENBANK SCHOOL
off Green Bank Lane, Northwich,
Cheshire CW8 1LD
Type: Co-educational Boarding
Only 6–18
Special needs: ASD **MLD SLD**
Wheelchair access: WA2

HEBDEN GREEN SCHOOL
Woodford Lane West, Winsford,
Cheshire CW7 4EJ
Type: Co-educational Day and
Boarding 2–19
Special needs: CP EPI HEA HI
PMLD SP&LD VI
Wheelchair access: WA1

HINDERTON SCHOOL
Capenhurst Lane, Ellesmere Port,
Cheshire CH65 7AQ
Type: Co-educational Day Only
3–11
Special needs: ASD SP&LD

OAKLANDS SCHOOL
Cheviot Square, Winsford,
Cheshire CW7 1NU
Type: Co-educational Day Only
11–16
Special needs: **MLD**

PARK LANE SCHOOL
Park Lane, Macclesfield,
Cheshire SK11 8JR
Website: www.parklane.school.
cheshire.org.uk
Type: Co-educational Day Only
2–19
Special needs: PMLD SLD
Wheelchair access: WA1

ROSEBANK SCHOOL
Townfield Lane, Northwich,
Cheshire CW8 4QP
Type: Co-educational Day Only
3–11
Special needs: ASD **ASP MLD**
SP&LD
Wheelchair access: WA2

THE RUSSETT SCHOOL
Middlehurst Avenue, Northwich,
Cheshire CW8 3BW
Type: Co-educational Day Only
2–19
Special needs: ASD DOW EPI HI
PMLD SLD VI
Wheelchair access: W

ST JOHN'S WOOD COMMUNITY SCHOOL
Knutsford, Cheshire WA16 8PA
Website: www.st-johns-school.
co.uk
Type: Co-educational Day Only
11–16
Special needs: BESD
Wheelchair access: WA2

SPRINGFIELD SCHOOL
Crewe Green Road, Crewe,
Cheshire CW1 5HS
Website: www.springfield.
cheshire.sch.uk
Type: Co-educational Day Only
3–19
Special needs: ASD DOW **PMLD SLD**
Wheelchair access: WA1

Halton Borough Council

Municipal Building
Kingsway
Widnes
Cheshire
WA8 7QF

ASHLEY SCHOOL
Cawfield Avenue, Widnes, Halton
WA8 7HG
Type: Co-educational Day Only
11–16
Special needs: **MLD**

BROOKFIELDS SCHOOL
Moorfield Road, Widnes, Halton
WA8 3JA
Type: Co-educational Day Only
3–11
Special needs: ASD PMLD SLD
Wheelchair access: WA1

CAVENDISH SCHOOL
Lincoln Close, Runcorn, Cheshire
WA7 4YX
Type: Co-educational Day Only
2–19
Special needs: ADHD ASD CP
EPI **PMLD SLD**
Wheelchair access: W

CHESNUT LODGE SCHOOL
Green Lane, Widnes, Cheshire
WA8 7HF
Website: www.
chesnutlodgeschool.co.uk
Type: Co-educational Day Only
2–16
Special needs: CP DYP EPI MLD
SP&LD VI
Wheelchair access: W

Warrington Education and Lifelong Learning Department

New Town House
Buttermarket Street
Warrington
Cheshire
WA1 2NJ

FOX WOOD SCHOOL
Chatfield Drive, Warrington,
Cheshire WA3 6QW
Type: Co-educational Day Only
4–19
Special needs: ASD **ASP PMLD SLD**

GRAPPENHALL RESIDENTIAL SCHOOL
Church Lane, Warrington,
Cheshire WA4 3EU
Type: Boys Boarding and Day
Special needs: ADD ADHD ASD
ASP **BESD** CB MLD SP&LD TOU

GREEN LANE SCHOOL
Green Lane, Warrington,
Cheshire WA1 4JL
Type: Co-educational Day Only
4–16
Special needs: ASD **MLD** SLD
Wheelchair access: WA2

CORNWALL

Cornwall Education Department

Treyew Road
Truro
Cornwall
TR1 3AY

CURNOW SCHOOL
Drump Road, Redruth, Cornwall
TR15 1LU
Website: www.curnow.cornwall.
sch.uk
Type: Co-educational Day Only
Special needs: **PMLD SLD**
Wheelchair access: WA2

NANCEALVERNE SCHOOL
Madron Road, Penzance,
Cornwall TR20 8TP
Type: Co-educational Day Only
2–19
Special needs: PMLD SLD
Wheelchair access: WA2

PENCALENICK SCHOOL
Truro, Cornwall TR1 1TE
Type: Co-educational Day Only
11–16
Special needs: **SLD**

CUMBRIA

Cumbria Education Service

5 Portland Square
Carlisle
CA1 1PU

GEORGE HASTWELL SCHOOL
Moor Tarn Lane, Barrow in
Furness, Cumbria LA14 3LW
Type: Co-educational Day Only
2–19
Special needs: PMLD SLD
Wheelchair access: WA1

MAYFIELD SCHOOL
Moresby, Whitehaven, Cumbria
CA28 8TU
Website: www.mayfieldcumbria.
org
Type: Co-educational Day Only
Special needs: PMLD **SLD**
Wheelchair access: WA1

SANDGATE SCHOOL
Sandylands Road, Kendal,
Cumbria LA9 6JG
Type: Co-educational Day Only
2–19
Special needs: ASD **ASP** BESD
CP EPI HI MLD **PMLD SLD** VI
Wheelchair access: WA1

SANDSIDE LODGE SCHOOL
Sandside Road, Ulverston,
Cumbria LA12 9EF
Type: Co-educational Day Only
2–19
Special needs: ASD **ASP** EPI HI
PMLD SLD SP&LD
Wheelchair access: WA1

DERBYSHIRE

Derby City Council

Corporation Street
Derby
DE1 2FS

IVY HOUSE SCHOOL
Moorway Lane, Derby,
Derbyshire DE23 7FS
Type: Co-educational Day Only
2–19
Special needs: PMLD SLD
Wheelchair access: WA1

ST ANDREW'S SCHOOL
St Andrew's View, Derby,
Derbyshire DE2 4EW
Website: www.standrewschool.
co.uk
Type: Co-educational Day and
Boarding 11–19
Special needs: ASD **SLD**
Wheelchair access: WA1

ST CLARE'S SCHOOL
Rough Heanor Road, Derby,
Derbyshire DE3 5AZ
Type: Co-educational Day Only
11–16
Special needs: ASD **BESD** HI
MLD SLD SP&LD

ST GILES SCHOOL
Hampshire Road, Derby,
Derbyshire DE21 6BT
Website: www.stgiles.derby.
sch.uk
Type: Co-educational Day Only
4–11
Special needs: **ADHD** ASD **ASP**
BESD CB CP DOW DYS EPI HI
IM **MLD PMLD SLD** SP&LD VI W
Wheelchair access: WA1

ST MARTIN'S SCHOOL
Wisgreaves Road, Derby,
Derbyshire DE2 8RQ
Type: Co-educational Day Only
11–16
Special needs: ADD ASD ASP
BESD DOW DYP DYS **MLD**
Wheelchair access: WA2

Derbyshire Education Offices

County Hall
Matlock
Derbyshire
DE4 3AG

ALFRETON PARK COMMUNITY SPECIAL SCHOOL
Wingfield Road, Alfreton,
Derbyshire DE55 7AL
Type: Co-educational Day Only
2–19
Special needs: ASD PMLD **SLD**
Wheelchair access: W

ASHGATE CROFT SCHOOL
Ashgate Road, Chesterfield,
Derbyshire S40 4BN
Type: Co-educational Day Only
2–19
Special needs: ASD BESD CP
DYS EPI HEA HI **MLD PMLD SLD**
SP&LD VI
Wheelchair access: WA1

BARNSTAPLE TUTORIAL UNIT (PRU)
St Johns Lane, Barnstaple,
Devon EX32 9DD
Type: Co-educational Day Only
Special needs: **BESD**

BENNERLEY FIELDS SCHOOL
Stratford Street, Ilkeston,
Derbyshire DE7 8QZ
Type: Co-educational Day Only
3–16
Special needs: ASD **ASP** BESD
DOW DYP DYS HI **MLD SLD**
SP&LD
Wheelchair access: W

BRACKENFIELD SCHOOL
Bracken Road, Nottingham,
Nottinghamshire NG10 4DA
Website: www.brackenfield.
derbsyhire.sch.uk
Type: Co-educational Day Only
5–16
Special needs: BESD MLD
Wheelchair access: WA1

THE DELVES SCHOOL
Hayes Lane, Swanwick,
Derbyshire DE55 1AR
Type: Co-educational 5–16
Special needs: ASD BESD MLD
SLD SP&LD

HOLBROOK CENTRE FOR AUTISM
Holbrook, Belper, Derbyshire
DE56 0TE
Type: Co-educational Day and
Boarding 5–19
Special needs: ASD **ASP** CB SLD

HOLLY HOUSE SCHOOL
Church Street North,
Chesterfield, Derbyshire S41 9QR
Type: Co-educational Day Only
4–11
Special needs: **BESD**

PEAK SCHOOL
Buxton Road, High Peak,
Derbyshire SK23 6ES
Type: Co-educational Boarding
and Day 2–19
Special needs: ASD **ASP** CP EPI
PMLD SLD
Wheelchair access: W

STANTON VALE
Thoresby Road, Nottingham,
Nottinghamshire NG10 3NP
Type: Co-educational Boarding
and Day 2–16
Special needs: CP
Wheelchair access: W

STUBBIN WOOD SCHOOL
Burlington Avenue, Mansfield,
Derbyshire NG20 9AD
Type: Co-educational Day Only
2–16
Special needs: ASD **ASP** BESD
MLD PMLD SLD SP&LD
Wheelchair access: WA1

DEVON

Devon County Council

County Hall
Topsham Road
Exeter
Devon
EX2 4QD

BARLEY LANE SCHOOL
Barley Lane, Exeter, Devon
EX4 1TA
Type: Co-educational Day Only
8–14
Special needs: **BESD**

BIDWELL BROOK SCHOOL
Shinner's Bridge, Dartington,
Devon TQ9 6JU
Website: www.bidwellbrook.
devon.sch.uk
Type: Co-educational Day Only
3–19
Special needs: ASD MLD **PMLD
SLD**
Wheelchair access: WA2

COURTLANDS SCHOOL
Widey Court, Plymouth, Devon
PL6 5JS
Type: Co-educational Day Only
Special needs: ADD ADHD ASP
MLD SP&LD

ELLEN TINKHAM SCHOOL
Hollow Lane, Exeter, Devon
EX1 3RW
Type: Co-educational Day Only
3–19
Special needs: ASD CP EPI HI
MLD **PMLD SLD** VI
Wheelchair access: WA1

HILL CREST SCHOOL
St John's Road, Exmouth, Devon
EX8 4ED
Type: Boys Boarding and Day
10–16
Special needs: **BESD**

THE LAMPARD COMMUNITY COLLEGE
St John's Lane, Barnstaple,
Devon EX32 9DD
Website: www.lampardschool.
co.uk
Type: Co-educational Day Only
7–16
Special needs: ASD **ASP DOW
MLD**
Wheelchair access: WA1

MARLAND SCHOOL
Torrington, Devon EX3 8QQ
Type: Boys Boarding Only 11–16
Special needs: ADD ADHD
BESD

MILL FORD SCHOOL
Rochford Crescent, Plymouth,
Devon PL5 2PY
Type: Co-educational Day Only
3–19
Special needs: ASD **PMLD SLD**
Wheelchair access: WA1

MILL WATER SCHOOL
Honiton Bottom Road, Honiton,
Devon EX14 2ER
Type: Co-educational Day Only
4–18

OAKLANDS PARK SCHOOL
John Nash Drive, Dawlish, Devon
EX7 9SF
Website: www.oaklandspark.
devon.sch.uk
Type: Co-educational Boarding
and Day 3–19
Special needs: ASD **ASP** CP EPI
PMLD **SLD**
Wheelchair access: W

PATHFIELD SCHOOL
Abbey Road, Barnstaple, Devon
EX31 1JU
Website: www.pathfield.devon.
sch.uk
Type: Co-educational Day Only
3–19
Special needs: ASD **ASP PMLD
SLD**
Wheelchair access: WA1

RATCLIFFE SCHOOL
John Nash Drive, Dawlish, Devon
EX7 9RZ
Website: www.dawlish-ratcliffe.
devon.sch.uk
Type: Co-educational Day and
Boarding 8–16
Special needs: ASD **ASP BESD**
Wheelchair access: WA3

SOUTHBROOK COLLEGE
Bishop Westall Road, Exeter,
Devon EX2 6JB
Website: www.southbrook.
devon.sch.uk
Type: Co-educational Day Only
7–16
Special needs: ASD **MLD**
Wheelchair access: WA1

Plymouth City Council

Civic Centre
Plymouth
PL1 2EW

BROOK GREEN CENTRE FOR LEARNING
Bodmin Road, Plymouth, Devon
PL5 4DZ
Type: Co-educational Day Only
11–16
Special needs: BESD **MLD**
Wheelchair access: WA1

DOWNHAM SCHOOL
Horn Lane, Plymouth, Devon
PL9 9BR
Type: Co-educational 3–16
Special needs: **SLD**
Wheelchair access: WA1

LONGCAUSE SCHOOL
Plympton, Plymouth, Devon
PL7 3JB
Type: Co-educational
Special needs: ASD **ASP MLD**

MOUNT TAMAR SCHOOL
Row Lane, Plymouth, Devon
PL5 2EF
Type: Co-educational Day Only
5–16
Special needs: **BESD**

WOODLANDS SCHOOL
Wood View Learning Community,
Devon PL6 5ES
Website: www.woodlands.
plymouth.sch.uk
Type: Co-educational Day Only
2–16 (Post 16 consultation
currently under way)
Wheelchair access: WA1
52-week care

Torbay Lifelong Learning and Culture Services Directorate

Oldway Mansion
Torquay Road
Paignton
Devon
TQ3 2TE

THE BICKNELL SCHOOL
Petersfield Road, Bournemouth,
Dorset BH7 6QP
Type: Boys Day and Boarding
7–16
Special needs: ADD ADHD ASP
BESD DYC DYP DYS SP&LD
TOU

LINWOOD SCHOOL
Alma Road, Bournemouth, Dorset
BH9 1AJ
Type: Co-educational Day Only
3–19
Special needs: ASD **ASP MLD
PMLD SLD**

DORSET

Dorset Education Offices

County Hall
Colliton Park
Dorchester
Dorset
DT1 1XJ

BEAUCROFT SCHOOL
Wimborne Road, Wimborne,
Dorset BH21 2SS
Type: Co-educational Day Only
4–16
Special needs: ASD ASP BESD
DOW EPI MLD SLD SP&LD VI
Wheelchair access: WA2

MOUNTJOY SCHOOL
Flood Lane, Bridport, Dorset
DT6 3QG
Website: www.mountjoy.dorset.
sch.uk
Type: Co-educational Day Only
2–19
Special needs: ASD **ASP** CP
DOW EPI HEA HI **PMLD** SLD
SP&LD VI
Wheelchair access: W

PENWITHEN SCHOOL
Winterborne Monkton,
Dorchester, Dorset DT2 9PS
Type: Co-educational Boarding
and Day 7–16
Special needs: **BESD**

WYVERN SCHOOL
Dorchester Road, Weymouth,
Dorset DT3 5AL
Website: www.wyvern.sch.uk
Type: Co-educational Day Only
2–19
Special needs: ASD PMLD SLD
Wheelchair access: WA1

YEWSTOCK SCHOOL
Honeymead Lane, Sturminster
Newton, Dorset DT10 1EW
Website: www.yewstock.sch.uk
Type: Co-educational Day Only
2–19
Special needs: ASD MLD PMLD
SLD
Wheelchair access: WA2

Borough of Poole

Room 159
Civic Centre
Poole
Dorset
BH15 2RU

LONGSPEE SCHOOL
Learoyd Road, Poole, Dorset
BH17 8PJ
Type: Co-educational Day Only
4–11
Special needs: ADD ADHD ASP
BESD CB

MONTACUTE SCHOOL
3 Canford Heath Road, Poole,
Dorset BH17 9NG
Website: www.montacute.poole.
sch.uk
Type: Co-educational Day Only
3–19
Special needs: ASD PMLD **SLD**
Wheelchair access: WA1

WINCHELSEA SCHOOL
Guernsey Road, Poole, Dorset
BH12 4LL
Type: Co-educational Day Only
3–16
Special needs: ASD **ASP MLD**
Wheelchair access: WA1

COUNTY DURHAM

Darlington Education Offices

2nd Floor
Town Hall
Darlington
County Durham
DL1 5QT

BEAUMONT HILL TECHNOLOGY COLLEGE & PRIMARY SCHOOL
Darlington Education Village, Darlington, County Durham DL1 2AN
Type: Co-educational Day Only 2–19
Special needs: ADHD ASD **ASP BESD** CP MLD **PMLD** SLD
Wheelchair access: WA1

Durham County Council

County Hall
County Durham
DH1 5UL

DENE VIEW SCHOOL
Cotsford Park, Peterlee, County Durham SR8 4SZ
Type: Co-educational Day Only 5–16
Special needs: **MLD**
Wheelchair access: W

DURHAM TRINITY SCHOOL
Flambard and Kirkham Premises, Durham, County Durham DH1 5TS
Type: Co-educational Day Only 2–19
Special needs: ASD **ASP MLD PMLD** SLD

ELEMORE HALL SCHOOL
Littletown, Sherburn, County Durham DH6 1QD
Website: www.elemore.co.uk
Type: Co-educational Boarding and Day
Special needs: **BESD**

GLEN DENE SCHOOL
Crawlaw Road, Peterlee, County Durham SR8 3BQ
Type: Co-educational Day Only 2–19
Special needs: ASD MLD PMLD SLD
Wheelchair access: W

HARE LAW SCHOOL
Catchgate, Stanley, County Durham DH9 8DT
Website: www.Harelaw.School@durham.gov.uk
Type: Co-educational Day Only 4–16
Special needs: ASD MLD SLD
Wheelchair access: W

THE MEADOWS SCHOOL
Whitworth, Spennymoor, County Durham DL16 7QW
Type: Co-educational Day Only 11–16

VILLA REAL SCHOOL
Villa Real Road, Consett, County Durham DH8 6BH
Website: www.villareal.durham.sch.uk
Type: Co-educational Day Only 2–19
Special needs: ADD ADHD ASD **ASP** BESD **CB** CP DOW EPI HEA IM **PMLD SLD** SP&LD VI
Wheelchair access: WA1

WALWORTH SCHOOL
Bluebell Way, Newton Aycliffe, County Durham DL5 7LP
Type: Co-educational Day and Boarding 5–11
Special needs: **ADD ADHD** ASP **BESD** MLD SP&LD

WARWICK ROAD SCHOOL
Warwick Road, Bishop Auckland, County Durham DL14 6LS
Type: Co-educational Day Only
Special needs: DYP DYS **MLD**

WINDLESTONE SCHOOL
Ferryhill, County Durham DL17 0HP
Website: www.windlestoneschool.com
Type: Co-educational Boarding and Day 11–16
Special needs: **BESD**
Wheelchair access: WA1

Hartlepool Borough Council

Civic Centre
Victoria Road
Hartlepool
Cleveland
TS24 8AY

CATCOTE SCHOOL
Catcote Road, Hartlepool TS25 4EZ
Type: Co-educational Day Only 11–19
Special needs: ASD **MLD PMLD SLD**
Wheelchair access: WA1

SPRINGWELL SCHOOL
Wiltshire Way, Hartlepool TS26 0TB
Website: www.oaveryspecialschool.com
Type: Co-educational Day Only 3–11
Special needs: ASD CP PMLD SLD

ESSEX

Essex County Council

County Hall
Market Road
Chelmsford
Essex
CM1 1LX

CASTLEDON SCHOOL
Bromfords Drive, Wickford, Essex
SS12 0PW
Type: Co-educational Day Only
5–16
Special needs: ASD **MLD**

CEDAR HALL SCHOOL
Hart Road, Benfleet, Essex
SS7 3UQ
Type: Co-educational Day Only
4–16
Special needs: **HI MLD** SP&LD
Wheelchair access: WA2

THE EDITH BORTHWICK
SCHOOL
Fennes Road, Braintree, Essex
CM7 5LA
Website: www.edithborthwick.
essex.sch.uk
Type: Co-educational Day Only
3–19
Special needs: ASD **ASP MLD**
PMLD SLD SP&LD
Wheelchair access: WA1

THE ENDEAVOUR SCHOOL
Hogarth Avenue, Brentwood,
Essex CM15 8BE
Website: www.endeavour.essex.
sch.uk
Type: Co-educational Day Only
5–16
Special needs: ADHD ASD ASP
DOW **MLD** SP&LD
Wheelchair access: WA2

GLENWOOD SCHOOL
Rushbottom Lane, Benfleet,
Essex SS7 4LW
Type: Co-educational Day Only
3–19
Special needs: ASD PMLD SLD
Wheelchair access: WA1

HARLOW FIELDS SCHOOL
Tendring Road, Harlow, Essex
CM18 6RN
Type: Co-educational Day Only
3–19
Special needs: ASD **ASP MLD**
PMLD SLD

THE HAYWARD SCHOOL
Maltese Road, Chelmsford,
Essex CM1 2PA
Type: Co-educational Day Only
5–16
Special needs: ADD ADHD ASD
ASP DOW DYP DYS **MLD** SP&LD

THE HEATH SCHOOL
Winstree Road, Colchester,
Essex CO3 5GE
Type: Boys Day and Boarding
11–16
Special needs: **BESD**
Wheelchair access: W

HOMESTEAD SCHOOL
School Road, Colchester, Essex
CO4 5PA
Type: Boys Boarding Only 14–19
Special needs: **BESD**

KINGSWODE HOE SCHOOL
Sussex Road, Colchester, Essex
CO3 3QJ
Type: Co-educational Day Only
5–16
Special needs: ADD ADHD ASD
BESD DOW DYC DYS EPI **MLD**
SP&LD
Wheelchair access: WA3

LEXDEN SPRINGS SCHOOL
Halstead Road, Colchester,
Essex CO3 9AB
Type: Co-educational Day Only
3–19
Special needs: ASD **ASP PMLD**
SLD
Wheelchair access: WA1

MARKET FIELD SCHOOL
School Road, Colchester, Essex
CO7 7ET
Type: Co-educational Day Only
5–16
Special needs: ASD **ASP** DOW
EPI **MLD** SLD SP&LD
Wheelchair access: WA1

OAKVIEW SCHOOL
Whitehills Road, Loughton, Essex
IG10 1TS
Type: Co-educational Day Only
3–19
Special needs: ASD **MLD SLD**
Wheelchair access: WA1

THE RAMSDEN HALL SCHOOL
Ramsden Heath, Billericay,
Essex CM11 1HN
Type: Boys Boarding Only
Special needs: **BESD**

SHOREFIELDS SCHOOL
Ogilvie House, Clacton, Essex
CO15 6HF
Type: Co-educational Day Only
3–19
Special needs: PMLD SLD
Wheelchair access: WA1

THRIFTWOOD SCHOOL
Slades Lane, Chelmsford, Essex
CM2 8RW
Type: Co-educational Day Only
5–16
Special needs: ADHD ASD ASP
CP DOW DYS **MLD** SP&LD
Wheelchair access: W

WELLS PARK SCHOOL
Lambourne Road, Chigwell,
Essex IG7 6NN
Type: Co-educational Boarding
Only 5–12
Special needs: **BESD**
Wheelchair access: W

WOODLANDS CAMPUS,
CNMSS
Patching Hall Lane, Chelmsford,
Essex CM1 4BX
Type: Co-educational Day Only
3–19
Special needs: ASD **ASP** PMLD
SLD
Wheelchair access: WA1

Southend-on-Sea Borough Council

5th Floor
Civic Centre
Victoria Avenue
Southend-on-Sea
SS2 6ER

KINGSDOWN SCHOOL
Snakes Lane, Southend-on-Sea,
Essex SS2 6XT
Type: Co-educational Day Only
Special needs: CP DOW EPI HEA
HI IM PMLD SLD VI
Wheelchair access: WA1

LANCASTER SCHOOL
Prittlewell Chase, Westcliff-on-
Sea, Essex SS0 0RT
Website: www.lancaster-school-
southend.co.uk
Type: Co-educational Day Only
14–19
Special needs: ASD CP HEA IM
PMLD SLD
Wheelchair access: WA1

PRIORY SCHOOL
Burr Hill Chase, Southend-on-
Sea, Essex SS2 6PE
Type: Co-educational Day Only
11–16
Special needs: **BESD**

THE ST CHRISTOPHER SCHOOL
Mountdale Gardens, Leigh-on-
Sea, Essex SS9 4AW
Website: www.tscs.southend.
sch.uk
Type: Co-educational Day Only
3–19
Special needs: **ADHD** ASD **ASP**
BESD DOW DYP DYS EPI HI
MLD SLD SP&LD
Wheelchair access: WA2
52-week care

ST NICHOLAS SCHOOL
Philpott Avenue, Southend-on-
Sea, Essex SS2 4RL
Type: Co-educational Day Only
11–16
Special needs: **ADD ADHD ASD
ASP BESD CB DOW DYC DYP
DYS EPI HEA HI** IM **MLD** SP&LD
TOU VI
Wheelchair access: WA3

Thurrock Council

New Road
Grays
Essex
RM17 6GF

KNIGHTSMEAD SCHOOL
Fortin Close, South Ockendon,
Essex RM15 5NH
Website: www.knightsmead.
thurrock.sch.uk
Type: Co-educational Day Only
3–19
Special needs: ASD **ASP PMLD
SLD**
Wheelchair access: W

TREETOPS SCHOOL
Buxton Road, Grays, Essex
RM16 2XN
Website: www.treetopsschool.
org
Type: Co-educational Day Only
3–16
Special needs: ADHD ASD MLD
SP&LD
Wheelchair access: WA1

WOODACRE SCHOOL
Erriff Drive, South Ockendon,
Essex RM15 5AY
Type: Co-educational Day Only
3–16
Special needs: CP DYP EPI MLD
PMLD SLD SP&LD
Wheelchair access: W

GLOUCESTERSHIRE

Gloucestershire LEA

Shire Hall
Westgate Street
Gloucester
Gloucestershire
GL1 2TG

ALDERMAN KNIGHT SCHOOL
Ashchurch Road, Tewkesbury,
Gloucestershire GL20 8JJ
Type: Co-educational Day Only
5–16
Special needs: **ASD** ASP BESD
DYS **EPI** HEA MLD SLD SP&LD
Wheelchair access: WA1

AMBERLEY RIDGE SCHOOL
Amberley, Stroud,
Gloucestershire GL5 5DB
Type: Co-educational Day and
Boarding
Special needs: **BESD**
Wheelchair access: W

BATTLEDOWN CENTRE FOR CHILDREN AND FAMILIES
Harp Hill, Cheltenham,
Gloucestershire GL52 6PZ
Website: www.battledown.gloucs.
sch.uk
Type: Co-educational Day Only
Special needs: ASD **ASP** BESD
CB CP DOW EPI HEA HI IM
PMLD SLD SP&LD VI
Wheelchair access: WA2

BELMONT SCHOOL
Warden Hill Road, Cheltenham, Gloucestershire GL51 3AT
Website: www.belmont.gloucs. sch.uk
Type: Co-educational Day Only 5–16
Special needs: ADD ADHD ASP **BESD MLD** SP&LD
Wheelchair access: WA2

BETTRIDGE SCHOOL
Warden Hill Road, Cheltenham, Gloucestershire GL51 3AT
Website: www.bettridge.org.uk
Type: Co-educational Day Only 2–19
Special needs: ASD DOW EPI PMLD **SLD** VI
Wheelchair access: W

CAM HOUSE SCHOOL
Drake Lane, Dursley, Gloucestershire GL11 5HD
Website: www. camhouseschool.ik.org
Type: Boys Boarding and Day 11–16
Special needs: **BESD**

COLN HOUSE SCHOOL
Horcott Road, Fairford, Gloucestershire GL7 4DB
Type: Co-educational Boarding and Day 9–16
Special needs: **BESD**

HEART OF THE FOREST COMMUNITY SPECIAL SCHOOL
Speech House, Coleford, Gloucestershire GL16 7EJ
Type: Co-educational Day Only 3–19
Special needs: ASD **DOW PMLD SLD**
Wheelchair access: WA1

THE MILESTONE SCHOOL
Longford Lane, Gloucestershire GL2 9EU
Type: Co-educational Day Only 2–16
Special needs: ADHD ASD **ASP** BESD CP DOW EPI **MLD PMLD SLD** VI
Wheelchair access: WA1

PATERNOSTER SCHOOL
Watermoor Road, Cirencester, Gloucestershire GL7 1JS
Website: www.paternoster. gloucs.ik.org
Type: Co-educational Day Only 2–16
Special needs: PMLD **SLD**
Wheelchair access: WA1

SANDFORD SCHOOL
Seven Springs, Cheltenham, Gloucestershire GL53 9NG
Type: Co-educational Day Only 6–16
Special needs: **BESD**

THE SHRUBBERIES SCHOOL
Oldends Lane, Stonehouse, Gloucestershire GL10 2DG
Website: www.shrubberies. gloucs.sch.uk
Type: Co-educational Day Only 2–19
Special needs: ASD **ASP PMLD SLD**
Wheelchair access: WA1

SOUTH GLOUCESTERSHIRE

South Gloucestershire Council Education Service

Bowling Hill
Chipping Sodbury
Bristol
BS37 6JX

CULVERHILL SCHOOL
Kelston Close, Yate, South Gloucestershire BS37 4SZ
Website: www.culverhillschool. ik.org
Type: Co-educational Day Only 7–16
Special needs: ADD ADHD ASD ASP BESD CP DOW DYP EPI HI **MLD** SP&LD VI
Wheelchair access: WA1

NEW SIBLANDS SCHOOL
Easton Hill Road, Thornbury, South Gloucestershire BS35 2JU
Type: Co-educational Day Only 2–19
Special needs: ASD **PMLD SLD**

WARMLEY PARK SCHOOL
Tower Road North, Bristol BS30 8XL
Website: www.warmleypark. org.uk
Type: Co-educational Day Only
Special needs: ASD **PMLD SLD**
Wheelchair access: WA1

HAMPSHIRE

Hampshire County Council

**The Castle
Winchester
Hampshire
SO23 8UG**

BASINGSTOKE SCHOOL PLUS
Pack Lane, Basingstoke,
Hampshire RG22 5TH
Type: Co-educational Day and
Boarding 10–16
Special needs: **BESD**

BAYCROFT SCHOOL
Gosport Road, Fareham,
Hampshire PO14 2AE
Type: Co-educational Day Only
11–16
Special needs: ASD **ASP MLD**

DOVE HOUSE SPECIAL SCHOOL
Sutton Road, Basingstoke,
Hampshire RG21 5SU
Type: Co-educational Day Only
11–16
Special needs: ASD **ASP MLD**

FOREST EDGE SPECIAL SCHOOL
Lydlynch Road, Southampton,
Hampshire SO40 3DW
Type: Co-educational Day Only
4–11
Special needs: ASD MLD SP&LD
Wheelchair access: WA1

GLENWOOD SPECIAL SCHOOL
Washington Road, Emsworth,
Hampshire PO10 7NN
Website: www.glenwood.hants.
sch.uk
Type: Co-educational Day Only
11–16
Special needs: **MLD**
Wheelchair access: WA2

HEATHFIELD SPECIAL SCHOOL
Oldbury Way, Fareham,
Hampshire PO14 3BN
Type: Co-educational Day Only
3–11
Special needs: ADHD ASD **ASP**
BESD CP DOW DYP EPI HEA HI
MLD SP&LD VI
Wheelchair access: WA1

HENRY TYNDALE SPECIAL SCHOOL
Ship Lane, Farnborough,
Hampshire GU14 8BX
Type: Co-educational Day Only
2–19
Special needs: ASD **ASP MLD
PMLD SLD**
Wheelchair access: WA1

HOLLYWATER SCHOOL
Mill Chase Road, Bordon,
Hampshire GU35 0HA
Type: Co-educational Day Only
2–19
Special needs: ADD ADHD ASD
ASP DOW EPI **MLD** PMLD **SLD**
TOU
Wheelchair access: WA1

ICKNIELD SPECIAL SCHOOL
River Way, Andover, Hampshire
SP11 6LT
Type: Co-educational Day Only
2–19
Special needs: ASD **ASP PMLD
SLD**
Wheelchair access: WA1

LAKESIDE SPECIAL SCHOOL
Winchester Road, Eastleigh,
Hampshire SO53 2DW
Type: Boarding and Day
Special needs: ADHD ASP **BESD**
SP&LD

LIMINGTON HOUSE SPECIAL SCHOOL
St Andrew's Road, Basingstoke,
Hampshire RG22 6PS
Type: Co-educational Day Only
2–19
Special needs: PMLD **SLD**

LORD WILSON SPECIAL SCHOOL
Coldeast Way, Southampton,
Hampshire SO31 7AT
Type: Boys 11–16

MAPLE RIDGE SPECIAL SCHOOL
Maple Crescent, Basingstoke,
Hampshire RG21 5SX
Type: Co-educational Day Only
4–11
Special needs: ASD **MLD**
Wheelchair access: W

THE MARK WAY SCHOOL
Bachelors Barn Road, Andover,
Hampshire SP10 1HR
Website: www.markway.hants.
sch.uk
Type: Co-educational Day Only
11–16
Special needs: **ADHD** ASD **ASP**
DYS HI **MLD** SP&LD
Wheelchair access: WA1

NORMAN GATE SPECIAL SCHOOL
Vigo Road, Andover, Hampshire
SP10 1JZ
Website: www.newnormangate.
ik.org
Type: Co-educational Day Only
2–11
Special needs: ASD MLD
Wheelchair access: W

OAK LODGE SCHOOL
Roman Road, Southampton,
Hampshire SO4 5RQ
Type: Co-educational Day Only
11–16
Special needs: ASD **MLD**
Wheelchair access: WA3

OSBORNE SPECIAL SCHOOL
Andover Road, Winchester,
Hampshire SO23 7BU
Type: Co-educational Boarding
and Day 11–19
Special needs: ADD ADHD ASD
ASP BESD CP DOW EPI HEA HI
MLD PMLD SLD SP&LD TOU
Wheelchair access: W

RACHEL MADOCKS
Eagle Avenue, Portsmouth,
Hampshire PO8 9XP
Type: Co-educational Day Only
2–19
Special needs: **PMLD SLD**
Wheelchair access: WA1

RIVERSIDE COMMUNITY SPECIAL SCHOOL
Scratchface Lane, Waterlooville,
Hampshire PO7 5QD
Website: www.riverside.hants.
sch.uk
Type: Co-educational 3–11
Special needs: VI
Wheelchair access: W

ST FRANCIS SPECIAL SCHOOL
Oldbury Way, Fareham,
Hampshire PO14 3BN
Type: Co-educational Day Only
2–19
Special needs: ASD **ASP** CP EPI
PMLD SLD
Wheelchair access: WA1

SALTERNS SPECIAL SCHOOL
Commercial Road, Southampton,
Hampshire SO40 3AF
Type: Co-educational Day Only
2–19
Special needs: ASD PMLD **SLD**
Wheelchair access: WA1

SAMUEL CODY SPECIALIST SPORTS COLLEGE
Lynchford Road, Farnborough,
Hampshire GU14 6BJ
Type: Co-educational Day Only
11–16
Special needs: ASD **MLD**
Wheelchair access: WA3

SAXON WOOD SPECIAL SCHOOL
Rooksdown, Basingstoke,
Hampshire RG24 9NH
Website: www.saxonwood.hants.
sch.uk
Type: Co-educational Day Only
2–11
Special needs: **CP EPI** HEA HI
IM MLD PMLD SLD VI
Wheelchair access: WA1

SHEPHERDS DOWN SCHOOL
Shepherds Lane, Winchester,
Hampshire SO21 2AJ
Type: Co-educational Day Only
4–11
Special needs: ASD **MLD PMLD SLD**
Wheelchair access: WA1

SUNDRIDGE SPECIAL SCHOOL
Cowplain, Hampshire PO8 8TR
Type: Boys Day Only 11–16
Special needs: **BESD**

WATERLOO SPECIAL SCHOOL
Warfield Avenue, Waterlooville,
Hampshire PO7 7JJ
Type: Co-educational Day Only
4–11
Special needs: **BESD**

WOLVERDENE SPECIAL SCHOOL
22 Love Lane, Andover,
Hampshire SP10 2AF
Type: Co-educational Day and
Boarding 4–11
Special needs: **BESD**

Portsmouth Education Authority

4th Floor Civic Offices
Guildhall Square
Portsmouth
Hampshire
PO1 2BG

CLIFFDALE PRIMARY SCHOOL
Battenburg Avenue, Portsmouth,
Hampshire PO2 0SN
Type: Co-educational Day Only
4–11
Special needs: ASD **ASP IM MLD SLD**
Wheelchair access: WA1

EAST SHORE SPECIAL SCHOOL
Eastern Road, Portsmouth,
Hampshire PO3 6EP
Type: Co-educational Day Only
2–19
Special needs: ASD DOW EPI
PMLD SLD
Wheelchair access: W

THE FUTCHER SCHOOL
Drayton Lane, Portsmouth,
Hampshire PO6 1HG

THE POLYGON SPECIAL SCHOOL
Handel Terrace, Southampton,
Hampshire SO1 2FH
Website: http://www.polygon.
southampton.sch.uk
Type: Boys Day Only 11–16
Special needs: ADD ADHD ASD
ASP **BESD**
Wheelchair access: WA2

REDWOOD PARK SCHOOL
Wembley Grove, Portsmouth,
Hampshire PO6 2RY
Type: Co-educational 11–16
Special needs: ASD **MLD**

VERMONT SPECIAL SCHOOL
Vermont Close, Southampton,
Hampshire SO1 7LT
Type: Boys Day Only 4–11
Special needs: ADD ADHD ASD
BESD MLD

WATERSIDE SCHOOL & UNIT
Tipner Lane, Portsmouth,
Hampshire PO2 8RA
Website: www.watersideschool.
com
Type: Co-educational Boarding
and Day 11–16
Special needs: ADD ADHD
BESD TOU
Wheelchair access: W

THE WILLOWS CENTRE FOR CHILDREN
Battenburg Avenue, Portsmouth,
Hampshire PO2 0SN
Website: www.
willowsnurseryschool.co.uk
Type: Co-educational Day Only
2–5
Special needs: ADD ADHD ASD
ASP BESD CP DOW DYP DYS
EPI HEA HI **MLD** SLD SP&LD VI
Wheelchair access: WA1

Southampton Lifelong Learning & Leisure Directorate

5th Floor
Frobisher House
Nelson Gate
Southampton
SO15 1BZ

THE CEDAR SPECIAL SCHOOL
Redbridge Lane, Southampton,
Hampshire SO16 0XN
Type: Co-educational 2–16
Wheelchair access: WA1

GREAT OAKS SCHOOL
Vermont Close, Southampton,
Hampshire SO16 7LT
Type: Co-educational Day Only
11–16
Special needs: ASD **ASP MLD
SLD**
Wheelchair access: WA1

NETLEY COURT SPECIAL SCHOOL
Victoria Road, Southampton,
Hampshire SO31 5DR
Type: Co-educational Day Only
4–11
Special needs: ASD **MLD SLD**
SP&LD

HEREFORDSHIRE

Herefordshire Council

PO Box 185
Blackfriars Street
Hereford
Herefordshire
HR4 9ZR

BLACKMARSTON SCHOOL
Honddu Close, Hereford,
Herefordshire HR2 7NX
Type: Co-educational Day Only
3–11
Special needs: **PMLD SLD**
Wheelchair access: WA1

THE BROOKFIELD SCHOOL
Grandstand Road, Herefordshire
HR4 9NG
Type: Co-educational Day Only
Special needs: **BESD** MLD

WESTFIELD SCHOOL
Westfield Walk, Leominster,
Herefordshire HR6 8HD
Website: www.westfield.hereford.
sch.uk
Type: Co-educational Day Only
4–19
Special needs: ASD PMLD **SLD**
Wheelchair access: WA1

HERTFORDSHIRE

Hertfordshire Children, Schools & Families

County Hall
Hertford
Hertfordshire
SG13 8DF

AMWELL VIEW SCHOOL
St Margarets, Stanstead Abbotts, Hertfordshire SG12 8EH
Type: Co-educational Day Only 2–19
Special needs: ASD **ASP** CP DOW EPI **PMLD SLD**
Wheelchair access: W

BATCHWOOD SCHOOL
Townsend Drive, St Albans, Hertfordshire AL3 5RP
Type: Co-educational Day Only 11–16
Special needs: **BESD**

BOXMOOR HOUSE SCHOOL
Box Lane, Hemel Hempstead, Hertfordshire HP3 0DF
Type: Boys Day and Boarding 11–16
Special needs: **BESD**

BRANDLES SCHOOL
Weston Way, Baldock, Hertfordshire SG7 6EY
Type: Boys 11–16
Special needs: **BESD**

BREAKSPEARE SCHOOL
Gallows Hill Lane, Abbots Langley, Hertfordshire WD5 0BU
Website: www.breakspeare. herts.sch.uk
Type: Co-educational Day Only 2–19
Wheelchair access: WA1

THE COLLETT SCHOOL
Lockers Park Lane, Hemel Hempstead, Hertfordshire HP1 1TQ
Website: www.thecollettschool. co.uk
Type: Co-educational Day Only 5–16
Special needs: ADHD ASD ASP CP DOW DYP EPI HI **MLD** SLD VI
Wheelchair access: WA2

COLNBROOK SCHOOL
Hayling Road, Watford, Hertfordshire WD19 7UY
Website: www.colnbrook.herts. sch.uk
Type: Co-educational Day Only 4–11
Special needs: ASD **MLD**

FALCONER SCHOOL
Falconer Road, Watford, Hertfordshire WD2 3AT
Type: Boys Day and Boarding 11–16
Special needs: **BESD**

GARSTON MANOR SCHOOL
Horseshoe Lane, Watford, Hertfordshire WD25 7HR
Type: Co-educational Day Only 11–16
Special needs: **MLD**

GREENSIDE SCHOOL
Shephall Green, Stevenage, Hertfordshire SG2 9XS
Type: Co-educational Day Only 2–19
Special needs: ASD **ASP PMLD SLD**
Wheelchair access: W

HAILEY HALL SCHOOL
Hailey Lane, Hertford, Hertfordshire SG13 7PB
Website: www.haileyhall.herts. sch.uk
Type: Boys Boarding and Day 11–16
Special needs: **BESD**

HAYWOOD GROVE
St Agnells Lane, Hemel Hempstead, Hertfordshire HP2 7BG
Type: Co-educational 5–11
Special needs: **BESD**

HEATHLANDS SCHOOL
Heathlands Drive, St Albans, Hertfordshire AL3 5AY
Website: www.heathlands.herts. sch.uk
Type: Co-educational Boarding and Day 2–18
Special needs: **HI**
Wheelchair access: WA2

KNIGHTSFIELD SCHOOL
Knightsfield, Welwyn Garden City, Hertfordshire AL8 7LW
Website: www.knightsfield.herts. sch.uk
Type: Co-educational Day and Boarding 11–18
Special needs: **HI**
Wheelchair access: WA1

LAKESIDE SCHOOL
Lemsford Lane, Welwyn Garden City, Hertfordshire AL8 6YN
Website: www.lakeside.herts. sch.uk
Type: Co-educational Day Only
Special needs: PMLD SLD
Wheelchair access: WA1

LARWOOD SCHOOL
Webb Rise, Stevenage, Hertfordshire SG1 5QU
Type: Co-educational Day and Boarding 4–11
Special needs: **ADD ADHD** ASD **ASP BESD**
Wheelchair access: WA2

LONSDALE SCHOOL
Webb Rise, Stevenage, Hertfordshire SG1 5QU
Type: Co-educational Day and Boarding 3–18
Special needs: HI **IM** VI
Wheelchair access: WA1

MEADOW WOOD SCHOOL
Coldharbour Lane, Watford, Hertfordshire WD2 3NU
Website: www.meadowwood. herts.sch.uk
Type: Co-educational Day Only 3–11
Special needs: **IM**
Wheelchair access: WA1

MIDDLETON SCHOOL
Walnut Tree Walk, Ware, Hertfordshire SG12 9PD
Type: Co-educational Day Only 4–11
Special needs: ASD **MLD**
Wheelchair access: WA1

PINEWOOD SCHOOL
Hoe Lane, Ware, Hertfordshire
SG12 9PB
Type: Co-educational 11–16
Special needs: **MLD**
Wheelchair access: WA1

ST LUKE'S SCHOOL
Crouch Hall Lane, Redbourn,
Hertfordshire AL3 7ET
Type: Co-educational Day Only
9–16
Special needs: ASD ASP HI **MLD**
Wheelchair access: WA1

SOUTHFIELD SCHOOL
Travellers Lane, Hatfield,
Hertfordshire AL10 8TJ
Type: Co-educational Day Only
4–11
Special needs: ASD **MLD**
Wheelchair access: WA1

THE VALLEY SCHOOL
Valley Way, Stevenage,
Hertfordshire SG2 9AB
Type: Co-educational Day Only
Special needs: **MLD**

WATLING VIEW SCHOOL
Watling View, St Albans,
Hertfordshire AL1 2NU
Website: www.watlingview@
thegrid.rog.uk
Type: Co-educational 2–19
Special needs: ASD PMLD SLD
Wheelchair access: WA1

WOODFIELD SCHOOL
Malmes Croft, Hemel
Hempstead, Hertfordshire
HP3 8RL
Type: Co-educational Day Only
5–19
Special needs: ASD SLD
Wheelchair access: W

WOOLGROVE SCHOOL
Pryor Way, Letchworth,
Hertfordshire SG6 2PT
Website: www.woolgrove.
org.uk
Type: Co-educational Day Only
5–11
Special needs: ASD **MLD**
Wheelchair access: WA1

ISLE OF WIGHT

Isle of Wight LEA

County Hall
Newport
Isle of Wight
PO30 1UD

MEDINA HOUSE SCHOOL
School Lane, Newport, Isle of
Wight PO30 2HS
Type: Co-educational Day Only
2–11
Special needs: ASD **ASP** BESD
CB **MLD** PMLD **SLD**
Wheelchair access: WA1

ST GEORGE'S SCHOOL
Watergate Road, Newport, Isle of
Wight PO30 1XW
Type: Co-educational Day Only
11–19
Special needs: **MLD PMLD SLD**
Wheelchair access: W

KENT

Kent County Council

Education & Learning
County Hall
Maidstone
Kent
ME14 1XQ

BOWER GROVE SCHOOL
Fant Lane, Maidstone, Kent
ME16 8NL
Website: www.bower-grove.
kent.sch.uk
Type: Co-educational Day Only
5–16
Special needs: ASD BESD DYP
MLD SP&LD
Wheelchair access: WA2

BROOMHILL BANK SCHOOL
Broomhill Road, Tunbridge Wells,
Kent TN3 0TB
Website: www.broomhill-bank.
kent.sch.uk
Type: Girls Boarding and Day
8–19
Special needs: **MLD** SP&LD

GRANGE PARK SCHOOL
Birling Road, Maidstone, Kent
ME19 5QA
Type: Co-educational Day Only
11–19
Special needs: **ASD ASP**
Wheelchair access: WA2

HARBOUR SCHOOL
Elms Vale Road, Dover, Kent
CT17 9PS
Website: www.harbour.kent.
sch.uk
Type: Co-educational Day Only
5–16
Special needs: **ADD ADHD** ASD
ASP BESD CB DOW DYP DYS
EPI HEA HI **MLD** SP&LD TOU VI

HIGHVIEW SCHOOL
Moat Farm Road, Folkestone,
Kent CT19 5DJ
Type: Co-educational Day Only
5–16
Special needs: **MLD**

IFIELD SCHOOL
Cedar Avenue, Gravesend, Kent
DA12 5JT
Type: Co-educational Day Only
4–19
Special needs: ASD DOW IM
MLD PMLD SP&LD
Wheelchair access: WA1

ISP RAINHAM
Old Church, Gillingham, Kent
ME8 8AY
Type: Co-educational Day Only
5–11
Special needs: **BESD**
Wheelchair access: WA3

LALEHAM GAP SCHOOL
Northdown Park Road, Margate,
Kent CT9 2TP
Type: Co-educational Boarding
and Day 5–16
Special needs: ASD **ASP** DYP
DYS SP&LD

MEADOWFIELD SCHOOL
Swantree Avenue, Sittingbourne,
Kent ME10 4NL
Type: Co-educational Day Only
5–19
Special needs: **SLD**

MILESTONE SCHOOL
Ash Road, Dartford, Kent
DA3 8JZ
Website:
www.milestone.kent.sch.uk
Type: Co-educational Day Only
2–19
Special needs: ASD **ASP PMLD**
SLD VI
Wheelchair access: WA1

OAKLEY SCHOOL
Pembury Road, Tunbridge Wells,
Kent TN2 4NE
Type: Co-educational Day Only
5–19
Special needs: **PMLD**
Wheelchair access: WA2

ORCHARD SCHOOL
Cambridge Road, Canterbury,
Kent CT1 3QQ
Website: www.orchard.ik.org
Type: Co-educational Day Only
11–16
Special needs: **MLD**
Wheelchair access: W

PORTAL HOUSE SCHOOL
Sea Street, Dover, Kent CT15 6AR
Type: Co-educational Day Only
11–16
Special needs: **BESD**
Wheelchair access: WA3

RIDGE VIEW SCHOOL
Cage Green Road, Tonbridge,
Kent TN10 4PT
Website: www.ridge-view.
kent.sch.uk
Type: Co-educational Day Only
2–19
Special needs: ASD **ASP** DOW
PMLD SLD
Wheelchair access: WA1

ROWHILL SCHOOL
Stock Lane, Dartford, Kent
DA2 7BZ
Website: www.rowhill.kent.sch.uk
Type: Co-educational Day Only
5–16
Special needs: **BESD**
Wheelchair access: WA1

ST ANTHONY'S SCHOOL
St Anthony's Way, Margate, Kent
CT9 3RA
Website: www.st-anthonys.
kent.sch.uk
Type: Co-educational Day Only
3–16
Special needs: BESD

STONE BAY SCHOOL
Stone Road, Broadstairs, Kent
CT10 1EB
Type: Boarding and Day
Special needs: ASD **ASP** CB
MLD SLD
Wheelchair access: WA3

VALENCE SCHOOL
Westerham, Kent TN16 1QN
Type: Co-educational Boarding
and Day 5–19
Special needs: CP EPI
Wheelchair access: WA1

WYVERN SCHOOL
Willesborough Site, Ashford, Kent
TN24 0QF
Type: Co-educational Day Only
5–19
Special needs: MLD SLD

**Medway Towns
Education and Leisure**

Civic Centre
Strood
Rochester
Kent
ME2 4AU

BRADFIELDS SCHOOL
Churchill Avenue, Chatham, Kent
ME5 0LB
Type: Co-educational Day Only
11–19
Special needs: ASD **MLD**
Wheelchair access: WA1

DANECOURT SCHOOL
Hotel Road, Gillingham, Kent
ME8 6AA
Type: Co-educational Day Only
4–11
Special needs: ADD ADHD ASD
ASP DOW **MLD** SLD SP&LD
Wheelchair access: WA1

LANCASHIRE

Blackburn with Darwen Council

King William Street
Town Hall
Blackburn
Lancashire
BB1 7DY

BROADLANDS SCHOOL
Roman Road, Blackburn,
Lancashire BB1 2LA
Type: Co-educational Day Only
3–5

CROSSHILL SCHOOL
Shadsworth Road, Blackburn,
Lancashire BB1 2HR
Type: Co-educational Day Only
11–16
Special needs: **MLD**
Wheelchair access: WA1

FERNHURST SCHOOL
Heys Lane, Blackburn,
Lancashire BB2 4NW

NEWFIELD SCHOOL
Roman Road, Blackburn,
Lancashire BB1 2LA
Type: Co-educational Day Only
2–19
Special needs: ASD **ASP PMLD**
SLD
Wheelchair access: WA1

SUNNYHURST CENTRE
Salisbury Road, Darwen,
Lancashire BB3 1HZ
Type: Co-educational Day Only
5–16

Blackpool Borough Council

PO Box 77
Town Hall
Blackpool
Lancashire
FY1 1AD

HIGHFURLONG SCHOOL
Blackpool Old Road, Blackpool,
Lancashire FY3 7LR

PARK SCHOOL
Whitegate Drive, Blackpool,
Lancashire FY3 9HF
Type: Co-educational Day Only
Special needs: **MLD**
Wheelchair access: W

Lancashire Education and Cultural Services Directorate

PO Box 78 County Hall
Fishergate
Preston
Lancashire
PR1 8XJ

ASTLEY PARK SCHOOL
Harrington Road, Chorley,
Lancashire PR7 1JZ
Type: Co-educational Day Only
4–16
Special needs: **MLD**
Wheelchair access: W

BEACON SCHOOL
Tanhouse Road, Skelmersdale,
Lancashire WN8 6BA
Type: Co-educational Day Only
5–16
Special needs: **BESD**

BLEASDALE HOUSE SCHOOL
Emesgate Lane, Carnforth,
Lancashire LA5 0RG
Type: Co-educational Boarding
and Day 2–19
Special needs: CP EPI HEA
PMLD SLD VI
Wheelchair access: WA1

BROADFIELD SCHOOL
Fielding Lane, Accrington,
Lancashire BB5 3BE
Type: Co-educational Day Only
Special needs: ASD **MLD** SLD
Wheelchair access: WA1

BROOKFIELD SCHOOL
Fouldrey Avenue, Poulton-le-
Fylde, Lancashire FY6 7HT
Type: Co-educational Day Only
11–16
Special needs: **BESD**
Wheelchair access: WA2

CALDER VIEW SCHOOL
March Street, Burnley,
Lancashire BB12 0BU
Type: Co-educational Day Only
4–16
Special needs: ASD ASP **MLD
SLD** SP&LD
Wheelchair access: W

THE COPPICE SCHOOL
Ash Grove, Preston, Lancashire
PR5 6GY
Type: Co-educational Day Only
2–19
Special needs: ASD CP PMLD
SLD VI
Wheelchair access: WA1

CRIBDEN HOUSE SCHOOL
Haslingden Road, Rossendale,
Lancashire BB4 6RX
Type: Co-educational Day Only
5–11
Special needs: **BESD**

GREAT ARLEY SCHOOL
Holly Road, Blackpool,
Lancashire FY5 4HH
Type: Co-educational 4–16
Special needs: **MLD**

HILLSIDE SPECIALIST
SCHOOL
Ribchester Road, Preston,
Lancashire PR3 3XB
Type: Co-educational Day Only
2–16
Special needs: ASD **ASP**

KINGSBURY SCHOOL
Skelmersdale, Lancashire
WN8 8EH
Website: www.kingsbury.lancs.
sch.uk
Type: Co-educational Day Only
2–11
Special needs: ASD MLD PMLD
SLD
Wheelchair access: WA2

THE LOYNE SPECIALIST
SCHOOL
Sefton Drive, Lancaster,
Lancashire LA1 2PZ
Website: www.loyneschool.
org.uk
Type: Co-educational Day Only
2–19
Special needs: ASD **ASP BESD
EPI HI PMLD SLD** VI
Wheelchair access: WA1

MAYFIELD SCHOOL
Gloucester Road, Chorley,
Lancashire PR7 3HN
Website: www.
mayfieldspecialschool.co.uk
Type: Co-educational Day Only
2–19
Special needs: ADD ADHD ASD
ASP BESD **CB** CP DOW DYP EPI
HEA HI IM **MLD PMLD SLD**
SP&LD TOU VI W

MOOR HEY SCHOOL
Far Croft, Preston, Lancashire
PR5 5SU
Type: Co-educational Day Only
5–16
Special needs: **MLD**

MOORBROOK SCHOOL
Ainslie Road, Preston,
Lancashire PR2 3DB
Type: Co-educational Day Only
11–16 .
Special needs: **BESD**

MOORLANDS VIEW SCHOOL
Manchester Road, Lancashire
BB1 5PQ
Type: Co-educational Day Only
11–16

MORECAMBE AND HEYSHAM
ROAD SCHOOL
Morecambe Road, Morecambe,
Lancashire LA3 3AB
Website: www.morecombe.
lancsngfl.ac.uk
Type: Co-educational Day Only
3–16
Special needs: ASD BESD DOW
HI **MLD** VI

NORTH CLIFFE SCHOOL
Blackburn Old Road, Blackburn,
Lancashire BB6 7UW
Type: Co-educational Day Only
5–16
Special needs: **MLD**
Wheelchair access: WA2

OAKFIELD HOUSE SCHOOL
Station Road, Preston,
Lancashire PR4 0YH
Website: www.
oakfieldhouseschool.co.uk
Type: Boys Day Only 6–11

PEAR TREE SCHOOL
29 Station Road, Kirkham,
Lancashire PR4 2HA
Type: Co-educational Day Only
2–19
Special needs: PMLD **SLD**
Wheelchair access: WA1

PENDLE COMMUNITY HIGH
SCHOOL AND COLLEGE
Gibfield Road, Colne, Lancashire
BB8 8JT
Type: Co-educational Day Only
11–19
Special needs: ADHD ASD **MLD
PMLD** SLD
Wheelchair access: WA1

RED MARSH SCHOOL
Holly Road, Blackpool,
Lancashire FY5 4HH
Website: www.redmarsh.
lancs.sch.uk
Type: Co-educational Day Only
2–19
Special needs: ASD PMLD **SLD**
Wheelchair access: WA1

ROYAL CROSS SCHOOL
Elswick Road, Preston,
Lancashire PR2 1NT
Website: www.royalcross.lancs.
sch.uk
Type: Co-educational Day Only
4–11
Special needs: **HI** SP&LD
Wheelchair access: WA1

TOR VIEW SCHOOL
Clod Lane, Haslingden,
Lancashire BB4 6LR
Website: www.torview.
lancsngfl.ac.uk
Type: Co-educational Day Only
4–19
Special needs: ADHD ASD **ASP
CB** DOW EPI **HEA** HI **MLD PMLD
SLD** VI
Wheelchair access: WA1

WENNINGTON HALL
Wennington, Lancashire LA2 8NS
Type: Boys Boarding and Day
Special needs: ADHD **BESD**
Wheelchair access: WA3

**WEST LANCASHIRE
COMMUNITY HIGH SCHOOL**
School Lane, Skelmersdale,
Lancashire WN8 8EH
Type: Co-educational Day Only
11–19
Special needs: ASD **ASP MLD
PMLD SLD** SP&LD
Wheelchair access: WA1

WHITE ASH SCHOOL
Thwaites Road, Accrington,
Lancashire BB5 4QG
Website: www.whiteash.
lancsngfl.ac.uk
Type: Co-educational Day Only
3–19
Special needs: **ASD** ASP CP
DOW EPI HI **PMLD SLD** SP&LD
VI
Wheelchair access: WA1

LEICESTERSHIRE

Leicester Education Department

**Marlborough House
38 Welford Place
Leicester
Leicestershire
LE2 7AA**

ASH FIELD SCHOOL
Broad Avenue, Leicester,
Leicestershire LE5 4PY
Type: Co-educational Day and
Boarding 14–19
Special needs: **CP** HI SP&LD VI
Wheelchair access: WA1

ELLESMERE COLLEGE
Ellesmere Road, Leicester,
Leicestershire LE3 1BE
Website: www.ellesmere.
leicester.sch.uk
Type: Co-educational Day Only
11–19
Special needs: **MLD**
Wheelchair access: WA2

KEYHAM LODGE SCHOOL
Keyham Lane, Leicester,
Leicestershire LE5 1FG
Type: Boys Day Only 11–16
Special needs: **BESD**

MILLGATE SCHOOL
18a Scott Street, Leicester,
Leicestershire LE2 6DW
Type: Boys Boarding and Day
11–16
Special needs: ADD ADHD
BESD
Wheelchair access: WA2

NETHER HALL SCHOOL
Netherhall Road, Leicester,
Leicestershire LE5 1DT
Type: Co-educational Day Only
5–19
Special needs: ASD **ASP PMLD
SLD**
Wheelchair access: WA1

OAKLANDS SCHOOL
Whitehall Road, Leicester,
Leicestershire LE5 6GJ
Type: Co-educational Day Only
5–11
Special needs: ASD DOW EPI
MLD SP&LD
Wheelchair access: W

WEST GATE SCHOOL
Glenfield Road, Leicester,
Leicestershire LE3 6DN
Website: www.westgate.
leicester.sch.uk
Type: Co-educational Day Only
5–19
Special needs: ADHD ASD **ASP
BCSD CP DOW** EPI **HI MLD
PMLD SLD** SP&LD VI
Wheelchair access: WA1

WESTERN PARK SCHOOL
Western Park, Leicester,
Leicestershire LE3 6HX
Type: Co-educational Day Only
Special needs: ADD ASP CP
DOW DYP EPI HEA HI SP&LD
TOU VI
Wheelchair access: W

Leicestershire Education Offices

**County Hall
Glenfield
Leicester
LE3 8RF**

ASHMOUNT SCHOOL
Ashmount, Loughborough,
Leicestershire LE11 2BG
Type: Co-educational Day Only
3–19
Special needs: ASD CP DOW EPI
PMLD **SLD**
Wheelchair access: WA1

BIRKETT HOUSE SPECIAL SCHOOL
Launceston Road, Magna,
Leicestershire LE18 2FZ
Type: Co-educational 5–19
Special needs: ASD CP DOW EPI
HI **PMLD SLD** SP&LD VI
Wheelchair access: WA1

DOROTHY GOODMAN SCHOOL
Stoke Road, Hinckley,
Leicestershire LE10 0EA
Website: www.
dorothygoodman.co.uk
Type: Co-educational Day Only
3–19
Special needs: ADHD ASD **ASP**
CB DOW EPI HEA **MLD PMLD
SLD**
Wheelchair access: WA1

FOREST WAY AREA SPECIAL SCHOOL
Warren Hius Road, Leicester,
Leicestershire LE67 4UU
Type: Co-educational Day Only
3–19
Special needs: ASD BESD CP
DOW EPI HEA HI **MLD** PMLD
SLD SP&LD VI
Wheelchair access: WA1

MAPLEWELL HALL SCHOOL
Maplewell Road, Loughborough,
Leicestershire LE12 8QY
Type: Co-educational Day Only
11–16
Special needs: ASD **MLD**
Wheelchair access: WA3

LINCOLNSHIRE

Lincolnshire County Council

**County Offices
Newland
Lincoln
Lincolnshire
LN1 1YQ**

AMBERGATE SCHOOL
Dysart Road, Grantham,
Lincolnshire NG31 7LP
Website: www.
ambergateschool.co.uk
Type: Co-educational 5–16
Special needs: **MLD**
Wheelchair access: W

THE ASH VILLA SPECIAL SCHOOL
Rauceby Hospital, Sleaford,
Lincolnshire NG34 8QA
Type: Co-educational Boarding
and Day 8–18
Special needs: ADD ADHD ASP
BESD HEA
Wheelchair access: W

THE ERESBY SCHOOL
Eresby Avenue, Spilsby,
Lincolnshire PE23 5HU
Type: Co-educational Day Only
2–19
Special needs: PMLD SLD
Wheelchair access: WA1

FORTUNA SCHOOL
Kingsdown Road, Lincoln,
Lincolnshire LN6 0FB
Type: Co-educational Day Only
Special needs: **BESD**
Wheelchair access: WA1

GARTH SCHOOL
Pinchbeck Road, Spalding,
Lincolnshire PE11 1QF
Website: www.
spaldingspecialschools.co.uk
Type: Co-educational Day Only
2–19
Special needs: ASD PMLD **SLD**
Wheelchair access: WA1

GOSBERTON HOUSE SCHOOL
Westhorpe Road, Spalding,
Lincolnshire PE11 4EW
Type: Co-educational Day Only
Special needs: ASD **ASP** MLD VI

JOHN FIELDING SCHOOL
Ashlawn Drive, Boston,
Lincolnshire PE21 9PX
Website: www.
johnfieldingschool.co.uk
Type: Co-educational Day Only
2–19
Special needs: **ASP DOW EPI
HEA HI IM PMLD SLD**
Wheelchair access: WA1

THE LADY JANE FRANKLIN SCHOOL
Partney Road, Spilsby,
Lincolnshire PE23 5EJ
Type: Co-educational Day Only
11–16
Special needs: ADD **ADHD** ASD
ASP BESD CB HEA
Wheelchair access: WA1

THE PHOENIX SCHOOL
Great North Road, Grantham,
Lincolnshire NG31 2LH

PRIORY SCHOOL
Neville Avenue, Spalding,
Lincolnshire PE11 2EH
Type: Co-educational Day Only
11–16
Special needs: ADD **ADHD** ASD
ASP BESD DOW **MLD**
Wheelchair access: WA2

QUEENS PARK SCHOOL
South Park, Lincoln, Lincolnshire
LN5 8EW
Website: www.
queensparkschool.net
Type: Co-educational Day Only
2–19
Special needs: ASD ASP CP
DOW HEA **PMLD SLD**
Wheelchair access: W

ST BERNARD'S SCHOOL
Wood Lane, Louth, Lincolnshire
LN11 8RS
Type: Co-educational Day and
Boarding 2–19
Special needs: **SLD**

ST CHRISTOPHER'S SCHOOL
Hykeham Road, Lincoln,
Lincolnshire LN6 8AR
Type: Co-educational 3–16

ST FRANCIS SPECIAL SCHOOL
Wickenby Crescent, Lincoln,
Lincolnshire LN1 3TJ
Type: Co-educational Day and
Boarding 2–19
Special needs: **CP** DOW EPI HEA
MLD
Wheelchair access: W

ST LAWRENCE SCHOOL
Bowl Alley Lane, Horncastle,
Lincolnshire LN9 5EJ
Type: Co-educational Day and
Boarding
Special needs: ASD DOW **MLD**
SP&LD VI
Wheelchair access: WA2

SANDON SCHOOL
Sandon Close, Grantham,
Lincolnshire NG31 9AX
Type: Co-educational Day Only
2–19
Special needs: ASD CP **DOW** EPI
PMLD SLD
Wheelchair access: W

WILLIAM HARRISON SPECIAL SCHOOL
Middlefield Lane, Gainsborough,
Lincolnshire DN21 1PU
Type: Co-educational Day Only
3–16
Special needs: ADD ADHD ASD
DOW EPI HI MLD SP&LD
Wheelchair access: WA1

THE WILLOUGHBY SCHOOL
South Road, Bourne, Lincolnshire
PE10 9JE
Type: Co-educational Day Only
2–19
Special needs: ASD **ASP** CP
DOW **PMLD SLD**
Wheelchair access: W

NORTH EAST LINCOLNSHIRE

North East Lincolnshire County Council

**Municipal Offices
Town Hall Square
Grimsby
North East Lincolnshire
DN31 1HU**

CAMBRIDGE PARK SCHOOL
Cambridge Road, Grimsby,
North East Lincolnshire DN34 5EB
Website: wwww.cambridgepark.
ne-lincs.sch.uk
Type: Co-educational Day Only
3–16
Special needs: ADD ASD **ASP**
BESD DOW DYP EPI HI **MLD**
SP&LD VI
Wheelchair access: WA1

HUMBERSTON PARK SCHOOL
St Thomas Close, Humberston,
North East Lincolnshire DN36 4HS
Website: uk.geocites.com/
matthewwinder/hpstest/
index.html
Type: Co-educational Day Only
3–19
Special needs: ASD PMLD **SLD**
Wheelchair access: WA1

NORTH LINCOLNSHIRE

North Lincolnshire Education Offices

Pittwood House
Ashby Road
Scunthorpe
North Lincolnshire
DN16 1AB

ST HUGH'S SCHOOL
Bushfield Road, Scunthorpe,
North Lincolnshire DN16 1NB
Type: Co-educational Day Only
11–19
Special needs: ADD ADHD ASD
ASP CP DOW EPI HEA HI **MLD**
PMLD **SLD** VI
Wheelchair access: WA1

ST LUKE'S PRIMARY SCHOOL
Burghley Road, Scunthorpe,
North Lincolnshire DN16 1JD
Type: Co-educational Day Only
3–11
Special needs: ADHD ASD CB
CP DOW EPI HI **MLD PMLD SLD**
VI
Wheelchair access: WA1

LONDON

Barnet LEA

The Burroughs
Hendon
London
NW4 4BG

MAPLEDOWN SCHOOL
Claremont Road, London
NW2 1TR
Website: www.
mapledownschool.org
Type: Co-educational Day Only
11–19
Special needs: PMLD SLD
Wheelchair access: WA1

NORTHWAY SCHOOL
The Fairway, London NW7 3HS
Type: Co-educational Day Only
5–11
Special needs: ASD **ASP** DOW
DYC DYS EPI HEA HI **MLD** TOU
VI
Wheelchair access: W

OAK LODGE SCHOOL
Heath View, London N2 0QY
Type: Co-educational Day Only
11–19
Special needs: ASD MLD
Wheelchair access: WA1

OAKLEIGH SCHOOL
Oakleigh Road North, London
N20 0DH
Type: Co-educational Day Only
2–11
Special needs: ASD PMLD **SLD**
Wheelchair access: WA1

Bexley Council

Education Offices
Hill View Drive
Welling
Kent
DA16 3RY

MARLBOROUGH SCHOOL
Marlborough Park Avenue,
Sidcup, Kent DA15 9DP
Type: Co-educational Day Only
11–19
Special needs: **PMLD SLD**
Wheelchair access: WA1

OAKWOOD SCHOOL
Woodside Road, Bexleyheath,
Kent DA7 6LB
Website: www.oakwood.bexley.
sch.uk
Type: Co-educational Day Only
11–16
Special needs: **BESD**

SHENSTONE SCHOOL
Old Road, Crayford, Kent
DA1 4DZ
Type: Co-educational Day Only
2–11
Special needs: ASD **ASP** CP
DOW EPI HI **PMLD SLD** VI
Wheelchair access: WA1

WESTBROOKE SCHOOL
South Gipsy Road, Welling, Kent
DA16 1JB
Type: Co-educational Day Only
5–11
Special needs: ASP **BESD**
Wheelchair access: WA2

WOODSIDE SCHOOL
Halt Robin Road, Belvedere, Kent
DA17 6DW
Type: Co-educational Day Only
5–16
Special needs: ADHD ASD **ASP**
HI **MLD** VI
Wheelchair access: WA3

Brent Council

Chesterfield House
9 Park Lane
Wembley
Middlesex
HA9 7RW

GROVE PARK SCHOOL
Grove Park, London NW9 0JY
Type: Co-educational Day Only
2–19
Special needs: CP EPI **HEA**
Wheelchair access: WA1

HAY LANE SCHOOL
Grove Park, London NW9 0JY
Type: Co-educational Day Only
2–19
Special needs: PMLD SLD
Wheelchair access: W

MANOR SCHOOL
Chamberlayne Road, London
NW10 3NT
Type: Co-educational Day Only
4–11
Special needs: ASD **ASP MLD**
SLD
Wheelchair access: WA2

VERNON HOUSE SCHOOL
Drury Way, London NW10 0NQ
Type: Co-educational 5–12
Special needs: **BESD**

WOODFIELD SCHOOL
Glenwood Avenue, London
NW9 7LY
Website: www.woodfield.
surrey.sch.uk
Type: Co-educational Day Only
11–16
Special needs: ASD **MLD** SP&LD
Wheelchair access: WA1

Bromley Education Offices

Civic Centre
Stockwell Close
Bromley
Kent
BR1 3UH

BURWOOD SCHOOL
Avalon Road, Orpington, Kent
BR6 9BD
Type: Boys Day Only 9–16

GLEBE SCHOOL
Hawes Lane, West Wickham,
Kent BR4 9AE
Website: www.glebe.bromley.
sch.uk
Type: Co-educational Day Only
11–16
Special needs: ASD **MLD**

**MARJORIE MCCLURE
SCHOOL**
Hawkwood Lane, Chislehurst,
Kent BR7 5PS
Type: Co-educational Day Only
3–19
Special needs: CP EPI HEA
Wheelchair access: W

RIVERSIDE SCHOOL
Main Road, Orpington, Kent
BR5 3HS
Type: Co-educational Day Only
4–19
Special needs: PMLD SLD
Wheelchair access: WA1

Camden LEA

Crowndale Centre
218–220 Eversholt Street
London
NW1 1BD

**BECKFORD PRIMARY
SCHOOL**
Dornfell Street, London NW6 1QL
Type: Co-educational Day Only
3–11

CHALCOT SCHOOL
Harmood Street, London
NW1 8DP
Website: www.chalcot.camden.
sch.uk
Type: Boys Day Only
Special needs: **BESD**

**CHRISTOPHER HATTON
PRIMARY SCHOOL**
38 Laystall Street, London
EC1R 4PQ
Type: Co-educational Day Only
3–11
Special needs: SP&LD

FRANK BARNES SCHOOL
Harley Road, London NW3 3BY
Website: www.fbarnes.camden.
sch.uk
Type: Co-educational Day Only
2–11
Special needs: **HI**

JACK TAYLOR SCHOOL
Ainsworth Way, London NW8 0SR
Type: Co-educational Day Only
5–19

**REGENTS PARK UNDER 5S
CENTRE**
Augustus Street, London
NW1 3TJ
Type: Co-educational Day Only
Special needs: ADD ADHD ASD
ASP BESD CB CP DOW DYC
DYP DYS EPI HEA HI IM MLD
PMLD SLD SP&LD TOU VI
Wheelchair access: W

**SOUTH CAMDEN COMMUNITY
SECONDARY SCHOOL**
Charrington Street, London
NW1 1RG
Website: www.sccs.camden.
sch.uk
Type: Co-educational Day Only
11–19
Wheelchair access: WA2

**SWISS COTTAGE SPECIALIST
SEN SCHOOL**
Avenue Road, London NW8 6HX
Website: www.
swisscottageschool.com
Type: Co-educational Day Only
2–16
Special needs: **MLD** SP&LD
Wheelchair access: WA1

City of Westminster LEA

PO Box 240, 14th Floor
Westminster City Hall
64 Victoria St
London
SW1E 6QP

COLLEGE PARK SCHOOL
Garway Road, London W2 4PH
Type: Co-educational Day Only
5–16
Special needs: **MLD**

QUEEN ELIZABETH II SCHOOL
Kennet Road, London W9 3LG
Type: Co-educational Day Only
5–19
Special needs: PMLD SLD
Wheelchair access: W

Croydon Education Department

Taberner House
Park Lane
Croydon
Surrey
CR9 1TP

BECKMEAD SCHOOL
Monks Orchard Road,
Beckenham, Surrey BR3 3BZ
Type: Boys Day Only
Special needs: **BESD**

BENSHAM MANOR SCHOOL
Ecclesbourne Road, Thornton
Heath, Surrey CR7 7BR
Website: www.benshammanor.
com
Type: Co-educational Day Only
11–16
Special needs: ASD **MLD**

PRIORY SCHOOL
Tennison Road, London
SE25 5RR
Type: Co-educational Day Only
12–19
Special needs: ASD DOW **SLD**
Wheelchair access: W

RED GATES SCHOOL
Farnborough Ave, South
Croydon, Surrey CR2 8HD
Website: www.redgates.croydon.
sch.uk
Type: Co-educational Day Only
4–12
Special needs: ASD **ASP PMLD
SLD**
Wheelchair access: WA1

ST GILES' SCHOOL
Pampisford Road, Croydon,
Surrey CR2 6DF
Type: Co-educational Day Only
4–19
Special needs: CP DYP EPI HEA
HI **IM PMLD** VI
Wheelchair access: WA1

ST NICHOLAS SCHOOL
Old Lodge Lane, Purley, Surrey
CR8 4DN
Type: Co-educational Day Only
4–11
Special needs: ASD **MLD**

TUDOR LODGE SCHOOL
Teaching Annexe, Purley, Surrey
CR8 3NA
Type: Co-educational Day Only
11–17
Special needs: ADD ADHD BESD
Wheelchair access: WA3

Ealing Education Offices

Perceval House
14–16 Uxbridge Road
Ealing
London
W5 2HL

BELVUE SCHOOL
Rowdell Road, Northolt,
Middlesex UB5 6AG
Website: www.belvueschool.org
Type: Co-educational Day Only
12–19
Special needs: ADD ASD BESD
CB **MLD** SLD SP&LD
Wheelchair access: W WA1

CASTLEBAR SCHOOL
Hathaway Gardens, London
W13 0DH
Website: www.castebar.ealing.
sch.uk
Type: Co-educational Day Only
3–11
Special needs: ASD **ASP** HI **MLD
SLD**
Wheelchair access: W

DURANTS SCHOOL
4 Pitfield Way, Enfield, Middlesex
EN3 5BY
Type: Co-educational Day Only
5–18
Special needs: SLD
Wheelchair access: WA3

JOHN CHILTON SCHOOL
Compton Crescent, Northolt,
Middlesex UB5 5LD
Type: Co-educational Day Only

MANDEVILLE SCHOOL
Eastcote Lane, Northolt,
Middlesex UB5 4HW
Type: Co-educational Day Only
2–11
Special needs: ASD **ASP PMLD
SLD**
Wheelchair access: WA1

ST ANN'S SCHOOL
Springfield Road, London W7 3JP
Type: Co-educational Day Only
Special needs: ASD **PMLD SLD**
Wheelchair access: WA1

SPRINGHALLOW SCHOOL
Compton Close, London W13 0JG
Type: Co-educational Day Only
3–16
Special needs: ASD **ASP**
Wheelchair access: W

Enfield Education Services

Civic Centre
Silver Street
Enfield
EN1 3XY

AYLANDS SCHOOL
Keswick Drive, Enfield,
Middlesex EN3 6NY

OAKTREE SCHOOL
Chase Side, London N14 4HN
Website: www.oaktree.enfield.
sch.uk
Type: Co-educational Day Only
5–19
Special needs: **MLD**

RUSSET HOUSE
11 Autumn Close, Enfield,
Middlesex EN1 4JA
Type: Co-educational Day Only
3–11
Special needs: ASD **ASP**
Wheelchair access: WA2

WAVERLEY SCHOOL
105 The Ride, Enfield, Middlesex
EN3 7DL
Type: Co-educational Day Only
3–19
Special needs: PMLD **SLD**
Wheelchair access: WA1

WEST LEA SCHOOL
Haslebury Road, London N9 9TU
Website: www.westleaschool.
co.uk
Type: Co-educational Day Only
4–17
Special needs: ADD ADHD **ASD**
ASP CP DYC DYP EPI **HEA** HI
SP&LD TOU VI
Wheelchair access: W

Greenwich Education Service

Wellington Street
Woolwich
London
SE18 6PW

CHARLTON SCHOOL
Charlton Park Road, London
SE7 8HX
Type: Co-educational Boarding
and Day
Special needs: **CP** EPI **PMLD**
SLD SP&LD
Wheelchair access: W

MOATBRIDGE SCHOOL
Eltham Palace Road, London
SE9 5LX
Type: Boys Day Only 11–16
Special needs: **BESD**
Wheelchair access: WA1

NEWHAVEN PRU SCHOOL
Newhaven Annexe, London
SE2 0HY
Type: Co-educational Day Only
11–17
Special needs: BESD

WATERSIDE SCHOOL
Robert Street, London SE18 7NB
Type: Co-educational Day Only
5–11

WILLOW DENE SCHOOL
Swingate Lane, London SE18 2JD
Website: www.willowdeneschool.
co.uk
Type: Co-educational Day Only
2–11
Special needs: ASD MLD PMLD
SLD
Wheelchair access: WA2

Hackney The Learning Trust

Reading Lane
Hackney
London
E8 1QG

CRUSOE HOUSE SCHOOL
Nile Street, London N1 7DR
Type: Boys Day Only
Special needs: **BESD**

DOWNSVIEW SCHOOL
Tiger Way, London E5 8QP
Type: Co-educational Day Only
5–16
Special needs: **MLD**

HORIZON SCHOOL
Wordsworth Road, London
N16 8BZ
Website: www.horizonschool.
co.uk
Type: Co-educational Day Only
11–16
Special needs: **MLD**

ICKBURGH SCHOOL
Ickburgh Road, London E5 8AD
Type: Co-educational Day Only
2–19
Special needs: PMLD SLD

STORMONT HOUSE SCHOOL
Downs Park Road, London
E5 8NP
Type: Co-educational 11–16
Special needs: HEA SP&LD

Hammersmith and Fulham Council

King Street
London
W6 9JU

CAMBRIDGE SCHOOL
Cambridge Grove, London
W6 0LB
Website: www.cambridge.lbhs.
sch.uk
Type: Co-educational 11–16
Special needs: **ADHD ASD** ASP
BESD MLD
Wheelchair access: WA2

GIBBS GREEN SCHOOL
Mund Street, London W14 9LY
Type: Co-educational Day Only
4–11
Special needs: **BESD**

JACK TIZARD SCHOOL
South Africa Road, London
W12 7PA
Website: www.jacktizard.lbhf.
sch.uk
Type: Co-educational Day Only
2–19
Special needs: CP EPI HEA
PMLD SLD VI W

QUEENSMILL SCHOOL
Clancarty Road, London
SW6 3AA
Type: Co-educational Day Only
3–11
Special needs: ASD **ASP**
Wheelchair access: WA1

WOODLANE HIGH SCHOOL
Du Cane Road, London W12 0TN
Website: www.woodlane.ibhf
Type: Co-educational Day Only
11–16
Special needs: **ASD** ASP **HEA**
SP&LD VI
Wheelchair access: WA1

Haringey Education Offices

Civic Centre
High Road
Wood Green
London
N22 8LE

BLANCHE NEVILE SCHOOL IN PARTNERSHIP WITH FORTISMERE SCHOOL
Burlington Road, London
N10 1NJ
Type: Co-educational Day Only
Special needs: **HI**

MOSELLE SPECIAL SCHOOL
Adams Road, London N17 6HW
Website: www.moselle.haringey.
sch.uk
Type: Co-educational Day Only
4–16
Special needs: ASD **ASP** BESD
DOW EPI **MLD SLD** SP&LD VI
Wheelchair access: WA2

VALE SPECIAL SCHOOL
c/o Northumberland Park
Community School, London
N17 0PG
Website: www.vale.haringey.
sch.uk
Type: Co-educational Day Only
2–19
Special needs: CP EPI **IM** SP&LD
Wheelchair access: WA1

WILLIAM C HARVEY SPECIAL SCHOOL
Adams Road, London N17 6HW
Website: www.haringey.gov.uk
Type: Co-educational Day Only
4–16
Special needs: PMLD SLD
Wheelchair access: WA1

Harrow Education Services

PO Box 22
Civic Centre
Harrow
Middlesex
HA1 2XF

ALEXANDRA SCHOOL
Alexandra Avenue, Harrow,
Middlesex HA2 9DX
Special needs: MLD

KINGSLEY HIGH SCHOOL
Whittlesea Road, Harrow Weald,
Middlesex HA3 6ND
Type: Co-educational Day Only
Special needs: **PMLD SLD**
Wheelchair access: WA1

SHAFTESBURY SCHOOL
Headstone Lane, Harrow,
Middlesex HA3 6LE
Type: Co-educational Day Only
11–18
Special needs: MLD
Wheelchair access: WA1

WOODLANDS SCHOOL
Whittlesea Road, Harrow,
Middlesex HA3 6LE
Type: Co-educational 3–11
Special needs: ASD **PMLD** SLD

Havering LEA

Town Hall
Main Road
Romford
Essex
RM1 3BB

CORBETS TEY SCHOOL
Harwood Hall Lane, Upminster,
Essex RM14 2YQ
Website: www.corbetsteyschool.
org.uk
Type: Co-educational Day Only
4–16
Special needs: ASD **MLD** SLD

DYCORTS SCHOOL
Settle Road, Romford, Essex
RM3 9YA
Type: Co-educational Day Only
3–16
Special needs: DYS EPI MLD
SP&LD
Wheelchair access: W

RAVENSBOURNE SCHOOL
Neave Crescent, Romford, Essex
RM3 8HN
Type: Co-educational Day Only
2–19
Special needs: ASD BESD CP
DOW DYS HEA **SLD** VI
Wheelchair access: W

London Borough of Hillingdon

Civic Centre
High Street
Uxbridge
Middlesex
UB8 1UW

CHANTRY SCHOOL
Falling Lane, West Drayton,
Middlesex UB7 8AB
Type: Co-educational Day Only
Special needs: **ADD ADHD**
BESD

GRANGEWOOD SCHOOL
Fore Street, Pinner, Middlesex
HA5 2JQ
Website: www.
grangewoodschool.co.uk
Type: Co-educational 3–11

HEDGEWOOD SCHOOL
Weymouth Road, Hayes,
Middlesex UB4 8NF
Type: Co-educational Day Only
Special needs: ASD **ASP** DOW
DYP HI **PMLD** VI

MEADOW HIGH SCHOOL
Royal Lane, Uxbridge, Middlesex
UB8 3QU
Website: www.meadowhigh.com
Type: Co-educational Day Only
11–18
Special needs: ASD **ASP MLD**
Wheelchair access: WA1

MOORCROFT SCHOOL
Bramble Close, Uxbridge,
Middlesex UB8 3BF
Website: www.moorcroft.
hillingdon.sch.uk
Type: Co-educational Day Only
11–19
Special needs: ASD PMLD **SLD**
Wheelchair access: WA1

THE WILLOWS SCHOOL
Stipularis Drive, Hayes,
Middlesex UB4 9QB
Website: www.hillingdon.gov.uk
Type: Co-educational Day Only
Special needs: **BESD**

Hounslow Council

Civic Centre
Lampton Road
Hounslow
Middlesex
TW3 4DN

THE CEDARS PRIMARY SCHOOL
High Street, Hounslow, Middlesex TW5 9RU
Website: www.cedars.hounslow.lgfl.net
Type: Co-educational Day Only 4–11
Special needs: **BESD**

LINDON BENNETT SCHOOL
Main Street, Hanworth, Middlesex TW13 6ST
Website: www.lgfl.net
Type: Co-educational Day Only 4–11
Special needs: ASD **PMLD SLD**
Wheelchair access: WA1

MARJORY KINNON SPECIAL SCHOOL
Hatton Road, Bedfont, Middlesex TW14 9QZ
Website: www.lgfl.net
Type: Co-educational Day Only 4–19
Special needs: ASD **MLD**
Wheelchair access: WA1

OAKLANDS SCHOOL
Woodlands Road, Isleworth, Middlesex TW7 6HD
Type: Co-educational Day Only 11–19
Special needs: PMLD **SLD**
Wheelchair access: W

SYON PARK SCHOOL
Twickenham Road, Isleworth, Middlesex TW7 6AU
Website: www.syonpark.hounslow.sch.uk
Type: Co-educational Day Only 11–16
Special needs: **BESD**

Islington Council

222 Upper Street
London
N1 1XR

THE BRIDGE SCHOOL & PROFESSIONAL TRAINING CENTRE
251 Hungerford Road, London N7 9LD
Website: www.thebridge.islington.sch.uk
Type: Co-educational Day Only 2–19
Special needs: ASD PMLD SLD
Wheelchair access: WA1

RICHARD CLOUDESLEY SCHOOL
Golden Lane, London EC1Y 0TJ
Type: Co-educational Day Only 2–18
Special needs: CP EPI SP&LD
Wheelchair access: W

SAMUEL RHODES SCHOOL
Richmond Avenue, London N1 0LS
Website: www.islington.gov.uk
Type: Co-educational Day Only 5–16
Special needs: **MLD**

The Royal Borough of Kensington & Chelsea

The Town Hall
Hornton Street
London
W8 7NX

PARKWOOD HALL SCHOOL
Beechenlea Lane, Swanley, Kent BR8 8DR
Website: www.parkwoodhall.rbkc.sch.uk
Type: Co-educational Boarding and Day 8–19
Special needs: ASD **DOW HEA MLD** SLD SP&LD

Kingston Upon Thames Education & Leisure Services

Guildhall 2
Kingston upon Thames
Surrey
KT1 1EU

BEDELSFORD SCHOOL
Grange Road, Kingston upon Thames, Surrey KT1 2QZ
Website: www.bedelsford.kingston.sch.uk
Type: Co-educational Day Only 2–16
Special needs: **CP** EPI HEA HI MLD **PMLD** VI
Wheelchair access: WA1

DYSART SCHOOL
190 Ewell Road, Surbiton, Surrey KT6 6HL
Website: www.dysartschool.org.uk
Type: Co-educational Day Only 4–19
Special needs: ASD **ASP** PMLD **SLD**
Wheelchair access: WA1

ST PHILIP'S SPECIAL SCHOOL
Harrow Close, Chessington, Surrey KT9 2HP
Type: Co-educational Day Only 10–19
Special needs: ASD **ASP** DOW **MLD**
Wheelchair access: WA3

Lambeth Council

Town Hall
Brixton Hill
London
SW2 1RW

ELM COURT SCHOOL
Elm Park, London SW2 2EF
Type: Co-educational Day Only 11–16
Special needs: ADD ADHD ASD BESD **MLD** SP&LD
Wheelchair access: WA1

LANSDOWNE SCHOOL
Argyll Close, London SW9 9QL
Type: Co-educational Day Only 5–16
Special needs: **MLD**

THE LIVITY SCHOOL
Mandrell Road, London SW2 5DW
Type: Co-educational Day Only
3–11
Special needs: ASD DOW PMLD
SLD
Wheelchair access: W

THE MICHAEL TIPPETT SCHOOL
Oakden Street, London
SE11 4UG
Type: Co-educational Day Only
11–19
Special needs: ASD PMLD SLD
Wheelchair access: WA1

TURNEY SCHOOL
Turney Road, London SE21 8LX
Website: www.turneyschool.
co.uk
Type: Co-educational 5–16
Special needs: ADD ADHD ASD
ASP DOW **MLD** SP&LD

London Borough of Lewisham

Town Hall
Catford
London
SE6 4RU

BRENT KNOLL SCHOOL
Mayow Road, London SE23 2XH
Type: Co-educational Day Only
4–16

GREENVALE SCHOOL
69 Perry Rise, London SE23 2QU
Type: Co-educational Day Only
11–19
Special needs: PMLD SLD
Wheelchair access: W

MEADOWGATE SCHOOL
Revelon Road, London SE4 2PR
Type: Co-educational Day Only
4–11
Special needs: ASD **ASP** MLD
Wheelchair access: W

NEW WOODLANDS SCHOOL (JMI)
49 Shroffold Road, Bromley, Kent
BR1 5PD
Type: Boys Day Only 5–11 (Key
Stage 3 11 – 14)
Special needs: **ADD ADHD**
BESD
Wheelchair access: WA1

PENDRAGON SCHOOL
Pendragon Road, Bromley, Kent
BR1 5LD
Website: www.pendragon.
lewisham.sch.uk
Type: Co-educational Day Only
11–16
Special needs: **MLD**

WATERGATE SCHOOL
Lushington Road, London
SE6 3WG
Website: www.watergate.
lewisham.sch.uk
Type: Co-educational Day Only
2–11
Special needs: PMLD **SLD**
Wheelchair access: W

London Borough of Merton

Merton Civic Centre
London Road
Morden
Surrey
SM4 5DX

CRICKET GREEN SCHOOL
Lower Green West, Mitcham,
Surrey CR4 3AF
Type: Co-educational Day Only
5–16
Special needs: ADHD ASD MLD
Wheelchair access: WA1

MELROSE SCHOOL
Church Road, Mitcham, Surrey
CR4 3BE
Type: Co-educational Day Only
9–16
Special needs: **BESD**

ST ANN'S SCHOOL
Bordesley Road, Morden, Surrey
SM4 5LT
Website: www.st-anns.merton.
sch.uk
Type: Co-educational Day Only
2–19
Special needs: ASD PMLD SLD
Wheelchair access: WA1

London Borough of Newham

Broadway House
High Street
Stratford
London
E15 1AJ

ELEANOR SMITH SCHOOL
North Street, London E13 9HN
Type: Co-educational Day Only
5–11
Special needs: **BESD**

JOHN F KENNEDY SCHOOL
Pitchford Street, London E15 4RZ
Type: Co-educational Day Only
2–19

Redbridge Education Services

Lynton House
255–259 High Road
Ilford
IG1 1NN

HATTON SCHOOL
Roding Lane South, Woodford
Green, Essex IG8 8EU
Type: Co-educational Day Only
3–11
Special needs: ASD **ASP MLD**
SP&LD

LITTLE HEATH SCHOOL
Hainault Road, Romford, Essex
RM6 5RX
Website: www.littleheath.
essex.sch.uk
Type: Co-educational Day Only
11–16
Special needs: ADD ADHD ASP
MLD SP&LD

NEW RUSH HALL SCHOOL
Fencepiece Road, Hainault,
Essex IG6 2LJ
Website: www.nrhs.redbridge.
sch.uk
Type: Co-educational Day Only
4–16
Special needs: **BESD**

NEWBRIDGE SCHOOL
Barley Lane Campus, Ilford,
Essex IG3 8XS
Website: www.newbridge.
redbridge.sch.uk
Type: Co-educational Day Only
2–19
Special needs: ASD **ASP** CP
MLD **PMLD SLD** VI
Wheelchair access: WA1

London Borough of Richmond upon Thames

Regal House, First Floor
London Road
Twickenham
Middlesex
TW1 3QB

CLARENDON SCHOOL
Hanworth Road, Hampton,
Middlesex TW12 3DH
Website: www.clarendon.
richmond.sch.uk
Type: Co-educational Day Only
7–16
Special needs: **MLD**
Wheelchair access: WA2

STRATHMORE SCHOOL
Meadlands Drive, Petersham,
Surrey TW10 7ED
Type: Co-educational Day Only
7–19
Special needs: ASD **ASP PMLD**
SLD
Wheelchair access: WA1

Southwark Education

John Smith House
144 – 152 Walworth Road
London
SE17 1JL

BEORMUND PRIMARY
SCHOOL
Crosby Row, London SE1 3PS
Website: www.
beormundschool.co.uk
Type: Co-educational Day Only
5–11
Special needs: **BESD**

BREDINGHURST SCHOOL
Stuart Road, London SE15 3AZ
Type: Boys Boarding and Day
Special needs: ADD ADHD
BESD

CHERRY GARDEN SPECIAL
PRIMARY SCHOOL
Macks Road, London SE16 3XU
Website: www.cherrygarden.
suffolk.sch.uk
Type: Co-educational Day Only
2–11
Special needs: ASD **ASP** CP EPI
HI PMLD **SLD** SP&LD VI
Wheelchair access: W

HAYMERLE'S SCHOOL
Haymerle Road, London
SE15 6SY
Type: Co-educational Day Only
5–11
Special needs: ADD ADHD ASD
BESD CP DOW DYP DYS EPI
HEA MLD SP&LD
Wheelchair access: W

HIGHSHORE SPECIAL
SCHOOL
Bellenden Road, London
SE15 5BB
Website: www.highshore.
southwark.sch.uk
Type: Co-educational Day Only
11–17
Special needs: ADD ADHD ASD
DOW DYC DYP DYS EPI IM **MLD**
SP&LD
Wheelchair access: WA1

SPA SCHOOL
Monnow Road, London SE1 5RN
Type: Co-educational 11–16
Special needs: ASD **ASP** MLD

TUKE SCHOOL
4 Woods Road, London SE15 2PX
Type: Co-educational Day Only
11–19
Special needs: ASD IM **PMLD**
SLD
Wheelchair access: WA2

Sutton Education Offices

The Grove
Carshalton
Surrey
SM5 3AL

CAREW MANOR SCHOOL
Church Road, Wallington, Surrey
SM6 7NH
Website: www.carewmanor.
org.uk
Type: Co-educational Day Only
7–16
Special needs: ASD ASP **MLD**
Wheelchair access: WA3

SHERWOOD PARK SCHOOL
Streeters Lane, Wallington,
Surrey SM6 7NP
Type: Co-educational Day Only
2–19
Special needs: ASD **ASP CP**
DOW PMLD SLD
Wheelchair access: WA1

WANDLE VALLEY SCHOOL
Welbeck Road, Carshalton,
Surrey SM5 1LW
Type: Co-educational Day Only
5–16
Special needs: **BESD**
Wheelchair access: WA2

Tower Hamlets Borough Council

Mulberry Place
5 Clove Crescent
London
E14 2BG

BEATRICE TATE SCHOOL
St Jude's Road, London E2 9RW
Website: www.beatricetate.
towerhamlets.sch.uk
Type: Co-educational Day Only
11–19
Special needs: CB DOW EPI HI
PMLD **SLD** VI
Wheelchair access: WA1

BOWDEN HOUSE
Firle Road, Seaford, East Sussex
BN25 2JB
Type: Boys Boarding Only 10–16
Special needs: **BESD**

CHERRY TREES SCHOOL
68 Campbell Road, London
E3 4EA
Type: Boys 5–11
Special needs: **BESD**

IAN MIKARDO HIGH SCHOOL
60 William Guy Gardens, London
E3 3LF
Type: Boys 11–16

PHOENIX SCHOOL
49 Bow Road, London E3 2AD
Website: www.phoenix.
towerhamlets.sch.uk
Type: Co-educational Day Only
2–16
Special needs: ASD **ASP** MLD
SP&LD
Wheelchair access: W

STEPHEN HAWKING SCHOOL
Brunton Place, London E14 7LL
Website: www.stephenhawking.
towerhamlets.sch.uk
Type: Co-educational Day Only
2–11
Special needs: **PMLD SLD**

Waltham Forest Council

Town Hall
Forest Road
London
E17 4JF

BELMONT PARK SCHOOL
Leyton Green Road, London
E10 6DB
Type: Co-educational 11–16

**BROOKFIELD HOUSE
SCHOOL**
Alders Avenue, Woodford Green,
Essex IG8 9PY
Type: Co-educational Day Only
2–16
Special needs: CP EPI **HEA** HI **IM**
Wheelchair access: WA1

ELSLEY SCHOOL
31 Elsley Road, London
SW11 5TZ
Type: Co-educational Day Only
5–11
Special needs: ADD ADHD
BESD MLD
Wheelchair access: W

JOSEPH CLARKE SCHOOL
Vincent Road, London E4 9PP
Type: Co-educational Day Only
2–19
Special needs: VI
Wheelchair access: W

**WHITEFIELD SCHOOL AND
CENTRE**
Macdonald Road, London
E17 4AZ
Website: www.whitefield.org.uk
Type: Co-educational Day Only
3–19
Special needs: ASD **ASP** CP
DOW DYP EPI HI MLD **PMLD**
SLD SP&LD VI
Wheelchair access: WA1

WILLIAM MORRIS SCHOOL
Folly Lane, London E17 5NT
Type: Co-educational Day Only
11–19
Special needs: ASD **ASP CB CP
EPI HEA HI MLD PMLD SLD**
SP&LD
Wheelchair access: WA1

Wandsworth LEA

The Town Hall
Wandsworth High Street
London
SW18 2PU

BRADSTOW SCHOOL
34 Dumpton Park Drive,
Broadstairs, Kent CT10 1RG
Website: www.bradstow.
wandsworth.sch.uk
Type: Co-educational Boarding
Only 5–19
Special needs: ASD **ASP** BESD
EPI **SLD**

GARRATT PARK SCHOOL
Waldron Road, London SW18 3SY
Website: www.garrattpark.
wandsworth.sch.uk
Type: Co-educational Day Only
11–17
Special needs: ADHD ASD BESD
DYC DYS HI MLD SP&LD VI
Wheelchair access: WA2

GREENMEAD SCHOOL
St Margaret's Crescent, London
SW15 6HL
Type: Co-educational Day Only
3–11
Special needs: **CP** MLD **PMLD**
SLD
Wheelchair access: WA1

LINDEN LODGE SCHOOL
61 Princes Way, London
SW19 6JB
Type: Co-educational Day and
Boarding 5–18
Special needs: VI

NIGHTINGALE SCHOOL
Beechcroft Road, London
SW17 7DF
Type: Boys Day Only
Special needs: **BESD**

OAK LODGE SCHOOL
101 Nightingale Lane, London
SW12 8NA
Website: www.oaklodge.
wandsworth.sch.uk
Type: Co-educational Boarding
and Day 11–19
Special needs: **HI**
Wheelchair access: WA3

PADDOCK SCHOOL
Priory Lane, London SW15 5RT
Website: www.lgfl.net
Type: Co-educational Day Only
3–19
Special needs: PMLD **SLD**
Wheelchair access: W

THE VINES SCHOOL
Forthbridge Road, London
SW11 5NX
Website: www.thevinesschool.
co.uk
Type: Co-educational Day Only
3–11
Special needs: ADHD ASD BESD
DOW HEA **MLD** VI
Wheelchair access: WA2

GREATER MANCHESTER

Bolton Education and Culture

Town Hall
Victoria Square
Bolton
Greater Manchester
BL1 1RU

FIRWOOD SCHOOL
Crompton Way, Bolton, Greater Manchester BL2 3AF
Type: Co-educational Day Only 11–19
Special needs: ASD **PMLD SLD**
Wheelchair access: WA1

GREEN FOLD SCHOOL
Highfield Road, Farnworth, Greater Manchester BL4 0RA
Type: Day Only 3–11
Special needs: ASD CP EPI **PMLD SLD**
Wheelchair access: WA1

LADYWOOD SCHOOL
Masefield Road, Bolton, Greater Manchester BL3 1NG
Type: Co-educational Day Only 4–11
Special needs: ASD MLD

LEVEN PARK SCHOOL
Stocks Park Drive, Bolton, Greater Manchester BL6 6DE
Type: Co-educational Day Only 11–16
Special needs: ADD ADHD **BESD** TOU
Wheelchair access: WA1

RUMWORTH SCHOOL
Armdale Road, Bolton, Greater Manchester BL3 4TP
Website: www.rumworth.sch.uk
Type: Co-educational Day Only 11–19
Special needs: ASD **MLD SLD**
Wheelchair access: WA1

THOMASSON MEMORIAL SCHOOL
Devonshire Road, Bolton, Greater Manchester BL1 4JP
Website: www.thomasson. bolton.sch.uk
Type: Co-educational Day Only 3–11
Special needs: **HI**
Wheelchair access: WA2

Bury Education & Culture Department

Athenaeum House
Market Street
Bury
Greater Manchester
BL9 0BN

CLOUGHSIDE
Bury New Road, Manchester, Greater Manchester M25 3BL
Type: Co-educational Day 12–18
Special needs: **Hospital School** BESD HI

ELMS BANK SPECIALIST ARTS COLLEGE
Ripon Avenue, Manchester, Greater Manchester M45 8PJ
Website: www.elmsbank.bury. sch.uk
Type: Co-educational Day Only 11–19
Special needs: ASD **MLD PMLD SLD**
Wheelchair access: WA1

MILLWOOD PRIMARY SPECIAL SCHOOL
Fletcher Fold Road, Bury, Greater Manchester BL9 9RX
Type: Co-educational Day Only 2–11
Special needs: ASD MLD PMLD SLD
Wheelchair access: WA1

Manchester Education Department

Overseas House
Quay Street
Manchester
M3 3BB

THE BIRCHES SPECIALIST SUPPORT SCHOOL
Newholme Road, Manchester, Greater Manchester M20 2XZ
Type: Co-educational Day Only 2–11
Special needs: BESD PMLD **SLD**
Wheelchair access: WA1

BUGLAWTON HALL
Buxton Road, Congleton, Cheshire CW12 3PQ
Type: Boys Day Only 8–16
Special needs: BESD

CAMBERWELL PARK SCHOOL
Bank House Road, Manchester, Greater Manchester M9 8LT
Type: Co-educational Day Only 2–11
Special needs: ASD BESD PMLD **SLD**
Wheelchair access: WA1

EWING SCHOOL
Central Road, Manchester, Greater Manchester M20 4ZA
Type: Co-educational Day Only 5–16
Special needs: SP&LD

GRANGE SCHOOL
77 Dickenson Road, Manchester, Greater Manchester M14 5AZ
Type: Co-educational Day Only 4–19
Special needs: ASD **ASP**
Wheelchair access: WA1

LANCASTERIAN SCHOOL
Elizabeth Slinger Road, Manchester, Greater Manchester M20 2XA
Type: Co-educational Day Only 2–16
Special needs: **CP HEA MLD SLD**
Wheelchair access: WA1

MEADE HILL SCHOOL
Middleton Road, Manchester,
Greater Manchester M8 4NB
Type: Co-educational Day Only
Special needs: ADD ADHD ASP
BESD DYP DYS HI MLD SP&LD
TOU

**MEDLOCK VALLEY HIGH
SCHOOL**
Palmerstone Street, Manchester,
Greater Manchester M12 6PT
Type: Co-educational Day Only
11–16
Special needs: MLD

MELLAND HIGH SCHOOL
Holmcroft Road, Manchester,
Greater Manchester M18 7NG
Type: Co-educational Day Only
11–19
Special needs: PMLD **SLD**
Wheelchair access: W

PIPER HILL SPECIAL SCHOOL
200 Yew Tree Lane, Manchester,
Greater Manchester M23 0FF
Type: Co-educational Day Only
11–19
Special needs: PMLD SLD
Wheelchair access: W

RICHMOND PARK SCHOOL
Cochrane Avenue, Manchester,
Greater Manchester M12 4FA
Website: web.ukonline.co.uk/
richmond-park
Type: Co-educational Day Only
Special needs: **MLD**

RODNEY HOUSE SCHOOL
388 Slade Lane, Manchester,
Greater Manchester M19 2HT
Type: Co-educational Day Only
2–7
Special needs: ASD **ASP** BESD
CP DOW EPI HEA HI MLD PMLD
SLD SP&LD TOU VI
Wheelchair access: W

ROUNDWOOD SCHOOL
Roundwood Road, Manchester,
Greater Manchester M22 4AB
Type: Day Only
Special needs: **MLD**

SOUTHERN CROSS SCHOOL
Barlow Hall Road, Manchester,
Greater Manchester M21 7JJ
Type: Co-educational Day Only
11–16
Special needs: **BESD**
Wheelchair access: WA2

WOODSIDE SPECIAL SCHOOL
Crossacres Road, Manchester,
Greater Manchester M22 5DR
Type: Co-educational Day Only
Special needs: **MLD**

Oldham Education and Culture

Civic Centre
West Street
Oldham
Greater Manchester
OL1 1UG

**BROWNHILL SPECIAL
SCHOOL**
Heights Lane, Rochdale,
Lancashire OL12 0PZ
Type: Co-educational Day Only
Special needs: **BESD**

HARDMAN FOLD SCHOOL
Dean Street, Failsworth, Greater
Manchester M35 0DQ
Type: Co-educational Day Only
11–16
Special needs: **BESD**

HILL TOP SCHOOL
Arncliffe Rise, Oldham, Greater
Manchester OL4 2LZ
Type: Co-educational Day Only
11–19
Special needs: ASD ASP DOW
SLD
Wheelchair access: W

**KINGFISHER COMMUNITY
SPECIAL SCHOOL**
Chadderton, Oldham, Greater
Manchester OL9 9QR
Type: Co-educational Day Only
2–11
Special needs: ASD BESD MLD
PMLD SLD SP&LD VI
Wheelchair access: W

MARLAND FOLD SCHOOL
Rosary Road, Oldham, Greater
Manchester OL8 2RP
Special needs: **MLD**

PARK DEAN SCHOOL
St Martin's Road, Oldham,
Greater Manchester OL8 2PZ
Type: Co-educational Day Only
11–19
Special needs: CP EPI HEA HI VI
Wheelchair access: W

SPRING BROOK SCHOOL
Heron Street, Oldham, Greater
Manchester OL8 4JD
Type: Co-educational Day Only
5–11
Special needs: **BESD**

Rochdale Metropolitan Borough Council

PO Box 39 Municipal Offices
Smith Street
Rochdale
Greater Manchester
OL16 1LQ

**ALDERMAN KAY SPECIAL
SCHOOL**
Tintern Road, Middleton, Greater
Manchester M24 6TQ
Type: Co-educational Day Only
5–16
Special needs: **BESD** DOW DYS
EPI HI **MLD SLD** SP&LD

**BIRTLE VIEW SPECIAL
SCHOOL**
George Street, Heywood, Greater
Manchester OL10 4PW

**HIGH BIRCH SPECIAL
SCHOOL (ADLINGTON UNIT)**
Bolton Road, Rochdale, Greater
Manchester OL11 4RA

INNES SPECIAL SCHOOL
Ings Lane, Rochdale, Greater
Manchester OL12 7AL
Website: www.innes.rochdale.
sch.uk
Type: Co-educational Day Only
5–19
Special needs: ASD **ASP** CP
DOW EPI HEA HI IM **PMLD SLD**
VI
Wheelchair access: WA1

RYDINGS SPECIAL SCHOOL
Great Howarth, Rochdale,
Greater Manchester OL12 9HJ
Type: Co-educational Day Only
3–16
Special needs: **BESD MLD SLD**
Wheelchair access: W

Salford Education and Leisure

Minerva House
Pendlebury Road
Salford
Greater Manchester
M27 4EQ

CHATSWORTH HIGH SCHOOL
Chatsworth High School, Salford, Greater Manchester M30 9DY
Type: Co-educational Day Only 11–19
Special needs: ASD EPI **PMLD SLD** SP&LD
Wheelchair access: WA1

IRWELL PARK HIGH
Britannia Street, Lancashire, Greater Manchester M6 6JB
Type: Co-educational 11–16

OAKWOOD HIGH SCHOOL
Chatsword Road, Eccles, Greater Manchester M30 9DY
Type: Co-educational Day Only 11–16

SPRINGWOOD PRIMARY SCHOOL
Barton Road, Manchester, Greater Manchester M27 5LP
Type: Co-educational 2–11

Stockport Metropolitan Borough Council

Education Services
Stopford House
Piccadilly
Stockport
SK1 3XE

CASTLE HIGH SCHOOL
Lapwing Lane, Stockport, Greater Manchester SK5 8LF
Website: www.
castlehill.stockport.sch.uk
Type: Co-educational Day Only 11–16
Special needs: **MLD**
Wheelchair access: WA2

HEATON SCHOOL
St James Road, Stockport, Greater Manchester SK4 4RE
Type: Co-educational Day Only 11–19
Special needs: ASD **PMLD SLD**
Wheelchair access: WA2

LISBURNE SCHOOL
Half Moon Lane, Stockport, Greater Manchester SK2 5LB
Type: Co-educational Day Only
Special needs: ASD DYP MLD SLD SP&LD

OAK GROVE SCHOOL
Matlock Road, Stockport, Greater Manchester SK8 3BU
Type: Co-educational Day Only 4–11

VALLEY SCHOOL
Whitehaven Road, Stockport, Greater Manchester SK7 1EN
Type: Co-educational Day Only 2–11 (with inclusive nursery)
Special needs: ASD PMLD SLD
Wheelchair access: WA1

WINDLEHURST SCHOOL
Windlehurst Lane, Stockport, Cheshire SK6 7HZ
Type: Co-educational Day Only
Special needs: **BESD**

Tameside LEA

Council Offices
Wellington Road
Ashton-under-Lyne
Lancashire
OL6 6DL

CROMWELL HIGH SCHOOL
Yew Tree Lane, Cheshire SK16 5BJ
Type: Co-educational Day Only 11–16
Special needs: PMLD **SLD**
Wheelchair access: WA1

DALE GROVE SCHOOL
Wilshaw Lane, Ashton-under-Lyne, Lancashire OL7 9RF
Type: Co-educational Day Only 5–16
Special needs: **BESD**

HAWTHORNS SCHOOL
Sunnyside Moss Campus, Audenshaw, Greater Manchester M34 5SF
Type: Co-educational Day Only 4–11
Special needs: **MLD**
Wheelchair access: WA1

OAKDALE SCHOOL & ACORN NURSERY
Cheetham Hill Road, Dukinfield, Greater Manchester SK16 5LD
Type: Co-educational Day Only 2–11
Special needs: ASD **PMLD SLD**
Wheelchair access: W

SAMUEL LAYCOCK SCHOOL
Mereside, Stalybridge, Cheshire SK15 1JF
Type: Co-educational Day Only 11–16
Special needs: **MLD**

Trafford Metropolitan Borough Council

Waterside House
Sale Waterside
Sale
M33 7ZF

BRENTWOOD SCHOOL
Brentwood Avenue, Altrincham, Greater Manchester WA14 1SR
Type: Co-educational Day Only
Special needs: ASD PMLD SLD
Wheelchair access: WA1

DELAMERE SCHOOL
Irlam Road, Urmston, Greater Manchester M41 6AP
Type: Co-educational Day Only
Special needs: ASD PMLD SLD
Wheelchair access: W

EGERTON HIGH SCHOOL
Kingsway Park, Urmston, Greater Manchester M41 7FZ
Type: Co-educational Day Only 11–16
Special needs: **BESD**
Wheelchair access: W

LONGFORD PARK SCHOOL
Longford Park, Stretford, Greater
Manchester M32 8PR
Website: www.longford.trafford.
sch.uk
Type: Co-educational Day Only
5–11
Special needs: ADD ADHD BESD
MLD

MANOR HIGH SCHOOL
Manor Avenue, Sale, Greater
Manchester M33 5JX
Type: Co-educational Day Only
11–18

PICTOR SCHOOL
Grove Lane, Altrincham, Greater
Manchester WA15 6PH
Type: Co-educational Day Only
2–11 (mixed gender)
Wheelchair access: WA1

Wigan Borough Council

Progress House
Westwood Park Drive
Wigan
Lancashire
WN3 4HH

**HIGHLEA SECONDARY
SCHOOL**
294 Mosley Common Road,
Worsley, Greater Manchester
M28 1DA
Website: www.
medinahouseschool.co.uk
Type: Co-educational Boarding
Only
Special needs: **BESD CP**

LANDGATE SCHOOL
Landgate Lane, Wigan, Greater
Manchester WN4 0EP

MERE OAKS SCHOOL
Boars Head, Wigan, Greater
Manchester WN1 2RF
Type: Co-educational Day Only
2–19
Wheelchair access: W

NEW GREEN HALL SCHOOL
Green Hall Close, Atherton,
Greater Manchester M46 9HP
Type: Co-educational Day Only
2–14
Special needs: **MLD**
Wheelchair access: WA1

OAKFIELD HIGH SCHOOL
Close Lane, Wigan, Greater
Manchester WN2 3SA
Website: www.oakfield.wigan.
sch.uk
Type: Co-educational Day Only
11–19
Special needs: **MLD**
Wheelchair access: WA2

WIGAN HOPE
Kelvin Grove, Wigan, Greater
Manchester WN3 6SP
Type: Co-educational Day Only
Special needs: PMLD SLD

WILLOW GROVE PRIMARY
Willow Grove, Wigan, Greater
Manchester WN4 9HP
Type: Co-educational Day Only
Special needs: ADHD **BESD** DYP
DYS
Wheelchair access: WA1

MERSEYSIDE

Knowsley Education Offices

Huyton Hey Road
Huyton
Knowsley
Merseyside
L36 5YH

**ALT BRIDGE SECONDARY
SUPPORT CENTRE**
Wellcroft Road, Knowsley,
Merseyside L36 7TA
Type: Co-educational Day Only
11–16
Special needs: ASP BESD HI
MLD SP&LD

THE ELMS SPECIAL SCHOOL
Whitethorn Drive, Stockbridge
Village, Merseyside L28 1RX
Type: Co-educational Day Only
2–19
Special needs: ASD **ASP** DOW
PMLD SLD
Wheelchair access: W

HIGHFIELD SCHOOL
Baileys Lane, Halewood,
Merseyside L26 0TY
Type: Co-educational Day Only
6–14
Special needs: **BESD**

**KNOWSLEY CENTRAL
PRIMARY SUPPORT CENTRE**
Knowsley, Merseyside L36 7SY
Special needs: ADD ASD DYS
MLD

**KNOWSLEY NORTHERN
PRIMARY SUPPORT CENTRE**
Bramcote Walk, Kirkby,
Merseyside L33 9UR
Type: Co-educational Day Only
Special needs: ASD BESD DYS
MLD SLD SP&LD
Wheelchair access: WA2

**KNOWSLEY SOUTHERN
PRIMARY SUPPORT CENTRE**
Arncliffe Road, Liverpool,
Merseyside L25 9QE
Type: Co-educational Day Only
3–11
Special needs: ADD ADHD ASD
ASP **BESD** CB DOW EPI HEA
MLD SLD SP&LD
Wheelchair access: WA1

SPRINGFIELD SPECIAL SCHOOL
Cawthorne Close, Kirkby, Merseyside L32 3XG
Website: www.springfield. knowsley.sch.uk
Type: Co-educational Day Only 2–19
Special needs: PMLD SLD
Wheelchair access: WA1

Liverpool Education Offices

2nd Floor Millennium House
Victoria Street
Liverpool
Merseyside
L1 8RF

ABBOTS LEA SCHOOL
Beaconsfield Road, Liverpool, Merseyside L25 6EE
Type: Co-educational Boarding and Day 5–19
Special needs: ASD **ASP**
Wheelchair access: WA1

ASHFIELD SCHOOL
Childwall Abbey Road, Liverpool, Merseyside L16 5EY
Type: Co-educational Day Only 11–16
Special needs: ADD ADHD ASD ASP DOW DYP DYS HEA HI **MLD SP&LD** TOU VI
Wheelchair access: WA3

BARLOWS PRIMARY SCHOOL (ASSESSMENT CENTRE)
Barlows Lane, Liverpool, Merseyside L9 9EH
Type: Co-educational Day Only 3–7
Special needs: ASD **BESD MLD** SLD SP&LD
Wheelchair access: WA1

CLIFFORD HOLROYDE CENTRE OF EXPERTISE
Thingwall Lane, Liverpool, Merseyside L14 7NX
Type: Co-educational Day Only 5–16
Special needs: **BESD**

ERNEST COOKSON SPECIAL SCHOOL
Mill Lane, Liverpool, Merseyside L12 7JA
Type: Boys Day Only
Special needs: **BESD**

GREENWAYS SCHOOL
Dingle Lane, Liverpool, Merseyside L8 9UB
Type: Co-educational Day Only 3–7
Special needs: ADD **ADHD ASD ASP** CB DYP EPI **MLD SLD** SP&LD TOU
Wheelchair access: WA1

HOPE SCHOOL
Naylorsfield Drive, Liverpool, Merseyside L27 0YD
Type: Boys Day Only 6–13
Special needs: **BESD**
Wheelchair access: WA2

LOWER LEE SPECIAL SCHOOL
Beaconsfield Road, Liverpool, Merseyside L25 6EF
Type: Boys Boarding Only 8–16
Special needs: **BESD**

MARGARET BEAVAN SCHOOL
Almonds Green, Liverpool, Merseyside L12 5HP
Type: Co-educational Day Only 5–16
Special needs: **MLD**

MEADOW BANK SPECIAL SCHOOL
Sherwoods Lane, Liverpool, Merseyside L10 1LW
Type: Co-educational Day Only 5–17
Special needs: **ADD** ASD **ASP** EPI **MLD** SP&LD

MERSEY VIEW SCHOOL
Minehead Road, Liverpool, Merseyside L17 6AX
Type: Co-educational Day Only 5–16
Special needs: **MLD**

MILLSTEAD SPECIAL NEEDS PRIMARY SCHOOL
Old Mill Lane, Liverpool, Merseyside L15 8LW
Type: Co-educational Day Only 2–11
Special needs: ASD PMLD **SLD**
Wheelchair access: W

PALMERSTON SCHOOL
Beaconsfield Road, Liverpool, Merseyside L25 6EE
Type: Co-educational Day Only 11–19
Special needs: ADD ADHD ASD ASP CP DOW DYP **EPI** HEA HI **PMLD SLD** SP&LD VI
Wheelchair access: W

PRINCES SCHOOL
Selborne Street, Liverpool, Merseyside L8 1YQ
Website: www.princesprimary. com
Type: Co-educational Day Only 2–11
Special needs: ASD **ASP PMLD SLD** SP&LD VI
Wheelchair access: WA1

REDBRIDGE HIGH SCHOOL
Sherwoods Lane, Liverpool, Merseyside L10 1LW
Type: Co-educational Day Only 11–19
Special needs: ASD **ASP PMLD SLD**
Wheelchair access: WA1

SANDFIELD PARK SCHOOL
Sandfield Walk, Liverpool, Merseyside L12 1LH
Type: Co-educational Day Only 11–19
Special needs: **CP EPI MLD** PMLD
Wheelchair access: WA1

WATERGATE SCHOOL
Upper Essex Street, Liverpool, Merseyside L8 6QB
Type: Co-educational Day Only 5–16
Special needs: MLD SP&LD

St Helens Education and Leisure Dept

The Rivington Centre
Rivington Road
St Helens
Merseyside
WA10 4ND

HURST SCHOOL
Hard Lane, St Helens, Merseyside WA10 6PN
Type: Co-educational Day Only
Special needs: **MLD** SP&LD

MILL GREEN SCHOOL
Mill Lane, Newton-le-Willows,
Merseyside WA12 8BG
Type: Co-educational Day Only
7–19
Special needs: ASD **PMLD SLD**
Wheelchair access: WA1

PENKFORD SCHOOL
Wharf Road, Newton-le-Willows,
Merseyside WA12 9XZ
Type: Co-educational Day Only
Special needs: **BESD MLD**
Wheelchair access: W

Sefton Council

Oriel Road
Bootle
Merseyside
L20 7AE

CROSBY HIGH SPECIALIST HUMANITIES COLLEGE
De Villiers Avenue, Crosby,
Merseyside L23 2TH
Type: Co-educational Day Only
12–16
Special needs: ADHD ASD BESD
MLD
Wheelchair access: W

MEREFIELD SPECIAL SCHOOL
Westminster Drive, Southport,
Merseyside PR8 2QZ
Type: Co-educational Day Only
3–19
Special needs: ASD **ASP PMLD
SLD**
Wheelchair access: WA1

NEWFIELD SPECIAL SCHOOL
Edge Lane, Liverpool,
Merseyside L23 4TG
Type: Co-educational Day Only
5–16
Special needs: ADD ADHD ASP
BESD DYP DYS EPI
Wheelchair access: WA1

PRESFIELD SPECIAL SCHOOL
Preston New Road, Southport,
Merseyside PR9 8PA
Type: Co-educational Day Only
11–19
Special needs: ASD **ASP MLD**
Wheelchair access: WA1

ROWAN PARK SCHOOL
Sterrix Lane, Litheland,
Merseyside L21 0DB
Type: Co-educational Day Only
Special needs: ASD **ASP** DOW
PMLD SLD SP&LD VI
Wheelchair access: W

Wirral Borough Council

Hamilton Building
Conway Street
Birkenhead
Wirral
CH41 4FD

CLARE MOUNT SCHOOL
Fender Lane, Wirral, Merseyside
CH46 9PA
Type: Co-educational Day Only
11–19
Special needs: **MLD** SLD
Wheelchair access: WA2

ELLERAY PARK SCHOOL
Elleray Park Road, Wallasey,
Merseyside CH45 0LH
Type: Co-educational Day Only
2–11
Special needs: ASD **ASP** CP
DOW DYP EPI HEA HI **PMLD
SLD** SP&LD VI
Wheelchair access: WA1

FOXFIELD SCHOOL
Douglas Drive, Wirral,
Merseyside CH46 6BT
Type: Co-educational Day Only
11–19
Special needs: ASD PMLD SLD
Wheelchair access: WA2

GILBROOK SCHOOL
Pilgrim Street, Birkenhead,
Merseyside CH41 5EH
Type: Co-educational Day Only
5–11
Special needs: **ADD ADHD
BESD**
Wheelchair access: W

HAYFIELD SCHOOL
Manor Drive, Wirral, Merseyside
CH49 4LN
Type: Co-educational
Special needs: ASD **ASP MLD**
SP&LD

KILGARTH SCHOOL
Cavendish Street, Birkenhead,
Merseyside CH41 8BA
Type: Boys Day Only 11–16
Special needs: **BESD**

THE LYNDALE SCHOOL
Wirral, Merseyside CH63 4JY
Type: Co-educational Day Only
2–11

MEADOWSIDE SCHOOL
Pool Lane, Birkenhead,
Merseyside CH49 5LA
Type: Co-educational Day Only
11–19
Special needs: ADHD ASD CP
DOW DYP EPI HEA IM MLD
PMLD SLD SP&LD VI
Wheelchair access: WA1

ORRETS MEADOW SCHOOL
Chapelhill Road, Birkenhead,
Merseyside CH46 9QQ
Type: Co-educational Day Only
7–11
Special needs: DYS

STANLEY SCHOOL
Pensby Road, Heswall,
Merseyside CH61 7UG
Type: Co-educational Day Only
2–11
Special needs: ASD **SLD**

MIDDLESBROUGH

Middlesbrough County Council

PO Box 99A
Town Hall
Middlesbrough
TS1 2QQ

BEVERLEY SCHOOL FOR CHILDREN WITH AUTISM
Beverley Road, Middlesbrough
TS4 3LQ
Website: www.beverleyautism.
ik.org
Type: Co-educational Day Only
3–19
Special needs: ASD **ASP**
Wheelchair access: WA2

HOLMWOOD SCHOOL
Saltersgill Avenue, Easterside,
Middlesbrough TS4 3PT
Website: www.
millenniumschools.co.uk
Type: Co-educational Day Only
Special needs: ADHD ASP **BESD
MLD**
Wheelchair access: WA1

PRIORY WOODS SCHOOL
Tothill Avenue, Middlesbrough
TS3 0RH
Type: Co-educational Day Only
4–19
Special needs: PMLD **SLD**
Wheelchair access: W

TOLLESBY SCHOOL
Saltersgill Avenue,
Middlesbrough TS4 3JS
Type: Co-educational Day Only
11–16
Special needs: **BESD** MLD

NORFOLK

Norfolk County Council

County Hall
Martineau Lane
Norwich
Norfolk
NR1 2DI

ALDERMAN JACKSON SPECIAL SCHOOL
Marsh Lane, King's Lynn, Norfolk
PE30 3AE
Type: Co-educational Day Only
2–19
Special needs: ASD **ASP CP
PMLD** SLD
Wheelchair access: WA1

CHAPEL ROAD SPECIAL SCHOOL
Chapel Road, Attleborough,
Norfolk NR17 2DS
Type: Co-educational 3–19
Special needs: ASD CB CP DOW
EPI HI **PMLD SLD** VI
Wheelchair access: WA1

THE CLARE SCHOOL
South Park Avenue, Norwich,
Norfolk NR4 7AU
Type: Co-educational Day Only
Special needs: HI **IM** SP&LD VI
Wheelchair access: WA1

EATON HALL SPECIAL SCHOOL
Pettus Road, Norwich, Norfolk
NR4 7BU
Type: Boys Boarding and Day
10–16
Special needs: **BESD**

THE ETHEL TIPPLE SCHOOL
Winston Churchill Drive, King's
Lynn, Norfolk PE30 4RP
Type: Co-educational 7–16
Special needs: **MLD**
Wheelchair access: WA1

FRED NICHOLSON SPECIAL SCHOOL
Westfield Road, Dereham,
Norfolk NR19 1BJ
Type: Co-educational Day and
Boarding 7–16
Special needs: **MLD**
Wheelchair access: W

HALL SPECIAL SCHOOL
St Faith's Road, Norwich, Norfolk
NR6 7AD
Type: Co-educational Day Only
3–19
Special needs: ASD CP DOW EPI
HCA HI IM **PMLD SLD** SP&LD VI
Wheelchair access: WA1

HARFORD MANOR SPECIAL SCHOOL
43 Ipswich Road, Norwich,
Norfolk NR2 2LN
Website: www.hardfordmanor.
norfolk.sch.uk
Type: Co-educational Day Only
3–19
Special needs: ASD PMLD SLD
Wheelchair access: WA1

JOHN GRANT SPECIAL SCHOOL
St George's Drive, Great
Yarmouth, Norfolk NR30 5QW
Type: Co-educational Day Only
3–19
Special needs: PMLD **SLD**
Wheelchair access: W

PARKSIDE SPECIAL SCHOOL
College Road, Norwich, Norfolk
NR2 3JA
Type: Co-educational Day Only
Special needs: **ADD ADHD ASD**
ASP BESD **DOW** EPI HI **MLD**
SP&LD TOU
Wheelchair access: WA1

**SHERINGHAM WOODFIELDS
SCHOOL**
Holt Road, Sheringham, Norfolk
NR26 8ND
Type: Co-educational Day Only
2–19
Special needs: PMLD **SLD**
Wheelchair access: WA1

**SIDESTRAND HALL SPECIAL
SCHOOL**
Cromer Road, Cromer, Norfolk
NR27 0NH
Type: Co-educational Boarding
and Day 7–16
Special needs: **MLD**

NORTHAMPTONSHIRE

Northamptonshire
Education Offices

**PO Box 216
John Dryden House
Northampton
Northamptonshire
NN4 7DD**

BILLING BROOK SCHOOL
Penistone Road, Northampton,
Northamptonshire NN3 8EZ
Type: Co-educational Day Only
2–16
Special needs: ASD **ASP MLD
SLD**

DEGRA HOUSE
67 Queens Park Parade,
Northampton, Northamptonshire
NN2 6LR
Type: Co-educational Day Only
11–16

FAIRFIELDS SCHOOL
Trinity Avenue, Northampton,
Northamptonshire NN2 6JN
Type: Co-educational Day Only
3–11
Special needs: ASD PMLD SLD
Wheelchair access: WA1

FRIARS SCHOOL
Friar's Close, Wellingborough,
Northamptonshire NN8 2LA
Website: www.friarsschool.ik.org
Type: Co-educational Day Only
11–19
Special needs: ASD **MLD** SLD
Wheelchair access: WA2

THE GATEWAY SCHOOL
St John's Road, Tiffield,
Northamptonshire NN12 8AA
Website: www.
thegatewayschool.ik.org
Type: Co-educational Day Only
11–18
Special needs: **ADD ADHD ASD**
ASP **BESD CB** TOU

**GREENFIELDS SCHOOL AND
SPORTS COLLEGE**
Harborough Road, Northampton,
Northamptonshire NN2 8LR
Type: Co-educational Day Only
11–19
Special needs: ASD **ASP PMLD
SLD**
Wheelchair access: WA1

ISEBROOK SCHOOL
Eastleigh Road, Kettering,
Northamptonshire NN15 6PT
Website: www.isebrook-school.
ik.org
Type: Co-educational Day Only
11–19
Special needs: ADHD ASD ASP
BESD CP DOW EPI HI **MLD** SLD
Wheelchair access: WA1

KINGSLEY SCHOOL
Churchill Way, Kettering,
Northamptonshire NN15 5DP
Website: www.kingsleyschool.
ik.org
Type: Co-educational Day Only
3–11
Special needs: ASD ASP CP
DOW EPI HI MLD PMLD SLD
SP&LD VI
Wheelchair access: WA1

MAPLEFIELDS SCHOOL
School Place, Corby,
Northamptonshire NN18 0QP
Website: www.maplefields.
northants.sch.uk
Type: Co-educational Day Only
5–16
Special needs: ADD ADHD
BESD

NORTHGATE SCHOOL
Arts College, Northampton,
Northamptonshire NN2 6LR
Website: www.northgate.ik.org
Type: Co-educational Day Only
11–16
Special needs: ADD ADHD ASD
ASP CP DOW DYP DYS EPI HI IM
MLD SLD SP&LD VI
Wheelchair access: WA1

THE ORCHARD SCHOOL
Beatrice Road, Kettering,
Northamptonshire NN16 9QR
Type: Co-educational Day Only
11–16
Special needs: **BESD**
Wheelchair access: W

WREN SPINNEY SCHOOL
Westover Road, Kettering,
Northamptonshire NN16 0AP
Type: Co-educational Day Only
11–19
Special needs: ASD CB **PMLD
SLD**
Wheelchair access: WA1

NORTHUMBERLAND

Northumberland Education Directorate

County Hall
Morpeth
Northumberland
NE61 2EF

ATKINSON HOUSE SCHOOL
North Terrace, Cramlington, Northumberland NE23 7EB
Type: Day Only
Special needs: ADD ADHD **BESD**

BARNDALE HOUSE SCHOOL
Barndale House, Alnwick, Northumberland NE66 1DQ
Type: Co-educational Day and Boarding 8–19
Special needs: **SLD**

CLEASWELL HILL SCHOOL
School Avenue, Choppington, Northumberland NE62 5DJ
Type: Co-educational Day Only 4–18
Special needs: ADD ADHD ASD ASP BESD DOW EPI HEA **MLD** SLD SP&LD TOU
Wheelchair access: WA2

COLLINGWOOD SCHOOL
Stobhillgate, Morpeth, Northumberland NE61 2HA
Type: Co-educational Day Only 4–16
Special needs: **MLD**
Wheelchair access: WA1

EAST HARTFORD SCHOOL
East Hartford, Cramlington, Northumberland NE23 9AR
Type: Co-educational Day Only 4–11
Special needs: ADHD ASD ASP **BESD** CB DOW DYP DYS **MLD** SLD

THE GROVE SCHOOL
Grove Gardens, Berwick Upon Tweed, Northumberland TD15 2EN
Type: Co-educational Day Only 3–19
Special needs: ASD DOW PMLD **SLD**
Wheelchair access: WA1

HILLCREST SCHOOL
East View Avenue, Cramlington, Northumberland NE23 9DY
Type: Co-educational Day Only 11–16
Wheelchair access: WA2

PRIORY SCHOOL
Dene Park, Hexham, Northumberland NE46 1HN
Type: Co-educational Day Only 3–19
Special needs: ASD **PMLD SLD**
Wheelchair access: WA1

NOTTINGHAMSHIRE

Nottingham City Council

Sandfield Centre
Lenton
Nottingham
Nottinghamshire
NG7 1HQ

ASPLEY WOOD SCHOOL
Robins Wood Road, Nottingham, Nottinghamshire NG8 3LD
Website: www.aspleywood.nottingham.sch.uk
Type: Co-educational Day Only 3–16
Special needs: **CP IM** VI
Wheelchair access: WA1

CARLTON DIGBY SCHOOL
Digby Avenue, Mapperley, Nottinghamshire NG3 6DS
Type: Co-educational Day Only 3–19
Special needs: ASD PMLD SLD
Wheelchair access: WA2

NETHERGATE SCHOOL
Swansdowne Drive, Nottingham, Nottinghamshire NG11 8HX
Type: Co-educational Day Only 5–16
Special needs: ADHD ASD BESD DOW DYP DYS EPI **MLD** SP&LD
Wheelchair access: W

ROSEHILL SCHOOL
St Matthias Road, Nottingham, Nottinghamshire NG3 2FE
Type: Co-educational Day Only 4–19
Special needs: ASD ASP

SHEPHERD SCHOOL
Harvey Road, Nottingham, Nottinghamshire NG8 3BB
Type: Co-educational Day Only 3–19
Special needs: ASD EPI PMLD SLD
Wheelchair access: W

WESTBURY SCHOOL
Chingford Road, Nottingham, Nottinghamshire NG8 3BT
Website: www.westburyschool.co.uk
Type: Co-educational Day Only 7–16
Special needs: **BESD**
Wheelchair access: W

WOODLANDS SCHOOL
Beechdale Road, Nottingham,
Nottinghamshire NG8 3EZ
Type: Co-educational Day Only
3–16
Special needs: ASD BESD MLD
SLD

Nottinghamshire County Council

County Hall
West Bridgford
Nottingham
Nottinghamshire
NG7 7QP

ASH LEA SCHOOL
Owthorpe Road, Nottingham,
Nottinghamshire NG12 3PA
Type: Co-educational Day Only
Special needs: **PMLD SLD**
Wheelchair access: WA1

BEECH HILL SCHOOL
Fairholme Drive, Mansfield,
Nottinghamshire NG19 6DX
Type: Co-educational 11–16
Special needs: ASD BESD **MLD**

BRACKEN HILL SCHOOL
Chartwell Road, Kirkby-in-
Ashfield, Nottinghamshire
NG17 7HZ
Type: Co-educational Day Only
3–19
Special needs: ADD ADHD ASD
ASP HEA MLD SLD SP&LD
Wheelchair access: WA2

DERRYMOUNT SCHOOL
Churchmoor Lane, Arnold,
Nottinghamshire NG5 8HN
Type: Co-educational Day Only
3–16
Special needs: ASD **ASP** BESD
CP EPI **HI MLD** SLD SP&LD VI

FOUNTAINDALE SCHOOL
Nottingham Road, Mansfield,
Nottinghamshire NG18 5BA
Type: Co-educational Boarding
and Day 3–19
Special needs: CP EPI HEA
SP&LD VI
Wheelchair access: W

FOXWOOD SCHOOL AND TECHNOLOGY COLLEGE
Derby Road, Nottinghamshire
NG9 3GF
Website: www.foxwood.sch.
dccl.net
Type: Co-educational Day Only
3–19
Special needs: ASD ASP MLD
Wheelchair access: WA1

FREYBURG SCHOOL
Duncanwood Lodge, Worksop,
Nottinghamshire S80 2BP
Type: Boys Day Only 12–15

NEWARK ORCHARD SCHOOL
Newark, Nottinghamshire
NG24 1JR
Website: www.newarkorchard.
notts.sch.uk
Type: Co-educational Day Only
3–19
Special needs: ASD **ASP PMLD
SLD**
Wheelchair access: WA2

REDGATE SCHOOL
Somersall Street, Mansfield,
Nottinghamshire NG19 6EL
Type: Co-educational Day Only
3–11
Special needs: **ADD ADHD** ASD
ASP EPI IM SLD

ST GILES SCHOOL
Babworth Road, Retford,
Nottinghamshire DN22 7NJ
Type: Co-educational Day Only
3–19
Special needs: ADD ADHD ASD
ASP BESD CP DOW EPI HI **MLD**
PMLD **SLD** VI
Wheelchair access: WA1

YEOMAN PARK SCHOOL
Park Hall Road, Mansfield,
Nottinghamshire NG19 8PS
Type: Co-educational Day Only
3–19
Special needs: ASD **ASP PMLD
SLD**
Wheelchair access: W

OXFORDSHIRE

Oxfordshire County Council

Macclesfield House
New Road
Oxford
OX1 1NA

BARDWELL SCHOOL
Hendon Place, Bicester, Oxfordshire OX26 4RZ
Type: Co-educational Day Only 2–19
Special needs: ASD **ASP** CP DOW EPI HI IM **PMLD SLD** SP&LD VI
Wheelchair access: WA1

BISHOPSWOOD SCHOOL
Grove Road, Berkshire RG4 9RJ
Website: www.bishopswood. oxon.sch.uk
Type: Co-educational Day Only 2–16
Special needs: ASD **ASP PMLD SLD** SP&LD VI
Wheelchair access: W

FITZWARYN SPECIAL SCHOOL
Denchworth Road, Wantage, Oxfordshire OX12 9ET
Type: Co-educational Day Only 3–16
Special needs: ASD **ASP MLD PMLD SLD**
Wheelchair access: WA2

FRANK WISE SCHOOL
Hornbeam Close, Banbury, Oxfordshire OX16 9RL
Website: www.frankwise.oxon. sch.uk
Type: Co-educational Day Only 2–16
Special needs: PMLD **SLD**
Wheelchair access: WA1

IFFLEY MEAD SPECIAL SCHOOL
Iffley Turn, Oxford, Oxfordshire OX4 4DU
Type: Day Only
Special needs: **MLD**
Wheelchair access: WA2

JOHN WATSON SPECIAL SCHOOL
Littleworth Road, Oxford, Oxfordshire OX33 1NN
Website: www. johnwatsonschool.co.uk
Type: Co-educational Day Only
Special needs: PMLD **SLD**
Wheelchair access: W

KINGFISHER SCHOOL
Radley Road, Abingdon, Oxfordshire OX14 3RR
Website: www.kingfisherschool. co.uk
Type: Co-educational Day Only 2–16
Special needs: MLD PMLD SLD
Wheelchair access: WA1

MABEL PRICHARD SPECIAL SCHOOL
St Nicholas Road, Littlemore, Oxfordshire OX4 4PN
Website: www.mabel-prichard. oxon-sch.uk
Type: Co-educational Day Only
Special needs: ASD CP DOW EPI HI PMLD SLD SP&LD VI
Wheelchair access: W

NORTHERN HOUSE SPECIAL SCHOOL
South Parade, Oxford, Oxfordshire OX2 7JN
Website: www. northernhouseschool.ik.org
Type: Co-educational Day Only 5–11
Special needs: ADD ADHD ASD ASP **BESD** DYS HI MLD SP&LD TOU VI
Wheelchair access: WA2

NORTHFIELD SPECIAL SCHOOL
Knights Road, Oxford, Oxfordshire OX4 6DQ
Type: Co-educational Day Only
Special needs: **BESD**

ORMEROD SPECIAL SCHOOL
Waynflete Road, Oxford, Oxfordshire OX3 8DD
Type: Co-educational Day Only 2–16
Special needs: ADHD ASD CP MLD SLD SP&LD VI
Wheelchair access: W

SPRINGFIELD SPECIAL SCHOOL
@ The Bronze Barrow, Witney, Oxfordshire OX28 1AR
Type: Co-educational Day Only 2–16
Special needs: PMLD **SLD**
Wheelchair access: WA1

WOODEATON MANOR SCHOOL
Woodeaton, Oxford, Oxfordshire OX3 9TS
Type: Co-educational Boarding and Day 12–16
Special needs: BESD EPI HI **MLD** VI

REDCAR AND CLEVELAND

Redcar & Cleveland

PO Box 83
Council Offices
Kirkleatham
Redcar and Cleveland
T510 1YA

KILTON THORPE SCHOOL
Marshall Drive, Brotton, Redcar
and Cleveland TS12 2UW
Type: Co-educational Day Only
3–19
Special needs: ASD **ASP MLD
PMLD** SLD SP&LD
Wheelchair access: W

KIRKLEATHAM HALL SCHOOL
Kirkleatham, Redcar, Redcar and
Cleveland TS10 4QR
Type: Co-educational Day Only
4–19
Special needs: ADHD ASD CP
DOW EPI HEA HI **PMLD SLD**
SP&LD VI
Wheelchair access: W

RUTLAND

Rutland County Council

Catmose
Oakham
Rutland
LE15 6HP

THE PARKS SCHOOL
Barleythorpe Road, Oakham,
Rutland LE15 6NR
Type: Co-educational Day Only
2–6
Special needs: ASD ASP BESD
CP DOW EPI HEA HI MLD PMLD
SLD SP&LD VI
Wheelchair access: WA2

SHROPSHIRE

Shropshire County Council

Shirehall
Abbey Foregate
Shrewsbury
Shropshire
SY2 6ND

ACCESS SCHOOL
Holbrook Villa Farm, Shrewsbury,
Shropshire SY4 3EW
Type: Co-educational Day Only
7–16

RUBICON
Smallbrook Lodge, Whitchurch,
Shropshire SY5 7AH
Type: Co-educational Day Only
11–19

SEVERNDALE SCHOOL
Hearne Way, Shrewsbury,
Shropshire SY2 5SL
Website: www.severndale.
shropshire.sch.uk
Type: Co-educational Day Only
Special needs: ASD **ASP MLD**
PMLD SLD
Wheelchair access: WA1

WOODLANDS SCHOOL
Tilley Green, Shrewsbury,
Shropshire SY4 5PJ
Type: Co-educational Day Only
11–16

Telford & Wrekin Education and Culture

Civic Offices
PO Box 440
Telford
Shropshire
TF3 4WF

THE BRIDGE SCHOOL
Waterloo Road, Telford,
Shropshire TF1 5NU
Type: Co-educational Day Only
2–19
Special needs: PMLD **SLD**
Wheelchair access: WA2

HAUGHTON SCHOOL
Queen Street, Telford, Shropshire
TF7 4BW
Type: 5–16
Wheelchair access: WA2

MOUNT GILBERT SCHOOL
Hinkshay Road, Telford,
Shropshire TF31 1DG
Type: Co-educational Day Only
11–15
Special needs: BESD

SOUTHALL SCHOOL
off Rowan Road, Telford,
Shropshire TF4 3PN
Type: Co-educational Day Only
5–16
Special needs: MLD

SOMERSET

Bath & North East Somerset Council

Education Services
Riverside
Temple Street
Bristol
BS31 1DN

FOSSE WAY SCHOOL
Longfellow Road, Bath, Bath &
North East Somerset BA3 3AL
Type: Co-educational Boarding
and Day 3–19
Special needs: ASD **ASP MLD**
SLD
Wheelchair access: WA2

THE LINK SPECIAL SCHOOL
Frome Road, Bath, Bath & North
East Somerset BA2 5RF
Type: Co-educational Day and
Boarding 4–16
Special needs: ADD ADHD
BESD CB DYC DYP DYS
Wheelchair access: WA1

SUMMERFIELD SCHOOL
Weston Park East, Bath, Bath &
North East Somerset BA1 2UY
Type: Co-educational Day Only
7–16
Special needs: BESD **MLD**
SP&LD

North Somerset County Council

Town Hall
Walliscote Grove
Weston-Super-Mare
North Somerset
BS23 1UJ

BAYTREE SCHOOL
The Campus, Weston-Super-
Mare, North Somerset BS24 7DX
Website: www.
baytreespecialschool.ik.org
Type: Co-educational Day Only
3–19
Special needs: ASD **ASP PMLD**
SLD
Wheelchair access: WA1

ELMWOOD SPECIAL SCHOOL
Hamp Avenue, Bridgwater, Somerset TA6 6AP
Type: Co-educational Day Only 4–16
Special needs: ASD BESD **MLD** SLD
Wheelchair access: WA1

ELSTAR (SEDGEMOOR)
Ashwell Park, Ilminster, Somerset TA19 9DX
Type: Girls Day Only 11–19

RAVENSWOOD SCHOOL
Pound Lane, Nailsea, North Somerset BS48 2NN
Website: www.ravenswood.n-somerset.sch.uk
Type: Co-educational Day Only 3–19
Special needs: ASD **ASP** DYC DYP DYS **MLD SLD**
Wheelchair access: WA2

WESTHAVEN SCHOOL
Ellesmere Road, Weston-Super-Mare, North Somerset BS23 4UT
Type: Co-educational Day Only 7–16
Special needs: ADHD ASD ASP BESD CP DYC DYP DYS EPI HI SP&LD VI
Wheelchair access: WA2

Somerset County Council

County Hall
Taunton
Somerset
TA1 4DY

AVALON SPECIAL SCHOOL
Brooks Road, Street, Somerset BA16 0PS
Type: Co-educational Day Only 2–19
Special needs: ASD ASP CP DOW DYP EPI **MLD PMLD SLD** SP&LD VI
Wheelchair access: W

CRITCHILL SCHOOL & LEARNING SUPPORT CENTRE
Nunney Road, Frome, Somerset BA11 4LB
Type: Co-educational Day Only 2–16
Special needs: ASD **ASP BESD CB DOW EPI HEA HI IM MLD PMLD SLD** SP&LD TOU VI W
Wheelchair access: W WA1 WA2

FAIRMEAD COMMUNITY SPECIAL SCHOOL
Mudford Road, Yeovil, Somerset BA21 4NZ
Type: Co-educational Day Only 4–16
Special needs: ADD ADHD ASD ASP BESD DOW DYP EPI HI IM **MLD** SP&LD TOU VI
Wheelchair access: WA1

FCL SCHOOL (FAMILIES CARE LIMITED)
Norton Fitzwarren, Taunton, Somerset TA2 6RQ
Type: Co-educational Day Only 9–16

FIVEWAYS SPECIAL SCHOOL
Victoria Road, Yeovil, Somerset BA21 5AZ
Type: Co-educational Day Only 4–19
Special needs: PMLD SLD
Wheelchair access: WA1

NEW HORIZON CENTRE SCHOOL
Bath House Farm, Taunton, Somerset TA6 5RH
Type: Co-educational Day Only 11–16

PENROSE SPECIAL SCHOOL
Albert Street, Bridgwater, Somerset TA6 7ET
Website: www.penrose.ik.org
Type: Co-educational Day Only 2–19
Special needs: ASD CP DOW EPI PMLD **SLD**
Wheelchair access: WA1

SELWORTHY SPECIAL SCHOOL
Selworthy Road, Taunton, Somerset TA2 8HD
Type: Co-educational Day Only 2–19
Special needs: ADD ADHD ASD **ASP** CP DOW EPI HEA HI IM MLD **PMLD SLD** VI
Wheelchair access: WA1

SKY COLLEGE
Pickeridge Close, Taunton, Somerset TA2 7HW
Website: www.skycollege.co.uk
Type: Boys Boarding and Day 11–16
Special needs: ADHD **BESD**

England – Staffordshire

STAFFORDSHIRE

Staffordshire County Council

Tipping Street
Stafford
Staffordshire
ST16 2DH

BLACKFRIARS SPECIAL SCHOOL
Priory Road, Newcastle under Lyme, Staffordshire ST5 2TF
Website: www.sln.org/blackfriars
Type: Co-educational 2–19
Special needs: **CP** DOW DYP EPI **HEA MLD** PMLD SLD SP&LD
Wheelchair access: WA1

CHASETOWN COMMUNITY SCHOOL
Church Street, Burntwood, Staffordshire WS7 3QL

CHERRY TREES SPECIAL SCHOOL
Giggetty Lane, Wolverhampton, West Midlands WV5 0AX
Type: Co-educational Day Only 2–11
Special needs: **PMLD SLD**
Wheelchair access: WA1

CICELY HAUGHTON SCHOOL
Westwood Manor, Stoke on Trent, Staffordshire ST9 0BX
Type: Boys Boarding and Day 5–11
Special needs: **BESD**

COPPICE SPECIAL SCHOOL
Abbots Way, Newcastle under Lyme, Staffordshire ST5 2EY
Type: Co-educational Day Only 3–16
Special needs: ASP MLD

CROWN SPECIAL SCHOOL
Bitham Lane, Burton upon Trent, Staffordshire DE13 0HB
Type: Co-educational Day Only 3–18
Special needs: ASD PMLD **SLD**
Wheelchair access: W

GREENHALL NURSERY
Second Avenue, Holmcroft, Staffordshire ST16 1PS
Type: Co-educational Day Only 2–5
Special needs: **CP** DYP EPI HEA HI IM MLD PMLD SLD SP&LD VI
Wheelchair access: WA1

HORTON LODGE SPECIAL SCHOOL
Rudyard, Leek, Staffordshire ST13 8RB
Type: Co-educational Day and Boarding 2–11
Special needs: CP SP&LD VI
Wheelchair access: W

LOXLEY HALL SPECIAL SCHOOL
Stafford Road, Uttoxeter, Staffordshire ST14 8RS
Type: Boys Boarding Only 10–16
Special needs: **BESD**

MARSHLANDS SPECIAL SCHOOL
Lansdowne Way, Stafford, Staffordshire ST17 4RD
Type: Co-educational Day Only 2–11
Special needs: **MLD** PMLD **SLD**
Wheelchair access: WA1

MEADOWS SPECIAL SCHOOL
High Street, Stoke on Trent, Staffordshire ST5 6BX
Type: Co-educational Day Only 3–19
Special needs: ASD ASP BESD DOW EPI HI **MLD** TOU VI
Wheelchair access: W

MERRYFIELDS SPECIAL SCHOOL
Hoon Avenue, Newcastle under Lyme, Staffordshire ST5 9NY
Type: Co-educational Day Only
Special needs: ASD **MLD** PMLD SLD

QUEEN'S CROFT COMMUNITY SCHOOL
Birmingham Road, Lichfield, Staffordshire WS13 6PJ
Website: www.queenscroft.staffs.sch.uk
Type: Co-educational Day Only 11–18
Wheelchair access: WA1

QUINCE TREE SPECIAL SCHOOL
Quince, Tamworth, Staffordshire B77 4EN
Type: Co-educational Day Only 2–19
Special needs: PMLD **SLD**
Wheelchair access: W

ROCKLANDS SPECIAL SCHOOL
Wissage Road, Lichfield, Staffordshire WS13 6SW
Type: Co-educational Day Only 2–11
Special needs: ASD ASP PMLD SLD

SAXON HILL SPECIAL SCHOOL
Kings Hill Road, Lichfield, Staffordshire WS14 9DE
Website: www.saxonhill.staffs.sch.uk
Type: Co-educational Day and Boarding 2–19
Special needs: **CP DYP EPI HEA HI IM PMLD** SP&LD VI
Wheelchair access: WA1

STRETTON COMMUNITY SPECIAL SCHOOL FEDERATION
Bitham Lane, Burton upon Trent, Staffordshire DE13 0HB
Type: Co-educational Day Only 4–18
Special needs: ASD **ASP MLD SLD**

TWO RIVERS HIGH SCHOOL
Torc Campus, Tamworth, Staffordshire B77 2HJ
Type: Co-educational Day Only 11–18
Special needs: **MLD SLD**
Wheelchair access: WA1

WIGHTWICK HALL SPECIAL SCHOOL
Tinacre Hill, Wolverhampton, West Midlands WV6 8DA
Type: Co-educational Day Only 11–19
Special needs: ASD MLD SP&LD
Wheelchair access: WA1

WILLIAM BAXTER SPECIAL SCHOOL
Stanley Road, Cannock, Staffordshire WS12 4JS
Type: Co-educational Day Only 11–19
Special needs: ADD ADHD ASD ASP BESD CP DOW DYP EPI HI IM **MLD** PMLD SP&LD VI
Wheelchair access: WA1

Stoke-on-Trent Education and Lifelong Learning

Civic Centre
Glebe Street
Stoke-on-Trent
Staffordshire
ST4 1HH

ABBEY HILL SPECIAL SCHOOL
Greasley Road, Stoke on Trent, Staffordshire ST2 8LB
Type: Co-educational Day Only 2–19
Special needs: ASD **ASP** BESD **MLD** SLD
Wheelchair access: WA1

AYNSLEY SPECIAL SCHOOL
Aynsley's Drive, Blythe Bridge, Stoke ST11 9HJ
Type: Co-educational Day Only
Special needs: ADHD ASD ASP BESD DOW **MLD**

HEATHFIELD SPECIAL SCHOOL
Chell Heath Road, Stoke on Trent, Stoke ST6 6PD
Type: Co-educational Day Only 2–16
Special needs: ASD DOW EPI PMLD **SLD** SP&LD
Wheelchair access: WA1

KEMBALL SPECIAL SCHOOL
Duke Street, Stoke ST4 3NR
Type: Co-educational Day Only 2–19
Special needs: PMLD SLD

MIDDLEHURST SPECIAL SCHOOL
Turnhurst Road, Stoke ST6 6NQ
Type: Co-educational Day Only 5–16
Special needs: BESD MLD SP&LD

STOCKTON-ON-TEES

Stockton-on-Tees Borough Council

PO Box 11
Church Road
Stockton-on-Tees
TS18 1LD

ABBEY HILL SCHOOL, TECHNOLOGY COLLEGE
Ketton Road, Stockton-on-Tees TS19 8BU
Type: Co-educational Day Only 11–19
Special needs: ADHD ASD **ASP** CP DOW DYP DYS EPI HEA HI **MLD PMLD SLD** SP&LD TOU VI
Wheelchair access: W

WESTLANDS ANNEXE
Mill Lane, Norton, Stockton-on-Tees TS20 1LG
Type: Co-educational Boarding 5–19
Special needs: **ASD BESD** MLD

SUFFOLK

Suffolk County Council

Endeavour House
Russell Road
Ipswich
Suffolk
IP1 2BX

THE ASHLEY SCHOOL

Ashley Downs, Lowestoft, Suffolk
NR32 4EU
Website: www.ashley.suffolk.
sch.uk
Type: Co-educational Day and
Boarding 7–16
Special needs: **MLD**

BEACON HILL SCHOOL

Stone Lodge Lane West, Ipswich,
Suffolk IP2 9HW
Type: Co-educational Day Only
5–16
Special needs: ASD **MLD**
Wheelchair access: WA1

BELSTEAD SCHOOL

Sprites Lane, Ipswich, Suffolk
IP8 3ND
Type: Co-educational Day Only
11–19
Special needs: ASD PMLD SLD
Wheelchair access: WA1

HEATHSIDE SCHOOL

Heath Road, Ipswich, Suffolk
IP4 5SN
Website: www.heathsideschool.
com
Type: Co-educational Day Only
Special needs: ASD **ASP** CB CP
EPI PMLD SLD W
Wheelchair access: WA1 WA2

HILLSIDE SCHOOL

Hitchcock Place, Sudbury,
Suffolk CO10 1NN
Website: www.hillsidespecial.
org.uk
Type: Co-educational Day Only
3–19
Special needs: **SLD**
Wheelchair access: W

PRIORY SCHOOL

Mount Road, Bury St Edmunds,
Suffolk 1P32 7BH
Type: Co-educational Day Only
9–16

THOMAS WOLSEY SCHOOL

642 Old Norwich Road, Ipswich,
Suffolk IP1 6LA
Type: Co-educational Day Only
3–19

WARREN SCHOOL

Clarkes Lane, Lowestoft, Suffolk
NR33 8HT
Type: Co-educational 3–19
Special needs: PMLD SLD
Wheelchair access: WA2

SURREY

Surrey County Council

Wood Street
Kingston upon Thames
Surrey
KT1 1AB

THE ABBEY SCHOOL

Menin Way, Farnham, Surrey
GU9 8DY
Website: www.abbey.surrey.
sch.uk
Type: Co-educational Day Only
10–16
Special needs: ASD **MLD**

BROOKLANDS SCHOOL

27 Wray Park Road, Reigate,
Surrey RH2 0DF
Type: Co-educational Day Only
2–11
Special needs: ASD DOW **PMLD
SLD**
Wheelchair access: WA2

CARWARDEN HOUSE COMMUNITY SCHOOL

118 Upper Chobham Road,
Camberley, Surrey GU15 1EJ
Website: www.carwardenhouse.
com
Type: Co-educational Day Only
11–19
Special needs: **MLD**
Wheelchair access: WA3

CLIFTON HILL SCHOOL

Chaldon Road, Caterham, Surrey
CR3 5PH
Website: www.clifton-hill.
surrey.sch.uk
Type: Co-educational Day Only
11–19
Special needs: **SLD**
Wheelchair access: WA1

FREEMANTLES SCHOOL

Pycroft Road, Chertsey, Surrey
KT16 9ER
Website: www.freemantles.
surrey.sch.uk
Type: Co-educational Day Only
4–14
Special needs: ASD **ASP**
Wheelchair access: WA2

GOSDEN HOUSE SCHOOL
Bramley, Guildford, Surrey
GU5 0AH
Website: www.gosdenhouse.
co.uk
Type: Co-educational Boarding
Only 5–16
Special needs: **MLD** SP&LD

**LIMPSFIELD GRANGE
SCHOOL**
89 Blue House Lane, Oxted,
Surrey RH8 0RZ
Type: Girls Boarding and Day
11–16
Special needs: ASD ASP DYP
DYS HEA IM SP&LD VI
Wheelchair access: WA2

LINDEN BRIDGE SCHOOL
Grafton Road, Worcester Park,
Surrey KT4 7JW
Type: Co-educational Boarding
and Day 4–19
Special needs: ASD **ASP**

MANOR MEAD SCHOOL
Laleham Road, Shepperton,
Surrey TW17 8EL
Type: Co-educational Day Only
Special needs: CP EPI PMLD
SLD
Wheelchair access: W

THE PARK SCHOOL
Onslow Crescent, Woking, Surrey
GU22 7AT
Type: Co-educational Day Only
11–16
Special needs: **MLD** SP&LD
Wheelchair access: WA1

PHILIP SOUTHCOTE SCHOOL
Addlestone, Surrey KT15 2QH
Website: www.philipsouthcote.
co.uk
Type: Co-educational Day Only
9–16
Special needs: HI **MLD**
Wheelchair access: WA1

POND MEADOW SCHOOL
Pond Meadow, Guildford, Surrey
GU2 6LG
Type: Co-educational Day Only
2–19
Special needs: PMLD SLD
Wheelchair access: W

PORTESBERY SCHOOL
Portesbery Road, Camberley,
Surrey GU15 3SZ
Type: Co-educational Day Only
2–19
Special needs: PMLD **SLD**

THE RIDGEWAY SCHOOL
14 Frensham Road, Farnham,
Surrey GU9 8HB
Type: Co-educational Day Only
2–19
Special needs: ASD CP DOW EPI
HI **PMLD SLD** VI
Wheelchair access: WA1

ST NICHOLAS SCHOOL
Taynton Drive, Redhill, Surrey
RH1 3PU
Type: Boys Boarding and Day
11–16
Special needs: BESD
Wheelchair access: WA3

STARHURST SCHOOL
Chart Lane South, Dorking,
Surrey RH5 4DB
Type: Boys Boarding and Day
11–16
Special needs: BESD

SIDLOW BRIDGE CENTRE
Ironsbottom Lane, Reigate,
Surrey RH2 8PP
Type: Co-educational Day Only
14–16
Special needs: **BESD**

SUNNYDOWN SCHOOL+
Portley House, Caterham, Surrey
CR3 5ED
Type: Boys Boarding and Day
11–16
Special needs: **DYS**

WALTON LEIGH SCHOOL
Queens Road, Walton-on-
Thames, Surrey KT12 5AB
Website: http://www.
waltonleighschool.org
Type: Co-educational Day Only
12–19
Special needs: ASD **PMLD SLD**
Wheelchair access: WA1

WEST HILL SCHOOL
Kingston Road, Leatherhead,
Surrey KT22 7PW
Type: Co-educational Day Only
9–16
Special needs: ASD **ASP MLD
SLD**
Wheelchair access: W

WEY HOUSE SCHOOL
Bramley, Guildford, Surrey
GU5 0BJ
Type: Boys Day and Boarding
7–11
Special needs: **BESD**
Wheelchair access: WA3

WISHMORE CROSS SCHOOL
Alpha Road, Chobham, Surrey
GU24 8NE
Type: Boys Boarding Only 11–16
Special needs: **BESD**

WOODFIELD SCHOOL
Sunstone Grove, Redhill, Surrey
RH1 3PR
Website: www.woodfield.
surrey.sch.uk
Type: Co-educational Day Only
9–16
Special needs: **MLD**
Wheelchair access: WA1

WOODLANDS SCHOOL
Fortyfoot Road, Leatherhead,
Surrey KT22 8RY
Type: Co-educational Day Only
2–19
Special needs: ASD **ASP PMLD
SLD**
Wheelchair access: WA1

EAST SUSSEX

Brighton & Hove Council

Kings House
Grand Avenue
Hove
East Sussex
BN3 2LS

ALTERNATIVE CENTRE FOR EDUCATION
Queensdown School Road, Brighton, East Sussex BN1 7LA
Type: Co-educational Day Only 11–16
Special needs: **BESD**

CEDAR CENTRE
Lynchet Road, Brighton, East Sussex BN1 7FP
Type: Co-educational Day Only
Special needs: **MLD**
Wheelchair access: WA2

DOWNS PARK SCHOOL
Foredown Road, Brighton, East Sussex BN41 2FU
Type: Co-educational Day Only 5–16
Special needs: ADHD ASD **ASP** DOW **MLD** SP&LD

DOWNS VIEW SCHOOL
Warren Road, Brighton, East Sussex BN2 6BB
Website: www.downsview. brighton-hove.sch.uk
Type: Co-educational Day Only 4–19
Special needs: ASD MLD PMLD SLD
Wheelchair access: WA1

HILLSIDE SCHOOL
Foredown Road, Brighton, East Sussex BN41 2FU
Website: www.hillside.brighton-hove.sch.uk
Type: Co-educational Day Only 4–16
Special needs: ASD PMLD **SLD**
Wheelchair access: WA1

PATCHAM HOUSE SCHOOL
7 Old London Road, Brighton, East Sussex BN1 8XR
Type: Co-educational Day Only 3–16
Special needs: ASP **CP** DYP EPI

East Sussex Education Department

PO Box 4, County Hall
St Annes Crescent
Lewes
East Sussex
BN7 1SG

GLYNE GAP SCHOOL
School Place, Bexhill-on-Sea, East Sussex TN40 2PU
Type: Co-educational Day Only 2–19
Special needs: ASD PMLD SLD
Wheelchair access: WA1

GROVE PARK SCHOOL
Church Road, Crowborough, East Sussex TN6 1BN
Type: Co-educational Day Only 3–19
Special needs: ASD MLD PMLD SLD
Wheelchair access: WA1

HAZEL COURT SCHOOL
Shinewater Lane, Eastbourne, East Sussex BN23 8AT
Type: Co-educational Day Only 11–19
Special needs: MLD PMLD SLD
Wheelchair access: WA1

THE LINDFIELD SCHOOL
Lindfield Road, Eastbourne, East Sussex BN22 0BQ
Type: Co-educational Day Only 10–16
Special needs: ADD ADHD ASD **ASP** DOW DYC DYS EPI HEA HI **MLD** SP&LD VI
Wheelchair access: WA1

NEW HORIZONS SCHOOL
Beauchamp Road, St Leonards-on-Sea, East Sussex TN38 9JU
Type: Co-educational Day Only 6–16
Special needs: ADD **ADHD** ASD ASP BESD CB
Wheelchair access: WA2

OAK GROVE COLLEGE
The Boulevard, Worthing, West Sussex BN13 1JX
Type: Co-educational Day Only 11–19
Special needs: ASD **ASP MLD PMLD SLD**
Wheelchair access: WA1

ST MARY'S SCHOOL
Horam, Heathfield, East Sussex TN21 0BT
Type: Co-educational Boarding and Day 11–19
Special needs: BESD MLD

SAXON MOUNT SCHOOL
Edinburgh Road, St Leonards-on-Sea, East Sussex TN38 8DA
Type: Co-educational Day Only 11–16
Special needs: ASD **MLD** SP&LD

THE SOUTH DOWNS COMMUNITY SPECIAL SCHOOL
Beechy Avenue, Eastbourne, East Sussex BN20 8NU
Website: www.southdowns. e-sussex.sch.uk
Type: Co-educational Day Only 4–11
Special needs: ADHD ASD **ASP** BESD CP DOW DYP EPI **MLD PMLD SLD** SP&LD

TORFIELD SCHOOL
Croft Road, Hastings, East Sussex TN34 3JT
Website: www.torfieldschool.net
Type: Co-educational Day Only 4–11
Special needs: ASD **ASP BESD CB** MLD SP&LD
Wheelchair access: WA2

WEST SUSSEX

West Sussex County Council

County Hall
West Street
Chichester
West Sussex
PO19 1RQ

ABBOTSFORD COMMUNITY SCHOOL
Cuckfield Road, Burgess Hill,
West Sussex RH15 8RE
Type: Boys Boarding and Day
7–16
Special needs: ADD ADHD ASD
ASP **BESD** DYS

CORNFIELD SCHOOL
Cornfield Close, Littlehampton,
West Sussex BN17 6HY
Website: www.cornfield.
w-sussex.sch.uk
Type: Co-educational Day Only
11–16
Special needs: **BESD**

COURT MEADOW SPECIAL SCHOOL
Hanlye Lane, Haywards Heath,
West Sussex RH17 5HN
Type: Co-educational Day Only
2–19
Special needs: ASD CB PMLD
SLD
Wheelchair access: WA1

FORDWATER SPECIAL SCHOOL
Summersdale Road, Chichester,
West Sussex PO19 6PP
Website: www.fordwater.
w-sussex.sch.uk
Type: Co-educational Day Only
2–19
Special needs: ASD **ASP PMLD
SLD**
Wheelchair access: W

HERONS DALE SPECIAL SCHOOL
Hawkins Crescent, Shoreham-by-
Sea, West Sussex BN43 6TN
Type: 4–16
Special needs: ASP **MLD**

LITTLEGREEN SPECIAL SCHOOL
Compton, Chichester, West
Sussex PO18 9NW
Website: www.littlegreen.
w-sussex.sch.uk
Type: Boys Boarding and Day
7–14
Special needs: ADD ADHD ASP
BESD TOU

MANOR GREEN COLLEGE
Lady Margaret Road, Crawley,
West Sussex RH11 0DX
Website: www.manorgreen-
college.w-sussex.sch.uk
Type: Co-educational Day Only
11–19
Special needs: ASD **MLD PMLD
SLD**
Wheelchair access: WA1

NEWICK HOUSE SPECIAL SCHOOL
Birchwood Grove Road, Burgess
Hill, West Sussex RH15 0DP
Website: www.newickhouse.
co.uk
Type: Co-educational Day Only
4–16
Special needs: ADD ADHD BESD
DOW DYP DYS EPI HEA HI **MLD**
SLD SP&LD
Wheelchair access: WA1

PALATINE SCHOOL
Palatine Road, Worthing, West
Sussex BN12 6JP
Website: www.palatine.org
Type: Co-educational Day Only
4–11
Special needs: ADD ADHD ASD
ASP CB **CP DOW** DYP EPI **HEA
IM MLD PMLD SLD** SP&LD
TOU W
Wheelchair access: W WA1 WA2

QUEEN ELIZABETH II SILVER JUBILEE SCHOOL
Comptons Lane, Horsham, West
Sussex RH13 5NW
Website: www.queenelizabeth2.
w-sussex.sch.uk
Type: Co-educational Day Only
2–19
Special needs: PMLD **SLD**
Wheelchair access: WA1
Non-maintained

ST ANTHONY'S SCHOOL
Woodlands Lane, Chichester,
West Sussex PO19 5PA
Website: www.st-anthonys.
w-sussex.sch.uk
Type: Co-educational Day Only
4–16
Special needs: ASD **ASP MLD**
SP&LD
Wheelchair access: WA1

TYNE AND WEAR

Gateshead Education Offices

Civic Centre
Regent Street
Gateshead
Tyne and Wear
NE8 1HH

THE CEDARS SCHOOL SPORTS COLLEGE
Ivy Lane, Gateshead,
Tyne and Wear NE9 6QD
Website: www.
cedarssportscollege.org.uk
Type: Co-educational Day Only
3–16
Special needs: **IM** SP&LD
Wheelchair access: WA1

DRYDEN SCHOOL
Shotley Gardens, Gateshead,
Tyne and Wear NE9 5UR
Type: Co-educational Day Only
Special needs: **PMLD SLD**
Wheelchair access: WA1

ESLINGTON PRIMARY SCHOOL
Hazel Road, Gateshead,
Tyne and Wear NE8 2EP
Type: Co-educational Day Only
5–11

FURROWFIELD SCHOOL
Senior Site, Whitehills Drive,
Gateshead, Tyne and Wear
NE10 9RZ
Type: Boys Day Only 11–16
Special needs: ADHD ASP **BESD**
DYP
Wheelchair access: WA1

GIBSIDE SCHOOL
Burnthouse Lane,
Newcastle upon Tyne,
Tyne and Wear NE16 5AT
Website: www.gibsideschool.org
Type: Co-educational 3–11
Special needs: ASD **ASP CP**
DOW PMLD SLD
Wheelchair access: WA1

HILL TOP SCHOOL
Wealcroft, Gateshead,
Tyne and Wear NE10 8LT
Type: Co-educational Day Only
Special needs: IM SP&LD VI
Wheelchair access: WA1

Newcastle City Council

Civic Centre
Barras Bridge
Newcastle upon Tyne
Tyne and Wear
NE1 8PU

GLEBE SCHOOL
Woodburn Drive, Whitley Bay,
Northumberland NE26 3HW
Type: Co-educational Day Only
4–11
Special needs: ASD **MLD** SP&LD
Wheelchair access: WA1

HADRIAN SCHOOL
Bertram Crescent,
Newcastle upon Tyne,
Tyne and Wear NE15 6PY
Website: www.hadrian.
newcastle.sch.uk
Type: Co-educational Day Only
2–11
Special needs: **PMLD SLD**
Wheelchair access: W

SIR CHARLES PARSONS SCHOOL
Westbourne Avenue, Newcastle
Upon Tyne, Tyne and Wear
NE6 4ED
Website: www.sircharlesparson.
newcastle.sch.uk
Type: Co-educational Day Only
11–19
Special needs: **PMLD SLD**
SP&LD
Wheelchair access: WA1

THOMAS BEWICK SCHOOL
Hillhead Parkway,
Newcastle upon Tyne,
Tyne and Wear NE5 1DS
Type: Co-educational Day and
Boarding 3–19
Special needs: ASD ASP MLD
SLD
Wheelchair access: WA1

TRINITY SCHOOL
Condercum Road, Newcastle
Upon Tyne, Tyne and Wear
NE4 8XJ
Type: Co-educational Boarding
7–16
Special needs: **BESD** SP&LD

North Tyneside Education Offices

Quadrant, The Silverlink North
Cobalt Business Park
North Tyneside
Tyne and Wear
NE27 0BY

PARKSIDE SCHOOL
Mullen Road, Wallsend,
Tyne and Wear NE28 9HA
Type: Co-educational Day Only
Special needs: ASD **SLD**

SILVERDALE SCHOOL
Langdale Gardens, Wallsend,
Tyne and Wear NE28 0HG
Type: Co-educational Day Only
Special needs: **BESD**
Wheelchair access: WA1

SOUTHLANDS SCHOOL
Beach Road, North Shields,
Tyne and Wear NE30 2QR
Type: Co-educational Day Only
11–17
Special needs: BESD **MLD**

WOODLAWN SCHOOL
Langley Avenue, Whitley Bay,
Tyne and Wear NE25 9DF
Website: www.woodlawn.org.uk
Type: Co-educational Day Only
2–16
Special needs: CP DYP HEA HI
IM SP&LD VI
Wheelchair access: WA1

South Tyneside Lifelong Learning & Leisure Directorate

**Town Hall and Civic Offices
South Shields
NE33 2RL**

BAMBURGH SCHOOL
Cautley Road, South Shields,
Tyne and Wear NE34 7TD
Type: Co-educational Day Only
2–17
Special needs: **ASD ASP HEA HI IM** SP&LD VI
Wheelchair access: WA1

EPINAY SCHOOL
Clervaux Terrace, Jarrow,
Tyne and Wear NE32 5UP
Website: www.epinay.org
Type: Co-educational Day Only
5–17
Special needs: BESD **MLD** SLD
Wheelchair access: WA2

GREENFIELDS SCHOOL
Victoria Road East, Hebburn,
Tyne and Wear NE31 1YQ
Type: Co-educational Day Only
2–19
Special needs: ASD IM **PMLD SLD** VI
Wheelchair access: WA1

MARGARET SUTTON SCHOOL
Ashley Road, South Shields,
Tyne and Wear NE34 0PF
Type: Co-educational Day Only
Special needs: **MLD**

OAKLEIGH GARDENS SCHOOL
Oakleigh Gardens, Nr
Sunderland, Tyne and Wear
SR6 7PT
Type: Co-educational Day Only
2–19
Special needs: **PMLD SLD**
Wheelchair access: W

Sunderland LEA

**PO Box 101, Civic Centre
Burdon Road
Sunderland
Tyne and Wear
SR2 7DN**

BARBARA PRIESTMAN SCHOOL
Meadowside, Sunderland,
Tyne and Wear SR2 7QN
Website: barbara.priestman.
org.uk
Type: Co-educational Day Only
Special needs: ASP VI

CASTLEGREEN COMMUNITY SCHOOL
Craigshaw Road, Sunderland,
Tyne and Wear SR5 3NF
Website: www.
millenniumschools.co.uk/pub/
sunderland/castlegreen/a.html
Type: Co-educational Day Only
11–19

COLUMBIA GRANGE SCHOOL
Oxclose Road, Washington,
Sunderland NE38 7NY
Website: www.
sunderlandschools.org/
columbiagrange
Type: Co-educational Day Only
2–11
Special needs: ASD **ASP** SLD
Wheelchair access: W
Non-maintained

DAVENPORT SCHOOL
Durham Road, Houghton-le-
Spring, Tyne and Wear DH5 8NF
Type: Co-educational Day Only
3–13
Special needs: ASD **ASP** MLD
PMLD **SLD**

FELSTEAD SCHOOL
Fordfield Road (North Side),
Sunderland, Tyne and Wear
SR4 0DA
Type: Co-educational Day Only
13–25
Special needs: BESD MLD

MAPLEWOOD SCHOOL
Redcar Road, Sunderland,
Tyne and Wear SR5 5PA
Type: Co-educational 4–11
Special needs: ADD ADHD ASD
ASP **BESD** TOU
Wheelchair access: WA1

PORTLAND SCHOOL
Weymouth Road, Sunderland,
Tyne and Wear SR3 2NQ
Website: www.portland-
school.co.uk
Type: Co-educational Day Only
11–19
Special needs: **PMLD SLD**
Wheelchair access: WA1

SPRINGWELL DENE SCHOOL
Swindon Road, Sunderland,
Tyne and Wear SR3 4EE
Type: Co-educational Day Only
Special needs: **BESD**

SUNNINGDALE SCHOOL
Shaftoe Road, Sunderland,
Tyne and Wear SR3 4HA
Type: Co-educational Day Only
2–11
Special needs: PMLD SLD
Wheelchair access: W

WELLBANK SCHOOL
Wellbank Road, Washington,
Tyne and Wear NE37 1NL
Type: Co-educational Day Only
3–13
Special needs: **MLD PMLD SLD**
Wheelchair access: W

WARWICKSHIRE

Warwickshire Education Offices

22 Northgate Street
Warwick
Warwickshire
CV34 4SR

BROOKE SCHOOL
Merttens Drive, Rugby,
Warwickshire CV22 7AE
Type: Co-educational Day Only
2–19
Special needs: MLD PMLD SLD
Wheelchair access: W

THE GRIFF SCHOOL
Coventry Road, Nuneaton,
Warwickshire CV10 7AX
Type: Co-educational Day Only
5–16
Special needs: **MLD**

OAKWOODS SCHOOLS
Morris Drive, Nuneaton,
Warwickshire CV11 4QH
Type: Co-educational 2–19
Special needs: **ADD ADHD ASD
ASP BESD CB CP DOW DYC
DYP DYS EPI HEA HI IM MLD
PMLD SLD** SP&LD VI
Wheelchair access: WA1

RIDGEWAY SCHOOL
Montague Road, Warwick,
Warwickshire CV34 5LW
Type: Co-educational Day Only
2–19
Special needs: ASD MLD PMLD
SLD
Wheelchair access: WA2

THE ROUND OAK SCHOOL
Pound Lane, Leamington Spa,
Warwickshire CV32 7RT
Type: Co-educational Day Only
5–16
Special needs: ADHD ASD BESD
DOW **MLD** SLD
Wheelchair access: WA2

WOODLANDS SCHOOL
Packington Lane, Coleshill,
West Midlands B46 3JE
Type: Co-educational Day Only
2–19
Special needs: ASD **ASP** BESD
MLD **PMLD SLD**
Wheelchair access: WA1

WEST MIDLANDS

Birmingham City Council

The Council House
Victoria Square
Birmingham
West Midlands
B1 1BB

BAGINTON FIELDS
Sedgemoor Road, Coventry,
West Midlands CV3 4EA
Type: Co-educational
Special needs: ADD ADHD ASD
ASP BESD CP DOW DYP EPI
MLD **PMLD SLD** SP&LD VI
Wheelchair access: WA1

BASKERVILLE SCHOOL
Fellows Lane, Birmingham,
West Midlands B17 9TS
Type: Co-educational Boarding
Only 11–19
Special needs: **ASD ASP**

BEAUFORT SCHOOL
16 Coleshill Road, Birmingham,
West Midlands B36 8AA
Type: Day Only 3–11
Special needs: **PMLD SLD**
Wheelchair access: WA1

BRAIDWOOD SCHOOL
Bromford Road, Birmingham,
West Midlands B36 8AF
Website: www.braidwoodonline.
org.uk
Type: Co-educational Day Only
11–18
Special needs: **HI**
Wheelchair access: WA1

BRAYS SCHOOL
Brays Road, Birmingham,
West Midlands B26 1NS
Website: www.brays.bham.
sch.uk
Type: Co-educational Day Only
2–11
Special needs: CP DOW EPI HEA
HI **IM** PMLD SLD SP&LD VI W
Wheelchair access: W WA1 WA2

BRIDGE SCHOOL
290 Reservoir Road,
Birmingham, West Midlands
B23 6DE
Type: Co-educational 2–11
Special needs: PMLD SLD

CALTHORPE SCHOOL AND SPORTS COLLEGE
Darwin Street, Birmingham,
West Midlands B12 0JJ
Website: www.calthorpe.
bham.sch.uk
Type: Co-educational Day Only
2–19
Special needs: ASD **ASP** BESD
DOW EPI HI **PMLD SLD** SP&LD
TOU VI
Wheelchair access: WA1

CHERRY OAK SCHOOL
60 Frederick Road, Birmingham,
West Midlands B29 6PB
Type: Co-educational Day Only
2–11
Special needs: ASD PMLD **SLD**
Wheelchair access: W

DAME ELLEN PINSENT SCHOOL
Ardencote Road, Birmingham,
West Midlands B13 0RW
Type: Co-educational Day Only
4–11
Special needs: ASD DOW **MLD**
SLD SP&LD

FOX HOLLIES SCHOOL AND PERFORMING ARTS COLLEGE
Highbury Community Campus,
Birmingham, West Midlands
B13 8QB
Type: Co-educational Day Only
11–19
Special needs: PMLD **SLD**
Wheelchair access: WA1

HALLMOOR SCHOOL
Hallmoor Road, Birmingham,
West Midlands B33 9QY
Type: Co-educational Day Only
4–19
Special needs: **MLD**

HAMILTON SCHOOL
Hamilton Road, Birmingham,
West Midlands B21 8AH
Type: Co-educational Day Only
4–11
Special needs: ASD ASP DOW
DYP EPI HI **MLD SLD** SP&LD

HUNTERS HILL
Spirehouse Lane, Bromsgrove,
West Midlands B60 1QD
Type: Co-educational Day Only
11–16

KINGSTANDING SCHOOL
Old Oscott Hill, Birmingham,
West Midlands B44 9SP
Type: Co-educational Day Only
11–19
Special needs: ASD **PMLD SLD**
SP&LD
Wheelchair access: W

LANGLEY SCHOOL
Lindridge Road, Sutton Coldfield,
West Midlands B75 7HU
Website: www.langley.bham.
sch.uk
Type: Co-educational Day Only
3–11
Special needs: ASD DOW **MLD**
SP&LD
Wheelchair access: WA1

LINDSWORTH (NORTH)
Monyhull Hall Road, Kings
Norton, Birmingham, West
Midlands B30 3QA
Type: Co-educational Boarding
11–16
Special needs: **BESD**

LINDSWORTH (SOUTH)
Monyhull Hall Road, Kings
Norton, West Midlands B30 3QA
Type: Co-educational 11–16
Special needs: **BESD**

LONGMOOR SCHOOL
Coppice View Road, Sutton
Coldfield, West Midlands B7 6UE
Website: longmoor.bham.sch.uk
Type: Co-educational Day and
Boarding 2–11
Special needs: ASD PMLD **SLD**

LONGWILL SCHOOL
Bell Hill, Birmingham,
West Midlands B31 1LD
Website: www.longwill.bham.
sch.uk
Type: Co-educational Day Only
2–11
Special needs: **HI**
Wheelchair access: WA1

MAYFIELD SCHOOL
Finch Road, Birmingham,
West Midlands B19 1HP
Type: Co-educational Day Only
2–19
Special needs: ADHD ASD **ASP**
BESD CP DOW EPI HI **PMLD
SLD**
Wheelchair access: WA1

PINES SCHOOL
Dreghorn Road, Birmingham,
West Midlands B36 8LL
Website: www.pines.bham.
sch.uk
Type: Co-educational Day Only
3–11
Special needs: ASD **ASP** SP&LD
Wheelchair access: W

PRIESTLEY SMITH SCHOOL
Perry Beeches Campus,
Birmingham, West Midlands
B42 2PY
Type: Co-educational Day Only
2–17
Special needs: ASD ASP CP DYS
HEA MLD VI
Wheelchair access: WA1

QUEENSBURY SCHOOL
Wood End Road, Birmingham,
West Midlands B24 8BL
Type: Co-educational Day Only
11–18
Special needs: **MLD**
Wheelchair access: WA2

SELLY OAK TRUST SCHOOL
Oak Tree Lane, Selly Oak,
West Midlands B29 6HZ
Website: www.sellyoak.bham.
sch.uk
Type: Co-educational Day Only
11–19
Special needs: **MLD**
Wheelchair access: WA2

SKILTS (RESIDENTIAL) SCHOOL
Gorcott Hill, Redditch,
West Midlands B98 9ET
Type: Boys Boarding and Day
4–12
Special needs: ADD **ADHD ASD**
ASP **BESD** DYS MLD

SPRINGFIELD HOUSE SCHOOL
Kenilworth Road, Solihull,
West Midlands B93 0AJ
Type: Co-educational Boarding
and Day 5–11
Special needs: ASD **BESD** MLD
Wheelchair access: WA3

TIVERTON SPECIAL SCHOOL
Rowington Close, Coventry,
West Midlands CV6 1PS
Type: Co-educational 3–11
Special needs: **SLD**
Wheelchair access: W

UFFCULME SCHOOL
Queensbridge Road,
Birmingham, West Midlands
B13 8QB
Website: www.uffculme.bham.
sch.uk
Type: Co-educational Day Only
3–13
Special needs: ASD ASP
Wheelchair access: WA3

VICTORIA SCHOOL
Bell Hill, Birmingham,
West Midlands B31 1LD
Type: Co-educational Day Only
2–19
Special needs: CP EPI HI MLD
PMLD SLD VI
Wheelchair access: W

WAINBODY WOOD SPECIAL SCHOOL
Stoneleigh Road, Coventry,
West Midlands CV4 7AB
Type: Co-educational Day Only
Special needs: **BESD**

WILSON STUART SCHOOL
Perry Common Road,
Birmingham, West Midlands
B23 7AT
Website: www.wilsonst.bham.
sch.uk
Type: Co-educational Day Only
2–19
Special needs: SP&LD
Wheelchair access: WA1

Coventry Education Offices

New Council Offices
Earl Street
Coventry
West Midlands
CV1 5RR

ALICE STEVENS SCHOOL
Ashington Grove, Coventry,
West Midlands CV3 4DE
Type: Co-educational Day Only
11–18
Special needs: **MLD**
Wheelchair access: W

CASTLE WOOD SCHOOL
Hawkesbury Fields site,
Coventry, West Midlands
CV2 1PL
Type: Co-educational Day Only
2–11
Special needs: PMLD **SLD**
Wheelchair access: W

CORLEY (COVENTRY) SCHOOL
Church Lane, Nr Coventry,
West Midlands CV7 8AZ
Type: Co-educational Day and Boarding
Special needs: ASD **ASP** MLD

DARTMOUTH SPECIAL SCHOOL
Tiverton Road, Coventry,
West Midlands CV2 3DN
Type: Boys Day Only 11–16
Special needs: ADD ADHD ASD **BESD** TOU
Wheelchair access: W

THE MEADOWS
Hawthorn Lane, Coventry,
West Midlands CV4 9PB
Type: Boys Day and Boarding
11–16
Special needs: **BESD**

SHERBOURNE FIELDS SCHOOL
Rowington Close, Coventry,
West Midlands CV6 1PR
Type: Co-educational Day Only
Special needs: ASD CP EPI **HEA HI IM** MLD PMLD SLD SP&LD VI
Wheelchair access: WA1

THREE SPIRES SCHOOL
Kingsbury Road, Coventry,
West Midlands CV6 1PJ
Type: Co-educational Day Only
3–11
Special needs: **MLD**

Dudley Directorate of Education & Lifelong Learning

Westox House
1 Trinity Road
Dudley
West Midlands
DY1 1JB

THE BRIER SPECIAL SCHOOL
Bromley Lane, Kingswinford,
West Midlands DY6 8QN
Type: Co-educational Day Only
4–16
Special needs: MLD SP&LD
Wheelchair access: WA1

HALESBURY SPECIAL SCHOOL
Feldon Lane, Halesowen,
West Midlands B62 9DR
Type: Co-educational Day Only
5–16
Special needs: ASP **MLD**

OLD PARK SCHOOL
Corbyn Road, Dudley,
West Midlands DY6 9AW
Type: Co-educational 3–19
Special needs: **SLD**
Wheelchair access: WA1

PENS MEADOW SCHOOL
Ridge Hill, Stourbridge,
West Midlands DY8 5ST
Type: Co-educational Day Only
3–19
Special needs: ASD PMLD **SLD**
Wheelchair access: WA2

ROSEWOOD SCHOOL
Overfield Road, Dudley,
West Midlands DY1 2NX
Website: www.rosewood.
dudley.gov.uk
Type: Boys Day Only 11–16
Special needs: **BESD**
Wheelchair access: W

THE SUTTON SCHOOL
Scotts Green Close, Dudley,
West Midlands DY1 2DU
Type: Co-educational Day Only
11–16
Special needs: **MLD**

THE WOODSETTON SPECIAL SCHOOL
Tipton Road, Dudley,
West Midlands DY3 1BY
Type: Co-educational Day Only
4–11
Special needs: ASD **MLD** SP&LD

Sandwell Education & Lifelong Learning

Shaftsbury House, 402 High Street
West Bromwich
Sandwell
West Midlands
B70 9LT

THE ORCHARD SCHOOL
Causeway Green Road, Oldbury,
West Midlands B68 8LD
Type: Co-educational Day Only
Special needs: ASD **CP PMLD SLD**
Wheelchair access: WA1

Solihull Education & Children's Services

PO Box 20
Council House
Solihull
West Midlands
B91 3QU

MERSTONE SCHOOL
Winward Way, Birmingham,
West Midlands B36 0VE
Type: Co-educational Day Only
2–18
Special needs: ASD **ASP** CP
DOW EPI **PMLD SLD**
Wheelchair access: W

REYNALDS CROSS SCHOOL
Kineton Green Road, Solihull,
West Midlands B92 7ER
Type: Co-educational Day Only
Special needs: PMLD SLD
Wheelchair access: WA1

Walsall Metropolitan Borough Council

Civic Centre
Darwall Street
Walsall
West Midlands
WS1 1DQ

CASTLE BUSINESS & ENTERPRISE COLLEGE
Odell Road, Walsall,
West Midlands WS3 2ED
Website: www.castle.walsall.
sch.uk
Type: Co-educational Day Only
4–19
Special needs: ASD **ASP** DOW
DYP **MLD** SLD SP&LD

DAW END SPECIAL SCHOOL
Floyds Lane, Walsall,
West Midlands WS4 1LF
Website: www.daw.end.walsall.
sch.uk
Type: Co-educational Day and
Boarding 5–16
Special needs: **BESD**
Wheelchair access: WA3

JANE LANE SCHOOL
Churchill Road, Walsall,
West Midlands WS2 0JH
Type: Co-educational Day Only
4–19
Special needs: **MLD**
Wheelchair access: W

MARY ELLIOT SPECIAL SCHOOL
Leamore Lane, Walsall,
West Midlands WS2 7NR
Website: www.mary-elliot.
walsall.sch.uk
Type: Co-educational Day Only
11–19
Special needs: ASD **PMLD SLD**
Wheelchair access: WA1

OAKWOOD SPECIAL SCHOOL
Druids Walk, Walsall,
West Midlands WS9 9JS
Website: www.oakwood.walsall.
sch.uk
Type: Co-educational Day Only
2–14
Special needs: ASD CP EPI HI
PMLD SLD VI
Wheelchair access: W

OLD HALL SPECIAL SCHOOL
Bentley Lane, Walsall,
West Midlands WS2 7LU
Website: www.oldhall.walsall.
sch.uk
Type: Co-educational Day Only
2–14
Special needs: **PMLD SLD**
Wheelchair access: WA1

Wolverhampton Lifelong Learning

Civic Centre
St Peter's Square
Wolverhampton
WV11 1RR

BROADMEADOW SPECIAL SCHOOL
Lansdowne Road,
Wolverhampton, West Midlands
WV1 4AL
Type: Co-educational Day Only
2–7
Special needs: ASD PMLD **SLD**
Wheelchair access: WA1

GREEN PARK SPECIAL SCHOOL
Green Park Avenue, Bilston,
West Midlands WV14 6EH
Type: Co-educational Day Only
5–19
Special needs: PMLD SLD
Wheelchair access: W

NEW PARK SCHOOL
Valley Park Campus,
Wolverhampton, West Midlands
WV6 0UB
Type: Co-educational Day Only
7–14
Special needs: **BESD**
Wheelchair access: WA2

PENN FIELDS SCHOOL
Birches Barn Road,
Wolverhampton, West Midlands
WV3 7BJ
Type: Co-educational Day Only
5–16
Special needs: ASD **BESD** HI
MLD SP&LD VI
Wheelchair access: W

PENN HALL SCHOOL
Vicarage Road, Wolverhampton,
West Midlands WV4 5HP
Website: www.penhall.co.uk
Type: Co-educational Day Only
3–19
Special needs: CP HEA HI **IM**
SP&LD VI
Wheelchair access: WA1

TETTENHALL WOOD SCHOOL
School Road, Wolverhampton,
West Midlands WV6 8EJ
Type: Co-educational Day Only
5–19
Special needs: ASD CP DOW
PMLD **SLD** SP&LD
Wheelchair access: WA2

WESTCROFT SCHOOL AND SPORTS COLLEGE
Greenacres Avenue,
Wolverhampton, West Midlands
WV10 8NZ
Website: www.westcroft.
wolverhampton.sch.uk
Type: Co-educational Day Only
5–8
Special needs: **MLD**
Wheelchair access: W

WILTSHIRE

Swindon Borough Council

Civic Offices
Euclid Street
Swindon
Wiltshire
SN1 2JH

BRIMBLE HILL SPECIAL SCHOOL
Tadpole Lane, Swindon, Wiltshire SN25 2NB
Type: Co-educational Day Only 2–11
Special needs: **SLD**
Wheelchair access: WA1

THE CHALET SPECIAL SCHOOL
Liden Drive, Swindon, Wiltshire SN3 6EX
Type: Co-educational Day Only 3–11
Special needs: ADHD ASD **ASP**
Wheelchair access: WA2

CROWDYS HILL SPECIAL SCHOOL
Jefferies Avenue, Swindon, Wiltshire SN2 7HJ
Type: Co-educational Day Only 11–16
Special needs: ADD ADHD ASD ASP HI **MLD** PMLD SLD
Wheelchair access: W

NYLAND SPECIAL SCHOOL
Nyland Road, Swindon, Wiltshire SN3 3RD
Type: Co-educational Day Only 5–11
Special needs: **ADD ADHD ASD ASP BESD CB** DYP DYS SP&LD TOU

ST LUKE'S SPECIAL SCHOOL
Cricklade Road, Swindon, Wiltshire SN2 7AS
Type: Co-educational Day Only 11–16
Special needs: **BESD**
Wheelchair access: W

UPLANDS SPECIAL SCHOOL
Leigh Road, Swindon, Wiltshire SN2 5DE
Type: Co-educational Day Only 11–19
Special needs: ASD **ASP** CP DOW **PMLD SLD**
Wheelchair access: W

Wiltshire County Council

County Hall
Bythesea Road
Trowbridge
Wiltshire
BA14 8JN

DOWNLAND SCHOOL
Downlands Road, Devizes, Wiltshire SN10 5EF
Type: Boys Boarding and Day 11–16
Special needs: ADHD ASP **BESD** DYS
Wheelchair access: WA3

EXETER HOUSE SPECIAL SCHOOL
Somerset Road, Salisbury, Wiltshire SP1 3BL
Type: Co-educational Day Only 2–19
Special needs: ASD PMLD SLD
Wheelchair access: W

LARKRISE SPECIAL SCHOOL
Ashton Street, Trowbridge, Wiltshire BA14 7EB
Type: Co-educational Day Only 3–19
Special needs: PMLD **SLD**

ROWDEFORD SPECIAL SCHOOL
Rowde, Devizes, Wiltshire SN10 2QQ
Type: Co-educational Day and Boarding 11–16
Special needs: **ADHD ASD ASP CP DOW DYP DYS EPI HEA HI IM MLD** SP&LD **TOU** VI
Wheelchair access: WA2

ST NICHOLAS SCHOOL
Malmesbury Road, Chippenham, Wiltshire SN15 1QF
Type: Co-educational Day Only 3–19
Special needs: ASD PMLD SLD

SPRINGFIELDS SPECIAL SCHOOL
Curzon Street, Calne, Wiltshire SN11 0DS
Type: Co-educational Boarding Only 10–17
Special needs: **BESD**

WORCESTERSHIRE

Worcestershire County Education Services Directorate

County Hall
Spetchley Road
Worcester
Worcestershire
WR5 2NP

THE ALEXANDER PATTERSON SCHOOL
Park Gate Road, Kidderminster,
Worcestershire DY10 3PU
Type: Co-educational Day Only
Special needs: ASD **ASP** BESD
MLD PMLD SP&LD
Wheelchair access: W

BLAKEBROOK SCHOOL
Bewdley Road, Kidderminster,
Worcestershire DY11 6RL
Type: Co-educational Day Only
Special needs: ASD PMLD **SLD**
Wheelchair access: W

CHADSGROVE SCHOOL & SPECIALIST SPORTS COLLEGE
Meadow Road, Bromsgrove,
Worcestershire B61 0JL
Website: www.
chadsgroveschool.co.uk
Type: Co-educational Day Only
2–19
Special needs: CP EPI HEA **IM**
PMLD VI
Wheelchair access: WA1

MANOR PARK SCHOOL
Turnpike Close, Worcester,
Worcestershire WR2 6AB
Website: www.manorparkschool.
worcs.sch.uk
Type: Co-educational Day Only
4–19
Special needs: PMLD **SLD**
Wheelchair access: WA2

PITCHEROAK SCHOOL
Willow Way, Redditch,
Worcestershire B97 6PQ
Type: Co-educational Day Only
2–18
Special needs: ASD **ASP MLD SLD**

REDGROVE UPPER SCHOOL
Shaw Lane, Bromsgrove,
Worcestershire B60 4EL
Type: Co-educational
Special needs: BESD

REGENCY HIGH SCHOOL
Carnforth Drive, Worcester,
Worcestershire WR4 9JL
Website: www.regency.worcs.
sch.uk
Type: Co-educational Day Only
11–19
Special needs: **BESD CB MLD**
PMLD **SLD**
Wheelchair access: WA1

RIVERSIDE UPPER SCHOOL
Thornloe Road, Worcester,
Worcestershire WR1 3HZ
Type: Co-educational Day Only
11–16
Special needs: BESD

STOURMINSTER SCHOOL
Comberton Road, Kidderminster,
Worcestershire DY10 3DX
Type: Co-educational 7–16
Special needs: ASD **MLD**
Wheelchair access: W

THORNTON HOUSE SCHOOL
Wylds Lane, Worcester,
Worcestershire WR5 1DR
Type: Co-educational Day Only
2–11
Special needs: ASD **MLD**
Wheelchair access: WA2

VALE OF EVESHAM SCHOOL
Four Pools Lane, Evesham,
Worcestershire WR11 1BN
Type: Co-educational Boarding
and Day 4–19
Special needs: ADD ADHD ASD
ASP DOW EPI HI **MLD PMLD**
SLD SP&LD
Wheelchair access: W

EAST RIDING OF YORKSHIRE

East Riding of Yorkshire

County Hall
Beverley
East Riding of Yorkshire
HU17 9BA

RIVERSIDE SCHOOL
Ainsty Street, Goole, East Riding
of Yorkshire DN14 5JS
Type: 4–16
Wheelchair access: WA1

Hull City Council

Guildhall
Hull
East Riding of Yorkshire
HU1 2AA

BRIDGEVIEW SCHOOL
Ferriby Road, Hessle, East Riding
of Yorkshire HU13 0HR
Type: Co-educational Day Only
6–16
Special needs: **BESD**

FREDERICK HOLMES SCHOOL
Inglemire Lane, Kingston upon
Hull, East Riding of Yorkshire
HU6 8JJ
Website: www.
frederickholmesschool.co.uk
Type: Co-educational Day Only
2–19
Special needs: **CP DOW IM
PMLD** SP&LD
Wheelchair access: WA1

GANTON SCHOOL
Springhead Lane, Hull, East
Riding of Yorkshire HU5 6YJ
Type: Co-educational Day Only
Special needs: ASD CP DOW EPI
PMLD SLD
Wheelchair access: W

KING'S MILL SCHOOL
Victoria Road, Driffield, East
Riding of Yorkshire YO25 7UG
Type: Co-educational Day and
Boarding 2–16
Special needs: PMLD **SLD**
Wheelchair access: WA1

NORTHCOTT SCHOOL
Dulverton Close, Kingston upon
Hull, East Riding of Yorkshire
HU7 4EL
Type: Co-educational Day Only
Special needs: ASD BESD EPI
HEA SP&LD

NORTH YORKSHIRE

North Yorkshire County Council

County Hall
Northallerton
North Yorkshire
DL7 8AE

APPLEFIELDS SCHOOL
Bad Bargain Lane, York,
North Yorkshire YO31 0LW
Website: www.applefields.york.
sch.uk
Type: Co-educational Day Only
11–19
Special needs: ASD MLD PMLD
SLD
Wheelchair access: WA1

BALIOL SCHOOL
Sedbergh, North Yorkshire
LA10 5LQ
Type: Boys Boarding Only 10–16
Special needs: ADHD ASP **BESD**
MLD

BROMPTON HALL SCHOOL
Brompton-by-Sawdon,
Scarborough, North Yorkshire
YO13 9BD
Type: Boys Boarding and Day
8–16
Special needs: ADHD ASP **BESD**
MLD

BROOKLANDS SCHOOL
Burnside Avenue, Skipton,
North Yorkshire BD23 2LX
Type: Co-educational Day Only
2–19
Special needs: **BESD DOW EPI
IM PMLD** SP&LD VI
Wheelchair access: WA1

DALES SCHOOL
Moreton-on-Swale, Northallerton,
North Yorkshire DL7 9QW
Type: Co-educational Day Only
2–19
Special needs: ASD **CP DOW**
PMLD SLD VI

THE FOREST SCHOOL
Park Lane, Knaresborough,
North Yorkshire HG5 0DQ
Website: www.theforestschool.
org.uk
Type: Co-educational Day Only
3–16
Special needs: ADD ADHD ASD
ASP BESD DOW **MLD** SLD
SP&LD
Wheelchair access: W

MOWBRAY SCHOOL
Masham Road, Bedale,
North Yorkshire DL8 2DS
Type: Co-educational Day Only
2–16
Special needs: ADHD ASD BESD
CP DOW **MLD** SLD SP&LD
Wheelchair access: WA1

NETHERSIDE HALL SCHOOL
Threshfield, Skipton,
North Yorkshire BD23 5PP
Type: Boys Boarding and Day
11–16
Special needs: ADD ADHD ASP
BESD DYP **DYS**

SPRINGHEAD SCHOOL
Barry's Lane, Scarborough,
North Yorkshire YO11 4HA
Website: www.
springheadschool.com
Type: Co-educational Day Only
2–19
Special needs: PMLD **SLD**
Wheelchair access: WA1

SPRINGWATER SCHOOL
High Street, Harrogate,
North Yorkshire HG2 7LW
Type: Co-educational Day Only
2–19
Special needs: ASD **ASP PMLD
SLD**
Wheelchair access: WA1

WELBURN HALL SCHOOL
Kirbymoorside, York,
North Yorkshire YO62 7HQ
Website: www.welburn-hall.
n-yorks.sch.uk
Type: Co-educational Boarding
and Day 8–18
Special needs: CP EPI HI MLD
SLD SP&LD VI
Wheelchair access: WA1

**York Education and
Leisure**

**10–12 George Hudson Street
York
North Yorkshire
YO1 1ZE**

FULFORD CROSS SCHOOL
Fulford Cross, York,
North Yorkshire YO1 4PB
Special needs: **MLD**

HOB MOOR OAKS SCHOOL
Green Lane, York, North Yorkshire
YO24 4PS
Type: Co-educational Day Only
2–11
Special needs: MLD PMLD SLD
Wheelchair access: WA1

NORTHFIELD SCHOOL
Beckfield Lane, York,
North Yorkshire YO26 5RQ
Type: Co-educational 5–16

SOUTH YORKSHIRE

Barnsley LEA

**Town Hall
Church Street
Barnsley
South Yorkshire
S70 2TA**

GREENACRE SCHOOL
Keresforth Hill Road, Barnsley,
South Yorkshire S70 6RG
Type: Co-educational Day Only
2–19
Special needs: ASD **ASP PMLD
SLD**
Wheelchair access: WA1

**Doncaster Education
Offices**

**The Council House
College Road
Doncaster
South Yorkshire
DN1 3AD**

**ANCHORAGE LOWER
SCHOOL**
Cusworth Lane, Doncaster,
South Yorkshire DN5 8JL
Type: Co-educational Day Only
4–12
Special needs: BESD **MLD**

ANCHORAGE UPPER SCHOOL
Barnsley Road, Doncaster,
South Yorkshire DN5 7UB
Type: Co-educational Day Only
13–16
Special needs: **MLD**

CEDAR SCHOOL
Cedar Road, Doncaster,
South Yorkshire DN4 9HT
Type: Co-educational Day Only
3–19
Special needs: **PMLD SLD**
Wheelchair access: WA1

CHASE SCHOOL
Ash Hill, Doncaster,
South Yorkshire DN7 6JH
Type: Co-educational Day Only
3–19
Special needs: ASD PMLD **SLD**
Wheelchair access: W

HEATHERWOOD SCHOOL
Leger Way, Doncaster,
South Yorkshire DN2 6HQ
Type: Co-educational Day Only
3–19
Special needs: HEA **IM PMLD**
SLD
Wheelchair access: WA1

PENNINE VIEW SCHOOL
Old Road, Doncaster,
South Yorkshire DN12 3LR
Type: Co-educational Day Only
6–16
Special needs: ADHD BESD
MLD SP&LD
Wheelchair access: WA2

ROSSINGTON HALL SCHOOL
Great North Road, Doncaster,
South Yorkshire DN11 0HS

Rotherham Education, Culture & Leisure Services

Norfolk House
Walker Place
Rotherham
South Yorkshire
S65 1UF

ABBEY SCHOOL
Little Common Lane, Rotherham,
South Yorkshire S61 2RA
Type: Co-educational Day Only
5–16
Special needs: **MLD**

GREEN ARBOUR SCHOOL
Locksley Drive, Rotherham,
South Yorkshire S66 9NT
Website: www.greenarbour.co.uk
Type: Co-educational Day Only
7–16
Special needs: ASD MLD SP&LD

HILLTOP SCHOOL
Larch Road, Rotherham,
South Yorkshire S66 8AZ
Website: www.hilltop.
rotherham.sch.uk
Type: Co-educational Day Only
2–19
Special needs: ASD **ASP** CP
DOW **PMLD SLD** VI
Wheelchair access: WA1

KELFORD SCHOOL
Oakdale Road, Rotherham,
South Yorkshire S61 2NU
Type: Co-educational Day Only
2–19
Special needs: ASD PMLD SLD
Wheelchair access: WA1

MILTON SCHOOL
Storey Street, Mexborough,
South Yorkshire S64 8QG
Type: Co-educational Day Only
4–16
Special needs: ASD **ASP MLD**
Wheelchair access: W

NEWMAN SCHOOL
East Bawtry Road, Rotherham,
South Yorkshire S60 2LX
Type: Co-educational Day Only
2–19
Special needs: CP
Wheelchair access: W

Sheffield City Council

Town Hall
Pinstone Street
Sheffield
South Yorkshire
S1 2HH

BENTS GREEN SECONDARY SCHOOL
Ringinglow Road, Sheffield,
South Yorkshire S11 7TB
Type: Co-educational Day and
Boarding
Special needs: ASD **ASP MLD**
SP&LD

BROAD ELMS SCHOOL
Broad Elms Lane, Sheffield,
South Yorkshire S11 9RQ
Type: Co-educational 4–11

DR JOHN WORRALL SCHOOL
Maltby Street, Sheffield,
South Yorkshire S9 2QA
Type: 5–16

EAST HILL SECONDARY SCHOOL
East Bank Road, Sheffield,
South Yorkshire S2 3PX
Website: www.easthill-sec.
sheffield.sch.uk
Type: Co-educational Day Only
11–16
Special needs: **MLD**
Wheelchair access: WA3

MOSSBROOK SCHOOL
Bochum Parkway, Sheffield,
South Yorkshire S8 8JR
Website: www.mossbrook.
sheffield.sch.uk
Type: Co-educational Day and
Boarding
Special needs: ASD **ASP** BESD
DOW EPI HEA **MLD SLD** SP&LD
Wheelchair access: W

NORFOLK PARK PRIMARY SCHOOL
Park Grange Road, Sheffield,
South Yorkshire S2 3QF
Type: Co-educational Day Only
2–11
Special needs: ASD **PMLD SLD**
Wheelchair access: W

THE ROWAN SCHOOL
4 Durvale Court, Sheffield,
South Yorkshire S17 3PT
Type: Co-educational Day Only
4–11
Special needs: ASD ASP SP&LD

TALBOT SECONDARY SCHOOL
Matthews Lane, Sheffield,
South Yorkshire S8 8JS
Type: Co-educational Day Only
11–19

WOOLLEY WOOD SCHOOL
Oaks Fold Road, Sheffield,
South Yorkshire S5 0TG
Type: Co-educational Day Only
3–10
Special needs: ASD **ASP PMLD
SLD**
Wheelchair access: WA1

WEST YORKSHIRE

Bradford Metropolitan District Council

City Hall
Bradford
West Yorkshire
BD1 1HY

BOLLING SCHOOL
Bradford, West Yorkshire BD4 7S4
Type: Co-educational Day Only 11–19
Special needs: ASD HEA **PMLD SLD** VI
Wheelchair access: WA1

BRAITHWAITE SCHOOL
Braithwaite Road, Keighley, West Yorkshire BD22 6PR
Type: Co-educational Day Only 2–19
Special needs: ASD ASP CP DOW DYS EPI **MLD** SLD SP&LD

BRANSHAW SCHOOL
Oakworth Road, Keighley, West Yorkshire BD21 1RA
Type: Co-educational Day Only 2–19
Special needs: ASD **ASP PMLD SLD**
Wheelchair access: WA2

CHAPEL GRANGE SCHOOL
Rhodesway, Bradford, West Yorkshire BD8 0DQ
Type: Co-educational Day Only 11–19
Special needs: ASD MLD PMLD **SLD**
Wheelchair access: WA2

GREENFIELD SCHOOL
Bradford, West Yorkshire BD10 8LU
Type: Co-educational Day Only 3–11
Special needs: ADHD ASD ASP SLD
Wheelchair access: WA1

HAYCLIFFE SCHOOL
Haycliffe Lane, Bradford, West Yorkshire BD5 9ET
Type: Co-educational Day Only 11–19
Special needs: ASD **ASP** BESD HI **MLD** SLD SP&LD VI
Wheelchair access: WA2

HEATON ROYDS SCHOOL
Redburn Drive, Shipley, West Yorkshire BD18 3AZ
Type: Co-educational Day Only 2–11
Special needs: EPI MLD **SLD** SP&LD

LISTER LANE SCHOOL
Lister Lane, Bradford, West Yorkshire BD2 4LL
Type: Co-educational Day Only 2–13
Special needs: **CP IM MLD** PMLD **SLD**
Wheelchair access: WA1

NETHERLANDS AVENUE SCHOOL
Netherlands Avenue, Bradford, West Yorkshire BD6 1EA
Type: Co-educational Day Only 2–11
Special needs: ASD **ASP MLD SLD** SP&LD

Calderdale Council

Crossley Street
Halifax
West Yorkshire
HX1 1UJ

HIGHBURY SCHOOL
Lower Edge Road, Brighouse, West Yorkshire HD6 3LD
Type: Co-educational Day Only
Special needs: ADD ADHD ASD **ASP** BESD **CP** DOW DYC DYP DYS **EPI** HEA **HI** MLD **PMLD SLD** SP&LD TOU VI
Wheelchair access: W

RAVENSCLIFFE HIGH SCHOOL AND SPORTS COLLEGE
Skircoat Green, Halifax, West Yorkshire HX3 0RZ
Type: Co-educational Day Only 11–19
Special needs: ASD CP **DOW** EPI HI **IM** MLD PMLD SLD SP&LD VI
Wheelchair access: WA2

WOOD BANK SPECIAL SCHOOL
Dene View, Halifax, West Yorkshire HX2 6PB
Website: www.woodbank. calderdale.sch.uk
Type: Co-educational Day Only 2–11
Special needs: ASD **ASP** CP **PMLD SLD**
Wheelchair access: WA1

Kirklees Education Service

8th Floor, Oldgate House
2 Oldgate
Huddersfield
West Yorkshire
HD1 6QW

FAIRFIELD SCHOOL
Dale Lane, Heckmondwike, West Yorkshire WF16 9PA
Type: Co-educational Day Only 3–19
Special needs: **PMLD SLD**
Wheelchair access: WA1

HARTSHEAD MOOR SCHOOL
Halifax Road, Cleckheaton, West Yorkshire BD19 6LP
Website: www. hartsheadmoorschool.org.uk
Type: Co-educational 5–16
Special needs: MLD
Wheelchair access: W

HIGHFIELDS SCHOOL
Cemetery Road, Huddersfield, West Yorkshire HD1 5NF
Type: Co-educational Day Only 3–19
Special needs: ASD **PMLD SLD**
Wheelchair access: W

LONGLEY SCHOOL
Dog Kennel Bank, Huddersfield,
West Yorkshire HD5 8JE
Type: Co-educational Day Only
5–16
Special needs: ADD ADHD ASD
ASP BESD CP DOW DYP DYS
EPI HEA HI **MLD** SP&LD VI
Wheelchair access: W

LYDGATE SCHOOL
Kirkroyds Lane, Huddersfield,
West Yorkshire HD7 7LS
Type: Co-educational Day Only
5–16
Special needs: **MLD**
Wheelchair access: WA1

**NORTONTHORPE HALL
SCHOOL**
Busker Lane, Huddersfield,
West Yorkshire HD8 9JU
Type: Co-educational Boarding
and Day 7–16
Special needs: **BESD**

RAVENSHALL SCHOOL
Ravensthorpe Road, Dewsbury,
West Yorkshire WF12 9EE
Website: www.ravenshallschool.
org.uk
Type: Co-educational Day Only
5–16
Special needs: ADHD BESD
DOW **MLD** SP&LD
Wheelchair access: WA1

TURNSHAWS SCHOOL
Turnshaws Avenue,
Huddersfield, West Yorkshire
HD8 0TJ
Website: www.cabletel-schools.
org.uk/turnshaws.special.school
Type: Co-educational Day Only
3–19
Special needs: ASD PMLD SLD
Wheelchair access: W

Leeds City Council

Civic Hall
Calverley Street
Leeds
West Yorkshire
LS1 1UR

BROOMFIELD SCHOOL
Broom Place, Leeds,
West Yorkshire LS10 3JP
Type: Co-educational Day Only
2–19
Special needs: ASD CP **MLD**
PMLD SLD VI
Wheelchair access: WA2

ELMETE CENTRAL BESD SILC
Elmete Lane, Leeds,
West Yorkshire LS8 2LJ
Type: Co-educational Day Only
11–16
Special needs: **BESD**

GREEN MEADOWS SCHOOL
Bradford Road, Guiseley,
West Yorkshire LS20 8PP
Type: Co-educational Day Only
2–19
Special needs: ASD **ASP** VI

**JOHN JAMIESON SCHOOL &
TECHNOLOGY COLLEGE**
Hollin Hill Drive, Leeds,
West Yorkshire LS8 2PW
Type: Co-educational Day Only
Special needs: CP HEA **MLD**
PMLD SLD SP&LD
Wheelchair access: WA1

**NW SPECIALIST INCLUSIVE
LEARNING CENTRE**
Tongue Lane, Leeds,
West Yorkshire LS6 4QD
Type: Co-educational Day Only
2–19
Special needs: EPI HI **PMLD** VI
Wheelchair access: W

WEST OAKS SCHOOL
Westwood Way, Leeds,
West Yorkshire LS23 6DX
Type: Co-educational Day Only
2–19
Special needs: ASD **ASP BESD**
CB DOW PMLD SLD
Wheelchair access: WA1

**WEST SILC – SPECIALIST
INCLUSIVE LEARNING
CENTRE**
Milestone Site, Stanningley,
West Yorkshire LS28 6HL
Type: Co-educational Day Only
2–19
Special needs: **MLD PMLD SLD**
Wheelchair access: WA1

Wakefield Metropolitan District Council

Town Hall
Wood Street
Wakefield
West Yorkshire
WF1 2HQ

THE FELKIRK SCHOOL
Highwell Hill Lane, Barnsley,
South Yorkshire S72 9DF
Type: Co-educational Boarding
and Day 11–16
Special needs: **BESD**

HIGHFIELD SCHOOL
Gawthorpe Lane, Ossett,
West Yorkshire WF5 9BS
Type: Co-educational Day Only
11–16
Special needs: ADD ADHD ASD
ASP **MLD** SLD VI
Wheelchair access: W

**KINGSLAND PRIMARY
SCHOOL**
Aberford Road, Wakefield,
West Yorkshire WF3 4BA
Website: www.kingsland.
wakefield.sch.uk
Type: Co-educational Day Only
2–11
Special needs: ASD **PMLD SLD**
Wheelchair access: WA1

OAKFIELD PARK SCHOOL
Barnsley Road, Wakefield,
West Yorkshire WF7 7DT
Type: Co-educational Day Only
11–19
Special needs: ASD **PMLD SLD**
Wheelchair access: WA1

**WAKEFIELD PATHWAYS
SCHOOL**
Poplar Avenue, Wakefield,
West Yorkshire WF10 3QJ
Type: Co-educational Day Only
4–11
Special needs: ASD

NORTHERN IRELAND

COUNTY ANTRIM

Belfast Area Education/ Library Board

40 Academy Street
Belfast
BT1 2NQ

CASTLE TOWER SCHOOL
22 Old Ballymoney Road, Ballymena, County Antrim BT43 6LX
Type: Co-educational Day Only 3–19
Special needs: **SLD**
Wheelchair access: WA1

CEDAR LODGE SPECIAL SCHOOL
Gray's Lane, Belfast, County Antrim BT36 7EB
Type: Co-educational Day Only 4–16
Special needs: ADHD ASD **ASP EPI HEA MLD** SP&LD
Wheelchair access: WA1

CLARAWOOD SCHOOL
Clarawood Park, Belfast, County Antrim BT5 6FR
Website: www.niyouthinfo.org
Type: Co-educational Day Only 8–11
Special needs: ADD ADHD ASP **BESD** DYP DYS MLD

DUNFANE SCHOOL
91 Fry's Road, Ballymena, County Antrim BT43 7EN
Type: Co-educational
Special needs: ADD BESD DOW DYP EPI MLD SP&LD VI
Wheelchair access: W

FLEMING FULTON SCHOOL
Upper Malone Road, Belfast, County Antrim BT9 6TY
Website: www.flemingfulton. org.uk
Type: Co-educational Day and Boarding 2–19
Special needs: **IM** SP&LD
Wheelchair access: WA1

GLENVEAGH SPECIAL SCHOOL
Harberton Park, Belfast, County Antrim BT9 6TX
Type: Co-educational Day Only
Special needs: ASD PMLD **SLD**

GREENWOOD HOUSE ASSESSMENT CENTRE
Greenwood Avenue, Belfast, County Antrim BT4 3JJ
Type: Co-educational Day Only 4–7
Special needs: ADD ADHD ASD ASP BESD DYS EPI HEA HI **MLD SLD** SP&LD VI
Wheelchair access: W

HARBERTON
Harberton Park, Belfast, County Antrim BT9 6TX
Special needs: ADD ADHD BESD DOW DYS MLD SP&LD
Wheelchair access: W

LOUGHSHORE EDUCATIONAL CENTRE
889 Shore Road, Belfast, County Antrim BT36 7DH
Type: Co-educational Day Only 11–17
Special needs: ADD ADHD ASD ASP BESD CB CP DYC DYP DYS EPI HI IM MLD TOU VI
Wheelchair access: W

MITCHELL HOUSE SPECIAL SCHOOL
Marmont, Belfast, County Antrim BT4 2GU
Type: Co-educational Day Only 3–19
Special needs: ASP CP EPI HEA MLD SP&LD
Wheelchair access: W

OAKWOOD SCHOOL ASSESSMENT CENTRE
Harberton Park, Belfast, County Antrim BT9 6TX
Type: Co-educational 3–8
Special needs: ASD BESD CP DOW EPI HEA HI PMLD SLD SP&LD VI
Wheelchair access: WA1

PARK EDUCATION RESOURCE CENTRE
145 Ravenhill Road, Belfast, County Antrim BT6 8GH
Type: Co-educational Day Only 11–19
Special needs: **MLD**

ST FRANCIS DE SALES SPECIAL SCHOOL
Beechmount Drive, Belfast, County Antrim BT12 7LU
Type: Co-educational Day Only

ST GERARD'S EDUCATION RESOURCE CENTRE
Upper Springfield Road, Belfast, County Antrim BT12 7QP
Type: Co-educational Day Only 4–16
Special needs: **MLD**

ST VINCENT'S CENTRE
6 Willowfield Drive, Belfast, County Antrim BT6 8HN

North Eastern Area Education & Library Board

Board Offices, County Hall
182 Galgorm Road
Ballymena
Co. Antrim
BT42 1HN

CASTLE TOWER SCHOOL
Beech Road Campus,
Ballymena, County Antrim
BT43 7EN
Type: Co-educational Day Only
3–11
Special needs: CP EPI HEA
Wheelchair access: WA2
52-week care

HILL CROFT SCHOOL
Abbot's Road, Newtownabbey,
County Antrim BT37 9RB
Type: Co-educational Day Only
Special needs: **SLD**
Wheelchair access: W

KILRONAN SCHOOL
46 Ballyronan Road, Magherafelt,
County Londonderry BT45 6EN
Website: www.kilronanschool.
co.uk
Type: Co-educational Day Only
3–19
Special needs: ASD CP DOW
PMLD **SLD**
Wheelchair access: WA1

RIVERSIDE SCHOOL
Fennel Road, Antrim, County
Antrim BT41 4PB
Type: Co-educational Day Only
3–19
Special needs: ASD EPI PMLD
SLD SP&LD

RODDENSVALE SCHOOL
The Roddens, Larne, County
Antrim BT40 1PU
Type: Co-educational Day Only
4–19
Special needs: IM **PMLD SLD**
Wheelchair access: WA1

ROSSTULLA SCHOOL
2–6 Jordanstown Road,
Newtownabbey, County Antrim
BT37 0QF
Type: Co-educational Day Only
4–17
Special needs: **MLD**
Wheelchair access: WA1

SANDELFORD SCHOOL
8 Rugby Avenue, Coleraine,
County Londonderry BT52 1JL
Type: Co-educational Day Only
Special needs: **SLD**

THORNFIELD SPECIAL SCHOOL
8–12 Jordanstown Road,
Newtownabbey, County Antrim
BT37 0QF
Type: Co-educational Day Only
Special needs: SP&LD
Wheelchair access: WA1

South Eastern Area Education & Library Board

Grahamsbridge Road
Dundonald
Belfast
County Antrim
BT16 2HS

ARDMORE HOUSE SCHOOL & SUPPORT SERVICE
95a Saul Street, Downpatrick,
County Down BT30 6NJ
Type: Co-educational Day Only
11–16
Special needs: **BESD**

BEECHLAWN SCHOOL
3 Dromore Road, Hillsborough,
County Down BT26 6PA
Website: www.beechlawnschool.
co.uk
Type: Co-educational Day Only
10–16
Special needs: ADHD ASD ASP
DYP **DYS MLD**
Wheelchair access: W

BROOKFIELD SCHOOL
65 Halfpenny Gate Road,
Craigavon, County Armagh
BT67 0HP
Website: www.brookfieldsch.
ik.org
Type: Co-educational Day Only
5–11
Special needs: ADD ASD **MLD**
SP&LD
Wheelchair access: WA1

CLIFTON SCHOOL
292A Old Belfast Road, Bangor,
County Down BT19 1RH
Type: Co-educational Day Only
3–19
Special needs: ASD **ASP** BESD
CB CP DOW EPI HI **PMLD SLD**
SP&LD VI
Wheelchair access: WA1

KILLARD HOUSE SCHOOL
North Road, Newtownards,
County Down BT23 3AP
Type: Girls Day Only 4–16
Special needs: MLD SLD SP&LD
Wheelchair access: WA3

KNOCKEVIN SCHOOL
29 Racecourse Hill, Downpatrick,
County Down BT30 6PU
Special needs: SLD

LAKEWOOD SPECIAL SCHOOL
169 Rathgael Road, Bangor,
County Down BT10 1TA
Type: Co-educational

LINDSAY SPECIAL SCHOOL
Foster Green Hospital, Belfast,
County Antrim BT8 4HD
Type: Co-educational Day and
Boarding 3–15
Special needs: **ADHD ASD** ASP
BESD DYP DYS HEA MLD

LONGSTONE SCHOOL
Millar's Lane, Belfast, County
Antrim BT16 0DA
Type: Co-educational Day Only
4–16
Special needs: BESD MLD
Wheelchair access: W

PARKVIEW SCHOOL
2 Brokerstown Road, Lisburn,
County Antrim BT28 2EE
Type: Co-educational Day Only
3–19
Special needs: ASD **ASP PMLD
SLD**
Wheelchair access: WA1

TOR BANK SCHOOL
718 Upper Newtownards Road,
Belfast, County Down BT16 1RG
Website: www.torbankschool.
org.uk
Type: Co-educational Day Only
3–19
Special needs: ADD ADHD ASD
ASP BESD CB CP DOW EPI HEA
HI IM MLD PMLD SLD SP&LD
TOU VI
Wheelchair access: WA2

COUNTY ARMAGH

Southern Education and Library Board

**3 Charlemont Place
The Mall
Armagh
County Armagh
BT61 9AX**

CEARA SCHOOL
Sloan Street, Craigavon, County
Armagh BT61 8NY
Website: www.cearaschool.com
Type: Co-educational 4–18

DONARD SCHOOL
Castlewellan Road, Banbridge,
County Down BT32 4XY
Type: Co-educational Day Only
Special needs: ASD **ASP BESD**
PMLD SLD
Wheelchair access: WA1

LISANALLY SPECIAL SCHOOL
85 Lisanally Lane, Armagh,
County Armagh BT61 7HF
Type: Co-educational Day Only
4–19
Special needs: ADD ADHD ASD
ASP BESD CP DOW DYP DYS
MLD PMLD SLD

RATHFRILAND HILL SCHOOL
Rathriland Road, Newry, County
Down BT34 1HU
Type: Co-educational Day Only
3–19
Special needs: ASD **ASP PMLD
SLD**

**SPERRINVIEW SPECIAL
SCHOOL**
8 Coalisland Road, Dungannon,
County Tyrone BT71 6FA
Website: www.sperrinview.ik.org
Type: Co-educational Day Only
3–19
Special needs: ASD **ASP** BESD
CB **CP DOW** EPI HEA HI IM
PMLD SLD SP&LD VI W
Wheelchair access: WA1

COUNTY TYRONE

Western Area Education and Library Board

1 Hospital Road
Omagh
County Tyrone
BT79 0AW

BELMONT HOUSE SCHOOL
Racecourse Road, Londonderry, County Londonderry BT48 7RE
Website: www.belmonthouse.lk.org
Type: Co-educational Day Only
3–19
Special needs: BESD **MLD** SP&LD

CRANNY SPECIAL SCHOOL
4a Deverney Road, Cranny, County Tyrone BT79 0JJ
Type: Co-educational Day Only
Special needs: ASD BESD CP DOW EPI HI **PMLD SLD** VI
Wheelchair access: W

ELMBROOK SCHOOL
Derrygonnelly, Enniskillen, County Fermanagh BT7 4AY
Type: Co-educational Day Only
4–19
Special needs: ASD **ASP** BESD CP **DOW** EPI HEA **PMLD SLD** SP&LD
Wheelchair access: WA1

ERNE SPECIAL SCHOOL
Derrygonnelly Road, Enniskillen, County Fermanagh BT74 7EY
Type: Co-educational Day Only
4–16
Special needs: **MLD**
Wheelchair access: W

FOYLE VIEW SCHOOL
15 Racecourse Road, Londonderry, County Londonderry BT48 7RB
Website: www.fofeview.com
Type: Co-educational Day Only
3–19
Special needs: ASD PMLD **SLD**
Wheelchair access: W

GLASVEY SPECIAL SCHOOL
15 Loughermore Road, Limavady, County Londonderry BT49 9PB
Type: Co-educational Day Only
3–19
Special needs: ASD BESD CP DYS EPI HEA HI **PMLD SLD** SP&LD VI
Wheelchair access: W

HEATHERBANK SCHOOL
17 Deverney Road, Omagh, County Tyrone BT79 0ND
Type: Co-educational Day Only
3–18
Special needs: **MLD SLD**
Wheelchair access: WA1

LIMEGROVE SCHOOL
2 Ballyquin Road, Limavady, County Londonderry BT49 9ET
Type: Co-educational Day Only
3–16
Special needs: BESD **MLD**

SCOTLAND

ABERDEENSHIRE

Aberdeen City Council

Summerhill Education Centre
Stronsay Drive
Aberdeen
AB15 6JA

ABERDEEN SCHOOL FOR THE DEAF
Sunnybank School, Aberdeen,
Aberdeenshire AB24 4NJ
Type: Co-educational Day Only
3–12
Special needs: **HI**
Wheelchair access: WA3

BEECHWOOD SCHOOL
Raeden Park Road, Aberdeen,
Aberdeenshire AB15 5PD
Type: Co-educational Day Only
5–18
Special needs: MLD SLD SP&LD
Wheelchair access: W

CORDYCE SPECIAL SCHOOL
Riverview Drive, Aberdeen,
Aberdeenshire AB21 7NF
Type: Co-educational Day Only
11–16
Special needs: **BESD**

HAZLEWOOD SCHOOL
Fernielea Road, Aberdeen,
Aberdeenshire AB15 6GU
Type: Co-educational Day Only
4–18
Special needs: ADHD ASD CP
DOW EPI HI MLD PMLD SLD
SP&LD VI
Wheelchair access: WA1

MARLPOOL SCHOOL
Cloverfield Gardens, Aberdeen,
Aberdeenshire AB21 9QN
Website: www.marlpool.ik.org
Type: Co-educational Day Only
Special needs: ADHD ASD **ASP**
CP DOW EPI IM **MLD SLD**
SP&LD VI
Wheelchair access: WA2

RAEDEN CENTRE
Mid-Stocket Road, Aberdeen,
Aberdeen City AB15 5PD
Type: Co-educational Day Only
3–5
Special needs: **ADHD** ASD **ASP**
CP DOW MLD PMLD
Wheelchair access: WA1

VISION SUPPORT SERVICE
Newhills School, Aberdeen,
Aberdeenshire AB21 9UB
Type: Co-educational Day Only
Special needs: VI
Wheelchair access: WA1

WOODLANDS SCHOOL
Regent Walk, Aberdeen,
Aberdeenshire AB24 1SX
Type: Co-educational Day Only
Special needs: **PMLD**
Wheelchair access: W

Aberdeenshire Council

Woodhill
Westburn
Aberdeen
AB16 5GB

THE ANNA RITCHIE SCHOOL
Grange Gardens, Peterhead,
Aberdeenshire AB42 2AP
Wheelchair access: WA2

BANKHEAD ACADEMY SEN BASE
Bankhead Avenue, Aberdeen,
Aberdeenshire AB21 9ES

CARRONHILL SCHOOL
Mill of Forest Road, Stonehaven,
Kincardineshire AB39 2G2
Type: Co-educational Day Only
3–18
Special needs: ASD **ASP PMLD SLD**
Wheelchair access: WA1

CENTRAL PRIMARY SCHOOL
St Peter Street, Peterhead,
Aberdeenshire AB42 1QD
Type: Co-educational Day Only
Special needs: SP&LD

ST ANDREW'S SCHOOL
St Andrew's Gardens, Inverurie,
Aberdeenshire AB51 3XT
Type: Co-educational Day Only
3–16
Special needs: ASD BESD CP
EPI HI MLD PMLD SLD SP&LD VI

ARGYLL AND BUTE

Argyll and Bute Council

Kilmory
Lochgilphead
Argyll and Bute
PA31 8RT

DRUMMORE DEVELOPMENT CENTRE
Soroba Road, Oban, Argyll and Bute PA34 4SB
Special needs: ASD DYS HI MLD PMLD SLD SP&LD

PARKLANDS SCHOOL
27 Charlotte Street, Helensburgh, Argyll and Bute G84 7EZ
Type: Co-educational Day Only 5–18
Special needs: ASD ASP DOW **PMLD SLD**
Wheelchair access: W

WHITEGATES LEARNING CENTRE
Lochgilphead, Argyll and Bute PA31 8SY

EAST AYRSHIRE

East Ayrshire Council

London Road
Kilmarnock
East Ayrshire
KA3 7BU

HILLSIDE SCHOOL
Dalgleish Avenue, Cumnock, East Ayrshire KA18 1QQ
Type: Co-educational Day Only 0–10
Special needs: ASD CP DOW DYP PMLD SLD
Wheelchair access: W

PARK SCHOOL
Grassyards Road, Kilmarnock, East Ayrshire KA3 7BB
Special needs: ASD BESD CP DOW DYP EPI MLD SP&LD
Wheelchair access: W

SOUTH PARK SCHOOL
38 Belmont Avenue, Ayr, South Ayrshire KA7 2NA
Type: Boys Day Only 3–16

WITCHHILL SCHOOL
Witch Road, Kilmarnock, East Ayrshire KA3 1JF
Type: Co-educational Day Only
Special needs: **PMLD**
Wheelchair access: WA1

WOODSTOCK SCHOOL
30 North Hamilton Street, Kilmarnock, East Ayrshire KA1 2QJ
Type: Co-educational Day Only 5–19
Special needs: ASD **SLD**
Wheelchair access: W

NORTH AYRSHIRE

North Ayrshire Council

Education Department
Cunninghame House
Irvine
Ayrshire
KA12 8EE

HAYSHOLM SCHOOL
Bank Street, Irvine, North Ayrshire KA12 0NE
Type: Co-educational Day Only 5–16

JAMES MACFARLANE SCHOOL
Dalry Road, Ardrossan, North Ayrshire KA22 7DQ
Type: Co-educational Day Only 2–18
Special needs: ASD **ASP** CP EPI **PMLD** SLD
Wheelchair access: W

JAMES REID SCHOOL
Primrose Place, Saltcoats, North Ayrshire KA21 6LH
Type: Co-educational Day Only 5–18
Special needs: **ADD** ADHD ASD ASP **BESD** CP DOW DYP DYS EPI HEA HI **MLD** SP&LD VI
Wheelchair access: W

STANECASTLE SCHOOL
Burns Crescent, Irvine, North
Ayrshire KA11 1AQ
Type: Co-educational Day Only
5–18
Special needs: ADHD ASD BESD
MLD SLD SP&LD VI
Wheelchair access: WA1

SOUTH AYRSHIRE

South Ayrshire Council

Educational Services
Wellington Square
Ayr
South Ayrshire
KA7 1DR

CRAIGPARK SCHOOL
Belmont Avenue, Ayr, South
Ayrshire KA7 2ND
Type: Co-educational Day Only
2–19
Special needs: CP DOW EPI
PMLD VI
Wheelchair access: WA1

INVERGARVEN SCHOOL
Henrietta Street, Girvan, South
Ayrshire KA26 9AL
Type: Co-educational Day Only

CLACKMANNANSHIRE

Clackmannanshire Council

Greenfield
Alloa
Clackmannanshire
FK10 2AD

FAIRFIELD SCHOOL
Pompee Road, Alloa,
Clackmannanshire FK10 3BX
Type: Co-educational Day Only
Special needs: **PMLD SLD**
Wheelchair access: WA1

LOCHIES SCHOOL
Gartmorn Road, Sauchie,
Clackmannanshire FK10 3PB
Type: Co-educational Day Only
5–12
Special needs: ADHD ASD **ASP**
BESD CP DOW DYP DYS EPI
SLD SP&LD
Wheelchair access: WA1

DUMFRIES & GALLOWAY

Dumfries and Galloway Council

Council Offices
English Street
Dumfries
Dumfries & Galloway
DG1 2DD

ELM BANK SCHOOL
Lovers Walk, Dumfries, Dumfries & Galloway DG1 1DP
Type: Co-educational Day Only
12–16
Special needs: **BESD**

LANGLANDS SCHOOL
Loreburn Park, Dumfries, Dumfries & Galloway DG1 1LS
Type: Co-educational Day Only
5–18
Special needs: ASD CB CP DOW EPI IM **PMLD** SLD SP&LD VI
Wheelchair access: WA1

STRANRAER ACADEMY
McMaster's Road, Stranraer, Dumfries & Galloway DG9 8BY
Website: www.schools.gabbitas.co.uk
Type: Co-educational Day Only
Special needs: ADHD **ASD** ASP BESD CP DOW DYP **DYS** EPI HEA HI **MLD** PMLD SLD SP&LD VI
Wheelchair access: W

DUNDEE

Dundee City Council

Floor 8, Tayside House
Crichton Street
Dundee
DD1 3RZ

KINGSPARK SCHOOL
5 Glenaffric Terrace, Dundee DD3 8HF
Type: Co-educational Day Only
5–18
Special needs: ASD CP EPI MLD PMLD SLD SP&LD
Wheelchair access: W

EAST DUNBARTONSHIRE

East Dunbartonshire LEA

Civic Way
Kirkintilloch
East Dunbartonshire
G66 4TJ

CAMPSIE VIEW SCHOOL
Boghead Road, Lenzie, East Dunbartonshire G66 4DR
Type: Co-educational Day Only
2–19
Special needs: ASD **ASP** CP DOW EPI **PMLD** SLD SP&LD VI
Wheelchair access: W

MERKLAND SCHOOL
Langmuir Road, Kirkintilloch, East Dunbartonshire G66 2QF
Type: Co-educational Day Only
5–18
Special needs: **MLD**
Wheelchair access: WA1

WEST DUNBARTONSHIRE

West Dunbartonshire Council

Garshake Road
Dumbarton
West Dunbartonshire
G82 3PU

CUNARD SCHOOL
Whitecrook, Clydebank, West
Dunbartonshire G81 1RQ
Type: Co-educational Day Only
5–12
Special needs: **BESD** SP&LD

KILPATRICK SCHOOL
Mountblow Road, Clydebank,
West Dunbartonshire G81 4SW
Type: Co-educational Day Only
Special needs: MLD PMLD SLD
Wheelchair access: W

FALKIRK

Falkirk LEA

McLaren House
Marchmont Avenue
Polmont
Falkirk
FK2 0NZ

CARRONGRANGE SCHOOL
Carrongrange Avenue, Falkirk
FK5 3BH
Type: Co-educational Day Only
11–18
Special needs: ASD **MLD** PMLD
SLD
Wheelchair access: WA1

DUNDAS DAY UNIT
Grangemouth, Falkirk FK3 9DL
Special needs: BESD

EDUCATION ASSESSMENT UNIT
Polmont, Falkirk FK2 0XS
Type: Co-educational Day Only
12–16
Special needs: **BESD**

FALKIRK DAY UNIT
Hope Street, Central FK1 4HA

TORWOOD SCHOOL
Stirling Road, Falkirk FK5 4SR
Type: Co-educational Day Only
Special needs: ASD CP DOW EPI
HEA SLD SP&LD
Wheelchair access: WA1

WINDSOR PARK SCHOOL
Bantaskine Road, Falkirk FK1 5HT
Type: Co-educational Day Only
4–18
Special needs: **HI** VI
Wheelchair access: WA1

FIFE

Fife Council

Auchterderran Centre
Woodend Road
Cardenden
Fife
KY5 0NE

HEADWELL SCHOOL
Headwell Avenue, Dunfermline,
Fife KY12 0JU
Type: Co-educational Day Only
5–18
Special needs: ASD **ASP EPI**

HYNDHEAD SCHOOL
Barncraig Street, Leven, Fife
KY8 1JE
Type: Co-educational Day Only
3–19
Special needs: ASD DOW EPI IM
PMLD SLD
Wheelchair access: WA2

JOHN FERGUS SCHOOL
Erskine Place, Glenrothes, Fife
KY7 4JB
Type: Co-educational Day Only
Special needs: ADD ASD **ASP**
BESD CP DOW EPI HI **PMLD**
SLD VI
Wheelchair access: WA1

KILMARON SCHOOL
Balgarvie Road, Cupar, Fife
KY15 4PE
Website: www.fife-ed.org.uk/
europe/k.Imaron
Type: Co-educational
Special needs: ASD ASP BESD
CP DOW EPI MLD PMLD **SLD**
Wheelchair access: W

LOCHGELLY NORTH SCHOOL
Lochgelly, Fife KY5 9PE
Type: Co-educational Day Only
4–19
Special needs: MLD PMLD SLD
Wheelchair access: W

ROBERT HENRYSON SCHOOL
Linburn Road, Dunfermline, Fife
KY11 4LD
Type: Co-educational Day Only
2–19
Special needs: ASD CP EPI HI
PMLD SLD VI
Wheelchair access: WA1

ROSSLYN SCHOOL
Viewforth Terrace, Kirkcaldy, Fife
KY1 3BP
Type: Co-educational Day Only
Special needs: ASD PMLD SLD
Wheelchair access: W

GLASGOW

East Renfrewshire Council

Eastwood Park
Rouken Glen Road
Giffnock
Glasgow
G46 6UG

ISOBEL MAIR SCHOOL
1a Drumby Cresent, Clarkston,
Glasgow G76 7HN

Glasgow City Council

Wheatley House
25 Cochrane Street
Merchant City
Glasgow
G1 1HL

ABERCORN SCHOOL
195 Garscube Road, Glasgow
G4 9QH
Type: Co-educational Day Only
11–18
Special needs: **MLD**

ASHCRAIG SCHOOL
100 Avenue End Road, Glasgow
G33 3SW
Type: Co-educational Day Only
12–19
Special needs: CP DYP EPI VI
Wheelchair access: WA1

BANNERMAN COMMUNICATION DISORDER UNIT
c/o Bannerman High, Glasgow
G69 7NS
Type: Boys Day Only 11–16
Special needs: ASD ASP

BROOMLEA SCHOOL
168 Broomhill Drive, Glasgow
G11 7NH
Type: Co-educational Day Only
2–12
Special needs: PMLD

CARNBOOTH SCHOOL
Carnbooth House, Glasgow
G76 9EG
Type: Co-educational Boarding
and Day
Special needs: HI VI
Wheelchair access: W

CARTVALE SCHOOL
80 Vicarfield Street, Glasgow
G51 2DF
Type: Boys Day Only 11–16
Special needs: **BESD**

CROFTCROIGHN SCHOOL
290 Mossvale Road, Glasgow
G33 5NY
Website: www.croftcroighn-pri.
glasgow.sch.uk
Type: Co-educational Day Only
2–11
Special needs: ASD CP EPI
PMLD SLD
Wheelchair access: W

**CROOKSTON LANGUAGE
UNIT**
c/o St Monica's Primary, Glasgow
G53 5SR
Special needs: SP&LD

**DARNLEY VISUAL
IMPAIRMENT UNIT**
c/o Darnley Primary, Glasgow
G53 7HT
Type: Co-educational Day Only
Special needs: VI

**DRUMCHAPEL LEARNING
CENTRE**
77 Hecla Avenue, Glasgow
G15 8LX

DRUMMORE SCHOOL
129 Drummore Road, Glasgow
G15 7NH
Type: Co-educational Day Only
5–12
Special needs: **MLD**

DUNTARVIE PRE-SCHOOL
c/o Cadder Primary, Glasgow
G23 5AR
Type: Co-educational Day Only
3–5
Special needs: ASD **ASP** SP&LD
Wheelchair access: WA3

EASTMUIR SCHOOL
211 Hallhill Road, Glasgow
G33 4QL
Type: Co-educational Day Only
4–11
Special needs: ASD **MLD**

GADBURN SCHOOL
70 Rockfield Road, Glasgow
G21 3DZ
Type: Co-educational Day Only
5–12
Special needs: **MLD**
Wheelchair access: W

HAMPDEN SCHOOL
80 Ardnahoe Avenue, Glasgow
G42 0DL
Type: Day Only
Special needs: ASD DOW EPI
PMLD SLD SP&LD
Wheelchair access: W

HOLLYBROOK SCHOOL
135 Hollybrook Street, Glasgow
G42 7HU
Type: Co-educational Day Only
12–19
Special needs: **MLD**

HOWFORD SCHOOL
487 Crookston Road, Glasgow
G53 7TX
Type: Co-educational Day Only
Special needs: ASD MLD
Wheelchair access: WA1

KELBOURNE SCHOOL
109 Hotspur Street, Glasgow
G20 8LH
Type: Co-educational Day Only
2–12
Special needs: **CP** EPI **HEA** MLD
SP&LD VI
Wheelchair access: WA1

KELVIN SCHOOL
69 Nairn Street, Glasgow G3 8SE
Type: Co-educational Day Only
Special needs: ASD BESD CP
EPI HEA HI MLD PMLD SLD
SP&LD VI
Wheelchair access: W

KENNYHILL SCHOOL
375 Cumbernauld Road,
Glasgow G31 3LP
Type: Co-educational Day Only
Special needs: **MLD**

KIRKRIGGS SCHOOL
500 Croftfoot Road, Glasgow
G45 0NJ
Type: Co-educational Day Only
Special needs: ADHD ASD CB
MLD SLD
Wheelchair access: WA2

LADYWELL SCHOOL
12A Victoria Park Drive South,
Glasgow G14 9RU
Type: Co-educational Day Only
12–16

LANGLANDS SCHOOL
100 Mallaig Road, Glasgow
G51 4PE
Type: Co-educational Day Only
2–12

LINBURN SCHOOL
77 Linburn Road, Glasgow
G52 4EX
Type: Co-educational Day Only
12–18
Special needs: PMLD SLD
Wheelchair access: WA1

MIDDLEFIELD SCHOOL
26 Partickhill Road, Glasgow
G11 5BP
Type: Co-educational Day and
Boarding 5–16
Special needs: **ASD ASP**

MILTON SCHOOL
6 Liddesdale Terrace, Glasgow
G22 7HL
Type: Co-educational Day Only
12–18

NEWHILLS SCHOOL
Newhills Road, Glasgow G33 4HJ
Type: Co-educational Day Only
12–18
Special needs: PMLD SLD
Wheelchair access: WA1

RICHMOND PARK SCHOOL
30 Logan Street, Glasgow
G5 0HP
Type: Co-educational Day Only
4–11
Special needs: CP EPI MLD
SP&LD

**ROSEPARK TUTORIAL
CENTRE**
Floor 2, Room 9, Glasgow
G11 7QZ

ROSEVALE SCHOOL
48 Scalpay Street, Glasgow
G22 7DD
Type: Co-educational Day Only
5–12

ROSSHALL ACADEMY
Visual Impairment Unit, Glasgow
G52 3PD
Type: Co-educational Day Only
12–18
Special needs: VI
Wheelchair access: WA2

ROYSTON LANGUAGE UNIT
c/o Royston Primary, Glasgow
G21 2NU
Type: Co-educational Day Only
5–8
Special needs: SP&LD

RUCHILL COMMUNICATION UNIT
Ruchill Primary School, Glasgow
G20 9HW
Type: Co-educational Day Only
1–7
Special needs: **ASD ASP**
Wheelchair access: WA3

ST AIDAN'S SCHOOL
255 Rigby Street, Glasgow
G32 6DJ
Type: Co-educational Day Only
Special needs: MLD
Wheelchair access: WA1

ST CHARLES' LANGUAGE UNIT
c/o St Charles' Primary, Glasgow
G20 6BG

ST JOAN OF ARC SCHOOL
722 Balmore Road, Glasgow
G22 6QS
Type: Co-educational Day Only
12–19
Special needs: **MLD**

ST JOSEPH'S HEARING IMPAIRED UNIT
c/o St Joseph's Primary, Glasgow
G4 9QX
Type: Co-educational Day Only
5–12 (SEN)
Special needs: **HI**

ST KEVIN'S SCHOOL
25 Fountainwell Road, Glasgow
G21 1TN
Type: Co-educational Day Only
5–12
Special needs: ASD **ASP BESD MLD** SP&LD
Wheelchair access: W

ST OSWALD'S SCHOOL
83 Brunton Street, Glasgow
G44 3NF
Type: Co-educational Day Only
Special needs: ADD ASD BESD
DOW DYS EPI **MLD**

ST RAYMOND'S SCHOOL
384 Drakemire Drive, Glasgow
G45 9SR
Type: Co-educational
Special needs: ADD ADHD ASD
BESD DOW DYP DYS EPI HI
MLD SP&LD
Wheelchair access: W

ST VINCENT'S (TOLLCROSS) SCHOOL
30 Fullarton Avenue, Glasgow
G32 8NJ
Type: Co-educational Day Only
2–18
Special needs: HI
Wheelchair access: W

TORYGLEN COMMUNICATION DISORDER UNIT
6 Drummreoch Place, Glasgow
G42 0ER
Type: Co-educational Day Only
Special needs: **ASD ASP**

HIGHLAND

The Highland Council

Glenurquhart Road
Inverness
Highland
IV3 5NX

DRUMMOND SCHOOL
Drummond Road, Inverness,
Highland IV2 4NZ
Type: Co-educational Day Only
2–19
Special needs: ADD ADHD ASD
ASP BESD CB CP DOW DYC
DYP DYS EPI HEA HI IM MLD
PMLD SLD SP&LD TOU VI
Wheelchair access: WA2

ST CLEMENT'S SCHOOL
Tulloch Street, Dingwall,
Highland IV15 9JZ
Type: Co-educational Day Only
3–19
Special needs: ASD **ASP CP DOW PMLD SLD**
Wheelchair access: W

ST DUTHUS SCHOOL
Old Academy, Tain, Highland
IV19 1ED
Type: Co-educational Day Only
3–19
Special needs: ASD **ASP** BESD
DOW **PMLD SLD**
Wheelchair access: W

INVERCLYDE

Inverclyde Education Services

105 Dalrymple Street
Greenock
Renfrewshire
Inverclyde
PA15 1HT

GARVEL SCHOOL
Chester Road, Greenock,
Inverclyde PA16 0TT
Type: Co-educational Day Only
2–11
Special needs: **HI**
Wheelchair access: W

GLENBURN SCHOOL
Inverkip Road, Greenock,
Inverclyde PA16 0QG
Type: Co-educational Day Only
Special needs: MLD SP&LD
Wheelchair access: W

LILYBANK SCHOOL
Birkmyre Avenue, Port Glasgow,
Inverclyde PA14 5AN
Type: Co-educational Day Only
5–18
Special needs: ASD CP DOW EPI
PMLD SLD
Wheelchair access: WA1

NORTH LANARKSHIRE

North Lanarkshire Council

Municipal Buildings
Kildonan Street
Coatbridge
North Lanarkshire
ML5 3BT

BOTHWELL PARK SCHOOL
Annan Street, Motherwell,
North Lanarkshire ML1 2DL
Type: Co-educational Day Only
12–18

CLYDEVIEW SCHOOL
Magna Street, Motherwell,
North Lanarkshire ML1 3QZ
Type: Co-educational Day Only
3–19
Special needs: **SLD** SP&LD

CRAIGHALBERT CENTRE
CUMBERNAULD
1 Craighalbert Way,
Cumbernauld, Glasgow G68 0LS
Website: www.craighalbert.
org.uk
Type: Co-educational Day Only
Special needs: **CP** EPI IM MLD
Wheelchair access: WA1

DRUMPARK SCHOOL
Coatbridge Road, Bargeddie,
North Lanarkshire G69 7TW
Type: Co-educational Day Only
3–18
Special needs: **MLD**
Wheelchair access: W

FALLSIDE SCHOOL
Sanderson Avenue, Uddingston,
North Lanarkshire G71 6JZ
Type: Co-educational Day Only
12–18

FIRPARK SCHOOL
Firpark Street, Motherwell,
North Lanarkshire ML1 2PR
Type: Co-educational Day Only
3–18
Special needs: ASD BESD CP
DOW DYP DYS EPI HI MLD **SLD**
SP&LD VI
Wheelchair access: W

GLENCRYAN SCHOOL
Greenfaulds Ring Road,
Cumbernauld, North Lanarkshire
G67 2XJ
Type: Co-educational Day Only
3–18
Special needs: ADD ASP DOW
DYC DYP DYS HEA HI MLD
SP&LD TOU VI
Wheelchair access: W

MAVISBANK SCHOOL
Mitchell Street, Airdrie,
North Lanarkshire ML6 0EB
Type: Co-educational 2–19
Special needs: **PMLD**
Wheelchair access: WA1

PENTLAND SCHOOL
Tay Street, Coatbridge,
North Lanarkshire ML5 2NA
Type: Co-educational Day Only
Special needs: **BESD**

PORTLAND HIGH SCHOOL
31 – 33 Kildonan Street,
Coatbridge, North Lanarkshire
ML5 3LG
Type: Co-educational Day Only
12–16

REDBURN SCHOOL
Mossknowe Building,
Cumbernauld, North Lanarkshire
G67 2EL
Type: Co-educational Day Only
2–19
Special needs: ASD BESD CP
DOW EPI PMLD SLD SP&LD VI
Wheelchair access: W

WILLOWBANK SCHOOL
299 Bank Street, Coatbridge,
North Lanarkshire ML5 1EG
Type: Co-educational Day Only
11–17
Special needs: **BESD**

SOUTH LANARKSHIRE

South Lanarkshire Education

Almada Street
Hamilton
ML3 0AA

CRAIGHEAD SCHOOL
Whistleberry Road, Hamilton,
South Lanarkshire ML3 0EG
Website: www.craigheadschool.
org
Type: Co-educational Day Only
5–18
Special needs: ASD ASP DYP
MLD SLD
Wheelchair access: WA1

GREENBURN SCHOOL
Maxwelton Avenue, East Kilbride,
South Lanarkshire G74 3DU
Type: Co-educational Day Only
1–19
Wheelchair access: W

HAMILTON SCHOOL FOR THE DEAF
Wellhall Road, Hamilton,
South Lanarkshire ML3 9UE
Type: Co-educational Day Only
3–11
Special needs: **HI**
Wheelchair access: WA1

KITTOCH SCHOOL
Livingstone Drive, East Kilbride,
South Lanarkshire G75 0AB
Type: Co-educational Day Only
3–5
Special needs: **BESD**

RIDGEPARK RESIDENTIAL SCHOOL
Mousebank Road, Lanark,
South Lanarkshire ML11 7RA

SANDERSON HIGH SCHOOL
High Common Road, East
Kilbride, South Lanarkshire
G74 2LX
Website: www.sanderson.
s-lanark.sch.uk
Type: Co-educational Day Only
11–18
Special needs: ADHD ASD ASP
CP DOW DYP EPI HI MLD PMLD
SLD SP&LD VI
Wheelchair access: WA1

VICTORIA PARK SCHOOL
Market Road, Carluke,
South Lanarkshire ML8 4BE
Type: Co-educational Day Only
3–18
Special needs: ASD BESD CP
DOW EPI PMLD SLD SP&LD VI
Wheelchair access: WA1

WEST MAINS SCHOOL
Logie Park, East Kilbride,
South Lanarkshire G74 4BU
Type: Co-educational Day Only
5–9
Special needs: SP&LD

LOTHIAN

Midlothian Council

Fairfield House
8 Lotham Road
Dalkeith
Midlothian
EH22 3ZG

CUIKEN HOUSE
150 Cuiken Terrace, Penicuik,
Lothian EH26 0AH
Wheelchair access: WA1

SALTERSGATE SCHOOL
3 Cousland Road, Dalkeith,
Lothian
Type: Co-educational Day Only
5–18
Special needs: ADD ASD BESD
DOW DYS EPI HEA MLD SLD
SP&LD
Wheelchair access: WA2

West Lothian LEA

Almondvale Boulevard
Livingston
West Lothian
EH54 6QP

BEATLIE SPECIAL SCHOOL
The Mall, Livingston, Lothian
EH54 5EJ
Type: Co-educational Day Only
3–16
Wheelchair access: WA1

BURNHOUSE SCHOOL
The Avenue, Whitburn, West
Lothian EH47 0BX
Type: Co-educational Day Only
10–16

**CEDARBANK SPECIAL
SCHOOL**
Cedarbank, Livingston, Lothian
EH54 6DR
Type: Co-educational Day Only
3–16

PINEWOOD SPECIAL SCHOOL
Elm Grove, Bathgate, West
Lothian EH47 7OX
Type: Co-educational Day Only
5–18

ORKNEY

Orkney Department of Education & Recreational Services

**Council Offices
Kirkwall
Orkney
KW15 1HP**

**GLAITNESS AURRIDA
SPECIAL SCHOOL**
Pickaquoy Road, Kirkwall,
Orkney KW15 1RP
Type: Co-educational Day and
Boarding 2–18
Special needs: MLD PMLD SLD
Wheelchair access: W

PERTH AND KINROSS

Perth & Kinross Council

**Education & Children's Service
Pullar House
35 Kinnoull Street
Perth
PH1 5GD**

GLEBE SCHOOL
Abbey Road, Perth, Perth and
Kinross PH2 6LW
Type: Co-educational Day and
Boarding 11–18
Special needs: **ADHD ASD ASP
CP DOW EPI IM PMLD SLD** VI
Wheelchair access: WA2

KERSLAND SCHOOL
Ben Nevis Road, Paisley,
Renfrewshire PA2 7BU
Website: www.kersland.sch.uk
Type: Co-educational Day Only
5–18
Special needs: ASD **SLD**
Wheelchair access: WA2

RENFREWSHIRE

Renfrewshire LEA

South Building
Cotton Street
Paisley
Renfrewshire
PA1 1LE

CLIPPENS SCHOOL
Brediland Road, Linwood,
Renfrewshire PA3 3RX
Type: Co-educational Day Only
5–19
Special needs: ASD CB **PMLD
SLD**
Wheelchair access: WA1

HUNTERHILL TUTORIAL CENTRE
Cartha Crescent, Paisley,
Renfrewshire PA2 7EL
Type: Boys Day Only 5–11
Special needs: ADD ADHD
BESD DYS

MARY RUSSELL SCHOOL
Hawkhead Road, Paisley,
Renfrewshire PA2 7BE
Type: Co-educational 5–18

ROXBURGHSHIRE

Scottish Borders Council

Newtown
St Boswell's
Melrose
Roxburghshire
TD6 0SA

BERWICKSHIRE HIGH SCHOOL SPECIAL UNIT
Duns, Scottish Borders
TD11 3QQ
Website: www.berwickshirehs.
org.uk
Type: Co-educational Day Only
Special needs: ASD CP MLD SLD
Wheelchair access: WA2

WILTON PRIMARY SCHOOL SPECIAL SCHOOL
Wellfield Road, Hawick, Scottish
Borders TD9 7EN
Website: www.wilton-pri.
scotborders.sch.uk
Type: Co-educational Day Only
5–13
Special needs: **ASD ASP** BESD
CP DOW DYS EPI **MLD PMLD
SLD**
Wheelchair access: WA1

STIRLING

Stirling Council

Room 213
Viewforth
Stirling
FK8 2ET

CHARLES BROWN SCHOOL
Fallin Primary School, Els Base, Fallin, Stirling FK7 7EJ
Website: www.fallin.primary. ik.org
Type: Co-educational Day Only
Wheelchair access: WA1

KILDEAN SCHOOL
Drip Road, Kildean, Stirling FK8 1RW
Type: Co-educational 3–12

WHINS OF MILTON SPECIAL SCHOOL
Fairhill Road, Stirling FK7 0LL
Type: Co-educational 6–12

WALES

ANGLESEY

Isle of Anglesey County Council

Fforddd Glanhfa
Llangefni
Anglesey
LL77 7TW

YSGOL Y BONT
The Industrial Estate, Anglesey
LL77 7JA
Type: Co-educational Day Only
3–19
Special needs: ASD ASP BESD
CP DOW DYP EPI HEA **PMLD
SLD** SP&LD TOU
Wheelchair access: WA1

BRIDGEND

Bridgend County Borough Council

Civic Offices
Angel Street
Bridgend
CF31 4WB

HERONSBRIDGE SCHOOL
Ewenny Road, Bridgend
CF31 3HT
Type: Co-educational Boarding
and Day 3–19
Special needs: ASD ASP CP
DOW EPI HI PMLD SLD SP&LD
VI
Wheelchair access: WA2

CAERPHILLY

Caerphilly County Borough Council

Caerphilly Road
Ystrad Mynach
Hengoed
Caerphilly
CF82 7EP

**TRINITY FIELDS SCHOOL &
RESOURCE CENTRE**
Caerphilly Road, Hengoed,
Caerphilly CF82 7XW
Website: www.schoolsite.edex.
net/1114
Type: Co-educational 3–19
Special needs: ADHD ASD **ASP**
CP DOW EPI HI **PMLD SLD** VI
Wheelchair access: WA1

CARDIFF

Cardiff County Council

County Hall
Atlantic Wharf
Cardiff
CF10 4UW

THE COURT SCHOOL
96a Station Road, Cardiff
CF4 5UX
Website: www.thecourtsp.cardiff.
sch.uk
Type: Co-educational Day Only
5–11
Special needs: **ADD ADHD ASD**
ASP **BESD CB** DYP **DYS** EPI
MLD SP&LD **TOU**
Wheelchair access: WA3

GREENHILL SCHOOL
Heol Brynglas, Cardiff CF4 6UJ
Type: Co-educational Day Only
11–16
Special needs: **BESD**
Wheelchair access: WA2

THE HOLLIES SCHOOL
Pentwyn Drive, Cardiff CF2 7XG
Type: Co-educational Day Only
3–11
Special needs: ADD ADHD ASD
ASP CP SP&LD
Wheelchair access: WA1

MEADOWBANK SCHOOL
Colwill Road, Cardiff CF14 2QQ
Type: Co-educational Day Only
4–11
Special needs: SP&LD
Wheelchair access: WA1

RIVERBANK SCHOOL
Vincent Road, Cardiff CF5 5AQ
Type: Co-educational Day Only
4–11
Special needs: ADHD ASD BESD
CP DOW DYP EPI HI **MLD SLD**
SP&LD

TY GWYN SCHOOL
Ty Gwyn Road, Cardiff CF23 5JG
Type: Co-educational Day Only
3–19
Special needs: **PMLD** SLD
Wheelchair access: W

WOODLANDS SCHOOL
Vincent Road, Cardiff CF5 5AQ
Type: Co-educational Day Only
11–19
Special needs: HI **MLD SLD**
Wheelchair access: W

CARMARTHENSHIRE

Carmarthenshire County Council

Education Headquarters
County Hall
Carmarthen
SA31 1JP

YSGOL HEOL GOFFA
Heol Goffa, Llanelli,
Carmarthenshire SA15 3LS
Type: Co-educational Day Only
3–19
Special needs: CP EPI **PMLD**
SLD
Wheelchair access: WA1

CONWY

Conwy County Borough Council

Bodlondeb
Conwy
LL32 8DU

YSGOL CEDAR COURT
65 Victoria Park, Colwyn Bay,
Conwy LL29 7AJ
Type: Co-educational Boarding
and Day 11–18
Special needs: **BESD**

YSGOL Y GOGARTH
Ffordd Nant y Gamar, Llandudno,
Conwy LL30 1YF
Type: Co-educational Boarding
and Day 3–19
Special needs: ADHD ASD ASP
CP DOW EPI HI PMLD **SLD**
SP&LD VI
Wheelchair access: WA1

DENBIGHSHIRE

Denbighshire Education Services

Canol Y Dre
Ruthin
Denbighshire
LL15 1QA

TIR MORFA SCHOOL (INF & JNR)
Rhyl Road, Rhuddlan,
Denbighshire LL18 2RN
Type: Co-educational Day Only
3–19
Special needs: ADD **BESD** DOW
EPI HI **MLD SLD** SP&LD VI
Wheelchair access: W

TIR MORFA SCHOOL (SENIORS)
Derwen Road, Rhyl,
Denbighshire LL18 2RN
Type: Co-educational Day Only
2–19
Special needs: **MLD SLD**

YSGOL PLAS BRONDYFFRYN
Park Street, Denbigh,
Denbighshire LL16 4RH
Website: www.denbighict.gov.
uk/ysgolplasbrondyffryn
Type: Co-educational Boarding
and Day 3–19
Special needs: **ASD ASP**
Wheelchair access: WA2

FLINTSHIRE

Flintshire LEA

County Hall
Mold
Flintshire
CH7 6NB

YSGOL BELMONT
Windmill Road, Buckley,
Flintshire CH7 3HA
Type: Co-educational Day Only
Special needs: CP EPI **MLD** SLD

YSGOL DELYN
Alexandra Road, Mold, Flintshire
CH7 1HJ
Type: Co-educational Day Only
2–19
Special needs: ADD ADHD ASD
ASP BESD CP DOW DYP DYS
EPI HI MLD **PMLD SLD**
SP&LD VI
Wheelchair access: W

YSGOL Y BRYN
King George Street, Shotton,
Flintshire CH5 1EA
Type: Co-educational Day Only
2–19
Special needs: ASD PMLD **SLD**
Wheelchair access: W

GWYNEDD

Gwynedd Council

County Offices
Shirehall Street
Caernarfon
Gwynedd
LL55 1SH

YSGOL COEDMENAI
Bangor, Gwynedd LL57 2RX
Type: Boys Day Only 9–15
Special needs: **BESD**

YSGOL HAFOD LON
Y Ffor, Pwllheli, Gwynedd
LL53 6UD
Type: Co-educational Day Only
4–19
Special needs: ADHD ASD **CP
DOW** EPI **PMLD** SLD SP&LD
Wheelchair access: W

YSGOL PENDALAR
Ffordd Bethel, Caernarfon,
Gwynedd LL55 1DU
Website: www.ysgolpendalar.org
Type: Co-educational Day Only
2–19
Special needs: ADHD ASD **ASP
CP DOW** EPI **PMLD SLD** SP&LD
Wheelchair access: WA1 WA2

MERTHYR TYDFIL

Merthyr Tydfil County Borough Council

Civic Centre
Castle Street
Avenue de Clichy
Merthyr Tydfil
CF47 8AN

GREENFIELD SPECIAL SCHOOL
Duffryn Road, Pentrebach,
Merthyr Tydfil CF48 4BJ
Type: Co-educational Day Only
2–19
Special needs: ASD **MLD PMLD SLD** SP&LD
Wheelchair access: W

MONMOUTHSHIRE

Monmouthshire County Council

County Hall
Torfaen
Cwmbran
Monmouthshire
NP44 2XH

MOUNTON HOUSE SCHOOL
Pwyllmeyric, Chepstow,
Monmouthshire NP16 6LA
Type: Boys Day and Boarding
11–16
Special needs: **BESD** MLD

NEATH PORT TALBOT

Neath Port Talbot Council

Civic Centre
Port Talbot
Neath Port Talbot
SA13 1PJ

YSGOL HENDRE SPECIAL SCHOOL
Main Road, Neath, Neath Port
Talbot SA10 7TY
Type: Co-educational Boarding
Only 11–16
Special needs: HI **MLD SLD** VI
Wheelchair access: WA2

NEWPORT

Newport LEA

Civic Centre
Newport
NP20 4UR

MAES EBBW SCHOOL
Maesglas Road, South Wales,
Newport NP20 3DG
Type: Co-educational Day Only
3–19
Special needs: ASD PMLD SLD
Wheelchair access: WA1

PEMBROKESHIRE

Pembrokeshire County Council

County Hall
Haverfordwest
Pembrokeshire
SA61 1TP

PORTFIELD SCHOOL
Portfield, Haverfordwest,
Pembrokeshire SA61 1BS
Type: Co-educational Day Only
3–19
Special needs: ASD CP EPI HI
PMLD SLD VI
Wheelchair access: WA1

POWYS

Powys Children, Families & Lifelong Learning Directorate

County Hall
Llandrindod Wells
Powys
LD1 5LG

BRYNLLYWARCH HALL SCHOOL
Kerry, Newtown, Powys SY16 4PB
Type: Co-educational Boarding
and Day
Special needs: ADD ASP **BESD
MLD**

YSGOL CEDEWAIN
Maesyrhandir, Newtown, Powys
SY16 1LH
Website: www.cedewain.powys.
sch.uk
Type: Co-educational Day Only
2–19
Special needs: ASD **ASP** PMLD
SLD SP&LD
Wheelchair access: WA1

YSGOL PENMAES
Canal Road, Brecon, Powys
LD3 7HL
Website: www.penmaes.powys.
sch.uk
Type: Co-educational Day and
Boarding 2–19
Special needs: ASD PMLD **SLD**
Wheelchair access: WA1

SWANSEA

Swansea Education Department

County Hall
Swansea
SA1 3SN

PEN-Y-BRYN SENIOR SCHOOL
Glasbury Road, Morriston,
Swansea SA6 7PA
Type: Co-educational Day and
Boarding 4–19
Special needs: ASD **MLD** SLD

YSGOL CRUG GLAS
Croft Street, Swansea SA1 1QA
Type: Co-educational 3–19
Special needs: **PMLD**
Wheelchair access: WA1

TORFAEN

Torfaen Education Offices

County Hall
Cwmbran
Torfaen
NP44 2WN

CROWNBRIDGE SCHOOL
Greenhill Road, Pontypool,
Torfaen NP4 5YW
Type: Co-educational Day Only
3–19
Special needs: ASD DOW PMLD
SLD SP&LD
Wheelchair access: W

VALE OF GLAMORGAN

Vale of Glamorgan Directorate of Learning and Development

Civic Offices
Holton Road
Barry
Vale of Glamorgan
CF63 4RU

ASHGROVE SCHOOL
Sully Road, Penarth, Vale of
Glamorgan CF64 2TP
Website: www.ashgroveschool.
btinternet.co.uk
Type: Day and Boarding
Special needs: ADD **ASD ASP**

YSGOL MAES DYFAN
Gibbonsdown Rise, Barry, Vale of
Glamorgan CF6 7QZ
Type: Co-educational Day Only
3–19
Special needs: **MLD SLD**
Wheelchair access: WA1

WREXHAM

Wrexham Education & Leisure Services Directorate

Ty Henblas
Queen's Square
Wrexham
LL13 8AZ

ST CHRISTOPHER SCHOOL
Stockwell Grove, Wrexham
LL13 7BW
Type: Co-educational Day Only
5–19
Special needs: ADD ADHD ASD
ASP **BESD** CP DOW DYC DYP
DYS HEA HI **MLD** PMLD **SLD**
SP&LD TOU VI
Wheelchair access: WA1

PART FOUR

Independent Mainstream Schools with Specialist Provision

4.1

Independent Mainstream Schools with Specialist Provision – An Introduction

As a parent, you have the best knowledge of your child's individual needs. You will want to consider whether he or she would be happy and able to thrive with appropriate help in a mainstream school, or whether a special school, with highly specialist facilities and resources, is more appropriate. You may feel that a special school will be best able to meet his or her needs. Alternatively, you may prefer your child to learn in a mainstream school environment if the right support is available.

The term 'mainstream school' is commonly used to describe any school that is not a special school. This would include schools that offer some specialist SEN provision.

In fact, the Education Act 1996 states that, for the purposes of operating the statutory framework for special educational needs, a mainstream school is any school that is not a special school *or* an independent school. City Technology Colleges, City Colleges for the Technology of the Arts, and Academies are independent schools, but are classified as 'mainstream' under the Act. These schools do not charge fees and are regulated by agreements with the Department for Education (DfE). They cater for children with SEN in a similar way to mainstream maintained schools.

To avoid confusion, and to tie in with common usage, 'mainstream' for the purposes of this section means independent schools (fee charging) that are not special schools. More specifically, this section deals with such independent schools that offer help for pupils with SEN. Many schools in this category offer assistance for pupils with specific learning difficulties, such as dyslexia, and are unlikely to be able to cater for children with severe emotional and behavioural difficulties. Most mainstream independent schools are not authorized to accept children with Statements of SEN, although the Secretary of State can give approval for the placement of an individual child with a Statement. This will of course vary from one school to another, as will the expertise and facilities available.

Some schools have extensive experience in providing SEN support. A few have a significant proportion of students with SEN and a dedicated unit in school staffed by qualified specialist teachers. Pupils may be withdrawn from certain lessons during the school day, during which time they receive specialist support. Some may offer differentiated work within the normal classroom. Others may be sympathetic to special needs but may not have the facilities to make any special provision. It is important to remember that in most cases schools will expect your child to meet the normal entry requirements for the school and to be able to cope in an ordinary school setting. However, where a special need amounts to a disability under the Disability Discrimination Act, the school will need to consider whether it is able to make reasonable adjustments to accommodate such needs, including the provision of extra support for which the school is entitled to charge a separate fee.

Parents should look at the individual school's admissions policy, SEN and disability policy and accessibility plan for details of the school's admission criteria and the provisions in place for children with SEN. All independent schools must now, by law, have such policies and plans in place and copies should be available on request.

If you are considering mainstream schools, it is important to find out exactly how these would meet your child's individual needs. To help you find out which schools in the directory are appropriate for your child, the support available at each school for each type of need is shown. If you are looking for schools that make provision for dyslexia, you may also find it helpful to consult the register of schools produced by CReSTeD (Council for the Registration of Schools Teaching Dyslexic Pupils) on page 495.

When contacting or visiting schools that interest you, you may wish to ask about the following points to help you make an assessment of the school's suitability:

Academic pace

Finding the right academic environment for your child is every bit as essential as finding a school that will provide the right level of SEN support. Ask to see examples of children's work. Where do leavers go? Is the school's overall thrust and ethos suitable for your child?

Experience and expertise in managing SEN

- How much experience has the school had of teaching children with needs or a spectrum of needs similar to your child's?

- How many such students are currently enrolled? What help do these students receive?

- What proportion of pupils in the school have SEN?

- Are staff qualified in SEN teaching?

- Does the school have full-time SEN teaching specialists or is teaching done on a part-time basis?

- What have been the destinations of recent leavers with SEN?

Meeting the needs of your child

- What strategy would the school suggest for meeting your child's needs? How many special lessons would your child have per week? How big are the groups for these lessons? Will your child have to give up another subject in order to have special lessons or will these be given outside normal lesson times? What will the lessons cover? Will there be additional support in class? If so, from whom?

- If Information Technology facilities are an important resource for your child, what can the school offer? Is there a dedicated area available? Are computers and laptops freely available for use?

- Will the school arrange for special arrangements during GCSE and/or A level examinations, if appropriate?

Communication with teachers and parents

- How will those in school, who are responsible for teaching and caring for your child, be kept informed of his or her needs and progress by the special needs department?

- How, and how often, will parents be kept in touch with progress and plans?

Wider needs

- It is equally important to check that your child's strengths and interests outside the classroom can be catered for. If he or she is good at music, sport, drama or has a special interest in, for example, outdoor pursuits or debating, will the school offer the right levels of encouragement and opportunities to develop these, either now or at a later stage?

- Similarly, what help and advice is given to senior school pupils about university entry and careers?

- Does your child have particular medical or dietary needs that must be provided for in school?

- Are there any religious considerations? If your family is of a faith different from that of the school, how will your child's faith be accommodated? Will he/she find it difficult to play a full part in school life?

- Does the school share your values as a parent? What are its policies with reference to discipline, bullying and drugs, and the extent of guidance given on Personal & Social Education (PSE)?

If you would like more personal help to find suitable mainstream schools for your child, contact Gabbitas, who can assist with independent educational assessment and selection of schools.

Gabbitas Educational Consultants
Norfolk House, 30 Charles II Street, London SW1Y 4AE
Tel: 020 7734 0161   Fax: 020 7437 1764
E-mail: info@gabbitas.co.uk   Website: www.gabbitas.co.uk

4.2

Notes on the Directory

Type of school

This directory comprises mainstream independent schools listed within the Department for Education Register of Independent Schools that have requested an entry in the Guide.

School entries

Each entry includes the school's contact details and a brief description to show pupil's gender, and age range and the type of accommodation available eg boarding and day. The information is intended as a guide only. For more details please contact schools direct.

Special needs provision

Provision is divided into three categories, as follows:

- Learning difficulties.
- Behavioural disorders/emotional and behavioural difficulties/challenging behaviour.
- Physical impairments/medical conditions.

Within each of these categories, each school has been asked to indicate: (a) the type of support provided; and (b) whether it currently has pupils who have been diagnosed with specific conditions, disorders or disabilities within that general category. It should be noted that the conditions, disorders and disabilities listed are not comprehensive and are offered as a guide only. To find out about provision for other types of special needs please make contact with schools.

Charging policy

Some forms of support may be provided within the school's standard fee. Others may be provided at the parents' or Local Authority's expense. For details of individual school policies please contact them individually.

Key to abbreviations used in the directory

Learning difficulties

Support provided:

CA   Some children with special needs receive help from classroom assistants

RA   There are currently very limited facilities for pupils with learning difficulties but reasonable adjustments can be made if necessary

SC   Some children with special needs are taught in separate classes for specific subjects

SNU   School has a dedicated Special Needs Unit, which provides specialist tuition on a one-to-one or small group basis by appropriately qualified teachers

WI   There is no dedicated Special Needs Unit but some children with special needs are withdrawn individually from certain lessons for one-to-one tuition

The school currently has pupils who have been diagnosed with:

DOW   Down's Syndrome
DYC   Dyscalculia
DYP   Dyspraxia
DYS   Dyslexia
MLD   Moderate Learning Difficulties

PMLD   Profound and Multiple Learning Difficulties
SLD   Severe Learning Difficulties
SP&LD   Speech and Language Difficulties

Behavioural disorders/emotional and behavioural difficulties/challenging behaviour

Support provided:

CA   Some children with behavioural problems receive help from classroom assistants

CO   Trained counsellors available for pupils

RA   There are currently very limited facilities for pupils with behavioural disorders but reasonable adjustments can be made if necessary

ST   Behaviour management strategies identified in school's behaviour management policy

TS   Staff trained in behaviour management available

The school currently has pupils who have been diagnosed with the following disorders:

ADD   Attention Deficit Disorder
ADHD   Attention Deficit Hyperactivity Disorder
ASD   Autism/Autistic Spectrum Disorder
ASP   Asperger's Syndrome

BESD   Behavioural, Emotional and Social Disorders
CB   Challenging Behaviour
TOU   Tourette's Syndrome

Physical impairments/Medical conditions

Support provided:

AT   Adapted timetable for children with health problems

BL	Materials can be provided in Braille	SL	Stairlifts
CA	Some children with behavioural problems receive help from classroom assistants	SM	Staff with medical training available
		TW	Accessible toilet and washing facilities
DS	Signing by staff and pupils	W	School has wheelchair access (unspecified)
HL	Hearing loops available		
IT	Specialist IT provision available	WA1	School is fully wheelchair accessible
RA	There are currently very limited facilities for pupils with physical impairments or medical conditions but reasonable adjustments can be made if necessary	WA2	Main teaching areas are wheelchair accessible
		WA3	No permanent access for wheelchairs; temporary ramps available

The school currently has pupils with the following impairments/medical conditions:

CP	Cerebral Palsy	HI	Hearing Impairment
EPI	Epilepsy	IM	Impaired Mobility
HEA	Health Problems (eg heart defect, asthma)	VI	Visual Impairment
		WU	Wheelchair Users

Symbols

+	Registered with CReSTeD (see Part 5.1)	*	School profile later in this section

4.3

Directory of Independent Mainstream Schools with Specialist Provision

England

BEDFORDSHIRE

MOORLANDS SCHOOL
Leagrave Hall, Luton,
Bedfordshire LU4 9LE
Website: www.moorlandsschool.
com
Type: Co-educational Day Only
2–11
Learning difficulties: DYS DYP
*Behavioural and emotional
disorders:* CA TS ST/ASD
Physical and medical conditions:
IT RA SM TW WA2/HEA

BERKSHIRE

THE ABBEY SCHOOL
17 Kendrick Road, Reading,
Berkshire RG1 5DZ
Website: www.theabbey.co.uk
Type: Girls Day Only 3–18
Learning difficulties: WI/DYS DYP
*Behavioural and emotional
disorders:* TS ST/ADD
Physical and medical conditions:
SL SM TW WA2/HEA

CEDARS SCHOOL
Church Road, Aldermaston,
Berkshire RG7 4LR
Website: www.thecedarsschool.
co.uk
Type: Co-educational Day Only
4–11
Learning difficulties: CA WI/DYS
Physical and medical conditions:
W

DOLPHIN SCHOOL
Waltham Road, Reading,
Berkshire RG10 0FR
Website: www.dolphinschool.
com
Type: Co-educational Day Only
3–13
Learning difficulties: WI/DYS
*Behavioural and emotional
disorders:* RA/ASP ASD
Physical and medical conditions:
RA

DOWNE HOUSE
Cold Ash, Thatcham, Berkshire
RG18 9JJ
Website: www.downehouse.net
Type: Girls Boarding and Day
11–18
Learning difficulties: SNU/DYS
DYP
*Behavioural and emotional
disorders:* RA
Physical and medical conditions:
RA/HEA HI

HERRIES SCHOOL
Dean Lane, Maidenhead,
Berkshire SL6 9BD
Website: www.herries.ws
Type: Co-educational Day Only
3–11
Learning difficulties: WI

HORRIS HILL SCHOOL
Newbury, Berkshire RG20 9DJ
Website: www.horrishill.com
Type: Boys Boarding and Day
7–13
Learning difficulties: SNU/MLD
DYS DYP
*Behavioural and emotional
disorders:* ADD
Physical and medical conditions:
SM/HI

HURST LODGE SCHOOL
Bagshot Road, Ascot, Berkshire
SL5 9JU
Website: www.hurstlodge.co.uk
Type: Co-educational Day and
Boarding 3–18 (Boys and Girls
3–18)
Learning difficulties: CA SC SNU
WI/MLD DYC DYS DYP
*Behavioural and emotional
disorders:* RA/ADD ADHD ASP
Physical and medical conditions:
AT RA/EPI HEA HI IM VI

MEADOWBROOK
MONTESSORI SCHOOL
Malt Hill, Bracknell, Berkshire
RG42 6JQ
Type: Co-educational Day Only
3–11
Learning difficulties: CA RA SNU/
MLD DYS
*Behavioural and emotional
disorders:* RA TS/ADHD ASP
ASD CB
Physical and medical conditions:
TW WA1 WA2

THE ORATORY SCHOOL
Reading, Berkshire RG8 0PJ
Website: www.oratory.co.uk
Type: Boys Day and Boarding
11–18
Learning difficulties: SNU/MLD
DYS DYP

OUR LADY'S
PREPARATORY SCHOOL
The Avenue, Crowthorne,
Berkshire RG45 6PB
Website: www.ourladysprep.
co.uk
Type: Co-educational Day Only
1–11

PAPPLEWICK SCHOOL
Windsor Road, Ascot, Berkshire
SL5 7LH
Website: www.papplewick.org.uk
Type: Boys Boarding and Day
6–13
Learning difficulties: WI/MLD
DYS
*Behavioural and emotional
disorders:* RA
Physical and medical conditions:
RA

ST ANDREW'S SCHOOL
Buckhold, Reading, Berkshire
RG8 8QA
Website: www.
standrewspangbourne.co.uk
Type: Co-educational Day and
Boarding 3–13
Learning difficulties: WI/DYS

ST BERNARD'S
PREPARATORY SCHOOL
Hawtrey Close, Slough, Berkshire
SL1 1TB
Website: www.st-bernards-prep.
slough.sch.uk
Type: Co-educational Day Only
3–11
Learning difficulties: CA WI/DYS
Physical and medical conditions:
TW WA2/HEA

ST GABRIEL'S
Sandleford Priory, Berkshire
RG20 9BD
Website: www.stgabriels.co.uk
Type: Girls Day Only 3–18 (Girls
3–18 Boys 3–7)
Learning difficulties: CA SNU/
MLD DYC DYS DYP
*Behavioural and emotional
disorders:* CA CO/ADD ASP
BESD
Physical and medical conditions:
AT CA RA SM TW/HEA

ST MARY'S SCHOOL, ASCOT

St Mary's Road, Ascot, Berkshire
SL5 9JF
Website: www.st-marys-ascot.
co.uk
Type: Girls Boarding and Day
11–18
Learning difficulties: WI/DYS DYP
Physical and medical conditions:
RA SM WA2/EPI HEA HI W

THORNGROVE SCHOOL

The Mount, Newbury, Berkshire
RG20 9PS
Website: www.thorngroveschool.
co.uk
Type: Co-educational Day Only
2–13
Learning difficulties: CA WI/DYS
DYP
*Behavioural and emotional
disorders:* RA
Physical and medical conditions:
RA/CP HEA

BRISTOL

BRISTOL CATHEDRAL SCHOOL

College Square, Bristol BS1 5TS
Website: www.bristolcathedral.
bristol.sch.uk
Type: Co-educational Day Only
10–18 (Co-ed VIth Form)
Learning difficulties: CA WI/DYS
DYP
*Behavioural and emotional
disorders:* RA/ADD ADHD ASP
TOU
Physical and medical conditions:
RA/HEA VI

CLIFTON COLLEGE

32 College Road, Bristol BS8 3JH
Website: www.cliftoncollegeuk.
com
Type: Co-educational Boarding
and Day 13–18
Learning difficulties: CA SNU/
DYC DYS DYP SP&LD
*Behavioural and emotional
disorders:* CO RA/ADD ASP
Physical and medical conditions:
RA WA3/HEA

CLIFTON COLLEGE PREPARATORY SCHOOL+

The Avenue, Bristol BS8 3HE
Website: www.cliftoncollegeuk.
com
Type: Co-educational Boarding
and Day 8–13
Learning difficulties: SNU/MLD
DYC DYS DYP
*Behavioural and emotional
disorders:* ST/ADD ASP BESD
Physical and medical conditions:
CA WA3/HEA HI VI

CLIFTON HIGH SCHOOL

College Road, Bristol BS8 3JD
Website: www.cliftonhigh.bristol.
sch.uk
Type: Co-educational Day and
Boarding 3–18
Learning difficulties: CA RA WI/
MLD DYC DYS DYP
*Behavioural and emotional
disorders:* CO
Physical and medical conditions:
AT BL HL IT RA SM WA3/HEA HI
VI

GRACEFIELD PREPARATORY SCHOOL

266 Overndale Road, Fishponds,
Bristol BS16 2RG
Website: www.gracefieldschool.
co.uk
Type: Co-educational Day Only
4–11
Learning difficulties: WI/MLD
*Behavioural and emotional
disorders:* TS
Physical and medical conditions:
WA3

OVERNDALE SCHOOL

Chapel Lane, Old Sodbury,
Bristol BS37 6NQ
Website: www.overndaleschool.
co.uk
Type: Co-educational Day Only
1–11
Learning difficulties: CA
*Behavioural and emotional
disorders:* TS ST

QUEEN ELIZABETH'S HOSPITAL

Berkeley Place, Bristol BS8 1JX
Website: www.qehbristol.co.uk
Type: Boys Day Only 7–18 (Sixth
Form International students are
welcome on a Guardianship
basis)
Learning difficulties: SNU/DYS
DYP
*Behavioural and emotional
disorders:* CO/ADD ADHD
Physical and medical conditions:
RA SM W/CP EPI HEA HI

THE RED MAIDS' SCHOOL

Westbury-on-Trym, Bristol
BS9 3AW
Website: www.redmaids.
co.uk
Type: Girls Day Only 11–18
Learning difficulties: CA SNU/
DYS
Physical and medical conditions:
CA SM TW/HEA VI

ST URSULA'S HIGH SCHOOL

Brecon Road, Westbury-on-Trym,
Bristol BS9 4DT
Website: www.st-ursulas.
bristol.sch.uk
Type: Co-educational Day Only
3–16
Learning difficulties: CA WI/MLD
DYS DYP
*Behavioural and emotional
disorders:* RA/ADD ADHD ASP
Physical and medical conditions:
CP HEA

TOCKINGTON MANOR SCHOOL

Tockington, Bristol BS32 4NY
Website: tockington.bristol.
sch.uk
Type: Co-educational Day and
Boarding 2–14
Learning difficulties: CA SC SNU/
DYS DYP

BUCKINGHAMSHIRE

AKELEY WOOD SCHOOL

Akeley Wood, Buckingham,
Buckinghamshire MK18 5AE
Website: www.
akeleywoodschool.co.uk
Type: Co-educational Day Only
3–18
Learning difficulties: SNU/MLD
DYS DYP
*Behavioural and emotional
disorders:* ADD ASP
Physical and medical conditions:
RA/HEA HI

DAIR HOUSE SCHOOL TRUST LTD

Bishops Blake, Farnham Royal,
Buckinghamshire SL2 3BY
Website: www.dairhouse.co.uk
Type: Co-educational Day Only
3–11
Learning difficulties: CA WI/DYS

GODSTOWE PREPARATORY SCHOOL

Shrubbery Road, High
Wycombe, Buckinghamshire
HP13 6PR
Website: www.godstowe.org
Type: Girls Day and Boarding
3–13 (Boys 3–8)
Learning difficulties: CA SC SNU/
MLD DOW DYC DYS DYP
*Behavioural and emotional
disorders:* CA CO/ADD ADHD
ASP ASD
Physical and medical conditions:
CA RA SM/CP EPI HEA HI

HIGH MARCH SCHOOL

23 Ledborough Lane,
Beaconsfield, Buckinghamshire
HP9 2PZ
Website: www.highmarch.co.uk
Type: Girls Day Only 3–11 (Boys
are only admitted into our Upper
Nursery class)
Learning difficulties: CA WI/DYC
DYS DYP
*Behavioural and emotional
disorders:* RA
Physical and medical conditions:
AT CA RA TW WA2/EPI HEA

MALTMAN'S GREEN SCHOOL

Maltmans Lane, Gerrards Cross,
Buckinghamshire SL9 8RR
Website: www.maltmansgreen.
com
Type: Girls Day Only 3–11
Learning difficulties: CA WI/MLD
DYS DYP
*Behavioural and emotional
disorders:* CO
Physical and medical conditions:
CA SM/HEA VI

ST TERESA'S CATHOLIC INDEPENDENT & NURSERY SCHOOL

Aylesbury Road, Princes
Risborough, Buckinghamshire
HP27 0JW
Website: www.st-teresas.
bucks.sch.uk
Type: Co-educational Day Only
3–11
Learning difficulties: CA WI/DYS
DYP
*Behavioural and emotional
disorders:* ADD ADHD ASP ASD
Physical and medical conditions:
CA TW WA2/HI

WYCOMBE ABBEY SCHOOL

High Wycombe,
Buckinghamshire HP11 1PE
Website: www.wycombeabbey.
com
Type: Girls Boarding and Day
11–18
Learning difficulties: SNU WI/
DYC DYS DYP
*Behavioural and emotional
disorders:* CO/ADHD
Physical and medical conditions:
RA SM TW WA3/EPI HEA

CAMBRIDGESHIRE

CAMBRIDGE CENTRE FOR SIXTH-FORM STUDIES
1 Salisbury Villas, Cambridge, Cambridgeshire CB1 2JF
Website: www.ccss.co.uk
Type: Co-educational Day and Boarding 15–21
Learning difficulties: CA RA/DYS DYP
Behavioural and emotional disorders: CA CO RA
Physical and medical conditions: RA SM/HEA

THE PERSE SCHOOL
Hills Road, Cambridge, Cambridgeshire CB2 8QF
Website: www.perse.co.uk
Type: Co-educational Day Only 11–18
Learning difficulties: CA SNU
Behavioural and emotional disorders: CO RA ST/ADD ADHD ASP
Physical and medical conditions: AT CA HL RA SM TW WA2 WA3/ EPI HEA VI

ST MARY'S JUNIOR SCHOOL
2 Brookside, Cambridge, Cambridgeshire CB2 1JE
Website: www. stmaryscambridge.co.uk
Type: Girls Day Only 4–11
Learning difficulties: CA/DYC DYS
Behavioural and emotional disorders: CA RA
Physical and medical conditions: HEA HI

SANCTON WOOD SCHOOL
2 St Paul's Road, Cambridge, Cambridgeshire CB1 2EZ
Website: www.sanctonwood. co.uk
Type: Co-educational Day Only 1–16
Learning difficulties: CA WI/DYC DYS DYP
Behavioural and emotional disorders: ASP TOU
Physical and medical conditions: AT HL RA/CP HEA HI VI

CHANNEL ISLANDS

ORMER HOUSE PREPARATORY SCHOOL
La Vallee, Alderney, Channel Islands GY9 3XA
Website: www.ormerhouse.com
Type: Co-educational Day Only 2–13
Physical and medical conditions: W/W

CHESHIRE

ABBEY GATE SCHOOL
Clare Avenue, Chester, Cheshire
CH2 3HR
Website: www.abbeygateschool.
org.uk
Type: Co-educational Day Only
3–11
Learning difficulties: CA WI/MLD
DYS DYP
*Behavioural and emotional
disorders:* CA TS ST/ADD ASD
Physical and medical conditions:
CA SM TW WA1 WA2/HEA HI VI

BRABYNS SCHOOL
34–36 Arkwright Road, Stockport,
Cheshire SK6 7DB
Website: www.
brabynsprepschool.co.uk
Type: Co-educational Day Only
2–11
Learning difficulties: RA WI/DYS
DYP
*Behavioural and emotional
disorders:* ASP
Physical and medical conditions:
EPI

CULCHETH HALL
Ashley Road, Altrincham,
Cheshire WA14 2LT
Website: www.culcheth-hall.
org.uk
Type: Girls Day Only 3–16 (Boys
2–4)
Learning difficulties: CA SC SNU/
DYC DYS DYP
*Behavioural and emotional
disorders:* CA TS/ADD ADHD
BESD
Physical and medical conditions:
AT CA/HEA

GREENBANK
PREPARATORY SCHOOL
Heathbank Road, Cheadle,
Cheshire SK8 6HU
Website: www.greenbankschool.
co.uk
Type: Co-educational Day Only
3–11
Learning difficulties: CA SC SNU/
MLD DYC DYS DYP
*Behavioural and emotional
disorders:* RA TS
Physical and medical conditions:
AT RA SM TW WA1 WA2/HEA

LORETO PREPARATORY
SCHOOL
Dunham Road, Altrincham,
Cheshire WA14 4GZ
Website: www.loretoprep.co.uk
Type: Co-educational Day Only
3–11 (Boys 4–7)
Learning difficulties: CA WI/MLD
DYS
*Behavioural and emotional
disorders:* CA ST
Physical and medical conditions:
CA TW WA2/CP EPI HEA HI IM W

NORTH CESTRIAN
GRAMMAR SCHOOL
Dunham Road, Altrincham,
Cheshire WA14 4AJ
Website: www.ncgs.co.uk
Type: Co-educational Day Only
11–18
Learning difficulties: CA WI/MLD
DYC DYS DYP
*Behavioural and emotional
disorders:* CA ST/ADD ADHD
ASP ASD BESD CB TOU
Physical and medical conditions:
CA SL SM TW W WA2/EPI HI W

RAMILLIES HALL
SCHOOL+
Ramillies Avenue, Cheadle,
Cheshire SK8 7AJ
Website: www.ramillieshall.co.uk
Type: Co-educational Day Only
Learning difficulties: CA SNU/
DYC DYS DYP
Physical and medical conditions:
CA RA/HI VI

TERRA NOVA SCHOOL
Holmes Chapel, Cheshire
CW4 8BT
Website: www.terranovaschool.
co.uk
Type: Co-educational Day and
Boarding 3–13
Learning difficulties: CA SNU WI/
DYC DYS DYP
*Behavioural and emotional
disorders:* RA/ADHD ASP
Physical and medical conditions:
RA SM W/HEA

CORNWALL

GEMS BOLITHO SCHOOL
Polwithen Road, Penzance,
Cornwall TR18 4JR
Website: www.bolithoschool.
co.uk
Type: Co-educational Day and
Boarding 4–18
Learning difficulties: CA SNU/
MLD DYC DYS DYP
*Behavioural and emotional
disorders:* CA/ADD ADHD ASP
Physical and medical conditions:
IT SM TW/HI

ROSELYON
St Blazey Road, Par, Cornwall
PL24 2HZ
Website: www.roselyon.cornwall.
sch.uk
Type: Co-educational Day Only
2–11
Learning difficulties: CA WI/MLD
DYS DYP
*Behavioural and emotional
disorders:* RA/ADD ADHD
Physical and medical conditions:
RA/HEA HI

ST IA SCHOOL
St Ives Road, St Ives, Cornwall
TR26 2SF
Website: www.st-ia.cornwall.
sch.uk
Type: Co-educational Day Only
4–8
Learning difficulties: RA WI
*Behavioural and emotional
disorders:* RA
Physical and medical conditions:
RA/HEA

ST JOSEPH'S SCHOOL
St Stephen's Hill, Launceston,
Cornwall PL15 8HN
Website: www.st-josephs.
cornwall.sch.uk
Type: Co-educational Day Only
3–16 (Boys 3–11)
Learning difficulties: SNU/MLD
DYS DYP
*Behavioural and emotional
disorders:* RA
Physical and medical conditions:
RA/HEA

ST PIRAN'S
PREPARATORY SCHOOL
14 Trelissick Road, Hayle,
Cornwall TR27 4HY
Website: www.stpirans.net
Type: Co-educational Day Only
3–16
Learning difficulties: CA WI/MLD
DYS
*Behavioural and emotional
disorders:* ST
Physical and medical conditions:
RA SM WA3/CP

CUMBRIA

LIME HOUSE SCHOOL+
Holm Hill, Carlisle, Cumbria
CA5 7BX
Website: www.
limehouseschool.co.uk
Type: Co-educational Boarding
and Day 4–18
Learning difficulties: CA SC SNU
WI/MLD DYS DYP
*Behavioural and emotional
disorders:* ADD ADHD ASP
Physical and medical conditions:
AT/HEA

ST BEES SCHOOL+
St Bees, Cumbria CA27 0DS
Website: www.st-bees-school.
org
Type: Co-educational Boarding
and Day 4–18
Learning difficulties: SNU WI/
DYC DYS DYP
*Behavioural and emotional
disorders:* RA/ADD ADHD BESD
Physical and medical conditions:
RA SM/EPI HEA VI

ST URSULAS CONVENT
SCHOOL
Burnfoot, Wigton, Cumbria
CA7 9HL
Website: www.stursulas.co.uk
Type: Co-educational Day Only
2–11
Learning difficulties: SNU/DYS
DYP
*Behavioural and emotional
disorders:* ASP ASD
Physical and medical conditions:
HEA

SEDBERGH JUNIOR SCHOOL
Danson House, Sedbergh, Cumbria LA10 5HG
Website: www.sedberghjuniorschool.org
Type: Co-educational Boarding and Day 4–13
Learning difficulties: CA SC SNU WI/MLD DYS DYP
Behavioural and emotional disorders: TS/ASP ASD
Physical and medical conditions: CA TW/HEA IM

SEDBERGH SCHOOL
Sedbergh, Cumbria LA10 5HG
Website: www.sedberghschool.org
Type: Co-educational Boarding and Day 14–18
Learning difficulties: SNU WI/DYS
Behavioural and emotional disorders: TS/ADD
Physical and medical conditions: RA SM/HEA HI VI

WINDERMERE SCHOOL
Windermere, Cumbria LA23 1NW
Website: www.windermereschool.co.uk
Type: Co-educational Boarding and Day 2–18
Learning difficulties: WI

DERBYSHIRE

BARLBOROUGH HALL SCHOOL
Barlborough, Chesterfield, Derbyshire S43 4TJ
Website: www.barlboroughhallschool.co.uk
Type: Co-educational Day Only 3–11
Learning difficulties: CA WI/DYS DYP
Physical and medical conditions: VI

DERBY HIGH SCHOOL
Hillsway, Derby, Derbyshire DE23 3DT
Website: www.derbyhigh.derby.sch.uk
Type: Co-educational Day Only 3–18
Learning difficulties: CA RA WI/DYC DYS DYP
Behavioural and emotional disorders: RA/ASD
Physical and medical conditions: RA/HEA

EMMANUEL SCHOOL
Juniper Lodge, Derby, Derbyshire DE22 1FP
Type: Co-educational Day Only 3–14
Learning difficulties: CA WI
Behavioural and emotional disorders: RA/ASP
Physical and medical conditions: RA WA3/HEA VI

GATEWAY CHRISTIAN SCHOOL
Moor Lane, Ilkeston, Derbyshire DE7 4PP
Website: www.gatewayschool.org.uk
Type: Co-educational Day Only 3–11
Learning difficulties: RA WI
Behavioural and emotional disorders: RA
Physical and medical conditions: RA/HEA

DEVON

KELLY COLLEGE PREPARATORY SCHOOL
Hazeldon House, Tavistock, Devon PL19 0JS
Website: www.kellycollegeprep.com
Type: Co-educational Day and Boarding 2–11
Learning difficulties: CA WI/DYS DYP
Behavioural and emotional disorders: ASD

KINGSLEY SCHOOL+
Kingsley School, Bideford, Devon EX39 3LY
Website: www.kingsleyschoolbideford.co.uk
Type: Co-educational Boarding and Day 11–18
Learning difficulties: SC SNU/DYS DYP

THE MAYNARD SCHOOL
Denmark Road, Exeter, Devon EX1 1SJ
Website: www.maynard.co.uk
Type: Girls Day Only 7–18 (A selective independent day school for girls aged 7–17.)
Learning difficulties: WI/DYS DYP
Behavioural and emotional disorders: CO
Physical and medical conditions: AT SM TW WA2/EPI HEA HI

ST CHRISTOPHER'S SCHOOL
Mount Barton, Totnes, Devon TQ9 6PF
Website: www.st-christophers.devon.sch.uk
Type: Co-educational Day Only 3–11
Learning difficulties: CA/MLD DYS DYP
Behavioural and emotional disorders: RA/ADHD ASD BESD
Physical and medical conditions: CA IT TW W WA1/HEA HI

ST MICHAEL'S
Tawstock Court, Barnstaple, Devon EX31 3HY
Type: Co-educational Day Only
Learning difficulties: CA SNU/MLD DOW DYS
Physical and medical conditions: TW/HI VI

TRINITY SCHOOL
Buckeridge Road, Teignmouth, Devon TQ14 8LY
Website: www.trinityschool.co.uk
Type: Co-educational Day and Boarding 4–20
Learning difficulties: CA SNU/MLD DYC DYS DYP
Behavioural and emotional disorders: CA CO TS ST/ADD ADHD ASP
Physical and medical conditions: CA IT SM TW WA2/HEA

WEST BUCKLAND PREPARATORY SCHOOL
Barnstaple, Devon EX32 0SX
Website: www.westbuckland.devon.sch.uk
Type: Co-educational Day and Boarding 3–11
Learning difficulties: CA RA/MLD DYC DYS DYP
Behavioural and emotional disorders: RA/ADD ADHD
Physical and medical conditions: CA SM TW W WA2/HEA VI

WEST BUCKLAND SCHOOL
Barnstaple, Devon EX32 0SX
Website: www.westbuckland.devon.sch.uk
Type: Co-educational Boarding and Day 3–18
Learning difficulties: CA SNU WI/DOW DYC DYS DYP
Behavioural and emotional disorders: CA CO RA TS ST/ADD ADHD ASP BESD
Physical and medical conditions: CA/EPI HEA HI VI

DORSET

BOURNEMOUTH COLLEGIATE PREP SCHOOL
40 St Osmund's Road, Poole, Dorset BH14 9JY
Website: www.bournemouthcollegiateschool.co.uk
Type: Co-educational Day Only 3–11
Physical and medical conditions: W

BOURNEMOUTH COLLEGIATE SCHOOL
College Road, Bournemouth, Dorset BH5 2DY
Website: www.bournemouthcollegiateschool.co.uk
Type: Co-educational Boarding and Day 11–18
Learning difficulties: SNU WI/DYC DYS
Physical and medical conditions: AT RA WA3/HEA

DORCHESTER PREPARATORY AND INDEPENDENT SCHOOLS

25/26 Icen Way, Dorchester, Dorset DT1 1EP
Website: www.dorchesterprepschool.co.uk
Type: Co-educational Day Only 3–18
Learning difficulties: CA WI/DYC DYS DYP
Behavioural and emotional disorders: RA/ADD ADHD ASP ASD
Physical and medical conditions: RA/HEA

MILTON ABBEY SCHOOL+

Blandford Forum, Dorset DT11 0BZ
Website: www.miltonabbey.co.uk
Type: Co-educational Boarding and Day 13–18
Learning difficulties: SNU/DYC DYS DYP SP&LD
Behavioural and emotional disorders: CO TS ST/ADD ADHD
Physical and medical conditions: RA/HEA HI

PORT REGIS PREPARATORY SCHOOL

Motcombe Park, Shaftesbury, Dorset SP7 9QA
Website: www.portregis.com
Type: Co-educational Boarding and Day 3–13
Learning difficulties: SNU WI/DYC DYS DYP
Behavioural and emotional disorders: CO/ADD ASP
Physical and medical conditions: DS HL RA SM TW/HEA HI

SHERBORNE SCHOOL

Abbey Road, Sherborne, Dorset DT9 3AP
Website: www.sherborne.org
Type: Boys Boarding and Day 13–18
Learning difficulties: SNU WI/MLD DYC DYS DYP
Physical and medical conditions: IT/EPI HEA HI VI

COUNTY DURHAM

POLAM HALL

Grange Road, Darlington, County Durham DL1 5PA
Website: www.polamhall.com
Type: Co-educational Boarding and Day 2–18 (Co-educational Junior School from age 2 to Year 4. Separate teaching Year 5 to Year 11. Co-educational Sixth Form)
Learning difficulties: CA SC SNU/MLD DYS DYP
Behavioural and emotional disorders: RA/ASP ASD
Physical and medical conditions: AT CA RA SM WA3/HEA HI

ESSEX

DAME BRADBURY'S SCHOOL
Ashdon Road, Saffron Walden, Essex CB10 2AL
Website: www.damebradburys.com
Type: Co-educational Day Only 3–11
Learning difficulties: CA RA/DYS DYP
Behavioural and emotional disorders: RA/ASD
Physical and medical conditions: RA/W

FELSTED SCHOOL
Felsted, Essex CM6 3LL
Website: www.felsted.org
Type: Co-educational Boarding and Day 13–18 (Felsted Prep School accepts day and boarding boys and girls from ages 4–12. Pupils are able to board from age 8.)
Learning difficulties: CA WI/DYS
Behavioural and emotional disorders: RA
Physical and medical conditions: AT CA IT RA SM TW WA2 WA3/EPI

ILFORD URSULINE PREPARATORY SCHOOL
2–4 Coventry Road, Ilford, Essex IG1 4QR
Website: www.ilfordursuline-prep.org.uk
Type: Girls Day Only 3–11
Learning difficulties: SNU/MLD DYS DYP
Behavioural and emotional disorders: TS/ADHD
Physical and medical conditions: TW WA2

LITTLEGARTH SCHOOL
Horkesley Park, Colchester, Essex CO6 4JR
Website: www.littlegarth.essex.sch.uk
Type: Co-educational Day Only 2–11
Learning difficulties: CA SNU WI/MLD DYC DYS DYP
Behavioural and emotional disorders: CA ST/ADD ADHD
Physical and medical conditions: CA IT RA SM TW WA3/HEA HI VI

RAPHAEL INDEPENDENT SCHOOL
Park Lane, Hornchurch, Essex RM11 1XY
Website: www.raphaelschool.com
Type: Co-educational Day Only 4–16
Learning difficulties: WI/DYS
Physical and medical conditions: RA

THORPE HALL SCHOOL
Wakering Road, Southend-on-Sea, Essex SS1 3RD
Website: www.thorpehall.southend.sch.uk
Type: Co-educational Day Only 2–16
Learning difficulties: CA SC WI/MLD DYC DYS DYP
Behavioural and emotional disorders: CA TS ST/ADD ADHD ASP ASD
Physical and medical conditions: CA HL SL SM TW WA2/EPI HEA

GLOUCESTERSHIRE

AIRTHRIE SCHOOL
27–29 Christchurch Road, Cheltenham, Gloucestershire GL50 2NY
Website: www.airthrie-school.co.uk
Type: Co-educational Day Only 3–11
Learning difficulties: CA SNU/DYS DYP
Physical and medical conditions: HEA VI

BREDON SCHOOL+
Pull Court, Tewkesbury, Gloucestershire GL20 6AH
Website: www.bredonschool.org
Type: Co-educational Boarding and Day 5–18
Learning difficulties: CA SNU/MLD DYC DYS DYP SP&LD
Behavioural and emotional disorders: CO TS/ADD
Physical and medical conditions: IT SL SM TW W WA2/HEA

CHELTENHAM COLLEGE
Bath Road, Cheltenham, Gloucestershire GL53 7LD
Website: www.cheltenhamcollege.org
Type: Co-educational Boarding and Day 13–18
Learning difficulties: WI

CHELTENHAM COLLEGE JUNIOR SCHOOL

Thirlestaine Road, Cheltenham, Gloucestershire GL53 7AB
Website: www.cheltcoll.gloucs. sch.uk
Type: Co-educational Boarding and Day 3–13
Learning difficulties: CA SNU/ DYS DYP SP&LD
Behavioural and emotional disorders: CA CO/ADD ADHD ASP
Physical and medical conditions: RA SM WA2

CHELTENHAM LADIES' COLLEGE

Bayshill Road, Cheltenham, Gloucestershire GL50 3EP
Website: www. cheltladiescollege.org
Type: Girls Boarding and Day 11–18
Learning difficulties: SNU WI/DYS DYP
Behavioural and emotional disorders: CO RA ST/ADD ADHD
Physical and medical conditions: AT IT RA SM TW W WA2 WA3/CP EPI HEA HI IM VI W

HATHEROP CASTLE SCHOOL

Hatherop, Cirencester, Gloucestershire GL7 3NB
Website: www.hatheropcastle. co.uk
Type: Co-educational Boarding and Day 2–13
Learning difficulties: SNU WI/ MLD
Behavioural and emotional disorders: ST

THE RICHARD PATE SCHOOL

Southern Road, Cheltenham, Gloucestershire GL53 9RP
Website: www.richardpate.co.uk
Type: Co-educational Day Only 3–11
Learning difficulties: CA SNU WI/ MLD DYS
Physical and medical conditions: CA TW WA2/CP EPI HEA VI

WESTONBIRT SCHOOL

Tetbury, Gloucestershire GL8 8QG
Website: www.westonbirt. gloucs.sch.uk
Type: Girls Boarding and Day 11–18
Learning difficulties: SNU/DYC DYS DYP
Physical and medical conditions: EPI HEA HI

WYCLIFFE COLLEGE+

Bath Road, Stonehouse, Gloucestershire GL10 2JQ
Website: www.wycliffe.co.uk
Type: Co-educational Boarding and Day 2–18
Learning difficulties: SNU WI/ DYC DYS DYP
Physical and medical conditions: RA

WYCLIFFE PREPARATORY SCHOOL+

Ryeford Hall, Stonehouse, Gloucestershire GL10 2LD
Website: www.wycliffe.co.uk
Type: Co-educational Boarding and Day 2–13
Learning difficulties: CA SNU WI/ DYC DYS DYP
Behavioural and emotional disorders: RA/ADD
Physical and medical conditions: CA RA SM/EPI HEA

HAMPSHIRE

DURLSTON COURT

Becton Lane, New Milton, Hampshire BH25 7AQ
Website: www.durlstoncourt. co.uk
Type: Co-educational Day Only 2–13
Learning difficulties: CA SNU/ MLD DYC DYS DYP
Behavioural and emotional disorders: ADHD
Physical and medical conditions: HEA

HORDLE WALHAMPTON SCHOOL+

Lymington, Hampshire SO41 5ZG
Website: www.hordlewalhampton. co.uk
Type: Co-educational Boarding and Day 2–13
Learning difficulties: CA SNU/ MLD DYS DYP
Behavioural and emotional disorders: ST/ASP
Physical and medical conditions: CA RA SM TW WA3/HEA HI

LORD WANDSWORTH COLLEGE

Hook, Hampshire RG29 1TB
Website: www.lordwandsworth. org
Type: Co-educational Boarding and Day 11–18
Learning difficulties: RA WI/DYS
Behavioural and emotional disorders: RA/ADD ASP
Physical and medical conditions: RA SM/EPI HEA

MAYVILLE HIGH SCHOOL+
35 St Simon's Road, Southsea,
Hampshire PO5 2PE
Website: www.mayvilleschool.
com
Type: Co-educational Day Only
Learning difficulties: SNU/DYS
DYP
*Behavioural and emotional
disorders:* ST/ADD ADHD ASP
ASD
Physical and medical conditions:
RA SM/HEA HI

THE PORTSMOUTH
GRAMMAR SCHOOL
High Street, Portsmouth,
Hampshire PO1 2LN
Website: www.pgs.org.uk
Type: Co-educational Day Only
2–18
Learning difficulties: WI

PORTSMOUTH HIGH
SCHOOL GDST
Kent Road, Southsea, Hampshire
PO5 3EQ
Website: www.portsmouthhigh.
co.uk
Type: Girls Day Only 3–18
Learning difficulties: WI/DYS DYP
Physical and medical conditions:
RA/HEA

ST NICHOLAS' SCHOOL
Redfields House, Redfields Lane,
Fleet, Hampshire GU52 0RF
Website: www.st-nicholas.
hants.sch.uk
Type: Girls Day Only 3–16 (Boys
3–7)
Learning difficulties: WI/DYS
Physical and medical conditions:
RA/HEA

SHERBORNE HOUSE
SCHOOL
Lakewood Road, Eastleigh,
Hampshire SO53 1EU
Website: www.sherbornehouse.
co.uk
Type: Co-educational Day Only
3–11
Learning difficulties: SNU/DYS

THE STROUD SCHOOL
Highwood House, Romsey,
Hampshire SO51 9ZH
Website: www.stroud-romsey.
com
Type: Co-educational Day Only
3–13
Learning difficulties: CA SNU/
MLD DYS
Physical and medical conditions:
RA

TWYFORD SCHOOL
Twyford, Winchester, Hampshire
SO21 1NW
Website: www.twyfordschool.
com
Type: Co-educational Day and
Boarding 3–13
Learning difficulties: SNU/DYS
Physical and medical conditions:
RA SM/HEA

WINCHESTER COLLEGE
College Street, Winchester,
Hampshire SO23 9NA
Website: www.
winchestercollege.org
Type: Boys Boarding and Day
13–18
Learning difficulties: SNU/DYC
DYS DYP
*Behavioural and emotional
disorders:* RA/ADD ADHD ASP
Physical and medical conditions:
VI

HERTFORDSHIRE

ABBOT'S HILL SCHOOL
Bunkers Lane, Hemel
Hempstead, Hertfordshire
HP3 8RP
Website: www.abbotshill.herts.
sch.uk
Type: Girls Day Only 3–16 (Boys
3–5)
Learning difficulties: CA SNU WI/
DYC DYS DYP
*Behavioural and emotional
disorders:* CO/ASP BESD
Physical and medical conditions:
IT SM/EPI HEA HI VI

EGERTON ROTHESAY
SCHOOL*
Durrants Lane, Berkhamsted,
Hertfordshire HP4 3UJ
Website: www.eger-roth.co.uk
Type: Co-educational Day Only
5–16
Learning difficulties: CA SC SNU/
MLD DYC DYS DYP SP&LD
*Behavioural and emotional
disorders:* ST/ADD ADHD ASP
ASD
Physical and medical conditions:
AT CA DS RA SM TW W WA3/CP
EPI HEA HI IM VI

HABERDASHERS' ASKE'S
BOYS' SCHOOL
Butterfly Lane, Elstree,
Hertfordshire WD6 3AF
Website: www.habsboys.org.uk
Type: Boys Day Only 5–18
Learning difficulties: RA/DYS
DYP
*Behavioural and emotional
disorders:* ADHD

HARESFOOT PREPARATORY SCHOOL
Chesham Road, Berkhamsted, Hertfordshire HP4 2SZ
Website: www.haresfoot.herts.sch.uk
Type: Co-educational Day Only (Children may join from 5 months of age into our Day Nursery.)
Learning difficulties: CA WI/DYS
Physical and medical conditions: CA RA/HEA HI IM

HIGH ELMS MANOR SCHOOL
High Elms Lane, Watford, Hertfordshire WD25 0JX
Website: http://www.highelmsmanorschool.com
Type: Co-educational Day Only
Learning difficulties: CA WI/MLD DYC DYS DYP
Behavioural and emotional disorders: RA/ADD ASP ASD
Physical and medical conditions: AT CA TW WA1 WA2/HEA HI W

KINGSHOTT SCHOOL
Hitchin, Hertfordshire SG4 7JX
Website: www.kingshottschool.co.uk
Type: Co-educational Day Only 4–13
Learning difficulties: DYS DYP
Physical and medical conditions: RA SM/HEA

NORFOLK LODGE MONTESSORI NURSERY
Dancers Hill Road, Barnet, Hertfordshire EN5 4RP
Website: www.norfolklodgeschool.co.uk
Type: Co-educational Day Only 1–4
Learning difficulties: RA
Behavioural and emotional disorders: RA
Physical and medical conditions: RA

THE PURCELL SCHOOL
Aldenham Road, Bushey, Hertfordshire WD23 2TS
Website: www.purcell-school.org
Type: Co-educational Day and Boarding 8–18
Behavioural and emotional disorders: CO RA/ASP
Physical and medical conditions: RA/VI

RICKMANSWORTH PNEU SCHOOL
88 The Drive, Rickmansworth, Hertfordshire WD3 4DU
Website: www.rickmansworthpneu.co.uk
Type: Girls Day Only 3–11
Learning difficulties: CA SNU/DYS DYP
Behavioural and emotional disorders: RA
Physical and medical conditions: HEA

ST CHRISTOPHER SCHOOL
Barrington Road, Letchworth Garden City, Hertfordshire SG6 3JZ
Website: www.stchris.co.uk
Type: Co-educational Boarding and Day 2–18
Learning difficulties: SNU/DYS DYP
Behavioural and emotional disorders: ASP
Physical and medical conditions: RA/EPI

ST EDMUND'S COLLEGE AND ST HUGH'S SCHOOL
Old Hall Green, Ware, Hertfordshire SG11 1DS
Website: www.stedmundscollege.org
Type: Co-educational Day and Boarding 3–18
Learning difficulties: CA WI/DYS DYP
Behavioural and emotional disorders: RA/ASP
Physical and medical conditions: IT SM TW WA2/EPI HEA HI VI

ST. HILDA'S SCHOOL
28 Douglas Road, Harpenden, Hertfordshire AL5 2ES
Website: www.sthildasharpenden.co.uk
Type: Girls Day Only 2–11
Learning difficulties: SC WI/DYC DYS DYP
Physical and medical conditions: W/HI

ST JOSEPH'S IN THE PARK
St Mary's Lane, Hertford, Hertfordshire SG14 2LX
Website: www.stjosephsinthepark.co.uk
Type: Co-educational Day Only 3–11
Learning difficulties: CA SC SNU/DYC DYS DYP
Behavioural and emotional disorders: ADD ADHD
Physical and medical conditions: CA/HEA HI

ISLE OF WIGHT

PRIORY SCHOOL
Alverstone Manor, Shanklin, Isle of Wight PO37 7JB
Type: Co-educational Day Only 2–18
Physical and medical conditions: W/W

RYDE SCHOOL
Queen's Road, Ryde, Isle of Wight PO33 3BE
Website: www.rydeschool.org.uk
Type: Co-educational Day and Boarding 3–18
Learning difficulties: SNU/DYC DYS DYP

KENT

ASHFORD SCHOOL
Ashford, Kent TN24 8PB
Website: www.ashfordschool. co.uk
Type: Co-educational Day and Boarding 3–18 (Co-ed 3–11)
Learning difficulties: CA SNU/ MLD DYS DYP
Behavioural and emotional disorders: CO RA/ADHD ASP ASD
Physical and medical conditions: RA SM W WA3/HEA

ASHGROVE SCHOOL
116 Widmore Road, Bromley, Kent BR1 3BE
Website: www.ashgrove.org.uk
Type: Co-educational Day Only 3–11
Learning difficulties: WI/DYS DYP

BABINGTON HOUSE SCHOOL
Grange Drive, Chislehurst, Kent BR7 5ES
Website: www.babingtonhouse. com
Type: Girls Day Only 3–16 (Boys 3–7)
Learning difficulties: CA WI/DYS DYP
Physical and medical conditions: RA/HI

BENENDEN SCHOOL
Cranbrook, Kent TN17 4AA
Website: www.benenden.kent. sch.uk
Type: Girls Boarding Only 11–18
Learning difficulties: SNU/DYS DYP
Behavioural and emotional disorders: RA
Physical and medical conditions: RA SM WA2/HEA HI VI

BRONTE SCHOOL
7 Pelham Road, Gravesend, Kent DA11 0HN
Website: www.bronteschool. co.uk
Type: Co-educational Day Only 3–11
Learning difficulties: CA SC/MLD DYS DYP
Behavioural and emotional disorders: CA/ADD ADHD ASP
Physical and medical conditions: CA RA SM WA3/HEA

DOVER COLLEGE
Effingham Crescent, Dover, Kent CT17 9RH
Website: www.dovercollege. org.uk
Type: Co-educational Boarding and Day 3–18
Learning difficulties: WI/DYS DYP
Physical and medical conditions: RA SM/HEA HI VI

DULWICH PREPARATORY SCHOOL, CRANBROOK
Coursehorn, Cranbrook, Kent TN17 3NP
Website: www.dcpskent.org
Type: Co-educational Day and Boarding 3–13
Learning difficulties: CA SNU WI/ DYS DYP
Behavioural and emotional disorders: ADHD ASP
Physical and medical conditions: IT RA W/EPI HEA IM

FARRINGTONS SCHOOL
Perry Street, Chislehurst, Kent BR7 6LR
Website: www.farringtons.org.uk
Type: Co-educational Day and Boarding 3–19
Learning difficulties: WI/MLD DYS DYP
Behavioural and emotional disorders: RA
Physical and medical conditions: RA SM WA3/EPI HEA HI VI

HARENC SCHOOL TRUST
167 Rectory Lane, Sidcup, Kent DA14 5BU
Website: www.harencschool. co.uk
Type: Boys Day Only 3–11
Learning difficulties: CA/MLD DYS DYP
Behavioural and emotional disorders: CA ST/ADD ASP
Physical and medical conditions: IT TW W WA2/HEA

HILDEN OAKS SCHOOL
38 Dry Hill Park Road, Tonbridge, Kent TN10 3BU
Website: www.hildenoaks.co.uk
Type: Co-educational Day Only
Learning difficulties: WI

KENT COLLEGE INFANT & JUNIOR SCHOOL
Vernon Holme, Canterbury, Kent CT2 9AQ
Website: www.kentcollege.com/ junior
Type: Co-educational Day and Boarding 3–11
Learning difficulties: SC SNU/ MLD DYC DYS DYP
Behavioural and emotional disorders: CA CO
Physical and medical conditions: TW WA3/HEA

KENT COLLEGE PEMBURY
Old Church Road, Tunbridge Wells, Kent TN2 4AX
Website: www.kent-college.co.uk
Type: Girls Boarding and Day 3–18
Learning difficulties: WI/DYC DYS DYP
Behavioural and emotional disorders: CO/ADD BESD
Physical and medical conditions: SM WA3/HEA

KING'S PREPARATORY SCHOOL
King Edward Road, Rochester, Kent ME1 1UB
Website: www.kings-school-rochester.co.uk
Type: Co-educational Day and Boarding 8–13
Learning difficulties: WI/DYS DYP

NORTHBOURNE PARK SCHOOL
Betteshanger, Deal, Kent CT14 0NW
Website: www.northbournepark. com
Type: Co-educational Day and Boarding 3–13
Learning difficulties: CA SNU/ DYC DYS DYP
Behavioural and emotional disorders: CO/ADD ADHD ASP ASD
Physical and medical conditions: CA RA/HEA HI VI

RUSSELL HOUSE SCHOOL
Station Road, Sevenoaks, Kent TN14 5QU
Website: www.russellhouse.kent. sch.uk
Type: Co-educational Day Only 2–11
Learning difficulties: WI/DYS DYP
Physical and medical conditions: WA1

ST FAITH'S AT ASH SCHOOL
5 The Street, Canterbury, Kent CT3 2HH
Type: Co-educational Day Only 3–11
Learning difficulties: CA RA WI/ DYS DYP
Behavioural and emotional disorders: CA RA ST/BESD
Physical and medical conditions: RA SM WA3/HEA HI

ST LAWRENCE COLLEGE
College Road, Ramsgate, Kent CT11 7AE
Website: www.slcuk.com
Type: Co-educational Boarding and Day 3–18
Learning difficulties: SNU/DYC DYS DYP
Behavioural and emotional disorders: ADD ADHD
Physical and medical conditions: RA SM/EPI HEA HI

ST LAWRENCE COLLEGE JUNIOR SCHOOL
College Road, Ramsgate, Kent CT11 7AF
Website: www.slcuk.com
Type: Co-educational Boarding and Day 3–11
Learning difficulties: CA WI/MLD DYS DYP
Behavioural and emotional disorders: CA RA TS ST/ASP ASD
Physical and medical conditions: RA SM WA3/HEA HI

ST MICHAEL'S SCHOOL
Otford Court, Sevenoaks, Kent TN14 5SA
Website: www.stmichaels-otford. co.uk
Type: Co-educational Day Only 2–13
Learning difficulties: WI

STEEPHILL INDEPENDENT SCHOOL
Castle Hill, Longfield, Kent DA3 7BG
Website: www.steephill.co.uk
Type: Co-educational Day Only 3–11
Learning difficulties: CA WI/MLD DYS
Behavioural and emotional disorders: RA ST
Physical and medical conditions: RA TW WA2

WALTHAMSTOW HALL
Hollybush Lane, Sevenoaks, Kent TN13 3UL
Website: www.walthamstow-hall. co.uk
Type: Girls Day Only 2–18
Learning difficulties: WI/DYC DYS DYP
Behavioural and emotional disorders: CO ST/ASP
Physical and medical conditions: AT SL SM TW/HEA

LANCASHIRE

ARNOLD SCHOOL
Lytham Road, Blackpool,
Lancashire FY4 1JG
Website: www.arnoldschool.com
Type: Co-educational Day Only
2–18
Learning difficulties: SNU WI/
MLD DYC DYS DYP
*Behavioural and emotional
disorders:* CA CO ST/ADD ADHD
BESD
Physical and medical conditions:
SL SM WA2/HEA HI

BURY GRAMMAR SCHOOL
BOYS
Tenterden Street, Bury,
Lancashire BL9 0HN
Website: www.bgsboys.co.uk
Type: Boys Day Only 7–18
Learning difficulties: RA/DYS
*Behavioural and emotional
disorders:* RA
Physical and medical conditions:
RA/EPI HEA HI

KING EDWARD VII AND
QUEEN MARY SCHOOL
Clifton Drive South, Lytham St
Annes, Lancashire FY8 1DT
Website: www.keqms.co.uk
Type: Co-educational Day Only
2–18
Learning difficulties: CA WI/DYC
DYS DYP
*Behavioural and emotional
disorders:* RA/ADD ADHD
Physical and medical conditions:
SM WA2/HEA VI

KIRKHAM GRAMMAR
SCHOOL
Ribby Road, Preston, Lancashire
PR4 2BH
Website: www.kirkhamgrammar.
co.uk
Type: Co-educational Boarding
and Day 3–18
Learning difficulties: SNU/DYC
DYS
Physical and medical conditions:
HEA

STONYHURST COLLEGE
Clitheroe, Lancashire BB7 9PZ
Website: www.stonyhurst.ac.uk
Type: Co-educational Boarding
and Day 13–18
Learning difficulties: SNU WI/
MLD DYC DYS DYP
*Behavioural and emotional
disorders:* CO ST/ADD ADHD
ASP
Physical and medical conditions:
SM WA3/EPI HEA HI

LEICESTERSHIRE

FAIRFIELD PREPARATORY
SCHOOL
Leicester Road, Loughborough,
Leicestershire LE11 2AE
Website: www.lesfairfield.org
Type: Co-educational Day Only
4–11
Learning difficulties: WI/DYS DYP
*Behavioural and emotional
disorders:* ASP
Physical and medical conditions:
SM TW WA2

LOUGHBOROUGH HIGH
SCHOOL
Burton Walks, Loughborough,
Leicestershire LE11 2DU
Website: www.leshigh.org
Type: Girls Day Only 11–18
Learning difficulties: RA WI/DYC
DYS DYP
Physical and medical conditions:
RA/EPI HEA HI VI

MANOR HOUSE SCHOOL
South Street, Ashby-de-la-Zouch,
Leicestershire LE65 1BR
Website: www.
manorhouseashby.co.uk
Type: Co-educational Day Only
4–16
Learning difficulties: CA SC WI/
DYC DYS DYP
*Behavioural and emotional
disorders:* RA/ADD ASP
Physical and medical conditions:
CA RA WA3/HEA HI VI

ST CRISPIN'S SCHOOL+
6 St Mary's Road, Leicester,
Leicestershire LE2 1XA
Website: members.aol.com/
bharrild/stcrispins
Type: Co-educational Day Only
3–16
Learning difficulties: CA RA SC
SNU WI/MLD DYC DYS DYP
*Behavioural and emotional
disorders:* CA TS ST/ADD ADHD
ASP BESD
Physical and medical conditions:
AT CA IT RA SL SM TW WA3/HEA
HI VI

LINCOLNSHIRE

KIRKSTONE HOUSE SCHOOL
Main Street, Bourne, Lincolnshire PE6 9PA
Website: www. kirkstonehouseschool.co.uk
Type: Co-educational Day Only 4–16
Learning difficulties: CA SNU WI/ MLD DYS DYP
Behavioural and emotional disorders: ADHD ASP ASD

ST HUGH'S SCHOOL
Cromwell Avenue, Woodhall Spa, Lincolnshire LN10 6TQ
Website: www.st-hughs. lincs.sch.uk
Type: Co-educational Boarding and Day 2–13
Learning difficulties: CA SNU WI/ MLD DYC DYS
Behavioural and emotional disorders: CA/ADD ADHD ASP ASD CB
Physical and medical conditions: CA IT SM TW WA2/HEA HI IM VI

ST MARY'S PREPARATORY SCHOOL
5 Pottergate, Lincoln, Lincolnshire LN2 1PH
Website: www.stmarysprep. co.uk
Type: Co-educational Day Only 2–11
Learning difficulties: CA SNU/ MLD DYS DYP
Behavioural and emotional disorders: RA/ASD
Physical and medical conditions: AT IT RA SM TW/CP HEA HI IM VI

LONDON

ALLEYN'S SCHOOL
Townley Road, London SE22 8SU
Website: www.alleyns.org.uk
Type: Co-educational Day Only 4–18
Learning difficulties: WI/DYC DYS DYP
Behavioural and emotional disorders: CO/ADD ASP TOU
Physical and medical conditions: RA SM TW/EPI HEA HI VI

ASTON HOUSE SCHOOL
1 Aston Road, London W5 2RL
Website: www.happychild.co.uk
Type: Co-educational Day Only 2–11
Learning difficulties: SNU/DYS DYP
Behavioural and emotional disorders: ST
Physical and medical conditions: CA SM TW WA3/HEA VI

AVENUE HOUSE SCHOOL
70 The Avenue, London W13 8LS
Website: www.avenuehouse.org
Type: Co-educational Day Only 3–11
Learning difficulties: RA WI/MLD DYS
Physical and medical conditions: RA SM WA3/HEA

BROOMWOOD HALL SCHOOL
68–74 Nightingale Lane, London SW12 8NR
Website: www.broomwood.co.uk
Type: Co-educational Day Only 4–13
Behavioural and emotional disorders: CA/ADD
Physical and medical conditions: IT RA SM TW

CAMERON HOUSE SCHOOL+
4 The Vale, London SW3 6AH
Website: www.cameronhouseschool.org
Type: Co-educational Day Only 4–11

CHANNING SCHOOL
London N6 5HF
Website: www.channing.co.uk
Type: Girls Day Only 4–18
Learning difficulties: WI/MLD DYS DYP
Behavioural and emotional disorders: ADHD
Physical and medical conditions: SM TW WA1 WA2/EPI HI IM

CHARTERHOUSE SQUARE SCHOOL
40 Charterhouse Square, London EC1M 6EA
Website: www. charterhousesquareschool.co.uk
Type: Co-educational Day Only 3–11
Learning difficulties: WI

DALLINGTON SCHOOL
8 Dallington Street, London EC1V 0BW
Website: www.dallingtonschool. co.uk
Type: Co-educational Day Only 3–11
Learning difficulties: CA/DYS DYP
Behavioural and emotional disorders: ST/ADD
Physical and medical conditions: RA/HEA HI

THE DOMINIE+
55 Warriner Gardens, London SW11 4DX
Website: www.thedominie.co.uk
Type: Co-educational Day Only 6–12
Learning difficulties: DYC DYS DYP
Behavioural and emotional disorders: ADHD
Physical and medical conditions: RA/HI

DUFF MILLER
59 Queen's Gate, London
SW7 5JP
Website: www.duffmiller.com
Type: Co-educational Day Only
14–19
Learning difficulties: WI/MLD
DYS DYP
*Behavioural and emotional
disorders:* ADD ADHD
Physical and medical conditions:
RA/EPI HEA VI

EATON HOUSE BELGRAVIA
3–5 Eaton Gate, London
SW1W 9BA
Website: www.
eatonhouseschools.com
Type: Boys Day Only 4–8
Learning difficulties: SNU WI/
MLD DYC DYS DYP
*Behavioural and emotional
disorders:* CA TS/BESD
Physical and medical conditions:
AT SM WA3/EPI

EATON HOUSE THE MANOR PREPARATORY
58 Clapham Common Northside,
London SW4 9RU
Website: www.
eatonhouseschools.com
Type: Boys Day Only 2–13
Learning difficulties: SNU WI/
DYC DYS DYP
*Behavioural and emotional
disorders:* CA RA/ADD ASP ASD
Physical and medical conditions:
CA

EATON HOUSE THE VALE
2 Elvaston Place, London
SW7 5QH
Website: www.
eatonhouseschools.com
Type: Co-educational Day Only
4–11
Learning difficulties: CA WI/MLD
*Behavioural and emotional
disorders:* TS
Physical and medical conditions:
RA

THE FALCONS SCHOOL FOR BOYS
2 Burnaby Gardens, London
W4 3DT
Website: www.falconschool.com
Type: Boys Day Only 3–8
Learning difficulties: CA WI
Physical and medical conditions:
RA/HEA

FINTON HOUSE SCHOOL
171 Trinity Road, London
SW17 7HL
Website: www.fintonhouse.org.uk
Type: Co-educational Day Only
4–11
Learning difficulties: CA SC SNU/
DOW DYC DYS DYP
*Behavioural and emotional
disorders:* RA/ASP ASD BESD
Physical and medical conditions:
CA DS HL RA SM TW WA3/HEA
HI VI

FRANCIS HOLLAND SCHOOL, SLOANE SQUARE SW1
39 Graham Terrace, London
SW1W 8JF
Website: www.fhs-sw1.org.uk
Type: Girls Day Only 4–18
Special needs: ADHD CP DYC
DYP DYS EPI HEA

GATEHOUSE SCHOOL
Sewardstone Road, London
E2 9JG
Website: www.gatehouseschool.
co.uk
Type: Co-educational Day Only
3–11
Learning difficulties: CA/DOW
DYS
Physical and medical conditions:
TW

THE HARRODIAN
Lonsdale Road, London
SW13 9QN
Website: www.harrodian.com
Type: Co-educational Day Only
5–18
Learning difficulties: SNU/DYC
DYS DYP

HEATH HOUSE PREPARATORY SCHOOL
37 Wemyss Road, London
SE3 0TG
Website: www.
heathhouseprepschool.com
Type: Co-educational Day Only
4–11
Physical and medical conditions:
W/W

LANSDOWNE COLLEGE
40–44 Bark Place, London
W2 4AT
Website: www.
lansdownecollege.com
Type: Co-educational Day Only
14–19 (Lansdowne is an
independent Sixth Form College
with a GCSE Department from
Year 10.)
Learning difficulties: RA/MLD
DYC DYS DYP
*Behavioural and emotional
disorders:* RA/ADD ADHD ASD
Physical and medical conditions:
RA WA3/EPI HEA

LION HOUSE SCHOOL
The Old Methodist Hall, London
SW15 6EH
Website: www.lionhouseschool.
co.uk
Type: Co-educational Day Only
3–8
Learning difficulties: CA WI/MLD
*Behavioural and emotional
disorders:* RA/ADD ASD
Physical and medical conditions:
AT CA IT TW WA2/HEA HI

MADNI GIRLS SCHOOL
Myrdle Street, London E1 1HL
Type: Girls Day Only 12–18
Learning difficulties: WI/DYC
*Behavioural and emotional
disorders:* RA
Physical and medical conditions:
WA3/HEA VI

MANDER PORTMAN WOODWARD
90–92 Queen's Gate, London
SW7 5AB
Website: www.mpw.co.uk
Type: Co-educational Day Only
14–19
Physical and medical conditions:
W/W

THE MONTESSORI HOUSE
5 Princes Avenue, London
N10 3LS
Website: www.montessori-house.
co.uk
Type: Co-educational Day Only
1–5
Learning difficulties: CA/MLD
*Behavioural and emotional
disorders:* CA/ASD
Physical and medical conditions:
CA/HEA

NORTHCOTE LODGE
SCHOOL
26 Bolingbroke Grove, London
SW11 6EL
Website: www.northcotelodge.
co.uk
Type: Boys Day Only 8–13
Learning difficulties: WI/DYC DYS
DYP
Physical and medical conditions:
RA SM/HEA

NOTTING HILL AND
EALING HIGH SCHOOL
GDST
2 Cleveland Road, London
W13 8AX
Website: www.gdst.net/nhehs
Type: Girls Day Only 4–18
Learning difficulties: WI/DYC DYS
DYP
*Behavioural and emotional
disorders:* RA/ADD ASP
Physical and medical conditions:
RA/HEA VI

PRIMROSE INDEPENDENT
SCHOOL
Congregational Church, London
N5 2TE
Type: Co-educational Day Only
2–11
Learning difficulties: WI/MLD
DOW DYS DYP
*Behavioural and emotional
disorders:* RA/ASP ASD
Physical and medical conditions:
AT CA/HEA

PUTNEY PARK SCHOOL
11 Woodborough Road, London
SW15 6PY
Website: www.putneypark.
london.sch.uk
Type: Co-educational Day Only
4–16
Learning difficulties: WI/DYC DYS
DYP
*Behavioural and emotional
disorders:* RA
Physical and medical conditions:
RA/EPI HEA

QUEEN'S GATE SCHOOL
133 Queen's Gate, London
SW7 5LE
Website: www.queensgate.org.uk
Type: Girls Day Only 4–18
Learning difficulties: DYC DYS
DYP
*Behavioural and emotional
disorders:* RA
Physical and medical conditions:
RA/HEA

THE ROCHE SCHOOL
11 Frogmore, London SW18 1HW
Website: www.therocheschool.
co.uk
Type: Co-educational Day Only
2–11
Learning difficulties: CA SC WI/
MLD DOW DYS DYP
*Behavioural and emotional
disorders:* ADD ADHD ASP ASD
Physical and medical conditions:
RA/IM

THE ROWANS SCHOOL
19 Drax Avenue, London
SW20 0EG
Website: www.kcs.org.uk
Type: Co-educational Day Only
3–8
Learning difficulties: WI
Physical and medical conditions:
RA/HEA

ST DUNSTAN'S COLLEGE
Stanstead Road, London SE6 4TY
Website: www.stdunstans.org.uk
Type: Co-educational Day Only
3–18
Learning difficulties: CA WI/DYC
DYS DYP
Physical and medical conditions:
RA/HI

ST JAMES JUNIOR
SCHOOL
Earsby Street, London W14 8SH
Website: www.stjamesjuniors.
co.uk
Type: Co-educational Day Only
4–11
Learning difficulties: WI/MLD

ST JOSEPH'S CONVENT
SCHOOL
59 Cambridge Park, London
E11 2PR
Type: Girls Day Only 3–11
Learning difficulties: CA SNU/
MLD
Physical and medical conditions:
HEA

ST MARGARET'S SCHOOL
18 Kidderpore Gardens, London
NW3 7SR
Website: www.st-margarets.
co.uk
Type: Girls Day Only 4–16
Learning difficulties: RA/MLD
DYC DYS DYP
*Behavioural and emotional
disorders:* CO
Physical and medical conditions:
HL SM W WA3

ST OLAVE'S
PREPARATORY SCHOOL
106–110 Southwood Road,
London SE9 3QS
Website: www.stolaves.org.uk
Type: Co-educational Day Only
3–11
Learning difficulties: SNU WI/SLD
DYS DYP

ST PAUL'S CATHEDRAL
SCHOOL
2 New Change, London
EC4M 9AD
Website: www.spcs.london.
sch.uk
Type: Co-educational Boarding
and Day 4–13
Learning difficulties: WI
Physical and medical conditions:
RA SM

STREATHAM & CLAPHAM HIGH SCHOOL
42 Abbotswood Road, London SW16 1AW
Website: www.gdst.net/streathamhigh
Type: Girls Day Only 3–18 (Boys 3–5)
Learning difficulties: CA SNU/DYC DYS DYP
Behavioural and emotional disorders: CA CO RA TS ST/ADD ASP ASD BESD CB
Physical and medical conditions: AT CA HL IT SM TW WA2/EPI HEA HI IM VI W

THAMES CHRISTIAN COLLEGE+
Wye Street, London SW11 2HB
Website: www.thameschristiancollege.org.uk
Type: Co-educational Day Only 11–16
Learning difficulties: CA WI/DYS DYP

UNIVERSITY COLLEGE SCHOOL
Frognal, London NW3 6XH
Website: www.ucs.org.uk
Type: Co-educational Day Only 11–18 (Boys aged 11–18 Girls aged 16–18 (Co-educational Sixth Form only))
Learning difficulties: MLD DYS
Behavioural and emotional disorders: CO
Physical and medical conditions: CA/VI

UNIVERSITY COLLEGE SCHOOL JUNIOR BRANCH
11 Holly Hill, London NW3 6QN
Website: www.ucs.org.uk
Type: Boys Day Only 7–11
Learning difficulties: DYS DYP
Behavioural and emotional disorders: CO/ADD ADHD ASP
Physical and medical conditions: RA/HI VI

WESTMINSTER ABBEY CHOIR SCHOOL
Dean's Yard, London SW1P 3NY
Website: www.westminster-abbey.org
Type: Boys Boarding Only 8–13
Learning difficulties: WI/DYS

WESTMINSTER CATHEDRAL CHOIR SCHOOL
Ambrosden Avenue, London SW1P 1QH
Website: www.choirschool.com
Type: Boys Boarding and Day 7–13
Learning difficulties: WI/DYS DYP
Behavioural and emotional disorders: RA/ADD
Physical and medical conditions: RA

WESTMINSTER TUTORS
86 Old Brompton Road, London SW7 3LQ
Website: www.westminstertutors.co.uk
Type: Co-educational Day Only 11–25
Learning difficulties: SC WI/MLD DYS DYP
Behavioural and emotional disorders: RA/ASP
Physical and medical conditions: AT RA/HEA

WETHERBY PREPARATORY SCHOOL
48 Bryanstan Square, London W1H 2EA
Website: www.wetherbyprep.co.uk
Type: Boys Day Only 8–13
Learning difficulties: DYS
Physical and medical conditions: RA

GREATER MANCHESTER

ABBEY COLLEGE
Cheapside, Manchester, Greater Manchester M2 4WG
Website: www.abbeymanchester.co.uk
Type: Co-educational Day Only 14–19
Behavioural and emotional disorders: ADHD
Physical and medical conditions: TW WA2

THE MANCHESTER GRAMMAR SCHOOL
Old Hall Lane, Manchester, Greater Manchester M13 0XT
Website: www.mgs.org
Type: Boys Day Only 9–18
Learning difficulties: RA WI/DYC DYS DYP
Behavioural and emotional disorders: RA/ADD ADHD ASD
Physical and medical conditions: RA/EPI HI VI W

WITHINGTON GIRLS' SCHOOL
100 Wellington Road, Manchester, Greater Manchester M14 6BL
Website: www.withington.manchester.sch.uk
Type: Girls Day Only 7–18
Learning difficulties: CA RA WI/DYC DYS DYP
Behavioural and emotional disorders: ADD
Physical and medical conditions: SM TW/HEA HI

MERSEYSIDE

MERCHANT TAYLORS' BOYS' SCHOOLS
Liverpool Road, Liverpool,
Merseyside L23 0QP
Website: www.merchanttaylors.
com
Type: Boys Day Only 4–18
Learning difficulties: CA SNU/
MLD DYC DYS DYP
*Behavioural and emotional
disorders:* TS ST/ADD ADHD ASP
ASD BESD CB
Physical and medical conditions:
IT SM/EPI HEA HI VI

STREATHAM HOUSE SCHOOL
Victoria Road West, Liverpool,
Merseyside L23 8UQ
Website: www.streathamhouse.
co.uk
Type: Co-educational Day Only
2–16 (Boys 2–11)
Learning difficulties: CA SC WI/
MLD DOW DYC DYS DYP
*Behavioural and emotional
disorders:* ADD ADHD ASD
Physical and medical conditions:
RA/HEA VI

MIDDLESEX

BUCKINGHAM COLLEGE SCHOOL
11–17 Hindes Road, Harrow,
Middlesex HA1 1SH
Website: www.buckcoll.org
Type: Boys Day Only 11–18 (Co-
ed VIth Form, but currently boys
only.)
Learning difficulties: CA SNU/
DYC DYS SP&LD
*Behavioural and emotional
disorders:* ADD ADHD ASP BESD
Physical and medical conditions:
AT RA/HEA

HAMPTON SCHOOL
Hanworth Road, Hampton,
Middlesex TW12 3HD
Website: www.hamptonschool.
org.uk
Type: Boys Day Only 11–18
Learning difficulties: SNU/DYS
DYP
*Behavioural and emotional
disorders:* CO TS ST/ADD ADHD
ASP ASD TOU
Physical and medical conditions:
AT CA SM TW W WA2/EPI HEA
HI VI

THE JOHN LYON SCHOOL
Middle Road, Harrow, Middlesex
HA2 0HN
Website: www.johnlyon.org
Type: Boys Day Only 11–18
Learning difficulties: CA SNU WI/
DYC DYS DYP
*Behavioural and emotional
disorders:* CA CO/ADD ASD
Physical and medical conditions:
SM/EPI VI

THE LADY ELEANOR HOLLES SCHOOL
102 Hanworth Road, Hampton,
Middlesex TW12 3HF
Website: www.lehs.org.uk
Type: Girls Day Only 7–18
Learning difficulties: WI/DYC DYS
DYP
*Behavioural and emotional
disorders:* CO/TOU
Physical and medical conditions:
RA SM TW WA1/EPI HEA VI

THE MALL SCHOOL
185 Hampton Road,
Twickenham, Middlesex
TW2 5NQ
Website: www.mall.richmond.
sch.uk
Type: Boys Day Only 4–13
Learning difficulties: CA RA WI/
DYS DYP
*Behavioural and emotional
disorders:* CA
Physical and medical conditions:
RA SM TW WA2/HEA

MERCHANT TAYLORS' SCHOOL
Sandy Lodge, Northwood,
Middlesex HA6 2HT
Website: www.mtsn.org.uk
Type: Boys Day Only 11–18
Learning difficulties: RA SNU/
DYS DYP
*Behavioural and emotional
disorders:* RA/ADD ADHD ASP
Physical and medical conditions:
RA WA3/CP EPI HEA HI

NORTHWOOD COLLEGE
Maxwell Road, Northwood,
Middlesex HA6 2YE
Website: www.northwoodcollege.
co.uk
Type: Girls Day Only 3–18
Learning difficulties: WI/DYS DYP
Physical and medical conditions:
CA RA/HEA HI IM VI

ST HELEN'S SCHOOL
Eastbury Road, Northwood,
Middlesex HA6 3AS
Website: www.sthn.co.uk
Type: Girls Day Only 3–18
Learning difficulties: WI/DYS
*Behavioural and emotional
disorders:* CO
Physical and medical conditions:
AT CA SM TW/EPI HEA HI

ST MARTIN'S SCHOOL
40 Moor Park Road, Northwood,
Middlesex HA6 2DJ
Website: www.stmartins.org.uk
Type: Boys Day Only 3–13
Learning difficulties: SC/DYC
DYS DYP
*Behavioural and emotional
disorders:* ST/ADHD ASP
Physical and medical conditions:
RA TW WA3/HEA

NORFOLK

BEESTON HALL SCHOOL
Cromer, Norfolk NR27 9NQ
Website: www.beestonhall.co.uk
Type: Co-educational Boarding
and Day 7–13
Learning difficulties: CA SNU/
MLD DYC DYS DYP
*Behavioural and emotional
disorders:* CA TS/ADD ASP
Physical and medical conditions:
CA SM TW/CP HEA HI IM

GLEBE HOUSE SCHOOL
2 Cromer Road, Hunstanton,
Norfolk PE36 6HW
Website: www.
glebehouseschool.co.uk
Type: Co-educational Boarding
and Day 4–13
Learning difficulties: CA WI/DYC
DYS DYP
*Behavioural and emotional
disorders:* RA
Physical and medical conditions:
RA

HETHERSETT OLD HALL
SCHOOL
Norwich Road, Norwich, Norfolk
NR9 3DW
Website: www.hohs.co.uk
Type: Co-educational Day and
Boarding 4–18 (Day boys
admitted aged 4–11 Day girls
admitted aged 4–18 Boarding
girls admitted aged 9–18 No
boys boarding)
Learning difficulties: SNU/MLD
DYS
*Behavioural and emotional
disorders:* RA/BESD
Physical and medical conditions:
CA SM TW WA2/I IEA IM

LANGLEY SCHOOL
Langley Park, Norwich, Norfolk
NR14 6BJ
Website: www.langleyschool.
co.uk
Type: Co-educational Boarding
and Day 10–18
Learning difficulties: SNU/DYC
DYS DYP
*Behavioural and emotional
disorders:* RA/ADD
Physical and medical conditions:
BL CA IT SM TW WA1/CP HEA IM
VI W

THE NEW ECCLES HALL
SCHOOL
Norwich, Norfolk NR16 2NZ
Website: www.neweccleshall.
com
Type: Co-educational Day and
Boarding 4–16
Learning difficulties: SC SNU/
DYC DYS DYP
*Behavioural and emotional
disorders:* RA ST/ADD ADHD
ASP ASD TOU
Physical and medical conditions:
AT CA IT RA SM/HEA HI IM

RIDDLESWORTH HALL+
Diss, Norfolk IP22 2TA
Website: www.riddlesworthhall.
com
Type: Co-educational Day and
Boarding 2–13 (Co-educational
boarding)
Learning difficulties: SNU/MLD
DYC DYS DYP
*Behavioural and emotional
disorders:* ST/ASD
Physical and medical conditions:
IT RA SM WA3/HEA

ST ANDREWS SCHOOL
Lower Common, East Runton,
Norfolk NR27 9PG
Type: Co-educational Day Only
6–12
Learning difficulties: MLD DYS
DYP
*Behavioural and emotional
disorders:* ASP ASD
Physical and medical conditions:
WA3

ST NICHOLAS HOUSE
KINDERGARTEN & PREP
SCHOOL
North Walsham, Norfolk
NR28 9AT
Website: www.stnicholashouse.
com
Type: Co-educational Day Only
3–11
Physical and medical conditions:
W/W

SACRED HEART SCHOOL
17 Mangate Street, Swaffham,
Norfolk PE37 7QW
Website: www.sacredheart.
norfolk.sch.uk
Type: Co-educational Day and
Boarding 3–16
Learning difficulties: CA SC/MLD
DYS DYP
*Behavioural and emotional
disorders:* ASP
Physical and medical conditions:
HI

TAVERHAM HALL PREPARATORY SCHOOL
Taverham Park, Norwich, Norfolk
NR8 6HU
Website: www.taverhamhall.
co.uk
Type: Co-educational Boarding
and Day 1–13
Learning difficulties: CA SNU WI/
DYS DYP
*Behavioural and emotional
disorders:* ST/ADD
Physical and medical conditions:
RA SM/EPI HEA

NORTHAMPTONSHIRE

GREAT HOUGHTON PREPARATORY SCHOOL
Great Houghton Hall,
Northampton, Northamptonshire
NN4 7AG
Website: www.ghps.co.uk
Type: Co-educational Day Only
1–13
Learning difficulties: CA SC SNU
WI/DYC DYS DYP
*Behavioural and emotional
disorders:* CA CO RA TS ST/ASP
ASD
Physical and medical conditions:
CA TW WA3/HEA VI

WINCHESTER HOUSE SCHOOL
High Street, Brackley,
Northamptonshire NN13 7AZ
Website: www.winchester-
house.org
Type: Co-educational Boarding
and Day 3–13
Learning difficulties: SNU WI

NORTHUMBERLAND

ROCK HALL SCHOOL
Rock, Alnwick, Northumberland
NE66 3SB
Website: www.rockhallschool.
com
Type: Co-educational Day Only
3–13
Learning difficulties: DYS
*Behavioural and emotional
disorders:* RA ST
Physical and medical conditions:
RA

NOTTINGHAMSHIRE

DAGFA HOUSE SCHOOL
57 Broadgate, Nottingham,
Nottinghamshire NG9 2FU
Website: www.dagfahouse.notts.
sch.uk
Type: Co-educational Day Only
2–16
Learning difficulties: CA WI/MLD
DYC DYS DYP
*Behavioural and emotional
disorders:* ASP ASD
Physical and medical conditions:
CA/HI VI

GREENHOLME SCHOOL
392 Derby Road, Nottingham,
Nottinghamshire NG7 2DX
Website: www.
greenholmeschool.co.uk
Type: Co-educational Day Only
3–11
Learning difficulties: WI

NOTTINGHAM HIGH SCHOOL
Waverley Mount, Nottingham,
Nottinghamshire NG7 4ED
Website: www.nottinghamhigh.
co.uk
Type: Boys Day Only 11–18
Learning difficulties: WI/DYC DYS
DYP
*Behavioural and emotional
disorders:* ST/ADD ADHD ASP
TOU
Physical and medical conditions:
RA/EPI HEA HI IM VI

PLUMTREE SCHOOL
Church Hill, Nottingham,
Nottinghamshire NG12 5ND
Website: www.plumtreeschool.
co.uk
Type: Co-educational Day Only
3–11
Physical and medical conditions:
W/W

RANBY HOUSE SCHOOL
Retford, Nottinghamshire
DN22 8HX
Website: www.
ranbyhouseschool.co.uk
Type: Co-educational Day and
Boarding 3–13
Learning difficulties: CA SC SNU/
MLD DOW DYC DYS DYP
*Behavioural and emotional
disorders:* CA RA ST/ADD ASP
ASD BESD CB
Physical and medical conditions:
CA IT SM WA2/HEA

SALTERFORD HOUSE SCHOOL
Salterford Lane, Nottingham,
Nottinghamshire NG14 6NZ
Website: www.
salterfordhouseschool.co.uk
Type: Co-educational Day Only
2–11
Learning difficulties: CA WI/MLD
DYS DYP
*Behavioural and emotional
disorders:* ST/ADHD ASP ASD
Physical and medical conditions:
RA WA2/HEA

WELLOW HOUSE SCHOOL
Newark, Nottinghamshire
NG22 0EA
Website: www.wellowhouse.
notts.sch.uk
Type: Co-educational Day and
Boarding 3–13
Learning difficulties: CA WI/DYS
Physical and medical conditions:
SM/EPI HEA

OXFORDSHIRE

THE CARRDUS SCHOOL
Overthorpe Hall, Banbury,
Oxfordshire OX17 2BS
Website: www.carrdusschool.
co.uk
Type: Girls Day Only 3–11 (Boys
3–8)
Learning difficulties: CA RA SC
WI
Physical and medical conditions:
WA3

CHERWELL COLLEGE
Greyfriars, Oxford, Oxfordshire OX1 1LD
Website: www.cherwell-college.co.uk
Type: Co-educational Boarding and Day (Focus on A-levels with the addition of A-level retake and final year GCSE, 16–19)
Learning difficulties: SC WI/MLD DYC DYS DYP
Behavioural and emotional disorders: CO/ADD ADHD
Physical and medical conditions: AT RA/HEA IM

CRANFORD HOUSE SCHOOL
Wallingford, Oxfordshire OX10 9HT
Website: www.cranford-house.org
Type: Co-educational Day Only 3–16 (Boys 3–7 Girls 3–16)
Learning difficulties: WI

DRAGON SCHOOL
Bardwell Road, Oxford, Oxfordshire OX2 6SS
Website: www.dragonschool.org
Type: Co-educational Boarding and Day 4–13
Learning difficulties: WI/DYC DYS DYP SP&LD
Behavioural and emotional disorders: CO RA/ADD ADHD ASP
Physical and medical conditions: RA SM TW WA2/HEA

FERNDALE PREPARATORY SCHOOL
5–7 Bromsgrove, Faringdon, Oxfordshire SN7 7JF
Website: www.ferndaleschool.co.uk
Type: Co-educational Day Only 3–11
Learning difficulties: CA WI/MLD DYS
Behavioural and emotional disorders: ADHD
Physical and medical conditions: RA WA3/EPI HEA HI VI

GREENE'S TUTORIAL COLLEGE
45 Pembroke Street, Oxford, Oxfordshire OX1 1BP
Website: www.greenes.org.uk
Type: Co-educational Day and Boarding 6–75 (Boarding (host families))
Learning difficulties: WI/MLD DYC DYS DYP
Behavioural and emotional disorders: RA/ADD ADHD ASP BESD
Physical and medical conditions: AT RA SM TW

THE MANOR PREPARATORY SCHOOL
Faringdon Road, Abingdon, Oxfordshire OX13 6LN
Website: www.manorprep.org
Type: Co-educational Day Only 2–11
Learning difficulties: CA SNU/DYC DYS DYP
Physical and medical conditions: AT CA HL SM TW W WA2/HEA HI VI

THE ORATORY PREPARATORY SCHOOL
Goring Heath, Reading, Oxfordshire RG8 7SF
Website: www.oratoryprep.org.uk
Type: Co-educational Day and Boarding 3–13
Learning difficulties: CA WI/DYC DYS DYP
Behavioural and emotional disorders: RA/ADD
Physical and medical conditions: CA TW WA1/HEA HI

OXFORD TUTORIAL COLLEGE
12 King Edward Street, Oxford, Oxfordshire OX1 4HT
Website: www.otc.ac.uk
Type: Co-educational Day and Boarding (16+)
Learning difficulties: SC WI/MLD DYS DYP
Behavioural and emotional disorders: RA/ADD ADHD BESD
Physical and medical conditions: AT RA WA3

ST HELEN & ST KATHARINE
Faringdon Road, Abingdon, Oxfordshire OX14 1BE
Website: www.shsk.org.uk
Type: Girls Day Only 9–18
Learning difficulties: WI/DYS
Behavioural and emotional disorders: CO/ADD ADHD
Physical and medical conditions: RA SM TW/EPI HEA HI

ST HUGH'S SCHOOL
Carswell Manor, Faringdon, Oxfordshire SN7 8PT
Website: www.st-hughs.co.uk
Type: Co-educational Boarding and Day 3–13
Learning difficulties: CA WI/MLD DYS DYP
Physical and medical conditions: HI

SHIPLAKE COLLEGE
Henley-on-Thames, Oxfordshire RG9 4BW
Website: www.shiplake.org.uk
Type: Co-educational Day and Boarding 11–18 (Day girls 16–18)
Learning difficulties: SNU/DYC DYS DYP
Behavioural and emotional disorders: ST
Physical and medical conditions: SM

SIBFORD SCHOOL+
Sibford Ferris, Banbury, Oxfordshire OX15 5QL
Website: www.sibford.oxon.sch.uk
Type: Co-educational Boarding and Day 4–18
Learning difficulties: CA SNU WI/DYC DYS DYP
Behavioural and emotional disorders: CO RA/ADD ADHD ASP ASD
Physical and medical conditions: CA RA SM/CP HEA IM

SUMMER FIELDS
Mayfield Road, Oxford,
Oxfordshire OX2 7EN
Website: www.summerfields.
oxon.sch.uk
Type: Boys Boarding and Day
7–13
Learning difficulties: SNU/MLD
DYC DYS DYP
*Behavioural and emotional
disorders:* CO RA/ADD ADHD
ASP BESD
Physical and medical conditions:
HL IT RA SM WA3/HEA HI

TUDOR HALL SCHOOL
Wykham Park, Banbury,
Oxfordshire OX16 9UR
Website: www.tudorhallschool.
com
Type: Girls Boarding and Day
11–18
Learning difficulties: SNU/DYC
DYS DYP SP&LD
*Behavioural and emotional
disorders:* CO
Physical and medical conditions:
CP EPI HEA

RUTLAND

BROOKE PRIORY SCHOOL
Station Approach, Oakham,
Rutland LE15 6QW
Website: www.brooke.rutland.
sch.uk
Type: Co-educational Day Only
2–11
Learning difficulties: CA WI/DYS
DYP
Physical and medical conditions:
CA SM TW W WA1 WA2/HEA

SHROPSHIRE

ADCOTE SCHOOL FOR GIRLS
Little Ness, Shrewsbury,
Shropshire SY4 2JY
Website: www.adcoteschool.
co.uk
Type: Girls Boarding and Day
4–18
Learning difficulties: CA SNU/
MLD DYS DYP
*Behavioural and emotional
disorders:* CA CO TS ST/ADHD
ASP ASD
Physical and medical conditions:
RA SM WA3

CASTLE HOUSE SCHOOL
Newport, Shropshire TF10 7JE
Website: www.
castlehouseschool.co.uk
Type: Co-educational Day Only
2–11
Learning difficulties: CA SC SNU
WI/MLD DYC DYS DYP SP&LD
*Behavioural and emotional
disorders:* ST/ADD ASP ASD
Physical and medical conditions:
CA RA SM WA3/HEA HI

DOWER HOUSE SCHOOL
Quatt, Bridgnorth, Shropshire
WV15 6QW
Website: www.
dowerhouseschool.co.uk
Type: Co-educational Day Only
2–11
Learning difficulties: WI

ELLESMERE COLLEGE+
Ellesmere, Shropshire SY12 9AB
Website: www.ellesmere.com
Type: Co-educational Boarding
and Day 7–18
Learning difficulties: SNU/DYC
DYS DYP
*Behavioural and emotional
disorders:* RA
Physical and medical conditions:
RA/HEA

MOOR PARK SCHOOL
Moor Park, Ludlow, Shropshire
SY8 4DZ
Website: www.moorpark.org.uk
Type: Co-educational Boarding
and Day 3–13
Learning difficulties: SNU/DYC
DYS DYP
*Behavioural and emotional
disorders:* CO/ADD ADHD ASP
Physical and medical conditions:
RA WA3/EPI HEA IM

MORETON HALL SCHOOL
Oswestry, Shropshire SY11 3EW
Website: www.moretonhall.org
Type: Girls Boarding and Day
3–18 (Boys 3–11)
Learning difficulties: SNU WI/
MLD DYC DYS DYP
*Behavioural and emotional
disorders:* CO ST
Physical and medical conditions:
IT SM TW WA3/HEA

THE OLD HALL SCHOOL
Stanley Road, Telford, Shropshire
TF1 3LB
Website: www.oldhall.co.uk
Type: Co-educational Day Only
4–11
Learning difficulties: SNU/DYC
DYS DYP
*Behavioural and emotional
disorders:* RA/ADD ADHD
Physical and medical conditions:
SM WA3

OSWESTRY SCHOOL BELLAN HOUSE
Bellan House, Oswestry,
Shropshire SY11 2ST
Website: www.oswestryschool.
org.uk
Type: Co-educational Day Only
2–9
Learning difficulties: SNU/DYS
DYP
*Behavioural and emotional
disorders:* RA/ADHD ASP
Physical and medical conditions:
RA/EPI

PRESTFELDE PREPARATORY SCHOOL
London Road, Shrewsbury,
Shropshire SY2 6NZ
Website: www.prestfelde.co.uk
Type: Co-educational Day and
Boarding 3–13
Learning difficulties: CA SNU/
DYS DYP
*Behavioural and emotional
disorders:* ADD ASP
Physical and medical conditions:
SM WA2/EPI HEA

WREKIN COLLEGE
Wellington, Shropshire TF1 3BH
Website: www.wrekincollege.
ac.uk
Type: Co-educational Boarding
and Day 11–19
Learning difficulties: RA WI/DYS
*Behavioural and emotional
disorders:* ADD ADHD ASP ASD

SOMERSET

CHARD SCHOOL
Fore Street, Chard, Somerset
TA20 1QA
Website: www.chardschool.ik.org
Type: Co-educational Day Only
2–11
Learning difficulties: CA WI/DYS
DYP
*Behavioural and emotional
disorders:* RA
Physical and medical conditions:
IT RA/VI

FARLEIGH FURTHER EDUCATION COLLEGE (FROME)
North Parade, Frome, Somerset
BA11 2AB
Website: www.priorygroup.com
Type: Co-educational Boarding
and Day 16–22
*Behavioural and emotional
disorders:* ASD
Physical and medical conditions:
WA3

KING'S BRUTON AND HAZLEGROVE+
Bruton, Somerset BA10 0ED
Website: www.kingsbruton.com
and hazlegrove.co.uk
Type: Mixed Residential and Day
2–18
Special needs: ADD ADHD ASP
CP DYC DYP DYS HEA VI

THE PARK SCHOOL
The Park, Yeovil, Somerset
BA20 1DH
Website: www.parkschool.com
Type: Co-educational Day and
Boarding 3–19
Learning difficulties: WI/MLD
DYS DYP
*Behavioural and emotional
disorders:* RA/ASP
Physical and medical conditions:
AT RA WA3/HEA

TAUNTON PREPARATORY SCHOOL
Staplegrove Road, Taunton,
Somerset TA2 6AE
Website: www.tauntonschool.
co.uk
Type: Co-educational Day and
Boarding 2–13
Learning difficulties: WI/DYC DYS
DYP
*Behavioural and emotional
disorders:* ST/ADD ADHD
Physical and medical conditions:
SM WA2

BATH & NORTH EAST SOMERSET

KINGSWOOD SCHOOL
Bath, Bath & North East Somerset
BA1 5RG
Website: www.kingswood.bath.
sch.uk
Type: Co-educational Boarding
and Day 3–18
Learning difficulties: RA WI/DYC
DYS DYP
Physical and medical conditions:
RA SM WA3/HEA

STAFFORDSHIRE

**ABBOTS BROMLEY
SCHOOL FOR GIRLS**
Abbots Bromley, Staffordshire
WS15 3BW
Website: www.abbotsbromley.
staffs.sch.uk
Type: Girls Boarding and Day
3–18
Learning difficulties: CA/MLD
SLD DYC DYS
Physical and medical conditions:
CA SM/VI

**BROOKLANDS SCHOOL &
LITTLE BROOKLANDS
NURSERY**
167 Eccleshall Road, Stafford,
Staffordshire ST16 1PD
Website: www.
brooklandsschool.com
Type: Co-educational Day Only
(0–3 year old children in Little
Brooklands Day Nursery total 63
in addition to main School total of
110.)
Learning difficulties: SNU/MLD
DYS
Physical and medical conditions:
VI

**LICHFIELD CATHEDRAL
SCHOOL**
The Close, Lichfield,
Staffordshire WS13 7LH
Website: www.
lichfieldcathedralschool.com
Type: Co-educational Day and
Boarding 3–16
Learning difficulties: SC SNU/
DYC DYS DYP
*Behavioural and emotional
disorders:* ST/ADD ASP CB
Physical and medical conditions:
CA SM WA3/HEA HI

**NEWCASTLE UNDER LYME
SCHOOL**
Mount Pleasant, Newcastle under
Lyme, Staffordshire ST5 1DB
Website: www.nuls.org.uk
Type: Co-educational Day Only
3–18
Learning difficulties: WI

**SMALLWOOD MANOR
PREPARATORY SCHOOL**
Uttoxeter, Staffordshire ST14 8NS
Website: www.smallwoodmanor.
co.uk
Type: Co-educational Day Only
2–11
Learning difficulties: CA WI/DYC
DYS DYP
Physical and medical conditions:
AT WA3/EPI HEA

STOCKTON-ON-TEES

RED HOUSE SCHOOL
36 The Green, Norton, Stockton-
on-Tees TS20 1DX
Website: www.redhouseschool.
co.uk
Type: Co-educational Day Only
3–16
Learning difficulties: RA WI/DYS
DYP
*Behavioural and emotional
disorders:* RA/ASP TOU
Physical and medical conditions:
RA/EPI

TEESSIDE HIGH SCHOOL
The Avenue, Eaglescliffe,
Stockton-on-Tees TS16 9AT
Website: www.teessidehigh.
co.uk
Type: Co-educational Day Only
3–18
Learning difficulties: RA WI/DYC
DYS DYP
*Behavioural and emotional
disorders:* RA ST/ADHD ASP
Physical and medical conditions:
RA/CP EPI HEA HI VI

SUFFOLK

THE ABBEY
The Prep School for Woodbridge
School, Woodbridge, Suffolk
IP12 1DS
Website: www.woodbridge.
suffolk.sch.uk/the_abbey
Type: Co-educational Day Only
4–11
Learning difficulties: WI/MLD
DYS
Physical and medical conditions:
TW WA?

MORETON HALL
PREPARATORY SCHOOL
Mount Road, Bury St Edmunds,
Suffolk IP32 7BJ
Website: www.moretonhall.net
Type: Co-educational Boarding
and Day 2–13
Learning difficulties: SC/MLD
DYS
*Behavioural and emotional
disorders:* RA
Physical and medical conditions:
CA SM TW WA3

ORWELL PARK
Ipswich, Suffolk IP10 0ER
Website: www.orwellpark.co.uk
Type: Co-educational Boarding
and Day 3–13
Learning difficulties: SNU/DYC
DYS DYP
*Behavioural and emotional
disorders:* RA/ADHD ASP
Physical and medical conditions:
RA WA3/EPI HEA

THE ROYAL HOSPITAL
SCHOOL
Holbrook, Ipswich, Suffolk
IP9 2RX
Website: www.
royalhospitalschool.org
Type: Co-educational Boarding
and Day 11–18
Learning difficulties: SNU WI/
MLD DYS DYP
*Behavioural and emotional
disorders:* CO RA
Physical and medical conditions:
RA SM WA2/EPI HEA

ST JOSEPH'S COLLEGE
Belstead Road, Ipswich, Suffolk
IP2 9DR
Website: www.stjos.co.uk
Type: Co-educational Day and
Boarding 2–18
Learning difficulties: CA WI/DYC
DYS DYP
*Behavioural and emotional
disorders:* RA ST/ADHD
Physical and medical conditions:
AT CA RA SL WA2/CP EPI HEA

SURREY

ABERDOUR
Brighton Road, Tadworth, Surrey
KT20 6AJ
Website: www.aberdourschool.
co.uk
Type: Co-educational Day Only
2–13
Learning difficulties: CA/DYC
DYS DYP
*Behavioural and emotional
disorders:* RA/ADD ADHD ASP
Physical and medical conditions:
RA SM/HEA

ALDRO SCHOOL
Lombard Street, Godalming,
Surrey GU8 6AS
Website: www.aldro.org
Type: Boys Boarding and Day
7–13
Learning difficulties: CA SNU WI/
MLD DYS DYP
*Behavioural and emotional
disorders:* RA/ADD ASP
Physical and medical conditions:
RA TW

BARFIELD SCHOOL AND NURSERY
Guildford Road, Farnham, Surrey
GU10 1PB
Website: www.barfieldschool.
com
Type: Co-educational Day Only
3–13
Learning difficulties: WI
Physical and medical conditions:
W

BISHOPSGATE SCHOOL
Englefield Green, Egham, Surrey
TW20 0YJ
Website: www.bishopsgate.
surrey.sch.uk
Type: Co-educational Day and
Boarding 2–13
Learning difficulties: SNU/DYC
DYS DYP
*Behavioural and emotional
disorders:* RA/ADHD
Physical and medical conditions:
TW WA2/EPI VI

BRAMLEY SCHOOL
Chequers Lane, Tadworth,
Surrey KT20 7ST
Website: www.bramleyschool.
co.uk
Type: Girls Day Only 3–11
Learning difficulties: CA WI/MLD
DYC DYS DYP
*Behavioural and emotional
disorders:* ST/ADD TOU
Physical and medical conditions:
IT SL SM TW W WA2/HEA

CAMBRIDGE TUTORS COLLEGE
Water Tower Hill, Croydon,
Surrey CR0 5SX
Website: www.ctc.ac.uk
Type: Co-educational Boarding
and Day 15–22
Learning difficulties: RA WI/MLD
DYS
Physical and medical conditions:
IT RA SM

CROYDON HIGH SCHOOL GDST
Old Farleigh Road, South
Croydon, Surrey CR2 8YB
Website: www.gdst.net/
croydonhigh
Type: Girls Day Only 3–18
Learning difficulties: RA/DYS
*Behavioural and emotional
disorders:* RA/ADHD ASD
Physical and medical conditions:
RA/HI

DOWNSEND SCHOOL
1 Leatherhead Road,
Leatherhead, Surrey KT22 8TJ
Website: www.downsend.co.uk
Type: Co-educational Day Only
2–13 (Children age 2–6 attend
one of our three Nursery & Pre-
Preparatory Departments or
Lodges, based in Ashtead,
Epsom & Leatherhead.)
Learning difficulties: CA SNU WI/
DYC DYS DYP
*Behavioural and emotional
disorders:* RA/ADD ADHD ASP
Physical and medical conditions:
RA W/HEA HI

DOWNSEND SCHOOL–ASHTEAD LODGE
22 Oakfield Road, Ashtead,
Surrey KT21 2RE
Website: www.downsend.co.uk
Type: Co-educational Day Only
2–6
Learning difficulties: RA WI
*Behavioural and emotional
disorders:* RA
Physical and medical conditions:
RA TW/HEA

EWELL CASTLE SCHOOL
Church Street, Epsom, Surrey
KT17 2AW
Website: www.ewellcastle.co.uk
Type: Co-educational Day Only
3–18 (Co-ed 3–11 Boys 3–18)
Learning difficulties: SC WI/DYC
DYS DYP
*Behavioural and emotional
disorders:* ADD ADHD ASP ASD
Physical and medical conditions:
AT RA/EPI HEA

FELTONFLEET SCHOOL
Cobham, Surrey KT11 1DR
Website: www.feltonfleet.co.uk
Type: Co-educational Boarding
and Day 3–13
Learning difficulties: WI/DYS DYP
*Behavioural and emotional
disorders:* ADHD
Physical and medical conditions:
HEA

HOE BRIDGE SCHOOL
Hoe Place, Woking, Surrey
GU22 8JE
Website: www.hoebridgeschool.
co.uk
Type: Co-educational Day Only
2–13
Learning difficulties: CA WI/DYS
DYP
*Behavioural and emotional
disorders:* CA RA/ADD ADHD
Physical and medical conditions:
RA SM TW WA2 WA3/HEA

KEW GREEN PREPARATORY SCHOOL
Layton House, Richmond, Surrey TW9 3AF
Website: www.kgps.co.uk
Type: Co-educational Day Only 4–11
Learning difficulties: CA SNU WI/MLD DYC DYS DYP
Behavioural and emotional disorders: CA CO TS ST/ADD CB
Physical and medical conditions: CA IT TW

LANESBOROUGH
Maori Road, Guildford, Surrey GU1 2EL
Website: www.lanesborough.surrey.sch.uk
Type: Boys Day Only 3–13
Learning difficulties: CA SNU WI/MLD DYS
Behavioural and emotional disorders: TS/ASP TOU
Physical and medical conditions: CA SM TW/HI

THE LARKS
19 Bluehouse Lane, Oxted, Surrey RH8 0AA
Website: http://www.the-larks.co.uk/
Type: Co-educational Day Only (Laverock site now used for The Larks Day care only–Laverocks now merged with Hazelwood.)
Learning difficulties: WI/DYS DYP
Behavioural and emotional disorders: ADHD
Physical and medical conditions: CA RA/HI

NEW LIFE CHRISTIAN SCHOOL
Cairo New Road, Croydon, Surrey CR0 1XP
Website: www.newlifecroydon/nlcs.co.uk
Type: Co-educational Day Only 4–11
Learning difficulties: WI

OAKFIELD SCHOOL
Coldharbour Road, Woking, Surrey GU22 8SJ
Website: www.oakfieldschool.co.uk
Type: Co-educational Day Only 3–16
Learning difficulties: WI/DYS DYP
Behavioural and emotional disorders: RA
Physical and medical conditions: RA

OAKHYRST GRANGE SCHOOL
160 Stanstead Road, Caterham, Surrey CR3 6AF
Website: www.oakhyrstgrangeschool.co.uk
Type: Co-educational Day Only 4–11
Learning difficulties: CA WI/DYS DYP
Behavioural and emotional disorders: ST/ASP
Physical and medical conditions: RA/HI VI

OLD VICARAGE SCHOOL
48 Richmond Hill, Richmond, Surrey TW10 6QX
Type: Girls Day Only 4–11
Learning difficulties: WI

PRIORY PREPARATORY SCHOOL
Bolters Lane, Banstead, Surrey SM7 2AJ
Website: www.prioryprep.co.uk
Type: Boys Day Only 2–13
Learning difficulties: CA WI/MLD DYC DYS DYP
Behavioural and emotional disorders: RA
Physical and medical conditions: CA RA SM TW WA3/HEA

REIGATE GRAMMAR SCHOOL
Reigate Road, Reigate, Surrey RH2 0QS
Website: www.reigategrammar.org
Type: Co-educational Day Only 11–18
Learning difficulties: CA/MLD DYS DYP
Behavioural and emotional disorders: ADHD ASP
Physical and medical conditions: CA SL SM WA2/EPI HEA HI

RIPLEY COURT SCHOOL
Rose Lane, Woking, Surrey GU23 6NE
Website: www.ripleycourt.co.uk
Type: Co-educational Day Only 3–13
Learning difficulties: WI/DYS DYP
Behavioural and emotional disorders: RA
Physical and medical conditions: RA SM/EPI HEA HI VI

ST DAVID'S SCHOOL
23 Woodcote Valley Road, Purley, Surrey CR8 3AL
Website: www.st-davidsschool.co.uk
Type: Co-educational Day Only 3–11
Learning difficulties: CA WI/DYC DYS DYP
Behavioural and emotional disorders: RA/ASP
Physical and medical conditions: CA RA SM TW/HEA VI

ST HILARY'S SCHOOL
Holloway Hill, Godalming, Surrey GU7 1RZ
Website: www.sthilarysschool.com
Type: Co-educational Day Only 1–11
Learning difficulties: CA SNU WI/DYS DYP
Physical and medical conditions: CA HL IT/HEA HI VI

ST JOHN'S SCHOOL
Epsom Road, Leatherhead, Surrey KT22 8SP
Website: www.stjohnsleatherhead.co.uk
Type: Co-educational Boarding and Day 13–18 (Co-ed VIth Form)
Learning difficulties: SNU WI/DYC DYS DYP
Behavioural and emotional disorders: CO/ADD ADHD ASP
Physical and medical conditions: SM TW WA2 WA3/EPI HEA HI

SEATON HOUSE SCHOOL
67 Banstead Road South, Sutton,
Surrey SM2 5LH
Website: www.seatonhouse.
sutton.sch.uk
Type: Girls Day Only 3–11 (Boys
3–5 Girls 3–11)
Learning difficulties: CA RA SC
WI/DYS DYP
*Behavioural and emotional
disorders:* RA
Physical and medical conditions:
RA/HEA

SUTTON HIGH SCHOOL GDST
55 Cheam Road, Sutton, Surrey
SM1 2AX
Website: www.gdst.net/
suttonhigh
Type: Girls Day Only 3–18
Learning difficulties: SC/MLD
DYS DYP
*Behavioural and emotional
disorders:* CO ST/BESD
Physical and medical conditions:
AT SM TW WA3/HEA HI

TRINITY SCHOOL
Shirley Park, Croydon, Surrey
CR9 7AT
Website: www.trinity-school.org
Type: Boys Day Only 10–18
(Boys 10–18 Girls 16–18)
Learning difficulties: WI/DYC DYS
DYP
*Behavioural and emotional
disorders:* CO/ADD ADHD ASP
ASD
Physical and medical conditions:
SL SM WA1/HEA VI

WOODCOTE HOUSE SCHOOL
Snow's Ride, Windlesham, Surrey
GU20 6PF
Website: www.
woodcotehouseschool.co.uk
Type: Boys Boarding and Day
7–14
Learning difficulties: SC SNU/
MLD DYC DYS DYP
*Behavioural and emotional
disorders:* RA/ADD ASP
Physical and medical conditions:
RA WA3

EAST SUSSEX

BRICKLEHURST MANOR PREPARATORY
Bardown Road, Wadhurst,
East Sussex TN5 7EL
Website: www.bricklehurst.co.uk
Type: Co-educational Day Only
3–11
Learning difficulties: CA SNU/
DYC DYS
Physical and medical conditions:
RA/HEA

EASTBOURNE COLLEGE
Old Wish Road, Eastbourne,
East Sussex BN21 4JY
Website: www.eastbourne-
college.co.uk
Type: Co-educational Boarding
and Day 13–18 (50% boarding /
50% day 60% boys / 40% girls)
Learning difficulties: MLD
Physical and medical conditions:
RA

LANCING COLLEGE PREPARATORY SCHOOL AT MOWDEN
The Droveway, Hove, East Sussex
BN3 6LU
Website: www.lancingprep.co.uk
Type: Co-educational Day Only
3–13
Learning difficulties: CA WI/DYS
*Behavioural and emotional
disorders:* RA/ADHD
Physical and medical conditions:
SM

ST ANDREW'S SCHOOL
Meads, Eastbourne, East Sussex
BN20 7RP
Website: www.androvian.co.uk
Type: Co-educational Boarding
and Day 2–13
Learning difficulties: CA SNU WI/
DYC DYS DYP
*Behavioural and emotional
disorders:* RA/ASP
Physical and medical conditions:
RA SM/HEA HI IM

ST CHRISTOPHER'S SCHOOL
33 New Church Road,
East Sussex BN3 4AD
Website: www.
stchristophershove.org.uk
Type: Co-educational Day Only
4–13
Learning difficulties: CA SNU WI/
MLD DYS
*Behavioural and emotional
disorders:* ST/ADHD ASP
Physical and medical conditions:
SM TW W WA2/HEA VI

WEST SUSSEX

BROADWATER MANOR SCHOOL
Broadwater Road, Worthing, West Sussex BN14 8HU
Website: www.broadwatermanor.com
Type: Co-educational Day Only 2–13
Learning difficulties: CA WI
Behavioural and emotional disorders: RA
Physical and medical conditions: RA/HEA

FONTHILL LODGE
Coombe Hill Road, East Grinstead, West Sussex RH19 4LY
Website: www.fonthill-lodge.co.uk
Type: Co-educational Day Only 2–11 (Single-sex ed 8–11)
Learning difficulties: CA WI/DYS DYP
Physical and medical conditions: CA RA SM TW W/HEA HI

HANDCROSS PARK SCHOOL
Handcross, Haywards Heath, West Sussex RH17 6HF
Website: www.handcrossparkschool.co.uk
Type: Co-educational Day and Boarding 2–13
Learning difficulties: CA SNU/MLD DYC DYS DYP
Behavioural and emotional disorders: CO TS/ADD ADHD
Physical and medical conditions: IT RA SM TW WA2/EPI HEA IM

WARWICKSHIRE

ARNOLD LODGE SCHOOL
Kenilworth Road, Leamington Spa, Warwickshire CV32 5TW
Type: Co-educational Day Only 3–13
Learning difficulties: WI/MLD DYC DYS DYP
Behavioural and emotional disorders: CO ST/ADD ADHD ASP
Physical and medical conditions: RA/EPI HEA HI VI

BILTON GRANGE
Rugby Road, Rugby, Warwickshire CV22 6QU
Website: www.biltongrange.co.uk
Type: Co-educational Boarding and Day 4–13
Learning difficulties: CA/MLD DYC DYS DYP
Behavioural and emotional disorders: CA CO TS/ADHD ASP ASD
Physical and medical conditions: CA RA SM/HEA VI

WEST MIDLANDS

BABLAKE SCHOOL
Coundon Road, Coventry, West Midlands CV1 4AU
Website: www.bablake.com
Type: Co-educational Day Only 11–19
Learning difficulties: SNU/DYS DYP
Physical and medical conditions: TW WA2

BIRCHFIELD SCHOOL
Wolverhampton, West Midlands WV7 3AF
Website: www.birchfieldschool.co.uk
Type: Co-educational Day and Boarding 4–13
Learning difficulties: CA SNU/MLD DYC DYS DYP
Behavioural and emotional disorders: RA TS ST/ADD ADHD ASP
Physical and medical conditions: AT RA SM TW WA3/HEA

DAVENPORT LODGE SCHOOL
21 Davenport Road, Coventry, West Midlands CV5 6QA
Website: www.davenportlodge.coventry.sch.uk
Type: Co-educational Day Only
Learning difficulties: CA WI/MLD DYS
Behavioural and emotional disorders: CA
Physical and medical conditions: TW W WA2

EDGBASTON HIGH SCHOOL FOR GIRLS
Westbourne Road, Birmingham, West Midlands B15 3TS
Website: www.edgbastonhigh. co.uk
Type: Girls Day Only 3–18
Learning difficulties: RA WI/DYC DYS DYP
Behavioural and emotional disorders: RA ST
Physical and medical conditions: AT HL IT SM TW WA2/CP EPI HEA HI IM

ELMHURST SCHOOL FOR DANCE
247–249 Bristol Road, Birmingham, West Midlands B5 7UH
Website: www.elmhurstdance. co.uk
Type: Co-educational Boarding and Day 11–19
Learning difficulties: RA WI/DYS DYP
Behavioural and emotional disorders: RA
Physical and medical conditions: SM TW W WA1 WA2/HI

HIGHCLARE SCHOOL
10 Sutton Road, Birmingham, West Midlands B23 6QL
Website: www.highclareschool. co.uk
Type: Co-educational Day Only 1–18 (Boys 1–12 & 16–18 (Boys are being accepted into Senior School from September 2011 from Year 7))
Learning difficulties: CA WI/DYS
Behavioural and emotional disorders: RA/ADD ADHD BESD
Physical and medical conditions: AT CA RA SM/HEA HI

KINGSWOOD SCHOOL
St James Place, Solihull, West Midlands B90 2BA
Website: www. kingswoodschool.co.uk
Type: Co-educational Day Only 2–11
Learning difficulties: CA SC SNU/ MLD DYC DYS DYP
Behavioural and emotional disorders: ADD ADHD ASP ASD
Physical and medical conditions: SM TW/VI

NORFOLK HOUSE SCHOOL
4 Norfolk Road, Birmingham, West Midlands B15 3PS
Type: Co-educational Day Only 3–11
Learning difficulties: RA WI
Behavioural and emotional disorders: RA
Physical and medical conditions: RA

PRIORY SCHOOL
39 Sir Harry's Road, Birmingham, West Midlands B15 2UR
Website: www.prioryschool.net
Type: Co-educational Day Only (Co-ed 1–11)
Learning difficulties: SNU/DYC DYS DYP

THE ROYAL WOLVERHAMPTON JUNIOR SCHOOL
Penn Road, Wolverhampton, West Midlands WV3 0EF
Website: www.theroyalschool. co.uk
Type: Co-educational Day and Boarding 2–11
Learning difficulties: CA RA SNU/ MLD DYC DYS DYP
Behavioural and emotional disorders: CA CO RA ST/ADHD CB
Physical and medical conditions: RA SM TW/HEA

RUCKLEIGH SCHOOL
17 Lode Lane, Solihull, West Midlands B91 2AB
Website: www.ruckleigh.co.uk
Type: Co-educational Day Only 3–11
Learning difficulties: CA RA WI/ DYS
Behavioural and emotional disorders: RA
Physical and medical conditions: RA/HEA

SAINT MARTIN'S SCHOOL
Malvern Hall, Solihull, West Midlands B91 3EN
Website: www.saintmartins-school.com
Type: Girls Day Only 3–18 (Girls may join the school from 2 years 9 months.)
Learning difficulties: CA SNU/ DYC DYS
Physical and medical conditions: AT SL TW W WA2/W

TETTENHALL COLLEGE+
Wood Road, Wolverhampton, West Midlands WV6 8QX
Website: www.tettenhallcollege. co.uk
Type: Co-educational Boarding and Day 2–18
Learning difficulties: CA SNU WI/ DYC DYS DYP SP&LD
Behavioural and emotional disorders: ADD ADHD ASD
Physical and medical conditions: RA SM/EPI HEA

WEST HOUSE SCHOOL
24 St James's Road, Birmingham, West Midlands B15 2NX
Website: www.westhouse.bham. sch.uk
Type: Boys Day Only 1–11 (Girls 1–4)
Learning difficulties: CA WI/MLD DYS
Behavioural and emotional disorders: CA ST/ADHD ASD TOU
Physical and medical conditions: RA TW/HEA

WOLVERHAMPTON GRAMMAR SCHOOL
Compton Road, Wolverhampton, West Midlands WV3 9RB
Website: www.wgs.org.uk
Type: Co-educational Day Only 10–18
Learning difficulties: CA SNU WI/ DYS DYP
Physical and medical conditions: TW WA2/IM

WILTSHIRE

CHAFYN GROVE SCHOOL
Bourne Avenue, Salisbury,
Wiltshire SP1 1LR
Website: www.chafyngrove.co.uk
Type: Co-educational Boarding
and Day 3–13
Learning difficulties: SNU/MLD
DYS DYP SP&LD
*Behavioural and emotional
disorders:* CO/ADD ADHD ASP
CB
Physical and medical conditions:
CA IT RA WA2/HEA HI

FARLEIGH FURTHER
EDUCATION COLLEGE
SWINDON
Fairview House, Swindon,
Wiltshire SN1 4AS
Website: www.priorygroup.com
Type: Co-educational Boarding
and Day 16–19
*Behavioural and emotional
disorders:* ASP ASD
Physical and medical conditions:
W

MEADOWPARK NURSERY
& PRE-PREP SCHOOL
Calcutt Street, Cricklade,
Wiltshire SN6 6BA
Website: www.
meadowparkschool.co.uk
Type: Co-educational Day Only
Learning difficulties: WI
Physical and medical conditions:
SM TW W

THE MILL SCHOOL
Whistley Road, Devizes, Wiltshire
SN10 5TE
Website: www.mill.wilts.sch.uk
Type: Co-educational Day Only
3–11
Learning difficulties: CA WI/DYS
Physical and medical conditions:
HEA

PRIOR PARK
PREPARATORY SCHOOL+
Calcutt Street, Cricklade,
Wiltshire SN6 6BB
Website: www.priorparkschools.
co.uk
Type: Co-educational Boarding
and Day 4–13
Learning difficulties: CA SNU WI/
DYC DYS DYP
Physical and medical conditions:
RA

SANDROYD SCHOOL
Rushmore, Salisbury, Wiltshire
SP5 5QD
Website: www.sandroyd.org
Type: Co-educational Boarding
and Day 7–13 (The Walled
Garden pre prep ages 2 1/2–7
years Sandroyd 7–13 years)
Learning difficulties: SNU/MLD
DYS DYP
*Behavioural and emotional
disorders:* ADD
Physical and medical conditions:
IT RA SM TW/HEA VI

SOUTH HILLS SCHOOL
Home Farm Road, Salisbury,
Wiltshire SP2 8PJ
Website: www.southhillsschool.
com
Type: Co-educational Day Only
Learning difficulties: CA WI/MLD
DOW
*Behavioural and emotional
disorders:* ST
Physical and medical conditions:
RA

STONAR SCHOOL
Cottles Park, Melksham, Wiltshire
SN12 8NT
Website: www.stonarschool.com
Type: Girls Boarding and Day
2–18
Learning difficulties: CA SNU/
MLD DYC DYS DYP
Physical and medical conditions:
AT CA RA SM/EPI HEA VI

WORCESTERSHIRE

BROMSGROVE PRE-PREPARATORY AND NURSERY SCHOOL
Avoncroft House, Bromsgrove, Worcestershire B60 4JS
Website: www.bromsgrove-school.co.uk
Type: Co-educational Day Only 2–7
Learning difficulties: CA RA WI/DYS DYP
Behavioural and emotional disorders: CA RA ST/ASP
Physical and medical conditions: RA/HEA HI VI

GREEN HILL SCHOOL
Evesham, Worcestershire WR11 4NG
Website: www.greenhillschool.co.uk
Type: Co-educational Day Only 3–13
Physical and medical conditions: W/W

HOLY TRINITY SCHOOL
Birmingham Road, Kidderminster, Worcestershire DY10 2BY
Website: www.holytrinity.co.uk
Type: Co-educational Day Only
Learning difficulties: CA WI/MLD DYS
Behavioural and emotional disorders: ASP
Physical and medical conditions: CA/EPI HEA HI IM

MALVERN ST JAMES
15 Avenue Road, Great Malvern, Worcestershire WR14 3BA
Website: www.malvernstjames.co.uk
Type: Girls Boarding and Day 4–18
Learning difficulties: SNU/MLD DYS DYP
Physical and medical conditions: SM TW WA1

RGS THE GRANGE
Grange Lane, Worcester, Worcestershire WR3 7RR
Website: www.rgsao.org
Type: Co-educational Day Only 2–11
Learning difficulties: CA WI/DYS DYP
Behavioural and emotional disorders: RA/ADD ADHD ASP TOU
Physical and medical conditions: WA2/EPI HEA HI

RGS WORCESTER & THE ALICE OTTLEY SCHOOL
Upper Tything, Worcester, Worcestershire WR1 1HP
Website: www.rgsao.org
Type: Co-educational Day Only 11–18
Learning difficulties: WI/DYC DYS DYP
Behavioural and emotional disorders: RA/ADD ADHD ASP TOU
Physical and medical conditions: RA/EPI HEA HI

WINTERFOLD HOUSE
Kidderminster, Worcestershire DY10 4PW
Website: www.winterfoldhouse.co.uk
Type: Co-educational Day Only 2–13
Learning difficulties: SNU/MLD
Behavioural and emotional disorders: RA
Physical and medical conditions: RA WA3

EAST RIDING OF YORKSHIRE

POCKLINGTON SCHOOL
West Green, Pocklington,
East Riding of Yorkshire
YO42 2NJ
Website: www.
pocklingtonschool.com
Type: Co-educational Boarding
and Day 7–18
Learning difficulties: SNU/DYS
*Behavioural and emotional
disorders:* RA
Physical and medical conditions:
RA SM/HEA

NORTH YORKSHIRE

AMPLEFORTH COLLEGE
York, North Yorkshire YO62 4ER
Website: www.college.
ampleforth.org.uk
Type: Co-educational Boarding
and Day 13–18
Learning difficulties: WI/DYC DYS
DYP
*Behavioural and emotional
disorders:* CO/ADD ADHD
Physical and medical conditions:
RA WA3/CP EPI

**AYSGARTH
PREPARATORY SCHOOL**
Newton-Le-Willows, Bedale,
North Yorkshire DL8 1TF
Website: www.aysgarthschool.
com
Type: Boys Day and Boarding
3–13 (Co-ed day 3–8)
Learning difficulties: CA SC SNU
WI/MLD DYC DYS DYP
*Behavioural and emotional
disorders:* RA/ADD ASP
Physical and medical conditions:
CA RA SM TW W WA3/HEA HI

BOOTHAM SCHOOL
York, North Yorkshire YO30 7BU
Website: www.boothamschool.
com
Type: Co-educational Boarding
and Day 11–18
Learning difficulties: CA WI/DYC
DYS DYP
*Behavioural and emotional
disorders:* CO ST/ASP ASD
BESD TOU
Physical and medical conditions:
CA SM TW WA2/CP EPI HEA

BRAMCOTE SCHOOL
Filey Road, Scarborough,
North Yorkshire YO11 2TT
Website: www.bramcoteschool.
com
Type: Co-educational Boarding
and Day 3–13
Learning difficulties: CA WI/MLD
DYC DYS DYP
*Behavioural and emotional
disorders:* CA/ADD ADHD ASP
Physical and medical conditions:
CA RA SM WA3/HEA

**HIGHFIELD
PREPARATORY SCHOOL**
Clarence Drive, Harrogate,
North Yorkshire HG1 2QG
Website: www.highfieldprep.
org.uk
Type: Co-educational Day and
Boarding 4–11
Learning difficulties: DYS

**LISVANE, SCARBOROUGH
COLLEGE JUNIOR
SCHOOL**
Filey Road, Scarborough,
North Yorkshire YO11 3BA
Website: www.
scarboroughcollege.co.uk
Type: Co-educational Day and
Boarding 3–11
Learning difficulties: CA SNU/
MLD DYS

MALSIS SCHOOL
Near Skipton, North Yorkshire
BD20 8DT
Website: www.malsis.com
Type: Co-educational Boarding
and Day 4–13
Learning difficulties: SNU/MLD
DYC DYS DYP
*Behavioural and emotional
disorders:* TS ST
Physical and medical conditions:
SM WA3/HEA

THE MOUNT SCHOOL
Dalton Terrace, York,
North Yorkshire YO24 4DD
Website: www.mountschoolyork.
co.uk
Type: Co-educational Day and
Boarding 3–18
Learning difficulties: CA WI/DYS
*Behavioural and emotional
disorders:* CO
Physical and medical conditions:
AT SM TW WA2/CP HEA IM

QUEEN MARY'S SCHOOL
Baldersby Park, Thirsk,
North Yorkshire YO7 3BZ
Website: www.queenmarys.org
Type: Girls Boarding and Day
2–16 (Boys 3–7)
Learning difficulties: SNU/MLD
DYS DYP
*Behavioural and emotional
disorders:* TS
Physical and medical conditions:
AT SM WA3/EPI

SOUTH YORKSHIRE

BIRKDALE SCHOOL
Oakholme Road, Sheffield,
South Yorkshire S10 3DH
Website: www.birkdaleschool.
org.uk
Type: Boys Day Only 4–18
(Co-ed VIth Form)
Learning difficulties: WI/DYS DYP
*Behavioural and emotional
disorders:* ADD
Physical and medical conditions:
HEA HI

WESTBOURNE SCHOOL
60 Westbourne Road, Sheffield,
South Yorkshire S10 2QT
Website: www.
westbourneschool.co.uk
Type: Co-educational Day Only
4–16
Learning difficulties: CA SC SNU/
MLD DYS
Physical and medical conditions:
EPI

WEST YORKSHIRE

**THE FROEBELIAN
SCHOOL**
Clarence Road, Leeds,
West Yorkshire LS18 4LB
Website: www.froebelian.co.uk
Type: Co-educational Day Only
3–11
Learning difficulties: CA RA WI/
DYS DYP
*Behavioural and emotional
disorders:* RA/ADD ASD
Physical and medical conditions:
RA/HEA

FULNECK SCHOOL+
Fulneck, Leeds, West Yorkshire
LS28 8DS
Website: www.fulneckschool.
co.uk
Type: Co-educational Day and
Boarding 3–18
Learning difficulties: CA SNU WI/
DYC DYS DYP
*Behavioural and emotional
disorders:* ADD ASP
Physical and medical conditions:
VI

MOORFIELD SCHOOL
Wharfedale Lodge, Ilkley,
West Yorkshire LS29 8RL
Website: www.moorfieldschool.
co.uk
Type: Girls Day Only 2–11
Learning difficulties: CA RA WI/
DYS
*Behavioural and emotional
disorders:* RA
Physical and medical conditions:
RA TW WA3/HEA

MOORLANDS SCHOOL

Foxhill Drive, Leeds,
West Yorkshire LS16 5PF
Website: www.moorlands-school.co.uk
Type: Co-educational Day Only
2–13
Learning difficulties: CA SNU/
MLD PMLD DOW DYS DYP
Physical and medical conditions:
IT TW WA3/HEA

THE RASTRICK INDEPENDENT SCHOOL

Ogden Lane, Brighouse,
West Yorkshire HD6 3HF
Website: www.rastrickschool.co.uk
Type: Co-educational Day Only
(Day pupils from birth to 16 years
of age.)
Learning difficulties: SNU WI/
MLD DYS DYP
*Behavioural and emotional
disorders:* TS ST/ASP
Physical and medical conditions:
AT IT RA WA3/EPI HEA HI

RICHMOND HOUSE SCHOOL

170 Otley Road, Leeds,
West Yorkshire LS16 5LG
Website: www.rhschool.org
Type: Co-educational Day Only
3–11
Learning difficulties: CA SC WI/
DYS DYP
*Behavioural and emotional
disorders:* RA ST
Physical and medical conditions:
CA RA TW WA3/IM

SUNNY HILL HOUSE SCHOOL

Wrenthorpe Lane, Wakefield,
West Yorkshire WF2 0QB
Website: www.silcoates.wakefield.sch.uk/
sunnyhillhouse.html
Type: Co-educational Day Only
2–7
Learning difficulties: CA WI

WOODHOUSE GROVE SCHOOL

Apperley Bridge, West Yorkshire
BD10 0NR
Website: www.woodhousegrove.co.uk
Type: Co-educational Boarding
and Day 11–18
Learning difficulties: SNU WI/DYS
DYP
*Behavioural and emotional
disorders:* ST/ADD ADHD ASP
Physical and medical conditions:
SM/CP EPI HEA HI

NORTHERN IRELAND

COUNTY DOWN

ROCKPORT SCHOOL
15 Rockport Road, Holywood,
County Down BT18 0DD
Website: www.rockportschool.
com
Type: Co-educational Boarding
and Day 3–16 (Boarding 7–13)
Learning difficulties: SNU WI/
DOW DYS
Physical and medical conditions:
HEA

COUNTY TYRONE

THE ROYAL SCHOOL DUNGANNON
1 Ranfurly Road, Dungannon,
County Tyrone BT71 6EG
Website: www.royaldungannon.
com
Type: Co-educational Day and
Boarding 11–19
Learning difficulties: RA WI/DYC
DYS DYP
*Behavioural and emotional
disorders:* CO RA/ADD
Physical and medical conditions:
CA SL SM TW WA2/EPI HEA HI VI
W

SCOTLAND

ABERDEENSHIRE

ST MARGARET'S SCHOOL FOR GIRLS
17 Albyn Place, Aberdeen,
Aberdeenshire AB10 1RU
Website: www.stmargaret.
aberdeen.sch.uk
Type: Girls Day Only 3–18 (Boys
3–5)
Learning difficulties: RA WI/DYS
DYP
*Behavioural and emotional
disorders:* RA/ADD ADHD ASP
Physical and medical conditions:
RA/EPI

ANGUS

HIGH SCHOOL OF DUNDEE
Euclid Crescent, Dundee, Angus
DD1 1HU
Website: www.
highschoolofdundee.org.uk
Type: Co-educational Day Only
5–18
Learning difficulties: CA SNU/
DYC DYS DYP
*Behavioural and emotional
disorders:* RA/ADD ADHD ASP
Physical and medical conditions:
RA/HEA HI VI

FIFE

ST LEONARDS SCHOOL
St Andrews, Fife KY16 9QJ
Website: www.stleonards-fife.org
Type: Co-educational Boarding
and Day 5–18
Learning difficulties: SNU WI/
MLD DYC DYS DYP
*Behavioural and emotional
disorders:* ADD ADHD ASP

GLASGOW

CRAIGHOLME SCHOOL
72 St. Andrew's Drive, Glasgow
G41 4HS
Website: www.craigholme.co.uk
Type: Girls Day Only 3–18 (Boys
3–5 in Nursery only)
Learning difficulties: RA WI/DYC
DYS DYP
*Behavioural and emotional
disorders:* RA/ASP ASD
Physical and medical conditions:
AT HL IT RA SM TW W WA3/EPI
HEA HI VI

**HUTCHESONS' GRAMMAR
SCHOOL**
21 Beaton Road, Glasgow
G41 4NW
Website: www.hutchesons.org
Type: Co-educational Day Only
5–18
Learning difficulties: WI/DYC DYS
DYP
*Behavioural and emotional
disorders:* RA/ADD ADHD ASP
ASD
Physical and medical conditions:
SM TW W WA2/EPI HEA HI IM VI

LOTHIAN

BELHAVEN HILL
Dunbar, Lothian EH42 1NN
Website: www.belhavenhill.com
Type: Co-educational Boarding
and Day 7–13
Learning difficulties: WI/DYS DYP
Physical and medical conditions:
TW WA2/HEA

DUNEDIN SCHOOL
Liberton Bank House, Edinburgh,
Lothian EH16 5TY
Website:
www.dunedin.edin.sch.uk
Type: Co-educational Day Only
10–17
Learning difficulties: CA SC SNU/
MLD DYC DYS DYP
*Behavioural and emotional
disorders:* CA CO TS ST/ASP
BESD
Physical and medical conditions:
CA IT TW W WA1 WA2/VI

**GEORGE WATSON'S
COLLEGE**
67–71 Colinton Road, Edinburgh,
Lothian EH10 5EG
Website: www.gwc.org.uk
Type: Co-educational Day Only
3–18
Learning difficulties: SNU WI/
DYC DYS DYP
*Behavioural and emotional
disorders:* ADD ADHD ASP ASD
Physical and medical conditions:
CA SM TW WA2/CP EPI HEA HI
IM VI W

**ST GEORGE'S SCHOOL
FOR GIRLS**
Garscube Terrace, Edinburgh,
Lothian EH12 6BG
Website: www.st-georges.
edin.sch.uk
Type: Girls Day and Boarding
1–18 (Boys 2–4)
Learning difficulties: CA RA SC
WI/MLD DYC DYS DYP
*Behavioural and emotional
disorders:* CO RA/ADD ASP
BESD
Physical and medical conditions:
AT BL CA HL IT SM TW WA2
WA3/EPI HEA HI IM VI

PERTH AND KINROSS

KILGRASTON+
Perth, Perth and Kinross PH2 9BQ
Website: www.kilgraston.com
Type: Girls Boarding and Day
2–18 (Boys day 2–9)
Learning difficulties: CA SNU WI/
DYC DYS DYP
Physical and medical conditions:
SM WA2/EPI

MORRISON'S ACADEMY
Ferntower Road, Crieff, Perth and
Kinross PH7 3AN
Website: www.
morrisonsacademy.org
Type: Co-educational Day Only
3–18
Learning difficulties: SNU/DYS
DYP
*Behavioural and emotional
disorders:* CO/ASP
Physical and medical conditions:
RA

STRATHALLAN SCHOOL
Perth, Perth and Kinross PH2 9EG
Website: www.strathallan.co.uk
Type: Co-educational Boarding
and Day 9–18 (Junior House for
Boys and Girls aged 9 to 13
Senior School for Boys and Girls
aged 13 to 18)
Learning difficulties: SNU/DYS
DYP SP&LD
*Behavioural and emotional
disorders:* RA/ADD ADHD ASP
Physical and medical conditions:
SM TW WA3/EPI HEA

RENFREWSHIRE

BELMONT HOUSE
Sandringham Avenue, Newton
Mearns, Renfrewshire G77 5DU
Website: www.belmontschool.
co.uk
Type: Co-educational Day Only
3–18
Learning difficulties: MLD DYS
DYP
*Behavioural and emotional
disorders:* ASP
Physical and medical conditions:
WA1

WALES

BRIDGEND

ST CLARE'S SCHOOL
Porthcawl, Bridgend CF36 5NR
Website: www.stclares-school.
co.uk
Type: Co-educational Day Only
3–18
Physical and medical conditions:
W

ST JOHN'S SCHOOL
Church Street, Porthcawl,
Bridgend CF36 5NP
Website: www.stjohnsschool-
porthcawl.com
Type: Co-educational Day Only
3–16
Learning difficulties: CA RA WI/
MLD DYS
*Behavioural and emotional
disorders:* RA TS

CARDIFF

HOWELL'S SCHOOL,
LLANDAFF GDST
Cardiff Road, Cardiff CF5 2YD
Website: www.howells-cardiff.
gdst.net
Type: Co-educational Day Only
3–18
Learning difficulties: RA WI/DYS
DYP
Physical and medical conditions:
RA WA3/HEA

CONWY

ST DAVID'S COLLEGE+
Llandudno, Conwy LL30 1RD
Website: www.stdavidscollege.
co.uk
Type: Co-educational Boarding
and Day 11–18
Learning difficulties: SNU/MLD
DYC DYS DYP
*Behavioural and emotional
disorders:* TS/ADD ADHD ASP

DENBIGHSHIRE

HOWELL'S SCHOOL
Denbigh, Denbighshire LL16 3EN
Website: www.howells.org
Type: Girls Boarding and Day
2–18
Learning difficulties: CA WI/MLD
DYS DYP
*Behavioural and emotional
disorders:* RA
Physical and medical conditions:
SM WA3/EPI HEA

MONMOUTHSHIRE

ST JOHN'S-ON-THE-HILL
Castleford Hill, Chepstow,
Monmouthshire NP16 7LE
Website: www.stjohnsonthehill.
co.uk
Type: Co-educational Boarding
and Day (Nursery from 3 months)
Learning difficulties: CA SNU/
MLD DYS DYP
*Behavioural and emotional
disorders:* RA/ASP
Physical and medical conditions:
RA SM/HEA

POWYS

CHRIST COLLEGE
Brecon, Powys LD3 8AF
Website: www.
christcollegebrecon.com
Type: Co-educational Boarding
and Day 11–18
Learning difficulties: WI/DYS
*Behavioural and emotional
disorders:* RA

SWANSEA

CRAIG-Y-NOS SCHOOL
Clyne Common, Bishoptston,
Swansea SA3 3JB
Website: www.craigynos.com
Type: Co-educational Day Only
2–11
Learning difficulties: CA WI/DYS
DYP
*Behavioural and emotional
disorders:* RA/ASP ASD
Physical and medical conditions:
CA RA/HEA IM

4.4

Profiles of Independent Mainstream Schools with Specialist Provision

Egerton Rothesay School

Durrants Lane, Berkhamsted, Hertfordshire HP4 3UJ
T: (01442) 865275 **F**: (01442) 864977 **E**: admin.dl@eger-roth.co.uk **W**: www.eger-roth.co.uk

Headteacher Mrs Nicola Boddam-Whetham
School status Co-educational independent
Religious denomination Christian
Member of ISA, ISC; **Accredited by** ISA
Special needs provision ADD, ADHD, **ASD**, **ASP**, **CP**, **DYC**,
DYP, **DYS**, **EPI**, HEA, HI, **IM**, **MLD**, SP&LD, VI, W
Age range 5–16
No of pupils 197; *Girls* 67; *Boys* 130
Average class size 9

A Very Different Education.

ERS is a school especially for the child who can benefit from additional support. This means delivering the best possible education for each child whilst providing them with a genuinely supportive framework that will help them to achieve their full potential.

We are an inclusive school, welcoming children with a wide range of abilities, from all faiths – or none – and from all cultures. We believe that learning should be enjoyable and rounded, being about preparing each child for life after school, as well as exams.

ERS focuses on students who have found, or would find it difficult to progress and succeed within another school. We have a range of specialist support, teachers and therapists who provide for a range of children whose additional needs may include Dyslexia, Dyspraxia, Speech, Language and Communication needs, Asperger and High Functioning Autism. Classes are grouped for individual requirements.

The school has an accepting atmosphere in which children feel understood and in which they do not feel 'different'. This boosts self confidence and aids the enrichment of learning.

Every child at Egerton Rothesay is seen as a unique person and an individual student. The school aims to make an excellent contribution to the life of each student ensuring that they can be supported in the way that they personally need to maximize their individual learning potential.

ERS provides a broad education whilst offering pupils a range of individually tailored strategies to enable each to access the curriculum.

Our aim is always to identify what we can do for your child, and then to work with our resources, and your support, so that we can help them to be successful. Our input can be for the child's whole school career, through to GCSE or simply on an interim basis to help refocus their progress, depending on their needs.

All learning and social activities take place within an environment offering exceptional pastoral care and whole person development that is driven and informed by the school's Christian foundation.

ERS is also more than just a local school. Students travel to the school from all locations, many using the comprehensive minibus service that the school runs over a 35 mile radius.

You are most welcome to come to the school to see if you think our approach would be right for your child. To arrange a visit please contact Liz Martin (01442 877060 or liz.martin@eger-roth.co.uk) or see our website: www.eger-roth.co.uk for more information.

4.5

Index of Independent Mainstream Schools

Abbreviations used in the index

LEARNING DIFFICULTIES

a) Support provided

SNU School has a dedicated Special Needs Unit which provides specialist tuition on a one-to-one or small group basis by appropriately qualified teachers

CA	Some children with special needs receive help from classroom assistants
RA	There are currently very limited facilities for pupils with learning difficulties but reasonable adjustments can be made if necessary
SC	Some children with special needs are taught in separate classes for specific subjects
WI	There is no dedicated Special Needs Unit but some children with special needs are withdrawn individually from certain lessons for one-to-one tuition

b) The school currently has pupils who have been diagnosed with:

DOW	Down's Syndrome
DYC	Dyscalculia
DYP	Dyspraxia
DYS	Dyslexia
MLD	Moderate Learning Difficulties
PMLD	Profound and Multiple Learning Difficulties
SLD	Severe Learning Difficulties
SP&LD	Speech and Language Difficulties

BEHAVIOURAL DISORDERS/EMOTIONAL AND BEHAVIOURAL DIFFICULTIES/ CHALLENGING BEHAVIOUR

a) Support provided:

CA	Some children with behavioural problems receive help from classroom assistants

CO   Trained counsellors available for pupils

RA   There are currently very limited facilities for pupils with behavioural disorders but reasonable adjustments can be made if necessary

ST   Behaviour management strategies identified in school's behaviour management policy

TS   Staff trained in behaviour management available

b) The school currently has pupils who have been diagnosed with the following disorders:

ADD   Attention Deficit Disorder

ADHD   Attention Deficit Hyperactivity Disorder

ASD   Autism/Autistic Spectrum Disorder

ASP   Asperger's Syndrome

BESD   Behavioural, Emotional and Social Disorders

CB   Challenging Behaviour

TOU   Tourette's Syndrome

PHYSICAL IMPAIRMENTS/MEDICAL CONDITIONS

a) Support provided:

AT   Adapted timetable for children with health problems

BL   Materials can be provided in Braille

CA   Some children receive help from classroom assistants

DS   Signing by staff and pupils

HL   Hearing loops available

IT   Specialist IT provision available

RA   There are currently very limited facilities for pupils with physical impairments or medical conditions but reasonable adjustments can be made if necessary.

SL   Stairlifts

SM   Staff with medical training available

TW   Accessible toilet and washing facilities

W   School has wheelchair access (unspecified)

WA1   School is fully wheelchair accessible

WA2   Main teaching areas are wheelchair accessible

WA3   No permanent access for wheelchairs, temporary ramps available

b) The school currently has pupils with the following impairments/medical conditions:

CP   Cerebral Palsy

EPI   Epilepsy

HEA   Health problems (eg heart defect, asthma)

HI   Hearing impairment

IM   Impaired mobility

VI   Visual impairment

WU   Wheelchair user

Learning difficulties

Support provided/Currenly have pupils diagnosed with learning difficulties

The Abbey, Woodbridge	WI/MLD DYS
Abbey Gate School, Chester	CA WI/MLD DYS DYP
The Abbey School, Reading	WI/DYS DYP
Abbot's Hill School, Hemel Hempstead	CA SNU WI/DYC DYS DYP
Abbots Bromley School for Girls, Abbots Bromley	CA/MLD SLD DYC DYS
Aberdour, Tadworth	CA/DYC DYS DYP
Adcote School for Girls, Shrewsbury	CA SNU/MLD DYS DYP
Airthrie School, Cheltenham	CA SNU/DYS DYP
Akeley Wood School, Buckingham	SNU/MLD DYS DYP
Aldro School, Godalming	CA SNU WI/MLD DYS DYP
Alleyn's School, London	WI/DYC DYS DYP
Ampleforth College, York	WI/DYC DYS DYP
Arnold Lodge School, Leamington Spa	WI/MLD DYC DYS DYP
Arnold School, Blackpool	SNU WI/MLD DYC DYS DYP
Ashford School, Ashford	CA SNU/MLD DYS DYP
Ashgrove School, Bromley	WI/DYS DYP
Aston House School, London	SNU/DYS DYP
Avenue House School, London	RA WI/MLD DYS
Aysgarth Preparatory School, Bedale	CA SC SNU WI/MLD DYC DYS DYP
Babington House School, Chislehurst	CA WI/DYS DYP
Bablake School, Coventry	SNU/DYS DYP
Barfield School and Nursery, Farnham	WI
Barlborough Hall School, Chesterfield	CA WI/DYS DYP
Beeston Hall School, Cromer	CA SNU/MLD DYC DYS DYP
Belhaven Hill, Dunbar	WI/DYS DYP
Benenden School, Cranbrook	SNU/DYS DYP
Bilton Grange, Rugby	CA/MLD DYC DYS DYP
Birchfield School, Wolverhampton	CA SNU/MLD DYC DYS DYP
Birkdale School, Sheffield	WI/DYS DYP
Bishopsgate School, Egham	SNU/DYC DYS DYP
Bootham School, York	CA WI/DYC DYS DYP
Bournemouth Collegiate School, Bournemouth	SNU WI/DYC DYS
Brabyns School, Stockport	RA WI/DYS DYP
Bramcote School, Scarborough	CA WI/MLD DYC DYS DYP
Bramley School, Tadworth	CA WI/MLD DYC DYS DYP
Bredon School, Tewkesbury	CA SNU/MLD DYC DYS DYP SP&LD
Bricklehurst Manor Preparatory, Wadhurst	CA SNU/DYC DYS
Bristol Cathedral School, Bristol	CA WI/DYS DYP
Broadwater Manor School, Worthing	CA WI
Bromsgrove Pre-preparatory and Nursery School, Bromsgrove	CA RA WI/DYS DYP
Bronte School, Gravesend	CA SC/MLD DYS DYP
Brooke Priory School, Oakham	CA WI/DYS DYP
Brooklands School & Little Brooklands Nursery, Stafford	SNU/MLD DYS

Buckingham College School, Harrow	CA SNU/DYC DYS SP&LD
Bury Grammar School Boys, Bury	RA/DYS
Cambridge Centre for Sixth-form Studies, Cambridge	CA RA/DYS DYP
Cambridge Tutors College, Croydon	RA WI/MLD DYS
The Carrdus School, Banbury	CA RA SC WI
Castle House School, Newport	CA SC SNU WI/MLD DYC DYS DYP SP&LD
Cedars School, Aldermaston	CA WI/DYS
Chafyn Grove School, Salisbury	SNU/MLD DYS DYP SP&LD
Channing School, London	WI/MLD DYS DYP
Chard School, Chard	CA WI/DYS DYP
Charterhouse Square School, London	WI
Cheltenham College, Cheltenham	WI
Cheltenham College Junior School, Cheltenham	CA SNU/DYS DYP SP&LD
Cheltenham Ladies' College, Cheltenham	SNU WI/DYS DYP
Cherwell College, Oxford	SC WI/MLD DYC DYS DYP
Christ College, Brecon	WI/DYS
Clifton College, Bristol	CA SNU/DYC DYS DYP SP&LD
Clifton College Preparatory School, Bristol	SNU/MLD DYC DYS DYP
Clifton High School, Bristol	CA RA WI/MLD DYC DYS DYP
Craig-y-Nos School, Bishoptston	CA WI/DYS DYP
Craigholme School, Glasgow	RA WI/DYC DYS DYP
Cranford House School, Wallingford	WI
Croydon High School GDST, South Croydon	RA/DYS
Culcheth Hall, Altrincham	CA SC SNU/DYC DYS DYP
Dagfa House School, Nottingham	CA WI/MLD DYC DYS DYP
Dair House School Trust Ltd, Farnham Royal	CA WI/DYS
Dallington School, London	CA/DYS DYP
Dame Bradbury's School, Saffron Walden	CA RA/DYS DYP
Davenport Lodge School, Coventry	CA WI/MLD DYS
Derby High School, Derby	CA RA WI/DYC DYS DYP
Dolphin School, Reading	WI/DYS
Dorchester Preparatory and Independent Schools, Dorchester	CA WI/DYC DYS DYP
Dover College, Dover	WI/DYS DYP
Dower House School, Bridgnorth	WI
Downe House, Thatcham	SNU/DYS DYP
Downsend School, Leatherhead	CA SNU WI/DYC DYS DYP
Downsend School – Ashtead Lodge, Ashtead	RA WI
Dragon School, Oxford	WI/DYC DYS DYP SP&LD
Duff Miller, London	WI/MLD DYS DYP
Dulwich Preparatory School, Cranbrook, Cranbrook	CA SNU WI/DYS DYP
Dunedin School, Edinburgh	CA SC SNU/MLD DYC DYS DYP
Durlston Court, New Milton	CA SNU/MLD DYC DYS DYP
Eaton House Belgravia, London	SNU WI/MLD DYC DYS DYP
Eaton House The Manor Preparatory, London	SNU WI/DYC DYS DYP
Eaton House The Vale, London	CA WI/MLD
Edgbaston High School for Girls, Birmingham	RA WI/DYC DYS DYP

Hurst Lodge School, Ascot	CA SC SNU WI/MLD DYC DYS DYP
Hutchesons' Grammar School, Glasgow	WI/DYC DYS DYP
Ilford Ursuline Preparatory School, Ilford	SNU/MLD DYS DYP
The John Lyon School, Harrow	CA SNU WI/DYC DYS DYP
Kelly College Preparatory School, Tavistock	CA WI/DYS DYP
Kent College Infant & Junior School, Canterbury	SC SNU/MLD DYC DYS DYP
Kent College Pembury, Tunbridge Wells	WI/DYC DYS DYP
Kew Green Preparatory School, Richmond	CA SNU WI/MLD DYC DYS DYP
Kilgraston, Perth	CA SNU WI/DYC DYS DYP
King Edward VII and Queen Mary School, Lytham St Annes	CA WI/DYC DYS DYP
King's College, Taunton	WI
King's Preparatory School, Rochester	WI/DYS DYP
KINGSLEY SCHOOL, Bideford	SC SNU/DYS DYP
Kingswood School, Solihull	CA SC SNU/MLD DYC DYS DYP
Kingswood School, Bath	RA WI/DYC DYS DYP
Kirkham Grammar School, Preston	SNU/DYC DYS
Kirkstone House School, Bourne	CA SNU WI/MLD DYS DYP
The Lady Eleanor Holles School, Hampton	WI/DYC DYS DYP
Lancing College Preparatory School at Mowden, Hove	CA WI/DYS
Lanesborough, Guildford	CA SNU WI/MLD DYS
Langley School, Norwich	SNU/DYC DYS DYP
Lansdowne College, London	RA/MLD DYC DYS DYP
The Larks, Oxted	WI/DYS DYP
Lichfield Cathedral School, Lichfield	SC SNU/DYC DYS DYP
Lime House School, Carlisle	CA SC SNU WI/MLD DYS DYP
Lion House School, London	CA WI/MLD
Lisvane, Scarborough College Junior School, Scarborough	CA SNU/MLD DYS
Littlegarth School, Colchester	CA SNU WI/MLD DYC DYS DYP
Lord Wandsworth College, Hook	RA WI/DYS
Loreto Preparatory School, Altrincham	CA WI/MLD DYS
Loughborough High School, Loughborough	RA WI/DYC DYS DYP
Madni Girls School, London	WI/DYC
The Mall School, Twickenham	CA RA WI/DYS DYP
Malsis School, Near Skipton	SNU/MLD DYC DYS DYP
Maltman's Green School, Gerrards Cross	CA WI/MLD DYS DYP
Malvern St James, Great Malvern	SNU/MLD DYS DYP
The Manchester Grammar School, Manchester	RA WI/DYC DYS DYP
Manor House School, Ashby-de-la-Zouch	CA SC WI/DYC DYS DYP
The Manor Preparatory School, Abingdon	CA SNU/DYC DYS DYP
The Maynard School, Exeter	WI/DYS DYP
Mayville High School, Southsea	SNU/DYS DYP
Meadowbrook Montessori School, Bracknell	CA RA SNU/MLD DYS
Meadowpark Nursery & Pre-Prep School, Cricklade	WI
Merchant Taylors' Boys' Schools, Liverpool	CA SNU/MLD DYC DYS DYP
Merchant Taylors' School, Northwood	RA SNU/DYS DYP
The Mill School, Devizes	CA WI/DYS

Milton Abbey School, Blandford Forum	SNU/DYC DYS DYP SP&LD
The Montessori House, London	CA/MLD
Moor Park School, Ludlow	SNU/DYC DYS DYP
Moorfield School, Ilkley	CA RA WI/DYS
Moorlands School, Leeds	CA SNU/MLD PMLD DOW DYS DYP
Moreton Hall Preparatory School, Bury St Edmunds	SC/MLD DYS
Moreton Hall School, Oswestry	SNU WI/MLD DYC DYS DYP
Morrison's Academy, Crieff	SNU/DYS DYP
The Mount School, York	CA WI/DYS
The New Eccles Hall School, Norwich	SC SNU/DYC DYS DYP
New Life Christian School, Croydon	WI
Newcastle-under-Lyme School, Newcastle-under-Lyme	WI
Norfolk House School, Birmingham	RA WI
Norfolk Lodge Montessori Nursery, Barnet	RA
North Cestrian Grammar School, Altrincham	CA WI/MLD DYC DYS DYP
Northbourne Park School, Deal	CA SNU/DYC DYS DYP
Northcote Lodge School, London	WI/DYC DYS DYP
Northwood College, Northwood	WI/DYS DYP
Notting Hill and Ealing High School GDST, London	WI/DYC DYS DYP
Nottingham High School, Nottingham	WI/DYC DYS DYP
Oakfield School, Woking	WI/DYS DYP
Oakhyrst Grange School, Caterham	CA WI/DYS DYP
The Old Hall School, Telford	SNU/DYC DYS DYP
Old Vicarage School, Richmond	WI
The Oratory Preparatory School, Reading	CA WI/DYC DYS DYP
The Oratory School, Reading	SNU/MLD DYS DYP
Orwell Park, Ipswich	SNU/DYC DYS DYP
Oswestry School Bellan House, Oswestry	SNU/DYS DYP
Overndale School, Old Sodbury	CA
Oxford Tutorial College, Oxford	SC WI/MLD DYS DYP
Papplewick School, Ascot	WI/MLD DYS
The Park School, Yeovil	WI/MLD DYS DYP
The Perse School, Cambridge	CA SNU
Pocklington School, Pocklington	SNU/DYS
Polam Hall, Darlington	CA SC SNU/MLD DYS DYP
Port Regis Preparatory School, Shaftesbury	SNU WI/DYC DYS DYP
The Portsmouth Grammar School, Portsmouth	WI
Portsmouth High School GDST, Southsea	WI/DYS DYP
Prestfelde Preparatory School, Shrewsbury	CA SNU/DYS DYP
Primrose Independent School, London	WI/MLD DOW DYS DYP
Prior Park Preparatory School, Cricklade	CA SNU WI/DYC DYS DYP
Priory Preparatory School, Banstead	CA WI/MLD DYC DYS DYP
Priory School, Birmingham	SNU/DYC DYS DYP
Putney Park School, London	WI/DYC DYS DYP
Queen Elizabeth's Hospital, Bristol	SNU/DYS DYP
Queen Mary's School, Thirsk	SNU/MLD DYS DYP

Ramillies Hall School, Cheadle | CA SNU/DYC DYS DYP
Ranby House School, Retford | CA SC SNU/MLD DOW DYC DYS DYP
Raphael Independent School, Hornchurch | WI/DYS
The Rastrick Independent School, Brighouse | SNU WI/MLD DYS DYP
Red House School, Norton | RA WI/DYS DYP
The Red Maids' School, Bristol | CA SNU/DYS
Reigate Grammar School, Reigate | CA/MLD DYS DYP
RGS The Grange, Worcester | CA WI/DYS DYP
RGS Worcester & The Alice Ottley School, Worcester | WI/DYC DYS DYP
The Richard Pate School, Cheltenham | CA SNU WI/MLD DYS
Richmond House School, Leeds | CA SC WI/DYS DYP
Rickmansworth PNEU School, Rickmansworth | CA SNU/DYS DYP
Riddlesworth Hall, Diss | SNU/MLD DYC DYS DYP
Ripley Court School, Woking | WI/DYS DYP
The Roche School, London | CA SC WI/MLD DOW DYS DYP
Rockport School, Holywood | SNU WI/DOW DYS
Roselyon, Par | CA WI/MLD DYS DYP
The Rowans School, London | WI
The Royal Hospital School, Ipswich | SNU WI/MLD DYS DYP
The Royal School Dungannon, Dungannon | RA WI/DYC DYS DYP
The Royal Wolverhampton Junior School, Wolverhampton | CA RA SNU/MLD DYC DYS DYP
Ruckleigh School, Solihull | CA RA WI/DYS
Russell House School, Sevenoaks | WI/DYS DYP
Ryde School, Ryde | SNU/DYC DYS DYP
St Andrew's School, Eastbourne | CA SNU WI/DYC DYS DYP
St Andrew's School, Reading | WI/DYS
St Bees School, St Bees | SNU WI/DYC DYS DYP
St Bernard's Preparatory School, Slough | CA WI/DYS
St Christopher School, Letchworth Garden City | SNU/DYS DYP
St Christopher's School, Hove | CA SNU WI/MLD DYS
St Christophers School, Totnes | CA/MLD DYS DYP
St Crispin's School, Leicester | CA RA SC SNU WI/MLD DYC DYS DYP
St David's College, Llandudno | SNU/MLD DYC DYS DYP
St David's School, Purley | CA WI/DYC DYS DYP
St Dunstan's College, London | CA WI/DYC DYS DYP
St Edmund's College and St Hugh's School, Ware | CA WI/DYS DYP
St Faith's at Ash School, Canterbury | CA RA WI/DYS DYP
St Gabriel's, Berkshire | CA SNU/MLD DYC DYS DYP
St George's School for Girls, Edinburgh | CA RA SC WI/MLD DYC DYS DYP
St Helen & St Katharine, Abingdon | WI/DYS
St Helen's School, Northwood | WI/DYS
St Hilary's School, Godalming | CA SNU WI/DYS DYP
St Hugh's School, Woodhall Spa | CA SNU WI/MLD DYC DYS
St Hugh's School, Faringdon | CA WI/MLD DYS DYP
St Ia School, St Ives | RA WI
St James Junior School, London | WI/MLD

St John's School, Leatherhead	SNU WI/DYC DYS DYP
St John's School, Porthcawl	CA RA WI/MLD DYS
St John's-on-the-Hill, Chepstow	CA SNU/MLD DYS DYP
St Joseph's College, Ipswich	CA WI/DYC DYS DYP
St Joseph's Convent School, London	CA SNU/MLD
St Joseph's In The Park, Hertford	CA SC SNU/DYC DYS DYP
St Joseph's School, Launceston	SNU/MLD DYS DYP
St Lawrence College, Ramsgate	SNU/DYC DYS DYP
St Lawrence College Junior School, Ramsgate	CA WI/MLD DYS DYP
St Leonards School, St Andrews	SNU WI/MLD DYC DYS DYP
St Margaret's School, London	RA/MLD DYC DYS DYP
St Margaret's School for Girls, Aberdeen	RA WI/DYS DYP
St Martin's School, Northwood	SC/DYC DYS DYP
St Mary's Junior School, Cambridge	CA/DYC DYS
St Mary's Preparatory School, Lincoln	CA SNU/MLD DYS DYP
St Mary's School, Ascot, Ascot	WI/DYS DYP
St Michael's, Barnstaple	CA SNU/MLD DOW DYS
St Michael's School, Sevenoaks	WI
St Nicholas' School, Fleet	WI/DYS
St Olave's Preparatory School, London	SNU WI/SLD DYS DYP
St Paul's Cathedral School, London	WI
St Piran's Preparatory School, Hayle	CA WI/MLD DYS
St Teresa's Catholic Independent & Nursery School, Princes Risborough	CA WI/DYS DYP
St Ursula's High School, Westbury-on-Trym	CA WI/MLD DYS DYP
St Ursulas Convent School, Wigton	SNU/DYS DYP
St. Hilda's School, Harpenden	SC WI/DYC DYS DYP
Sacred Heart School, Swaffham	CA SC/MLD DYS DYP
Steephill Independent School, Longfield	CA WI/MLD DYS
Saint Martin's School, Solihull	CA SNU/DYC DYS
Salterford House School, Nottingham	CA WI/MLD DYS DYP
Sancton Wood School, Cambridge	CA WI/DYC DYS DYP
Sandroyd School, Salisbury	SNU/MLD DYS DYP
Stonar School, Melksham	CA SNU/MLD DYC DYS DYP
Stonyhurst College, Clitheroe	SNU WI/MLD DYC DYS DYP
Strathallan School, Perth	SNU/DYS DYP SP&LD
Streatham & Clapham High School, London	CA SNU/DYC DYS DYP
Streatham House School, Liverpool	CA SC WI/MLD DOW DYC DYS DYP
The Stroud School, Romsey	CA SNU/MLD DYS
Seaton House School, Sutton	CA RA SC WI/DYS DYP
Sedbergh Junior School, Sedbergh	CA SC SNU WI/MLD DYS DYP
Sedbergh School, Sedbergh	SNU WI/DYS
Sherborne House School, Eastleigh	SNU/DYS
Sherborne School, Sherborne	SNU WI/MLD DYC DYS DYP
Shiplake College, Henley-on-Thames	SNU/DYC DYS DYP
Sibford School, Banbury	CA SNU WI/DYC DYS DYP
Smallwood Manor Preparatory School, Uttoxeter	CA WI/DYC DYS DYP

South Hills School, Salisbury	CA WI/MLD DOW
Summer Fields, Oxford	SNU/MLD DYC DYS DYP
Sunny Hill House School, Wakefield	CA WI
Sutton High School GDST, Sutton	SC/MLD DYS DYP
Taunton Preparatory School, Taunton	WI/DYC DYS DYP
Taverham Hall Preparatory School, Norwich	CA SNU WI/DYS DYP
Teesside High School, Eaglescliffe	RA WI/DYC DYS DYP
Terra Nova School, Holmes Chapel	CA SNU WI/DYC DYS DYP
Tettenhall College, Wolverhampton	CA SNU WI/DYC DYS DYP SP&LD
Thames Christian College, London	CA WI/DYS DYP
Thorngrove School, Newbury	CA WI/DYS DYP
Thorpe Hall School, Southend-on-Sea	CA SC WI/MLD DYC DYS DYP
Tockington Manor School, Tockington	CA SC SNU/DYS DYP
Trinity School, Croydon	WI/DYC DYS DYP
Trinity School, Teignmouth	CA SNU/MLD DYC DYS DYP
Tudor Hall School, Banbury	SNU/DYC DYS DYP SP&LD
Twyford School, Winchester	SNU/DYS
Walthamstow Hall, Sevenoaks	WI/DYC DYS DYP
Wellow House School, Newark	CA WI/DYS
West Buckland Preparatory School, Barnstaple	CA RA/MLD DYC DYS DYP
West Buckland School, Barnstaple	CA SNU WI/DOW DYC DYS DYP
West House School, Birmingham	CA WI/MLD DYS
Westbourne School, Sheffield	CA SC SNU/MLD DYS
Westminster Abbey Choir School, London	WI/DYS
Westminster Cathedral Choir School, London	WI/DYS DYP
Westminster Tutors, London	SC WI/MLD DYS DYP
Westonbirt School, Tetbury	SNU/DYC DYS DYP
Winchester College, Winchester	SNU/DYC DYS DYP
Winchester House School, Brackley	SNU WI
Windermere School, Windermere	WI
Winterfold House, Kidderminster	SNU/MLD
Withington Girls' School, Manchester	CA RA WI/DYC DYS DYP
Wolverhampton Grammar School, Wolverhampton	CA SNU WI/DYS DYP
Woodcote House School, Windlesham	SC SNU/MLD DYC DYS DYP
Woodhouse Grove School, Apperley Bridge	SNU WI/DYS DYP
Wrekin College, Shropshire	RA WI/DYS
Wycliffe College, Stonehouse	SNU WI/DYC DYS DYP
Wycliffe Preparatory School, Stonehouse	CA SNU WI/DYC DYS DYP
Wycombe Abbey School, High Wycombe	SNU WI/DYC DYS DYP

Behavioural and emotional disorders

Support provided/Currenly have pupils diagnosed with disorders

Abbey Gate School, Chester	CA TS ST/ADD ASD
The Abbey School, Reading	TS ST/ADD
Abbot's Hill School, Hemel Hempstead	CO/ASP BESD

Downe House, Thatcham	RA
Downsend School, Leatherhead	RA/ADD ADHD ASP
Downsend School – Ashtead Lodge, Ashtead	RA
Dragon School, Oxford	CO RA/ADD ADHD ASP
Dunedin School, Edinburgh	CA CO TS ST/ASP BESD
Eaton House Belgravia, London	CA TS/BESD
Eaton House The Manor Preparatory, London	CA RA/ADD ASP ASD
Eaton House The Vale, London	TS
Edgbaston High School for Girls, Birmingham	RA ST
Ellesmere College, Ellesmere	RA
Elmhurst School for Dance, Birmingham	RA
Emmanuel School, Derby	RA/ASP
Farringtons School, Chislehurst	RA
Felsted School, Felsted	RA
Finton House School, London	RA/ASP ASD BESD
The Froebelian School, Leeds	RA/ADD ASD
Gateway Christian School, Ilkeston	RA
Gems Bolitho School, Penzance	CA/ADD ADHD ASP
Glebe House School, Hunstanton	RA
Godstowe Preparatory School, High Wycombe	CA CO/ADD ADHD ASP ASD
Gracefield Preparatory School, Fishponds	TS
Great Houghton Preparatory School, Northampton	CA CO RA TS ST/ASP ASD
Greenbank Preparatory School, Cheadle	RA TS
Greene's Tutorial College, Oxford	RA/ADD ADHD ASP BESD
Hampton School, Hampton	CO TS ST/ADD ADHD ASP ASD TOU
Handcross Park School, Haywards Heath	CO TS/ADD ADHD
Harenc School Trust, Sidcup	CA ST/ADD ASP
Hatherop Castle School, Cirencester	ST
Hethersett Old Hall School, Norwich	RA/BESD
High Elms Manor School, Watford	RA/ADD ASP ASD
High March School, Beaconsfield	RA
High School of Dundee, Dundee	RA/ADD ADHD ASP
Highclare School, Birmingham	RA/ADD ADHD BESD
Hoe Bridge School, Woking	CA RA/ADD ADHD
Hordle Walhampton School, Lymington	ST/ASP
Howell's School, Denbigh	RA
Hurst Lodge School, Ascot	RA/ADD ADHD ASP
Hutchesons' Grammar School, Glasgow	RA/ADD ADHD ASP ASD
Ilford Ursuline Preparatory School, Ilford	TS/ADHD
The John Lyon School, Harrow	CA CO/ADD ASD
Kent College Infant & Junior School, Canterbury	CA CO
Kent College Pembury, Tunbridge Wells	CO/ADD BESD
Kew Green Preparatory School, Richmond	CA CO TS ST/ADD CB
King Edward VII and Queen Mary School, Lytham St Annes	RA/ADD ADHD
The Lady Eleanor Holles School, Hampton	CO/TOU
Lancing College Preparatory School at Mowden, Hove	RA/ADHD

Pocklington School, Pocklington	RA
Polam Hall, Darlington	RA/ASP ASD
Port Regis Preparatory School, Shaftesbury	CO/ADD ASP
Primrose Independent School, London	RA/ASP ASD
Priory Preparatory School, Banstead	RA
The Purcell School, Bushey	CO RA/ASP
Putney Park School, London	RA
Queen Elizabeth's Hospital, Bristol	CO/ADD ADHD
Queen Mary's School, Thirsk	TS
Queen's Gate School, London	RA
Ranby House School, Retford	CA RA ST/ADD ASP ASD BESD CB
The Rastrick Independent School, Brighouse	TS ST/ASP
Red House School, Norton	RA/ASP TOU
RGS The Grange, Worcester	RA/ADD ADHD ASP TOU
RGS Worcester & The Alice Ottley School, Worcester	RA/ADD ADHD ASP TOU
Richmond House School, Leeds	RA ST
Rickmansworth PNEU School, Rickmansworth	RA
Riddlesworth Hall, Diss	ST/ASD
Ripley Court School, Woking	RA
Rock Hall School, Alnwick	RA ST
Roselyon, Par	RA/ADD ADHD
The Royal Hospital School, Ipswich	CO RA
The Royal School Dungannon, Dungannon	CO RA/ADD
The Royal Wolverhampton Junior School, Wolverhampton	CA CO RA ST/ADHD CB
Ruckleigh School, Solihull	RA
St Andrew's School, Eastbourne	RA/ASP
St Bees School, St Bees	RA/ADD ADHD BESD
St Christopher's School, Hove	ST/ADHD ASP
St Christophers School, Totnes	RA/ADHD ASD BESD
St Crispin's School, Leicester	CA TS ST/ADD ADHD ASP BESD
St David's College, Llandudno	TS/ADD ADHD ASP
St David's School, Purley	RA/ASP
St Edmund's College and St Hugh's School, Ware	RA/ASP
St Faith's at Ash School, Canterbury	CA RA ST/BESD
St Gabriel's, Berkshire	CA CO/ADD ASP BESD
St George's School for Girls, Edinburgh	CO RA/ADD ASP BESD
St Helen & St Katharine, Abingdon	CO/ADD ADHD
St Helen's School, Northwood	CO
St Hugh's School, Woodhall Spa	CA/ADD ADHD ASP ASD CB
St Ia School, St Ives	RA
St John's School, Leatherhead	CO/ADD ADHD ASP
St John's School, Porthcawl	RA TS
St John's-on-the-Hill, Chepstow	RA/ASP
St Joseph's College, Ipswich	RA ST/ADHD
St Joseph's School, Launceston	RA
St Lawrence College Junior School, Ramsgate	CA RA TS ST/ASP ASD

St Margaret's School, London	CO
St Margaret's School for Girls, Aberdeen	RA/ADD ADHD ASP
St Martin's School, Northwood	ST/ADHD ASP
St Mary's Junior School, Cambridge	CA RA
St Mary's Preparatory School, Lincoln	RA/ASD
St Piran's Preparatory School, Hayle	ST
St Ursula's High School, Westbury-on-Trym	RA/ADD ADHD ASP
Steephill Independent School, Longfield	RA ST
Salterford House School, Nottingham	ST/ADHD ASP ASD
Stonyhurst College, Clitheroe	CO ST/ADD ADHD ASP
Strathallan School, Perth	RA/ADD ADHD ASP
Streatham & Clapham High School, London	CA CO RA TS ST/ADD ASP ASD BESD CB
Seaton House School, Sutton	RA
Sedbergh Junior School, Sedbergh	TS/ASP ASD
Sedbergh School, Sedbergh	TS/ADD
Shiplake College, Henley-on-Thames	ST
Sibford School, Banbury	CO RA/ADD ADHD ASP ASD
South Hills School, Salisbury	ST
Summer Fields, Oxford	CO RA/ADD ADHD ASP BESD
Sutton High School GDST, Sutton	CO ST/BESD
Taunton Preparatory School, Taunton	ST/ADD ADHD
Taverham Hall Preparatory School, Norwich	ST/ADD
Teesside High School, Eaglescliffe	RA ST/ADHD ASP
Terra Nova School, Holmes Chapel	RA/ADHD ASP
Thorngrove School, Newbury	RA
Thorpe Hall School, Southend-on-Sea	CA TS ST/ADD ADHD ASP ASD
Trinity School, Croydon	CO/ADD ADHD ASP ASD
Trinity School, Teignmouth	CA CO TS ST/ADD ADHD ASP
Tudor Hall School, Banbury	CO
University College School, London	CO
University College School Junior Branch, London	CO/ADD ADHD ASP
Walthamstow Hall, Sevenoaks	CO ST/ASP
West Buckland Preparatory School, Barnstaple	RA/ADD ADHD
West Buckland School, Barnstaple	CA CO RA TS ST/ADD ADHD ASP BESD
West House School, Birmingham	CA ST/ADHD ASD TOU
Westminster Cathedral Choir School, London	RA/ADD
Westminster Tutors, London	RA/ASP
Winchester College, Winchester	RA/ADD ADHD ASP
Winterfold House, Kidderminster	RA
Woodcote House School, Windlesham	RA/ADD ASP
Woodhouse Grove School, Apperley Bridge	ST/ADD ADHD ASP
Wycliffe Preparatory School, Stonehouse	RA/ADD
Wycombe Abbey School, High Wycombe	CO/ADHD

Independent Mainstream Schools with Specialist Provision

Physical and medical conditions

Support provided/Currenly have pupils with impairments or medical conditions

The Abbey, WOODBRIDGE	TW WA2
Abbey College, Manchester	TW WA2
Abbey Gate School, Chester	CA SM TW WA1 WA2/HEA HI VI
The Abbey School, Reading	SL SM TW WA2/HEA
Abbot's Hill School, Hemel Hempstead	IT SM/EPI HEA HI VI
Abbots Bromley School for Girls, Abbots Bromley	CA SM/VI
Aberdour, Tadworth	RA SM/HEA
Adcote School for Girls, Shrewsbury	RA SM WA3
Akeley Wood School, Buckingham	RA/HEA HI
Aldro School, Godalming	RA TW
Alleyn's School, London	RA SM TW/EPI HEA HI VI
Ampleforth College, York	RA WA3/CP EPI
Arnold Lodge School, Leamington Spa	RA/EPI HEA HI VI
Arnold School, Blackpool	SL SM WA2/HEA HI
Ashford School, Ashford	RA SM W WA3/HEA
Aston House School, London	CA SM TW WA3/HEA VI
Avenue House School, London	RA SM WA3/HEA
Aysgarth Preparatory School, Bedale	CA RA SM TW W WA3/HEA HI
Babington House School, Chislehurst	RA/HI
Bablake School, Coventry	TW WA2
Barfield School and Nursery, Farnham	W
Beeston Hall School, Cromer	CA SM TW/CP HEA HI IM
Belhaven Hill, Dunbar	TW WA2/HEA
Belmont House, Newton Mearns	WA1
Benenden School, Cranbrook	RA SM WA2/HEA HI VI
Bilton Grange, Rugby	CA RA SM/HEA VI
Birchfield School, Wolverhampton	AT RA SM TW WA3/HEA
Bishopsgate School, Egham	TW WA2/EPI VI
Bootham School, York	CA SM TW WA2/CP EPI HEA
Bournemouth Collegiate Prep School, Poole	W
Bournemouth Collegiate School, Bournemouth	AT RA WA3/HEA
Bramcote School, Scarborough	CA RA SM WA3/HEA
Bramley School, Tadworth	IT SL SM TW W WA2/HEA
Bredon School, Tewkesbury	IT SL SM TW W WA2/HEA
Bricklehurst Manor Preparatory, Wadhurst	RA/HEA
Bristol Cathedral School, Bristol	RA/HEA VI
Broadwater Manor School, Worthing	RA/HEA
Bromsgrove Pre-preparatory and Nursery School, Bromsgrove	RA/HEA HI VI
Bronte School, Gravesend	CA RA SM WA3/HEA
Brooke Priory School, Oakham	CA SM TW W WA1 WA2/HEA
Broomwood Hall School, London	IT RA SM TW
Buckingham College School, Harrow	AT RA/HEA
Bury Grammar School Boys, Bury	RA/EPI HEA HI

Cambridge Centre for Sixth-form Studies, Cambridge	RA SM/HEA
Cambridge Tutors College, Croydon	IT RA SM
The Carrdus School, Banbury	WA3
Castle House School, Newport	CA RA SM WA3/HEA HI
Cedars School, Aldermaston	W
Chafyn Grove School, Salisbury	CA IT RA WA2/HEA HI
Channing School, London	SM TW WA1 WA2/EPI HI IM
Chard School, Chard	IT RA/VI
Cheltenham College Junior School, Cheltenham	RA SM WA2
Cheltenham Ladies' College, Cheltenham	AT IT RA SM TW W WA2 WA3/CP EPI HEA HI IM VI W
Cherwell College, Oxford	AT RA/HEA IM
Clifton College, Bristol	RA WA3/HEA
Clifton College Preparatory School, Bristol	CA WA3/HEA HI VI
Clifton High School, Bristol	AT BL HL IT RA SM WA3/HEA HI VI
Craig-y-Nos School, Bishoptston	CA RA/HEA IM
Craigholme School, Glasgow	AT HL IT RA SM TW W WA3/EPI HEA HI VI
Croydon High School GDST, South Croydon	RA/HI
Culcheth Hall, Altrincham	AT CA/HEA
Dagfa House School, Nottingham	CA/HI VI
Dallington School, London	RA/HEA HI
Dame Bradbury's School, Saffron Walden	RA/W
Davenport Lodge School, Coventry	TW W WA2
Derby High School, Derby	RA/HEA
Dolphin School, Reading	RA
The Dominie, London	RA/HI
Dorchester Preparatory and Independent Schools, Dorchester	RA/HEA
Dover College, Dover	RA SM/HEA HI VI
Downe House, Thatcham	RA/HEA HI
Downsend School, Leatherhead	RA W/HEA HI
Downsend School – Ashtead Lodge, Ashtead	RA TW/HEA
Dragon School, Oxford	RA SM TW WA2/HEA
Duff Miller, London	RA/EPI HEA VI
Dulwich Preparatory School, Cranbrook, Cranbrook	IT RA W/EPI HEA IM
Dunedin School, Edinburgh	CA IT TW W WA1 WA2/VI
Eastbourne College, Eastbourne	RA
Eaton House Belgravia, London	AT SM WA3/EPI
Eaton House The Manor Preparatory, London	CA
Eaton House The Vale, London	RA
Edgbaston High School for Girls, Birmingham	AT HL IT SM TW WA2/CP EPI HEA HI IM
Ellesmere College, Ellesmere	RA/HEA
Elmhurst School for Dance, Birmingham	SM TW W WA1 WA2/HI
Emmanuel School, Derby	RA WA3/HEA VI
Ewell Castle School, Epsom	AT RA/EPI HEA
Fairfield Preparatory School, Loughborough	SM TW WA2
The Falcons School for Boys, London	RA/HEA

Farleigh Further Education College (Frome), Frome	WA3
Farleigh Further Education College Swindon, Swindon	W
Farringtons School, Chislehurst	RA SM WA3/EPI HEA HI VI
Felsted School, Felsted	AT CA IT RA SM TW WA2 WA3/EPI
Ferndale Preparatory School, Faringdon	RA WA3/EPI HEA HI VI
Finton House School, London	CA DS HL RA SM TW WA3/HEA HI VI
Fonthill Lodge, East Grinstead	CA RA SM TW W/HEA HI
The Froebelian School, Leeds	RA/HEA
Gatehouse School, London	TW
Gateway Christian School, Ilkeston	RA/HEA
Gems Bolitho School, Penzance	IT SM TW/HI
George Watson's College, Edinburgh	CA SM TW WA2/CP EPI HEA HI IM VI W
Glebe House School, Hunstanton	RA
Godstowe Preparatory School, High Wycombe	CA RA SM/CP EPI HEA HI
Gracefield Preparatory School, Fishponds	WA3
Great Houghton Preparatory School, Northampton	CA TW WA3/HEA VI
Green Hill School, Evesham	W/W
Greenbank Preparatory School, Cheadle	AT RA SM TW WA1 WA2/HEA
Greene's Tutorial College, Oxford	AT RA SM TW
Hampton School, Hampton	AT CA SM TW W WA2/EPI HEA HI VI
Handcross Park School, Haywards Heath	IT RA SM TW WA2/EPI HEA IM
Harenc School Trust, Sidcup	IT TW W WA2/HEA
Haresfoot Preparatory School, Berkhamsted	CA RA/HEA HI IM
Hazlegrove Preparatory School, Yeovil	SM TW/HEA HI
Heath House Preparatory School, London	W/W
Hethersett Old Hall School, Norwich	CA SM TW WA2/HEA IM
High Elms Manor School, Watford	AT CA TW WA1 WA2/HEA HI W
High March School, Beaconsfield	AT CA RA TW WA2/EPI HEA
High School of Dundee, Dundee	RA/HEA HI VI
Highclare School, Birmingham	AT CA RA SM/HEA HI
Hoe Bridge School, Woking	RA SM TW WA2 WA3/HEA
Holy Trinity School, Kidderminster	CA/EPI HEA HI IM
Hordle Walhampton School, Lymington	CA RA SM TW WA3/HEA HI
Horris Hill School, Newbury	SM/HI
Howell's School, Denbigh	SM WA3/EPI HEA
Howell's School, Llandaff GDST, Cardiff	RA WA3/HEA
Hurst Lodge School, Ascot	AT RA/EPI HEA HI IM VI
Hutchesons' Grammar School, Glasgow	SM TW W WA2/EPI HEA HI IM VI
Ilford Ursuline Preparatory School, Ilford	TW WA2
The John Lyon School, Harrow	SM/EPI VI
Kent College Infant & Junior School, Canterbury	TW WA3/HEA
Kent College Pembury, Tunbridge Wells	SM WA3/HEA
Kew Green Preparatory School, Richmond	CA IT TW
Kilgraston, Perth	SM WA2/EPI
King Edward VII and Queen Mary School, Lytham St Annes	SM WA2/HEA VI
King's College, Taunton	W

The Rowans School, London	RA/HEA
The Royal Hospital School, Ipswich	RA SM WA2/EPI HEA
The Royal School Dungannon, Dungannon	CA SL SM TW WA2/EPI HEA HI VI W
The Royal Wolverhampton Junior School, Wolverhampton	RA SM TW/HEA
Ruckleigh School, Solihull	RA/HEA
Russell House School, Sevenoaks	WA1
St Andrew's School, Eastbourne	RA SM/HEA HI IM
St Andrews School, East Runton	WA3
St Bees School, St Bees	RA SM/EPI HEA VI
St Bernard's Preparatory School, Slough	TW WA2/HEA
St Christopher School, Letchworth Garden City	RA/EPI
St Christopher's School, Hove	SM TW W WA2/HEA VI
St Christophers School, Totnes	CA IT TW W WA1/HEA HI
St Clare's School, Porthcawl	W
St Crispin's School, Leicester	AT CA IT RA SL SM TW WA3/HEA HI VI
St David's School, Purley	CA RA SM TW/HEA VI
St Dunstan's College, London	RA/HI
St Edmund's College and St Hugh's School, Ware	IT SM TW WA2/EPI HEA HI VI
St Faith's at Ash School, Canterbury	RA SM WA3/HEA HI
St Gabriel's, Berkshire	AT CA RA SM TW/HEA
St George's School for Girls, Edinburgh	AT BL CA HL IT SM TW WA2 WA3/EPI HEA HI IM VI
St Helen & St Katharine, Abingdon	RA SM TW/EPI HEA HI
St Helen's School, Northwood	AT CA SM TW/EPI HEA HI
St Hilary's School, Godalming	CA HL IT/HEA HI VI
St Hugh's School, Woodhall Spa	CA IT SM TW WA2/HEA HI IM VI
St Ia School, St Ives	RA/HEA
St John's School, Leatherhead	SM TW WA2 WA3/EPI HEA HI
St John's-on-the-Hill, Chepstow	RA SM/HEA
St Joseph's College, Ipswich	AT CA RA SL WA2/CP EPI HEA
St Joseph's In The Park, Hertford	CA/HEA HI
St Joseph's School, Launceston	RA/HEA
St Lawrence College, Ramsgate	RA SM/EPI HEA HI
St Lawrence College Junior School, Ramsgate	RA SM WA3/HEA HI
St Margaret's School, London	HL SM W WA3
St Margaret's School for Girls, Aberdeen	RA/EPI
St Martin's School, Northwood	RA TW WA3/HEA
St Mary's Preparatory School, Lincoln	AT IT RA SM TW/CP HEA HI IM VI
St Mary's School, Ascot, Ascot	RA SM WA2/EPI HEA HI W
St Michael's, Barnstaple	TW/HI VI
St Nicholas House Kindergarten & Prep School, North Walsham	W/W
St Nicholas' School, Fleet	RA/HEA
St Paul's Cathedral School, London	RA SM
St Piran's Preparatory School, Hayle	RA SM WA3/CP
St Teresa's Catholic Independent & Nursery School, Princes Risborough	CA TW WA2/HI
St. Hilda's School, Harpenden	W/HI

School	Provision
Steephill Independent School, Longfield	RA TW WA2
Saint Martin's School, Solihull	AT SL TW W WA2/W
Salterford House School, Nottingham	RA WA2/HEA
Sancton Wood School, Cambridge	AT HL RA/CP HEA HI VI
Sandroyd School, Salisbury	IT RA SM TW/HEA VI
Stonar School, Melksham	AT CA RA SM/EPI HEA VI
Stonyhurst College, Clitheroe	SM WA3/EPI HEA HI
Strathallan School, Perth	SM TW WA3/EPI HEA
Streatham & Clapham High School, London	AT CA HL IT SM TW WA2/EPI HEA HI IM VI W
Streatham House School, Liverpool	RA/HEA VI
The Stroud School, Romsey	RA
Seaton House School, Sutton	RA/HEA
Sedbergh Junior School, Sedbergh	CA TW/HEA IM
Sedbergh School, Sedbergh	RA SM/HEA HI VI
Sherborne School, Sherborne	IT/EPI HEA HI VI
Shiplake College, Henley-on-Thames	SM
Sibford School, Banbury	CA RA SM/CP HEA IM
Smallwood Manor Preparatory School, Uttoxeter	AT WA3/EPI HEA
South Hills School, Salisbury	RA
Summer Fields, Oxford	HL IT RA SM WA3/HEA HI
Sutton High School GDST, Sutton	AT SM TW WA3/HEA HI
Taunton Preparatory School, Taunton	SM WA2
Taverham Hall Preparatory School, Norwich	RA SM/EPI HEA
Teesside High School, Eaglescliffe	RA/CP EPI HEA HI VI
Terra Nova School, Holmes Chapel	RA SM W/HEA
Tettenhall College, Wolverhampton	RA SM/EPI HEA
Thorngrove School, Newbury	RA/CP HEA
Thorpe Hall School, Southend-on-Sea	CA HL SL SM TW WA2/EPI HEA
Trinity School, Croydon	SL SM WA1/HEA VI
Trinity School, Teignmouth	CA IT SM TW WA2/HEA
Twyford School, Winchester	RA SM/HEA
University College School, London	CA/VI
University College School Junior Branch, London	RA/HI VI
Walthamstow Hall, Sevenoaks	AT SL SM TW/HEA
Wellow House School, Newark	SM/EPI HEA
West Buckland Preparatory School, Barnstaple	CA SM TW W WA2/HEA VI
West Buckland School, Barnstaple	CA/EPI HEA HI VI
West House School, Birmingham	RA TW/HEA
Westminster Cathedral Choir School, London	RA
Westminster Tutors, London	AT RA/HEA
Wetherby Preparatory School, London	RA
Winterfold House, Kidderminster	RA WA3
Withington Girls' School, Manchester	SM TW/HEA HI
Wolverhampton Grammar School, Wolverhampton	TW WA2/IM
Woodcote House School, Windlesham	RA WA3
Woodhouse Grove School, Apperley Bridge	SM/CP EPI HEA HI

PART FIVE

Reference Section

Council for the Registration of Schools Teaching Dyslexic Pupils (CReSTeD)

Registered charity number 1052103

CReSTeD (The Council for the Registration of Schools Teaching Dyslexic Pupils) produces an annual register of schools that provide for children with specific learning difficulties (dyslexia). CReSTeD is still concerned mainly with dyslexia provision, but dyslexia rarely exists in isolation and so we now also include dyspraxia, dyscalculia, ADD and pragmatic and semantic language difficulties.

The aim is to help parents and those who advise them to choose a school that has been approved to published criteria. CReSTeD was established in 1989 and works alongside the British Dyslexia Association and Dyslexia Action. Schools wishing to be included in the Register are visited by a CReSTeD consultant, whose report is considered by the CReSTeD Council before registration can be finalized.

Consulting the Register should enable parents to decide which schools they wish to approach for further information. Students with SpLD have a variety of difficulties and so have a wide range of special needs. An equally wide range of teaching approaches is necessary. CReSTeD has therefore grouped schools together under six broad categories, which are designed to help parents match their child's needs to an appropriate philosophy and provision.

The six categories of schools are described below:

- *Dyslexia Specialist Provision (DSP) Schools.* The school is established primarily to teach pupils with dyslexia. The curriculum and timetable are designed to meet specific needs in a holistic, coordinated manner, with a significant number of teaching staff holding nationally recognized qualifications in teaching dyslexic pupils.
- *Specialist Provision Schools (SPS).* The school is established primarily to teach pupils with SpLD. The curriculum and timetable are designed to meet specific needs in a holistic, coordinated manner with a significant number of staff qualified in teaching dyslexic pupils.

- *Dyslexia Unit (DU).* The school has a designated unit or centre that provides specialist tuition on a small group or individual basis, according to need. The unit or centre is an adequately resourced teaching area under the management of a senior specialist teacher, who coordinates the work of other specialist teachers and ensures ongoing liaison with all mainstream teachers. This senior specialist teacher will probably have head of department status, and will certainly have significant input into the curriculum design and delivery.
- *Specialist Classes (SC).* Schools where SpLD pupils are taught in separate classes within the school for some lessons, most probably English and mathematics. These are taught by teachers with qualifications in teaching SpLD pupils. These teachers are deemed responsible for communicating with the pupils' other subject teachers.
- *Withdrawal System (WS).* Schools where SpLD pupils are withdrawn from appropriately selected lessons for specialist tuition from a teacher qualified in teaching SpLD pupils. There is ongoing communication between mainstream and specialist teachers.
- *Maintained Sector (MS).* Maintained schools where the school supports dyslexic pupils to access the curriculum, where there is a system of identifying dyslexic pupils, and where there is a withdrawal system for individualized literacy support. There is a positive ongoing communication between mainstream and SEN staff, and the Senior Management Team (SMT).

NB listings below contain details of DSP, DU, SC and WS schools only.

A school in one category may also offer the sort of care found in a different, less intensive category. For example, a Dyslexia Unit category school may offer a Withdrawal System. If a school seems appropriate in other ways, parents should check directly with the school.

CReSTeD examines the adequacy of the school's provision for SpLD pupils. The school is likely to have been inspected by Ofsted (or its equivalent) for both the education and boarding provision. Such reports, which may be obtainable from the school, deal with many statutory matters including Criminal Record Bureau checks. Information obtained from these statutory reports assist with the production of the CReSTeD consultant's report on a school.

Schools listed have chosen to be visited and registered. They are normally revisited at three-yearly intervals.

A copy of the Register, together with further information about CReSTeD, may be obtained by contacting CReSTeD on 01242 604852, by e-mail at admin@crested.org.uk, or by writing to The Administrator, Greygarth, Litttleworth, Winchcombe, Cheltenham GL54 5BT. Alternatively, visit the website at www.crested.org.uk.

Dyslexia Specialist Provision Schools – DSP

Abingdon House School
4–6 Abingdon Road, London W8 6AF
Tel: (0845) 230 0426
Fax: (0845) 230 0426

E-mail: ahs@abingdonhouseschool.co.uk
Independent; city; day
50 boys and girls 4–11

Appleford School
Shrewton, Salisbury, Wiltshire SP3 4HL
Tel: (01980) 621020
Fax: (01980) 621366
E-mail: secretary@appleford.wilts.sch.uk
Independent; rural; boarding, weekly
boarding and day
90 boys and girls 7–13

Brown's School
Cannock House, Hawstead Lane, Chelsfield,
Orpington, Kent BR6 7PH
Tel: (01689) 876816
Fax: (01689) 827118
E-mail: info@brownsschool.co.uk
Independent; rural; day
40 boys and girls 7–12

Calder House School
Colerne, Bath, Wiltshire SN14 8BN
Tel: (01225) 742329
Fax: (01225) 742329
E-mail: head@calderhouseschool.co.uk
Independent; village; day
50 boys and girls 5–13

The Dominie
55 Warriner Gardens, London SW11 2DX
Tel: (020) 7720 8783
E-mail: lrdominie@aol.com
Independent; city; day
32 boys and girls 6–13

Edington and Shapwick School
Shapwick Manor, Shapwick, Bridgwater,
Somerset TA7 9JN
Tel: (01458) 210384
Fax: (01458) 210384
E-mail: shapwick@edingtonshapwick.co.uk
Independent; rural; boarding, weekly
boarding and day
170 boys and girls 8–18

Fairley House School
30 Causton Street, London SW1P 4AU
Tel: (020) 7976 5456
Fax: (020) 7976 5905
E-mail: office@fairleyhouse.org.uk
Independent; city; day
159 boys and girls 5–14

Frewen College
Brickwall, Northiam, Rye, East Sussex
TN31 6NL
Tel: (01797) 252494
Fax: (01797) 252567
E-mail: office@frewencollege.org
Independent; village; boarding; day
95 boys 5–16

Knowl Hill School
School Lane, Pirbright, Surrey GU24 0JN
Tel: (01483) 797032
Fax: (01483) 797641
E-mail: info@knowlhill.org.uk
Independent; village; day
45 boys and girls 7–16

Mark College
Mark, Highbridge, Somerset TA9 4NP
Tel: (01278) 641632
Fax: (01278) 641426
E-mail: markcollege@priorygroup.com
Independent; rural; boarding, weekly
boarding and day
90 boys 10–19

The Moat School
Bishop's Avenue, London SW6 6EG
Tel: (020) 7610 9018
Fax: (020) 7610 9098
E-mail: office@moatschool.org.uk
Independent; city; day
90 boys and girls 11–16

Moon Hall College and Burys Court
Flanchford Road, Leigh, Reigate
Surrey RH2 8RE
Tel: (01306) 611372
Fax: (01306) 611037
E-mail: enquiries@buryscourtschool.co.uk
Independent; rural; day
85 boys and girls 7–16

Moon Hall School
Pasturewood Road, Holmbury St Mary
Dorking, Surrey RH5 6LQ
Tel: (01306) 731464
E-mail: enquiries@moonhallschool.co.uk
Independent; rural; weekly boarding and day
100 boys and girls 7–13

More House School
Moons Hill, Frensham, Farnham, Surrey
GU10 3AP
Tel: (01252) 792303
Fax: (01252) 797601
E-mail: schooloffice@
   morehouseschool.co.uk
Independent; rural; boarding, weekly
boarding and day
275 boys 9–18

Northease Manor School
Rodmell, Lewes, East Sussex BN7 3EY
Tel: (01273) 472915
Fax: (01273) 472202
E-mail: office@northease.co.uk
Independent; rural; weekly boarding and day
85 boys and girls 10–17

Nunnykirk Centre for Dyslexia
Netherwitton, Morpeth, Northumberland
NE61 4PB
Tel: (01670) 772685
Fax: (01670) 772434
E-mail: secretary@nunnykirk.co.uk
Non-maintained special school; rural; weekly
boarding and day
45 boys and girls 9–18

St David's College
Llandudno
Conwy LL30 1RD
Tel: (01492) 875974
Fax: (01492) 870383
E-mail: headmaster@
   stdavidscollege.co.uk
Independent; rural; boarding; weekly
boarding and day
250 boys and girls 11–18

Stanbridge Earls School
Stanbridge Lane, Romsey, Hampshire
SO51 0ZS
Tel: (01794) 529400
Fax: (01794) 511201
E-mail: admin@stanbridgeearls.co.uk
Independent; rural; boarding and day
170 boys and girls 10–19

Sunnydown School
Portley House, 152 Whyteleafe Road,
Caterham, Surrey CR3 5ED
Tel: (01883) 342281
Fax: (01883) 341342
E-mail: head@sunnydown.surrey.sch.uk
Local authority; edge of town; weekly
boarding and day
70 boys 11–16

Trinity School
13 New Road, Rochester, Kent ME1 1BG
Tel: (01634) 812233
Fax: (01634) 812233
E-mail: admin@trinityschoolrochester.co.uk
Independent; town; day
50 boys and girls 6–16

The Unicorn School
20 Marcham Road
Abingdon, Oxfordshire OX14 1AA
Tel: (01235) 530222
Fax: (01235) 530222
E-mail: info@unicorndyslexia.co.uk
Independent; town; day
67 boys and girls 6–13

Dyslexia Unit – DU

Avon House School
490 High Road, Woodford Green, Essex
IG8 0PN
Tel: (020) 8504 1749
Fax: (020) 8505 5337
E-mail: avonhousedyslexiacentre@msn.com
Independent; edge of town; day
210 boys and girls 2–11

Barnardiston Hall Preparatory School
Hall Road, Barnardiston, Haverhill, Suffolk
CB9 7TG
Tel: (01440) 786316
Fax: (01440) 786355
E-mail: lesley@barnardiston-hall.co.uk
Independent; rural; boarding, weekly
boarding and day
225 boys and girls 2–13

Bethany School
Curtisden Green, Goudhurst, Cranbrook,
Kent TN17 1LB
Tel: (01580) 211273
Fax: (01580) 211151
E-mail: admin@bethanyschool.org.uk
Independent; rural; weekly boarding and day
420 boys and girls 11–19

Bloxham School
Bloxham, near Banbury, Oxfordshire
OX15 4PE
Tel: (01295) 720222
Fax: (01295) 721897
E-mail: registrar@bloxhamschool.com
Independent; rural; boarding, weekly
boarding and day
410 boys and girls 11–18

Bredon School
Pull Court, Bushley, Tewkesbury,
Gloucestershire GL20 6AH
Tel: (01684) 293156
Fax: (01684) 298008
E-mail: enquiries@bredonschool.co.uk
Independent; rural; boarding, weekly
boarding and day
245 boys and girls 7–18

Centre Academy
92 St John's Hill, Battersea, London
SW11 1SH
Tel: (020) 7738 2344
Fax: (020) 7738 9862
E-mail: admin@centreacademylondon.eu
    or info@centreacademy.net
Independent; city; day
70 boys and girls 7–19

Clayesmore Preparatory School
Iwerne Minster, Blandford Forum, Dorset
DT11 8PH
Tel: (01747) 811707
Fax: (01747) 811692
E-mail: admissions@clayesmore.com
Independent; village; boarding and day
260 boys and girls 2½–13

Clayesmore School
Iwerne Minster, Blandford Forum, Dorset
DT11 8LL
Tel: (01747) 812122
Fax: (01747) 813187
E-mail: hmsec@clayesmore.com
Independent; rural; boarding and day
375 boys and girls 13–18

Clifton College Preparatory School

The Avenue, Clifton, Bristol BS8 3HE
Tel: (0117) 315 7502
Fax: (0117) 315 7504
E-mail: admissions@
  clifton-college.avon.sch.uk
Independent; edge of town; boarding,
weekly boarding and day
400 boys and girls 8–13

Cobham Hall

Cobham, Gravesend, Kent DA12 3BL
Tel: (01474) 823371
Fax: (01474) 825902
E-mail: enquiries@cobhamhall.com
Independent; rural; boarding and day
180 girls 11–18

Danes Hill School

Leatherhead Road, Oxshott, Surrey
KT22 0JG
Tel: (01372) 842509
Fax: (01372) 844452
E-mail: lel@daneshill.surrey.sch.uk
Independent; rural; day
880 boys and girls 3–13

Ellesmere College

Ellesmere, Shropshire SY12 9AB
Tel: (01691) 622321
Fax: (01691) 623286
E-mail: hmsecretary@ellesmere.com
Independent; rural; boarding and day
550 boys and girls 8–18

Ercall Wood Technology College

Golf Links Lane, Wellington, Telford,
Shropshire TF1 2DU
Tel: (01952) 387300
E-mail: admin@admin.ercall-online.org.uk
Local authority; town; day
850 boys and girls 11–16

Finborough School

The Hall, Great Finborough, Stowmarket,
Suffolk IP14 3EF
Tel: (01449) 773600
Fax: (01449) 773601
E-mail: admin@finborough.suffolk.sch.uk
Independent; village; boarding, weekly
boarding and day
225 boys and girls 2½–18

Fulneck School

Fulneck, Pudsey, Leeds, West Yorkshire
LS28 8DS
Tel: (0113) 257 0235
Fax: (0113) 255 7316
E-mail: general@fulneckschool.co.uk
Independent; semi-rural; boarding, weekly
boarding and day
390 boys and girls 3–18

Hazlegrove School, King's Bruton Preparatory School

Sparkford, Yeovil, Somerset BA22 7JH
Tel: (01963) 440314
Fax: (01963) 440569
E-mail: office@hazlegrove.co.uk
Independent; rural; boarding and day
370 boys and girls 2–13

Holmwood House School

Lexden, Colchester, Essex CO3 9ST
Tel: (01206) 574305
Fax: (01206) 768269
E-mail: hst@holmwood.essex.sch.uk
Independent; edge of town; weekly boarding
and day
420 boys and girls 4–13

Hordle Walhampton School

Lymington, Hampshire SO41 5ZG
Tel: (01590) 672013
Fax: (01590) 678498
E-mail: office@hordlewalhampton.co.uk
Independent; rural; boarding, weekly
boarding and day
210 boys and girls 7–13

Kingham Hill School
Kingham, Chipping Norton, Oxfordshire
OX7 6TH
Tel: (01608) 658999
Fax: (01608) 658658
E-mail: admissions@
kingham-hill.oxon.sch.uk
Independent; rural; boarding, weekly
boarding and day
260 boys and girls 11–18

King's School
Bruton, Somerset BA10 0ED
Tel: (01749) 814200
Fax: (01749) 813426
E-mail: office@kingsbruton.com
Independent; rural; boarding and day
340 boys and girls 13–18

Kingsley School Bideford
(previously Grenville College)
Northdown Road, Bideford
Devon EX39 3LY
Tel: (01237) 426200
E-mail: admissions@
kingsleyschoolbideford.co.uk
Independent; rural town; boarding and day
300 boys and girls 11–18

Kingswood College Trust
Scarisbrick Hall, Southport Road, Ormskirk,
Lancashire L40 9RQ
Tel: (01704) 880200
Fax: (01704) 880032
E-mail: admin@kingswoodcollege.co.uk
Independent; rural; day
180 boys and girls 2½–19

Kingswood House School
56 West Hill, Epsom, Surrey KT19 8LG
Tel: (01372) 723590
Fax: (01372) 749081
E-mail: office@kingswoodhouse.org
Independent; urban; day
200 boys 3–13, girls 3–7

Lime House School
Holm Hill, Dalston, Carlisle, Cumbria CA5
7BX
Tel: (01228) 710225
Fax: (01228) 710508
E-mail: lhsoffice@aol.com
Independent; rural; boarding and day
230 boys and girls 4–18

Malvern St James
15 Avenue Road, Malvern, Worcestershire
WR14 3BA
Tel: (01684) 892288
Fax: (01684) 566204
E-mail: admin@malvernstjames.co.uk
Independent; semi-rural; boarding, weekly
boarding and day
380 girls 7–18

Mayville High School
35 St Simon's Road, Southsea, Hampshire
PO5 2PE
Tel: (02392) 734847
Fax: (02392) 293649
E-mail: mayvillehighschool@talk21.com
Independent; city; day
470 boys and girls 1–16

Merton House School
Abbot's Park, Chester CH1 4BD
Tel: (01244) 377165
Fax: (01244) 374569
E-mail: secretary@
mertonhousechester.co.uk
Independent; city; day
100 boys and girls 2½–11

Monkton Combe School
Monkton Combe, Bath BA22 7HG
Tel: (01225) 721102
Fax: (01225) 721181
E-mail: principal@monkton.org.uk
Independent; village; boarding and day
345 boys and girls 11–18

Mostyn House School
Parkgate, South Wirral, Cheshire CH64 6SG
Tel: (0151) 336 1010
Fax: (0151) 353 1040
E-mail: enquiries@mostynhouse.co.uk
Independent; semi-rural; day
230 boys and girls 4–18

Moyles Court School
Moyles Court, Ringwood, Hampshire
BH24 3NR
Tel: (01425) 472856
Fax: (01425) 474715
E-mail: info@moylescourt.co.uk
Independent; rural; boarding and day
180 boys and girls 4–16

Newlands School
Eastbourne Road, Seaford, Sussex
BN25 4NP
Tel: (01323) 892334/490000
Fax: (01323) 898420
E-mail: enquiries@newlands-school.com
Independent; edge of town; boarding and
day
280 boys and girls 2½–18

Ramillies Hall School
Ramillies Avenue, Cheadle Hulme, Cheshire
SK8 7AJ
Tel: (0161) 485 3804
Fax: (0161) 486 6021
E-mail: study@ramillieshall.co.uk
Independent; edge of town; boarding,
weekly boarding and day
100 boys and girls 4–16

Riddlesworth Hall Preparatory School
Diss, Norfolk IP22 2TA
Tel: (01953) 681246
Fax: (01953) 688124
E-mail: rhps@riddlesworthhall.com
Independent; rural; boarding, weekly
boarding and day
80 boys and girls 7–13

St Bees School
St Bees, Cumbria CA27 0DS
Tel: (01946) 828000
Fax: (01946) 823657
E-mail: mailbox@st-bees-school.co.uk
Independent; village; boarding, weekly
boarding and day
300 boys and girls 11–18

Sibford School
Sibford Ferris, Banbury, Oxfordshire
OX15 5QL
Tel: (01295) 781200
Fax: (01295) 781204
E-mail: admissions@sibfordschool.co.uk
Independent; rural; boarding, weekly
boarding and day
395 boys and girls 5–18

Sidcot School
Winscombe, North Somerset BS25 1PD
Tel: (01934) 843102
Fax: (01934) 844181
E-mail: info@sidcot.org.uk
Independent; rural; boarding and day
520 boys and girls 3–18

Slindon College
Slindon House, Arundel, West Sussex
BN18 0RH
Tel: (01243) 814320
Fax: (01243) 814702
E-mail: registrar@slindoncollege.co.uk
Independent; village; boarding, weekly
boarding and day
110 boys 9–16

Tettenhall College
Wood Road, Tettenhall, Wolverhampton,
West Midlands WV6 8QX
Tel: (01902) 751119
Fax: (01902) 741940
E-mail: head@tettcoll.co.uk
Independent; urban; boarding, weekly
boarding and day
495 boys and girls 2–18

Wycliffe College
Bath Road, Stonehouse, Gloucestershire
GL10 2JQ
Tel: (01453) 822432
Fax: (01453) 827634
E-mail: senior@wycliffe.co.uk
Independent; rural; boarding and day
415 boys and girls 13–18

Wycliffe Preparatory School
Ryeford Hall, Stonehouse, Gloucestershire
GL10 2LD
Tel: (01453) 820470
Fax: (01453) 825604
E-mail: prep@wycliffe.co.uk
Independent; rural; boarding and day
330 boys and girls 2½–13

Specialist Classes – SC

Bruern Abbey School
Chesterton House, Chesterton, Oxfordshire
OX26 1UY
Tel: (01869) 242448
Fax: (01869) 243949
E-mail: secretary@bruernabbey.org
Independent; rural; weekly boarding and day
55 boys 8–13

Mount Carmel Preparatory School
1 Aughton Park Drive, Aughton
Ormskirk, Lancashire L39 5BU
Tel: (01695) 473254
E-mail: head@mountcarmel.me.uk
Independent; town; day
65 boys and girls 4–11

St Crispin's School
6 St Mary's Road, Leicester LE2 1XA
Tel: (0116) 270 7648
Fax: (0116) 270 9647
E-mail: enquiries@stcrispins.co.uk
Independent; city; day
130 boys and girls 3–16

Withdrawal System – WS

Dowdales School
Nelson Street, Dalton in Furness, Cumbria
LA15 8AH
Tel: (01229) 897911
Fax: (01229) 897913
E-mail: office@dowdales.cumbria.sch.uk
Local authority; rural; day
1,100 boys and girls 11–16

Kilgraston School
Bridge of Earn, Perthshire PH2 9BQ
Tel: (01738) 812257
Fax: (01738) 813410
E-mail: headoffice@kilgraston.com
Independent; rural; weekly boarding and day
255 pupils, girls 5–18, boys 5–13

King's School Rochester
Satis House, Boley Hill,
Rochester, Kent ME1 1TE
Tel: (01634) 888555
Fax: (01634) 888505
E-mail: walker@
    kings-school-rochester.co.uk
Independent; city; boarding, weekly
boarding and day
550 boys and girls 8–18

Milton Abbey School
Blandford Forum, Dorset DT11 0BZ
Tel: (01258) 880484
Fax: (01258) 881910
E-mail: info@miltonabbey.co.uk
Independent; rural; boarding and day
215 boys 13–18, girls 16–18

North London International School
Friern Barnet Road
London N11 3DR
Tel: (020) 8920 0600
Fax: (020) 8368 3220
E-mail: admissions@nlis.org
Independent; city; day
380 boys and girls 2–18

Our Lady's Convent School
Burton Street, Loughborough,
Leicestershire LE11 2DT
Tel: (01509) 263901
E-mail: office@olcs.leics.sch.uk
Independent; edge of town; boarding and
day
200 boys and girls 7–13

Prior Park Preparatory School
Calcutt Street, Cricklade, Wiltshire SN6 6BB
Tel: (01793) 750275
Fax: (01793) 750910
E-mail: officepriorparkprep@
    priorpark.co.uk
Independent; edge of town; boarding,
weekly boarding and day
200 boys and girls 7–13

Putney Park School
11 Woodborough Road, Putney, London
SW15 6PY
Tel: (020) 8788 8316
Fax: (020) 8780 2376
E-mail: office@putneypark.london.sch.uk
Independent; city; day
260 boys and girls (girls 4–16 boys 4–8)

Thames Christian College
Wye Street, Battersea, London SW11 2HB
Tel: (020) 7228 3933
Fax: (020) 7924 1112
E-mail: info@
    thameschristiancollege.org.uk
Independent; city; day
100 boys and girls 11–16

Ysgol Aberconwy
Morfa Drive, Conwy, LL32 8ED
Tel: (01492) 593243
Fax: (01492) 592537
E-mail: bettym@aberconwy.conwy.sch.uk
Local authority; coastal town; day
1,155 boys and girls 11–18

Ysgol Rhydygors
Llanstephan Road, Johnstown, Carmarthen
SA31 3NQ
Tel: (01267) 231171
Fax: (01267) 220336
E-mail: head.rhydygors@ysgolccc.org.uk
Local authority Special School; semi-rural;
weekly boarding
45 boys and girls 7–16

Useful Addresses and Associations

Action for Blind People
14–16 Verney Road
London SE16 3DZ
Tel: (020) 7635 4800
Freephone Helpline: (0800) 915 4666
Fax: (020) 7635 4900

Action for Blind People provides free and confidential support for blind and partially sighted people in all aspects of their lives. One call to Action ensures that visually impaired people receive help with anything from finding a job, applying for benefit, housing issues, aids and adaptations, holiday breaks or information on local services. We also offer advice to people who have a visually impaired friend or family member. Whatever the need, Action can help.

Action for Sick Children
32b Buxton Road
High Lane
Stockport SK6 8BH
Helpline: (0800) 074 4519
Website: www.actionforsickchildren.org
Contact: Pamela Barnes, Chairman

Offers support and advice for the parents of sick children. Aims to join parents and professionals in promoting high-quality health care for children in hospital and at home.

Services include: publications, research and a branch network which offers advice and support.

ADDISS
PO Box 340
Edgware
Middlesex HA8 9HL
Tel: (020) 8952 2800
Fax: (020) 8952 2909
E-mail: info@addiss.co.uk

The National Attention Deficit Disorder Information and Support Service provides people-friendly information and resources to anyone who needs assistance – parents, sufferers, teachers or health professionals.

Advice Service Capability Scotland (ASCS)
11 Ellersly Road
Edinburgh EH12 6HY
Tel: (0131) 313 5510
Textphone: (0131) 346 2529
Fax: (0131) 346 1681
E-mail: ascs@capability-scotland.org.uk
Website: www.capability-scotland.org.uk

Capability Scotland will be a major ally in supporting disabled people to achieve full equality and to have choice and control of their lives by 2020. Capability Scotland provides flexible services to children, young people and adults with a range of disabilities and their families and carers. These include community living, day and residential services, employment services, respite/short breaks, education and learning, family support and activities, and disability equality training. ASCS (Advice Service Capability Scotland) is a national disability advice and information service. ASCS has a small lending library, which can be used by anyone living in Scotland.

Advisory Centre for Education (ACE) Ltd
1C Aberdeen Studios
22 Highbury Grove
London N5 2DQ
Exclusion Advice: (0808) 800 0327 Mon–Fri 10 am–5 pm
General Advice: (0808) 800 5793 Mon–Fri 10 am–5 pm
Exclusive Info Line: (020) 7704 9822 (24hr)
E-mail: enquiries@ace-ed.org.uk
Website: www.ace-ed.org.uk

The Advisory Centre for Education is an independent national education advice centre that offers free and confidential telephone advice to parents every weekday from 10 am to 5 pm on the above numbers. ACE helps explain the state school system, formal procedures, and aspects of education law, particularly in the areas of admission and exclusion appeals, and special educational needs issues. ACE has a full range of publications described in a free publication leaflet and offers training to parents' groups, governors, LEA officers and teachers. Contact the business line 020 8354 8318 for these services, e-mail ACE at enquiries@ace-ed.org.uk or write to ACE at the above address. Information on all these issues is also available on the ACE website www.ace-ed.org.uk, which is currently being updated.

Afasic
Olive House, 1st Floor
20 Bowling Green Lane
London EC1R 0BD

Admin: (020) 7490 9410
Helpline: (0845) 355 5577/
(020) 7490 9420
E-mail: info@afasic.org.uk
Website: www.afasic.org.uk

Afasic represents children and young adults with speech, language and communication difficulties and supports and provides information to parents/carers and professionals.

Association of Educational Psychologists

26 The Avenue
Durham DH1 4ED
Tel: (0191) 384 9512
Fax: (0191) 386 5287
E-mail: aep@aep.org.uk
Website: www.aep.org.uk
Secretary: Charles Ward

The AEP is the independently certificated trade union and professional association for educational psychologists. It represents the professional and employment interests of 93% of qualified educational psychologists working in the United Kingdom, most of whom work for local government. It is the only professional association or trade union in the UK organized exclusively by and for educational psychologists. The AEP is unequivocally the voice of the educational psychology profession and has just over 3,000 members.

Association of National Specialist Colleges (NATSPEC)

39 Sanders Road
Quorn
Loughborough
Leicestershire LE12 8JN
Tel/Fax: (01509) 554357
E-mail: kevin.obrien43@ntlworld.com
Website: www.natspec.org.uk
Chief Executive: Kevin O'Brien

NATSPEC member colleges seek to offer the widest choice of innovative, high-quality, cost-effective and appropriate further education and training, in residential or day settings, for young people and adults with learning difficulties and/or disabilities.

Association for Spina Bifida and Hydrocephalus (ASBAH)

ASBAH House
42 Park Road
Peterborough PE1 2UQ
Helpline: (0845) 450 7755
Fax: (01733) 555985
E-mail: helpline@asbah.org
Website: www.asbah.org
Executive Director: Ms Jackie Bland, MA

ASBAH provides information, advice and support for people with spina bifida and/or hydrocephalus, and their families, carers and professionals.

Autism Independent UK

(formerly The Society for the Autistically Handicapped – SFTAH)
199–203 Blandford Avenue
Kettering
Northants NN16 9AT
Tel: (01536) 523274
Fax: (01536) 523274
E-mail: autism@autismuk.com
Website: www.autismuk.com

Training, housing, information, free membership via the website.

Beat: beating eating disorders

Wensum House
103 Prince of Wales Road
Norwich
Norfolk NR1 1DW
Admin: (0300) 123 3355
Helpline: (0845) 634 1414
Mon–Fri 10.30 am–8.30 pm, Sat 1–4.30 pm
Youth Helpline: (0845) 634 7650
Mon–Fri 4–8.30 pm, Sat 1–4.30 pm
(18 years and under)

Fax: (01603) 664915
E-mail: info@b-eat.co.uk
Website: www.b-eat.co.uk

Beat is the leading UK-wide charity providing information, help and support for people affected by eating disorders – anorexia, bulimia nervosa and binge eating disorder. Details of local contacts are freely available to the caller ringing our helpline. Beat services and support include:

● Helplines: national telephone, e-mail and text helplines.
● Self Help: UK-wide network of groups run by volunteers.
● Information: a website at www.b-eat.co.uk, leaflets and literature for individuals and organizations, details and contacts for treatment services in the UK.
● Training: courses and conferences for health, education and social care staff.
● Media: information and resources for journalists and broadcasters.

● Research: support for academic and clinical studies, and research trials.

Beat's vision is that Eating Disorders will be beaten.

The Bobath Centre for Children with Cerebral Palsy
(Registered Charity No 229663)
250 East End Road
London N2 8AU
Tel: (020) 8444 3355
Fax: (020) 8444 3399

The Bobath treatment concept was developed by Dr and Mrs Bobath in the 1940s and is a holistic interdisciplinary approach involving occupational physio- and speech and language therapists. Treatment is provided on an individual basis (outpatient only), and therapists teach parents and carers how to continue therapy at home/or in school. A letter of referral is required from the child's consultant paediatrician or general

practitioner giving full medical history and birth details. Letters should be addressed to the Appointments and Funding Manager. On the basis of this information an application for funding may be made to the NHS. When the Centre has been notified in writing that its fees will be met, a consultation or course of treatment will be offered. If you would like further information, this may be obtained from the Appointments and Funding Manager. The Centre organizes postgraduate training courses in the Bobath treatment approach for physio-, occupational and speech and language therapists who are working with children who have cerebral palsy.

Details may be obtained from the Training Co-ordinator.

Further information is available on the website (www.bobath.org.uk).

BREAK Charity

(Registered Charity No 286650)
Davison House
1 Montague Road
Sheringham
Norfolk NR26 8WN
Tel: (01263) 822161
Fax: (01263) 822181
E-mail: office@break-charity.org
Website: www.break-charity.org
Contact: Guest Bookings Administrator

BREAK provides fully supported holidays, short breaks and respite care for children and adults with learning disabilities and other special needs, including those with high level needs and challenging behaviours, on the north Norfolk coast.

Full 24-hour care and a varied holiday programme, including outings, are provided. Special dietary requirements can be met. The Centre is fully accessible with numerous aids and adaptations, heated indoor swimming pool and adapted bus with wheelchair lift. BREAK also has two fully accessible wheelchair-friendly chalets for families with special needs, providing a low-cost self-catering holiday in the West Country. Please contact us to find out more.

Breakthrough Deaf/Hearing Integration

Alangale House
The Close
West Hill Campus
Bristol Road
Birmingham B29 6LN
Tel: (0121) 472 6447
Fax: (0121) 471 4368

British Association of Teachers of the Deaf (BATOD)

Tel: (0845) 643 5181
E-mail: secretary@batod.org.uk
Website: www.batod.org.uk
Secretary: Mr Paul Simpson

The British Association of Teachers of the Deaf (BATOD) is the only Association representing the interests of Teachers of the Deaf in the UK. BATOD promotes excellence in the education of all deaf children, young people and adults and safeguards the interests of Teachers of the Deaf. Nationally, conferences are organized to develop the professional expertise of Association members and to promote issues connected with the education of deaf children. There are seven Regions, which organize workshops and activities locally. Courses and conferences are open to non-members. Associate membership is open to those who are not qualified Teachers of the Deaf.

British Deaf Association

10th Floor
Coventry Point
Market Way
Coventry CV1 1EA
Tel (voice): (02476) 550 936
Textphone: (02476) 550 393
Videophone: 841 297 143
Fax: (02476) 221 541

E-mail: helpline@bda.org.uk
Website: www.bda.org.uk

British Dyslexia Association
Unit 8, Bracknell Beeches
Old Bracknell Lane
Bracknell RG12 7BW
Tel: (0845) 251 9003
Helpline: (0845) 251 9002
Fax: (0845) 251 9005
E-mail: admin@bdadyslexia.org.uk
Helpline e-mail: helpline@
    bdadyslexia.org.uk
Website: www.bdadyslexia.org.uk
Helpline/Information Service 10 am–12.45 pm
& 2 pm–4.45 pm weekdays

bibic
Knowle Hall
Bridgwater
Somerset TA7 8PJ
Tel: (01278) 684060
E-mail: info@bibic.org.uk
Website: www.bibic.org.uk
Director of Family Services: Vivienne
Streeter

bibic exists to maximize the potential of
children with learning difficulties affecting
their sensory communication, social, motor
and learning abilities.
Working with parents and carers, bibic has a
valuable support system that offers time to
talk, expert advice and practical help.
Individual programmes are produced to
improve the quality of life for the whole family
unit. Therapists teach the child's parents or
carers how to help their child's development
with carefully tailored holistic programmes
and a comprehensive nutrition programme.
Progress is carefully monitored and
programmes are adjusted as and when
necessary.

British Institute of Learning Disabilities (BILD)
Campion House
Green Street
Kidderminster
Worcestershire DY10 1JL
Tel: (01562) 723010
Fax: (01562) 723029
E-mail: enquiries@bild.org.uk
Website: www.bild.org.uk

BILD works towards improving the
quality of life of people with learning
disabilities.

The British Kidney Patient Association (BKPA)
3 The Windmills, St Mary's Close
Turk Street, Alton GU34 1EF
Tel: (01420) 541424
Fax: (01420) 89438
E-mail: info@britishkidney-pa.co.uk
Website: www.britishkidney-pa.co.uk
Contact: Ms Rosemary Macri

The BKPA was founded in 1975 by Elizabeth
Ward, whose son was diagnosed with kidney
failure at the age of 13 years. At that time there
was no national association concerned with
the plight of Britain's kidney patients. Now
kidney patients can turn to the BKPA for
support, advice and, perhaps more
importantly, financial help and a much
needed break with their families.
The work of the BKPA falls roughly into two
halves engendered by two quite separate
needs: on the one hand the material and
physical needs of the patients and their
relatives, and on the other the necessity to
lobby for more and improved facilities and
increased governmental funding, so that all
parents may benefit from improvements in
technology and pharmaceutical
achievements.

British Psychological Society
48 Princess Road East
Leicester LE1 7DR
Tel: (0116) 254 9568

The British Psychological Society is the
professional body incorporated by Royal

Charter to maintain standards for the profession of psychology in the United Kingdom. The *Directory of Chartered Psychologists*, published by the Society, contains the names and addresses of Chartered Educational Psychologists who can provide services for parents and children with Special Educational Needs.

British Retinitis Pigmentosa Society
PO Box 350
Buckingham
Buckinghamshire MK18 1GZ
Tel: (01280) 821334
Helpline: (0845) 123 2354
Fax: (01280) 815900
E-mail: info@brps.org.uk
Website: www.brps.org.uk

The British Stammering Association
15 Old Ford Road
London E2 9PJ
Tel: (020) 8983 1003 (3 lines)
Helpline: (0845) 603 2001
Fax: (020) 8983 3591
E-mail: ch@stammering.org
Website: www.stammering.org
Schools' Liaison Officer Tel/Fax:
(01606) 77374 (Visits and training arranged without charge)

The BSA is the largest charity in Europe helping children who stammer. It provides free information for parents, teenagers and teachers, and a helpline is available to discuss specific problems. It also offers a mail-order service on specialist publications and a video pack for teachers.
Training courses for teachers are held across the country, giving advice on how to help and support pupils who stammer. The BSA has produced three CDs to support pupils who stammer in school. Details of its services can be found on its website at www.stammering.org.

Brittle Bone Society
Great Paterson House
30 Guthrie Street
Dundee DD1 5BS
Tel: (01382) 204446
Helpline: (0800) 0282459
Fax: (01382) 206771
E-mail: bbs@brittlebone.org
Website: www.brittlebone.org

The Society provides advice, encouragement and practical help for anyone affected by Osteogenesis Imperfecta (brittle bones).

Centre for Studies on Inclusive Education (CSIE)
New Redland Building
Coldharbour Lane
Frenchay
Bristol BS16 1QU
Tel: (0117) 328 4007
Fax: (0117) 328 4005
Website: www.csie.org.uk

An independent education centre supporting inclusion and challenging exclusion.
Publishes the *Index for Inclusion*, which helps schools break down barriers to learning and participation for all pupils.
Advice and publications for parents wishing their children with special needs to be included in mainstream schools.

Cerebra – For Brain Injured Children and Young People
Lyric Building
King Street
Carmarthen SA31 1BD
Tel: (0800) 323 1159
Helpline: (0800) 328 1159
Fax: (01267) 244213
E-mail: info@cerebra.org.uk
Website: www.cerebra.org.uk

Our Parent Support team provides free information, contact services and legal advice. Cerebra also funds research into causes, prevention, evidence-based treatments and therapies. A grant scheme provides respite holidays, equipment and necessities not available elsewhere. The postal lending library stocks books, sensory toys, CD ROMS and videos. A bulletin is published quarterly.

The Child Psychotherapy Trust
Star House
104–108 Grafton Road
London NW5 4BD
Tel: (020) 7284 1355
Fax: (020) 7284 2755
E-mail: info@psychotherapy.org.uk
Website:
www.childpsychotherapytrust.org.uk

Launched in 1987, the Child Psychotherapy Trust is a national charity dedicated to increasing the number of child psychotherapists available throughout the UK to treat emotionally damaged children, adolescents and their families. It is convinced of the benefits of treating emotional difficulties early, before they become entrenched.
The Trust publishes a range of material including a series of *Understanding Childhood* leaflets, written by child psychotherapists, for parents, carers and people working with children and families, which aim to promote understanding of children's emotional health, development and behaviour. It also publishes a newsletter available for £10 per year. The Trust supports and manages various outreach projects, but does not itself offer psychotherapy or referral services.

Children's Legal Centre
University of Essex
Wivenhoe Park
Colchester
Essex CO4 3SQ
Tel: (01206) 877910 General Enquiries
Fax: (01206) 877963
E-mail: clc@essex.ac.uk
Website: www.childrenslegalcentre.com

The Children's Legal Centre is a unique, independent national charity concerned with law and policy affecting children and young people. It opened in 1981 as the major UK project for the International Year of the Child and is staffed by lawyers and professionals with expertise in child law.
For general information regarding legislation affecting children, young people and their families, please look up our website or ring the Child Law Advice Line Freephone (0808) 802 0008 between 9.00 am and 5.00 pm.
The Centre's Education Law and Advocacy Unit holds a national education law contract to provide free legal advice and assistance from the Community Legal Service Direct. Opening hours: Monday–Friday, 9.30 am– 5 pm. We can provide advice on all aspects of education law, including: exclusions; special educational needs; admissions to school; school transport; bullying; home education; education negligence; human rights claims; Secretary of State complaints; Local Government Ombudsman complaints; and judicial reviews.
Education Law Advice Line: 0845 345 4345.
The Children's Legal Centre produces a number of user-friendly legal guides and a monthly journal called *childRIGHT*. For more information, contact our publications office on 01206 877920.

CLAPA (Cleft Lip and Palate Association)
1st Floor, Green Man Tower
332b Goswell Road
London EC1V 7LQ
Tel: (020) 7833 4883
Fax: (020) 7833 5999
E-mail: info@clapa.com
Website: www.clapa.com
Chief Executive: Gareth Davies

CLAPA was set up in 1979 as a partnership between parents and professionals involved with the treatment of cleft lip and/or palate to provide specialist support for parents, the growing child, the adolescent and the adult. As well as practical parent-to-parent support services, CLAPA runs a helpline, dispatches feeding equipment, publishes a range of information leaflets, organizes workshops for health professionals and, through its 50 branches, raises money towards facilities for local hospital treatment.

Colostomy Association

2 London Road
East Street
Reading
Berkshire RG1 4QL
Tel: (0118) 939 1537
Helpline: (0800) 328 4257
E-mail: cass@colostomyassociation.org.uk
Website: www.colostomyassociation.org.uk

Community Link
MacMillan Cancer Support

89 Albert Embankment
London SE1 7UQ
Cancerline: (0808) 808 2020
Fax: (020) 7840 7841
Website: www.macmillan.org.uk

Community Link provides free confidential support services for people affected by cancer, and is part of national cancer charity Macmillan Cancer Support. Community Link works with UK cancer self-help and support groups, to help people with cancer, their families and carers, offering emotional and practical support close to home.

Contact a Family

209–211 City Road
London EC1V 1JN
Tel: (020) 7608 8700
Helpline: (0808) 808 3555
(Mon–Fri, 10 am–4 pm; Mon 5.30–7.30 pm)
Textphone: (0808) 808 3556
Fax: (020) 7608 8701
E-mail: info@cafamily.org.uk
Website: www.cafamily.org.uk

Contact a Family is the only UK-wide charity providing advice, information and support to parents of all disabled children – no matter what their health condition. We enable parents to get in contact with other families through a family linking service, both on a local and national basis.

Our freephone helpline provides a one-stop-shop for families of children with disabilities, offering advice on welfare rights, community care issues, education needs and a listening ear with access to interpreters. We have a number of local, regional and national offices plus volunteer family workers around the UK. Part of our service is to provide information to professionals and development advice to support groups.

We also work to influence services and have campaigns that aim to improve the quality of life for families with disabled children.

Our wide range of publications for parents and professionals includes *The Contact a Family Directory – Specific Conditions, Rare Disorders and UK Family Support Groups*. Price £35 (new edition every year). Most of our information materials can be found on our website, others will need to be ordered.

Cornelia de Lange Syndrome Foundation UK

The Gate House
104 Lodge Lane
Grays
Essex RM16 2UL
Tel: (01375) 376439
E-mail: info@cdls.org.uk
Website: www.cdls.org.uk
General Manager: Jacquie Griffin

The CdLS Foundation exists to ensure early and accurate diagnosis of CdLS nationwide. It promotes research into the causes and manifestations of the syndrome and helps people with a diagnosis of CdLS to make informed decisions throughout their lifetimes. The foundation has a helpline and also produces booklets and other information packs about the condition, which are sent to carers and professionals to spread awareness and provide basic information about CdLS. There is a quarterly newsletter, which covers new stories about research developments and family news.

development of curricula and examinations in communication skills.

CACDP offers certification in British Sign Language, Lipspeaking, Communication with Deafblind People and Deaf Awareness, and carries out the selection, training, monitoring and registration of examiners.

The Council for the Advancement of Communication with Deaf People
Durham University Science Park
Block 4, Stockton Road
Durham DH1 3UZ
Tel: (0191) 383 1155
Textphone: (0191) 383 7915
Fax: (0191) 383 7914
E-mail: durham@cacdp.org.uk
Website: www.cacdp.org.uk
Chief Executive: Miranda Pickersgill

CACDP aims to improve communication between deaf and hearing people by the

CReSTeD (Council for the Registration of Schools Teaching Dyslexic Pupils)
(Registered Charity No 1052103)
Greygarth
Littleworth
Winchcombe
Cheltenham GL54 5BT
Tel/Fax: (01242) 604852
Administrator: Ms Christine Hancock

The CReSTeD Register provides information to parents and those who advise them on choosing schools for children with SpLD (dyslexia). Working alongside the British

Dyslexia Association and Dyslexia Action, CReSTeD was established in 1989 to produce a list of suitable schools, both maintained and independent. All schools listed have been through an establishment registration procedure, including a visit by a CReSTeD-selected consultant. For a list of schools see pages 495–504.

Cystic Fibrosis Trust

11 London Road
Bromley
Kent BR1 1BY
Tel: (020) 8464 7211
Helpline: (0300) 373 1000
Fax: (020) 8313 0472
E-mail: enquiries@cftrust.org.uk
Website: www.cftrust.org.uk

The Cystic Fibrosis Trust is the UK's only national charity dedicated to all aspects of Cystic Fibrosis (CF). The CF Trust funds research aimed at treating the symptoms of, and finding an effective treatment for, Cystic Fibrosis. It also aims to ensure appropriate healthcare for those with CF and provides information, advice and practical support for people with Cystic Fibrosis and their families across the UK.

deafPLUS

BVSC, The Centre for Voluntary Action
138 Digbeth
Birmingham
West Midlands B5 6DR
Tel: (0121) 643 4343
Textphone: (0121) 525 3092
Fax: (0121) 643 4541
E-mail: julia.pitt@deafPLUS.org
Website: www.deafPLUS.org
Advocacy Officer: Julia Pitt

Disability Alliance

Universal House
88–94 Wentworth Street
London E1 7SA

Office (minicom available):
(020) 7247 8776
Fax: (020) 7247 8765
Open 10 am–4 pm
Website: www.disabilityalliance.org

Disability Alliance is committed to breaking the link between disability and poverty. It provides information about social security benefits to disabled people, their carers and advisers through publications (including the annual *Disability Rights Handbook* that is available from May each year). Other recent titles include *The ESA Guide* and *Benefit Appeals*. Free briefings and factsheets are available from their website. It campaigns for improvements to the social security system.

The Disability Law Service
39–45 Cavell Street
London E1 2BP
Tel: (020) 7791 9800
Minicom: (020) 7791 9801
Fax: (020) 7790 9802
E-mail: advice@dls.org.uk

Provides a broad range of free legal advice and assistance on post-18 education and other areas for disabled people, their families and carers, including community care, employment welfare, benefits and disability discrimination.

Disability Sports Events
Belle Vue Centre
Longsight
Manchester M12 5GL
Tel: (0161) 953 2499
Fax: (0161) 953 2420
E-mail: info@dse.org.uk
Website: www.disabilitysport.org.uk

DSE is the Events arm of the English Federation of Disability Sport (EFDS). DSE develops sporting opportunities for disabled people to compete in a range of sports. DSE coordinate regional and national championships for disabled people to compete in a range of sports, including Mini Games for children aged 6–12 through to National Junior Swimming and Athletics.

Disabled Living Foundation
380–384 Harrow Road
London W9 2HU

The Disability Rights Handbook
A must for all special needs staff

A fully comprehensive guide to benefits and tax credits for disabled children and young people, including:

Disability Living Allowance
Employment and Allowance Support
Child tax credit
Child benefit
Financing studies – grants and loans
Income support
Incapacity benefit
Help for carers
Community care/Residential care
How to challenge decisions
Housing benefit and much, much more

This book is essential for anyone working with
16–19-year olds

Published May 2011. Price £28.50 (postfree) or £14.00 (postfree) for people on benefit. Also available on CD price £34.50
ISBN: 978-1-903335-53-6
Order now by sending payment by cheque or postal order to:
Disability Alliance
Universal House,
88–94 Wentworth Street,
London E1 7SA

Please allow 21 days for delivery
Registered Charity number 1063115

Helpline: (0845) 130 9177
Tel: (020) 7432 8009
Fax: (020) 7266 2922
E-mail: advice@dlf.org.uk
Website: www.dlf.org.uk
Head of Services: Sue Clements

The Disabled Living Foundation is a national charity, which provides free and impartial advice and information on equipment to enable disabled and older people to manage daily living activities. Its services are open to all: disabled people, carers, relatives, students and professionals.

The organization runs a telephone, letter and e-mail enquiry service and an equipment demonstration centre. It also publishes a range of fact sheets.

Dogs for the Disabled
(Registered Charity No 1092960)
The Frances Hay Centre
Blacklocks Hill
Banbury

Oxon OX17 2BS
Tel: (01295) 252600
Fax: (01295) 252668
E-mail: info@dogsforthedisabled.org

Specially selected dogs are trained as assistance dogs to perform tasks that adults and children with disabilities find difficult or impossible. We also provide services for families with a child with autism. Practical tasks include retrieving articles (eg TV remote), opening and closing doors, activating light switches, helping people to get undressed, help with rising from a chair or walking independently of other aids. Dogs are trained to suit individual needs, and provide independence, security and companionship.

Down's Syndrome Association
Langdon Down Centre
2a Langdon Park
Teddington TW11 9PS
Tel: (0845) 230 0372

Down's Syndrome Association
Education Support Packs for Mainstream and Special Schools

The *Education Support Packs* are a comprehensive and practical resource, with versions, for mainstream schools and also for special schools that include or are thinking about including children with Down's syndrome.

Unlike existing resources, the *Education Support Packs* are unique in being designed to meet the needs of hard-pressed teaching professionals with little time or specialist knowledge of Down's syndrome. Drawing on the huge professional experience of their creators, they include information on a range of topics such as dealing with challenging behaviour, methods for improving literacy, numeracy and communication plus a wide range of curriculum-based differentiated teaching materials.

The *Education Support Packs* are available to download free from the Down's Syndrome Association website **www.downs-syndrome.org.uk** or can be ordered from our national office at at £10 per copy for the mainstream pack and £10 or £25 for the special schools one, including P&P.

Fax: (0845) 230 0373
E-mail: info@downs-syndrome.org.uk
Website: www.downs-syndrome.org.uk

The Down's Syndrome Association is the only charity in the country which works exclusively with people with Down's syndrome. It exists to provide support, information and advice to people with Down's syndrome, their parents/carers, families and those professionals who work with them. The Association has a network of affiliated parent-led support groups, a national office and resource centres in Teddington and offices in Belfast and Cardiff. It is a national charity covering England, Wales and Northern Ireland.

Down's Syndrome Scotland

158–160 Balgreen Road
Edinburgh EH11 3AU
Tel: (0131) 313 4225
Fax: (0131) 313 4285
E-mail: info@dsscotland.org.uk
Website: www.dsscotland.org.uk

Down's Syndrome Scotland provides information and support to people with Down's syndrome, parents, carers and professionals. We also produce a wide range of publications and deliver first class training.

Dyslexia Action

Park House
Wick Road
Egham
Surrey TW20 0HH
Tel: (01784) 222300
Fax: (01784) 222333
E-mail: info@dyslexiaaction.org.uk
Website: www.dyslexiaaction.org.uk
Chief Executive: Shirley Cramer

Dyslexia Action is a national charity and the UK's leading provider of services and support for people with dyslexia and literary difficulties. We specialize in assessment,

teaching and training. We also develop and distribute teaching materials and undertake research.

Dyslexia Action is the largest supplier of specialist training in this field and is committed to improving public policy and practice. We partner with schools, LEAs, colleges, universities, employers, voluntary sector organizations and Government to improve the quality and quantity of help for people with dyslexia and specific learning difficulties.

Our services are available through 26 centres and 160 teaching locations around the UK. Over half a million people benefit from our work each year.

Dyspraxia Foundation

(Registered Charity No 1058352)
8 West Alley
Hitchin
Herts SG5 1EG
Tel: (01462) 455016
Helpline: (01462) 454986
Fax: (01462) 455052
E-mail:
dyspraxia@dyspraxiafoundation.org.uk
Website: www.dyspraxiafoundation.org.uk

Objectives: The objects of the Dyspraxia Foundation are: to support individuals and families affected by dyspraxia; to promote better diagnostic and treatment facilities for those who have dyspraxia; to help professionals in health and education to assist those with dyspraxia; to promote awareness and understanding of dyspraxia.

Services provided: publishes leaflets, booklets, books and guides for parents, those who have dyspraxia and professionals; organizes conferences and talks about dyspraxia and related topics for parents, carers and professionals.

Local support groups: for details of Parent Volunteer Local Support Groups, if available, please contact the National Office.

Membership: various subscription categories. Details available from the National Office.

Electronic Aids for the Blind
Suite 14, 71–75 High Street
Chislehurst
Kent BR7 5AG
Tel: (020) 8295 3636
Fax: (020) 8295 3737

A national charity helping blind and partially sighted people of all ages to achieve their fullest potential by awarding partial grants and arranging fund-raising appeals to third parties to purchase specialist or suitably adapted equipment for personal use where no statutory obligations exist and where there is financial hardship.

emPOWER
c/o Limbless Association
Rehabilitation Centre
Queen Mary's Hospital
Roehampton Lane
London SW15 5PR
Tel: (020) 8788 1777
Fax: (020) 8788 3444
E-mail: enquiries@empowernet.org
Website: www.empowernet.org

A consortium of users of prosthetics, orthotics, wheelchairs and electronic assistive technology which campaigns for a 'natural look' based on individual needs.

ENABLE Scotland
2nd Floor, 146 Argyle Street
Glasgow G2 8BL
Tel: (0141) 226 4541
Fax: (0141) 204 4398
E-mail: info@enable.org.uk
Website: www.enable.org.uk

ENABLE Scotland can provide information about issues affecting children with learning

disabilities in Scotland. It has a network of local branches across Scotland offering mutual support to parents and runs a range of services, including supported living, employment training and support, flexible support service and family-based respite care.

Epilepsy Action
New Anstey House
Gate Way Drive
Yeadon
Leeds LS19 7XY
Tel: (0113) 210 8800
Helpline: (0808) 800 5050
Fax: (0113) 391 0300
E-mail: epilepsy@epilepsy.org.uk
Website: www.epilepsy.org.uk

Epilepsy Action is the largest member-led epilepsy organization in the UK. We are committed to supporting the needs of people with epilepsy, by working with individuals, families, carers and professionals to increase awareness and understanding of the condition. Our services to support people with epilepsy in education include a free telephone and e-mail helpline, and a network of local branches. Epilepsy Action produces online resources for professionals and families, and information packs for schools.

Epilepsy Scotland
48 Govan Road
Glasgow G51 1JL
Tel: (0141) 427 4911
Helpline: (0808) 800 2200
Fax: (0141) 419 1709
E-mail: enquiries@epilepsy
scotland.org.uk
Website: www.epilepsyscotland.org.uk

Epilepsy Scotland lobbies policymakers for better policies and services to meet local needs, and campaigns against the stigma of epilepsy by raising public awareness.

Services include relevant literature and information on epilepsy, a video library, an interactive website, and a freephone helpline for people with epilepsy, their families, carers and professionals. Epilepsy Scotland provides training courses in epilepsy management and offers a community support service for adults with epilepsy and additional community care needs. We support a network of groups throughout Scotland.

Equality and Human Rights Commission
PRLL – GHUX – CTRX
Arndale House
Arndale Centre
Manchester M4 3EQ
Tel: (0845) 604 6610
Fax: (0845) 604 6630
E-mail: englandhelpline@
equalityhumanrights.com
Website: www.drc-gb.org

European Agency for Development in Special Needs Education
Østre
Stationsvej 33
DK-5000 Odense C
Denmark
Tel: +45 64 41 00 20
Fax: +45 64 41 23 03
E-mail: secretariat@european-agency.org
Website: www.european-agency.org

Family Fund
Unit 4, Alpha Court
Monks Cross Drive
Huntington
York YO32 9WN
Tel: (01904) 621115
Textphone: (01904) 658085
Low-cost line: (0845) 130 4542
Fax: (01904) 652625
E-mail: info@familyfund.org.uk
Website: www.familyfund.org.uk

The purpose of the Family Fund is to ease the stress on families who care for severely disabled children aged 17 and under, by providing grants and information related to the care of the child.

The Foundation for Conductive Education
The National Institute of Conductive Education
Cannon Hill House
Russell Road, Moseley
Birmingham B13 8RD
Tel: (0121) 449 1569
Fax: (0121) 449 1611
E-mail: foundation@conductive-education.org.uk
Website: www.conductive-education.org.uk
Monday–Friday, 9 am–5 pm
Director of Fundraising and Marketing:
Treena Jones

A national charity formed in 1986 'to establish and develop the science and skill of Conductive Education in the UK'.
The National Institute of Conductive Education provides direct services to children and adults with motor disorders, such as cerebral palsy and dyspraxia in children and Parkinson's disease, multiple sclerosis, stroke or head injury in adults. Through a system of positive teaching and learning support, Conductive Education maximizes participants' control over bodily movement in ways that are relevant to daily living.
The National Institute also undertakes research and offers a comprehensive range of professionally oriented, skills-based training courses at all levels, including the BA (Hons) Conductive Education degree in conjunction with the University of Wolverhampton. Covers UK and overseas.

Fragile X Society
53 Winchelsea Lane
Hastings TN35 4LG
Tel: (01424) 813147
Contact: Mrs Lesley Walker

Friends of Landau-Kleffner Syndrome
3 Stone Buildings
Lincoln's Inn
London WC2A 3XL
E-mail: info@friendsoflks.com
Website: www.friendsoflks.com

The Guide Dogs for the Blind Association
Hillfields
Burghfield Common
Reading RG7 3YG
Tel: (01189) 835555
E-mail: guidedogs@guidedogs.org.uk
Website: www.guidedogs.org.uk
Contact: Chris Dyson

Hearing Aided Young Adults
7–11 Armstrong Road
London W3 7JL
Tel: (020) 8743 1110
Fax: (020) 8742 9043

Hearing Concern
95 Gray's Inn Road
London WC1X 8TX
Tel: (020) 7740 9871
SMS: (07624) 809978
Fax: (020) 7740 9872
Helpline: (0845) 074 4600
E-mail: info@hearingconcern.org.uk
Website: www.hearingconcern.org.uk

Hearing Concern is a people-centred charity offering one-to-one support, advice, access and inclusion to all deaf and hard of hearing people whose main mode of communication is speech.

Helen Arkell Dyslexia Centre
Frensham
Farnham
Surrey GU10 3BW
Tel: (01252) 792400

Fax: (01252) 795669
E-mail: enquiries@arkellcentre.org.uk
Website: www.arkellcentre.org.uk
Principal: Mrs Bernadette McLean

A registered charity providing comprehensive help and care for children and adults with specific learning difficulties, including assessment, tuition, speech and language therapy, and short courses, as well as teacher training and schools support. Financial help is available. Specialist books on dyslexia for parents and teachers are available by mail order.

Henshaw's Society for Blind People
Atherton House
89–92 Talbot Road
Old Trafford
Manchester M16 0GS
Tel: (0161) 872 1234
Fax: (0161) 848 9889
E-mail: childrenfamiliesmcr@ henshaws.org.uk
Website: www.henshaws.org.uk

Henshaw's give expert care, advice and support to children and families affected by sight loss – right where it's needed most. We run this service across the North West, offering a wide range of support services for children and parents who are blind and visually impaired. Working together, we enable and encourage children and parents to live to the full – building the skill they need, to get the future they want.

Hyperactive Children's Support Group (HACSG)
71 Whyke Lane
Chichester
West Sussex PO19 7PD
Tel: (01243) 539966
E-mail: hyperactive@hacsg.org.uk
Website: www.hacsg.org.uk
Contact: Mrs Sally Bunday

The HACSG provides ideas and information to parents, carers and professionals seeking help for ADHD/Hyperactive children and young people. Non-drug therapies are our main interest. Free introductory pack available on request.

I CAN
8 Wakely Street
London EC1V 7QE
Tel: (0845) 225 4071
Fax: (0845) 225 4072
E-mail: info@ican.org.uk
Website: www.talkingpoint.org.uk and www.ican.org.uk

I CAN is the children's communication charity. It works to develop speech, language and communication skills for all children, with a particular focus on children who find communication hard.
I CAN works to ensure all people who have a responsibility to children, either directly or indirectly, from parent to teachers to policy makers, understand the importance of good communication skills. It does this through:

- Information, training, support and online resources for children, families and professionals.
- Direct service provision through two schools for children with severe and complex disabilities, and a network of early years provisions.
- Consultancy and outreach services through I CAN's Early Talk and Primary Talk programmes and Communications Skills Centres.
- Raising awareness through campaigns such as Make Chatter Matter and through initiatives such as the Chatterbox Challenge.
- Campaigning to place communication skills at the heart of children's policy.

Independent Panel for Special Education Advice
6 Carlow Mews
Woodbridge
Suffolk
IP12 1EA
Advice Line: (0800) 018 4016
Admin: (01394) 384711
Chief Executive: Angie Lee-Foster

IPSEA offers free and independent advice and support to parents of children with special educational needs, including free advice on LEAs' legal duties towards children with SEN, home visits where necessary, free support and possible representation for those parents appealing to the Special Educational Needs Tribunal, and free second opinions on a child's needs and the provision required to meet those needs.

The Institute for Neuro-Physiological Psychology
1 Stanley Street
Chester
Cheshire CH1 2LR
Tel: (01244) 311414
E-mail: mail@inpp.org.uk
Founder: Peter Blythe
Director: Sally Goddard-Blythe

Established in 1975 to carry out research into the effects of central nervous system dysfunctions on children with learning difficulties, and to develop appropriate CNS remedial and rehabilitation programmes. INPP can diagnose what underlies dyslexia, dyspraxia and other specific learning difficulties, and then devise an appropriate physical correction programme to be done each day at home or school. The children are regularly monitored, and as the basic causes are corrected they begin to benefit from teaching and the educational process. INPP also runs several courses for other professionals in the identification, assessment and remediation of neuro-developmental difficulties.

LDA
Abbeygate House
East Road
Cambridge CB1 1DB
Tel: (0845) 120 4776
Fax: (0800) 783 8648

LDA offers an extensive selection of innovative, high-quality resources to make teaching easier and learning a lot more fun. LDA aims to help every child achieve their best in a fun and inclusive learning environment. Working hard to find and develop new and exciting products to help children with special needs or additional support requirements to reach their full potential, LDA's range encompasses everything from language, literacy and inclusion to maths, motor skills and PSHE.

Learning and Teaching Scotland
The Optima
58 Robertson Street
Glasgow G2 8DU
Tel: (0141) 282 5000
Fax: (0141) 282 5050
E-mail: enquiries@LTScotland.org.uk
Website: www.LTScotland.org.uk

Learning and Teaching Scotland is a national public body sponsored by the Scottish Government. LT Scotland's remit is to provide advice, support, resources and staff development that enhance the quality of educational experiences in Scotland, with a view to improving attainment and achievement for all and promoting lifelong learning. It combines expertise on the school and pre-school curriculum and on the use of information and communications technology (ICT) in education and lifelong learning. LT Scotland is actively involved in software and internet development and multimedia production of educational resources.

Leber's Optic Neuropathy Trust
13 Palmar Road
Maidstone
Kent ME16 0DL
Tel: (01622) 751025
Contact: Mrs T Handscombe

Lennox-Gastaut Support Group
9 South View
Burrough on the Hill
Melton Mowbray LE14 2JJ
Tel: (01664) 454305
E-mail: andrew.gibson15@
   btopenworld.com
Contact: Andrew Gibson

Leukaemia CARE
One Birch Court
Blackpole East
Worcester WR3 8SG
Tel: (01905) 755977
Fax: (01905) 755166
CARE Line: (0800) 169 6680
E-mail: info@leukaemiacare.org.uk
Website: www.leukaemiacare.org.uk
Fundraising website:
www.raise4leukaemia.org.uk
Administration: Stephanie Whitehouse

Leukaemia CARE is a national charity that
provides care and support to patients, their
families and carers during the difficult journey
through the diagnosis and treatment of blood
and lymphatic cancers. Leukaemia CARE
provides the only dedicated freephone care
line for patients and their families that enables
people to discuss their feelings, concerns
and emotions at such a difficult period of time.

Limbless Association
Queen Mary's Hospital
Roehampton Lane
London SW15 5PR
Tel: (020) 8788 1777
Fax: (020) 8788 3444
E-mail: enquiries@limbless-association.org
Website: www.limbless-association.org

Information on a disabled football team, run in
cooperation with Chelsea Football Club, also
available.

**The London Centre for Children with
Cerebral Palsy**
54 Muswell Hill
London N10 3ST
Tel: (020) 8444 7242

Provides Conductive Education for children
with cerebral palsy, and courses for
professionals working with children in
mainstream education who have cerebral
palsy.

**LOOK – National Federation of Families
with Visually Impaired Children**
c/o Queen Alexandra College
49 Court Oak Road
Harborne
Birmingham B17 9TG
Tel: (0121) 428 5038
Fax: (0121) 427 9800
E-mail: steve@look-uk.org
Website: www.look-uk.org

LOOK provides information, support and
advice to families of visually impaired
children.

Lowe's Syndrome Association
29 Gleneagles Drive
Penwortham
Preston
Lancashire PR1 0JT
Tel: (01772) 745070
E-mail: info@lowesyndrome.org
Contact: David and Julie Oliver

The Makaton Charity
Manor House
46 London Road
Blackwater
Surrey GU17 0AA

Tel: (01276) 606760
Fax: (01276) 36725
E-mail: info@makaton.org
Website: www.makaton.org

Makaton is a language programme that provides basic means of communication and encourages the development of language and literacy skills in children and adults with learning and communication difficulties. The Makaton Charity provides training and advice for parents, carers and professionals who wish to use Makaton through a national network of local and regional tutors. A wide range of resource materials is also available from the Makaton Charity: these include books of signs and symbols, DVDs, computer databases and a family support helpline.

Marfan Association UK
Rochester House
5 Aldershot Road
Fleet
Hampshire GU51 3NG
Tel: (01252) 810472

Fax: (01252) 810473
Chairman/Support Coordinator:
Mrs Diane L Rust

Marfan syndrome is an inherited disorder of connective tissue, which may affect the eyes, skeleton, lungs, heart and blood vessels and may be life-threatening. The Marfan Association UK exists to support those with the condition, providing educational material about Marfan syndrome for both medical and lay sectors and encouraging research projects.

MIND (The Mental Health Charity)
15–19 Broadway
London E15 4BQ
Tel: (020) 8219 2122
Information Line: (0845) 766 0163
E-mail: info@mind.org.uk
Website: www.mind.org.uk
Chief Executive: Paul Farmer

Mind has been speaking out for better mental health for over 60 years and is now the

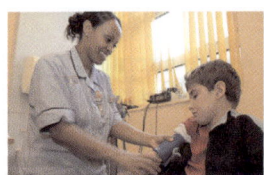

More than 60,000 people in the UK have a muscle disease or related condition. The Muscular Dystrophy Campaign is the only national UK charity focusing on all muscle disease. We have pioneered the search for treatments and cures since 1959, and are dedicated to improving the lives of all people affected. We provide:

- An Information and Support Line - **freephone 0800 652 6352**
- A team of MDC Care Advisors
- Free information prepared by doctors, clinicians and healthcare professionals
- Expert medical care at five muscle centres
- Links to condition specific support groups

020 7803 4800   **info@muscular-dystrophy.org**   **www.muscular-dystrophy.org**

Registered Charity No. 205395

leading mental health charity in England and Wales. We work in partnership with around 200 local Mind associations to improve the lives of people with experience of mental distress.

Muscular Dystrophy Campaign
4th FLoor, 61 Southwark Street
London SE1 0HL
Tel: (020) 7803 4800
Fax: (020) 7401 3495
Freephone: (0800) 652 6352
E-mail: info@muscular-dystrophy.org
Website: www.muscular-dystrophy.org

The Muscular Dystrophy Campaign is the national charity funding research into treatments and cures for the muscular dystrophies and allied muscle wasting conditions. The Campaign also supports adults and children affected by these conditions with expert clinical care and grants towards equipment. The charity relies on voluntary donations to fund its work.

National Association for Gifted Children
Suite 14, Challenge House
Sherwood Drive

Bletchley
Milton Keynes MK3 6DP
Tel: (0845) 450 0295
Helpline: (0845) 450 0221
Fax: (0870) 770 3219
E-mail: amazingchildren@ nagcbritain.org.uk
Website: www.nagcbritain.org.uk

NAGC provides services and support to gifted children, their families and those involved in their education through its information service, branch activities, counselling services and in-service training. It works to increase awareness and understanding of the social, emotional and education needs of gifted children and to improve provision.

National Association of Independent and Non-Maintained Special Schools (NAIMS)
Action for Children
Penhurst School
New Street
Chipping Norton
Oxfordshire OX7 5LN
Tel: (01608) 642559
Fax: (01608) 647029
E-mail: stephen-bb@nch.org.uk
Principal: Mr S Bajdala-Brown

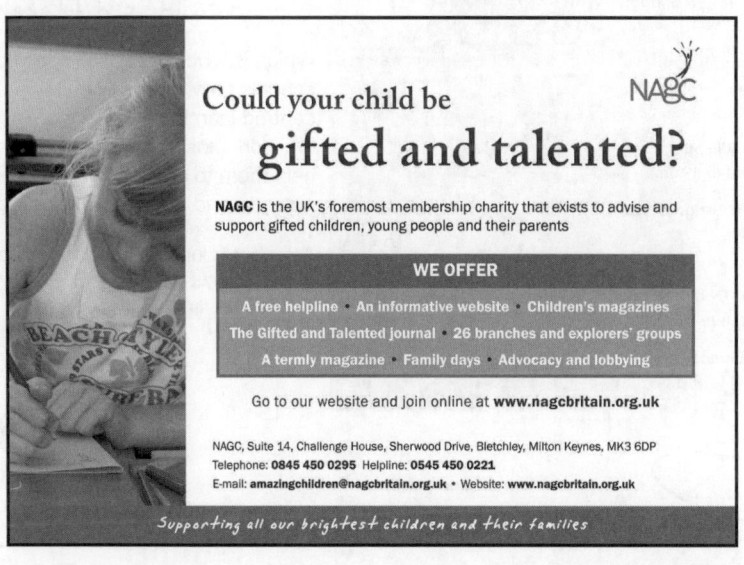

nasen

nasen House
4/5 Amber Business Village
Amber Close
Amington
Tamworth B77 4RP
Tel: (01827) 311500
Fax: (01827) 313005
E-mail: welcome@nasen.org.uk
Contact: Ms Beverley Walters

Nasen is the leading UK professional association embracing all special and additional educational needs and disabilities, promoting the education, training, development and support of all those working within this field. Membership of nasen is an invaluable source of advice, support and practical solutions, offering an exclusive and vital range of benefits that support teachers, governors, teaching assistants and the entire education support network to deliver high quality inclusive practice. Benefits include fresh and creative education resources, dynamic conferences and seminars with world-class speakers, an inspirational

professional development programme, plus print and online journals and magazines, exhibitions and access to recently completed research. Nasen also contributes greatly and has a strong influence on policy and practice in the area of special educational needs through consultation and joint projects with other professional bodies.

The National Autistic Society

393 City Road
London EC1V 1NG
Tel: (020) 7833 2299
Helpline: (0845) 070 4004
Mon–Fri, 10 am–4 pm
Fax: (020) 7833 9666
E-mail: nas@nas.org.uk
Website: www.autism.org.uk

The National Autistic Society is the UK's leading charity for people affected by autism. For more than 40 years we have worked to help children and young people across the autism spectrum enjoy their lives and reach their goals. A well-rounded education, tailored to the needs of the individual, can

make all the difference. It gives them the best start and paves the way for a full and meaningful adult life.

In working with families and carers, no other specialist provider offers more education services across the autism spectrum. Our provision varies from day through to weekly, termly and full 52-week boarding.

National Deaf Children's Society

15 Dufferin Street
London EC1Y 8UR
Tel: (020) 7490 8656 (voice & text)
Freephone Helpline: (0808) 800 8880 (voice & text) Open Mon–Fri, 9.30 am–5 pm, Sat 9.30 am–12 noon
Fax: (020) 7251 5020
E-mail: helpline@ndcs.org.uk
Website: www.ndcs.org.uk

The National Deaf Children's Society (NDCS) is the national charity dedicated to creating a world without barriers for deaf children and young people. NDCS is an organization of families, parents and carers, and provides emotional and practical support through our Freephone Helpline, network of trained support workers, wide range of other support services including an audiologist and technology team, and our publications and website. We have free membership for parents and carers, and for the professionals who support deaf children. NDCS can also help with welfare rights, benefit claims and making education choices. Events and activities are free to members.

The National Eczema Society

Hill House, Highgate Hill
London N19 5NA
Helpline: (0870) 241 3604
Fax: (020) 7281 6395
E-mail: helpline@eczema.org
Website: www.eczema.org

National Reye's Syndrome Foundation of the UK

15 Nicholas Gardens
Pyrford
Woking
Surrey GU22 8SD
Tel: (01932) 346843
E-mail: Gordon.Denney@ukgateway.net
Website: www.reyessyndrome.co.uk
Contact: Mr Gordon Denney

Reye's syndrome is a children's disease that affects the liver and brain. It is an acute disorder that affects children when they seem to be recovering from a viral illness. The latest advice from the Medicines and Healthcare Products Regulatory Agency requires all aspirin products to carry a warning that

The National Deaf Children's Society (NDCS) is the national charity dedicated to creating a world without barriers for deaf children and young people. There are over 35,000 deaf children in the UK and three more babies are born deaf every day. NDCS represents the interests and campaigns for the rights of all deaf children and young people from birth until they reach independence.

NDCS provides vital support to deaf children and their families in all aspects of their lives. The charity offers clear balanced information to support parents in helping their deaf child reach their full potential. This support is provided through a Freephone Helpline, a network of family officers and a range of family events. NDCS also holds activity events for deaf children and young people to help them develop confidence.

Contact the NDCS:
The National Deaf Children's Society
15 Dufferin Street, London EC1Y 8UR
Freephone Helpline: 0808 800 8880 (voice/ text)
  open Mon-Fri, 10am–5pm
Fax: 020 7251 5020
E-mail: helpline@ndcs.org.uk
Visit our website: www.ndcs.org.uk

every deaf child

children under 16 should not take aspirin because of a possible link with Reye's syndrome. The National Reye's Syndrome Foundation of the United Kingdom was formed to provide funds for research into the cause, treatment, cure and prevention of Reye's syndrome and Reye-like illnesses, to inform both the public and medical communities, and to provide support for parents whose children have suffered from the disease.

The National Society for Epilepsy
Chesham Lane
Chalfont St Peter
Buckinghamshire SL9 0RJ
Tel: (01494) 601300
Helpline: (01494) 601 400 Mon–Fri (national rate) 10 am–4 pm
Fax: (01494) 871927
Website: www.epilepsynse.org.uk

The National Society for Epilepsy (NSE) is the UK's leading epilepsy charity. We provide:

- specialist medical and residential services for adults with epilepsy;
- Information resources including leaflets, books and DVDs on the medical, psychological and social aspects of living with epilepsy;
- information about epilepsy from our website (www.epilepsy.org.uk);
- a confidential helpline for anyone wanting to know more about epilepsy, with information, written resources and emotional support. Helpline: 01494 604 400 (Mon–Fri, 10am–4pm);
- trained volunteers who provide information about epilepsy in healthcare settings, and deliver a Schools Awareness Programme;
- customized training including epilepsy awareness courses and epilepsy awareness and rectal diazepam training;
- fundraising events and opportunities;
- an Associate Membership scheme giving

people the opportunity to keep up to date with information about epilepsy and support our work.

Network 81
1–7 Woodfield Terrace
Chapel Hill
Stansted
Essex CM24 8AJ
Tel: (0845) 077 4055
Fax: (0845) 077 4057
E-mail: network81@btconnect.com
Website: www.network81.org
Administrator: Val Rosier

Network 81 offers practical help and support to parents throughout all stages of assessment and Statementing as outlined in the Education Act 1996 and Code of Practice 2001. Our national helpline offers an individual service linked to a national network of local contacts. We can also offer advice and information on the organization of assessment in schools and give guidelines on how to choose a school.
Network 81 produces a range of literature aimed at familiarizing parents with the assessment and Statementing procedures. Many parents found our *Network 81's Parents' Guide* particularly useful. We also run extensive training programmes for parents and those working with parents.

The Neurofibromatosis Association
Quayside House
38 High Street
Kingston upon Thames KT1 1HL
Tel: (020) 8439 1234
Helpline: (0845) 602 4173
Monday and Wednesday 9 am–4 pm
Tuesday 9 am–12 pm
Fax: (020) 8439 1200
E-mail: nfa@zetnet.co.uk;
info@nfauk.org
Website: www.nfauk.org

Newlife Foundation for Disabled Children
Newlife Centre
Hemlock Way
Cannock
Staffordshire WS11 7GF
Tel: (01543) 468888
Fax: (01543) 468999
E-mail: info@newlifecharity.co.uk
Website: www.newlifecharity.co.uk

OAASIS (Office for Advice, Assistance, Support and Information on Special Needs)
Brock House
Grigg Lane
Brockenhurst
Hampshire SO42 7RE
Helpline: (01590) 622880
Fax: (01590) 622687
E-mail: oaasis@cambiangroup.com
Website: www.oaasis.co.uk
Administrator: Andrea Woodbridge

Anyone can contact us on any aspect of SEN and we will offer help, support, advice. People contact us on a wide range of issues from a new diagnosis, help when things are going wrong at school, advice on educational rights, where to find legal advice, looking for an appropriate special school or college. OAASIS has 36 information sheets, some First Guide publications for more in-depth knowledge, pocket/wallet sized cards to explain a condition to members of the public. OAASIS can also provide details of independent special schools and colleges for autism, Asperger Syndrome, SEBD, therapeutic needs and other learning difficulties; respite/holidays and supported living/adult homes for autism and Asperger Syndrome and much more.

Ohdo Syndrome Family Network
36 Borrowdale Avenue
Gatley
Cheadle SK8 4QF
Tel: (0161) 428 8583
E-mail: patseville@btinternet.com

Paget Gorman Society
(Registered Charity No 1008041)
2 Dowlands Bungalows
Dowlands Lane
Smallfield
Surrey RH6 9SD
Tel: (01342) 842308
E-mail: pru.phillips@googlemail.com
Website: www.pgss.org

Advice and information for parents and professionals concerned with speech and language-impaired children. The Society runs courses in Paget Gorman Signed Speech (PGSS). Publications and a video are available.

Parents for Inclusion
336 Brixton Road
London SW9 7AA
Tel (business line): (020) 7738 3888
Helpline: (0800) 652 3145
Minicom: (020) 7582 5333
Fax: (020) 7735 3828
E-mail: info@parentsforinclusion.org
Website: www.parentsforinclusion.org

Parents helping parents so that disabled children can learn, make friends and have a voice in ordinary school and throughout life. We are a national charity based in London.

The Partially Sighted Society
7/9 Bennetthorpe
Doncaster DN2 6AA
Tel: (0844) 477 4966
Fax: (0844) 477 4969
E-mail: info@partsight.org.uk
Website: www.partsight.org.uk

Mail order for heavy lined paper, books and advisory service.

Perthes Association
PO Box 773
Guildford
Surrey GU1 1XN

Tel (Admin): (01483) 534431
Helpline: (01483) 306637
E-mail: admin@perthes.org.uk
Website: www.perthes.co.uk

The Association advises families of children suffering from Perthes' disease and associated conditions in all parts of the British Isles and abroad. Perthes' disease (a potentially crippling disease of the hip) is a form of osteochondritis, which affects 5.5 per 100,000 children (mainly boys) between the ages of 2 and 15 years. Perthes Association volunteers are at the end of the telephone line for any worried or distressed parents, and will visit them if possible or put them in touch with a family living locally.

The Physical and Sensory Service
The Education Centre
Church Street
Pensnett
Dudley
West Midlands DY5 4EY
Tel: (01384) 818007
Fax: (01384) 814241
E-mail: pss.ed@dudley.gov.uk
Website: www.dudley.gov.uk

The Physical and Sensory Service provides a range of services to children, parents and educational establishments. A team of specialist teachers provides support, advice and, where appropriate, specialist resource materials to children who have a physical disability or sensory impairment.

Prader-Willi Syndrome Association (UK)
125a London Road
Derby DE1 2QQ
Tel: (01332) 365676 Monday–Friday
9.30 am–3.30 pm, answerphone at other times
Fax: (01332) 360401
E-mail: admin@pwsa.co.uk
Website: www.pwsa.co.uk

Rathbone
Head Office
Churchgate House
56 Oxford Street
Manchester M1 6EU
Special Education Advice Line:
(0800) 085 4528
Fax: (0161) 238 6356

A national charity supporting parents of children with special educational needs to help them reach their potential and get the best education throughout their time at school. The service is available to parents for whom English is a second language and we provide information and advice in the following languages: Urdu, Hindi, Punjabi, Gujerati and Bengali. Outreach service is also available throughout the North-West.

REACH Charity Ltd – Association for Children with Upper Limb Deficiency
PO Box 54
Helston
Cornwall TR13 8WD
Tel: (0845) 130 6225
Fax: (0845) 130 0262
E-mail: reach@reach.org
Website: www.reach.org.uk

Each year, there are babies born in the UK missing part of one or both arms and hands. 'Reach' aims to provide affected families with the opportunity to get together, share experiences and information on what to do (or not to do) and where to go for advice regarding treatment.
The Management Committee comprises 'Reach' parents who give their time voluntarily with one full time paid administrator.
'Reach' organizes family meetings, confidence building events, provides one-handed recorders, helps with grants for computer equipment for children with no hands, adaptations to sports equipment, bicycles, cars, or musical instruments.

Please, pause and consider the effect on a child with one or no hands in a two handed society.

RNID, for Deaf and Hard of Hearing People
19–23 Featherstone Street
London EC1Y 8SL
Tel: (0808) 808 0123 – Helpline
Textphone: (0808) 808 9000 – Helpline
Fax: (020) 7296 8199
E-mail: informationline@rnid.org.uk
Website: www.rnid.org.uk
Chief Executive: Dr John Low

RNID is the largest charity representing the 9 million deaf and hard of hearing people in the UK. As a membership charity, we aim to achieve a radically better quality of life for deaf and hard of hearing people. We do this by campaigning and lobbying vigorously, by raising awareness of deafness and hearing loss, and by providing services and through social, medical and technical research.

Royal Association for Disability and Rehabilitation (RADAR)
12 City Forum
250 City Road
London EC1V 8AF
Tel: (020) 7250 3222
Minicom: (020) 7250 4119
E-mail: radar@radar.org.uk
Website: www.radar.org.uk

Information on all aspects of disability.

Royal College of Speech and Language Therapists
2 White Hart Yard
London SE1 1NX
Tel: (020) 7378 1200
Fax: (020) 7403 7254

Royal Mencap Society
Caron Lane – Head of Advice & Information Service
4 Swan Courtyard
Coventry Road, Charles Edward Road

Birmingham B26 1BU
Tel: (0121) 707 7877
Helpline: (0808) 808 1111
E-mail: help@mencap.org.uk
Website: www.mencap.org.uk
Chairman: Brian Baldock CBE
Chief Executive: Jo Williams CBE

Royal MENCAP Society is a registered charity that offers services to adults and children with learning disabilities. We offer help and advice on Benefits, Housing and Employment via the Helpline tel: 0808 808 1111.
Helplines are open from Monday to Friday, 9.30 am–4.30 pm; Wednesday, subject to change (open am, closed pm). Language Line is also used.
Office is open from Monday to Friday (9 am–5 pm) 0121 707 7877. This Helpline covers England only.
Wales Helpline: 0808 8000 300.
Northern Ireland Helpline: 08457 636 227.
We offer help and advice to anyone or we can signpost them in the right direction. We can also provide information and support for leisure, recreational services (Getaway Clubs), residential services and holidays.

The Royal National Institute of Blind People (RNIB)
105 Judd Street
London WC1H 9NE
Helpline: (0845) 766 9999
(Open 9 am–5 pm Monday to Friday, on Wednesdays the Helpline is open 9 am–4 pm. Messages can be left on our answer phone outside these hours.)
E-mail: e&einformation@rnib.org.uk
Website: www.rnib.org.uk
Chief Executive: Lesley-Anne Alexander

RNIB offers support to all children with sight problems, including those who have other special needs too. It also supports families because of the crucial role they play in the education and development of their child. In addition, RNIB provides information, resources and training for the many professionals from education, health and social services who work with them.

Rubinstein Taybi Syndrome Support Group
162 Buckfield Road
Leominster
Herefordshire HR6 8HF
Tel: (01568) 616149
Contact: Mrs Rosemary Robertson

To offer support to families and carers and provide information about the condition.

SCOPE
Scope Response
PO Box 833
Milton Keynes MK12 5NY
Tel: (0808) 800 3333
Text: SCOPE plus your message to 80039. Texts are free to sender.
E-mail: response@scope.org.uk
Website: www.scope.org.uk

Scope is the UK's leading disability charity. Our focus is on children and adults with cerebral palsy and people living with other severe and complex impairments. Our vision is a world where disabled people have the same opportunities to fulfil their life ambitions as non-disabled people.

Scottish Centre for Children with Motor Impairments
Craighalbert Centre
1 Craighalbert Way
Cumbernauld
Glasgow G68 0LS
Tel: (01236) 456100
Fax: (01236) 736889
E-mail: sccmi@craighalbert.org.uk
Website: www.craighalbert.org.uk

Grant-aided school for children 0–8 with motor impairments, combining principles of

Conductive Education with the Scottish curriculum.

The Scottish Society for Autism
New Struan School
Bradbury Campus
100 Smithfield loan
Alloa
Clackmannanshire FK10 1NP
Tel: (01259) 222000
Fax: (01259) 724239
E-mail: newstruan@
autism-in-scotland.org.uk
Website: www.autism-in-scotland.org.uk

SSA is the leading provider of services for autism in Scotland. It runs New Struan School, the only accredited school for autism in Scotland (both residential and day pupils); residential and specialist day services for adults; the only respite care centre for autism in the UK; nationwide family support services; training for carers and professionals; support self-help groups and local societies; and

produces information and a members' magazine. SSA undertakes community care assessments and gives guidance on diagnosis, assessment and care management. Advice on all aspects of autism is available from SSA's professional staff.

Scottish Spina Bifida Association
The Dan Young Building
6 Craighalbert Way
Cumbernauld
Glasgow G68 0LS
Tel: (01236) 794500
Fax: (01236) 736435
Chief Executive: Andrew H D Wynd
PA to CEO: Julie Snaddon
Services and Development Manager:
Diane Waugh

The Scottish Spina Bifida Association seeks to increase public awareness and understanding of individuals with spina bifida/hydrocephalus and allied disorders. It aims to support all those affected to identify

their needs and to empower them to make informed choices and decisions.

Scottish Support for Learning Association
(Registered Charity No SC026546)
11 Mayshand Road
Loanhead
EH20 9HJ
Tel: (0141) 883 6134
E-mail: info@ssla.org.uk
Website: www.ssla.org.uk
Contact: Sheena Richardson

SENNAC: Special Educational Needs – National Advisory Council
Pett Archive & Study Centre
Toddington
Cheltenham
Gloucestershire GL54 5DP
Hon General Secretary: Mr John Cross

Sense, The National Deafblind & Rubella Association
101 Pentonville Road
London N1 9LG
Tel: (0845) 127 0060
Fax: (0845) 127 0061
Minicom: (0845) 127 0062
E-mail: enquiries@sense.org.uk
Website: www.sense.org.uk

Sense is the national voluntary organization supporting and campaigning for people who are deafblind, their families, their carers, and professionals who work with them. People of all ages and with widely varying conditions use Sense's specialist services. Founded as a parents' self-help group in 1955, Sense is now the leading national organization working with deafblind people.
Sense:
- offers advice, help and information to deafblind people and their families;
- supports families through a national network and local branches;
- runs a holiday programme for deafblind children and adults;
- provides education, residential, respite and day services;
- offers training and consultancy.

Sense Scotland
TouchBase
43 Middlesex Street
Glasgow G41 1EF
Tel: (0141) 429 0294
Fax: (0141) 429 0295
E-mail: info@sensescotland.org.uk
Website: www.sensescotland.org.uk

Sense Scotland works with children and adults who have communication support needs because of deafblindness, sensory impairment, learning or physical disability. They lead in communication and innovative support services for people who are marginalized because of challenging behaviour, health care and continuity across age groups. Sense Scotland works closely with families and colleagues from health, education and social work.
Services include:
- family advisory services;
- community living and support for adults;
- support services for adults and for children;
- residential short breaks for adults and children;
- art development and outdoor education work for children and adults;
- practice training for professionals;
- assessments;
- representations, consultation and policy development;
- health and general information enquiry services.

Sense West
9a Birkdale Avenue
Off Heeley Road
Selly Oak
Birmingham B29 6UB
Tel: (0121) 415 2723 (voice and text)
Fax: (0121) 472 2723

Sense West provides a regional advisory service to families, deafblind people and professionals working with them, an adult service department offering a range of residential provision and learning opportunities based on individual need for deafblind and multiple disabled sensory-impaired adults, and a Training and Consultancy Service offering advice, assessment and training to people involved with the education and care of deafblind children and adults. They also provide day services based in Birmingham and Exeter, an Outreach service, both Communicator-Guide service and Intervenor Service (in the Midlands and South West) and an information service.

The Sequal Trust
(Special Equipment and Aids for Living)
3 Ploughmans Corner
Wharf Road
Ellesmere
Shropshire SY12 0EJ
Tel/Fax: (01691) 624222

A national charity which fundraises to supply communication aids to those people with speech, movement or learning difficulties, on a lifelong loan basis. Registration fee is £20 for life membership. There is no age limit for application, but an assessment of need is required from a health care professional and applicants need to be on a low income or solely in receipt of benefits.

The SIGNALONG Group
Stratford House
Waterside Court
Neptune Way
Rochester
Kent ME2 4NZ
Tel: (0845) 450 8422
Website: www.signalong.org.uk

SIGNALONG is a sign-supporting system based on British Sign Language intended to promote communication in learning disabilities and autism. The charity has devised a uniform method of presenting signs with drawings and descriptions, and has published the widest range of illustrated signs in Britain, catering for all ages and abilities. Resources are available in paper and electronic format. Manuals contain full signing instructions, but training and advice are also provided, both by SIGNALONG staff and by independent accredited tutors. SIGNALONG works with other organizations to develop symbol resources and to promote total communication to enable understanding and expression of choice.

Skill – National Bureau for
Students with Disabilities
Unit 3, Floor 3
Radisson Court
219 Long Lane
London SE1 4PR
Tel: (020) 7450 0620
Fax: (020) 7450 0650
Information Service:
(0800) 328 5050, (0800) 068 2422
(Info Service Textphone)
Tuesdays 11.30 am–1.30 pm,
Thursdays 1.30 pm–3.30 pm
E-mail: info@skill.org.uk
Website: www.skill.org.uk
Director: Barbara Waters

Skill is a national voluntary organization that promotes opportunities for young people and adults with any kind of impairment or learning difficulty – in further, higher and adult education, work-based learning, entry to employment and volunteering.

Social Emotional and Behavioural
Difficulties Association
Room 211, The Triangle
Exchange Square
Manchester M4 3TR
Tel: (0161) 240 2418

Fax: (0161) 838 5601
E-mail: admin@sebda.org
Website: www.sebda.org
Executive Director: Dr Ted Cole

SEBDA provides accredited training and supports professionals working with children with behavioural difficulties.

Special Needs Advisory Project Cymru (SNAP)
10 Cooper's Yard
Curran Road
Cardiff CF10 5NB
Tel: (029) 2038 4868
Fax: (029) 2038 8776
E-mail: snapcym@aol.com.uk

SNAP Cymru offers information and support to families of children and young people who have, or may have, special educational needs/disability.

Tourette Syndrome (UK) Association (trading as Tourettes Action)
Southbank House
Black Prince Road
London SE1 7SJ
Tel: (020) 7798 2356
Helpline: (0845) 458 1252
E-mail: help@tourettes-action.org.uk
Website: www.tourettes-action.org.uk

A Registered Charity dedicated to:
- providing support;
- educating, informing and campaigning;
- promoting medical research on behalf of all those affected by TS.

Tuberous Sclerosis Association
PO Box 12979
Barnt Green
Birmingham B45 5AN
Tel/Fax: (0121) 445 6970
E-mail: diane.sanson@ tuberous-sclerosis.com

Website: www.tuberous-sclerosis.org
Contact: Mrs Diane Sanson

Offers support to people with tuberous sclerosis and their families or carers. Promoting education, publicity and information to increase awareness and understanding. There are Specialist Advisers to advise on any problems relating to TS. The TSA also organizes regional and national meetings and conferences and operates a Benevolent Fund. There are a number of specialist Clinics around the country.

Vision Aid
Registered Charity No. 518641
PO Box 2211
Deane
Bolton BL6 9FW
Tel: (01204) 64265
E-mail: visionaiduk@aol.com

Williams Syndrome Foundation Ltd
161 High Street
Tonbridge TN9 1BX

Tel: (01732) 365152
Fax: (01732) 360178
E-mail: John.Nelson-wsfoundation@btinternet.com
Website: www.williams-syndrome.org.uk

YoungMinds
48–50 St John Street
London EC1M 4DG
Tel: (020) 7336 8445
Tel (Parents Information Service): (0808) 802 5544
Fax (office): (020) 7336 8446
E-mail: enquiries@youngminds.org.uk
Website: www.youngminds.org.uk

YoungMinds is the UK's leading charity committed to improving the emotional well-being and mental health of children and young people, and empowering their parents and carers. We also offer a range of intensive training and consultancy solutions for professionals who work with children, aimed at increasing knowledge and understanding of CAMHS.

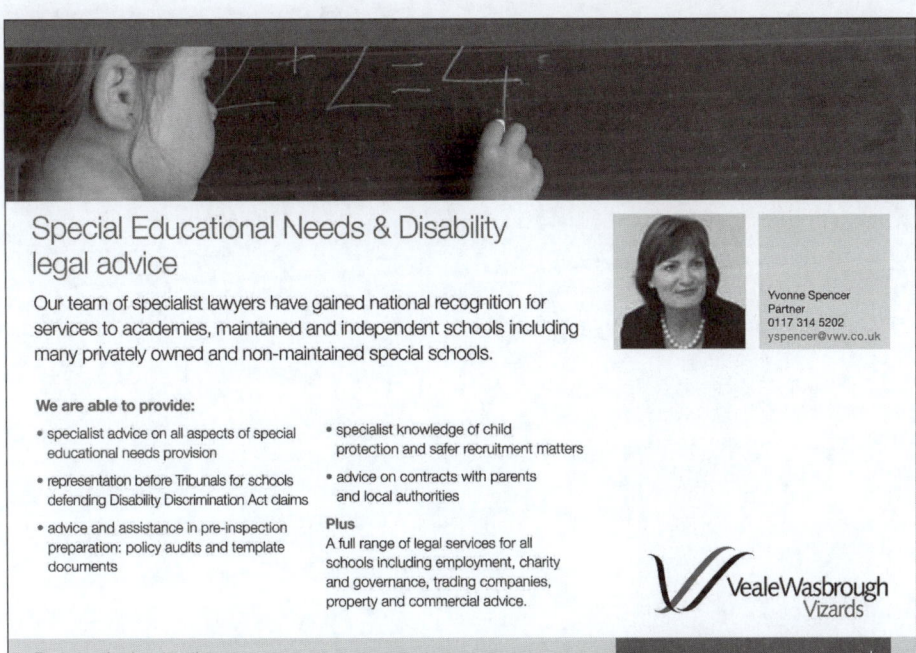

5.3

Bibliography

The following list has been compiled with the kind assistance of editorial contributors and offers suggested further reading on many aspects of special educational needs.

General

'The Code of Practice for the Identification and Assessment of SEN'

'Special Educational Needs: A guide for parents'

'Meeting Special Educational Needs – A programme of action'

'Meeting Special Educational Needs – A programme of action' – a summary, also available in braille, on audio-cassette and in British Sign Language

All the above publications are available from the Department for Education (DFE)
Tel: 0845 602 2260

'Young Adults with Special Needs: Assessment, Law and Practice – Caught in the Acts'
John Friel
Jessica Kingsley Publishers
ISBN: 9781853022319

'Network 81 Parents' Guide'
Network 81, 1–7 Woodfield Terrace
Chapel Hill, Stansted, Essex CM24 8AJ
Tel: 0870 770 3306
£8.50

'How and Why Children Fail'
Edited by Ved Varma, Foreword by James Hemming
Jessica Kingsley Publishers
ISBN: 9781853021862
£17.95

'Special Education Handbook'
Advisory Centre for Education (ACE)
Tel: 020 7704 3370
ISBN: 187 067231 3
£17.99

Supporting Support Assistants & Supporting Special Educational Needs

'Supporting Support Assistants – A practical handbook for SENCOs in mainstream primary and secondary schools'
Stephanie Lorenz, 1996

'Supporting Special Educational Needs in Secondary School Classrooms'
Jane Lovey
David Fulton Publishers, 2002
ISBN: 1853468320
£19.99

'Tribunal Toolkit'
Advisory Centre for Education
Tel: 020 7704 3370

'Taking Action: Your Child's Right to Special
Education – The definitive guide for parents,
teachers, advocates and advice workers'
J White and I Rubain, 2000
Questions Publishing Co Ltd
ISBN: 184 190010 9

'Disability Rights Handbook'
A guide to rights, benefits and services for all
people with disabilities and their families
Disability Alliance
Universal House
88–94 Wentworth Street, London E1 7SA
Tel: 020 7247 8776
Fax: 020 7247 8765
ISBN: 1 9033 35383
£25.00 or £10.00 for people on benefit

'Children First'
Royal Association for Disability and
Rehabilitation (RADAR)
Publications Department
12 City Forum, 250 City Road
London EC1V 8AF

'Children in Difficulty: A guide to
understanding and helping'
J Elliot and M Place
RoutledgeFalmer, 2004
ISBN: 0415 325 447
£19.99

'Hope for the Journey – Helping children
through good times and bad. Story building
for parents, teacher and therapist'
C R Snyder, D McDermott, W Cook and
M A Rapoff
Percheron Press, 2002
ISBN: 0971242704
£17.21

'Spelling: Remedial strategies'
Diane Montgomery
Cassell, 1997
ISBN: 0304329746

'Understanding and Supporting Children
with Emotional or Behavioural Difficulties'
Edited by P Cooper
Jessica Kingsley, 1999
ISBN: 9781853026669

For students aged 16+ with disabilities

'After Age 16 – What next?': Please log on to:
www.after16.org.uk
Family Fund, Unit 4, Alpha Court
Monks Cross Drive
Huntingdon YO32 9WN
Tel: 01904 621115

'COPE: Directory of Post-16 Residential
Education and Training for Young People'
Helen Evans, Tessa Doe, Debbie Stec and
Hilary Jones
Lifetime Publishing, 2006
ISBN: 0904979114
£36.99

'The Association of National Specialist
Colleges Directory'
A directory of colleges with specialist
provision for disabled students: please log
on to www.natspec.org.uk
Chief Executive: Kevin O'Brien
39 Sanders Road
Quorn, Loughborough
Leicestershire LE12 8JN
Tel: 01509 5543573

'Youthaid Guide to Training and Benefits for
Young People'
Published by Youthaid, 322 St John Street
London EC1V 4NT
Tel: 020 7833 8499
E-mail: youthaid@gn.apc.org
ISBN: 1907658202
£6.00

'Your Future Needs Assessment'
(Scotland Only)
Published by the Special Needs Forum of

Children in Scotland
Contact: Children in Scotland
5 Shandwick Place, Edinburgh EH2 4RG
Tel: 0131 228 8484
Fax: 0131 228 8585
£2.95

A range of publications covering all aspects
of education for disabled students is
available from Skill, The National Bureau for
Students with Disabilities
Chapter House, 18–20 Crucifix Lane
London SE1 3JW
Tel: 0800 328 5050 (voice) or
0800 068 2422 (text)

Higher education

'UCAS Handbook'
Available from UCAS or careers offices.

'UCAS Helpline'
Tel: 01242 227788
Minicom: 01242 225857
Website: www.ucas.ac.uk

'The Big Offical UCAS Guide to University
and College Entrance'
UCAS Sheedon and Ward

'Into HE: A guide to higher education for
people with disabilities'
Skill, Unit 3, Floor 3, Radisson Court,
219 Long Lane, London SE1 4PR
London SE1 3JW
Tel: 0800 328 5050 (voice) or
0800 068 2422 (text)

ADD/ADHD

'The Difficult Child'
Stanley Turecki
Bantam Books, 2000
ISBN: 0553380362
£8.66

'Is Your Child Hyperactive, Inattentive,
Impulsive, Distractible: Helping the
ADD/hyperactive child'
Stephen Garber, Marianne Daniels Garber
and Robyn Spizman
Villard Books, Random House, 1995
ISBN: 067975945X
£9.72

'Power Parenting for Children with ADD'
Grad L Flick
Prentice-Hall International, 1996
ISBN: 0876288778
£12.99

'Beyond Ritalin'
Stephen Garber, Marianne Daniels Garber
and Robyn Spizman
Harper Perennial, 1997
ISBN: 006977256
£7.10

'Taking Charge of ADHD'
Russell Barkley
Guildford Press, 2000
ISBN: 1572306009
£14.50

Autism/Asperger's syndrome

'The Autistic Spectrum: A guide for parents
and professionals'
Lorna Wing
Constable and Robinson, 2002
ISBN: 1841196746

'The Complete Guide to Asperger's
Syndrome'
Tony Attwood
Jessica Kingsley Publishers, 2006
ISBN: 9781843104957

'Autism and Asperger syndrome'
Simon Baron-Cohen
Oxford University Press, 2008
ISBN: 9786198504900

'Parenting a child with Asperger syndrome:
200 tips and strategies'
Brenda Boyd
Jessica Kingsley Publishers, 2003
ISBN: 9781843101376

'Teaching young children with autism
spectrum disorders to learn: a practical
guide for parents and staff in mainstream
schools and nurseries'
Liz Hannah
The National Autistic Society, 2001
ISBN: 9781899280322

'How to help your autistic spectrum child:
practical ways to make life run smoothly'
J Brealy and B Davies
White Ladder Press, 2006
ISBN: 9781905410057

A wide selection of resources for people
affected by autism and professionals are
available from The National Autistic Society.
See our online shop www.autism.org.uk/shop
393 City Road, London EC1V 1NG
Tel: 020 7833 2299
E-mail: nas@nas.org.uk
Website: www.autism.org.uk
Helpline: 0845 070 4004 (Mon–Fri,
10am–4pm)

Cerebral palsy

A range of publications on cerebral palsy is
available from SCOPE.
SCOPE Response
PO Box 833
Milton Keynes MK12 5NY
Tel: 0808 800 3333
Fax: 01908 321051
E-mail: response@scope.org.uk

'The Cerebral Palsy Handbook'
Marion Stanton
Vermilion, 2002
ISBN: 0091876761

'My Perfect Son has Cerebral Palsy: A
mother's guide of helpful hints'
Marie A Kennedy
1st Books Library, 2001
ISBN: 0759609543

Cystic fibrosis

A range of publications on cystic fibrosis is
available from the Cystic Fibrosis Trust,
either by post or from the Trust's website.
11 London Road
Bromley
Kent BR1 1BY
Tel: 020 8464 7211
Fax: 020 8313 0472
E-mail enquiries@cftrust.org.uk
Website: www.cfrust.org.uk

Deafness and hearing impairment

A range of publications on childhood
deafness is available from the National
Deaf Children's Society.
15 Dufferin Street
London EC1Y 8PD
Tel: 020 7251 5020

'Issues In Deaf Education'
S Gregory et al
David Fulton Publishers, 1998
ISBN: 1853465127

Down's syndrome

'Down's Syndrome – The facts'
Mark Selikowitz
Oxford University Press, 2004
ISBN: 0192626620
£13.00

'A Parent's Guide to Down's Syndrome'
Siegfried M Pueschel
Brookes Publishing Co, 2000
ISBN: 1557664528

'The Down's Syndrome Handbook: A
practical guide for parents and carers'
Dr Richard Newton

Vermilion Publishing, 2004
ISBN: 0091884306

'Down's Syndrome – An Introduction for
Parents and Carers'
Cliff Cunningham
Souvenir Press
3rd edition, 2006
ISBN: 0285636979

Dyscalculia

'The Trouble with Maths'
Steve Chinn
RoutledgeFalmer
ISBN: 0415324984
£24.99

'Mathematics for Dyslexics:
Including Dyscalculia'
3rd edition
Chinn and Ashcroft
Wiley
ISBN: 0470026928
£26.99

'Sum Hope 2 – Dealing with Dyscalculia'
Steve Chinn
Souvenir Press
ISBN: 9780285637986
£12.99

The 'What to do when you can't . . .' series of
five numeracy books
Steve Chinn, 2010
Egon Publishers

'Working with Dyscalculia'
Ann Henderson, Fil Came and Mel Brough
Learning Works, 2003
ISBN: 0953105520

'Dyscalculia Guidance'
B Butterworth and D Yeo
NFER – Nelson, 2004
ISBN: 0708711529

Dyslexia

For parents:

'Dyslexia: A parent's survival guide'
C Ostler
Ammonite Books, 1999
ISBN: 1869866134

'Overcoming Dyslexia (A straightforward
guide for families and teachers)'
B Hornsby
Macdonald & Co
ISBN: 0091813204

'The Scars of Dyslexia (Eight case studies in
emotional reactions)'
J Edwards
Cassell, 1995
ISBN: 0304329444

'Susan's Story (An autobiographical account
of my struggle with words)'
S Hampshire
Corgi, 1990
ISBN: 0552135860

'This Book Does not Make Sens, Cens, Sns,
Scens, Sense'
J Auger
Better Books

'Reversals'
E Simpson
Gollancz

Dyslexia – General

'Dyslexia: 100 years on'
T & E Miles
Open University Press, 1999
ISBN: 0335200346

'Dyslexia in Children'
Fawcett & Nicholson
Harvester Wheatsheaf

'The Pattern of Difficulties'
T R Miles
Whurr

'Developmental Dyslexia'
M E Thompson
Whurr

'Dyslexia'
2nd edition
M J Snowling
Blackwell

'Dyslexia: Speech and Language:
A practitioner's handbook' 2nd edition
Snowling & Stackhouse
Whurr

'Psychological Assessment of Dyslexia'
M Turner
Whurr

'Specific Learning Difficulties (Dyslexia):
Challenges & responses'
Pumfrey & Reason
Routledge

'Dyslexia: A practitioner's handbook'
Gavin Reid
Wiley
ISBN: 0471973912

'The Routledge Companion to Dyslexia'
Gavin Reid (Ed)
Routledge, 2009
ISBN: 9780415430791

Teaching

'Dyslexia in Practice – A guide for teachers'
Edited by Janet Townsend and Martin Turner
Kluwer, 2000
ISBN: 0306462516
        0306462524 (pbk)

'Dyslexia: A teaching handbook'
Thompson & Watkins
Whurr
ISBN: 1861560397

'Learning Difficulties in
Reading & Writing'
NFER Nelson

'Specific Learning Difficulties (Dyslexia): A
teacher's guide'
Crombie M
Jordanhill College of Education

'Dealing with Dyslexia'
Heaton & Winterson
Better Books, 1996
ISBN: 1897635575

'Children with Special Learning Difficulties'
Tansley & Pankhurst
NFER Nelson

'Reading Writing & Dyslexia:
A cognitive analysis'
Ellis A
Lawrence Erlbaum, 1993
ISBN: 0863773079

'Instrumental Music for Dyslexics:
A teaching handbook'
S Ogelthorpe
Whurr

'Overcoming Dyslexia:
A practical handbook for the classroom'
Broomfield & Combley
Whurr

Resources

'Learning to Learn'
S Malone
Nasen
ISBN: 1874784434

'Alpha to Omega'
Hornsby & Shear

Heinemann, 1999
ISBN: 0435103881

'Spotlight on Words'
G Aitken
Robinswood Press, 1970
ISBN: 1869981510

'Easy Type'
R Kinloch
Egon Publishers, 1994
ISBN: 0905858905

'New Phonic Blending Kit'
Learning Materials Ltd

For the older student:

'Help for the Dyslexic Adolescent'
E G Stirling
St David's College, Llandudno

'Use Your Head'
T Buzan
BBC, 1999
ISBN: 056337103X

'Study Skills: A pupil's survival guide'
C Ostler
Ammonite Books

'Adult Dyslexia: Assessment,
counselling and training'
McLoughlin, Fitzgibbon & Young
Whurr, 1993
ISBN: 1897635354

'Dyslexia at College'
D Gilroy & T Miles
Routledge, 1995
ISBN: 0415127785

A range of teaching and learning resources
for parents, adults, teachers and
psychologists are available from Dyslexia
Action.
Park House
Wick Road
Egham
Surrey TW20 0HH
Tel: 01784 222300
Fax: 01784 222333
E-mail: info@dyslexiaaction.org.uk
Website: www.dyslexiaaction.org.uk

'How to Detect and Manage Dyslexia'
P Ott
Heinemann, 1997
ISBN: 0435104195

'Living with Dyslexia'
B Riddick
Routledge, 1997
ISBN: 0415125014

'The Dyslexia Handbook'
A series of articles on different aspects of
dyslexia
British Dyslexia Association
ISBN: 1872653316

Dyslexia

'Developmental Dyspraxia'
2nd Edition, 1999
Madeleine Portwood
ISBN: 1853465739
£21.50 + p&p

'Take Time'
Mary Nash-Wortham and Jean Hunt
£13.95 + p&p

'Dyspraxia – Developmental Co-ordination
Disorder'
Amanda Kirby
Souvenir Press Ltd, 1994
ISBN: 0285635123
£13.50 + p&p

All the above are available from
The Dyspraxia Foundation
8 West Alley, Hitchin
Hertfordshire SG5 1EG
Tel: 01462 455016
Fax: 01462 455052
Website: www.dyspraxiafoundation.org.uk

Epilepsy

Articles:

'Epilepsy'
Jill Parkinson and Mike Johnson
Continuum
ISBN: 0826487483

'Epilepsy, Learning and Behaviour
in Children'
F M Besal
In 'Epilepsia' 1995 36 1:58–63
Raven Press, New York

'Established antiepileptic drugs'
M Brodie *et al*
In 'Seizure' 1997 6:159–174

'Behaviour problems in children with
new-onset epilepsy'
D W Dunn *et al*
In 'Seizure' 1997 4:283–287

'Educational Attainment in Children
and Young People with Epilepsy'
P Thomson
In 'Epilepsy and Education –
A medical symposium on changing attitudes
to epilepsy in education'
Edited by Jolyon Oxley and Gregory Stores
Labaz Sanofi UK
London 1986

Gifted children

'Challenge of the Able Child'
David George
David Fulton Publishers
ISBN: 1853463469
£12.99

'Supporting the Child of Exceptional Ability at
Home and at School'
S Leyden
David Fulton, 2002
ISBN: 1853468789

The National Association for Gifted Children
(NAGC) publishes a range of resources,
publications and newsletters for its
members.
Contact the NAGC
Suite 14
Challenge House
Sherwood Drive
Bletchley
Milton Keynes MK3 6DP
Helpline: 0845 450 0221
Monday–Friday 9.15 am–4 pm
General Enquiries: 0845 450 0295
Fax: 0870 7703219
Email: amazingchildren@nagcbritain.org.uk
Website: www.nagcbritain.org.uk

'Able, Gifted and Talented'
Janet Bates and Sarah Munday
£7.99

'Gifted Children: A guide for parents and
professionals'
Kate Distin (Ed)
Jessica Kingsley
Available from NAGC at £15 inc p&p

'Discovering and Developing Talent in
Schools: An Inclusive Approach'
Better, Gray-Fow
NACE/ David Fulton, 2005
£17.00

'Exceptionally Gifted Children 2nd Edition'
Miraca Gross
Routledge-Falmer, 2004
£23.99

'Learning Without Limits'
Susan Hart
Open University Press, 2004
£20.99

'Gifted Young Children: A guide for teachers
and parents' 2nd edition
Louise Porter
Open University Press, 2005
£21.99

'Gifted and Talented in the Early Years'
Margaret Sutherland
Paul Chapman, 2005
£16.99

'Too Clever by Half: A fair deal for gifted children'
C Winstanley
Trentham Books, 2004
£18.99

Leukaemia

'Living with Leukaemia'
Patsy Westcott
Hodder Wayland, 2002
ISBN: 0750241616

Childhood Leukaemia: The facts (The Facts Series)'
John S Lilleyman
Oxford University Press, 2000
ISBN: 019263142X

Muscular dystrophy

'Muscular Dystrophy: The facts'
Alan E H Emery
Oxford University Press, 2000
ISBN: 0192632175

'Childhealth Care Nursing: Concepts, theories and practice'
Edited by B Carter and A K Dearmun
Blackwell Scientific, 1995
ISBN: 0632036893
£19.99

'Inclusive Education for Children with Muscular Dystrophy and other Neuromuscular Conditions'
Guidance for Primary and Secondary schools is available from the
Muscular Dystrophy Campaign, 2nd edition
61 Southwark Street, London SE1 0HL
Tel: 020 7803 4800
www.muscular-dystrophy.org

'Wheelchair Provisions for Children and Adults with Muscular Dystrophy and other Neuromuscular Conditions'
A comprehensive guidance aimed at helping staff plan appropriate wheelchair and seating provision for both children and adults with a neuromuscular condition. Although primarily aimed at Wheelchair Service staff, it can also be a useful resource of best practice for users, parents, carers and other health professionals.
Muscular Dystrophy Campaign
61 Southwark Street
London SE1 0HL
Tel: 020 7803 4800
www.muscular-dystrophy.org
Free:
A guide for families with a newly diagnosed child.
A guide for families with a child aged 5–12.
Materials for children, including siblings and classmates.

Speech and language difficulties

AFASIC Publications

'Supporting Your Child's Speech and Language': 12 booklets – price from £1 to £2 each, full set £15.00, plus p&p

'Glossary Sheets on Speech and Language Impairments': 28 individual sheets that explain terms used to describe children with speech and language impairments (50p each, £10.00 for the full set), plus p&p

'Accessing Speech and Language Therapy for your Child – A guide to the law'
£3.00, plus p&p

'Children and Young People with Speech and Language Impairments in Mainstream Secondary Schools'
£3.00, plus p&p

'Choosing a School – An AFASIC guide to educational options for children with speech and language impairments'
£3.00, plus p&p

Resources

'How to Identify and Support Children with Speech and Language Difficulties'
£9.99, plus p&p

'Understanding Children with Dyspraxia/ DCD in the Early Years'
£10.00, plus p&p

'Language & Literacy: Joining together' (special price) £4.00, plus £9.00 p&p

All the above publications are available from AFASIC –
1st Floor
120 Bowling Green Lane
London EC1R 0BD
Tel: 020 7490 9410
Fax: 020 7251 2834
Website: www.afasic.org.uk

Spina bifida and hydrocephalus

'Teaching the Student with Spina Bifida'
Fern L Rowley-Keith & Donald H Reigel
Paul Brookes Publishing Co
ISBN: 10557660646

'Living with Spina Bifida'
Adrian Sandler MP
University of North Carolina Press, 2004
Obtainable from Trevor Brown Associates
Tel: 020 7388 8500
ISBN: 1080782352X
£14.95

'Spinabilities: A young person's guide to spina bifida'
Edited by Marlene Lutkenhoff
Woodbine House (USA) &
Sonya Oppenheimer
Woodbine House Inc., USA, 1997

ISBN: 0933139867
£12.99

'Hydrocephalus – Its implications for teaching and learning'
ASBAH, Peterborough, 2008
ISBN: 090 6687128

'Current Concepts in Spina Bifida and Hydrocephalus'
Carys Bannister & Brian Tew
MacKeith Press
Distributed by
Blackwell Scientific Publishers
ISBN: 0901260916

'LINK'
Quarterly magazine of ASBAH obtainable from ASBAH House
Titles available from ASBAH
42 Park Road
Peterborough PE1 2UQ
Tel: 0845 450 7755
Fax: 01733 555985
E-mail: helpline@asbah.org

To view the full range of publications produced by ASBAH visit www.asbah.org

Gilles de la Tourette syndrome

'Tourette Syndrome: The facts'
Mary Robertson and Simon Baron-Cohen
Oxford University Press, 1998
ISBN: 019852398X
£9.99

'Teaching the Tiger: A handbook for individuals involved in the education of students with attention deficit disorders, Tourette syndrome or obsessive-compulsive disorder'
Marilyn P Dornbush & Sheryl K Pruitt
Hope Press, 1995
ISBN: 1878267345
£18.37

'Tourette Syndrome'
Amber Carroll, Mary Robertson
David Fulton Publishers, 2000
ISBN: 1853466565

Visual impairment

'Visibility', 'eye contact', 'Curriculum Close-Up', 'Book Sales Catalogue'

'Visibility' focuses primarily on the education of visually impaired children and young people who attend mainstream schools or colleges; 'eye contact' focuses on the education of visually impaired children with additional disabilities. Both journals are published three times a year by RNIB (Royal National Institute for the Blind). Annual Subscription: £10.50 (UK), £15.00 (overseas) for each journal.
To subscribe contact:
RNIB Customer Services
PO Box 173
Peterborough PE2 6WS
Tel: 0845 702 3153
E-mail: cservices@rnib.org.uk

'Curriculum Close-Up' is a free termly newsletter for anyone involved in the education of blind and partially sighted children. Each issue focuses on a different subject. For your free subscription contact:
Suzy McDonald
Curriculum Information Officer
RNIB
58–72 John Bright Street
Birmingham B1 1BN
Tel: 0121 665 4223
E-mail: suzy.mcdonald@rnib.org.uk

'Book Sales Catalogue' offers a wide range of publications about education and employment in the field of sight problems. More than 350 different titles are available through mail order, including books, videos and other materials.

For your copy contact:
RNIB Customer Services
PO Box 173
Peterborough PE2 6WS
Tel: 0845 702 3153
E-mail: cservices@rnib.org.uk

Insight magazine:
Essential reading for parents, teachers, teaching assistants and health and social care professionals working with children and young people with sight problems, including those with complex needs. Includes free photocopiable supplements full of practical tips on making lessons accessible for all learners with sight problems. Published by RNIB six times a year. Visit: rnib.org.uk/insightmagazine for up-to-date subscription details.

Products and publications:
RNIB supplies a range of adapted games and learning materials specially designed for children with sight loss including those with additional disabilities. We publish a range of books, magazines, leaflets, videos and DVDs for parents and professionals.
Visit: rnib.org.uk/shop.
Parents and professionals can keep up to date with publications about sight loss and complex needs from RNIB and publishers around the world by subscribing to RNIB's free eNewsletter at: rnib.org.uk/booksforprofessionals.

Useful publications:
Visit RNIB Online Shop to browse and purchase the following publications, and more, at rnib.org.uk/shop or contact RNIB Customer Services on tel: 0303 123 9999; e-mail: cservices@rnib.org.uk.

'Count Me In'
A DVD promoting the inclusion, achievement and involvement of blind and partially

sighted children including those with complex needs in a range of early years, mainstream and special school settings.
RNIB, 2009

'Learning Together' (second edition)
A creative approach to learning for children with multiple disabilities and a visual impairment.
Mary Lee and Linda MacWilliam
RNIB, 2003

'Focus on Foundation' (second edition)
Packed with practical ideas for the successful inclusion of children with sight loss in early year's settings including reception classes.
RNIB, 2008
ISBN: 9781858789170

'Which Way'
An early years guide for parents of children with sight problems who have additional complex communication, learning or physical needs.
RNIB, 2002
ISBN: 1 85878 527 8

'Exploring Quality'
How to audit, review and profile your school's provision for pupils who have multiple disabilities and visual impairment.
Judy Bell and Lucy Naish
RNIB, 2005
ISBN: 1 85878 653 3

'Exploring Access in Mainstream'
How to audit your mainstream school environment, focusing on the needs of children who have multiple disabilities and visual impairment.
Judy Bell, Louise Clunies-Ross and Lucy Naish
RNIB, 2004
ISBN: 1 85878 630 4

5·4

Glossary of Abbreviations

Special needs support provided (independent mainstream schools)

Learning difficulties

CA   Some children with special needs receive help from classroom assistants

RA   There are currently very limited facilities for pupils with learning difficulties but reasonable adjustments can be made if necessary

SC   Some children with special needs are taught in separate classes for specific subjects

SNU   School has a dedicated Special Needs Unit, which provides specialist tuition on a one-to-one or small group basis by appropriately qualified teachers

WI   There is no dedicated Special Needs Unit but some children with special needs are withdrawn individually from certain lessons for one-to-one tuition

Behavioural disorders/emotional and behavioural difficulties/challenging behaviour

CA   Some children with behavioural problems receive help from classroom assistants

CO   Trained counsellors available for pupils

RA   There are currently very limited facilities for pupils with behavioural disorders but reasonable

adjustments can be made if necessary

ST   Behaviour management strategies identified in school's behaviour management policy

TS   Staff trained in behaviour management available

Physical impairments/medical conditions

AT   Adapted timetable for children with health problems

BL   Materials can be provided in Braille

CA   Some children receive help from classroom assistants

DS   Signing by staff and pupils

HL	Hearing loops available	TW	Accessible toilet and washing facilities
IT	Specialist IT provision available	W	School has wheelchair access (unspecified)
RA	There are currently very limited facilities for pupils with physical impairments or medical conditions but reasonable adjustments can be made if necessary	WA1	School is fully wheelchair accessible
		WA2	Main teaching areas are wheelchair accessible
SL	Stairlifts	WA3	No permanent access for wheelchairs; temporary ramps available
SM	Staff with medical training available		

Special needs

ADD	Attention Deficit Disorder
ADHD	Attention Deficit Hyperactivity Disorder
ASD	Autistic Spectrum Disorder
ASP	Asperger's Syndrome
BESD	Behavioural, Emotional and Social Disorders
CB	Challenging Behaviour
CP	Cerebral Palsy
DOW	Down's Syndrome
DYC	Dyscalculia
DYP	Dyspraxia
DYS	Dyslexia
EPI	Epilepsy
HEA	Health Problems (eg heart defect, asthma)
HI	Hearing Impairment
IM	Impaired Mobility
MLD	Moderate Learning Difficulties
PMLD	Profound and Multiple Learning Difficulties
SLD	Severe Learning Difficulties
SP&LD	Speech and Language Difficulties
TOU	Tourette's Syndrome
VI	Visual Impairment
WU	Wheelchair User

Associations and accrediting bodies

ALI	Action Learning Institute
AOC	Association of Colleges
ARC	Association for Residential Care
AWCEBD	The Association of Workers for Children with Emotional and Behavioural Difficulties
BDA	The British Dyslexia Association
BILD	British Institute of Learning Disabilities

BSA	Boarding Schools Association
CES	Catholic Education Service
CReSTeD	Council for the Registration of Schools Teaching Dyslexic Pupils
ECIS	European Council of International Schools
EQUALS	Entitlement and Quality Education for Pupils with Severe Learning Difficulties
FEFC	Further Education Funding Council
GBA	Governing Bodies Association
HMC	The Headmasters' and Headmistresses' Conference
IAPS	The Independent Association of Prep Schools
ISA	The Independent Schools Association
ISC	The Independent Schools Council
ISI	The Independent Schools Inspectorate
JEC	Joint Epilepsy Council
LSC	Learning & Skills Council
NAES	National Association of EBD Schools
NAIMS	The National Association for Independent and Non-maintained Schools
NAS	National Autistic Society
NASEN	The National Association for Special Educational Needs
NASS	The National Association for Voluntary and Non-maintained Special Schools
NATSPEC	The National Association of Specialist Colleges
NCSE	National Council for Special Education
NCVO	National Council of Voluntary Organisations
NFAC	National Federation of Access Centres
OCR	Oxford, Cambridge and RSA Examinations
OPSIS	National Association for the Education, Training and Support of Blind and Partially Sighted People
SHMIS	The Society of Headmasters and Headmistresses of Independent Schools
SRCON	Surrey Regional Colleges Network
TSC	Training Standards Council
WJEC	Welsh Joint Education Committee

Main Index

P

Q

T

U

V

W

Y